PREACHING THROUGH THE BIBLE

BY
JOSEPH PARKER

VOL. 1

GENESIS

BAKER BOOK HOUSE
Grand Rapids, Michigan

Standard Book Number: 8010-6888-6

Library of Congress Catalog Card Number: 59-10860

Reprinted 1971 by
Baker Book House Company

Originally printed
under the title,
The People's Bible

PREFACE.

THIS is not a Bible Commentary in the usual sense of that term. It is a pastor's commentary upon such portions of Holy Scripture as are of obvious and immediate importance to the growth of the soul in Divine wisdom, and is, therefore, not intended to take the place of the verbal and critical commentaries which so ably represent the latest phases of Christian erudition. Instead of going minutely through any book verse by verse, the first object will be to discover its governing idea or principal purpose, and to make that clear by taking out of the book, say twelve, twenty, or thirty instances most strikingly illustrative of the writer's intention. For example, some such order as the following (always held to be variable of course) may be adopted :—

GENESIS : A book of *Beginnings* : the beginning of Creation ; the beginning of Humanity ; the beginning of Family life ; the beginning of Disobedience ; a kind of daybreak book ; a wondrous dawn ; an hour of revelation and vision. To get hold of *this* idea is to get a thorough insight into the book of Genesis.

EXODUS : Phases of *Providence* : in leadership, in national deliverances, in organisation, in codified human life, in all the mystery of human training and discipline, showing how the tabernacle of God is with men upon earth : a refuge, a judgment, a symbol. To master *this* idea is to seize the very spirit of the book of Exodus.

LEVITICUS : Religious *Mechanics* : the Mechanics of Sin-reckoning ; the Mechanics of Sacrifice ; the Mechanics of Intercession ; the Mechanics of Purification ; the higher meaning of all these intricate and costly formalities ; the unprofitableness of bodily exercise ; the revelation and development of true Sacrifice.

So with all the other books. We must discover the genius or purpose of each book, and elucidate and magnify it by the strongest illustrative instances. As for detail, it is abundantly and satisfactorily treated in critical commentaries devoted to the study of language, custom, antiquity, and science. The purpose of the People's Bible is pastoral; it aims so to bring all readers under the moral sovereignty of the sacred Book as to arm them against temptation, enrich them with solid comfort, and fortify them with the wisdom of God.

We assume an immense responsibility in claiming that any book is a final and authoritative standard in faith and morals. We place the book itself in an awful position. We separate it from all other books; we make sceptical criticism a profane offence, and devout obedience an essential element of spiritual character. The mind has simply to receive, the will has simply to obey, the heart has simply to trust. The book is to us verily as God himself. Are we, in nineteenth-century light, to stand by such a position, or to abandon it? Is the Bible still to stand alone, and to demand the obeisance of all other books; is the dream-book to stand in the harvest-fields of literature and to receive the homage of the bending sheaves? In reply, I would rather avail myself of the limited responsibility of a personal testimony, than even appear to involve others by the use of terms often difficult or impossible to fix in rigid definition. At the risk of a verbal paradox, I will embolden myself to say that the older I grow the more inspired the Bible seems to become. You know my meaning. The book enlarges like a heightening sky. You also know my meaning when I say that there is only one book in the world which can prove the inspiration of the Bible, and that is the Bible itself. Possibly in our early reading of the Scriptures we put ourselves into a false relation to the book by taking with us some preconceived notion or theory of inspiration, and trying to make the Bible exactly fit our mechanical orthodoxy. This was like timing the sun by our chronometers, instead of timing our chrono-meters by the sun. What wonder if we have lost much by this process ? What wonder if the supposed orthodoxy has originated the real scepticism ? Inspiration, like its Author, is a term which has no equivalent in other words and therefore can have no complete theory. Strange as it may appear, there are some words which lexicography cannot break up into explanatory syllables, and amongst them the word *Inspiration* holds a foremost place. We must *feel* some meanings, as blind men feel the morning light. Illustrations of inspiration we can have ; also reverent suggestions respecting it ; also such confirmations as arise from coincidence, unity, purpose, and issue,— here, indeed, is the most inviting and productive field of devout and even intellectual research ; but to say authori-tatively where Inspiration begins, where it ends, how it operates, what it involves, where it separates itself from genius, how it burned for brief day in shepherd or king, fisherman or tentmaker, and then was withdrawn to heaven, nevermore to glow upon earth, would be to have the very inspiration which is said to have completed itself in revelation. The Bible addresses every aspect and every necessity of my nature ; it is my own biography ; I seem to have read it in some other world ; we are old friends ; the breathing of Eternity is in us both, and we have happened together, to our mutual joy, on this rough shore of time. I never know how great a Book it is until I try to do without it, then the heart aches ; then the eyes are put out with the great tears of grief ; then the house is no home of mine ; then life sinks under an infinite load of weariness. In great moods of moral exul-tation I cannot stoop to the unworthy fray of intellectual encounter, to compare theories, to discuss contradictory scepticisms, and to institute comparisons between the cleverness which baffles me and the faith which impels me to service.

But has Inspiration really ceased out of the Church?
Is the Holy Spirit but a term in ancient theology? **Is**
he not the *abiding* Paraclete? Jesus Christ distinctly
promised that the Paraclete should abide " for ever," and
can he be in the heart without inspiring the whole range
of the mind? I have no doubt as to the continuance of
Inspiration in the Church, for it seems to me to be the
one gift which must, of gracious necessity, abide for ever
—the gift, indeed, without which the Church could not
exist. But the gift is not always to be used in one direction. There are inspired *readers* as certainly as there are
inspired writers. " There is a spirit in man, and **the**
inspiration of the Almighty giveth him understanding,"
in the deep and true reading of the Word. I am not
alarmed by the perils which must instantly suggest themselves to apprehensive minds, though some of those perils,
viewed from unequal distances, are unquestionably por-
tentous in outline. The gift of inspired reading is the
gift of the whole believing and suppliant Church. There
is no inspired *class* in the Church, Divinely marked off for
special reverence and remuneration ; indeed, it seems to
me that the so-called priests are the *only* uninspired
followers—the mere craftsmen and pensioners—of the
Church ; they are " shepherds that cannot understand :
they all look to their own way, every one for his gain,
from his quarter." " Let them alone : they be blind leaders
of the blind." You need not, therefore, fear that I am
pointing to a priestly class. The kind of inspiration I
mean can be had for the asking by all humble souls.
" If ye then, being evil, know how to give good gifts
unto your children : how much more shall your heavenly
Father give the Holy Spirit to them that ask him ? "
The proof of such inspiration will be found less in
intellectual splendour than in spiritual docility and child-
like obedience ; we shall be unconscious of the shining
of our face, but shall know that in our hearts there
is a great softness of love, a holy yearning after our

Father's perfectness; we shall be most inspired when we are most teachable; we may be sure that the purpose of the Holy Spirit is being accomplished within us when we say, "Speak, Lord, for thy servant heareth," and ask him, beside whom are the two anointed ones, not to withhold his revelation from babe-like souls. Verily, Inspiration hath not ceased. Let us pray for an inspired ministry: in other words, that all ministers may be blessed with a double portion of the Holy Spirit. This is our protection against priestism. This will sanctify every man, body, soul, and spirit, and make the whole Church the living temple of the Holy Ghost. When ministers are Divinely inspired their public reading of the Scriptures will be an exposition; every accent will be as a tongue of fire, and every emphasis will give new hints of meaning. The inspired writers wait for inspired readers. How the Holy Book leaps, so to say, in recognition of the sacred touch and the loving glance! Inspired reading gives us a Bible which cannot be taken from us; not a mechanical Bible, which cunning hands can disjoint; not an artificial Bible, which relies upon scattered proof-texts;—but a living revelation: a voice which awakens faithful echoes in the heart; a self-attesting book; its own mystery and its own lamp; without beginning or end; an infinite surprise: an infinite benediction. Have no fear that the Ark of the Testimony will be taken. We lose our inspiration when we lose our Faith, and then we are the subjects of irrational panic. Rather say, "Come up, ye horses; and rage, ye chariots; and let the mighty men come forth, . . . for Pharaoh, king of Egypt, is but a noise." Theories and dogmas, propositions and controversies, orthodoxies and heterodoxies, come and go, but the Word of the Lord abideth for ever, "surely as Tabor is among the mountains, and as Carmel by the sea."

One word as to the highest qualification alike of a commentator and a reader. I have the more confidence in pointing out this qualification, for the reason that the

profoundest of Biblical scholars will be the first to maintain its supremacy.   Without that qualification we must
for ever stand as strangers outside the Bible, but with it
the soul may speak, as it were, face to face with God.
The critical expositor has his well-defined field of service
within whose lines he can render incalculable help to the
cause of Christ, yet this wide field rather increases than
diminishes the area within which the meek and lowly
spirit, the broken and humble heart, can read the deepest
meaning of the Divine word.   With a theology so vast,
so sublime, yet so practical, calling us to all that is mysterious and ghostly in adoration, summoning the soul into
the inmost sanctuary of the Invisible God—without a
shape on which to rest the affrighted eye, or a line on
which to lay the trembling hand ; calling us onward and
upward through a silence that makes our very breathing
a conscious trespass, and through a light from which our
very purity shrinks in shame,—with a theology so practical
as to search our hidden life as with fire, to test our
standards and balances, to bring our words to judgment,
and to track our daily course with the criticism of God,
—with a theology demanding personal incarnation in
fellowship and service, charging us with the sacred trust
of representing Christ to a hostile world, and constantly
charging us to prove the reality of our faith by the sincerity of our love,—with such a theology handed to us by
inspired penmen for exposition and exemplification, who
does not see that high above all other qualifications—
even prophecy, tongues, mysteries, and all knowledge
—must stand in holy isolation and solitary privilege
the PURE HEART that alone can see God !

CONTENTS.

Up to this point an endeavour has been made to prepare the mind for the study of the still higher mysteries. Assuming this to have been in a measure successful, the book proceeds thus :—

Then follows an Essay upon

The whole of the above argument, instead of being based on the assumption that there *is* a God, raises the inquiry, Here is a Universe,—here is a Society,—here is a Book,—how are they to be accounted for? Hence the practical rather than the metaphysical tone of the reasoning. The first verse in Genesis suggests this discussion. Instead, however, of placing this discussion formally under a given chapter and verse, I have thought it better to regard it as arising from the whole spirit and structure of the Bible, as, in my opinion, it unquestionably does. My hope is that the mere chapter-and-verse method of proof will be increasingly distrusted and discarded, and that it will be replaced by such a conception of the genius and temper of the whole Bible as to render at least the narrowest forms of heresy simply impossible.

GENESIS . . . .

In order to present different aspects of the same truths without disturbing the main line of the study there are given in distinguishing type various outlines under the title of NOTES FOR PREACHERS . . . 118—126

That a book which began with the Creation of the heaven and the earth should end with the coffining of Joseph, is a circumstance which not only suggests but necessitates the incompleteness of the record. We are evidently entitled to expect a continuation. We are not meant to be satisfied with Genesis. It is but a beginning ; not a mechanical beginning which can be arbitrarily determined, but a vital germ whose development can be suppressed only by ignorance or violence. So, whilst we pause, we pause in an attitude of confident expectation.

HANDFULS OF PURPOSE" . . . .

Texts and subjects whose treatment could not be taken up in direct historical sequence.

I. "Ye shall be as gods" (Gen. iii. 5).

II. "God took him" (Gen. v. 24).

III. "The place of the altar which he made there at the first" (Gen. xiii. 4).

IV. "And his sons Isaac and Ishmael buried him" (Gen. xxv. 9).

V. "I have learned by experience" (Gen. xxx. 27).

VI. "And Laban called it Jegar-Sahadutha, but Jacob called it Galeed" (Gen. xxxi. 47).

VII. "The sun rose upon him" (Gen. xxxii. 31).

VIII. "And Esau said I have enough, my brother Gen. xxxiii. 9).

IX. "Gad, a troop shall overcome him, but he shall overcome at the last" (Gen. xlix. 19).

X. "And when Joseph's brethren saw that their father was dead, they said, Joseph will peradventure hate us, and will certainly requite us all the evil which we did unto him" (Gen. l. 15).

PANORAMA OF GENESIS . . . . .

THE PEOPLE'S BIBLE.

PRAYER FOR WISDOM.

FATHER OF SPIRITS, we can never see thee; but in our hearts we feel thy touch, a touch of humbled almightiness and a nearness as of light. We love thee more than we can ever tell. We go out after thee as if by right, and as if by sweet necessity. Every morning come to us before the sun rises, and every night watch us till the stars die out. Make all things remind us of thy presence, all beauty, all light, all music, all action; then our life will be large and our inheritance will be infinite wealth. We feel that we have not yet begun to live. Now and then a great throb of life makes us feel somewhat of our possibilities; yea, even as if we had begun our immortality and set our feet on heaven's land. Then we fall back, and sin, and lie, and long for that which is wholly forbidden. Oh, the torture of this wild contradiction! We are mad with agony that cannot be borne. Our cheeks burn with shame hotter than any fire of our kindling. Then we would that some Lazarus might be sent with cooling water from the brooks above to stay the infinite torment, but no human answer comes to the crying of our pain. We now come to thyself, for with thee is all the mercy of the Cross. "God be merciful unto us, sinners," and give us the sweet peace which follows Divine pardon. Blessed Saviour, thy fragrant name makes the whole Bible smell as a garden of rare flowers; to-day we open the Book, that we may walk with thee and hear thy voice and see the wonders which are hidden in the little letter. We would not go a step without thee, for then verily we would go out of the garden into the bare wilderness. Tell us all the meaning of this sacred writing. Make Moses breathe like a living teacher, that he may hold us by the enchantment of thy own name. May the old book become the very newest of writing, because the inspiring Spirit inspires us who read it. Carry forward our knowledge into wisdom, for knowledge puffeth up and kills like a letter which is not understood. Holy One, now hear us. Trinity in heaven, dwell in our hearts as in temples made ready for the holy presence, and may we live so well that we may seem to have lived long. We want to nestle in thy bosom. We want to touch thee. We want—oh, thou knowest all; why should we not take refuge in all-speaking silence? Amen.

INTRODUCTORY.

WE are just about to open the Bible, and to fix our eyes upon the very miracle of books. It is a great occasion— a critical hour, full of possibilities beyond present imagining, and big with issues which the day of judgment can alone disclose. My conviction deepens that the Bible is the most modern of books, that is to say, it is the history of the very time which is passing over us; it contains every man's biography; it is full of the passion and tragedy, the love and sacrifice, which we know to be the substantial history of the day. The morning newspaper, apparently so fresh and novel, is but a reprint of Moses and the prophets, with some slight difference in incident and colour, but with no difference whatever of moral substance and meaning. So fully persuaded am I of all that is meant by this view that I am prepared to risk the claim for inspiration on the part of the Bible upon it. The Bible is proving its inspiration by the facts which make up both our spiritual experience and our exterior history, or if it is not actually and obviously doing so, it is under- mining that claim and hastening its doom as a mere superstition. It is of small consequence to me to know who wrote the Bible, when it was written, what has become of the manuscripts or under what circumstances the book was determined as to shape, size, and limits. Here it is: it is a book, and a book with a history, and for my purpose it is enough to find out what the book actually says to my life, my heart, my conscience, and all my higher faculties, and to judge it, not by some official standard, but by the recognised and most solemn facts which make up human history. That is my ground, and I claim for it the sanction of reason. The Bible asks for no privilege in the matter of judgment : its bold appeal is to the highest court of immediate fact and experience. Even in its deepest mysteries, it is mysteri- ously human and in no sense superstitiously Divine. My purpose is to make all this clear, and so make the Bible doubly ours, not something held because an irresponsible authority has charged it upon us, but because we have at last a book which knows us, puts our thoughts into words, fills up our need, and teaches us the only prayers which even God can answer. No book can stand upon its mere venerableness except for literary purposes, that is, as a curiosity or a book of academical exercise and test. Whatever rules living men must itself be living, and whatever rules them profoundly and lastingly must have corresponding depth and durableness in itself.

Let us agree as to the spirit in which we must enter upon those sacred studies. We must rid our minds of all prejudice, and let the book have ample opportunity to make its own impression. We cannot mistake the music of truth. If we rashly begin high up amongst the wordless mysteries, we shall certainly be dazed, and probably be filled with the spirit of unbelief. We must begin on the ground we know—the moral ground, the region of standards, equities, and obligations, and go on from point to point until we enter the upper regions where silence is better than speech. I must ask you, even in our first studies, to be very quiet for a long time, to avoid mental effervescence and the impetuosity of that rude cleverness which rushes to conclusions, and always misses principal meanings. "Put off thy shoes from off thy feet; for the place whereon thou standest is holy ground." We must, indeed, judge the book in some degree by the spirit which it demands on the part of its readers. If for a moment it can tolerate irreverence, it is no book of God's. It must devour the frivolous man, yea, even with fire unquenchable, and cast into outer darkness the man who would pry with mental jauntiness into its secret. There need not be any ostentation about the repulse, as if arising from mere pride or vindicating an arbitrary superiority; the repulse must come without show of pique, come as from eternity, and overwhelm with unnameable and immeasurable force. The Bible has no revelation to make to unbiblical minds. It will only speak to the lowly and the helpless, the contrite and the sore in heart. Oh, but this book can be so dumb and can look so blank! It will spread no table for mere daintiness of taste, but will find a whole festival for thorough and expectant hunger. If we come in any other spirit, let us go away at once, that we may escape the pain of humiliation and disappointment; there is really nothing for us in the Bible; it was never meant for us; as well go into the unexplored wilderness to find our father's house, or dig in the earth to find the gate of heaven "Open thou mine eyes, that I may behold wondrous things out of thy law." Thou who didst write the book for man, prepare man to read the book ; give him the sensitive heart, the apt mind, and the obedient and most loyal will; then shall the book hold all things true, and be unto the soul as the very library of God.

This day I seem to begin my life work, the very thing that expresses my supreme purpose and highest hope. A holy fire glows in my expanding heart as I dwell upon the holy task and all its endless issues. The translation of the Bible which we need from time to time is not a merely grammatical exercise, or a discussion of various readings and ancient authorities. Grammar we must have if we are to have speech, but the grammar being settled, the higher translation has yet to begin. What is that higher translation ? It is such a rendering of the Divine Word as will meet all human need, elevate all human desire, and sanctify all human endeavour ; such a rendering as will show that everything has been provided for in the Bible that human life can ever need or hope for. If we are asked, Why not lecture upon modern events ? the answer is that there are no modern events to lecture upon in any sense which supersedes the Bible. As well try to make a new earth as to make a new book : we make new fields, new gardens, new crops, but the earth abideth the same for ever ; and that is precisely what we do with books—they all grow upon the old soil of the Bible; they look new, they are superficially new, they are bought and sold as new; but the Word of the Lord abideth for ever, and man's work is but the labour of a brief day. How much farther have we got than Adam and Eve, man and woman, strength and beauty, the temptation and the sin, the felt nakedness and the sheepskin covering? Not an inch. Cain still lives in Cain*ism*. The world is still bringing deluges upon its own sinful head. Abram is still going forth in quest of a land flowing with milk and honey. Yea, old Eden still blooms, and men are trying to pass the guarding fire and live again as if by force of arms amid its trees and rivers and haunts of green beauty and softness. How to get back to that garden is the problem of all time and the despair of all ambition. There are some who try to be modern and even original, by reading Tennyson in the pulpit in preference to Isaiah, but in doing so they receive no encouragement from Tennyson himself. These small madnesses are not wholly inexplicable; they have a look of cleverness, and they minister, without the vulgarity of seeming to do so, to the vanity of the madman himself. But there is no durableness in such tricks. A month kills them, or six months at the most drags them into contempt. Isaiah waits, and Isaiah calmly comes to the front again, comes with the stately peace of eternal right. On this conviction I shall endeavour to found myself in carrying out my life-work in this Bible. Nor will it be any strain upon me so to act, for I see everything in the Bible—all law in the Pentateuch, all history in the prophets, all music in the Psalms, all imaginative literature in the parables, all dream and hope and Divinely ordered tumult in the grand Apocalypse. God forbid we should ever accept the sophism that the Bible is a text-book for preachers, and nothing more: it is the people's book: it belongs to the human heart in all days and places. Just in proportion as this can be made clear will the Bible regain its primacy in literature, and secure the homage of an admiring and grateful world. Its protectors will be innumerable—the poor man, the working man, the sorrowing man, the suffering woman, the little child, these will lay down their lives for it, and think the sacrifice too small.

Thus the Bible, like its Author, is not the I WAS, but the I AM—the Immediate, the Present, the Ever-Now; quite a contradiction in mere words, but a perfect consistency in highest life and thought.

It is indeed pitiable, something quite absurdly vain, to hear a certain kind of people making out by lame violence, which they mistake for forcible reasoning, that the Bible is an old-world book, a rag out of fashion, not a garment fit for this day's wearing. Some knavish preachers are not ashamed to do this: they have lived on the dear old book, it has kept them and their families in food and lodging these last thirty years, and yet they have nothing good to say about it; they like better the last book which they do not understand, or the last novel, which is as hemlock or cruel strychnine to the soul. Thieves they be, knaves with pulpit robes reluctantly thrown over their thievish breasts. Beware of them. They are clever liars, swindlers who look too innocent to be quite guiltless, hirelings who hunger for the pelf. Nay, the black indictment does not end there. They are killers of men; bandits who thrust weapons into souls and slay the young, the unsuspecting, and the frank. I could respect, in some grim way, the vulgar infidel who blasphemes openly and on purpose, and rejoices in his pitiful bellowing, mistaking the very blatancy for courage; but the man in the pulpit who insults the Bible on which he lives, and wriggles out of the professions by which he climbed to the pulpit he dishonours, I charge with worse crimes than those which blackened Barabbas or damned Iscariot. I call for men who will honour the Bible, men of all-seeing purity of heart, men who deliver the messages of God with the tenderness of Christ.

More Bible is what is wanted; fuller reading of the book itself, and a much freer application of it to the facts of daily life. I have not hesitated to say that life itself is the deepest and truest comment upon the Bible, and that in the Bible absolutely everything is to be found in germ and outline. The Bible must be dashed out of the hand of the priest, and put into the hands of the people. I will not have it that the Bible is a mystery book in the sense of being only accessible by experts; it is the people's book, as the firmament is the people's firmament and the air is the people's air. Of course the scientific man has his own view of the sky and his own way of examining the air, yet the poorest dunce may look up into the solemn heights and the meanest drudge drink in the living air. Many people could make more of the sky itself than of a learned lecture upon it, and a mountain breeze could be appreciated when a chemical analysis would be misunderstood. It is so with the Bible. Let the people themselves read "Moses and the prophets," not send for a priest to read for them, but sit down to the sacred task and spell out its infinite thought. Men who can help us to do this—not do this for us—are our true friends. They are the ministers of Christ, and our servants for Christ's sake. They know the true use of the Bible, and prove the inspiration of the book by showing how all life responds to its voice and confirms its moral demands. When they fail to do this they fall from their high vocation and grieve the Spirit of God.

INSPIRATION.

ACCORDING to the teaching of both Testaments, a few men seem to have been Divinely inspired either to speak, or to put into a written form, what was communicated to them as the truth of God. This inspiration was, we are led to believe, accorded to but a few, not one of whom, however, so far as we can learn, ever brought moral discredit upon his solemn and august vocation. Some of them had been even profligate in iniquity *before* their inspiration; but having spoken the word of God, they appear to have been purified as by a holy fire. That their number was but small is rather an argument in favour of their claim than otherwise, when we consider what is evident in all the highest energy and form of life known amongst ourselves. Few men, for example, have been inspired (qualified) to write the intermediate bible of civilisation—that exciting and often tragical book which interposes between the volume of nature and the volume of spiritual testimony. There are but few historians, few poets, few aphorists. Yet the few do not speak for themselves alone : they represent human nature, and establish their right to supremacy and homage in proportion as they speak not the jargon of a class, but the universal language of humanity. Inspiration does not separate David and Paul from the human race : it lifts the human race to a high pinnacle of honour and expectation. The Divine inspiration of one man presupposes a corresponding degree of Divine inspiration (actual or possible) in all other men. Few, indeed, may have been inspired to *speak* the Word, but all have been inspired to *feel* it. Is inspiration, as commonly understood, given to but a few ? So is wealth, so is poetry, so is courage, so is art, so is wisdom. The key of the chamber is given to one keeper, but the chamber itself is to be opened for the entrance of the whole world. "Why should David or Paul have been more inspired than I am?" is a peevish inquiry, wanting as much in reason as in dignity, and finding its natural completion in the profane inquiry—" Why is *God* more Divine than I am ? " It is the kind of question which vexes human life with the most pitiful discontent. It brings with it a brood worthy of itself. Why should Homer have been more poetical ? Why should Plato have been more philosophical ? Why should Euclid have been more mathematical ? It will be answered that their supremacy is held only until a higher genius can successfully dispute it, and that Moses and John should be allowed to hold theirs on the same condition. Be it so ! Where do Moses and John deprecate a challenge of their personal supremacy ? Yet common justice will insist that if the inspiration of the Biblical writers be challenged, *the rival inspiration must cover the whole of the original ground,* for it must be borne in mind that not only do the Biblical writers touch upon some subjects which may be treated by ordinary sagacity and learning, but they distinctly touch subjects which are connected with the innermost life and secret of the universe. It will not be enough, then, to limit the competition to the production of felicitous proverbs or artistic parables ; there must be a moral purity, an intellectual grasp, a spiritual insight and sympathy, which shall so combine as to represent the same mastery and familiarity in relation to the invisible and supernatural which are to be found in the inspired Testaments. Then will arise a farther question. Supposing something like an equality in the breadth and tone of the rival revelations, we must know in what direction they respectively move in affecting the practical life of mankind. Does the one move towards reverie, self-content, spiritual isolation ? Does the other impel in the direction of philanthropy, sacrifice, worship ? These are inquiries which can be definitively settled.

But the complaint is not so much that a *few* writers should have claimed Divine inspiration as that their authority should bind the religious faith of all men through all time. It is the idea of apparent despotism in doctrine that is strongly resented. Is the grievance substantial or imaginary ? It should be observed that the Bible opens its revelation without any preliminary contract with the reader either as to a limit of faith or a degree of authority. The believers in inspiration may possibly have themselves to charge with a grave mistake upon this important point, for it might be supposed by any one who has attended to the controversy without carefully reading the Bible itself that the book has upon its very forefront a distinct statement of its Divine inspiration and authority, which must be accepted without question or murmur. Nothing can be farther from the fact. As to a formal claim of inspiration, there is no more of it in the opening of Genesis than there is in the opening of the Metamorphosis. Were the Bible put into the hands of a scholarly and critical pagan without one word of introduction or comment, he would be a long time in discovering any tittle of a formal claim on the part of the book to be considered inspired and authoritative. He would at once be struck by the loftiness and firmness of its tone, and might be led so far as to say, "This man could not have spoken more boldly had the very gods themselves addressed him from the heavens"; or he might attribute the boldness to the quality of a language peculiar for pomp and sublimity; but he would not be either humbled or embarrassed by a preliminary demand for the surrender of his judgment or his life. The inspiration of the Bible grows upon a man much as a consciousness of his own intellectual and spiritual life grows upon him. This higher consciousness is often sudden in its development. It would seem that in a moment—preceded, it may be, by a long, though more or less unconscious, preparation —an initial lifetime is thrown off and a new spiritual citizenship is established. In this way the slave of dictionaries sometimes rises into a master of languages, the slow cipherer into a philosophical arithmetician, and the cautious student of politics into a sagacious statesman. The line of separation is invisible, almost imaginary, yet it divides experiences that are most diverse. In some such way the Bible has suddenly elevated itself from a school book to a revelation, and men have felt that they could not set it again in the rank of common writings without a sense of serious moral loss. They have not foreseen the result of their reading. At first they yielded to a merely literary fascination; by-and-by moral sympathy was touched in some degree; curiosity was excited; then came wonder, and after wonder came uncertainty, like a keen pain in the heart; then came a sentence like this to test the faith and to ripen the strange experience into Christian joy : " Holy men of old spake as they were moved by the Holy Ghost " ; and with that sentence came a responsibility which put the reader into a new and solemn relation to the book.

If the Bible is Divinely inspired, it follows that it is Divinely authoritative. Inspiration and authority must stand or fall together. Consider what it is that is professedly revealed. What is it? It is not history ; it is not cosmogony ; it is not ethnology ; it is not even a code of morals. It is worth while, then, to pause a moment, that we may get the full emphasis of the answer. The supreme revelation that is made in the Bible is the revelation of GOD. Everything else belongs to the region of detail. The Divine personality is the vital and all-embracing revelation. Creation may suggest it, the curious interweaving and combination of daily events may point towards it as towards a possibility, but the Bible distinctly reveals it as the secret of all things. But the Bible, having made this revelation, cannot stop there. The term *God* includes all other terms. It is not a high symbol in abstract reasoning, or the almost aërial line which the metaphysician is content to begin with : it is the all-controlling factor in regions visible and invisible—it is this, or it is nothing. The moment, therefore, that the question of Divine Fatherhood or Rulership is raised, all the great questions covered by the term *humanity* are raised along with it, and by their very urgency they may easily create a clamour unfavourable to the consideration of their most important bearings. It is better, therefore, to reason downward from the quiet and solemn heights of the Divine personality than to struggle upwards through all the controversy and bewilderment of human interests. If the Bible declares the true idea of God, it must presumptively give the true doctrine of human nature. God must be self-declared. Man has no instruments that can measure the Divine power, or search out the Divine wisdom. But *how* is God to grant a revelation of himself? Christian theology answers,—By the inspiration of chosen men who shall be his instruments for this special purpose. Instantly that inspiration becomes thus individualised a great difficulty arises—the very difficulty which has been pointed out in the Divine incarnation : we look at the Divine mystery through the human medium, and instead of fixing the mind upon the inspiring Spirit, we fix it upon the inspired man.

It is thus that loss is incurred, and that disadvantage is inflicted upon the subjects of inspiration. To speak, for example, of the inspiration of *David*, is to limit a Divine quantity by a human personality; and the danger (almost inevitable) is that the mind be fixed upon the term *David* rather than upon the term *inspiration*. We must enlarge the minor term if we can; and how is this to be done but by speaking, not of the inspiration of Moses or David, Ezekiel, or John, but of the inspiration of *humanity*, the individuals themselves being nothing but the points of contact at which a Divine action is set up? Much is gained by this elimination of the personal element. Inspiration is greater than personality. Instead of speaking of the authority of *Paul*, we are to speak of the authority of *truth*: Paul may, indeed, have been chosen as the medium of utterance, but the utterer is God. It is mere peevishness, or perhaps defiance, which chafes at the authority of a *man*; that is not the question at all; assent is sought to the proposition that the eternal authority of God has been declared through human instrumentality. In what other way could it have been declared? Is there any other way so free from the vulgarity of sensationalism, so rational, so philosophical, so ennobling, so sublime? No homage is offered to Moses, to David, or to Paul. The Bible, in all its Divine elements, would be unimpaired were the names of its human penmen removed. Yet those names are of peculiar value in humanising a volume which requires softening shadows to mitigate its unique glories. The writers never obtrude their personal dignity; they never conceal their personal weaknesses; the word of the Lord is a burden to them, and is often accepted with hesitation and misgiving. But what if there be slips or other faults in the work of the inspired men? In one sense, so much the better; in the sense, for example, that these are imperfections which actually beget confidence—superficial imperfections which give all the advantage of contrast to work that is known to be solid and enduring. The musician is limited by his instrument. Though he may have ravished a world by his strains, he could be almost angry with the instrument which has failed to express the still finer tones which madden him with indescribable joy. In the matter of inspiration the Almighty proposed to dwell in houses of clay; what wonder if they were unequal to such a Presence?

We have said that the Divine inspiration of one man presupposes a corresponding degree of Divine inspiration (actual or possible) in all other men. The inspiration of speech presupposes the inspiration of hearing, true listening being much more than an exercise of a merely physical function. If few men know how to speak, fewer still know how to listen. Men are preoccupied; voices of prejudice, interest, self-worship, never cease to besiege the ear of the soul : add to these a drowsiness hardly distinguishable from a temptation, and a persistent appeal from the whole external estate of life, and the difficulty of spiritual hearing will be no longer a mystery. The universal inspiration comes through a quickening and sanctifying action upon the *moral sense* of mankind. The one thing which that moral sense never did accomplish is *the discovery of God.* In its most exalted and energetic moods it got no farther than an inscription to the Unknown Power,—a long way, too,—a sublime distance, verily,—still not a Bible, but a marble slab.

That the Biblical revelation of God does not instantly satisfy every mind, and bring into unanimity the religious sentiment of the world, is a self-destructive argument as applied against the doctrine of Divine inspiration. It proves too much. Where is there unanimity upon any subject which challenges alike the intellectual and moral attention of mankind ? Not only so ; the Bible itself anticipates the very difficulty, and mourns with pathetic lamentation that the disclosure of God has been received with incredulity or resentment. If it be suggested that such a revelation should have been given as would at once, by its copiousness and brilliance, have established itself in the confidence of the world, the suggestion proceeds in forgetfulness of the fact that that very confidence itself has been warped and vitiated, and is no longer the simple and honest love which is the secret of spiritual sympathy and interpretation. How to recover the idea of God was the problem. The Bible distinctly undertakes its solution, and in so doing claims authoritatively to be known, not as a volume of history, a code of morals, a treatise on philosophy, but as the one written Book of *God.*

Inspiration had at the very outset to encounter the difficulty of *language*, inasmuch as there was no speech common to the whole world. The world has a common heart, a common nature, a common instinct, but not a common tongue. Even in the same language words constantly vary in expressiveness and value : not only does time change their application and their limits, but they actually convey different meanings to different minds ; and there is not always an interpreter at hand to draw the line of exact signification and prevent confusion and controversy. A word may not seem precisely the same thing to any two men, though it may be well known to both of them in a rough sense, which may suffice for ordinary purposes. How to express an eternal quantity through a mutable language ! This is in another form the precise difficulty of the Incarnation, for what flesh is to spirit speech is to thought. The difficulty has never been wholly overcome—certainly not in the Incarnation, for Jesus Christ was despised and rejected of men ; and certainly not in the Bible, for it has provoked more controversy, fiercer and bitterer too, than any other book in all literature. It should be noted, too, that the very objections which from the beginning have been urged against Christ have also been pressed against the Bible—objections relating to form, to structure, to origin, to apparent contradiction, and to manifest insufficiency to meet the demands of the situation. In both cases human expectation was set at nought, and something was offered which could not but mortify the pride of the receiver. We must, then, go beyond forms, symbols, and measurable quantities, and find the meaning of inspiration in elevation and purity of thought, in the scrupulousness and magnanimity of moral instinct, in the ennobling and all-hoping charity by which our best life is distinguished, and ceasing all pedantic strife about mere *words*, must cast ourselves with reverence and holy joy upon the eternal *Word*.

So far we have looked at inspiration as a *doctrine* ; if we are to estimate its value as a *fact*, we must get at least a general notion of the principal characteristics of the particular book on behalf of which inspiration is claimed. In this and the succeeding chapter we shall move within what may be called extra-theological limits, for a purpose which will be disclosed as we proceed. At the outset, we must strongly deny that any man could *à priori* have told the proper scope and tone of a book Divinely inspired. It is one thing to have the book, and to reason backwards; it is another to be called upon, in its absence, to say exactly what an inspired revelation should be. We have to found an opinion upon a particular book, and it will be entirely for the book itself to prove its own inspiration. The Bible must do what every other book must do, that is to say, it must make its own place in the world ; let it prove its inspiration by inspiring its readers ; let it show its heavenliness by the amount of heaven which it sets up on earth ; if it fail by these tests, any attempt to uphold it by organised authority is absurd and hopeless. The object of this chapter is to gather into one view three or four marked charac- teristics of the book, simply regarded as a literary composition, and to ask the reader to assign them some value in the argument. At first, we open the Bible for critical, and not for theological purposes, and at once we encounter the difficulty arising from a profusion of peculiar and startling characteristics.

1. The Bible is undoubtedly marked by *a wonderful reserve of power*. Its writers nowhere betray any sign of exhaustion, nor do they display the slightest wish to make the most of their materials in a literary point of view. There are single chapters which any writer could easily have elaborated into a volume. The rule seems to have been to say everything in the fewest possible words. The Bible abounds in indications, brief, vivid, and multitudinous, and is, hence, pre-eminently a text-book. We wonder that the writers do not say more, yet we feel that even in their brevity they have said more than any other men have ever said. They have marvellous skill in perspective. They excite the greatest expectations, and then teach the readers whom they have thus almost frenzied that such expectations are to be held as a discipline, and not to be pushed to a premature fulfilment. The great ambition of other sacred books seems to be to do everything : they put a key into every lock, under every enigma they write at least a conjectural answer, they determine the attitudes and services proper to every hour of the day, and whatever intellectual energy they have is apparently expressible in letter and symbol. They resemble the finite in an ambitious determination to represent the infinite, whereas the Bible repre- sents the infinite in a condescending endeavour to find expression in the finite. The Bible is a perpetual beginning, rich in its immediate satisfactions, but richer still in its promises. Through every revelation there is a hint of another revelation yet to

come. The Bible has a wonderful firmament, out of which the light comes, and the rain, and from which the key of heaven may at any moment drop. Its earth is very legible; its firmament is an eternal mystery. Is this, then, the kind of book which is presumably worthy of a high origin ? In this reserve of power has it any resemblance to the book of physical nature ? In Bashan are there not more acorns than oaks ? Under quiet exteriors are there any fierce energies ? Is there anywhere a sign of exhaustion, as if the creation were almost equal to the Creator ? Completeness may be a sign of weakness. Omnipotence has no final line. When the artist says that he can add nothing further to his picture, he confesses the limitation of his power : the attainment of his ideal is the signature of his weakness. The Bible is full of gaps, of unfinished pictures, of jagged and broken outlines; in the artistic sense of the word there is no perfection—the question is whether there is sufficient astronomic force to overcome all surface inequalities, and to secure the velocity which is rest and the friction which is light. The theologian must determine this, rather than the critic.

2. The Bible grapples with *the highest subjects* which can engage the attention of mankind. A professedly inspired book treating of mere trifles, or of points which are but of secondary interest, would have been the very cruelty of irony. The Bible advances instantly to the highest lines of spiritual inquiry : God, creation, invisible worlds, sin, death, immortality, are its familiar themes. But more important than the fact of its grappling with such subjects is its peculiar method of treating them. Its approach, so to speak, is invariably from the higher side : the Bible *reveals*, it does not *suggest*; it *declares*, it does not *investigate*; all the surprise is on the side of the reader, never on the side of the writer. Looked at in the light of presumptive inspiration, this is precisely the proper result. If God has spoken at all, he must have spoken positively and authoritatively. The *tone* of the Bible is emphatically immodest and exaggerated if it is the tone of mere inquirers or speculators ; on the other hand, it is the only tone (so far as we can judge) that befits the supremacy and condescension of God. The imperative mood, which is seemly in a king, is brusque in an equal and impertinent in an inferior. This is the mood of the Bible. Though its subjects are innumerable,

there is no incertitude in its statement of any one of them ; more, indeed, might have been stated as it appears to our impatience, but more may mean less, as excess of light is equivalent to darkness. The Bible tone is such as befits inspiration, but it is an obvious and fatal mistake if it is *vox et præterea nihil.* Even ordinary men may secure respect when they speak subjunctively, but when they speak imperatively they become ridiculous and contemptible. It is not difficult to distinguish between a bray and a roar.

The precision and weight of the tone will be seen to be the more remarkable when the peculiarity of the revelation is considered. The Bible seems to have a line without a limit. In nature, we seem to be bounded by the horizon ; yet who has measured its diameter, or laid his hand upon the sky line ? We move towards it, yet we never get away from the centre. It is the same with the Divine revelation. Its sky line recedes as we advance. The limit is visible yet unapproachable. We can get to the end of the chapters, yet we never get to the end of the book. The Bible combines a wide liberty with a conspicuous and sacred law of trespass. Its words of promise are rich in incentive and solace ; thus :—"I have many things to say unto you, but ye cannot bear them now " ; " We know in part, and we prophesy in part, but when that which is perfect is come, then that which is in part shall be done away " ; " It doth not yet appear what we shall be " ; " Hereafter ye shall see " ; " When Christ, who is our life, shall appear, then shall ye also appear with him in glory." By such words (were there no other) the Bible separates itself from all other books which claim to convey such sacred communications.

3. Not only does the Bible grapple with the greatest subjects, and pronounce upon them with dogmatic precision and emphasis ; *it so discloses its subjects as to demand the interest of all nations through all time.* The Bible insists upon being the Book of the whole world. It does this, too, in a very wonderful manner. At first it makes no claim as to circulation. By-and-by it becomes a book of much importance to a particular people. Farther on, its language increases in copiousness and boldness. Finally, it declares its leaves to be for the healing of the nations. The change of tone as between the Old Testament and the New is one

of the most remarkable phenomena in all literature. There is a steady, though often imperceptible, movement from the local to the universal : in the Old Testament there is an antiquity which makes one solemn ; so gigantic, so silent, so irreparable, are the ruins of empire, ritual, and fortune ; there we find the thick moss, the biting canker, the seal of death ; and all this strangely interspersed with beauty which must live for ever : in the New Testament there is all the stir of modern life—enterprise, revolution, progress. Men are moving from land to land, speaking in all languages, publishing one Name, and bearing one grim symbol. Is such a movement in keeping with the presumptive inspiration of the book ? The Old Testament having reached the height of sublimity, what eminence remained for the new ? After thunder and pomp, resounding trumpets and tramp of mailed men, there came gentleness and beauty, purity and nobleness, pardon and love. Is such a line of development in keeping with the presumptive inspiration of the book ? What could be more daring than to displace a soldier by a missionary ? This is an anti-climax in history, unless, indeed, it be " the foolishness of God."

Looking at great breadths of history, it is evident that the believers in the Abesta, the Veda, and even the Koran, have not been careful to create a system of world-wide propagation of their respective faiths. Little beyond a military spasm in the case of the last of them has been attempted in this direction. But the believers in the Bible have been impelled to translate it into all languages and to send it into all regions. The Bible has, as a mere matter of fact, forced its way where no other book has ever gone ; and as for the variety of intellect which it has interested in its fortunes, no other writing can bear comparison with it. The coldest and the most ardent temperaments have alike sought to extend its influence : the richest learning and the most splendid eloquence have felt honoured in its service, and the most valorous men have hazarded their lives to publish its contents in hostile lands. They have done this because of the effect of Bible teaching upon their hearts ; necessity was laid upon them, and out of this necessity came their highest joy. Such facts, which can be verified without trouble, show how true it is that the Bible so discloses its subjects as to claim the homage

of all nations through all time. This consideration is evidently of
some value as a practical test of the presumptive inspiration of
the book. If nature be recalled as a witness, we shall be told
that *universality* characterises all the great gifts of God, and
therefore will probably mark any revelation which professes to
have been indited by his Spirit.

4. The Bible contains *the most startling proposition as to the
destruction of sin.* In some respects this is its supreme peculiarity.
The action which the Bible proposes is infinitely more remarkable on the *Divine* side than on the human. How to take *sin*
out of the world is the problem. Let the mind dwell upon the
terms for a moment that their import may be felt. *How* is sin
to be met, overcome, ultimately and for ever destroyed ? By a
poor human struggle ? By self-ablution ? By self-mutilation ?
Is sin to be taken away only by taking away the *sinner ?* What
originality would there be in so obvious and coarse a method ?
The question is how to save the man and destroy the sin, and
the answer to an inquiry so vital cannot but be waited for with
anxious impatience ! In the midst of speculative debate upon the
point, the Bible comes forward with this startling answer : *God
himself will die, the just for the unjust !* If this be not the supreme
blasphemy, it is the very Gospel of God ! One or other it certainly is. It is not an answer that can be spoken of with indifference. As a human suggestion it is utter madness. It is salvation
that is contemplated in the terms of the inquiry, but how can
salvation come by death ? Observe, this immediate argument
does not touch the theology of the proposition ; it is wholly concerned with the mere facts which lie upon the very surface of the
inquiry, the most tragical of which is the proposition that the
just should die for the unjust, and that by the shedding of blood
should come the remission of sins. It is enough, in this connection, that we merely point it out, with the humble confession,
indeed, that if it be not the most awful of all irony, and therefore the most sinful of all sins, it is the most affecting doctrine
that ever appealed to the human heart ! There it is, however,
and the student must deal with it. If he gives it the go-by, he
instantly disqualifies himself for this high investigation ; he flees
from difficulty, and becomes a mere trifler in controversy. If he
takes it up seriously, he may possibly find that it gives articulate

ness to emotions that have long troubled his own heart with a kind of pleasurable pain—the pain of suffering and death, that he might make a way for the pardon and restoration of his own sinning child. The child may never have measured his own sin until he has seen the agony of his father's wounded love. But here we are touching points beyond our argument. This, suffice it now to say, is a mystery not to be illuminated by words—any heart that has suffered much through the sinfulness of others will catch some far-off hint of its meaning; for the rest, there is no interpretation possible to us.

5. The Bible is marked by *a marvellous combination of sublimity and condescension alike as to subject and to method of treatment.* There are heights from which descent would seem to be impossible, and there are familiarities which are apparently too minute and common to permit of return to the highest dignity. Yet the return, in both directions, is made with an ease which, even in a literary point of view, is undoubtedly wonderful, as if the heights and the depths were in reality but one plane to the invisible and ruling Spirit. If astronomic motion smooths the mountainous and rugged surface of earth, what if spiritual velocity make one line of things which to us are high and low, sublime and approachable? What a book is the Bible in the mere matter of variety of contents! Everything seems to be in it : poem, narrative, music, friendship, personal news, national intelligence, judgment, battle, prayer, song, anathema, and benediction. The bush is common enough, but what of the fire which makes the shepherd turn aside ? The bread is such as has been used at supper, yet presently it will become the body of Christ ! Paul is almost in heaven, yet in the very height of his anticipations he asks for his parchments and his cloak, and he knows exactly where both were left. Whole pages are taken up with obscure names, and more is told of a genealogy than of the day of judgment. Stories are half told, and the night falls before we can tell where the victory lay. Where is there anything to correspond with this ? Not in any book, certainly, but in actual life there is the selfsame thing over again without the loss of one line. If the sun could print for us what he sees on any day in the year, he would print a second edition of the Bible. We should have it all over again, including perhaps something even of creation itself, with its light, its

ascending and descending waters, its trees bringing forth each after its kind, its sunny day, its starry night; but the humanity would be the same, still more vividly—family life, love, fear, envy, covetousness, magnanimity; chosen people and alien lands; temples warm with the fire of the Lord, and houses of vain and corrupt idolatry; the noise of war and the song of peace; shepherds keeping their flocks, and soldiers listening for the foe; David in the wilderness and Jonah on the sea; weird dreams, spectral hands on the wall, baffled magicians, and truth-telling prophets; psalms for which no music is good enough, and proverbs that glisten with wit. All these, and more, we should have on every or any day in the year if the sun could but print as well as shine! This is just the Bible. It is a page torn out of the great volume of human life, only torn by the hand of God, and annotated by his Spirit. What is the daily newspaper but a revised translation of the Bible, often, indeed, with God left out in the spelling, though he cannot be left out in reality? Take to-morrow's paper in one hand and the Bible in the other, and see if the paper be not full of repetitions and if there be not something like an echo in all its utterances.

Other indications might be made, but these will do in the meantime, as indicating at least a basis of judgment. Here is a book which is marked by a wonderful reserve of power, which grapples with the greatest subjects which can engage the attention of mankind, which so grapples with them as to demand (under sanctions, too) the attention of all men through all time, which offers the most startling proposition for the removal of sin, and which is marked by a marvellous combination of sublimity and condescension, alike as to subject and to method of treatment. Is such a book, judging by these characteristics, likely to sustain any claim to be an inspired and authoritative revelation of the will of God? We only ask for a *primâ facie* case. If such a case be granted, probably a careful and honest perusal of the Bible will follow, and this will be something gained.

THE SPIRITUAL ORGAN.

" ANY tyro can see the facts for himself if he is provided with those not rare articles a nettle and a microscope." These words are Mr. Huxley's. But why the microscope? Suppose the "tyro" should be provided with "a nettle" only? These inquiries point in a direction which materialists are unwilling to pursue in all its bearings and applications. The introduction of the microscope is an admission that even the keenest eyes cannot see certain substances, forms, and movements without the aid of optical instruments. Great store is to be set by this admission, for it requires in material investigation precisely what is demanded in spiritual inquiry. Suppose that one of Mr. Huxley's students should insist upon examining the nettle without the aid of the microscope, and should declare that he is unable to verify Mr. Huxley's observations? Mr. Huxley would properly reply that the inner structure and life of the nettle could not be seen by the naked eye, for they are microscopically " discerned." Common-sense would confirm the justness of this answer, and hold the student disentitled to pronounce any opinion upon the question. Now this is precisely what St. Paul does in treating the subject of spiritual investigation ; he says that such an investigation cannot be conducted without an organ of which the microscope is a good emblem : " The natural man receiveth not the things of the Spirit of God : for they are foolishness unto him ; neither can he know them, because they are spiritually discerned "—the student without the microscope cannot fully or scientifically examine the plant, neither can any inquirer discern and understand " the things of the Spirit of God," without a spiritual organ adapted to the difficulty of the investigation.

It will be remembered that Mr. Huxley desiderated for the ear something equivalent in service to the use of the microscope ; thus : " The wonderful noonday silence of a tropical forest is, after all, due only to the dulness of our hearing ; and could our ears catch the murmurs of these tiny Mäelstroms as they whirl in the innumerable myriads of living cells which constitute each tree, we should be stunned as with the roar of a great city." If Mr. Huxley could discover an instrument which could do for the ear what the microscope does for the eye, he would be entitled to claim attention to it, and to insist that no judgment respecting the air of a tropical forest was of any scientific value that was not formed by the aid of such instrument. This, again, is precisely the ground taken in the Bible; thus: "He that hath ears to hear, let him hear"—"They have ears to hear and hear not." There is hearing *and* hearing. Let two men listen to the same music; the one shall be held as by a spell, and the other shall become weary and impatient: to the one man the music is a revelation, to the other is a mere noise. In such a case whose judgment would be taken in valuing the music? An artist judging the controversy would say, This is not ordinary music; it is rich in unusual combinations; it cannot be received by the untrained or unsympathetic ear; it can be discerned only by the very spirit of music itself. Such an explanation would be allowed as valid and satisfactory, and the opposing opinion, formed without natural or scientific capability, would be held to be impertinent and worthless. It is just so that St. Paul talks upon Christian subjects. He insists that spiritual things must be compared with spiritual; that the natural man receiveth not the things of the Spirit of God; that such things are actually foolishness unto the natural man, so much so that he can neither receive them nor understand them, for they are spiritually discerned: he also explains why the Gospel is not seen with equal clearness by all men. "If our gospel be hid, it is hid to them that are lost: in whom the god of this world hath blinded the minds of them which believe not, lest the light of the glorious gospel of Christ, who is the image of God, should shine unto them"; and as to his own knowledge of the Gospel, St. Paul says, "I neither received it of man, neither was I taught it, but by the revelation of Jesus Christ." So steadfastly does he stand to it that a spiritual microscope or organ is needed. He allows natural wit, sagacity, penetration, no place in this investigation: the gift is special; the power comes down from God. It will, of course, be easy to deny St. Paul's authority, but mere denial amounts to nothing. In his turn St. Paul might deny the authority of the musical interpreter, and treat with contempt every canon by which painting or eloquence is judged. If we cannot see the organism of a nettle without a microscope, can we see " the things of the Spirit of God " without special illumination ? A man who will not give an opinion upon the exact structure of a grass blade without the help of a microscope ought to be the last man to deny the need of a spiritual organon for the interpretation of spiritual realities. Mr. Huxley will reply that the results of microscopic inquiry are self-illustrative and self-proving ; but that is a mere accident of the case, arising from the fact that the thing examined is itself visible : but when did a microscope reveal a thought, or follow all the excitement of a passion ? Yet thought and passion are susceptible of intellectual and moral analysis. Men understand each other by common sympathies. The mere mathematician does not understand the poet. Silence and speech may be mutual mysteries. Strangers who never saw each other may prove to be kindred in soul. Call it sympathy, affinity, spiritual faculty, or what you may, there is the fact that some kind of organon is needed for the fullest interpretation of all life that is marked by depth and richness. St. Paul gives this fact its spiritual application, or its application to the study of spiritual questions ; he says there is a witness of the Spirit—a Divine shining in the heart—a birth— without which no man can see the kingdom of God. What is there unreasonable in this view, or improbable ? What if religion itself be the instrument through which we read the things of the Spirit of God ?

Another illustration supplied by science itself will point in the same direction. There are two shining surfaces afar off ; they are both equally bright : viewed by the naked eye, there is no difference between them. Now examine them through the polariscope, and the one will show itself to be fire, and the other merely a reflection—not one spark of fire or ray of light in it ! So much for the medium of observation. Yet when Christianity teaches that a special organ is needed for the interpretation of spiritual things, the materialist demurs and objects. Science itself being witness, the most piercing eye needs microscopic help ; yet science is occasionally unjust enough to deny to others what is indispensable to itself. St. John attributes spiritual knowledge to "an unction from the Holy One," and St. Paul teaches the same doctrine in words very clear and strong : "Since the beginning of the world men have not heard, nor perceived by the ear, neither hath the eye seen it, O God, beside thee, what he hath prepared for him that waiteth for him" (Isa. lxiv. 4), . . . "*but God hath revealed it unto us by his Spirit : for the Spirit searcheth all things, yea, the deep things of God*" (1 Cor. ii. 10). Such words show that the difficulty of spiritual interpretation was felt long before modern scientists propounded their non-spiritual theories, and they show also that the difficulty was met in the only practicable way, namely, by requiring a spiritual organ for the interpretation of spiritual personalities and doctrines. Christian thinkers might have been troubled if no provision had been made for the treatment of this materialistic objection, for then it would have seemed as if " the whole armour of God " was short of one weapon ; but the folly was answered before the fool had spoken, that no one might imagine he had gotten an advantage against God.

It may be difficult to express in one word the nature of this spiritual organ, impossible, indeed, unless we go to Jesus Christ, who came to reveal the Father. He will give us the universal term. In the Old Testament we have hints, broken and scattered lights, of which we can make little that is complete and final, but in the sayings of Jesus and the writings which grew out of them we find terms which cover all things. In the New Testament there is one answer to all the great questions which excite human thinking; thus : What is God ? God is *love.* What is the greatest commandment ? Thou shalt *love.* To whom will God reveal himself ? " He that *loveth* me shall be loved of my Father, and I will love him, and will manifest myself to him." Love is the universal language—the child knows it, and the savage ; it blesses earth, and is the very heavenliness of heaven. Not only so ; it is the secret of all success, as it is the inspiration of all labour. And more still, it is not only true of Jesus that manifestation follows love ; it is equally true of all ordinary things, and therefore presumptively true of spiritual illumination and progress. It may be helpful to the main argument to dwell upon this thought for a moment. To whom will any earnest *man* most unreservedly manifest himself ? To a friend or to an enemy ?

To a cold critic or a sympathetic listener? Let two of his acquaintances or even kinsfolk be equally intelligent and honest, yet let one of them excel the other in tenderness or appreciativeness, in that one indescribable element which expresses itself in welcome and hospitality—not the welcome of ceremony, or the hospitality of bread—and to which of them will he manifest most of his inner life? He will in effect use the words of Jesus Christ, "I will manifest myself to him that loveth me." This is the testimony of universal experience. To whom will *nature* reveal itself—the sea, the hill, the light? To the clown or to the poet? The poet gets something out of "the meanest flower that blows." Appreciation creates for itself new heavens and a new earth. The wise listener hears music in the wind, the stream, and the twitter of unfamed birds. What does the clown hear, or the sordid man? Noises without order, tongues unknown and uninterpreted. Nature says precisely what Jesus Christ says— "I will manifest myself to him that loveth me." Illustrations are afforded by every aspect of life. We get out of nature and art what we ourselves bring to them. The Royal Academy is a show of coloured canvas, or a church of lofty and sacred genius, according to the capacity, the sympathy, or the reverence of the observer; any dog may see the canvas, but only a painter or a poet can see the picture. We have here, then, a continuance of the same reasonableness that marked the use of instruments, and in addition we have a tender graciousness expressed in the fact that the organ is a simple and universal faculty, which every man holds as part of his very manhood, and which he can exercise under all possible conditions of life.

A remarkable expression, in harmony with this interpretation of love, is used by St. Paul in his epistle to the Romans: "The carnal mind is enmity against God; for it is not subject to the law of God, neither indeed can be"; enmity is set in opposition to love, and carnality in opposition to spiritual-mindedness. The carnal mind is not only enmity against godliness, or some modification or form of religion; it is enmity against *God*— the controversy is not with a fraction, but with the whole number. But the carnal mind! is not that a remarkable contradiction in terms? Not in terms only, but also in actual life, for the anomaly is known to every observer of human

nature. Mind may be so overpowered by the gratification of
animal appetites as to become the minor quantity in manhood,
the body so overgrown as almost to have absorbed the soul.
Where this is the case the very idea of *God* is repugnant, because
that idea necessitates government, discipline, responsibility, all of
which, again, are founded upon absolute and infinite holiness.
Such a mind is at perpetual enmity against God : it is not subject
to the law of God (carrying the ideas of government, discipline,
and responsibility), neither indeed can be ; " They that are in
the flesh cannot please God "—·" The world cannot receive the
Spirit of truth, because it seeth him not, neither knoweth him."
More than the gratification of bodily appetites is involved in
being "in the flesh" or having "the carnal mind." Self-gratification is a wide term ; it is interchangeable with self-trust, self-
sufficiency, self-completeness, or self-idolatry. Such selfhood
always exists to the exclusion of spirituality ; it is enmity against
God, and, properly understood, it is enmity against human nature
and against society. The reasonableness of this ought to be
acknowledged by scientists even of the most irreligious class, for
the moment they touch any medium or instrument of observation
they acknowledge their own incompleteness, and their consequent
need of help. The self-satisfied mind is enmity against science as
much as against religion. It declares its own sufficiency, and by
so much it declines offers of illumination or advancement. St.
Paul, therefore, was stating a universal truth when he said that
" the carnal mind is enmity against God." Docility is one of the
first conditions of improvement, but docility and self-sufficiency
are incompatible ; there is a controversy between them, and
according to the settlement of that contention will be the spirit
and character of the future man.

From these observations it will be seen that in declining the
leadership of the materialists we justify ourselves by denying
their qualification to judge spiritual questions. Intellectual
vigour as applied in one direction accounts for nothing in such
qualification : "Having eyes, they see not ; having ears, they hear
not ; and having hearts, they do not understand." Among them
that are born of women there may not have appeared men of
greater intellectual capacity, but he that is least in the kingdom
of God is greater than their chief or king. Evidently so, for it is

a higher kingdom altogether, involving destinies and conferring advantages which cannot be described in comparative terms. The great error which scientists have committed is having, *as such,* taken upon themselves to give any opinion upon spiritual subjects ; and religious men would commit a similar error if, *as such,* they undertook to pronounce judgment upon purely scientific questions. A man who has familiarised himself with the organism of a nettle is not *therefore* entitled to give an opinion upon the inspiration of the Bible, any more than is a man who can compose a sermon *therefore* qualified to criticise a painting. Scientists, too, may avail themselves of the very questionable advantage of supposing themselves able to ignore religion, whereas religious men are bound by their very loyalty to the Christian faith to encourage and applaud the progress of science, and to turn such progress into an occasion of religious thankfulness. Scientists have at present the charm of novelty, almost romance, whilst religious thinkers are reposing upon truths ripened and mellowed by centuries, yet capable of adaptation to the demands of current experience and progress. Controversy between science and religion is wholly out of place, and was not begun by religion. Science, falsely so called, and vain philosophy have been consistently condemned by Christian apostles, but the very terms show reverence for what is true and solid both in the one and in the other. Probably that controversy will not be allayed until the relationships (as distinguished from the dogmas) of religion and science be adjusted. Science marks but a single province of human inquiry, and (not impossibly) is as at present pursued limited to one section of one world ; religion, on the other hand, touches the whole circle of human life, and rules the spirit and habitudes of all worlds. To compare the universal with the limited is to be unjust to both, and to exalt the limited above the universal is to replace the sun with a private lamp. Religion and science has each its peculiar mystery ; and if the one is to be avoided or discredited on account of its difficulties, the other must fall by the rigour of the same law.

In his " Synthetic Philosophy (First Principles)" Mr. Herbert Spencer concludes an elaborate and able chapter on ultimate religious ideas with a remarkable suggestion bearing upon this argument. Having expounded a good many theories, and shown the insufficiency of a good many hypotheses, he says, "Thus the mystery which all religions recognise turns out to be a far more transcendent mystery than any of them suspect—not a relative, but an absolute mystery. . . . The Power which the universe manifests to us is utterly inscrutable." In a theologian this tone would have been regarded as dogmatic; certainly its modesty is well hidden by its decisive vigour. But is the doctrine true? So far as the Bible is concerned, it is *not* true that the absolute inscrutableness of the Power was unsuspected. On the contrary, it is affirmed in manifold terms, and specially declared by Jesus Christ. "No man knoweth the Father save the Son"; "No man hath seen God at any time"; "No man can see God and live." A recollection of such sentences would have modified the breadth of the foregoing assertion, and brought down its argumentative value to its proper nothingness. We have already pointed out that this is a question of *revelation*; the inscrutableness is granted ("Who can find out God, or know the Almighty unto perfection?"), but the distinct revelation is also affirmed by Jesus Christ, and that affirmation has created for itself too great an influence in the world to be simply ignored. At the risk of retraversing a few steps, it may be well to recall the emphasis of that affirmation, "The only begotten Son, which is in the bosom of the Father, he hath declared him"; "No man knoweth the Father, save the Son, and he to whomsoever the Son will reveal him"; "I have manifested thy name unto the men which thou gavest me out of the world"; "As the Father knoweth me, even so know I the Father"; "If ye had known me, ye should have known my Father also." With declarations such as these before us, identified with a name upon which a Church is founded, and supported by a character whose purity and beneficence have excited the wonder of the world, is it fair on the part of any philosopher to dwell upon the inscrutableness of God as if no revelation had at all events been professed? If Mr. Herbert Spencer had never heard of the Christian faith, he could only have stopped where he has done so; but with that faith before him, he was bound to respect it, at least on intellectual grounds. We insist that it be remembered that Mr. Herbert Spencer has not treated the Christian argument, con-

sidered as an anticipation of his own theory, and that therefore
the paganism of his logic should not be taken for more than it is
worth.

Looking at the whole ground thus traversed, two convictions
have been strengthened by the anti-Christian argument :—
First, that the theoretical exclusion of the spiritual element,
instead of diminishing the mystery of human life, greatly and
painfully increases it. Viewing the whole question as lying
within the province of reason, it is to us *easier* to believe that
behind all visible things there is an infinite and eternal Spirit
than to believe that all things are self-existent, self-dependent,
and wholly material. Our opinion upon this point has been
clearly expressed by the author just quoted —" The atheistic
theory is not only absolutely unthinkable, but even if it were
thinkable, would not be a solution: the assertion that the universe
is self-existent does not really carry us a step beyond the
cognition of its present existence, and so leaves us with a mere
restatement of the mystery." Reason itself is more satisfied with
the theory of an independent origin and a supreme rule than
with the theory of no origin and no supremacy. If any man
could make good a proposition to give us a doctrine of the
universe without mystery, and that would satisfy all the inquiries
of reason, he would come into the discussion with immense
advantage ; but instead of such a proposition, we are invited to
accept a theory which treats a part as if it were the whole, and
offers no answer to the wonder and the sorrow of human life. If
the Bible were removed from civilisation, it would leave more
mystery behind it than it would take away, with this difference, too : that whilst without it we should have mystery cold,
dark, and despairing, with it we have mystery relieved by light
and accompanied by the most pathetic and comforting promises.
It cannot be too constantly remembered that the Bible itself
fully recognises its own mysteries, and never once asks to be
accepted on the ground that it removes every difficulty from
human thinking, and renders it impossible for the human intellect to confound itself by impious speculation. From beginning
to end there is mystery in the Bible, but is it not just such
mystery as the awfulness of eternity might be supposed to throw

upon the narrow and troubled way of time? Is not a man a mystery to a child? And being such, is his existence to be denied or his superiority to be questioned? The child himself is a mystery, and the man is but a continuation of the same difficulty. There is a mystery that is natural and proper, even necessary, so to say; and there may be a mystery which is simply arbitrary, or a mystery to those only who refuse to avail themselves of proffered light. Is there any monotony so intolerable as life would be without mystery? Every day brings its own secret, and the surprise of the coming hour is often its keenest joy. Properly understood, it may be that mystery is but the longer word for mercy. We are drawn forward by the mighty and often gracious power of the *unknown*. What is beyond the next curve on the road? May not to-morrow open our prison door? By such questioning is melancholy kept at bay, and weakness preserved from despair. All our life is set in mystery, from the cradle to the grave : education, enterprise, art, wit, poetry, music, are all caught in the same cloud, a cloud often dark, yet with fringes of light and rents through which the blue is seen. Reduce the universe to a self-existent, self-ruling, and self-terminating machine, and still there will remain the mysteries : How came it to be? By what means is it kept together? How did we come into it? What is the final appeal of right against wrong? And what is there, if anything, beyond death? Materialism is deficient in compass : it cannot comprehend the whole case : its analysis of a leaf is admirable, but it is lost amidst the secrets of the heart—it creates more mysteries than it removes, and in the long run it aggravates itself into the greatest mystery of all.

Second, the non-spiritual argument has strengthened the conviction that any creed which discourages the pure aspirations or destroys the honourable hopes of mankind is presumptively untrue. It will not be denied that in the human heart there is a " pleasing hope, a fond desire, a longing after immortality." This aspiration brings the most elevating and chastening influences to bear upon human thinking and human activity, and is, on that account, likely to be the expression of a profound spiritual reality. Its extinction would not only leave a great void in the heart; it would also remove encouragements and restraints which are needful to the highest development of strength and the most healthful discipline of character. Granted that goodness should be valued and pursued for its own sake, yet goodness itself is impaired alike in quality and in quantity by being withdrawn from the infinite relationships and bearings which are recognised by Christianity ; it is degraded within measurable and even variable limits, and is in danger of being treated with cunning manipulation and used for selfish purposes. Not only so ; immunities are granted to vice, so long as it is wily enough to escape the clutches of the law, by assuring the vicious man that when he has played out his last trick he is as well off as the man who has vainly troubled himself with a conscience, seeing that they both pass into everlasting darkness and silence. If in the common affairs of life men are moved by hope, it is but a fuller application of the same law which is found in the influence of Christian aspiration, the one being the limited, the other the unlimited term. Besides this, any doctrine that promises the universal establishment of righteousness—which asserts the coming of judgment upon every form of evil, and the raising up of every virtue that has been trampled upon—commends itself to the understanding and the conscience of man as a doctrine that is presumptively true. It is, in fact, the one doctrine that is needed as the inspiration of honest men and the defence of all holy and generous interests. Under its authority and consolation men can wait hopefully, and whilst they are waiting they can urge the judgments of God upon the attention of evil-doers. Withdraw this doctrine, and it is impossible to deny that a great loss has been inflicted upon the human family, a loss which must be the more keenly felt because all the arrangements of civilised society have been pointed in the very direction of its truthfulness, that is to say, society has been aiming, in all its encouragements of virtue and all its repressions of vice, to generate a social religion, and establish a commonwealth in which reprobacy shall be reduced to a minimum. But these local attempts have been founded upon what appeared to be a universal authority, and have drawn their sanctions from it. Deny that authority or impair it, and you loosen the bonds of social organisation, and discourage every hope of perfect union and world-wide peace. Christian doctrine cannot be simply ignored or banished. It has wrought itself too thoroughly into the living tissue of society to be removed without necessitating the most intricate and serious consequences. Not only will there be required a reconstruction of society as it exists in Christendom, but every man who has been moved by Christian aspiration will, so to speak, have to divest himself of his old consciousness, and start his whole life from a new centre; in a word, he will have to give the lie to himself, and put to silence all the voices of his own nature which have hitherto been to him as the echoes of the voice of God.

With that wonderful completeness which we have pointed out as belonging to the Bible, the very ground of scientists, so far as they dwell upon the materiality and limitations of human life, has been anticipated in the pages of revelation. It was not reserved for the microscope to find out man's weakness, or to teach him to look to the plants of the field for types of his frailty and perishableness. It might be supposed, from much that has passed under our review, that not until quite recently was it known that there is a protoplasm common to man and to the fading grass; a quotation or two will show how mistaken would be this supposition : "As for man, his days are as grass : as a flower of the field, so he flourisheth. For the wind passeth over it, and it is gone; and the place thereof shall know it no more"; "He cometh forth as a flower, and is cut down"; "We all do fade as a leaf." The Bible does not leave man without humiliation as to the tenure of earthly life : The Lord "knoweth our frame; he remembereth that we are dust"; "He remembered that they were but flesh; a wind that passeth away, and cometh not again"; "What is your life? It is even a vapour, that appeareth for a little time, and then vanisheth away." Humiliation enough, long before Mr. Huxley came "with those not rare articles a nettle and a microscope." On the other hand, the Bible never fails to magnify the inner and better life of man, thus : "The world passeth away, and the lust thereof : but he that doeth the will of God abideth for ever"; "Thou hast made him a little lower than the angels, and hast crowned him with glory and honour"; "As we have borne the image of the earthy, we shall also bear the image of the heavenly"; "It doth not yet appear what we shall be; we shall be like him; for we shall see him as he is"; "We know, that if our earthly house of this tabernacle were dissolved, we have a building of God, an house not made with hands, eternal in the heavens."

Dr. Tyndall, whose writings cannot be read without the highest advantage, does, indeed, allow that something more than pure materialism is needed to meet the whole circle of human want. With great beauty, he says : "The circle of human nature is not complete without the arc of feeling and emotion. The lilies of the field have a value for us beyond their botanical ones—a certain lightening of the heart accompanies the declaration that 'Solomon in all his glory was not arrayed like one of these.' The sound of the village bell which comes mellowed from the valley to the traveller upon the hill has a value beyond its acoustical one. The setting sun, when it mantles with the bloom of roses the Alpine snows, has a value beyond its optical one. Round about the intellect sweeps the horizon of emotions from which all our noblest impulses are derived." Yet, in the face of these admissions, Dr. Tyndall would, unless we greatly misinterpret his meaning, take special care to exclude theology as a possible help to the full satisfaction of human nature. It is not to the theologian, but the poet, that he extends the hand of welcome: "I think the poet will have a great part to play in the future of the world. To him it is given for a long time to come to fill those stores which the recession of the theologic tide has left exposed; to him, when he rightly understands his mission and does not flinch from the tonic discipline which it assuredly demands, we have a right to look for that heightening and brightening of life which so many of us need. He ought to be the interpreter of that power which, as

'Jehovah, Jove, or Lord,'

has hitherto filled and strengthened the human heart." Such an admission has meaning in it, and hope, notwithstanding the dislike, latent rather than fully expressed, of theological study and suggestion. There are not wanting men, whose intellectual power Dr. Tyndall himself would be the first to recognise and honour, who believe that the "Poet" has already come with the "interpretation," and the solace. What if they be right? Dr.

Tyndall is longing for a poet; other men, whom he would cal¹ great and good, think that in Jesus Christ they have found the " Interpreter " of that power which has been named " Jehovah, Jove, or Lord." Certainly Jesus called him by the name of Father, and spoke much of his love and care. No tenderer words were ever spoken; no deeper words ever challenged intellectual attention; and as for noble deeds, his life is full of them. What the " poet " can do more than Jesus did in the interpretation of God, we cannot even imagine. When he blessed little children, and gave lost women a new beginning of life ; when he brought the prodigal home, and delivered the poor from the spoiler; and did all this as the will of his Father,—it is not to be wondered at that some bruised and despairing hearts should have taken him as their Poet, their Teacher, and their Lord. It seemed as if he was the very Refuge which men needed, and a very present help in time of trouble. His voice always sounded as if it *might* have been God's own ; there was so much pathos in it, so much real lovingkindness, and such a sounding of something far off and unknown. Possibly, too, those outcast women may have seen further than some proud thinkers, and have known through their very sin and its mortal pain more of Christ's real nature than could ever be known by self-righteousness and supposed infallibility. Shall we, then, cast off this Man thoughtlessly, and bear our sorrow in darkness, until a poet come with new songs and unheard rhythms ? The question is serious enough, and much may depend upon the answer. We believe that poets will come generation after generation until the end of time, but we have no hope that any of them will call God by a tenderer name than Father, or propose a higher obedience than purity and love.

PRAYER.

ALMIGHTY GOD, teach us thy greatness through thy goodness, lest we be affrighted, and become as men in whom there is no strength. We would see thy glory, but our eyes could not bear the light; may we therefore see thy mercy, and become accustomed to the milder glory. Show us that thy pity is great, that thy love itself is glorious, and thus, little by little, as we are able to bear it, do thou continue and complete the revelation of thyself to our wondering and grateful hearts. Thou dost grow upon us like an increasing light; continue so to do until there be in us no darkness at all, our whole life beautiful with the presence of thy glory, cleansed and purified by the fire of thy righteousness.

We bless thee for thy great care over us: our bones are thine; thou dost set them down one by one in thy record book: the very hairs of our head are all numbered; thou dost count our steps and hedge about our way, and with manifold defences and innumerable ministries dost thou train us in this ever-wonderful life. We cannot tell what to-morrow may bring forth; therefore dost thou call upon us to crowd our energy into the present moment, and make it hot with noble and strenuous endeavour to be good and to do right. Help us to dismiss to-morrow from our thoughts; may it have no place in our dreamings; may we be men of to-day, urgent and rapid as those who are upon the king's business.

Thou hast given us houses to dwell in; thou dost spread our table morning, noon, and night; a hundred springs of joy and comfort thou dost cause to burst forth around us. Thou dost keep the roof upon our head, even when the storm breaks upon it with utmost fury. Behold, thou dost kindle our fire; thy hand is round about the light of our lamp. We therefore still bless thee with new hymns and ever-enlarging and heightening songs; yea, our whole life would become one swelling psalm, rising unto heaven, expressing our daily love, our continual and inviolable trust. By the grace of God we are what we are. Thou didst fill up the pit into which our feet had well nigh fallen. Thou didst bring down the high places which made us fear—behold, thou didst smite the mighty archers of Kedar, and make those who boasted themselves therein as hirelings who had but a year to live. Thou rulest the ragings of the sea; thou makest stars that fit the darkness of the night; thou dost cause thy chariot wheels to become eyes, fierce amid their brightness, to all pursuing enemies; thou dost find a path for us in the wilderness, and rivers break out in unexpected places. Thou art worthy to receive from us glory and power and majesty and riches; hear the ascriptions of our burning gratitude and return the same into our hearts as heavenly benedictions.

We bless thee that we are here, for this is none other than the house of

God and the gate of heaven. We know the language of the place; it has become as our native tongue by its familiar tenderness. Behold, here we meet a great cloud of witnesses, the sainted and honoured dead who are round about the throne, and are looking on with eyes that never tire nor sleep. The Lord grant unto us all the power and inspiration of the most sacred memories that gather around the holy place! We remember our sin, but in the presence of thy grace it is as nothing. Where sin abounds grace doth much more abound. Thou dost cause life to overflow death, and immortality thou dost cause to outshine all the mean lustre of this present moment. So thou dost meet our sin with the infinite grace that is in Christ Jesus. The blood of Jesus Christ, thy Son, cleanseth from all sin. We leave our burden at the Cross; we shall never find it more.

Hear the hearts that are full of prayer, that cannot utter their desires because of the vehemency of their secret emotion. Hear the parent who wonders where the wanderer is, and would offer him a thousand welcomes if he would return. Hear the mother who must live in her sighs, because she dare not put them into speech, so keen and poignant her yearnings after those who are out of the way. Hear thou the unuttered desires of the penitent, the man who would return if he could find some secret door by which to come stealthily into his father's dishonoured house; find such a way for him thyself, this very day, and make this the birthday of his soul, the beginning of a blessed immortality. Hear us for our loved ones who are sick, mighty Physician, tender Nurse, go into all our sick chambers, and by the brightness of thy presence bring healing to the souls that must soon quit their tenements of clay.

The Lord look upon the old man tottering over his staff and looking into his grave; the Lord's own fingers touch the cheek of the babe cooing and crowing in his cradle; the Lord's eyes be for good upon the bent old woman, who has seen the measure of her time and longs for the city of rest! The Lord break the bones of every evil man and turn his counsel into night and confusion and trouble, and bring him thereby not to ruin, but to contrition! The Lord unsettle the foundations of every iniquitous throne; the Lord baffle the decrees and the counsels of every wicked empire and prosper every man that endeavours to do good with simplicity and earnestness!

The Lord hear us in these things! We are always in his arms; may he now draw us still more closely to his heart! Amen.

THE UNKNOWABLE GOD.

"God is great, and we know him not."—JOB xxxvi. 26.

GOD—Unknown, Unknowable; even so, yet not the less the one Reality, and the one Energy of the universe. What it is possible to *know* it must be possible to explain, to put into an equal number of words, which, being all set together, sum themselves into the exact measure of the thing that is known. What can be known can of course be contained by the faculty which knows it. The vessel is of necessity larger than its contents. It, then, any faculty of mine knows God, that faculty contains God, and is in that sense larger than God, which is impossible and absurd. Whatever I can know is, by the very fact that I can know it, less than I am ; bigger, it may be, as to mere size in length and breadth, a huge disc that glares with light, or a globe flying fast, yet with speed that can be set down in so many ciphers or lines of ciphers on a child's slate, so clearly that we can say : It is so much an hour the great wings fly, and not one mile more. What is that but mere bigness, an appeal to our easily excited wonder, a Size that shakes our pride and bids us mind our ways, or a weight may fall upon us from the sky ? It is nothing but infinitised mud, nothing but an ascertainable quantity and intensity of fire—a wide and high stair leading to nothing !

Unknown—Unknowable. Thanks. I am tired of the Known and the Knowable, tired of saying this star is fifty millions of miles in circumference, that star is ninety millions of miles farther off than the moon, and yonder planet is five million times larger than the earth. It is mere gossip in polysyllables, getting importance by hugeness, something that would never be named in inches, and that owes its fame to the word *millions*. It is so that men want to make a mouthful of God ! A great mouthful, no doubt, say even to the extent of super-millions squared and cubed into a whole slateful of ciphers, but pro-nounceable in words ! Failing this, they suppose they have destroyed him by saying he is Unknowable and Unknown. It makes me glad to think he is ! That any One or any Thing should be unknowable and should yet invite and stimulate inquiry is educationally most hopeful. O soul of mine, there are grand times in store for thee ! I cannot rattle my staff against the world's boundary wall, and say, The End !—Poor staff ! It thrusts itself into a cloud ; it goes over the edge ; it is like to be pulled out of my hand by gravitation from another centre stronger than the earth's core, a gravitation that pulls even the earth itself and keeps it from reeling and falling. Yes, prying staff, thou canst touch nothing but a most ghostly emptiness. Soul of man, if thou wouldst truly see—see the Boundless, see the Possible, see God—go into the dark when and where the darkness is thickest. That is the mighty and solemn sanctuary of vision. The light is vulgar in some uses. It shows the mean and vexing detail of space and life with too gross a palpableness, and frets the sensitiveness of the eyes. I must find the healing darkness that has never been measured off into millions and paraded as a nameable quantity of surprise and mystery. *Deus absconditus.* God hideth himself, oftenest in the light; he *touches* the soul in the gloom and vastness of night, and the soul, being true in its intent and wish, answers the touch without a shudder or a blush. It is even so that God comes to me. He does not come through man's high argument, a flash of human wit, a sudden and audacious answer to an infinite enigma, or a toilsome reply to some high mental challenge. His path is through the pathless darkness—without a footprint to show where he stepped; through the forest of the night he comes; and when he comes the brightness is all within! My God—unknown and unknowable—cannot be chained as a Prisoner of logic, or delivered into the custody of a theological proposition, or figured into literal art. Shame be the portion of those who have given him a setting within the points of the compass, who have robed him in cloth of their own weaving, and surnamed him at the bidding of their cold and narrow fancy! For myself, I know that I cannot know him, that I have a joy wider than knowledge, a conception that domes itself above my best thinking, as the sky domes itself in infinite pomp and lustre above the earth whose beauty it creates. God! God! God! best defined when undefined; a Fire that may not be touched; a Life too great for shape or image; a Love for which there is no equal name. Who is he? God. What is he? God. Of whom begotten? God. He is at once the question and the answer, the self-balance, the All.

We have tried to build our way up to him by using many words with some cunning and skill. We have thought to tempt him into our cognition by the free use of flattering adjectives. Surely, said we, he will pour his heart's wine into the golden goblets which we hold to catch the sacred stream. We have called him Creator, Sovereign, Father; then Infinite Creator, Eternal Sovereign, Gracious Father, as if we could build up our word-bricks to heaven and surprise the Unknown and the Unknowable in his solitude, and look upon him face to face. We have come near to blasphemy herein. What wonder had we been thrust through with a dart! We have thought our Yesterday roomy enough to hold God's Eternity, and have offered him with every show of abounding sufficiency the hospitality of our ever-changing words as a medium of revelation. *Our* words! Words that come and go like unstable fashions. Words that die of very age; words that cannot be accepted unanimously in all their suggestions and relations even by two men. Into these words we have invited God, and because he cannot come into them but as a devouring fire, we have stood back in offence and unbelief. God! God! God! ever hidden, ever present, ever distant, ever near; a Ghost, a Breath, making the knees knock in terror, ripping open a grave at the very feet of our pleasure, a mocking laugh at the feast, filling all space like the light, yet leaving room for all his creatures; a Terror, a Hope—Undefinable, Unknow able, Irresistible, Immeasurable. God is a Spirit!

Undefinable, Unknown, Unknowable, Invisible, Incomprehen-sible, grim negatives, emptinesses that deceive us by their vast hollowness, and nothing more, are these surly words. The wrong word is to blame for the wrong conclusion. We have chosen the very worst word in our haste, and have needlessly humbled ourselves in doing so. We have made a wall of the word when we might have made it into six wings, twain to cover the face, twain to cover the feet, and twain with which to fly. Instead of Unknowable, Invisible, Incomprehensible, say Super-knowable, Supervisible, Supercomprehensible, and at once the right point of view is reached and the mystery is made luminous. From the *Un*knowable I turn away humiliated and discouraged; from the *Super*knowable I return humbled, yet inspired. The *Un*knowable says: Fool, why bruise thy knuckles in knocking at the final granite as if it were a door that could be opened? The *Super*knowable says: There is something larger than thy intelli-gence; a Secret, a Force, a Beginning, a God! Evermore is the difficulty in the lame *word* and not in the solemn truth. We make no progress in religion whilst we keep to our crippled feet; in its higher aspects and questionings it is not a road to walk upon, it is an open firmament to fly in. Alas for his progress who mistakes crutches for wings! Yet this absurdity has so recommended itself to our coldness as to win the name of prudence, sobriety, and self-suppression. We have lost the broad and mighty pinions that found their way to heaven's gate, and the eye of burning love that looked steadfastly into the sacred cloud. We have now taken to walking, and our lame feet pick their uncertain way over such stones as Unknown, Unknowable, Invisible, Incomprehensible, and we finish our toilsome journey exactly where we began it. Enthusiasm sees God. Love sees God. Fire sees God. But we have escaped the revealing, because sympathetic, fire, and have built our prudent religion upon the sand. On the sand! Think of it! So we go to it, and walk around it, and measure it, and break it up into propositions, and placard it on church walls, and fight about it with infinite clamour and some spitefulness. My soul, amid all Unknowableness, Incomprehensibleness, and other vain and pompous nothings, hold fast to the faith that thou canst *know* God, and yet know nothing merely *about* him; know him by love and pureness, and not know *about* him by intellectual art or theological craft.

Invisible! This is what the Bible itself says. The invisibleness of God is not a scientific discovery; it is a Biblical revelation; it is a part of the Bible. "No man hath seen God at any time"— "No man can see God and live." This is the difficulty of all life, and the higher the life the higher the difficulty. No man can see *himself* and live! He can see his incarnation, but his very *self*— the pulse that makes him a man—he has never seen, he can never see! Anatomy says it has never found the soul, and adds, "Therefore there is no soul." The reasoning o'erleaps itself and takes away its own life by rude violence. Has anatomy found *Genius*? Has the surgical knife opened the chamber in which *Music* sings and seen the Singer? Or has anatomy laid its finger upon *Imagination* and held it up, saying, "Behold, the mighty wizard"? But if there is no soul, simply because anatomy has never found one, then there is no genius, no music, no imagination, no chivalry, no honour, no sympathy, because the surgeon's knife has failed to come upon them in wounding and hacking the human frame! Anatomise the dead poet and the dead ass, and you will find as much genius in the one as in the other; *therefore* there is no genius! Who that valued his life would set his foot on such a bridge as that rickety "therefore"? But some men will venture upon any bridge that seems to lead away from God ; a very simple anatomy will find the reason ; it is because " they DO NOT LIKE to retain God in their hearts "—it is not because of intellectual superiority, but because of moral distaste. An internal cancer accounts for this invincible aversion.

Unknown ; Unknowable ; truly, yet not on that account un-usable and unprofitable. That is a vital distinction. The master of science humbly avows that he has not a theory of magnetism ; does he therefore ignore it, or decline to inquire into its uses ? Does he reverently write its name with a big M, and run away from it shaken and whitened by a great fear ? Verily he is no such fool. He actually *uses* what he does not *understand*. I will accept his example and bring it to bear upon the religious life. I do not scientifically know God ; the solemn term does not come within the analysis which is available to me ; God is great, and I know him not : yet the term has its practical *uses* in life, and into those broad and obvious uses all men may inquire. What part does the God of the Bible play in the life of the man who accepts him and obeys him with all the inspiration and•diligence of love ? Any creed that does not come down easily into the daily life to purify and direct it is by so much imperfect and useless. I cannot read the Bible without seeing that God (as there revealed) has ever moved his believers in the direction of *courage* and *sacrifice*. These two terms are multitudinous, involving others of kindred quality, and spreading themselves over the whole space of the upper life. In the direction of courage, not mere animal courage, for then the argument might be matched by gods many, yet still *gods*, though their names be spelt without capitals ; but *moral* courage, noble heroism, fierce rebuke of personal and national corruption, sublime and pathetic judgment of all good and all evil. The God-idea made mean men valiant soldier-prophets ; it broadened the piping voice of the timid inquirer into the thunder of the national teacher and leader ; for brass it brought gold, and for iron silver, and for wood brass, and for stones iron ; instead of the thorn it brought up the fir-tree, and instead of the brier the myrtle-tree, and it made the bush burn with fire. Wherever the God-idea took complete possession of the mind every faculty was lifted up to a new capacity, and borne on to heroic attempts and conquests. The saints who received it subdued kingdoms, wrought righteousness, obtained promises, stopped the mouths of lions; quenched the violence of fire, out of weakness were made strong, waxed valiant in fight, turned to flight the armies of the aliens.   Any idea that so inspired in man life and hope is to be examined with reverent care.   The *quality* of the courage determines its value, and the value of the idea which excited and sustained it.   What is true of the courage is true also of the *sacrifice* which has ever followed the acceptance of the God-idea.   Not the showy and fanatical sacrifice of mere blood-letting; many a Juggernaut, great and small, drinks the blood of his devotees; but spiritual discipline, self-renunciation, the esteeming of others better than one's self, such a suppression of the self-thought as to amount to an obliteration of every motive and purpose that can be measured by any single personality, such are the practical *uses* of the God-idea. It is not a barren sentiment.   It is not a coloured vapour or a scented incense, lulling the brain into partial stupor or agitating it with mocking dreams : it arouses courage ; it necessitates self sacrifice; it touches the imagination as with fire; it gives a wide and solemn outlook to the whole nature ; it gives a deeper tone to every thought; it sanctifies the universe ; it makes heaven possible.   Unknown—Unknowable.   Yes, but not therefore unusable or unprofitable.

Say this God was dreamed by human genius.   Be it so.   Make him a creature of *fancy*.   What then ?   The man who made, or dreamed, or otherwise projected *such* a God must be the author of some *other* work of equal or approximate importance.   Produce it !   That is the sensible reply to so bold a blasphemy. Singular if man has made a Jehovah and then has taken to the drudgery of making oil paintings, and ink poems, and huts to live in.   Where is the congruity ?   A man says he kindled the *sun*, and when asked for his proof he strikes a *match* which the wind blows out !   Is the evidence sufficient ?   Or a man says that he has covered the earth with all the green and gold of summer, and, when challenged to prove it, he produces a wax flower which melts in his hands !   Is the proof convincing ?   The God of the Bible calls for the *production* of other gods—gods wooden, gods stony, gods ill-bred, gods well-shaped, and done up skilfully for market uses; from his heavens he laughs at them, and from his high throne he holds them in derision. He is not afraid of competitive gods. They try to climb to his sublimity, and only get high enough to break their necks in a sharp fall. Again and again I demand that the second effort of human genius bear some obvious relation to the first. The sculptor accepts the challenge, so does the painter, so does the musician; why should the Jehovah-dreamer be an exception to the common rule of confirmation and proof? We wait for the evidence. We insist upon having it; and, that we may not waste our time in idle expectancy, we will meanwhile call upon God, saying, " Our Father which art in heaven, Hallowed be thy name. Thy kingdom come. Thy will be done in earth, as it is in heaven!"

PRAYER.

O THOU who didst never begin and who canst never end, **All in all,** more than heart can dream or tongue can tell, we are now about to speak of thee, and to tell the nothing that we know. Thou canst make our hearts burn within us; that burning shall be the purification of our souls and the chief comfort of our lives. Come to us, not in terror, but in love, not in the wrath which shakes the universe, but in the pity which saves the world. We have heard the crashing of thy thunder and would never hear it any more; henceforward do thou mercifully be unto us as the silent dew or the quiet light, and our souls shall live in thy forbearance. Jesus, save us! Jesus, cleanse us! Blood of the Lamb, take our sins away! God of gods and Lord of lords, by the showing of thyself make the universe look small and make our life a throb of thine own eternity. Deliver us from mistaken notions concerning thyself, and let us see all thy love in Christ Jesus thy dear Son. Surely thou art our heart's perplexity by reason of thy mystery, and our heart's supreme delight by reason of thy continual grace. We know that we have wronged thee by our mistaken views of thy character, yet dost thou gently correct us by many revelations of power and grace. Continue thy holy ministry in our hearts until all dross is burnt away and there is left only the fine gold of true wisdom. O Christ, cleanse us! Holy Spirit, make us like unto God himself! Amen.

THE PERSONAL GOD.

"The Lord God, even my God."—I CHRON. xxviii. 20.

EVERY man has what practically amounts to a god of his own. That is to say, he has a conception of God which no other mind has seized, and that conception forms the living centre of his personal religion. There are several gods in Christendom which I have renounced, and against which every honest man should, from any point of view, inveigh with strong indignation. Three examples occur to me at this moment. (1) There is a god that specifically foreordains so many people to be saved and so many to be lost; this god calls upon all men to be saved, well knowing that the call will neither be heard nor answered, because of an arbitrary decree which he himself has issued. This god I abhor and renounce, and I treat his power with scorn and defiance. No such god could ever secure my confidence or tempt me into other than mocking prayer. (2) Then there is another god, in many respects the exact contrary of this. He is infinitely soft; he is "all tears"; he is constantly misspending his love and complaining of the daily waste; his life is a tumultuous sentiment, rushing like an unbanked river into any swamp that will receive it and turn it into fetid and barren greenness. This god I pity and avoid. There is further (3) a kind of gentleman-god who is the refined and respectable patron of a certain type of churches. He never attends any other place of worship; he is nothing if not genteel; he submits himself sabbatically to the mild encomiums of sundry feeble persons who use him for professional purposes and never make any vulgar or exciting allusions to him.

My God is wholly unlike these three idols. Were there but these three to choose from, I should in very deed be a godless man. My heart goes out towards another God, about whom I will say what little I can, the most being less than nothing, and the highest love being but dead coldness when spoken in the words of man. What I know about this God I have learned solely from the Son of the carpenter. He seemed to be a long time in saying anything about God. The first time he spoke of him, except by way of quotation, he did not call him God, or Lord, or Most High, or Eternal; he called him "your Father which is in heaven"! Not that he disavowed the more solemn name, for the next time he turned to the topic he said "God's throne." After long companionship with the Son of the carpenter, and even much loving intimacy with his most secret heart, I have come to know something about this Father who has a throne, and this God who is a Father.

Intellectually my God is as unthinkable as mathematically the horizon is immeasurable. We can lay one end of the tape upon the earth, but we cannot lay the other end on the horizon, yet the horizon is visible, and is just—*yonder*! But because God is unthinkable it does not follow that he is not to be thought about. The fatal mistake of some thinkers seems to lie just there. The unthinkable is not something contrary to thought, but is something above thought, as the immeasurable is not a quantity which disproves figures, but exceeds them. Astronomy gives us a universe whose orbit is so stupendous that any section of any circle ever measured by mathematics appears upon its circumference as merely a straight line. An unthinkable universe, yet objectively here, undeniable, most palpable, and not wholly without use! I like to think about it until thought falls into a dream, and the dream is too grand for words and becomes a dumbly religious amazement. If I think only of my own parish, I become small; of my own country only, a selfish patriot; of the universe, I heighten with the infinite idea. This experience has its inexpressible counterpart in religion. I am incomplete and restless without God. I grope for him in a great darkness, and my heart is pained with bitter crying and a very agony of desire. You must give me a God, or I will create one. Idolatry is philosophical; in its most tragic bloodiness it is but the desperation of a life that is nearly Divine. The God and Father of Jesus Christ fills me with ineffable satisfaction, not that he falls wholly within the lines of my intellectual capacity, but is as the sun which fills the earth with its glory and yet holds in reserve infinitely more than the earth can receive. It is open to others to call this phantasy on my part. I might call it phantasy, too, and endeavour to quench it, but that I am the better for it, coming out of the enrapturing reverie as I do with a sacred contempt for all meanness and a burning desire to help and bless all other human life. Such a phantasy is not without substance, and therefore is no phantasy, though seeming to be such to men whose intellectual guests are always less than themselves. If it perished like a cloud, I might value it at the price of a cloud, but so long as it constrains me to do good, to think nobly, to give generously, and to suffer patiently, I must encourage it, though it be called by no other name than phantasy.

Another thought. It is a mistake to suppose that knowledge comes to us solely through what are known as intellectual processes. Some things we know intuitively, some sympathetically, some experimentally. Some knowledge is, so to say, startled into us by sudden distress or sudden joy. No image or superscription of reasoning is upon it, yet it rules us like a revelation, and it is consciously at the peril of a great loss that we refuse it place and utterance in our life. As human education is something both before school and after it—the school being merely a bracket in the opening of youth—so knowledge, in its highest reach and quality, comes before reasoning and continues after it, without any law or measure which science has yet determined. I put it down, therefore, as one line in my creed that man's knowledge is not the product or issue of his intellect alone.

The most powerful—may I not say the most tremendous ?—hold which God has upon me is in a moral direction. He is in very deed a holy God. He cannot look upon sin with the least degree of allowance. He gives me a final standard of right and wrong. If I could get rid of this God, I could easily get rid of all inconvenient morality. He will not allow me to yield to the temptation of circumstances, or to pit one suggestion against another in any argument whose conclusions would fraudulently enrich me, or separate my individual benefit from the security and completeness of the broad commonwealth. There is a law of righteousness in his mouth, a sword of justice is in his hand, and the whole royalty of his throne is set against all selfishness and corruption. This is my God. He is the continual torment of my sin, and the continual hope of my penitence. I am a better man with him than I could possibly be without him, and that is a test which no false religion can bear. Without him my morality would be a calculation, a public attitude, or a social investment; it might often have the semblance of the rarest virtue, and for all purposes of casual criticism might successfully float through the passing hour : but a vital and invincible morality it would not be; it would not wear well; any unequal strain might break it, and show the inner craft of an artificial exterior.

These two aspects of God give me all that I need in the way of intellectual speculation and moral rest. My mind is filled with the grandeur of the conception, and its highest moods are promised an ever-enlarging delight and satisfaction. On the other hand, I find the rest which every mind must ardently desire when looking at the collisions and tumults of all time. I feel that the end is not yet, and that my judgment would be as a word spoken out of season. More than this, I am assured that the world must be more to its Maker than ever it can be to me, and therefore that if he can keep the sunny roof over its stormy scenes, it would be imbecility and impiety on my part to complain of its inequalities and misadventures. I rest in the almightiness of God, and my patience is ennobled into a religion by the confidence that all things are working together by measures and compensations which must result in universal contentment and rest. Again and again, therefore, I am shown that my creed is not a phantasm, but a reality, not a dream which pleases one set of my powers, but a discipline that puts upon me great strains and summons me to gracious labours.

This Unthinkable and Holy God I humbly receive from Jesus Christ, the Son of the carpenter. " He only hath revealed him." He claims that he came from the bosom of the Father, and my experience of his grand and ever-ennobling teaching confirms the probability of his having done so. More than this : so far as the human intellect can go, Jesus Christ is not, in his word and works, distinguishable from God. Whether beyond the point attainable by the mind any inequality discovers itself we cannot now know. To my mind Jesus Christ is one with God. His words are unfathomable in meaning, though direct and immediate in the holy uses of comfort and illumination. More and more do I grow in the conviction that any God that cannot be made immediately available by the very simplest descriptions or definitions is neither the Father nor the Saviour of men. Though he be great, yet must he have respect unto the lowly ; to the lowly he must accommodate himself in his revelations, and in no wise must he shut himself up as the monopoly of professional interpretation or sacerdotal pretension. These conditions are all realised in the God of Jesus Christ. God is love. God is light. God is life. God is a Spirit. God is Father. No other God ever admitted of such easy translation into the speech of men. This is MY God.

GOD, THE EXPLANATION OF ALL THINGS.

IF you ask me how I know that there is a God, if I tell you in reply that the Bible says so, you may very well be dissatisfied with the answer. You would indeed be entitled to say, "That may be so, but who gave the Bible authority to say anything of the kind ? " I should be reasoning in a circle if I should find that there was a God because the Bible said so, and that there was a revelation because God had inspired it. That would be wholly a circular movement, altogether inadequate, and wholly mocking and unsatisfactory. As a Christian teacher, I set forth no such plea. I do not begin at a metaphysical point at all. The method of argument which I shall apply to the whole line of Christian evidence in this discourse is this : Here are certain facts ; account for them. In other words, here is a lock ; open it. Instead of saying, "There is a God ; go out and prove it," I will say, "Here are certain facts, ten thousand strong ; account for them." Instead of saying that there is a Providence watching over us all, I will say, "Here is my life—you know it : strange mysterious, tumultuous, many-coloured : comedy having its laugh cut short by sudden tragedy, tragedy startled into momentary relaxation by unexpected comedy : diversity of temper, engagement, habitude, destiny—here are the facts ; account for, them." Instead of saying to you, "There is a book which is inspired," I shall say nothing of the kind. I shall, as a literary surveyor, go over the book and report upon it to you. I will tell you what the book is, in its contents, in its spirit, in its history, in its purpose, and I shall ask you to account for it. So I am not going to ask any favour of any man. I am not going even to ask you to admit a metaphysical axiom, saying, "Let it be granted, so and so " ; I shall take the facts, you shall find them, and I will pile them up one on the top of another, and ask you what the next step is.

Now this is the purely scientific method. We begin with facts, and we ask for the explanation--no man can object to that. You can leave them unaccounted for? No, not as a scientific man. Unaccounted for! Any fool could do that, but you are a man of knowledge. You can go up to a certain point and then wheel round and leave the explanation unattempted? No. Let the vulgar do that. Let men of science be fearless. The challenge of the Nazarene called Christ was, "Knock, ask, seek; batter the door till it opens." That is my Leader, my fearless, chivalrous Master. I will bind you, therefore, to be scientific right through and through; you shall not cease when you like; you shall not shut up the school when you think it time to go, but you shall keep it open as long as there is a single ray of light in the western sky. The spirit of the age says, "Prove all things, push the scientific inquiry to its utmost extent, be deterred by nothing, ask and demand the answer." I accept the challenge, and I ask, if you have gathered the facts together, how do you account for them? How does the sun come to shine? How do men come to different lots and destinies in life? How comes it that there is no man who has seen the wind? Why has no cunning hand made a glass that can show to-morrow? You see I am dealing strictly with facts. I have botanists, geologists, astronomers, sociologists, and a whole host of others running to every point of the compass to bring in facts. I am waiting till they get them all completed, and when they are complete, I shall say, "Account for them." That, I take it, is practical.

Now, as a mere matter of fact, some persons have ventured to say, "The facts of the universe, its coherence, magnitude, colour, light, beauty, proportion, harmony, utility—the facts of the universe, put them under what names you please, are to be accounted for by the doctrine, In the beginning, God." Do I take the answer, finally, simply, because it happens to have been given? Nothing of the sort. A certain kind of mind might say, "If we say that God made all things, the question will arise, Who made God?" So be it: it is a very proper question; push it, urge it, repeat it, and get an answer if you can. Do you think I am to be frightened, as a Christian teacher, by the suggestion that if I say God made all things, somebody will say, Who made God? It is a grand question; repeat it, urge it, vehemently and wisely, when you have got the reply, make it known.

But there is a way of treating the suggestion which seems to me to be rational, and most practical. You say God made all things, that God is omnipotent, omniscient, omnipresent, merciful, wise, and kind beyond all human conceptions of his attributes. Do I believe you because you say so, or because the Bible says so? No. What do I do? I try whether the answer covers the question, and does so satisfactorily. You have been abroad, and you have somehow lost your key, and you cannot open the lock under which all your travelling possessions are. A friend says, "Here is a bunch of keys for you." You can take three courses in reference to that bunch of keys. You can say, "Where does the whitesmith live, what is his name, and how came he to be a whitesmith, that made those keys?" That would be a very philosophical inquiry to make. Or you may say, "By what authority did any man presume to make a bunch of keys? Who gave him liberty to do so?" That would be a magnificent assertion of the independence of the human mind. Or you can try the keys. That would be most humbling, but very common sense. I propose to try the key; if it fits, I will keep it. I am simply dealing with the suggestion now as a suggestion. Does Omnipotence even seem to account for creation? Does Providence even seem to account for what is seen in daily life? Does Infinite Love even seem to account for the sparing of many who have outraged all obligation and honour? Is there anything in life—anything of injustice, disparity, inequality—to justify the suggestion that there must be a final judgment and an allotment of rewards and punishments? I confess that the suggestion is equal to the occasion, and that no other suggestion, theory, hypothesis, or conjecture—I am treating it simply under these categories, you observe—so completely covers the whole case as the doctrine that in the beginning, God—and that God creates, rules, sustains, and redeems. I therefore take your suggestion, and say "Better than any other it accounts for the facts."

Suppose it should be objected that this suggestion still leaves a good many inquiries to be answered, what then? So does science. It is not as if any one theory accounted for everything The scientific man comes to a point at which he says, "I stop there." The religious man comes to a point at which he says the same thing, the difference being that the scientific man has explained nothing, accounted for nothing, beyond the most visible and limited line. The religious man suggests a Father, a Ruler, a Sovereign, and has found it somewhere written, that is yet to be tested, that what we know not now we shall know hereafter. Taking the two suggestions simply as such, I say the one is larger than the other—deeper, grander; touches points in my life left untouched by the other, and therefore by so much it is worthy of further investigation.

Take this same illustration of the lock and key. Do I say I believe that this key will open the lock because I have been told it will? Certainly not; that would be foolish reasoning indeed. I put the key into the lock and turn it, and thus my faith stands upon fact. This is exactly what I do with the suggestion, In the beginning, God. I retain my manhood, what I call my independence—no book is allowed to take this from me; every book that is good addresses these facts in me, consults and honours them, and therefore I open the book, called pre-eminently *The* Book, and it says, "In the beginning, God." I take the suggestion as a rational man; in the first place it is only a suggestion : by-and-by it may grow into a revelation.

I have a great and cunningly contrived lock called the universe, and the question is how to open it. I cannot tell. It is a grand lock, and I should like to open it. The Bible says, "I can give you the key of that lock." Then I say, "You are a bold book, and boldness is an attribute of truth." Do I stop there and say I believe there is a key because I have read a book which says there is one? Verily, no. I say to the book, whatever its name may be, "Where is the key?" When the Bible says, "The key is God, omnipotent, omniscient, omnipresent, righteous, merciful, holy, just, brighter than the light, more patient than motherhood, more pitiful than fatherhood, full of compassion, and most longsuffering," I take the key, I press it into the lock, I find that it opens the lock, wholly and easily—what do I do? I kiss the book, I love it, I call it God's book, I meditate therein day and night. Have you a better reason? Let me have it : I will try it exactly in the same way—only it must cover all the ground, it must be available night and day, it must not be subject to climatic changes, it must not succumb to atmospheric effects, it must keep time on the Alps, and keep time in the valleys—must that suggestion of yours. I wait for it. It shall be treated with the profoundest respect.

But suppose it should be further said, "That may be the happiest intellectual suggestion yet given ; it may be the brightest intellectual guess which even genius in its most inspiring and elated moods has suggested. But it may be only an intellectual suggestion, and its originality may be one day eclipsed." Very good ; I anticipate that objection, thus : If this book gave me only an intellectual idea of the construction and government of the universe, I dare not accept any intellectual answer as final. Intellect is never self-complete. If it were only a clever guess— the cleverest guess—I should suspect it on account of its very ability. How then am I seconded and backed in use of this key ? I will tell you. The Bible does not allow itself to be thus easily nonsuited in the court of human investigation, by the suggestion that it is very clever, a very brilliant reply, a magnificent guess, and nothing more. The answer of the Bible is not a merely intellectual success. What kind of God does the Bible bring to open the lock of the universe? A moral God—a God who lays a moral claim upon me—a God who is pained by my intellectual admiration of him, if it be limited within its own lines—a God that makes my intellectual assent to his being an aggravation of my blasphemy if I rest there. This is a wondrous key : it is a key which says, "You must keep me, night and day, and never go anywhere without me, and you must only do that which is right, pure, true, honourable, and just." It is not a successful intellectual reply, that, that God is the key that fits the universe; here is a moral God, a God that says, "You must do justly and love mercy—be true, upright, honourable, sincere, holy." There is no intellectual answer that I could not wriggle out of. Here is a moral enclosure that keeps me within a prison, from which I cannot escape argumentatively : an enclosure which becomes the widest liberty if I accept it sympathetically. Thus the intellectual satisfaction is magnified into moral service, and the command is, Thou shalt love the key, Thou shalt love the Lord thy God with all thy heart, with all thy soul, with all thy mind, and with all thy strength. So that, you see, what was at

first an intellectual answer to an intellectual difficulty grows into
a moral suggestion with a supreme claim upon everything that
makes you a man. Completeness is the test of the highest logic.

Why, then, have we not seen God? Because you can never
see anything that is really great. No man can see God and live.
No man can see life; you can see its effects. Why, no man ever
paints the sun. He does try his brush upon the meaner moon—
he may paint sunlight—solar effects—but what man ever took
acreage enough of canvas to paint that great white wheel the
sun? No man hath seen God; no man hath seen himself! Life
always comes in incarnations. It takes a garment within which
it conceals itself, and from within which it performs its wonders.
You kiss your child's cheek; you cannot kiss its soul. "I have,"
says one man, "gone up and down the earth with scientific
weapons and instruments, and I cannot find God anywhere. In
fact, I have taken the human body to pieces, and I cannot find the
soul; therefore there is no soul." My reasoning would be, "You
cannot find the soul, and therefore presumptively there is a soul
to be found." So differently do we view the same things.
Thus, if you cannot find the soul, no more can you find intelligence; therefore there is no intelligence. Beautiful logic; very
rapid. True, I have taken a man to pieces, and I can find no soul
in him. Very good; dissect Shakespeare from head to foot, and
find the genius in him. You cannot; therefore there is no genius.
A short and easy method with the poet. I will take this organ to
pieces, great stops, little stops, all sorts of pipes and reeds and
flutes, and I will fill the floor of this church with them, and say,
'You call that a musical instrument; will you be kind enough to
point out where the music is?" Take the bellows to pieces to
find the air, take the man to pieces to find the soul, dissect the
universe to find God. Your methods are wrong; your whole
scheme of genius is out of joint.

Why have we not seen God? Let me ask you with what
instruments could you have looked at him—what instruments
have you equal to the inquiry and investigation? "We have
eyes." Are you sure of that? "Quite sure of that." Is there
anything in that drop of water trembling on that pin point?
"Nothing in the world." I tell you there is a whole busy population in there. You say that is impossible. But you have eyes?

"Yes." Use them. "I do, and there is nothing in that drop of water." Now take this glass. Through the microscope you see all that large busy energetic population, and you lay down the glass, saying that you never could have thought it. Why have you not seen God? Have you seen the wind? No. There is no wind. You must admit that reasoning. You have not seen it; therefore there is none; reasoning is proof triumphant. You have not seen it. You are up early in the morning, and you are out all day; you live and work in the open air; you have not seen the wind; therefore there is none. Magnificent—as reasoning. There is a piece of iron; here is something in my hand towards which that piece of iron runs; you see the iron coming; see? I cannot see the magnetism between what is in my hand and the iron which is drawn, but it is the invisible that is doing it.

Having all these facts before me, it becomes easy for me to believe the words, No man hath seen God at any time; no man can see God and live. Why cannot I see God? I cannot see my own thought. Why cannot I see God? I cannot see a single motive that impels me. When, therefore, the preacher tells me that the invisible is the greatest, I say, I know that it is so down here in my own little life, at all events. Therefore it is not unlikely to be so in the higher liberties and spaces of the universe. You are travelling across the sea. What is there between you and the Atlantic Ocean? A plank an inch thick. Why don't you take a knife and cut that plank in two, and go into the sea? You could do it; physically yes, morally no. What keeps you back? The invisible. What do you mean by the invisible? Reason, reflection, sense of the value of life, consciousness of the responsibility—these things that have never been seen, that are altogether intangible and imponderable; these are the mighty forces that hold you back as an inviolable leash. Knowing these facts, when the Christian teacher says to me, "It is so on a larger scale; all things are under the Divine government of an invisible Being," I answer it is not unlikely to be so, seeing that within my own sphere of action the invisible is supreme.

I feel, therefore, in this introductory discourse—understand that it is merely introductory—that I am standing on the most solid ground when I occupy the position with which I began namely, here is the universe, large, radiant, complete, narmonic, grand ; account for it. I have listened to all the various reasons which have been given. How far is the reason good ? I have not treated any one of the answers higher than that; I have taken them simply in an intellectual way. No answer so completely covers the whole case, no answer leaves so little to be explained, no answer brings so profound and gracious a comfort to my mind and heart as the answer, " In the beginning, God." When a fuller answer comes I will accept it.

I have not seen God, but God was manifest in the flesh, just as my thought was. There is nothing mysterious in that. The Word was made flesh, and dwelt among us ; so was your motive. There is nothing crushingly and blindingly mysterious in the suggestion that the Word, Thought, the Logos, was made flesh. So must it be with every Logos, with every high thought, with every poet's dream. It must find a Bethlehem where it shall be born, and the stars must lead to it. No man hath seen God at any time ; the only begotten Son that is in the bosom of the Father, he hath revealed him. Blessed are they that have not seen and yet have believed. We are obliged to do that in the lower ranks and lines of life. Oh that we might do it in the higher ranges and the nobler studies of the universe !

We have seen that there are two ways of proceeding about this great proposition that there is a God. The first and unsatisfactory one is to endeavour intellectually to prove it, which has never been done, and never can be done, so far as I see at present. The second method is to say, Here are certain things round about us—facts, realities—which we cannot deny, and about whose existence there is no dispute ; account for them. We have adopted the second method in this argument.

When the algebraist says, " Let x equal the unknown quantity," I could interrupt him, and say, " First prove the x," but that would be a very foolish interruption. I allow him to use his x, and I await the solution which comes from his use of that symbolic letter. Well, I say, allow me to say, " Let God equal the unknown quantity," and you wait till I have carried that assumption through the whole universe so far as it is accessible to us. When I hand in my solution it will be time for you to examine and critcise it. Here is the universe—vast, radiant, marvellous in combinations and processes. Here is my life, many-coloured, swift in movement, rapid in its combinations—tragical, comical, wondrous life. Account for these things. And the Christian teacher says he has endeavoured to account for them, and that no word so completely meets all the necessities of the case, so completely answers all difficulties, relieves all mysteries, as the word *God*. He says, "If I leave that word unspoken, I leave everything loose, incoherent, self-contradictory. If I pronounce that word with the reverence and love of the heart, I find a centre into which all things are gathered up, in which all things are fastened, out of which all things radiate with precision and utility and dignity. I find in God, personal, ever present, all-loving, the best solution of the things that are round about me, and all the things which constitute myself." Now we cannot allow him to escape with that answer only. We must go a little further into his conception of this term *God*. If it be a term only, then one term may be answered by another. We must take his term to pieces, and by a careful and just analysis, we may find what it comprehends and involves.

What do you mean when you say "God"? A thousand things. No two men mean the same thing when they say "God," and the mischief is that there should be persons who suppose that all men should mean exactly the same thing when they use the greatest terms that are in human speech. You mean the same thing when you say "clock," when you say "door," or "road," or "river." These are little terms, and they fall within simple and easy meanings. But when you say "child," what do you mean? "Man," what is the limit? "God" . . . ? You must not insist upon men caging the infinite, or laying bars of iron upon the immeasurable. There is a function which imagination alone can discharge—high, reverent, self-restrained, chastened but ever vigilant and urgent imagination. One man says, "When I think of God, I think of the sum total of being, the life fount out of which all living streams flow. He is not to be expressed or defined in words; he is spirit acting on spirit, the wondrous mighty All; he is to be thought about rather than spoken of. I worship him in silence; I look up, but do not speak; the mean words of man do but debase and vulgarise the infinite." His exhortation to me is, "Stand under that conception as thou dost stand under the firmament, and take what is given thee of spiritual light and warmth and rain, and be dumb."

Now, this is a man in whose religion there is no detail; he is religious in the gross. If you begin to make propositions to him, you insult his veneration. He would as soon think of parcelling out the firmament into private acres as of dividing and sub-dividing the infinite thought into small theological propositions. In support of such a view there is very much to be said. It ennobles and dignifies the mind; it silences many vain and foolish speeches; it kills the sectarianism which is built upon peculiar interpretations or audacious guesses; it is religion in the gross, a grand silence, an eloquent speechlessness. It is a look that prays; it is an attitude that worships. The Church wants none of book or man called priest or teacher. It stands outside of all these things, overwhelmed by the vastness of its own conception, trembling, speechless, before the wordless Infinite.

Another man says, "When I think of God, I think of him as a person, as a magnified man, an infinite extension of myself. I can lay hold of him in no other way. I could not join the thinking of that man whom you have just described. I must have a concrete, personal, individual God. When I think of such a God, I think of myself infinitised. I am a germ, he the full fruition. For example, if you ask me to define heaven, how can I do it but by glorifying the earth? I cannot create a new universe; I can but multiply that which is round about me. So if you ask me to define heaven, I will go to the garden on a summer day, when the flowers are most beauteous and fragrant; I will say, Multiply that sight by infinitude, and you have paradise. I will go into a place where the music is most transporting and ravishing, where you have musical instruments of all sorts, touched by fingers of magic, by fingers of fire, and I will say, Listen; multiply that by infinitude, and you have heaven. So when I think of God, I say, Find a man at his best, purest, and noblest estate; find a man of the highest genius and the fullest inspiration; invest him with all possible attributes of excellence. When you have done so, multiply him by infinity, and you begin to get my notion of God."

This is a simpler conception than the first; yet it is warranted by the whole letter and spirit of Holy Scripture. It is warranted,

however, only as a convenience and help to the human understanding. It is a figurative representation of an otherwise
incomprehensible fact. When God condescends to be called a
person, it is an act of incarnation on his part, a miraculous
conception, a new and daily humiliation of his majesty. The
word *person* can never express the idea *God.* Yet it is a
needful term, as indicating the very least that God can make
himself. If the theologian contents himself by saying, " God is a
person ; turn over the page and go over to the next lesson," he is
a fool. God is a person. He calls himself such that I may get
hold of him ; he tabernacles himself in this short word that I
may speak to him. It is a word I would not give up ; it is
needful to my conception of the Divine nature. It signifies
individuality as distinguished from immensity, a living and
loving heart as distinguished from indifference and the sublimity
of immovableness. It means *Father.* There the human heart
rests.

But if you ask me what I personally mean by God, I mean
neither of these two things alone. I mean more. I am a
Christian teacher. As such I have a special revelation on which
I rely. He is God beyond all knowledge, merciful and gracious,
patient even unto longsuffering, watching us with an eye never
closed in sleep, caring for us with all care, redeeming us with
blood, training us for a grand and abiding hereafter. He is more
than God, more than God and Father. He is to me the God and
Father of our Lord Jesus Christ. So that, as a Christian thinker,
I go to Christ for the interpretation of God, and for the uses
which are to be made of that interpretation. I leave the realm of
speculation, I come out of the cloud, I sit down beside Jesus, and
say to him, " Show me the Father by showing me thyself. Let
me lay my hand upon his heart by laying it upon thine."

Now, if I go to Jesus Christ for my interpretation, and the
uses that are to be made of that interpretation, what shall I find ?
I shall find a Man who was constantly and essentially godly.
The one thing which Jesus Christ wished to do in his life, in his
youth, was his Father's business. When he last spoke, that
night when the mortal terror seized his life, he wanted to do
his Father's will. That is godliness. At twelve he says, " Wist
ye not that I must be about my Father's business ? " At mid-

night he said, "Not my will, but thine be done." That is the
way to prove God—to live in him, to be ruled by him, to
breathe his spirit. Mark the infinite reasonableness of this.
Given such a God as Jesus Christ revealed, he must be the
supreme thought of the mind and the all-absorbing joy of the
soul.

Religion thus judged is not a duty. No man can be religious
as a mere obligation if he would be religious in the Christian
sense. Religion must not be something *upon* a man; it must be
something *in* a man, that shall become the man himself. Hard
at first, becoming more easy and gladsome as the days roll on.
His music must be this : "I delight to do thy will, O God. My
delight is in the law of the Lord. I delight in the law of the
Lord after the inward man. I will delight myself in thy
commandments which I have loved." That is the spirit of
religion. Do you go to church because it is your duty to go?
Then I do not wonder at you being late, because a man hates
duty. Do you go to church because it is your duty to go? Then
I do not wonder at you longing to get out of it again, for duty is
always hard if included within itself, without outlook, or fire, or
poetry, or equal motive behind it. At first it may have somewhat
of the nature of discipline in it. You are learning music; you
touch your instrument, and the instrument speaks back as if it
were insulted. Why? Because it did not know your fingers,
and though your fingers did not mean to be at all rude to the
great eloquent angel, yet they touched it roughly, and the sound
was a sound of resentment. Put into English, it meant, "Hands
off." Then, oh, the looking at the notes and at the keys, and at the
keys and at the notes, and the twisting and the beginning again,
and the going back, and the exclamations of self-disgust, and the
determinations never to try again! Still you persevered, and
one day you touched the instrument like a friend, and the
instrument answered you like a friend. From that hour it was
your delight, not your duty, to go and hold sweet long fellowship with that instrument.

You are learning a language; you say you would like to learn
it without going through the grammar. I daresay you would :
that is an old wish, and most human. But the strange alphabet,
the everlasting declensions, the whole regiments and armies and

phalanxes of irregulars and exceptions—who can face them? You persevere, and some day you hear a speaker of that language address you, and you know what he said, and, oh, the boyish joy, oh, the childlike gladness! You run to your best friend and say, "He spoke to me in German, and I quite understood him." From that moment your German was a delight to you—if ever such a language can be a delight to any mortal intellect. But it is first hard, and then easier, and then gladsome. So with this church-going and Bible-reading and religious service; it is at first somewhat perhaps of the nature of duty and obligation—you feel that you are in an imperative mood and cannot well escape from it, and so you have to conjugate backwards until you get into the lighter and more genial moods—but at last it is a delight, and the word *commandment* itself but too sweetly indicates the gladness and the rapture with which you render religious service.

If I study God under the direction of Jesus Christ, and following his example, I shall be quite childlike in my spirit in relation to the Father. Jesus Christ was a Son in the Father's house. Beloved, what manner of love hath the Father bestowed on us that we should be called the sons of God! I want to be led into this higher music, namely, my Father's business, my Father's way, my Father's house, my Father's pleasure. When I can say so,

> "I'll bid farewell to every fear,
> And wipe my weeping eyes."

When God is only an intellectual conception to me, my life is an intellectual weariness, my toil a manual drudgery, but when he says, "I am thy Father, and thou art my child," and I seize the notion, then all the days of the week are absorbed in a bright calm Sabbath that comes like a sanctuary and a defence around my soul.

But my unbelief will not let me seize all this enjoyment of God. My unbelief will not let God be Father; my unbelief says to me—for unbelief is an awful theologian—"Look here"—and I look at its grim, hard face—"God will be a kind of Father to you by-and-by if you will do certain things, which it is impossible for you to do." Poor gospel, mean gospel! Faith says, "See here; God is your Father; whatever you may be, he changeth

not. Mean, miserable, sinful head, heart, hand, foot, soiled
through and through, God is still your Father, and he is longing
for you to come home again.   He is grieved by your sin; as a
Father he will pardon your guilt, as a Father he will watch
over your going out and your coming in; as a Father he undertakes your redemption—look to him and live." That is a grander
speech; I know speeches that are true : we all do that.   When
unbelief says to me, "God will be your Father under such and
such conditions, which it is impossible for you to fulfil," I know
that unbelief is telling me a lie; the voice is false, the tone is
undivine. When faith says to me, "Child, thy Father calls thee,"
something within me answers like an echo to a voice, and I know
the Gospel to be true.

Then what is it that hinders me fully and entirely enjoying
all this revelation of God and resting upon him wholly ?   If I
have to be frank with you, the answer will be a mournful one.
I could gild it; I will not.   The reason I do not fully, with
absoluteness of realisation, enjoy this revelation of God in Christ
is, after it there comes a demand which I find it painful to fulfil;
I first of all have to go to a Sinai : the ten commandments are
handed to me written in stone.   I walk on ; precepts and statutes
are written upon the rock and upon the tree : are being uttered
in the wind and trumpeted in the thunder.   Religion, as revealed
by Christ, is not a pleasant dream or an intellectual luxury ; it is
the supreme command, it is the absolute claim of God.   If I have
to be religious in Jesus Christ's sense, accepting his definition of
God, I shall have no time for myself, I shall have no money of
my own, I shall have no friends of my own picking, I shall have
no feast that he will not claim to be at, I dare touch no wine that
he does not first drink—I dare not even go into a wilderness
without taking his lamp with me—and these things the incomplete, shattered human will hates.   Selfishness says, "Give me
a little of my own, I do not care how little, only let it be mine.
Give me half a day in the month, give me ten shillings a week,
let me go into this door and into that—only do, and I ask no
more."   But Jesus Christ says, "No—not a moment, not a penny,
not an entrance, not a single thought thine own."   And yet he
says his yoke is easy and his burden is light.   So it is, like the
music and the language I have now spoken about. Rightly

taken to, the preliminaries rightly undergone, in the grace and strength of Heaven, the outcome will indeed be blessed.

So I return to my starting point, and say I have two courses open to me about this matter. I can have a god of my own imagining; I can go to my fancy for a god, or I can accept the God that is revealed in the Holy Scriptures. You go to your fancy for a god; let me ask you a plain question: Is your fancy a very likely quarter in which to find a very adequate divinity? You mock the poor idolater who makes a god out of a tree; I want you to see you are doing exactly the same thing, minus the tree. Nay, the idolater has a god of his fancy; he says, "I must make this into something visible": you have a god in your fancy, and you dare not make him visible; you cannot, no manger would cradle him, no Magi from the far East would trim their lamps and bind their sandals and handle their staves to find him. It takes the true God to come down into flesh; no other dare venture on the meanness. Besides, if you made your god, you could unmake him.

I conclude, therefore, by saying—finishing thus the first part of my discourse—that, given the universe, given human life, given the whole scheme of things as now known to us, to account for them, no other solution so fully satisfies my intelligence and my heart as the solution—God. Given the solution, God, no interpretation of that term, pantheistic as including the great sum total, deistic as including a general but not special providence, can satisfy my heart. I find the only interpretation of God I can rely upon and rest in is the interpretation given by Jesus Christ. With that I will fight my fight in time; with that I will face the great unknown.

We have agreed, for the purposes of this argument, not to endeavour to prove intellectually the existence of God. We have, indeed, gone so far as to say that that is impossible. The finite cannot prove the infinite; it would, indeed, be a self-stultification of terms. The infinite must reveal itself to the finite; the finite can never either find out or prove it. What then? Our course was to take the facts as we find them, and having massed those facts before us, to put this inquiry concerning the whole of them: How are these facts to be accounted for? We say nothing about

God at the beginning. We do not dogmatically and authoritatively say, "There is a God, and you must believe it." We are
content for the purposes of this study to leave God out of the
question altogether at the beginning, and to go with men of
science wherever they may take us, and when we have completed
their circle, to ask the question I have just put, namely, How are
all these most wonderful things to be accounted for?

Let us look at human society. Having acquainted ourselves
somewhat with its constitution, with what I may call the very
mystery of its being, let us continue to urge the inquiry, How
is it to be explained or accounted for? You have upon the
face of the earth what is called human society, an organic sum
total, which time does not destroy, which contention, antagonism,
and strife of the fiercest kind only helps to expand and to consolidate. Time uses his scythe, Death goes forth to his black
harvest, the whole earth seems to be ripped and scarred with
tombs, and yet on the green earth there is a greater society to-
day than there ever was. How is it to be accounted for? By
its order, by its sympathy, by its brotherly love, by its spiritual
graces? You do not ask me to answer that ridiculous interroga-
tion. No two men are exactly alike, no two interests are precisely
identical; everywhere the thing that strikes you is difference,
contrast, incompatibility, and yet you can no more hinder the
progress of this society, or reduce it to nothingness, than you can
impede a planet or dissolve a star. This society is a continual
mystery. It is a batch, a chaos, of inconsistencies. You say it
must kill itself, yet it lives on, more prosperous and influential
year by year. Might has sometimes had right so utterly in its
power that you have said right can never survive. Yet right
has thriven in adversity, and clothed itself with new beauty in the
fire. Human society seems always to have had a razor at its
throat, but never yet has it taken its own life. Account for it.
Society is marked by contrasts that appear to be in themselves
full of peril, and fraught with danger that can neither be mitigated
nor avoided. What think ye? Society is divided into master
and servant. What society, looked at philosophically, could live
under such a division as that only? Why do you not bridge over
the difference? Why do you not make all men equal? Why
do you not lift up that which is far down, that all may become on

a level, one having no higher and better rights than another? You meet in congress; you print programmes; you have discussions. Why do you not level up and make all equal? Society is divided into learned and ignorant. Why does not the ignorant man read books and make himself learned? You have refined and vulgar. Why does not the vulgar man go to school and put on refinement, if he cannot put it *in*? These are questions that you can dismiss with an easy, airy lightness if you like, but if you do so, you abandon the scientific spirit, and you have no right any longer to claim a status amongst the most ardent and interrogative intelligence of the day.

Then look at the moral distinctions you have in society. You have every variety of temper, purpose, desire, sensibility, and service. You have the brave man whose face is a battle; you have the coward that skulks out of the light, the generous and the mean, the unsuspecting and the distrustful, the earnest soul that prays for the race like an intercessor, and the villain whose life never heightened and softened into a prayer for any human soul. Account for these things. On yonder hillside you have such a lot of dear, bright, romping little children; they never could be sad; that is the sun of the world. Arguing from what I see on that stirring side of the hill, I should say the world is heaven. On the other side of the hill you have the old man sighing for home, the bad man ending a wild day in a wilder night; you have the blind, who only know of morning by hearsay, the dumb, the imbecile; and on and on the exciting panorama stretches and palpitates until the eye is dim with watching. Account for these things—for progress amid collision, for rest amid strife, for solidity amid earthquake and whirlwind. Tell me how it is that society, drunk, mad, with a razor at its throat, cannot commit suicide.

Now I hold that this is as much matter of purely scientific interest as the formation of rocks or the distribution of plants. One student says, "I am an inquirer into physical manhood." I reply, "I am a student of social manhood." We are both scientific inquirers. I cannot allow that the man who has a small sharp knife in his hand for the purpose of cutting human sinews is a scientific student, at the expense of the man who is studying social humanity and asking how it coheres, increases, and advances. This, however, in passing.

Now look at your own individual life, and thus bring the mystery nearer home. You have no control over your birth. In the name and fear of God, I say that if I had been asked if I would have been born into this world, I should have said No. I am not here of my own will, yet I dare not go out. Born a little infant, of whom the priest says, "Of such is the kingdom of heaven," I may go out into hell. I did not ask to come in, I dare not pray to go out, except with reserves and calculations that diminish the prayer into a skulking request. You work, you learn, you suffer; you fight and lose the battle, you run and lose the race; you are just going to drink the cup of joy, and an invisible hand dashes it out of your grasp. The child that is to be your mainstay and comfort, that is to draw down the lids of your eyes at last, and say, "God bless you!" even after you have just gone, dies first. The man who never prays beats you hollow at every game you play. You touch the rock, and it melts into water; another man with foot that never trod the altar stair touches the water, and it hardens into rock again, and he builds his castle upon its stony base. How is it? Is he a scientific man who comes with his brows bound with botanical specimens, and he not a scientific man who comes up from society asking urgently with tears in his voice, with much doubt in his tone, and great sad wonder, "How is it? can it be explained? what is the *rationale* of this marvellous incoherent cohesion, this self-contradictory society"?

Then see your power and your weakness. You cannot do the things you want to do. From finger tip to finger tip you are under seven feet in length. If I offered you the sun in the heavens to put out your fingers a sixteenth of an inch further, you could not. You are full of yesterday; you are no wiser than a dog about to-morrow. We say, "When the historian comes, how will he view such and such circumstances?"—that is, a man who is clever in turning over dusty pages, and making out small print, and getting together forgotten things. I say, "When is the prophet coming who can read to-morrow?" and the dreary answer, more an echo than a voice, is, "Never."

How do we account for these things? Suppose we say it is chance. Magnificent answer—satisfying every fool to satiety— chance! I ask if that would satisfy any intelligent man amongst you. The man who can believe that all I have now described, and all which is related thereto, is the work of chance, has a greater capacity of belief than any heathen that ever swallowed ten thousand gods. Look how the suggestion of chance degrades us. Have we not power to protect ourselves against chance ? We protect ourselves against infection ; why do we not get up a limited liability company for the protection of one another against this mad dog, chance ? We are clever; why not apply our ingenuity in this direction ? What is the good of your building bridges, and laying telegraphs, and lighting electric flames, and doing all manner of wonderful things, if you cannot conquer chance and chain him to a kennel ? Are you going to sit down under the plague of chance ? Why do we not assemble in solemn congress, and get the upper hand of a power that makes everything else so uncertain ? Let us, however, renounce the name of chance as rather short, and, on the whole, somewhat silly, and let us give it a nobler name, and call all that we have now seen " the operation of the law of averages." I am sure that must console every breaking heart. At once you will feel that we have hit upon the profoundest solution of the mysteries that becloud and embarrass and agonise this frail human life. But if Presbyter is Priest writ large, the law of average is chance turned into a polysyllable, and nothing more. How are we to account for these things ?

Suppose a man should say, " Let us not account for them." Then I should charge him with being wanting in the scientific spirit, which says, " We want to know ; we want to find out ; we must be true to the line of our inquiry."

Upon this matter you go to what is called Church, and addressing the man who stands up in the pulpit, you say to him, " Sir, how do you account for what is called Society, with all its tragedy and comedy, its strife, contention, loss, pain, joy, risk, madness, and yet wondrousness of genius and power ? How do you account for the child dying, for the good man suffering, and for the knave prospering ? What have you to say about blood problems like these ? I am tired of hearing trifles discussed." I answer, " In the beginning, God. These things are not what they seem ; you have not seen all; above all, under all, around all, there is a mysterious, benign, judicial, gracious Providence. The

time of full solution is not yet; we are in the thick of dust and
smoke; a great fight is going on; the meaning will be read out to
you by-and-by." What is his answer to me? He says, "Without
calling upon you for any merely intellectual defence of that
suggestion, I feel that it ought to be, that it must be, true." I
cannot, however, rest with that concession; in the meantime
it is excellent; it gives me a standing ground with the man, but
nothing more. Observe how this method of reasoning operates.
If you start from the point—there is a God; go and find him—
then all the mysteries of society will be so many objections to the
theory. If you commence at the other end—see, here is society;
account for it—then you are not lost amid all the details of the
case, but you' catch its spiritual genius, its moral afflatus and
spirit, and lifting yourself above all that is of the nature of
mere detail, you say, with a reverent spirit, "How is it?"
The answer is, "God."

But if we give the answer: "God," the difficulties appear to
remain. Children die; good men suffer; bad men prosper; the
scroll in the hand of weary pensive Time is still written all over
with mourning, lamentation, and woe. How are we to reconcile
such facts with the doctrine of an all-wise, all-powerful, and all-
gracious Providence? I will give you the answer. How does
the Bible, regarding it as simply a book without a name, treat
such inquiries, or regard such differences? First, it recognises
them, and by so much it commits itself to some explanation.
The Bible does not slur over the difficulties of human life: no
book is so explicit and minute and emphatic in its delineation of
human life, human suffering, and human discipline. Sometimes
when I open my Bible it seems to be nothing but one long, heavy
groan over human sin and human woe. So we have to deal
with a book that comes down amongst us and says, "Yes, the
difficulties you speak about are real; they are not to be ignored,
and no trifling answer will cover them." So far, so good.

In the next place, the Bible traces these evils to their cause.
It may be wrong, or it may be right, but it does not blink the
question, "What is the reason?" It says, "This is the reason:
sin is the explanation of moral crookedness on the part of man.
The breach of faith, the suicide of integrity, the rebellious off-
taking of the robe of innocence and taking on the nakedness of

shame—this is the explanation." I claim nothing for the answer, further than it does attempt to go to the root of the matter, and give a cause for what occasions us so much just and bewildering perplexity.

In the next place, the Bible points out the highest uses of many of the sufferings which afflict human society. The Bible does not give them up in despair : the Bible does not limit those sufferings within the area of their immediate operation. The Bible says to me, " The wound is very deep, but it may be healed ; the suffering is very keen, but it is for thy chastening and purification. The disappointment is very bitter, but there is a deep and gracious meaning in it, and behind it; wait for the explanation. Accept these perplexities in a reproachful, pining spirit, and they will aggravate themselves and become tenfold more difficult of endurance ; receive them in the right spirit, saying, ' God reigns ; God loves me ; God means good by me : he makes stars in the darkness ; he intends all these things to bring out of my life wine that has not yet been crushed out of the grapes of my heart '— speak so, and what now afflicts thee may become a root of joy and a spring of pleasure." I take that answer : I say there is in it sympathy ; there is no attempt to evade the difficulty, there is no effort made to mitigate my own apprehension of the magnitude and terribleness of these sufferings : they are all recognised ; their case is stated, their possible highest uses are indicated.

And then the Bible not only recognises these evils, traces their cause, and indicates some of their uses ; it predicts their consummation and their extinction. It is not afraid of them. The Bible says, " Sorrow may endure for a night ; joy cometh in the morning." The Bible says, " All these things are but for a moment, if you bring to bear upon them the power of an endless life. Your light affliction is but for a moment, if you look at things not seen." " Jesus Christ came into the world," says the Bible, " to put an end to these things, and to reconcile all things unto himself, and he will do it." There is no break in the emphasis ; there is no halting in the Biblical prophecy ; it goes straight through like a king, like a God. When I compare these answers with the suggestion of chance and the law of averages, I feel that the true science is in the Biblical reply, and not in the false conjecture. Here then, I rest, till some better solution be given me. I quiet myself in God. "Not my will, but thine be done." The details vex me; the great universal and unchangeable principle consoles and sustains me.

Crossing the great deep at night, lying sleeplessly and perhaps painfully in your berth, longing for the light, without much hope that it will bring you comfort, what hear you? The surge of the water, the moan of the wind, and the tinkle of a bell. That bell has no sooner told its little tale of time than a voice in a sing-song tone says, "All's well, all's well." It is the man on the look-out. You say, "How can all be well when I am not sleeping? how can all be well when I am sick and in pain? how can all be well when I am not at home and the children are longing for me?" There is a higher law than your sleeplessness, your pain, and your child's desire for your presence. Within those limits you are right; all is not well; but in the higher sphere that takes in a larger area and commands a wider outlook, all's well, all's well. So it is with this marvellous mystery, this strange Providence. "I am sick, and tired, and heart-broken, misunderstood, and belied, and slandered, and ill-fed, and battered down," saith the Christian man, but the angel on the look-out says, "All's well, all's well." The vessel has her face straight home, and the sea is yielding to give her passage-way. "All's well, all's well." And at last, at home,

> "Above the rest this note shall swell,
> My Jesus hath done all things well."

When I compare this reply with chance and law of averages, I feel that the Bible has got the scientific answer, the grand philosophy. So my song shall be :—

> "O Lord, how happy should I be
> If I could cast my care on thee,
> If I from self could rest,
> And feel at heart that One above
> In perfect wisdom, perfect love,
> Is working for the best!"

Men, brethren, and fathers, this is the answer of the Bible. I wait for a more magnificent reply.

———

I have finally to apply the argument to the book which is

called the Book of God. I shall report first upon the Old Testament; I am to do it simply as a literary surveyor, not as a theologian, not as a sceptic. I assume that you have appointed me to prove the book; to look over it for you, and to tell you what is in it, and to give you a general notion of its genius and scheme. You will understand, therefore, that I am now about to act the part of a literary surveyor, whose business it will be to draw you a general outline of the book, and to tell you something about its principal contents. Having got the plan fully on the table before us, I shall repeat the question which constitutes the staple of this whole argument, namely, How is such a book to be accounted for?

I may just mention to you, in the first instance, that as a literary surveyor, I have thought it to be my duty to read the book. I am certain that many persons on hearing that will be secretly surprised, for nowadays there is a keen and all but infinite intuition which knows a book without reading it. Not having attained to that high grace, I am obliged to begin at the beginning, and read my book straight through, like a drudge. I have done that for you. You will be surprised how very few people have ever done so. If you press them upon the point, they will say that no doubt they must have done so when they were at school. Others will say that there can be no doubt that, as children, they may have gone through, at all events, the principal part of the book; so you have halting and crippled talk of that kind. Where is the man who can say—as every man is bound to say, who is going to give anything like a complete and responsible opinion —" I have read the book straight on, from ' In the beginning God created the heaven and the earth,' to the benediction in the book of the Revelation of St. John the Divine"? The man who has done so has a right to have some opinion about the volume. Having myself, therefore, as your literary surveyor, just gone over the whole field, from the very beginning to the very end, I am here to report to you something about the book, and having handed in my report, I shall not be content for you to pigeon-hole it, and to say you will look at it by-and-by when you have a more convenient season. I shall ask you to remunerate me for my toil by giving an opinion, a decision, promptly; and the question I shall urge upon you with importunity and vehemence will be, "How can you account for such a book as the Bible?" Now let us go to work.

First of all, I am struck with what we should call the utter want of scientific or artistic arrangement in the putting together of the book. Nobody seems to have cared much how it was put together. It has not been edited, it has been huddled; there is no trace of a literary plan; no editor or architect could have been employed in putting together the various parts. Man after man appears to have written just what he pleased, and the parts seem to have been thrown together anyhow. I dare not put out a book so badly arranged, but here it is, with all its imperfections on its head. There is no preface; there is no index; there is no table of contents. Here and there—in fact, all over the face of the book—strange hands have scribbled something by which they have meant to indicate the contents of the book, but the men themselves have written, as it appears to me, when they pleased, how they pleased, as much as they pleased, and have allowed other people to add little bits here and there, and the book has come together in the night time, when nobody could tell exactly how it was, to tumble into such rough coherence as it may claim. There is not the slightest attempt to secure beauty or uniformity of outline. Things that belong to one another are not put together. Some are here, some there, and some otherwhere, and a good many are half put: are suggested rather than stated. There is a great deal of cloud and mystery and incompleteness. I was not surprised at this, because I had, just before reading the book, been spending a few years in endeavouring to put together another book, called Nature, and I was quite struck with the resemblance between the book written and the book unwritten. When I went out to the fields of nature, I said, "Now, all the ferns will grow together, all the oaks will be set in a row, all the birds will be distributed, will be caged in with little golden clouds they cannot escape, and all things will be done in order." Just the contrary. I seemed to find the ferns anyhow. As I got farther and farther into the secret, I began to see that under the disorder there was an order, subtle and complete. When I went from Kew Gardens into the great forest of nature, I said, God made Kew, and some blundering fools have made the forest. I said, Kew does credit to God. so nicely trimmed, so carefully swept, so critically labelled. Ah, said I, this is worthy of a God ; but the tangled forests, the solitary places, the growth unregistered, untrimmed, unscheduled, growing without tabulation —what could I say but that some wild beast of a man had been there, making order disorder, and turning scheme and plan and cosmos into chaos and darkness ?

When I went to the Zoological Gardens, I said, Now you see this is worthy of a God : all nicely caged in, all the places ticketed ; a man knows here where he is, but as to nature—a jungle and forest and wilderness and rock and crag and ravine and deep river and tortuous way. But I saw that the book unwritten and the book written were marvellously alike in this ; there was a kind of fearless genius, of dauntless spirit, that rose up out of the chaos, and said, " Mend me, if you can," and I was, therefore, as a literary surveyor, touched into a momentary glow by what I thought was the independent fearlessness and fierceness of a disorder that set itself up to rank with sun and star and milky way. I found the Botanical Gardens were made by man at so much a day, the Zoological Gardens the same. I found that any extent of botanical and zoological arrangement could be effected for so much a day. There is no science in nature, there is no theology in the Bible ; but as nature supplies all the material upon which science operates, so the Bible supplies all the material which theology puts together, often with the hands of a clumsy artisan, and nearly always with the beggarly spirit of a bigot.

The next thing that struck me in reading your book was that it makes no pretence whatever to be restrained by what is called taste or delicacy. There are many things in it that cannot be read aloud, thank God. There are some things which little children are not permitted to read. Ah me ! how foolishly we treat those who are of the kingdom of heaven ! The book moves calmly and without shame right on, amid the miscellaneousness of our life. It looks like fire ; who can corrupt fire ? It has a spirit of absolute and incorruptible purity. The Bible makes no apology, draws no curtain, makes no excuse, never turns aside to stammer or to blush ; on it goes : taking life as it is, and describing it without flattery or fear. It strikes me as very like what I have seen ir the other book, unwritten. The Bible is true to the very root and reality of things. The book does not ignore facts with a goody-goody blindness, but faces them, names them, proposes remedies for them, and searches into the root and core of the whole of them. No man in this country dare publish certain separate chapters of the Bible, and show them in his window. How then? They are right in their setting. Pick them out with a foul spirit, and they are foul; let them alone in the order and rhythm which God has appointed, and we cannot do without them. Evil be to him that evil thinks. These things belong to a greater whole; they must not be detached; the part that would be intolerable is essential to the whole that is beautiful.

The third thing that I have to report to you, as your literary surveyor, is that this book was written by some thirty or forty people, who, generally speaking, never saw one another, and who were probably unaware, speaking generally, that other people were writing parts of the book. Some of them lived a thousand years and more apart. Hardly any of them had what we should now call schooling or education; some had very much, some had none. There was one grand old man—I like his pen, shaggy and strong; it makes a crashing noise as it writes—who was very highly learned, and another was a rough-handed, horny-fleshed man, who kept a secretary, whom he never paid, to put down such blundering remarks as occurred to his fisherman's lips. One was very great, clothed with clouds, crowned with starlights, and another was an unlearned and ignorant man, and they have put their contributions to this book all within the same covers. There they are to-day, and the literary beauties of the Bible have been praised by men of letters. Many of the compositions are bold, grand, elevating, thrilling; some of them have never been excelled in simple pathos and in profound sympathy. I report this as a fact.

Add to these considerations the further fact that this book never shirks any great question. It does not content itself with trifles; it is not a book that offers little mincing guesses to little riddles—it gives an answer, whether right or wrong I do not now say, but, as a matter of fact, it does give an answer to the highest questions that can engage the human mind. By so much it commits itself—by so much it comes into open court in the broad daytime, and says, "Cross-examine me"—by so much it gives a cross-examiner an immense advantage over it; its utterances, and confessions, and statements are so broad and unreserved, he would be an unskilled cross-examiner who could not torture a witness so frank and open-mouthed. In the very forefront it has a God; its very first sentence is illuminated and sanctified by an awful name. The Bible does not grope after God in reverent or audacious speculation—it declares him, reveals him, asserts him. The Bible does not say, "Now, let it be granted, merely for the sake of argument, that there is a God"; but boldly it begins, "In the beginning God created the heaven and the earth." It next addresses itself to man, and enlarges upon his career and destiny. The Bible accounts for him; the Bible says, "I will tell you when you were made, and how, and all about you." The Bible says, "I will account for the tumult and disorder, and incoherence and ruin: I know the mournful secret." For these things it gives no superficial name; it speaks a new word. It gives to dumb unconsciousness a speech which that unconsciousness claims as most expressive. The Bible says, "Sirs, all these tragedies, tumults, tempests, agonies, ruins, griefs, deaths, all come out of *sin.*" The answer may be right, the answer may be wrong—I am only telling you that the Bible does not shirk the question. It has a short, sharp, piercing answer: it does not hide itself in a high cloud, where you cannot get at it; it comes flap down on the plain dust and says, with face of fire and tongue of passion, "This is sin." By so much it puts itself into my power. It does not address me from an altitude I cannot attain; it puts its feet, so to speak, in my own footprints, and tells me the cause of my distress and bitterness of soul.

The Bible does not content itself with drawing a line around one world or one day. It takes in the future; it has a great horizon; its straight lines do form an angle, Euclid notwithstanding. Ay, marvellous is that. The old geometrician tells me that straight lines do not form an angle, and he is right within his little limits. But if I look at two straight lines, say two rows of trees, or two rows of houses, if they be long enough, they seem to get together, or there would be no poetry in the world. It is that forming the far-off perspective, that mingling of things so far separate, that gives the world its genius and its literature. So the B.ble looks down the common rows and lines of things, and brings in the future, a haze, a mist, a golden cloud, a strange mingling of things, out of which shall come what it calls heaven.

The Bible is not a book that can only tell you what is the matter with you. Any doctor can do that. The Bible is a hopeful book ; its music seems to come out of Almightiness, and to fill all space with its enraptured strains. It foretells the levelling of the high hills and the lifting up of the valleys, the outstraightening of the crooked lines. The Bible is most jubilant in tone. With a trumpet of thunder it tells that the King is coming. Nor is this animation to be accounted for by high spirits that are momentary and transient. The Bible deals with the saddest facts in human life first, and out of its treatment of these facts comes the shouting of infinite joy. The Bible deals with the most ghastly and tragic human fact of sin. Never does it say "Peace, peace," when there is no peace. Its policy is not "Forgive and forget and say nothing more about it." Never does it make light of iniquity. It says, " Stand, till I dig a hell for it, and fill it with unquenchable fire."

The Bible does not say, "If there has been sin in the world, punish it." Any gaoler can punish a thief ; how to redeem him, cure him, make him honest, that is the problem the Bible undertakes to solve. The magistrate arms himself with little rods and instruments of torture and punishment, and he says, " Hand over the thieves and rascals to me, and I will see what can be done with them." Nothing. Punishment is failure ; punishment is vile surgery. What does God do ? This book says—I am simply reporting upon it—" I show unto you a more excellent way." Punishment we must have for social uses, but punishment is never regenerative. Punishment does not re-make or re-create or restore the soul. You must have atonement. How ? By blood. Whose blood ? The blood of the innocent. The injurer can never die sacrificially, expiatorily—he can only die like a condemned dog. Who is to suffer, then, that forgiveness may be possible ? The innocent, the injured. The future of the afflicted land will have to be redeemed through the suffering of the sons of God, through the night sweats of blood the light may not look upon, but there will come that sweet, great spirit of love afterwards that will say, "Father, forgive them ; they know not what they do." You will never say it out of your own intelligence; you will never say it out of your consciousness; you will never say it out of your selfishness; you can only say it when the nails run into you and the blood gushes from your smitten side. If thou hast not been among those agonies, thou art a poor fool and not fit to read words that have any sense in them.

The Bible does not come to me and say, "You are a sinner," only; it says, "You are a sinner, and I can save you. Behold the Lamb of God that taketh away the sin of the world. God so loved the world, that he gave his only begotten Son, that whosoever believeth in him might not perish, but have everlasting life. The blood of Jesus Christ cleanseth from all sin." You can vulgarise these answers, or you can make them sublime. They are the answers of this book. The Bible is not afraid to say that God died. No other book ever parted with its god in death. The Bible is not afraid to say that sin is the supreme difficulty of God, a difficulty not to be met by the miracle of power, but to be counteracted by the greater miracle of sacrifice.

I have to report that your book reveals God in a very singular manner. It does not shut up God in eternity ; it makes him a man, it gives him a human name, it finds a cradle for him in Bethlehem and an altar on Calvary ; it represents him as hungering, thirsting, sleeping, rejoicing, weeping. Does it bring him into contempt ? No further than you can bring fire into contempt. Fire will be treated most familiarly up to a given point, but beyond that—hands off! That is how it is with God. Fire loosed from the sun will come into your kitchen and cook your food, in the friendliest way ; fire will go upstairs into the nursery and keep the little children warm all day and not refuse to burn all night. When there is sickness in the house, fire says, "Take me into the sick-chamber ; I will make pictures for the ailing one; I will throw shadows on the wall; I will warm the air"—it will be friendly with all possible generosity and grace. Now make free with it, trifle with it ; down goes your house. Say, "Thou dost come into my kitchen and nursery and sick-chamber; now let us be friends, and let us take away all restrictions and limitations," and one hot cinder brings your castle to the ground. No trifling. Friendliness? Yes. Trifling? No. So my great God Christ. Who so gentle? who so humble? who so meek in heart? No house too mean for him to enter, no food too coarse for him to bless, no sin too vile for him to pardon; yet does he answer rulers with silence, and astound death by resurrection.

I have to report that this book never flatters or courts any reader,—does not wish to make itself popular. It announces its laws and urges its claims most inexorably—compromise and concession it will never make; with authority and emphasis it never ceases to speak. Other books ask to be read, plead for opportunity, beg to be heard; I have passed thousands of them through my hands as a literary surveyor, and they all begin, in effect, "Courteous reader, will you be so indulgent as to pay attention to me? Will you oblige me by reading half-a-dozen pages?" This book never. It tells every man that he is a sinner: to every man it preaches the humiliating doctrine of self-helplessness. At first it makes enemies. It sends a sword in the earth; it kindles a fire in families. When the proud man comes to it, it says, "Hands off; you are bad." When the rich man says, "Let me look at you," it says, "Woe unto ye that trust in riches." When the self-righteous man comes with long lean fingers, and touches it with cold marrow, it says, "O ye generation of vipers!" It takes the wise in their own craftiness, and the answers of great men it returns as the replies of fools. Yet it leaves no class of human experience unprovided for. It has a gospel for the penitent and a promise for the hopeless, a blessing for little children, a solace for hearts broken with grief. It has texts which the poorest memory can recollect; it has "jewels five words long that sparkle on the forefinger of all time." It has arguments to arrest the most powerful mind, promises which must be whispered, psalms in which the thunder might take part, judgments which strike us dumb with fear.

Now, sirs, that is my report. I will next treat of the New Testament, for you especially, but my report is so far complete. Now account for the book. If any of you should say to me, having heard these things, "Truly this is the book of him who made the heaven and the earth," I should say, "Amen." If any of you should say, "A book that inspires must itself be inspired," I should say, "The argument is unanswerable."

I now propose to give you an idea of the structure and bearing of the New Testament, and then to ask you, How do you account for such a book written under such circumstances?

Now, there was a Man in history—nobody doubts his reality as a historical personage—called Jesus Christ, who lived a certain life, who had round about him a certain number of disciples, part of whom undertook to give to the world a biographical and spiritual description of their Master. How would that life be written? I should say, first of all, the oldest disciple will write the first part of it, and that would be natural. In fact, I do not see how there can be any escape from an appointment of that sort. The senior disciple, the first man called by his Lord, will, of course, know more about him than anybody else could possibly know, and, therefore, he will write the first portion of the life. Then there were two other men with whom Christ was very familiar; their names were James and John. James will follow the first disciple, as a matter of course; then John will conclude the whole testimony; and thus we shall have the three favourites in actual life, also the three favourites in literary appointments, and the biography of Christ will be threefold, and its authorship will be by Peter, James, and John. So you think? You are wrong, wholly. The first disciple is not permitted to write a word of the life of his Master, nor is the second whom you have named, James; and the third undertakes to do a work which I will presently describe. Matthew and John were of the first twelve; Mark and Luke were not. So we are to have two lives written from the inside and two lives written from the outside. Where there is such an openness, where such a challenge to variety of gift, recollection, power, genius, I want you to see that there must also have been a certain indestructible consciousness of the truth and reality of the things that were about to be narrated. If all the disciples had been of the first twelve, we might have said there is something like a literary conspiracy there; but two of them are of the twelve, and two are not of the twelve; two of them write from a more or less interior view, and the other two from a more or less external view.

Now look at the characteristics. The first man is called Matthew. He was a man of business; he was a commercial man; he was a tax-gatherer, a publican; he had to do with figures, with marking down accounts, with taking a statement of this man and of that man, embracing many particulars. He was a kind of commercial literary character. Now when he comes to write a book, is he faithful to these characteristics, or is he so completely changed that he himself actually would not know his own individuality? He is precisely in literature what he was in business—a man of action. In Matthew's Gospel you have action following action right swiftly, and also you have in Matthew the longest reports of the discourses which Jesus Christ delivered. He was a man of action, and he was a man also used to the pen. He took down statements and objections and all kinds of different things which he heard in the prosecution of his business, and he is precisely and minutely faithful to those characteristics when he comes to contribute his share to the literature of the Master whom he served.

Now Mark was a different kind of man. There was not so much activity in his disposition and life. He was a quiet, observant man, nearly always in the background. When he came to the front, he very soon regretted having done so, and fell back again into the shadows. He was one of a large number of persons—not active, enterprising, valorous, hardly ever seen at the front, and yet necessary to the completeness of the construction of human society. What do we find in Mark's Gospel, then? Exactly what we should expect to find from such a man. There is no other Gospel that exhibits so clear and complete a power of observation as Mark's Gospel exhibits. Hence I find in Mark an account of Christ's gestures, how he stood, especially of Christ's looks—those silent, all-meaning looks. Mark seems to have kept his eye upon the eyes of his Lord. It is in Mark I read how he looked, how he observed, how he stood, how he sighed—precisely the characteristics you would have expected from all that is known of Mark's general disposition and turn of mind. He is not a monstrosity in literature; he is alike when he stands back in the shadow and when he represents his picture of the Lord Jesus Christ. And yet who can tell how much Mark was indebted to another? Who was that other?

That other was the first disciple. Mark was the secretary of Peter. Mark wrote very much at Peter's dictation, and who could have told Mark so much about the looks of Christ as Peter could tell him? The supreme look of Christ was directed to Peter; that look broke Peter's heart; and who could tell how quietly and pathetically, with great tears in his eyes and great sobs in his voice, Peter directed Mark's attention to those wonderful and revealing looks of the all-seeing eyes of the Lord, and especially of that last look which went to Peter's heart and broke it? How strange a retribution, how singular that the first disciple should be ordered back, and that the first disciple's *interpres*, or secretary, or clerk, should be sent forth to the very front! How like what we do know in Providence ourselves! Who can tell whether this book was not also written by the hand that is writing the literature of our daily life—so strange, so mixed, so tragical, so startling, so unlike everything that we ourselves ever have written, or could write? I suggest the thought; I do not give an authoritative reply.

Luke was a physician, a man who had been long years at school, a literary man, accustomed to observe closely, to ask critical questions, and to listen for the answers. Do we find anything in his Gospel to correspond with that kind of training? Exactly what corresponds to it, nothing more and nothing less. Hence, in Luke, you have so long accounts of the diseases which our Lord cured; you have a completeness which you might have expected from a scholarly and literary man. Luke, in fact, begins his Gospel by saying that, as many persons had undertaken to give a life of Christ, he himself would undertake to write a life, beginning at the very beginning, and setting forth in order the things which occurred in that life—just what you would expect from a man who had been at school, from a skilled pen, from a literary mind. I point this out as part of the evidence, and leave you to form your own opinion as to its value.

Now we come to one of the first twelve, John, and John is unlike all the other three. John does not pay so much attention to events as to thoughts. He is not so careful about the alphabet as about the literature. John was deeply religious; he lay on the bosom of his Lord; he was the disciple whom Jesus loved. How, then, did he do his work? Precisely in conformity with these characteristics. In John we find the deep things of God. He takes us beyond mere fact and incident, and reveals the eternal light and the infinite love. He makes us acquainted with the heart of Christ; he binds up the whole meaning and purpose of God in the short but immeasurable word Love. It is just the Gospel one would have expected from the man who reclined on his Lord's heart, and who seemed to hear the beatings of that inward life. I point this out also simply as a fact in the record; it is for you to think about it. Matthew could not have written John's Gospel. If Matthew had read John's Gospel, he would have been astounded by it, so differently may the self-same thing be represented, so immeasurable is the infinite, so impossible is it for any one mind to grasp the whole truth and any one eye to see all the beauty of that which is Divine and eternal. I should not wonder if Matthew had almost questioned the reality of John's Gospel, simply because John goes beyond the letter and beyond the event into infinite meanings and poetical interpretations. He had that high and Divine imagination which magnifies things little and mean and vulgar until they become great and grand and sublime. Mark could not have written John's Gospel; only John himself knew the mystery of this music; only John could venture into those high sanctuaries and repeat in spiritual speech the music of the Gospel of the Logos. In John's great heart was the secret of the Lord. John's scholarship was not of the letter; it was the light of genius, it was the quiet and holy miracle of sympathy, it was the triumph of love. This is the secret of all true and deep interpretation. You cannot teach a man to be an expositor of Scripture. This kind is not learned in the schools; it is learned in secret with Christ; so that the great expositor of the Scriptures is born and not made. It is in him; it is not put into him by man. As we love we read deeply; as we pray we see farthest; as we shut out the world by closing our eyelids, so do we enlarge the world and see the brightest and Divinest things in God's creation.

This, then, is the book you have to deal with, written by four different men, written by two who were of the first number of the twelve and by two who were not included in that select society, bearing upon it all the characteristics of the individual writers. Where, then, is Peter, the senior disciple, the man

who first gave Christ companionship? Has he no place in the
book? Was he lifted up only to be laughed at, and then to be
dropped into oblivion? Is it so that Christ treats those who
first come to him and obey his voice in life? No, no. We
expected Peter to be first; he is first—at the other end. Was it
not mercy that spared him from being in the first four? Was it
not pity that spared him from writing the story of his own
shame? Think for a moment. How could he have written one
of the four accounts of the life of Christ? How perplexed and
bewildered he must have been all through because he saw the
end from the beginning of his undertaking! Was it not mercy, I
repeat, that spared him that test? Now, Paul could tell the story
of his hostility and antagonism. Why? It was intellectual.
Not only so—so far as it was moral—he could say about it,
"Because I did it ignorantly in unbelief, I verily thought I was
doing God service in all this open opposition." But Peter had
no such plea; no such excuse could have occurred to the senior
disciple. He deliberately, and with profane language, denied his
Master. He said, "I know not the man." He went forth and
wept out his very heart in great scalding tears in secret, and
when the life came to be written, that merciful Master said, "He
cannot be in the first four; he would have to tell all that shocking
tragic story; let that be told by others; he shall have his place;
let him wait."

The Lord is most merciful even when we least expect it. Did
we but know it, there is always mercy in the very thing which
we regret most. When we are kept in the background it is
mercy that appoints our lot. There is something in it we cannot
understand. If I say, "Why am I not of the first four? I can
find no reason for not being there; I am older, abler, better,
stronger than any of them; why am I not there?" hear thy
Lord saying unto thee, "Because of my mercy. Something
would occur thou dost not fully foresee; the background is thy
place just now. I appoint the lot and the estate of man; if thou
art at the front or at the back, it is my doing." The Lord exalteth
and the Lord abaseth, and men's lives are not thrown together by
mishap and by chance and by lottery. There is a Divinity in all
this masonry and shaping and upbuilding. Thou shalt have thy
place. It is not man that is keeping you back. You are fretting

and chafing in secret because you are not in the head place; it is not men that are keeping you down; they could not do so. God knows that it is better for you and me to be where we are than to be elsewhere. Wait in the prison till Pharaoh sends for thee, poor injured one. Wait in the stable till the Lord sends for thee, thou complaining colt. Wait on the Lord, I say, and know that thy place is not of thine own carving and forcing, is not a birth and expression of thine own foolish and selfish urgency, and that the bounds of our habitation are fixed by God.

Is Peter wholly overlooked and allowed to drop out of view? No; Peter's record is in the book; he has his own place; he writes two letters which no other man could have written; they are the letters of a penitent. His pen is dipped in the blood of a broken heart, and truly the music is grand in massiveness and passion. He takes his place without a murmur; even in the arranging of the book, with which he had nothing to do, he seems to be in his right place. The others were first; he comes last; the pinnacle hath an honour as well as the foundation. The Evangelists have written, the acts of the apostles have been recorded, Paul has argued, James has lectured; and when they are all done the old disciple comes forward, to be followed by the only man who could complete the new and final revelation of God's love. There is a rhythm in this order which is not mechanical, or, to change the figure, the stones thus placed were set up by him who built all things, and he who built all things is God. It is not every hand that has skill to write a programme; it is not every man who is equally clever at all points. There is a genius of order, and that genius of order is wonderfully honoured in the very succession of the books of the New Testament. I want to hear what Peter has to say. He is kept back from view till they are all done, and when they have all laid their pens down, he says, " I will write you what I know of this great Christ," and Peter's epistles are full of the blood of Christ. It is Peter who calls it "precious blood"; it is Peter who sets it above silver and gold and all corruptible things; it is he who magnifies the Cross of Christ and the blood of Christ with the pathos that can only come out of a heart not lightly wounded on the surface, but struck through and through with the darts of the enemy.

Read the book in the light of these suggestions, and when you have so read it tell me how you are to account for it.

Now, resuming the thread of the last discourse and completing it in a moment, let me ask, What was Jesus Christ's relation to the whole—to the Old Testament, the writings that were said to be inspired? He had a very difficult part to play with that book, in the hands of those who were the leaders and teachers of the people. He came forward, and he said, " I observe those books in your hands ; all that they contain is sufficient to guide men to God." Where was his mission—what did he come to do? Again and again he said, " There is enough in these books to lead you to God " ; so then what work was set out for him to accomplish? He said, " Search the Scriptures, for they are they which testify of me." When a man asked him the way of salvation, he said, " How readest thou ? what is written in the law ? " When a man cried from hell that some one might be sent to his father's house to convert his five brethren, the answer was, " They have Moses and the prophets ; let them hear them : if they hear not Moses and the prophets, neither will they be persuaded though one rose from the dead." So he made his task most difficult. He said, " There is enough in those writings to enlighten the mind and lead the heart to the Eternal Father," and then he claimed that every jot and tittle in those writings bore entirely upon himself. He set himself forth as the interpretation and completeness of everything that was written. So the book is there, and the Man is there, and judgment is called for. This Man never smoothed down difficulties, but rather seemed to create them, to suggest points of challenge and comparison. There was no fear in his mind and heart : he spoke like a man who was addressing himself to a great question, every point of which he had fully comprehended. Not only so—he is not merely general in his application of the Old Testament to himself : he is minute and special and particular. So he takes up the volume of Isaiah ; he finds the place where it is written, " The Spirit of the Lord God is upon me, because the Lord hath anointed me to preach good tidings unto the meek, unto the poor, and to those that are bound and are heavy-laden." He closes the book, hands it to the minister, and says, " I am he of whom the prophet did thus write.' He says, " The stone which the builders rejected, the same is become the head stone of the corner." He applies, therefore, not the whole Scriptures only, but minute and separate portions of the whole record, to himself, so that men who might have been bewildered by a great breadth of application had the opportunity of testing him very severely at special points which he himself indicated as crucial and final.

Then he gave unity to the book. We thought that as it had been the work of some thirty or forty men, it was more or less incoherent—we were to make of it what we could—it was something built at different ages and periods of the world's history, and one part had next to no relation to the other. Jesus Christ said, "All these books are one; I am the all-uniting and all-illuminating centre; you can trace every mystery in the Scriptures to me; you can find the fulfilment of every hopeful prophecy in my kingdom. Where shadows startle you, I am behind them; where types and symbols perplex you, you will find their meaning in my ministry and priesthood." So the book is not many, but one : from beginning to end it is the revelation of our Lord Jesus Christ. We upon whom the ends of the age have come are not to read the book to find what meaning we can put upon it : the meaning is settled, and it is Christ, and Christ only. The creation means Christ; the promise to shattered man in Eden means Christ; the sacrifices and all the ceremonies of Judaism mean Christ; the music of Israel's sweetest harp means Christ; the light that gleams and burns in prophecy means Christ; the Song of songs rolls its tender strain around Christ; the burdens of the later seers were burdens of Christ. No page did Christ disclaim; no prophet did Christ disown; he appropriated all names and figures and symbols of beauty : he was the Root and the Offspring of David, he was the Bright and Morning Star, he was the Flower of Jesse and the Plant of Renown, he was the Rose of Sharon and the Lily of the Valley, he was the Shepherd of the Flock, and the Redeemer of those who were in the hand of the enemy; he had not where to lay his head, yet he was perfumed with the powders of the merchants. He sat on the well of Jacob weary with his journey, yet his chariot was of the wood of Lebanon. His face was marred more than any man's, yet to the eyes of love his countenance was white and ruddy, and among ten thousand he was chief. He was thirsty, yet he knew the nations were preparing for him spiced wine of the pomegranate. He was despised and rejected of men, yet he filled the firmament as One who was to be the Desire of all nations. What wonder, then, that when he met the distressed ones going to Emmaus, and when he heard the complaint of their ignorance and their sigh of suppressed dismay, he began at Moses and all the prophets and expounded to them in all the Scriptures the things concerning himself?

We are invited now to read the Bible in the light of the suggestion that it all means Christ, all its ends are to be bound up in Christ, all its difficulties and mysteries are to find their solution in the Son of God. As he proceeded, would God we had been there to hear the wondrous word! The hearts of the dejected burned within them. That is the secret of inspiration; that is how you know whether the Bible is inspired or not—does it make your heart burn—does it inspire you? If so, the cause must be equal to the effect. Christ therefore began at Moses and the prophets and the Psalms, and expounded unto the disciples in all the Scriptures the things concerning himself. No other man dare have claimed so tattered a book; no other man dare have said, "All these writings, by so many different hands, and at so many periods of the world's history, converge as to their meaning and fulfilment in my person and ministry." We should have needed a neater book, a smaller and completer treatise; but he takes in all the varied writing, all the tumultuous and miscellaneous literature, and he says, "I bind it into one unity and compose it into one unique and indestructible system of my personality and my ministry." He put the key into the drooping hands of the men walking to Emmaus; at its touch the lock sprang back, and a liberty wide as heaven came in place of their limitation and distress. When therefore I read this book, I now read it as a complete book: I take Christ with me from the beginning to the end. When the writing is very hard, the reading very difficult to my ignorance, and I want information, I will wait until I see Christ himself, and then I may have some hard questions to put to him—hard to me, not to him—everything is hard to a man who cannot see one hour ahead—but what can be hard to him who breathes eternity and the measure of whose strength is infinite?

Without Christ the Bible is chaos; with Christ it is order, and music, and light.

Hitherto we have been discussing what may be called the negative side of the great questions which have come under our consideration. We now advance to consider the positive aspect of these great inquiries and problems.

In the Bible you find men who say positively that God has spoken to them, and has told them to speak to other people in his name. They do not merely *suppose* that God has spoken to them; they say they have received messages from his mouth, that his hand touched their lips, and that they have spoken the very words which he told them to deliver. Now, on the face of it, this is an astounding declaration. It has no counterpart in our own experience, we imagine. Judging by ourselves, by all our communications with the unseen world and the Divine intelligence, we should say that no such action ever took place in any human instance. Let us consider that a moment. If a man were to arise, and say, "God came to me last night, touched my mouth, and gave me a certain message. He asked me what I saw; I told him what appeared to me in the visions of the soul, and the consequence of it all is that he has sent me to you this morning to speak directly and positively in his name." I ask you, as a Christian assembly, how you would receive that man. You would unhesitatingly pronounce him a fanatic or a lunatic. There is not a soul here, probably, that would regard that man as other than in some degree insane. Yet we who would so speak about a contemporary gather reverently, and, we believe, with intelligent adoration and hopefulness, around a book which says in every tittle of it, "God wrote me; God spoke me; God endorsed me." Is it antiquity that we are worshipping? Is it old English terminology that gets the better of our veneration, and makes us think that this book is Divine, and this spelling is holier than all other orthography? Or is it (let the heart answer and the intelligence speak) a deep, solemn, childlike conviction that in the Bible we have God's own plainly declared word, and that it is all we require for earth and time, for heaven and eternity? I ask you to consider that question, lest you should be labouring under some delusion. Let us be healthy in our thinking, let us be sound and real in our intercourse and convictions, and then we may expect to enjoy all that belongs to sound health, to robust intelligence, to complete and earnest conviction.

Consider the times in which the Bible writers lived, as compared with our own days. Consider the all but infinite silence of their intellectual region. Is there any silence anywhere now? The air is full of noise; silence is a banished spirit, a historic angel. We live amid the dinning clatter of the fussiest civilisation that ever prevailed. That may account for a good deal that is peculiar in our thinking. Every wheel creaks, every footstep has an echo; the noise is so rude and deafening that some of its more tired victims long for the release of that wide land where the wicked cease from troubling and the weary are at rest. There seems to have been no noise in the old times—the Bible days—but now there is no quietness. One has a fiery tongue, another a prophecy, another a patent, another a telegraph, another a telephone. Great buildings are put up, in which men place cunning samples of machinery; science and travel outrun one another for their respective prizes; it is all fuss, noise, rivalry neck-and-neck work. It is enough to make God speechless. How can he be heard amid the uproar of our unintelligent and urgent fuss? He built a pulpit; he meant that pulpit to be wide as the horizon, high as heaven. We have made it six feet long by four and a half, and have told men to build a little, fussy, noisy thing outside it called a platform, where sweltering rhetoricians encounter the continual peril of rhetorical suicide. God said it was to be all pulpit, all church; men were to preach in the pulpit and sing in it, and be glad in it; it was to be the greatest and grandest thing under the stars. Now we lock it up; now we diminish its dimensions; now we say that certain things are more becoming the platform than the pulpit. Ah me! Every morning has its snowfall of newspapers, every evening its special editions and its latest telegrams. There is a financial pandemonium on the exchange, and a theological Bedlam in the church. Every man knows now everything better than everybody else and uses the speech of infallibility in protesting that he is the humblest of creatures. The whole air is lacerated by the cries of human turbulence; cursing and praying, lying and

preaching, oaths and brawls, songs of hell and psalms of heaven,
heighten and aggravate the swelling discord. What wonder if,
amid all this, we say, " God hath not spoken; there is no God
to speak " ? We have filled the atmosphere with dust, and we
have made the dust move by the breath of our noise until it has
become quite a storm, and then, having created all this tempest of
violence round about us, we wonder who ever can believe that
God has spoken to the human race. To whom does God speak—
to the blustering maniac, or to the trembling worshipper? He
says, " To this man will I look: to the man who is humble
and of a contrite heart, who trembleth at my word."

Consider the times in which the Bible writers lived. Contrast
their times with ours. Their days were long, calm, lighted up
clearly to the very last; their shadow was a kind of secondary
light. The old Bible man went straight up to heaven in spirit,
and asked God what he was to do, and God told him. The altar
fire never went out; the Bible saint took his battle orders direct
from God—stored away his banner in God's sanctuary till he
wanted it again. The great prophets waited daily at the gate of
heaven, and panted for God as the hart panteth for the water-
brooks. You can hardly imaginatively conceive the difference
between those times and our own. It was the day of silence;
God's going was heard in the wind; the clouds were the dust of
his feet; the silence was too deep and grand to be the hush of
human making; it was the very peace of God, the solemn quietness of infinite rest. Things were then seen in their Divine
relations, not in their human contractions and meanness. Then
there were no guide books to the mountains that are round about
Jerusalem; there are now. Now the British excursionist asks,
" How high is that hill ? "—the hill about which the Psalmist
said, " As the mountains are round about Jerusalem, so the Lord
is round about his people." In the two voices you have the two
revelations. The English excursionist, with his month's holiday
heavily on his hands, asks about the geological formation
of the hills concerning which the old man said, " The strength
of the hills is his also "—a greater and holier comment.
Oh, if Moses could now go to Sinai, and see the kind of
people that are taken there, the whole thing would be explained. The grand old prophet, grim as the rock, with his

torrent of beard grey as foam, would look up for God; and if we were there, we should be putting little pieces of stones in small wallets, and buying the wood that saw Christ's tears, with Hebrew inscriptions on it, and placing the same in our drawing-rooms. The times explain everything: fuss, and excursion, and noise, and rattle, and panic, and dissolution, and bank failure, and bankruptcy, and political crises, and agonies of all sorts and kinds, making the air a great swirl and torment; and the long-ago yesterday, when the mountain was petrified poetry, when the rocks were unhewn altars, when the hills were libraries, and the winds great mighty organs that could thunder and tremble and wail and cry.

The Bible man saw the religious aspect of material nature; the present-day man sees the material aspect of supposedly Divine things. We linger now where the prophets wept and prayed, and ask when the steamboat leaves, and when the train comes in, and we are the men who want to drag down the heavens, and make trade with the stars. Which is to be the rule, the old faith or the present unbelief? The ancient heroism or the present self-idolatry? Moses went up the mountains alone and in solitude, Ezekiel paced the way of the river alone, Isaiah saw the King in his beauty when there was nobody with him, and long before the city had lighted its daily fire, Daniel had thrown up his window eastward, and communed with the infinite, silent Holy Spirit. Do you know what silence is? You cannot know it in the city. I saw it, if I may so say, in the depths and on the heights of the grand Simplon Pass. There and then I understood the Bible! No human creature to be seen, no human voice to be heard, no human habitation to be descried; the great rocks, the clouds brilliant in their untainted bloom, the scream of birds, the warbling of the stream as it made its way down the deep ravine to some broader water, the snow here, yonder, notwithstanding the fierce glow of an all but intolerable sun—alone—there I felt that if I did not make a noise with my own going, the silence would speak to me like a ghost. I understood it then. But the moment one other traveller came, the spell was broken, the church dissolved, and the Simplon Pass became a common way.

How can I help myself in that same direction? By such

solitude as is possible to me, by getting into quietness and silence, by being alone a good deal. If thou dost live only on the street, amid the rattle of bad pianos and the chatter of worse talkers, then thou dost know nothing of all the old mystery that made the Bible. When you are most alone, you will have most of God. We have been growing in the human direction. There is nothing more unlike the Bible than our newspaper to-day: it is all event and rattle and procession and march and noise and battle—and lies. We have come into a material age : we are developing the mountains. The old men made altars of them and developed themselves. That is the difference ; that the explanation. Do I complain ? No. The pendulum must go both ways, or it is not swinging right. You must have the Divine period, and you must have the human period ; the spiritual and the material. Both have their places in this great mystery of human development ; only do not say that the one is complete without the other. We need the Bible ; we need the daily news- paper as well now. We need all the Biblical prayer ; we need all the present-day industry and ingenuity and enterprise and thrift and skill. Do not separate the one from the other : it is the pendulum's oscillation—not this point and not that, but the complete, geometric, regular swing that ticks off your moments, and tells you how the ages are being spent.

It is thus you must read the Bible. The Bible is two books. You say the Bible contradicts itself. So it does—within the narrow, little, miserable limits which men put down for their judgments. There is Calvinism in the Bible ? Yes. And Arminianism ? Yes. There is one man in the Bible who says, " Faith—faith—faith," and another who says, " Works—works— works,"—are they both right ? Both are perfectly right. So in the old time we had the quietness and the silence, the rich psalm and the noble prayer, and the heroic self-sacrifice ; to-day we have energy, industry, mechanical contrivance, great engineer- ing skill : we are all busy from morn till eve, so busy that we resent intrusion—we have no time to talk about aught but the business of the immediate hour. And both states of life, properly understood and rightly treated, go to make up God's meaning of human history and human destiny.

The little peddling question which many men would like me

to answer, if I could, is this : How did God speak to the prophets
—did he speak to them face to face and visibly ? How far were
the prophets inspired—were the very words, the very spelling,
the punctuation even, given to the prophets—is every comma in
the Bible an inspired comma, or is the semicolon more inspired
than the comma? The little question of a little mind. The men
who ask such questions are not in earnest : they are not blood
questions, they are surface inquiries, they are of the nature of
gossip and twaddle, they do not come up out of the burning,
aching heart. What does that heart ask? Another kind of
question altogether. The question which I put to the Bible, and
about the Bible, is this: Do you inspire me ? If so, you are
yourself inspired. I enlarge that question in justice to the Bible,
because there may be something in me that prevents the full
expression of the inspiration that is in the Holy Bible, and I ask,
What has the Bible done in those lands which have read it most
and loved it most ? Does the reading of the Bible ennoble man,
lift up the mind, quicken the imagination, re-enkindle the best
hopes, sustain the holiest ambitions ? Does the Bible lead me to
undo the heavy burden, to feed the hungry, clothe the naked,
visit the sick ? Does the Bible give me all the inspiration of its
own infinite charity ? If so, the inspiration of the Bible is an
undoubted and absolute fact. You judge the tree by its fruits,
and you do well; judge the book by the results which come
from its careful, patient reading, and from the arduous endeavours
to give practical interpretation to its most sacred and difficult
precepts.

How is it that God does not write a Bible now ? How is it
that God does not make another sun now ? Is the old sun worn
out ? Why does not God write an addendum to the Bible ?
What addendum could he write ? He has spoken upon every
great subject, and he has told us everything needful to their
understanding and out-living. You cannot mention one great
theme on which there is not more written than we have yet
studied or carried out. I will tell you when the addendum
will come, as I have told you aforetime. I can give the
very day and date on which you will receive a new Bible.
When the old one has been literally and spiritually obeyed,
when its injunctions have all been carried out in their spirit and

meaning, when the present Bible is exhausted as to its spiritual interpretation, its intellectual enlightenment, and its moral demands. When we can honestly go to the Lord who wrote the Bible, and say, "We have done it all; we have completed the curriculum of duty and service; there is not a letter in it which we have not fulfilled," then he will hand us the second volume of his gracious revelation.

Instead of saying, "There is a God; go and find him" or instead of saying, "We can intellectually prove that there is a God," we have started the argument from the exactly opposite point. Our course of inquiry has lain along this line, namely, "Here is the universe; how do you account for it? Here is human life, with its tragedy and comedy, its multitudinousness, yet its unity, its disorder and chaos, and yet its organisation, society scattered all over the face of the globe, always in contention, yet always in progress—how do you account for it? Here is the Bible, written by some thirty or forty people, who lived in different ages, some of whom had no idea of what the others had written, some of whom could have had no idea as to what the others would write—a book without preface and without index, which is to-day working such mighty wonders in the thinking and in the general culture and civilisation of the globe—how do you account for it?" That is the argument which we have been endeavouring to elaborate.

We have found that one Person at least has risen, and said, "The universe, life, the Bible, Christ, all that is great, mysterious, solemn, beautiful, is to be accounted for by the words, In the beginning, God." Now the question arises, and comes up, indeed, for some sort of settlement—When you say *God*, do you not simply add one mystery to a great number already in existence? Do you not rather increase the light, or the darkness, as the case may be? Might it not be as intelligible to say, "The universe is to be accounted for by a great Secret"? Might it not even to some be as intelligible to say, "All things are to be accounted for by an inscrutable power called A B C"? Do we not simply mention a name, and leave the mystery exactly where we find it? That is the question I propose now to discuss—I hope, in some degree, to settle.

My first answer is that, in saying, In the beginning, God, we do not use a name only. Otherwise, then A, B, C might be just as intelligible, yet as useful, as the other letters, G, O, D. We do not, however, use a name only; we go far beyond a mere appellation. We have not a name only, but a character, and upon the quality of that character does the settlement depend. There is a very full revelation of the character of God given in the Bible, and it is so given as to come down to our own level, so that human reason can look at it, can look at what may be called even its extreme points. The character is not written upon the radiant clouds and in characters too minute for human vision to decipher. God is so delineated in the Bible as to be in our streets, in our houses, to be actually in the sanctuary of our own consciousness, so that human reason can look at him and consider the character which is portrayed, and pronounce almost complete and authoritative judgment upon it. Not only is this true. There is another fact which, in my estimation, has much to do with the whole consideration of this question. Not only is the character of God delineated in the Bible, and not only is it such a character as no human imagination, in my opinion, could have conceived, but it is precisely such a character as human imagination has been incessantly and vainly endeavouring to get rid of. I have, therefore, now to state the character of God as revealed in the Bible, and to ask you to follow me attentively in the portrayal, and to ask at last whether such a God could have sprung out of merely human fancy.

In the Bible God is represented as being at once the mightiest, and, in some respects, the weakest of all beings. Observe the self-contradiction and the consequent audacity, if not blasphemy, of the conception. Supposing that the human mind could have conceived of God as the mightiest of all beings, it did not lie within that imagination to conceive him also as the weakest, because the one idea would, in human reasoning, of necessity exclude the other. He is God over all, omniscient, infinite in strength and in skill, yet the meanest human heart can shut him out. The heaven and the heaven of heavens cannot contain him, yet he will enter the broken heart, and take up his habitation in the contrite spirit. Angels and archangels adore him, seraph and cherub burn and glow in his presence, and do obeisance to his power, yet my human heart and yours can shut him out, and cause him to say, wet with midnight dew, cold with nocturnal chill, " Behold, I stand at the door and knock ; if any man open the door, I will come in." This is the conception. I ask you whether it is a conception possible to the human mind. One or the other might be, but to conjoin the two, to clothe him with omnipotence, yet to keep him outside the heart door, unable to open it, is a kind of conception not native, so far as I know of human literature, to the human mind.

More than this ; God works along the line of his weakness, and continually shows his humiliation, when he might work along the line of his strength, and show the grandeur and terribleness of his majesty. How is he represented in the Bible ? He has thunderbolts in his uplifted hand. He has tears in his pitying eyes. What human imagination could conceive the two ideas ? He counteth the number of the stars, and because he is great in power, not one faileth, yet his vineyard is full of thorns and briers, and the tower thereof is thrown down. He doeth as he pleaseth amongst the armies of heaven, yet the husbandmen shut him out of his own fields and slay his Son with the sword. He is clothed with honour and majesty, yet he is grieved, afflicted, disappointed, sore in heart. The question is, Could any human imagination have conceived these two self-contradictory and mutually excluding ideas ? Given the possibility that one of them could have arisen in the human mind, who can account for the miracle that the precisely opposite idea and conception also occurred to the same intelligence ?

Not only so—the mystery grows. God himself voluntarily and lovingly spares the very race that rejects and dishonours him. He preserves and nourishes and entreats a sinful race, when he might enjoy unbroken and ineffable delight with the spirits that have kept their first estate. Why bear with a race of rebels ? You would not. Why not crush them, and dwell with the unfallen and loyal hosts of the heavenly world ? Yet sinners are spared, the life of mischief-makers is prolonged, rebels are pitied, and tokens of love are given to them by the God who has a sword and thunderbolts, and lightnings, and judgments, and maledictions, and the key of hell. How is this ? Has human imagination raised itself to this infinite compassion, spared a sinful world, and in the poetry of its highest moods redeemed a race by an ideal atonement? Is it possible? If human imagination has done this transcendent work, it must have done some other work which will be in proportion to its infinite excellence. Where is that other and competing work? We have a right to demand it; we do demand it. We pit an author against himself; we say, this was his early work, this the work of his middle period, and these are the productions of his declining years. We can never compare him with any other artist; he himself alone may be his parallel. If we have therefore this rule of reasoning amongst ourselves in other matters, why not apply it in this higher inquiry? I press it. If human imagination has conceived this God, where is the next and competing work which that human imagination has produced? If this conception is the work of human imagination, then human imagination has been declining ever since. It began with a glorious dream; it has ended in nightmare and insanity. Tell me that the architect who built St. Peter's in Rome has nothing else to show than a series of dog-kennels to prove that he built the swelling dome and magnificent walls of that great church; could I believe it? I should doubt it. So that when you tell me that this God is a human fancy, I ask for human fancy number two and three and four, that I may pit the artist against himself, and ask the dreamer for a succession of his dreams, that I may know how far he can justify himself by the multiplicity and variety of his work.

More than this: we have in the Bible a God who has created a scheme of providence which, viewed in such portion as is visible within the horizon of time, afflicts the human mind with a sense of utter confusion and utter inability on its part to bring it into order and peace. The Bible acknowledges that righteousness is thrown down in the streets, that the wicked are not in trouble as other men, that they have more than heart could wish; yet it asserts that God is all-powerful, that he is presiding over a vast and complicated scheme of things, that he rules an economy of laws, and forces, and compensations, out of which, as out of primeval chaos, he will bring light and order, beauty and rest. The Bible asserts this in the face of appearances which would cover both the theory and the theorist with utter ridicule and contempt. How dare human imagination create a conception which is falsified by everyday life and by our own little experience? What fool is he who sets up a theory which every fact on the streets overthrows, condemns, and despises? This is what the Bible does; it sets God upon the circle of the earth, it puts the reins of the universe into his hands, it tells us that all things are working together for good, it begs us to give God time that he may sweep the whole cycle of his own thought and movement, and it declares that all these conflicting forces shall be caught up in a grand astronomic movement that shall sphere them like stars, and make them glow, and burn, and revolve like completed constellations of light. Is it in the power of human genius to conceive two such contradictory ideas?

Now these considerations, accumulating themselves as they now begin to do into an impossibility as against the claims of human imagination, are further strengthened by the fact that, notwithstanding all these appearances of weakness, disorder, defeat, and humiliation, the God of the Bible never lowers the standard of righteousness, and never makes unequal and undignified terms with his enemies. He never says, " I must lower the standard if you will not come up to it." He never says, " Then I must be the party that shall make all the concessions, and we will change the whole moral standard in order to accommodate ourselves to human imbecility and pollution." Never. The standard is purity of heart, absolute righteousness, holiness without which no man shall see the Lord. So then, according to the theory that the God of the Bible is a human imagination, we have a corrupt humanity, known to be such by personal consciousness and universal observation and experience—we have a corrupt humanity conceiving an incorruptible Divinity, an unholy heart projecting out of its own thoughts an infinitely holy God, an imagination the feebleness of whose wing is proved by every other effort it has made, soaring into the very heaven of heavens, unwearied by the infinite distance, undazzled by the essential light, dictating a description of God in terms the sublimity of whose eloquence is only surpassed by the fascination of their music; and, having performed once for all this miracle of miracles, it subsides not only into commonplace intellectually, but into confusion and rebellion morally. Can you believe in such a possibility? Then, indeed, greater is your faith than the religion of Christ asks it to be.

There have been many gods and lords, have there not? Yes, many, of the human imagination, as pagan literature so abundantly testifies; but they betray their origin so obviously as to do away with the necessity of serious argument. We can see how they came to be, we can weigh them and measure them; we can account for them, and, as Sir William Hamilton said, "A God that can be understood is not a God at all." But even here we must be just: even such gods as we find in heathendom may be distorted figures of an original revelation, the broken memories of a sacred vision in ages far off. For God has never left himself without witness, and it is one of the charges against the men who have been unfaithful to this witness that when they knew God, they glorified him not as God, neither were thankful; but became vain in their imaginations, and their foolish heart was darkened: professing themselves to be wise, they became fools, and changed the glory of the incorruptible God into an image made like to corruptible man, and to birds, and to four-footed beasts, and creeping things. Truly such gods come easily enough within the scope of human imagination, so disennobled are they by their grotesqueness, so debased by sensuality, so discredited by shortsightedness; nay, more, such gods themselves are the best answers to the impious theory that the God of the Bible is the outcome of the imagination of man.

So you see when we give God as the explanation of all things, we do not use a mere name: we use a name that indicates a character, a spirit, and it is by this character that we wish the suggestion—calling it no more in the meantime—that God created the heaven and the earth and rules our life to be estimated and valued. The men of natural science to-day tell us that there is a secret, and they reverentially spell the word *secret* with a capital S. So far, so good. They tell us that there is a power, with a capital P, unknown, with a capital U—religion in typography, a kind of small altar made by large capitals. So far, I repeat, so good. Wherever I find a man who can spell secret, referring to some power in the universe he cannot under-stand, with a capital S, I find the beginning of the life that is right. Despair of no man who has a feeling of veneration; find a man who cannot look upon a sunset without tears coming into his eyes, and you find a man who may not be far from the kingdom of God. Find a man who in the presence of death is silent, and his speechlessness may be a kind of negative religion. I am not content with *Secret,* though so typographically honoured. The Bible says there is a secret, and the answer to it is Father, Saviour, Redeemer, Lord. Are these but so many words? Every one of these words is a character, and that character has direct and immediate relation to our life, and that character clothes itself with abasements which bring it within our vision, and subject it even to our critical inquiry and estimate. It is a great thing to do.

The argument, then, briefly stands thus. The God of the Bible is so consistent, the same at the last as at the first, though ages intervened between the delineations given by the earliest writers and those given by the latest—so majestic yet so condescending, so righteous yet so clement, so immediately and minutely identified with human affairs, yet so infinitely raised above their debasement and contamination—so wholly unlike every other conception of the human mind, that human credulity itself is simply staggered by the suggestion that such a God was born in the imagination of man. This then is where I rest. I claim no finality; I scorn no other man's thinking. I had a universe given to me to account for. One man told me it was to be accounted for by chance, and I felt—I *felt*—that he was a fool. I had human life given to me to account for, in all zones and climes, in all ages and seas and lands. I studied it. One man told me it was to be accounted for by the law of averages, and I felt that he was a fool. I had the Bible to account for. I read it straight through, and I was told by one man that it happened to come together just as it is, that there is no purpose in it, no organic or spiritual genius and unity, and that it is a gathering up of fragments that have no mutual relation, and as I read the thing, as it got into me and made my blood tingle, I felt that he, too, was a fool. Then I came to this revelation, " In the beginning, God "—God not a name only, but a character, a spirit, a life, a reality : God is light, God is love, God is Saviour, God blessed for evermore, King of kings, Lord of lords, and I *felt* that the answer was grand enough to be true.

GENESIS.

THIS is a book of beginnings. Do not force the mind to immediate opinions
upon it ; let it tell out every bar of its new music, until the soul, startled by
the unfamiliar tones, has become acquainted with the far-off melody and
been brought to love its repetition in the hope that repetition may itself
become a kind of interpretation. The mind ought not to rush with heedless-
ness or violence upon a book like Genesis, if only for the one reason that
it is Genesis, and not Finis. Nor is there any sound reasoning in the easy
philosophy which says that the Hebrew language, or other Eastern speech,
is given to hyperbole, or such wealth of expression as is inconsistent with
literal exactitude or arithmetical precision. What is exactitude ? What
is precision ? In the expression of religious thought is that the right
language which rebukes imagination and makes a final standard of the
alphabet, or is that the right language which contemns its own inability to
overtake the sacred meaning, and seeks by what is called exaggeration to
express what is inexpressible ? The Hebrew language is as certainly a
Divine creation as is the mouth of man. " Who hath made man's mouth ? "
In whatever degree other and later languages may be indebted to the invention of grammarians, I cannot but find in the Hebrew tongue an instrument
bearing special witness to the Divine hand. Its very amplitude is part of
the fulness of all other things. It is a speech, bearing seed after its own
kind, a language from which all other language has been deduced without
impoverishing the original abundance. We must not, therefore, evade many
a difficulty under the easy plea that Oriental languages are pictorial, re-
dundant, imaginative, or hyperbolical. God himself is to our poor thought
the great hyperbole. The universe must be an infinite exaggeration to any
single part of its own entirety. The truly religious reason and emotion
carries us up to a region where exaggeration is impossible, where passion is
temperance, where madness is composure, where every word in human
speech must be crushed into one syllable with which to begin the utterance
of the unutterable. If we degrade ourselves into merely literal critics, we
disqualify ourselves to judge religious truth ; yet this is what men have
done of set purpose, and with some show of mental vanity, actually boasting
that in the suppression of feeling they would begin the study of God.
Hence we have seen a huge literary apparatus in place of the shadow of an
Altar clothed with radiant clouds, and a thousand critics in place of an
innumerable company of worshippers. In religious study there is but one
thing better than speech, and that is silence. If we have speech, it must be
great speech. Words must come like strong rivers too deep to be noisy

and not like shallow brooks that fret the ear with petulant self-consciousness. It is so the Divine Hebrew speech flows through the Church; "the river of God is full of water," a most plentiful stream, worthy of the Fountain whence it flows, worthy of the Throne whither it returns.

Gen. i. 1-25.

1. In the beginning (of all things) God created the heaven (the Hebrew word for "heaven" is always plural) and the earth.

2. And the earth was without form (desolate), and void; and darkness was upon the face of the deep. And the Spirit of God moved (brooded, rather than fluttered or hovered) upon the face of the waters.

3. And God said (commanded), Let there be light: and there was light.

4. And God saw the light, that it was good: and God divided the light from the darkness.

5. And God called the light Day, and the darkness he called Night. And the evening and the morning were the first day (period of time).

6. And God said, Let there be a firmament (expanse or expansion) in the midst of the waters, and let it divide the waters from the waters.

7. And God made the firmament, and divided the waters which were under the firmament from the waters which were above the firmament: and it was so.

8. And God called the firmament Heaven. And the evening and the morning were the second day.

9. And God said, Let the waters under the heaven be gathered together unto one place, and let the dry land appear: and it was so.

10. And God called the dry land Earth; and the gathering together of the waters called he Seas: and God saw that it was good.

11. And God said, Let the earth bring forth grass, the herb yielding seed, and the fruit tree yielding fruit after his kind, whose seed is in itself, upon the earth: and it was so.

12. And the earth brought forth grass (the first calling forth of life upon the earth), and herb yielding seed after his kind, and the tree yielding fruit, whose seed was in itself, after his kind: and God saw that it was good.

13. And the evening and the morning were the third day.

14. And God said, Let there be lights (luminaries or light-bearers) in the firmament of the heaven to divide the day from the night; and let them be for signs, and for seasons, and for days, and years:

15. And let them be for lights in the firmament of the heaven to give light upon the earth: and it was so.

16. And God made (the word is "made," not "created," pointing to different methods of construction) two great lights; the greater light to rule the day, and the lesser light to rule the night: he made the stars also.

17. And God set them in the firmament of the heaven to give light upon the earth,

18. And to rule over the day and over the night, and to divide the light from the darkness: and God saw that it was good.

19. And the evening and the morning were the fourth day.

20. And God said, Let the waters bring forth abundantly the moving

creature that hath life, and fowl that may fly above the earth in the open firmament (the concave vault) of heaven.

21. And God created great whales, and every living creature that moveth, which the waters brought forth abundantly, after their kind, and every winged fowl after his kind : and God saw that it was good.

22. And God blessed them saying, Be fruitful, and multiply, and fill the waters in the seas, and let fowl multiply in the earth.

23. And the evening and the morning were the fifth day.

24. And God said, Let the earth bring forth the living creature after his kind, cattle (grass-eating), and creeping thing (worms, insects, and reptiles), and beast (carnivorous) of the earth after his kind : and it was so.

25. And God made the beast of the earth after his kind, and cattle after their kind, and everything that creepeth upon the earth after his kind : and God saw that it was good.

THE UNBEGINNING BEGINNING.

WAS ever the mind so staggered and so humiliated as by this first chapter of Genesis ! The mind is plunged into infinite depths, and driven up into infinite heights, and forced with irresistible violence across infinite breadths, and then is asked by mechanical critics what it thinks of it all ! Why, of course, it cannot think. It is in the whirl of an infinite amazement; it is humbled, abashed, and stupefied utterly. The action never pauses for a moment; how busy are the days, and how active the night in star-lighting; in the waters is a great stir of life; the woods are burning with colour ; the earth is alive with things that creep ; the air vibrates with the clap of wings. Then we are called upon to say what we think of it all ! Why, what do we know about it ? We have only seen it upon paper—upon a scroll that twists and crinkles under the burden it has to carry, and that writhes because of the torment of a secret it can never tell. What do we think of it all ? First tell me what have we *seen* of it all. Nothing ! Who has seen the sun, been around him on every side, passed through his provinces, scaled his mountains, trembled in his solitudes ? Who has acquainted himself with the stars, every one of them, great and small ; the planets with their belts and rings, and the treasure hidden in their central caskets—the innumerable stars—unmeasured and immeasurable thoroughfares of glory—steeps of worlds—ocean after ocean of constellations—a way white as milk—figures as of lions and winged creatures—timid stars, timid because so small ;

burning stars, only kept from destroying us because of distance—
stars that could swallow up our sun without adding a beam to
their own splendour or a sprinkling of dust to their own magnitude—what do we think of them all ? Especially of those we
have never seen ; the starry kingdoms that glow beyond every
horizon that has dawned upon our dreams ; every system the
centre of some other system ; their revolutions an eternity, their
space an infinity !

What, indeed, do we know about our own earth ? Nothing
worth naming ! We have chipped the rocks here and there,
and drawn diagrams which we have sold to children, and paid
carpenters for drawers to keep spars in ; we have made maps of
the world which we are always readjusting and recolouring :
we have called common things by uncommon names ; but who
knows anything about the earth ? Who has walked over all the
ocean beds and acquainted himself with all the mystery of the
sea ? Who has stood a yard from the shore of his own little
world, and watched the tiny boat voyaging over the sea of space ?
Who has seen both hemispheres at once ? Who has been in both
hemispheres on the same day ? Who can make the wind blow
from the east or west ? What is the wind ? Ay, poor idiot-
philosopher, hot with carrying huge burdens of polysyllables,
tell me what is the wind, and thy answer shall be the root of
another question. Our wisdom is like a tree growing only
questions, a hard fruit, hard to reach, hard to use.

A marvellous harmony, too, there is in the statement of *cause*
no guessing or supposing or humble suggestion ; on the contrary,
a definite and thrilling asseveration: hear it :—" God created "—
" And God said "—" And God saw "—" And God called "—" And
God made "—" And God set "—" And God blessed "—GOD !
That is the cause : Personality, Mind, Purpose, Government—
these are the ideas which the bold writer puts before everything
and above everything. The mysteries of the creation are but
shadows of the mystery of the Creator. How curious is the
variety of mind ! Some minds instantly fix upon the heavenly
bodies, and get credit for being astronomers ; others upon plants
and flowers, and get credit for being botanists ; others upon
beasts and birds, and get credit for being naturalists—all such

minds are supposed to be very scientific and very able : but when another type of mind seizes upon the term GOD, the highest term of all, it is sneered at as theological, with a strong tinge of fanaticism. It seems to me that the theologian has undertaken the highest task of all, and that, compared with his work, all other work is child's play. But God is unknowable. So is nature ; so is to-morrow ; so is man; so is space. Or, if you will have it, let us say that, in the degree in which nature is knowable, God is knowable ; when science advances religion goes along with it ; science builds the altar at which religion prays. If nature is great, God must (reasonably and analogously) be greater; if nature displays wisdom, God must be wiser; if nature indicates power, it indicates it in such a degree as to make God all-powerful. Thus the first chapter of Genesis might have been written backwards—" The heaven and the earth had a beginning : the earth was without form and void ; order came, and light, and night and day, and a great firmament, and all the host of life, and everything so good, so beautiful, so beneficent, as to be worthy of the name of GOD." The other method of statement is infinitely grander, and indeed infinitely simpler. As Christian reasoners we adopt it, as Christian worshippers. Instead of the infantile statement—" Here is a picture which must have had a painter," we name the Artist and credit him with the picture. If we remove the term GOD from this chapter, we leave behind a mystery of darkness ; when we reinsert the term GOD we import the nobler mystery of light. In a very plain sense there is, so far as the visible creation is concerned, less mystery *with* a Creator than *without* one. Here, then, is the Christian standpoint, and here the Christian resting ground— God the mighty and holy Maker of all things. If the things them- selves were not here, we might have some difficulty about God, but these things embody him, represent him, make him, in some degree, manifest to our naked eyes. We must not be afraid, or ashamed even, of true Deism. It is irrational, not merely senti- mental, to poetise the moon and ignore the sun which she modestly reflects. What is *God* to us ? Does he live ? Is he only an aggregation of sublime epithets ? Or, do we live and move and have our being in him ? Do not let us trouble the mind with vain endeavours to define God ; on the contrary, let us guard the mind against what may too narrowly be described as "intelligent conceptions" of God, for thereby we may not lift up our intelligence to God, but drag down God to our intelligence, and so become our own idolaters. To think that it is in our power to think of GOD is to come under the influence of what may, without infinite watchfulness of the heart, become the most insidious temptation that can assail the human mind. The most intelligent conception of God would seem to me to be that God cannot be intellectually conceived. We *feel after* him. He is recognised by the heart. Whenever he comes within the lines of reason it is by a condescension so complete as almost of necessity to mislead reason, as if the dewdrop should suppose it holds the sun which it only reflects. We bow down before God. We cannot see God and live. God is great, and we know him not. A wonderful thing it was for any mind, supposing it to be but a finite thought, to introduce the word GOD into human speech. If we could think ourselves out of our familiarities back to beginnings, we should find in the introduction of this word something like a miracle in language. Once uttered, once written, it is immediately recognised as the word which the ages have been waiting for, and the mind is apt to imagine that it always knew the word, and that the word is part and parcel of its own quality—a kind of ingratitude not unknown even in strictly human education and intercourse. Yet once suggested (we should say revealed), how strong are the commendations it brings with it! Truly, things do look as if they might have been brought about by a personal and sovereign Mind. They are so wonderfully made, so balanced, so rounded, so interdependent; so huge, yet so safe; so small, yet each cared for and fed as if it were an only child; so long-continued, too, age after age, that time has no more dial space to write figures upon that will tell all the tale of duration. Yes; now that some one has put into the mind the idea of God, we cannot get rid of it. "The heavens declare the glory of God; and the firmament sheweth his handiwork. Day unto day uttereth speech, and night unto night sheweth knowledge." Reason is not humbled by this confession, but ennobled by it. Reason itself says, It must be so! Reason takes off its sandals and lays down its crook, saying, Surely this is holy ground! Reason is a worshipper. Reason has seen space, and inferred the Infinite; reason has seen duration, and inferred the Eternal; a voice has whispered into the ear of reason the mysterious word GOD, and reason cannot silence the solemn music. " The fool hath said in his heart, There is no God," but the world has not accepted the fool's speech. Crime has endeavoured to upset law, yet is there infinite quietness in the order of creation. The heathen have raged and the people imagined a vain thing, yet has their rage died like a wind, and their pride been broken as a potter's vessel. Here, then, we stand. We accept the idea—GOD. We did not create it, we have tried to destroy it, yet there it is—a great light, a solemn darkness, a temple of mystery, " a deep where all our thoughts are drowned."

The practical effect of this faith has been most remarkable and confirmatory. A mysterious and gracious process of identification has completed itself in the purest and loftiest affections of the heart; so I should now have to give up a God that has involved himself in my thinking, not only with all time and space, not only with life and destiny, as they project themselves on horizons far away, but with this day's duty, with all immediate obligation, sacrifice, service, and character. GOD is not now a symbol of an imaginary kind, whose action, in my thinking, I can suspend without loss of light and force ; he has become—account for it as you may—the ruling power of my life, the moral centre of my conduct, the thought which penetrates, inspires, and sanctifies me. The ease or difficulty with which a man can surrender GOD depends, if I may so say, upon the use to which he has become accustomed to put the mysterious term. If GOD has been but a nebulous and speechless dream—a veneration without a corresponding morality—the act of surrender will be as indefinite as itself. But in our case, as Christian believers and Christian teachers, GOD is in every part of our life ; he has manifested himself to us ; he has taken up his abode with us ; the Spirit of his Son is in our hearts, crying, Abba, Father ; he searches us and tries us ; he acts directly and judicially upon every motive ; he guides us with his eye ; he besets us behind and before, and lays his hand upon us ; to him our hearts aspire in instinctive as well as in reasoned prayer ; the spontaneous

outstretching of our hands is towards his holy temple, if haply
we may touch his strength, and feel secure because he is almighty;
when we do wrong our eyes are darkened as with a cloud, and
when we do well our hearts feel upon them the light of a smile.
That is our case now; in such circumstances surrender would
be destruction. We have, if I may so put it, gone too far in our
use of God to turn away from him and yet retain our identity
intact. "We live and move and have our being in God." We
have passed the merely argumentative stage. "God dwelleth in
us, and his love is perfected in us." "Our fellowship is with
the Father, and with his Son Jesus Christ." Whilst God was
but an incipient thought—a possible superstition of the mind—
we might have crushed the embryo; but we have heard a voice,
and opened the door, and God has come in and has supped with
us, and we with him. We are now, so to speak, involved in
God, complicated with him; "partakers of the Divine nature,"
"partakers of his holiness." "Of him are we in Christ Jesus,
who of God is made unto us wisdom, and righteousness,
and sanctification, and redemption." Though our minds cannot
grasp his infinity, our hearts can feel his love; though our imagination cannot search his understanding, our conscience can
respond to his righteousness; though we cannot explain, we can
pray. Thus, God has laid hold of our highest nature, though
apparently our intellect stands in rebuke, abashed before him.
There are, therefore, moral considerations in any proposed surrender, as well as considerations of a merely intellectual kind,
and whilst the intellectual considerations are on no account to
be lowered in value and dignity, the considerations which turn
towards conscience and character, which construct society upon
a religious and therefore responsible basis, and insist upon
making daily conduct itself into a kind of daily worship, can only,
in my view, be relaxed at the peril of the very morality they aim
to express   I rest in what I believe to be the Christian conception of God. It fills and satisfies, it comforts and inspires my
best nature. My reason bows before it. My conscience accepts
it. My heart is thankful for it; my whole soul grows towards
strength and completeness under its hallowing benediction. I
feel that it must be right, because it enables me to pity sin, to
be kind to the unthankful and the evil, to find in every man a

brother, and to bow down with all the nations of the world, saying, " Our Father, which art in heaven."

Yes, now I look at things, they *might* have been made by God . they are vast enough, splendid enough, and harmonious enough. I do not particularly mind if they did come out of germs, molecules, and plasms which naked eyes cannot see. Very likely. They are the more wonderful for that. I never supposed that God drove up the worlds into their places like infinite loads drawn by infinite horses. " Germs " is quite notion enough for me. The kingdom of heaven itself is like unto a grain of mustard seed, and *that* kingdom is infinitely larger than all the constellations put together. As I look upon that kingdom the constellations fade into pale sparks as if by conscious contrast. Once creation looked big—quite an enormous and awful bulk—but now that I have seen him by whom, for whom, and through whom, it was made, the stars are but pin points and the great circle but a dim shadow because of the glorious majesty of his Godhead. Matter lessens as thought enlarges, and so along this line we find the comforting truth that death is by reason of increasing life " swallowed up in victory." This would seem to be the evolution through which Biblical thought itself has passed. David considered the heavens, the moon, and the stars, and wondered that God should make account of the son of man. Peter, a man in every way likely to be impressed by bulk and force and radiance, having been with Jesus and learned of him—having seen the white flame on Tabor which Saul afterwards saw at the gate of Damascus—looked upon the infinite pomp, and predicted the noise of its departure and the smoke of its dissolution.

This marvellous development of what may be called contempt for inferior things, how magnificent soever their exterior, is characteristic of the whole process of spiritual growth, and is, indeed, a test of its progress and healthiness. A remarkable instance is found in the Apostle Paul. A mind so capacious and energetic could have glorified any sphere of human activity, yet gathering together all the privileges of ancestry, all the dignities of office all the temptations of sense, he burned them all on the altar of the Cross, and counted their sacrifice a gain.

So much depends upon what may be called the uppermost principle or force in a man's nature. Where it is commercial, markets are universes and prices are the only recognised poetry; where it is love of physical science, the visible creation is the mind's ample heaven; where it is patriotism, the country is the only sanctuary worth saving; where it is theological, the universe is but a spark, all space is but a bubble, time has no measurable proportion to unbeginning and unending duration—the one absorbing and inspiring thought is GOD. Hence the infinite raptures of Christian experience, hence triumph over every pain which cruelty can inflict, hence the shout of victory in the very presence of death. So even thus early in our studies of the Bible—even in this architectural and almost experimental Genesis—we come upon some of the ultimate truths of practical Christianity. Are we still impressed by bulk? Is the visible creation still so huge and important a thing? Is the eye still amazed by the pomp of the nocturnal sky and the radiance of summer noondays? Or have we passed the era of childish wonder and arithmetical computation, and entered into the temple of worship and seen the Maker whose presence annihilates all things made? The creation is for children; the sanctuary is for men: matter is for the senses; thought is for the soul. This is the sign of growth. By this we know just where we are on the Divine scale. If we are still only gaping at Size and Light, we are but in a rudimentary state; we should have passed beyond this long ago, and should now be in a region that has no boundaries, in a kingdom without sun or moon, without night, without sea, without temple, where precious stones are thrust into the foundations, and gold is trodden upon as the pavement, and the one glory is "the throne of God and of the Lamb." If we have not passed into this new Jerusalem, we have been idling away our time in laborious frivolity, heaping up the wind and gathering the waters into sieves.

Gen. i. 26–31.

26. And God said, Let us make man in our image (deliberation enhances dignity), after our likeness: and let them have dominion over the fish of the sea, and over the fowl of the air, and over the cattle, and over all the earth, and over every creeping thing that creepeth upon the earth.

27. So God created man (the Adam) in his own image; in the image of God created he him; male and female created he them.

28. And God blessed them (wished them well, a home word, the beginning of home!), and God said unto them, Be fruitful, and multiply, and replenish (utilise it) the earth (one sphere at a time), and subdue it: and have dominion over the fish of the sea, and over the fowl of the air, and over every living thing that moveth upon the earth.

29. And God said (the granting of a Divine charter), Behold, I have given you every herb bearing seed, which is upon the face of all the earth, and every tree, in the which is the fruit of a tree yielding seed; to you it shall be for meat.

30. And to every beast of the earth, and to every fowl of the air, and to every thing that creepeth upon the earth, wherein there is life, I have given every green herb for meat: and it was so.

31. And God saw everything that he had made, and, behold, it was very good (lo! very good!). And the evening and the morning were the sixth day.

THE MAKING OF MAN.

THERE is surely no bolder sentence in all human speech. It takes an infinite liberty with God! It is blasphemy if it is not truth. We have been accustomed to look at the statement so much from the human point that we have forgotten how deeply the Divine character itself is implicated. To tell us that all the signboards in Italy were painted by Raphael is simply to dishonour and bitterly humiliate the great artist. We should resent the suggestion that Beethoven or Handel is the author of all the noise that passes under the name of music. Yet we say, God made *man*! Look at man, and repeat the audacity if you dare! Lying, drunken, selfish man; plotting, scheming, cruel man; foolish, vain, babbling man; prodigal man, wandering in wildernesses in search of the impossible, sneaking in forbidden places with the crouch of a criminal, putting his finger in human blood and musing as to its probable price per gallon—did God make *man*? Not merely make him in some rough outline way, but make him in the Divine image and likeness as an other-self, a limited and shadowed divinity? Verily, then, a strange image is God's! Leering, gibing, mocking image; a painted mask; a vizor meant to deceive. See where cunning lurks in its own well-managed wrinkle—see how cold selfishness puts out the genial warmth of eyes that should have beamed with kindness; hear how mean motives have taken the music out of voices that

should have expressed most trustful frankness : then look at
the body, misshapen, defiled, degraded, rheum in every joint,
specks of corruption in the warm currents of the blood, leprosy
making the skin loathsome, the whole body tottering under the
burden of the invisible but inseparable companionship of death !
Is this the image, is this the likeness of God ? Or, take man at
his best estate, what is he but a temporary success in art—
clothier's art, schoolmaster's art, fashion's art ? He cannot see
into to-morrow ; he imperfectly remembers what happened
yesterday ; he is crammed for the occasion, made great for the
little battle, careful about the night air, dainty as to his digestion,
sensitive to praise or blame, preaching gospels and living blasphemies, praying with forced words, whilst his truant mind is
away in the thick of markets or the complexity of contending
interests. Is this the image of God ? Is this incarnate deity ?
Is this Heaven's lame success in self-reproduction ? Oh, how we
burn under the sharp questioning ! How we retire into our
proper nothingness, and beg that no more words may fall upon
us like whetted spears ! Yet there are the facts. There are the
men themselves. Write on the low brow—" the image and
likeness of God " ; write on the idiot's leering face—" the image
and likeness of God " ; write on the sensualist's porcine face—
" the image and likeness of God " ; write on the puppet's
powdered and painted countenance—" the image and likeness of
God "—do this, and then say how infinite is the mockery, how
infinite the lie !

Yet here is the text. Here is the distinct assurance that
God created man in his own image and likeness ; in the image of
God created he him. This is enough to ruin any Bible. This
is enough to dethrone God. Within narrow limits any man
would be justified in saying, If man is made in the image
of God, I will not worship a God who bears such an
image. There would be some logic in this curt reasoning,
supposing the whole case to be on the surface and to be
within measurable points. So God exists to our imagination
under the inexpressible disadvantage of being represented by
ourselves. When we wonder about him we revert to our own
constitution. When we pray to him we feel as if engaged in
some mysterious process of self-consultation. When we reason

about him the foot of the ladder of our reasoning stands squarely on the base of our own nature. Yet, so to say, how otherwise could we get at God? Without some sort of incarnation we could have no starting point. We should be hopelessly aiming to seize the horizon or to hear messages from worlds where our language is not known. So we are driven back upon ourselves —not ourselves as outwardly seen and publicly interpreted, but our inner selves, the very secret and mystery of our soul's reality

Ay; we are now nearing the point. We have not been talking about the right "man" at all. The 'man" is within the man; the "man" is not any one man; the "man" is Humanity. God is no more the man we know than the man himself is the body we see. Now we come where words are of little use, and where the literal mind will stumble as in the dark. Truly we are now passing the gates of a sanctuary, and the silence is most eloquent. We have never seen man; he has been seen only by his Maker! As to spirit and temper and action, we are bankrupts and criminals. But the sinner is greater than the sin. We cannot see him; but God sees him; yes, and God loves him in all the shame and ruin. This is the mystery of grace. This is the pity out of which came blood, redemption, forgiveness, and all the power and glory of the Gospel. Arguing from the outside, that is, from appearance and action, and from such motive as admits of outward expression, it is easy to ridicule the notion that God made man in his own image. But arguing from other facts, it is impossible, with any intellectual or moral satisfaction, to account for man on any other theory than that he is the direct creation of God. If I think of sin only, I exclude God from the responsibility of having made man; but when I think of repentance, prayer, love, sacrifice, I say, Surely this is God! this is Eternity! When I see the sinner run into sin, I feel as if he might have been made by the devil; but when he stands still and bethinks himself; when the hot tears fill his eyes; when he sighs towards heaven a sigh of bitterness and true penitence; when, looking round to assure himself of absolute solitude, he falls down to pray without words; *then* I see a dim outline of the image and likeness in which he was created. In that solemn hour I begin to see *man*—the man that accounts for the Cross, the man who grieved God, the man who brought down the Christ. You have often seen that man in yourselves. Sometimes you have felt such stirrings of soul, such heavenly and heavenward impulses, such pureness of love, such outleaping of holy passion towards God and all godliness, that you have thought yourselves to be *worth* saving, even at the cost of blood ! There was no vanity in such thought, no self-exaggeration ; there was a claim of eternal kinship, a cry as of a child who felt that the Father cared for its sin and its sorrow.

Thus everything depends as usual on the point of view, and as usual we are in the first instance always tempted to take the narrow and unworthy standing ground. We have to be actually driven to high conceptions and to the true rendering of things. We are so dull of sight, so nearly deaf, so almost soulless, by reason of some great calamity which has unmade and uncrowned us, that we miss the genius and poetry of things. In everything surely there is a touch of God, could we but see the finger-print. There is some connection between the differently coloured juices of things—between the milk of the wheat stalk and the blood which has given Calvary its fame—could we but see it. O those blind eyes of ours ! they make one mistake after another ; they let God go past without seeing any outline of a presence ; they turn day into a spoiled night. Yet sometimes we get glimpses that beasts can never get. Sometimes at a bound we leave the wisest brutes down in the clay to which they belong, and listen at doors concealed by light. The first man in the Bible saw little enough, but how much the last man saw ! What a difference between the Adam of Genesis and the John of the Apocalypse ! It is easy to believe that John was made in the image and likeness of God. What eyes the man had, and ears, and power of dreaming great dreams, and in how sublime contempt he held all things called great on earth ! He saw doors opened in heaven ; he was summoned as by a trumpet to see things which must be hereafter ; he saw the throned One like a jasper and a sardine stone, and a rainbow about the throne, in sight like unto an emerald : wondrous visions rewarded the gaze of wondrous eyes—lightnings and thunderings and seven lamps of fire burning before the throne—books of mysteries, harps, and golden vials full of odours, a rider with a bow and a crown, who went forth conquering and to conquer, white robes, golden censers, an angel with a face like the sun and his feet as pillars of fire, and a lamb as it had been slain ! Look at *that* seer, if you would know in whose image and likeness man was created and made. Is there no similar apocalypse even in our narrowed experience ? Are we not as truly one in the book of Revelation as we are one in the book of Genesis ? When the poet dreams, the ploughman dreams. When the poet creates for his soul's highest utterance a new speech, the dumb man has a claim by right of descent to the new wealth of eloquence. When, therefore, I want to know who I am and what I was meant to be, I will not only read the book of Genesis, but peruse with the enchantment of kindred and sympathy the marvels of the infinite Apocalypse.

We cannot think of God having made man without also thinking of the responsibility which is created by that solemn act. God accepts the responsibility of his own administration. Righteousness at the heart of things, and righteousness which will yet vindicate itself, is a conviction which we cannot surrender. It is indeed a solemn fact that we were no parties to our own creation. We are not responsible for our own existence. Let us carefully and steadily fasten the mind upon this astounding fact. God made us, yet we disobey him ; God made us, yet we grieve him ; God made us, yet we are not godly. How is that ? There is no answer to the question in mere argument. For my part I simply wait. I begin to feel that, without the power of sinning, I could not be a man. As for the rest, I hide myself in Christ. I go where he goes. He has told me more than any other teacher has ever done, and he says he has more to tell me. I acknowledge the mystery ; I feel the darkness ; I tremble in the tumult ; but I look to Christ to bring all things into light, and crown all things with peace. This is what we call the Christian standpoint, and I deliberately and gratefully occupy it. God will answer for himself. He will not be hard upon me, for he knoweth my frame, he remembereth that I am but dust ; he will not despise me because he made me in his image and likeness. Strange, too, as it may appear, 1 enjoy the weird charm of life's great mystery, as a traveller might enjoy a road full of sudden turnings and possible surprises, preferring such a road to the weary, straight line, miles long, and white with hot dust. I have room enough to pray in. 1 have room enough to suffer in. By-and-by I shall have large space, and day without night to work in. We have yet to die ; that we have never done. We have to cross the river—the cold, black, sullen river. Wait for that, and let us talk on the other side. Keep many a question standing over for heaven's eternal sunshine.

If we would see God's conception of man, we must look upon the face of his Son—him of whom he said, " This is my beloved Son, in whom I am well pleased." That is man ; that is the ideal humanity. It is useless to look in any other direction for God's purpose and thought. God does not ask us to imitate even our most perfect fellow-creature, except in so far as that fellow-creature imitates and exemplifies Christ. Do not let us mock one another, and tauntingly ask if we are made in the image and like-ness of God ; but let us steadfastly gaze on Christ, marking the perfectness of his lineaments, the harmony of his attributes, the sublimity of his purpose, and then, pointing to him in his solitude of beauty and holiness, we may exclaim, " Behold the image of God ! " We must not judge Christ by what we know of man ; we must judge man by what we know of Christ. Very wide indeed and very beneficent is the application of this thought; its right and fearless application would regenerate social judgment and fellowship ; its acceptance would destroy all social contempt, and elevate all social thinking. We should find out the greatest man in every social grade, and judge every man and honour every man in that grade on that greatest man's account. We have unfortu-nately reversed this process of judgment, and have even begrudged the renown of the one on account of the obscurity of the many Here, by analogy, whose remoteness is apparent rather than real. we touch the mystery of human greatness as represented by the majesty of Christ. The poorest man should say, " *Christ* was a man ! " The slave should say, " Frederick Douglass was a slave ! " The blacksmith should say, " Elihu Burritt was a blacksmith ! "

The tentmaker should say, "Paul was a tentmaker!" Thus, the lowest should dwell under the shadow of the highest, not the highest be reminded of the lowliness of his origin or the obscurity of his class. He carries up his class along with him. He shows that class what its members may be and do. He is their typical man, their crowned and glorified brother. It is the same on an infinite scale with the Man Christ Jesus. Look to him if you would see the image and likeness of God. Look to him if you would estimate the value of man. We have to bear his image ; we have to be what he is. Look at him, and say, each of you, *That* is what I have to be like !

Wonderful in pathos is the appeal which results from all these considerations. That appeal is to be felt rather than expressed in words. Man is God's child ; man bears a signature Divine. Great things are expected of man : reasoning which approaches the quality of a revelation ; service which requires Almightiness alone to exceed it ; love that courts the agony of sacrifice ; purity hard to distinguish from the holiness of God.

NOTES FOR PREACHERS.

MAN naturally asks for *some* account of the world in which he lives. Was the world *always* in existence? If not always in existence, how did it *begin* to be? Did the sun make itself? These are not *presumptuous* questions. We have a right to ask them—the right which arises from our intelligence, and justifies our progress in knowledge. The *steam engine* did not make itself; did the sun? *Dwelling houses* did not make themselves; did the stars? The child's *coat* did not make itself; did the child's *soul*? If it is legitimate to reason from the known to the unknown, and to establish an *à fortiori* argument in relation to common phenomena, why not also legitimate in reference to the higher subjects which are within the province of reason? At present we wish to know how the heavens and the earth came into existence, and we find in the text an answer which is *simple, sublime, and sufficient*, and is therefore likely to be *right*.

I. The answer is SIMPLE. There is no attempt at learned analysis or elaborate exposition. A child may understand the answer. It is direct, positive, complete. Could it have been *more* simple? Try any *other* form of words, and see if a purer simplicity be possible. Observe the value of *simplicity* when regarded as bearing upon the *grandest* events. The question is not who made a *house*, but who made a *world*, and not who made *one* world, but who made *all* worlds; and to this question the answer is, *God* made them. There is great risk in returning a *simple* answer to a *profound* nquiry, because when simplicity is not the last result of knowledge, it is mere *imbecility*.

II. The answer is SUBLIME. *God!* God *created!* (1) Sublime because far-reaching in point of *time*: in the BEGINNING! Science would have attempted a fact; religion has given a *truth*. If any inquirer can fix a *date*, he is not forbidden to do so. Dates are for children. (2) Sublime because connecting the *material* with the *spiritual*. There is, then, something more than dust in the universe. Behind all shapes there is a living image. Every atom bears a superscription. It is something surely to have the name of *God* associated with all things great and small that are around us. Nature thus becomes a materialised *thought*. The wind is the breath of God. The thunder is a note from the music of his speech. (3) Sublime because evidently revealing, as nothing else could have done, the *power and wisdom* of the Most High. All these things were *created*; they were called into existence, and therefore must be less than God, who so called them; and if *less*, how great must their *Creator* be! We justly infer the greatness of the *artist* from the greatness of his *pictures*. Judge *God* by the same standard.

III. The answer is SUFFICIENT. It might have been both simple and sublime, and yet not have reached the point of adequacy. Draw a straight line, and you may describe it as simple, yet who would think of calling it *sublime*? Look at the rising sun pouring floods of light upon the dewy landscape: it is undoubtedly sublime, but is it credible that the landscape was *created* by the sun? We must have simplicity which reaches the point of sublimity, and sublimity which sufficiently covers every demand of the case. The sufficiency of the answer is manifest: Time is a drop of Eternity; Nature is the handiwork of God; Matter is the creation of Mind; God is over all blessed for evermore! This is enough. In proportion as we exclude God from the operation, we increase *difficulty*. Atheism never simplifies. Negation works in darkness.

The answer of the text to the problem of creation is simple, sublime, and sufficient, in relation—(1) *To the inductions of geology.* Assume that the heavens and the earth have existed for ages which arithmetic cannot number, what then? It was in the *beginning* that God's work was done! (2) *To the theory of evolution.* Assume that in some time incalculably past there was but the minutest *germ*, what then? Who created the germ? If man cannot create an oak, can he create an *acorn*?

There are some practical inferences suggested by these reflections.

First: If God *created* all things, then all things are under his *government.* This assurance should give rest and hope to the religious inquirer. Be right with the Creator, and thou hast nothing to fear from creation.

Second: If God created the heavens and the earth, then the heavens and the earth may be studied *religiously.* Science need not be atheistic. Scientific inquiry will be most successful when most *religious.* This is reasonable. Know the writer if you would really know his works. Know the Creator if you would profoundly and accurately know creation. The highest study is spiritual. We may know nature, and yet know nothing of God. The tailor knows my figure; does he therefore know my *soul*?

Third: If God created all things, then it is reasonable that he should *take an interest* in the things which he created. Analogy suggests this. Scripture confirms it. "He causeth the grass to grow for the cattle, and herb for the service of man." "He giveth to the beast his food, and to the young ravens which cry." "He looketh on the earth, and it trembleth; he toucheth the hills, and they smoke."

What has been said of creation may be said in a still loftier sense of redemption. The answer of God to the sin of the world is simple, sublime, sufficient. "God so loved the world," etc. This shows the *unity* of the works of God. All created things are made to be the ministers of man. For man the sun shines, the rain falls, the seasons revolve. "If God so clothe the grass of the field," etc.

And God said, Let there be light.
And God said, Let there be a firmament.
And God said, Let the waters under the heaven be gathered together.
And God said, Let there be lights.
And God said, Let the waters bring forth abundantly.
And God said, Let the earth bring forth the living creature.
And God said, Let us make man.

IT is not to discuss the mere science, so called, of creation that these words are put together in the form of a text. We are not about to analyse light, or discuss the chemistry of water, or the progress of animal life. It is not by these methods that we can get anything like a complete grasp of the idea of creation. The chemist works along his own brilliant line of discovery and exposition; the astronomer has his special field to explore; the geologist has a well-defined sphere to occupy. It is manifest, however, that not one of these men can tell the *whole* tale, and make a complete story of creation. Another man is wanted. A man who, though not necessarily going into formal science, sees the whole idea, and speaks of it in its unity. This man is the *theologian*. He is not a chemist, an astronomer, a geologist, a botanist —he is more: he speaks of circles, not of segments; of principles, not of facts; of causes and purposes rather than of effects and appearances. Not that the latter are excluded from his study, but that they are so wisely included in it as to be put in their proper places.

We may see the meaning of this more clearly by taking other ground. Take the idea of the political state. At the head of affairs set the prime minister; now it is obviously possible that in the cabinet over which he presides there may be men very much better qualified than himself for the various departmental services. He may not be half so good a financier as the chancellor of the exchequer; he may be ill-qualified to administer the affairs of the admiralty, or of the poor law board; he may be ignorant of many of the details of the postal service; he may be utterly incapable of giving a sound opinion upon any legal question,—yet his is the supreme mind in the cabinet! The cabinet would be disorganised were his influence to be withdrawn. In an emphatic sense he is a *states*man: he carries in his mind the state as *a whole:* with an intellectual energy and rapidity known only to the highest genius, he collects the sense of all his counsellors, he settles their advices into their proper proportions, and by the peculiar inspiration which makes him their master, he takes care that the part is never mistaken for the whole. Observe, each man may actually be abler in some point than his chief, yet not one of all the brilliant staff would dispute the supremacy of that chief's mind. It is one thing to be a politician, another to be a statesman.

Apply the illustration to the case in hand. The theologian does not, in his proper character, deal with mere departments. One man is superior to him in chemistry; another may actually laugh at his astronomy or geology; a third may despise him when he talks about animal or botanical physiology, —yet he may know more of the *wholeness* of creation than any of them, and may give the ablest of them the password which opens the central secret of the universe. The aurist studies the ear, and the oculist the eye, others devote themselves to special studies of the human frame, but there is another and completer man to whom we hasten when the mystery of *life* itself becomes a pain which may end in death. That other and completer man would himself send sufferers of special maladies to men who had made those maladies the subject of exclusive study, yet in his knowledge of the mystery of life he might excel them all.

In some such way would we hint at the proper position of the theologian. He may or may not be a chemist ; he may or may not know some particular science; but if he be a Divinely inspired theologian—not a mere sciolist in Divinity, a pedant in letters—he will see farther than any other man, he will hear voices which others do not hear, and will be able to shape the politics of class students into the sublime and inclusive statesmanship of a sacred philosophy.

What, then, so far as we can gather from the words before us, has Biblical theology to say about creation, material and human ?

I. THAT CREATION IS AN EXPRESSION OF GOD'S MIND. It is the embodiment of an idea. It is the form of a thought. Theology says that creation has a beginning, and that it began at the bidding of God. Theology says, You see the heavens ? They are the work of God's fingers. You see the moon and the stars ? God ordained them : all things are set in their places by the hand of God. He laid the foundations of the earth, and covered it with the deep as with a garment. When he uttereth his voice, there is a multitude of waters in the heavens, and he causeth the vapours to ascend from the ends of the earth ; he maketh lightnings with rain, and bringeth forth the wind out of his treasures. You see the cedars of Lebanon ? God planted them. You see the moon ? God set her for seasons. You behold the sun ? Though he be the king of day, yet he knoweth his going down. You see the high hills ? God hath made in them a refuge for the wild goats. You see the fir-trees ? God hath found in them a house for the stork. " O Lord, how manifold are thy works ! in wisdom hast thou made them all : the earth is full of thy riches." Now this is very unscientific in its form of expression, yet it is the declaration of theology. Theology could not speak otherwise. Theology would dwarf itself if it went into formal statement of so-called scientific truth. But what does theology do ? She sends the chemist on her errands, she calls the astronomer to consider the heavens, and sends the geologist to read the story of the rocks. They are not rebels ; they are friends and allies and chosen servants. Yet not one of them could by any possibility do the *whole* work. The geologist and the astronomer talk different languages. The chemist and the botanist but dimly comprehend each other. It is the theologian that must call them to a common council, and proclaim their conclusions in a universal tongue.

Granted that there is mystery in the doctrine that all things were created by the word of God. This is not denied. It is felt, indeed, to be a necessity of the case. On the other hand, whatever mystery may be on the side of theology, *there is nothing but mystery* on the side of atheism.

II. That creation, being an expression of God's mind, MAY FORM THE BASIS FOR THE CONSIDERATION OF GOD'S PERSONALITY AND CHARACTER. If we see something of the artist in his work, we may see something of the Creator in creation. The works of God proclaim his eternal and incommunicable *sovereignty*. "Who hath directed the Spirit of the Lord, or being his counsellor, hath taught him? With whom took he counsel, and who instructed him, and taught him in the path of judgment, and taught him knowledge, and showed to him the way of understanding?" Thus men are put back : they are ordered off beyond the burning line which lies around the dread sovereignty of God. If a man would trespass that line, he would encounter the thunder of questions which would make him quail : "Where wast thou when I laid the foundations of the earth?" "Hast thou commanded the morning since thy days, and caused the dayspring to know his place?" "Hast thou entered into the springs of the sea? or hast thou walked in the search of the depth?" "Have the gates of death been opened unto thee? or hast thou seen the doors of the shadow of death?" "Where is the way where light dwelleth?" "Hast thou entered into the treasures of the snow?" "Canst thou bind the sweet influences of Pleiades, or loose the bands of Orion? Canst thou bring forth Mazzaroth in his season? or canst thou guide Arcturus, with his sons?" And still the questions would come like the shocks of a rising storm, until the proudest speculator might quake with fear, and totter into darkness that he might hide the shame of his pride. As a mere matter of fact, man cannot approach the dignity of having himself *created* anything. He is an inquirer, a speculator, a calculator, a talker, but not a *creator*. He can *talk about* creation. He can reckon the velocity of light, and the speed of a few stars. He can go out for a day to geologise and botanise ; but all the while a secret has mocked him, and an inscrutable power has defied the strength of his arm. The theologian says, that secret is God, that power is Omnipotence.

There is more than sovereignty ; there is *beneficence*. "While the earth remaineth, seedtime and harvest, and cold and heat, and summer and winter, and day and night shall not cease." " He sendeth springs into the valleys, which run among the hills. They give drink to every beast of the field ; the wild asses quench their thirst. By them shall the fowls of the heaven have their habitation, which sing among the branches." "He hath not left himself without witness, in that he did good, and gave us rain from heaven, and fruitful seasons, filling our hearts with food and gladness.' "Thou openest thine hand, and satisfiest the desire of every living thing." "Thou openest thine hand ; they are filled with good." " He giveth to the beast his food, and to the young ravens which cry." This is a step downwards, yet a step upwards. Over all is the dread sovereignty of God—that sovereignty stoops to us in love to save our life, to spread our table, and to dry our tears ; it comes down, yet in the very condescension of its majesty it adds a new ray to its lustre. The theologian says, This is *God's* care , this is the love of the *Father* ; this bounty is an expression of the *heart* of *God.* It is not a freak of what is called *nature* ; it is not a sunny chance ; it is a purpose, a sign of love, a direct gift from God's own heart.

III That God's word is its own security for fulfilment. God said, Let there be, and there was. "He spake, and it was done ; he commanded, and it stood fast." "By the word of the Lord were the heavens made, and all the host of them by the breath of his mouth." This is the word which alone can ultimately prevail. "As the rain cometh down from heaven, and returneth not thither," etc. We see what it is in the *natural* world; we shall see what it is in the *spiritual*. "I am the Lord; I will speak, and the word that I will speak shall come to pass." "The word of God liveth and abideth for ~ver." "Heaven and earth shall pass away, but my word shall not pass away." "For ever, O Lord, thy word is settled in heaven." "God is not a man, that he should lie; neither the son of man, that he should repent: hath he said, and shall he not do it? or hath he spoken, and shall he not make it good?" "What his soul desireth, even that he doeth."

This is of infinite importance—(1) As the *hope* of righteousness; (2) as the *inevitable doom* of wickedness.

IV. That the word which accounts for the existence of *Nature* accounts also for the existence of *Man*. "Know ye not that the Lord, he is God? it is he that made us, and not we ourselves." "O Lord, thou art our Father; we are the clay, and thou our Potter; and we are the work of thy hand." "Have we not all one Father? hath not one God created us?" "We are the offspring of God." "In him we live, and move, and have our being."

See what a great system of *unity* is hereby established. He who made the *sun* made *me* !

How to *begin* to write the Bible must have been a question of great difficulty. The beginning which is given here commends itself as peculiarly sublime. Regard it as you please, as literal, historical, parabolical, it is unquestionably marked by adequate energy and magnificence of style. Judging from the method of the writer, I should at once say, the aim of this man is not to tell with scientific precision the natural history of creation; he has some other undeclared purpose in view. He finds that he must say *something* about the house before he says anything about the tenant, but he feels that that something must be the least possible. Hence we have this rugged but majestic account. In reading this wonderful chapter we must receive several memorable impressions :—

First : *This account of creation is deeply religious,* and from this fact I infer that the whole book of which it is the opening chapter is intended to be a religious and not a scientific revelation. If a natural philosopher had under-taken to write an account of the earth, he would have begun in a totally different tone, and he would have been justified in so doing. A work on geography that began with the analysis of a psalm or prayer would be justly considered as going out of its proper sphere, and in all probability we should regard its unseasonable piety as a subtraction from its scientific value. The object of Moses is simply and absolutely *religious.* We do not say that a man is an atheist because he writes upon geology without announcing a religious creed. So we ought not to say that a man is an ignoramus because he writes a religious book without any pretence to scientific learning. This man is resolved on reading all things from the God-side; he will read them downwards, not upwards; he will begin at the fountain, not at the stream; and in claiming to do this he is evidently exercising a legitimate discretion, and he must justify its exercise by the results which he secures. Our life may be read from an outside standpoint, and therefore we are glad to hear the testimony of the anatomist, the physiologist, and the physician; they have a right to speak, and they have a right to be heard : our life may also be read from an internal standpoint, and therefore we are glad to hear the psychologist, the metaphysician, the theologian. Let us listen to them all. We may need all the help they can severally and jointly give us. Now Moses says, I am going to write the history of the world as a *theologian* ; I deliberately and distinctly assume a theological standpoint, and my meaning you may catch from my first tone— ' In the beginning God created the heaven and the earth." How he will conduct the discussion we cannot at this moment tell. He may have made a mistake in supposing that it can be conducted from this point at all. But in common fairness give him time. The disgrace and the shame will be his, not ours, if he fail, so the least we can do is to let him have all the scope he asks for. It does not follow because another writer proposes to give the history of creation without any reference to God that therefore he will inevitably and completely succeed. Even an atheist may be sometimes wrong ! I ask fair play for both godly and godless writers ; let each write his Bible, and the God that answereth by fire, let him be God !

Instead, therefore, of boggling at this first chapter of Genesis, I read it as its writer meant it to be read, and I reserve the right of critical revision after I have fully mastered what he has really written. From the intensity of his religious tone, I am bound to infer that this man is going to tell me in the simplest and directest manner all he can tell about creation, or all he thinks it needful to tell in order to get a sufficient background for the story which it is his main purpose to relate. He does not lay claim to any consideration which I need hesitate to yield. He does not say, "I am inspired, what I say is said with Divine and final authority, and you must accept it or be lost in outer darkness for ever." He says nothing about inspiration. He does not lay claim to one tittle of authority. In a plain, abrupt, urgent manner he begins his stupendous task. I am charmed with his directness. I feel that if the story had to be told at all, it is begun in the best possible manner. If the writer had beaten around the bush in laborious literary circumlocution, I should have suspected him ; he would have been a mere book-maker, a clever artiste in the use of words ; but he begins at once, as with a *creative* fiat, the tone being worthy of the brilliant occasion. I bespeak for him, then, a fair hearing.

Second : *This account of creation evidently admits of much elucidation and expansion.* This it has unquestionably received. Moses does not say, "I have told you everything, and if any man shall ever arise to make a note or comment upon my words, he is to be regarded as a liar and a thief." Certainly not. He gives rather a rough outline which is to be filled up as life advances. He says in effect, "This is the text ; now let the commentators come with their notes." The geologist has come, and he says, "Read this word *beginning* as if it referred to incalculable time " ; and there is no reason why his suggestion should not be adopted. In the next place he says, "Read this word *day* as if it meant a great number of ages " ; very good, we read it exactly so, and it does us no harm. Then other men of science arise to say, "Don't suppose that the heavens and the earth were made exactly as you see them ; they came out of a germ, an atom, a molecule," and I answer, So be it : God did not make a tottering old man exactly as we see him ; he did not make the trees and flowers exactly as we see them ; and if it is the same with the heavens and the earth, so be it. "They came partly by friction," says the scientist. Very good, I reply ; what is friction and who made it ? "Rotation had something to do with it." Possibly so, I answer ; what is rotation and who started it ? "Origin of species," whispers another. Very good, I answer ; what is origin and when did it originate ? Instead of resenting these suggestions, I am thankful for them. I put them all together, and I find the difference between Moses and his scientific commentators to be that Moses worked synthetically and they worked analytically, that is, Moses put all things together, and the sum total was God ; his opposing commentators take things all to pieces, and the sum total is a circumference without a centre. It is uncertain whether geologists contradict Moses, but it is positively certain beyond all doubt that geologists contradict one another. Still this contradiction may be the very friction out of which the light and warmth of truth will come. So that the commentators be but honest and sober-minded men, I welcome all they have to say and if they be otherwise, they will have to eat their own words, and other pain no man need wish them. This first chapter of Genesis is like an acorn, for out of it have come great forests of literature ; it must have some pith in it, and sap, and force, for verily its fertility is nothing less than a miracle.

Third : This account of creation, though leaving so much to be elucidated, is in harmony with fact in a sufficient degree to *give us confidence in the things which remain to be illustrated.* In almost every verse there is something which we know to be true as a mere matter of fact, and therefore we are prepared to believe that what is hazy may yet be shown to be full of stars as bright and large as the nearer planets which we call facts. Undoubtedly we have day and night, sea and dry land, grass and herbs and fruit-trees, and undoubtedly there is a light that rules the day, and another light that rules the night ; the waters, too, are full of moving creatures, and fowls have the liberty of the open firmament. So it was no poet's creation that Moses looked at, but the plain grand universe just as we see it and touch it. It was bold of him to think that it had a "beginning"; *that* was an original idea, very startling and most graphic. He does not say that God had a beginning ! Observe that, if you please ! How easy to have suggested that God and the universe are both eternal ! Instead of doing this (a comparatively easy thing, escaping endless questioning), he says the heavens and the earth had a beginning, and therefore have a history more or less traceable. If he had said, "God, man, and matter are all eternal, but I will take up the history of man at a given point and follow it down to recent times," he would have made easy work for himself. But he makes difficulty ! He opens the way for a thousand objections ! This is satisfactory to my mind. It is a boldness that corresponds to the valour of truth as we know it. It may be, then, that we have got hold of the right guide after all ! All I ask is that he be not interrupted until he has come to the very last word of his story.

Fourth: *There is a special grandeur in the account which is here given of the origin of man.* In the twenty-sixth verse, the tone quite changes. Even the imperative mood softens somewhat, as if in an infinitely subtle way (far out of the reach of words) man's own consent had been sought to his own creation. "Let us make man"—"make," as if little by little, a long process in the course of which man becomes a party to his own making! Nor is this suggestion so wide of the mark as might at first appear. Is man not even *now* in process of being "made"? Must not all the members of the "US" work upon him in order to complete him and give him the last touch of imperishable beauty? The Father has shaped him; the Son has redeemed him; the Spirit is now regenerating and sanctifying him; manifold ministries are now working upon him, to the end that he may "come to a PERFECT MAN, unto the measure of the stature of the fulness of Christ." As it were, arbitrarily and sovereignly, the dust was shaped into human form, an upright thing that had wonderful powers and still more wonderful latent possibilities. But is not all Biblical history an appeal to this upright thing to *be* a man? Is not the Gospel of Christ the good news that he may *have* life, yea eternal life, and enter upon a destiny of immeasurable progress and ineffable felicity? What, I ask again, if man is still *in process of being made?* What if our present selves have to be shed as blossoms to make way for the fruit? In this sense the building of manhood may well take as long as the building of the rocks. It is a fearful thought, most solemn, yet most humbling, that we may be but a stratum on which other strata have to lie until the last line is laid down, and God's ideal of humanity is realised. Or take it the other and pleasanter way, which all Scripture would seem to sanction, namely, man was made a living soul, that is, every man was intended to live, and has capacities which will enable him to receive life in its largest and Divinest sense; this is, indeed, his unique and glorious characteristic, his point of infinite departure from the beasts that perish. But he can destroy himself! He can choose death rather than life. Now it is in this very choice that man is really "made." The appeal is, Will ye *be* a man? Will you *have* life? Jesus Christ says, "I am come that ye might have life." Thus, as I said with apparent self-contradiction, man is asked to be a party to his own creation—to consent to be himself! "Ye will not come unto me that ye might have life." "This is life eternal, to know thee the only true God, and Jesus Christ, whom thou hast sent." Glorious to me is this idea (so like all we know of the Divine goodness) of asking man whether he will accept life and be like God, or whether he will choose death and darkness for ever. God does not say to man, "I will make you immortal and indestructible whether you will or not; live for ever you shall." No; he makes him capable of living; he constitutes him with a view to immortality; he urges, beseeches, implores him to work out this grand purpose, assuring him, with infinite pathos, that he has no pleasure in the death of the sinner, but would rather that he should LIVE. A doctrine this which in my view simplifies and glorifies human history as related in the Bible. Life and death are not set before any *beast*; but life and death are distinctly set before *man*—he can live, he was meant to live, he is besought to live; the whole scheme of Providence and redemption is arranged to help him to live—why, then, will ye die?

Gen. ii. 1-3.

"Thus the heavens and the earth were finished, and all the host of them.
And on the seventh day God ended his work which he had made; and he
rested on the seventh day from all his work which he had made. And God
blessed the seventh day, and sanctified it : because that in it he had rested
from all his work which God created and made."

ADAM, EDEN, AND EVE.

SIMPLE and honest is this as the speech of a little child ! A
child tells you things in lumps and mouthfuls, and hurries
on to conclusions in a manner quite its own and not despicable.
But was Moses a child? Exactly that and nothing more in
book-writing. He had no forerunners to study, no models to
copy, no high grammatical authorities to consult. Strange that
men should be hard upon him in matters literary, when they
have been so long at school and he was never at school at all !

But was he not inspired? Certainly he was—an inspired
child, or he never would have written as he did. There is a
Divine grace in his style which makes men ask, Whose image
and superscription is this?

He says God *rested*. Is not that a sweet child's notion? He
knew no other term, no long-syllabled emptiness, and he thought
the term just the right one for the place. So it is. It is a word
that touches our sympathy and makes us rest too. I feel that
I need rest after reading the first chapter of Genesis ; it is so
energetic, so full, so urgent ! It is really beautiful after you have
seen the foam and heard the roar of Niagara to go away into one
of the quiet green spots near at hand ; we seem to rest the
stunned ear. And what a cataract is this first chapter of Genesis !
How suns, and stars, and firmaments, and seas, and mighty living
things move in quick and even terrible succession ! *And God
rested*, says Moses. Not that God was tired, but his work was
done—the last beauty glowed tenderly on the picture like a smile
of contented love If Moses had said that "The Infinite having

caused this emanation called the universe to settle into harmonic proportions," and so forth, I should have turned away from him in disgust, for it would have been the strut of the peacock, and I have no liking for that air. It is best as it is. It even brings God near to us in a kind of human sympathy : commanding, creating, setting fast the orbs and rocks ; he is far enough away from us ; but when he *rests* he seems to be close at hand and to know what our own weariness is.

And he blessed the seventh day. And long afterwards Jesus blessed the bread. The work of each was done. Jesus died before he was nailed to the Cross; no man took his life from him ; he laid it down of himself. You remember when? When he said in Gethsemane, "Not my will, but thine be done " ; *then* he died. The remainder was but a Jews' murder, a highwayman's conquest. God saw everything that he had made, and, behold, it was very good ; and Jesus, too, shall see of the travail of his soul and be satisfied. Thus the *end* shall be good ; the process may be rugged and severe, but the end will be bright and tenderly calm.

" These are the generations of the heavens and of the earth when they were created, in the day that the Lord God made the earth and the heavens, and every plant of the field before it was in the earth, and every herb of the field before it grew : for the Lord God had not caused it to rain upon the earth, and there was not a man to till the ground. But there went up a mist from the earth, and watered the whole face of the ground. And the Lord God formed man of the dust of the ground (signifying man's feeble- ness), and breathed into his nostrils the breath of life (a direct gift from God) ; and man became a living soul.

" And the Lord God planted a garden eastward in Eden (Paradise is a Persian name for an enclosed park) ; and there he put the man whom he had formed. And out of the ground made the Lord God to grow every tree (the ancients admired trees rather than landscapes) that is pleasant to the sight, and good for food ; the tree of life also in the midst of the garden, and the tree of knowledge of good and evil. And a river went out of Eden (Eden means pleasure ground) to water the garden ; and from thence it was parted, and became into four heads. The name of the first is Pison : that is it which compasseth the whole land of Havilah, where there is gold ; and the gold of that land is good : there is bdellium and the onyx stone. And the name of the second river is Gihon : the same is it that compasseth the whole land of Ethiopia. And the name of the third river is Hiddekel : that is it which goeth toward the east of Assyria. And the fourth river is Euphrates. And the Lord God took the man, and put him into the garden of Eden to dress it and to keep it " (4-15).

Here begins that great system of Divine and human co-operation which is still in progress. There were trees, plants, herbs, and flowers, but a gardener was wanted to get out of the earth everything that the earth could yield. By planting, and transplanting, and replanting, you may turn a coarse tree into a rare botanical specimen—you may refine it by development. So man got something for his own pains, and became a sort of secondary creator! This was almost too much for him. He began to think that he had done nearly everything himself, quite forgetting who gave him the germs, the tools, the skill, and the time. It is so easy for you junior partners in old city firms to think that the "house" would have been nowhere if you had not gone into partnership! But really and truly, odd as it may seem, there *was* a "house" before you took it up and glorified it.

What a chance had man in beginning life as a gardener! Beginning life in the open sunny air, without even a hothouse to try his temper! Surely he ought to have done something better than he did. The air was pure, the climate was bright, the soil was kindly : you had but to "tickle it with a spade and it laughed in flowers." And a river in the grounds! Woe to those who have their water far to fetch! But here in the garden is the stream, so broad that the moment it is liberated from the sacred place it divides itself into four evangelists, carrying everywhere the odours of Eden and the offer of kindly help. Surely, then, man was well housed to begin with. He did not begin life as a beggar. He farmed his own God-given land, without disease, or disability, or taxation to fret him ; yet what did he make of the fruitful inheritance? Did the roots turn to poison in his mouth, and the flowers hang their heads in shame when his shadow fell on them? We shall see.

"And the Lord God commanded the man, saying, Of every tree of the garden thou mayest freely eat : but of the tree of the knowledge of good and evil, thou shalt not eat of it : for in the day that thou eatest thereof thou shalt surely die" (vv. 16, 17).

There need not, I think, be any reasonable difficulty in finding out the meaning of these trees. Make the statement historical, or make it parabolical, and it comes much to the same thing. It means that there is a permanent line separating obedience from disobedience; that all created life is limited; and that whoever breaketh through a hedge a serpent shall bite him. These trees were not traps set to catch the man; they were necessities of the case. They showed him where to stop. Wonderful, truly, that if he touched the tree of mystery he should *die!* Yes, and it is grandly and solemnly true. It is so with life. Let life alone if you would live. Receive it as a mystery, and it will bless you; degrade it, abuse it, and it will slay you in great wrath. It is the same with *light.* Pluck the sun, and you will be lost in darkness; let the sun alone in his far-off ministry, and you shall never want day and summer. It is the same with *music.* Open the organ, that you may read its secret, and it will fall into silence; touch it on the appointed keys, and it will never tire in answering your sympathetic appeals. It is so difficult to be satisfied with the little we have and the little we know. We want to see over the hedge. We long to withdraw the screen that is everywhere trembling around us. We torture these little pulses of ours to tell us what they are, and how they were set a-ticking in their warm prisons. No man ever saw his own heart! There it is, knocking in his side, as if it wanted to come out; but if you let it out, it can return to its work no more! It seems to be only the skin that covers the pulse; but, though seemingly so near, it is really so far!

"*In the day that thou eatest thereof thou shalt surely die,*" said the Almighty. This is not a threat. It is not a defiance or a challenge. It is a revelation; it is a warning! When you tell your child not to touch the fire or it will be burned, you do not threaten the child: you warn it in love, and solely for its own good. Foolish would the child be if it asked why there should be any fire; and foolish are we, with high aggravations, when we ask why God should have set the tree of life and the tree of knowledge in Eden. These trees are in every family. Yes; they are in every family, because they are in every heart! How near is death! One act, and we cease to live. This is true—physically, morally, socially: one act—one step between us and death!

*And the Lord God said, It is not good that the man should be alone; I will make him an helpmeet for him. And out of the ground the Lord God formed every beast of the field, and every fowl of the air; and brought them unto Adam to see what he would call them: and whatsoever Adam called every living creature, that was the name thereof.   And Adam gave names to all cattle, and to the fowl of the air, and to every beast of the field ; but for Adam there was not found an helpmeet for him.   And the Lord God caused a deep sleep to fall upon Adam, and he slept : and he took one of his ribs, and closed up the flesh instead thereof ; and the rib, which the Lord God had taken from man, made he a woman, and brought her unto the man.   And Adam said, This is now bone of my bones, and flesh of my flesh : she shall be called Woman, because she was taken out of Man. Therefore shall a man leave his father and his mother, and shall cleave unto his wife : and they shall be one flesh.   And they were both naked, the man and his wife, and were not ashamed " (vv. 18-25).

God has always been thinking what would be for the man's good.   How, then, does God propose to meet loneliness ?   By making another man ?   Why, when he made a man to keep Cain company, Cain killed him !   It would seem to be one of the deepest laws of human nature that man must kill man, and that the only chance of keeping society together is by the marvellous influence of woman.   For man to be alone means suicide ; for two men to be together means homicide ; woman alone can keep society moving and healthful.   The woman and the little child are the saviours of social order at this day all over the world. For woman to be alone is as bad as for man to be alone.   Safety is in contrast, and in mutual complement.

Reverence for womanhood will save any civilisation from decay. Beautiful and very tender is this notion of throwing man into a deep sleep to take a rib from him as the starting-point of a blessed companionship.   So much is always being done for us when we are in states of unconsciousness !   We do not get our best blessings by our own fussiness and clever contrivance : they come we know not how.   They are sweet surprises ; they are born of the spirit, and are as untraceable as the veerings of the wind.   This is the course of true love, and of marriages that are made in heaven. You cannot by searching, and advertising, and scheming find out a companion for the lonely soul.   She will come upon you unconsciously.   You will know her by a mark in the forehead which none but yourself can read.   The moment you see her the soul will say, " Behold the bride ! " and you, leaving your father and your mother, shall cleave unto your own wife, and you shall be one for ever.   "A good wife is from the Lord." He who made the lock will also make the key.   "This also cometh forth from the Lord of hosts, which is wonderful in counsel and excellent in working."

God rested from all his work on the seventh day, and yet he had not made woman! In making her he seems to have begun again. Can Omniscience have afterthoughts! Could this deed not have been brought within the seven days? Better think of it as a deed which makes a space for itself so special as to have a separate numbering in the list; nay, as to be itself the beginning of a list, illustrious and immortal. O woman, love thy Maker! Thou art the most wonderful instrument he made in the earth; see to it that the music of thy life be all given to his holy praise.

Gen. iii. 1-5.

"Now the serpent was more subtil than any beast of the field which the Lord God had made. And he said unto the woman, Yea, hath God said, Ye shall not eat of every tree of the garden? And the woman said unto the serpent, We may eat of the fruit of the trees of the garden : but of the fruit of the tree which is in the midst of the garden, God hath said, Ye shall not eat of it, neither shall ye touch it, lest ye die. And the serpent said unto the woman, Ye shall not surely die : for God doth know that in the day ye eat thereof, then your eyes shall be opened, and ye shall be as gods, knowing good and evil."

THE WOMAN, THE SERPENT, AND THE FALL.

WHAT a vain wrangling of words there has been about this serpent talking! I pass by that altogether, and settle myself on the unquestionable fact that the woman did actually eat of the fruit and that human nature has ever since suffered from the effects of her doing so. Evidently *something* has disagreed with the world. We do not trust, love, honour, and help one another; we are selfish, mean, irascible, unforgiving; we know that our respectability is the thinnest part about us and that the faintest scratch will touch the wolf. If, when I am most conscious of this, some one should say to me, "This is the serpent's work," I should answer, "Very likely." That is how I should take it in my highest moods; the natural history difficulty would never occur to me in the holy excitement of my moral anger. The serpent itself is the best comment upon the text. Look at it : glittering, lithe, cunning, cold, smooth, poisonous—truly, it looks as if it *might* have done it ! I don't think the lion could, or the elephant, the eagle, or the ox ; but the serpent brings with it a high probability of baseness and mischief. Then, again, what do you mean by talking ? Is there no talking but what is done by the tongue ? Men talk with their eyes, their hands, their shoulders, their attitudes—and sometimes we say, " He said as plainly as if he had spoken," when the man in question has adopted a clever posture or an eloquent action of the eye. So a single suggestion may start a long train of reasoning, and we justly charge upon that suggestion all the consequences that have flowed from it.

A clever serpent, truly, to begin using words in a double sense ! That is pre-eminently a serpent-like trick. Observe how the word *die* is played upon. It is used by the serpent in the sense of dropping down dead, or violently departing out of this world ; whereas the meaning, as we all know by bitter experience, is infinitely deeper. We lose our life when we lose our innocence ; we are dead when we are guilty ; we are in hell when we are in shame. Death does not take a long time to come upon us ; it comes in the very day of our sin—" in the day that thou eatest thereof thou shalt surely die."

" And when the woman saw that the tree was good for food, and that it was pleasant to the eyes, and a tree to be desired to make one wise, she took of the fruit thereof, and did eat, and gave also unto her husband with her ; and he did eat. And the eyes of them both were opened, and they knew that they were naked ; and they sewed fig-leaves together, and made themselves aprons " (vv. 6, 7).

A beautiful gate it is that opens upon ruin ! It is well shaped, well painted, and the word *Welcome* illuminates it in vivid letters. We have all eaten of this tree, and we eat of it every day. A thing looks nice and therefore we take it ; a sound is very pleasant and therefore we listen to it ; an action promises pleasure and therefore we do it. When did ever a man do anything because it looked hard, uninviting, and severe ? When did he drink much gall ? or when did he eat much of the bitter aloes ? His temptation does not lie in that direction, but contrariwise ; it is when the tree is " pleasant to the eyes " that he rushes upon it with suicidal frenzy. Offer to him *pleasure*, and you may lead him like a sheep to the slaughter. Now *every* appetite of man points in the direction of pleasure, and every appetite pleads to be satisfied. To satisfy it and yet control it is the supreme trial of life. It cries, Give, give; and if you give it one inch of undue liberty it will drag you down to the chambers of death.

Wonderful in its depth of meaning is this expression, *" the eyes of them both were opened" !* They saw before; no new organs of vision were created; yet they saw what they had never seen, as we ourselves have done. Temptation blinds us, guilt opens our eyes; temptation is night, guilt is morning. In guilt we see ourselves, we see our hideousness, we see our baseness: we see hell!

" Their eyes were opened," and they saw that their character was gone! You can throw away a character in one act, as you throw away a stone. Can you go after it and recover it? Never! You may get something back by penitence and strife, but not the holy thing exactly as it was. A stone that is thrown along the road you may recover, but a stone thrown at night time into the sea who can get back again!

" They sewed fig-leaves together and made themselves aprons." And this we have been doing ever since! We try to replace nature by art. When we have lost the garment sent from heaven we try to replace it with one woven from earth. But our deformity shows through the finest robe! The robe may be ample, brilliant, luxurious, but the cripple shows through its gorgeous folds. Ever since this fig-leaf sewing, life has become a question of clothes.

The legs of the lame are not to be made equal by the tailor. Clothes are irreligious. Clothes are liars. Clothes are letters of credit, but they are forgeries. The clever tailor is only a clever impostor, and the best-dressed man is the most successful hypocrite. Of course we blame the climate for being cold, and we say we must use the bounties of providence: yes, yes, but all this is secondary talk: primarily, clothes are the trappings of guilt.

And now let us follow the development of the story. The Lord came into the garden in the cool of the day (v. 8), and Adam and his wife hid themselves among the trees of the garden.

So there is a consistency in sin : they hid themselves from one
another ; hid themselves from the presence of the Lord. Sin is
the only separating power. Goodness loves the light. Innocence
is as a bird that follows the bidding of the sun When your
little child runs away from you, either you are an unlovely parent,
or the child has been doing something wrong.

Adam was afraid of the Lord ! (v. 10). Afraid of him who
had made the beautiful garden, the majestic river, the sun, and
the moon and the stars ! How unnatural ! Instead of running
to the Lord, and crying mightily to him in pain and agony of
soul, he shrank away into shady places and trembled in fear
and shame. We do the same thing to-day. We flee from God.
Having done some deed of wrong, we do not throw ourselves in
utter humiliation before the Lord, crying for his mercy and
promising better life : we stand behind a tree, thinking that he
will pass by without seeing us. This sin makes a fool of a man
as well as a criminal : it makes him ridiculous as well as guilty.
It makes its own judgment day !

"And the man said, The woman whom thou gavest to be with me, she
gave me of the tree, and I did eat" (v. 12).

And much Adam has been blamed for so saying, yet it was
the plain fact, and about as good a thing as there was to be said.
It would be a mean thing *now* for a man to blame a woman, but
in this case Adam was really blaming himself. Besides, we
sometimes pay a compliment to the very person whom we seem
to blame. Our action is this : " Can it be wrong to do what
such a person told me to do ? Is not the person the best apology
for the deed ? If I cannot believe an angel, whom am I to
believe ? " You say that Adam blamed the woman, but he
blamed God still more, if there was really any blaming at all
in the case, which is doubtful. The man cured of his blindness
did not *blame* Jesus when he said—" He that put clay upon
mine eyes, the same said unto me, Wash in the pool of Siloam."
Besides, who are we that we should scowl upon Adam ? Whatever Adam did, *we* did ; Adam was not an individual only, he
was the type of manhood. And even if he were not, there is
not a man amongst us who would not skulk out of his guilt at
the expense of the fairest woman or sweetest child that ever

breathed. " He that is without s n let him cast the first stone."
A woman would do infinitely more for a man than any man
would do for a woman.

Then come the penal clauses, and it is wonderful how the
curse is tempered with mercy, so much so indeed that it is difficult to tell whether there is not more blessing than cursing in the
sentence. The seed of the woman is to be mighty enough to
crush the serpent ; and the ground is to be difficult of tillage
for *man's sake.* Hard agriculture is a blessing. To get harvests
for nothing would be a pitiless curse indeed. To be sentenced
to " hard labour " is really a blessing to great criminals ; it breaks
in upon the moodiness that would become despair ; it taxes
invention ; it keeps the blood moving ; it rouses energy. Many
a man has been *made* by the very hardness of his task. But
terrible are the words—" *unto dust shalt thou return.*" According
to these words it is plainly stated that man was to be exactly
what he was before he was made at all,—he was to be dead
dust, by reason of his sin. Whether any way of escape can be
found out remains to be seen. The *law* is plain ; whether *mercy*
can modify it will be revealed as we proceed in the wondrous
story. Perhaps there may yet be made a Man within a man,
a Spirit within a body, a Son within a slave. That would be
glorious, surely ! Night has fallen upon the guilty pair, but in
the night there are stars, large, bright, like tender eyes shining
through the darkness,—perhaps these stars will lead on to a
manger, a Child, a Saviour !

Then come words which no man can fully understand, about
Adam becoming as God, and about the cherubim and the flaming
sword keeping the way of the tree of life. Yet, though there
be much mystery, there is also some warm light, and what there
is of such light is as a glint of summer kindling upon the desolate
scene. Observe, the tree of life was not cut down ; nor was it
withdrawn from the trees of the field,—no, the tabernacle of
God was left with men upon the earth. Well was the way
watched until the time should come for approach : strait is the
gate and narrow is the way that leadeth unto life, yet men may
travel now up to the blessed tree and take the fruit of immortality ! God has never taught us to set little store by life. He has
always watched it and guarded it as with hosts of armed angels.

It is not to be wantonly plucked. It is God's choice gift. He has, too, alway kept the line very distinct between himself and his creatures,—" *the man is become as one of us, to know good and evil;* " not *really* as " one of us," but *imaginatively* so ; he thinks he now knows all that there is to be known, but this imagination must be corrected by the imposition of high discipline : he thinks he has discovered the sham and failure of things and found out the scheme of God ; he must be undeceived ; throw a skin upon his back, drive him out of the garden, keep the tree of life, and let him learn by long and bitter experience that there is no short road to dominion and immortality.

PRAYER.

ALMIGHTY GOD, though thou art unsearchable, yet in Jesus Christ we have seen the brightness of thy face. We have long sought for thee, but thou didst not come closely to us in all the works of thy hands ; we said, Surely we shall find God in the light, and his face will shine upon us through the congregation of the stars ; we have gone forward, but thou wast not there ; backward, but we could not perceive thee ; on the left hand where thou dost work but we could not behold thee ; thou didst hide thyself on the right hand, so that our eye could not see thee. We heard that thy way was in the sea and thy path in the great waters, but in all the floods we did not hear the voice for which our hearts longed in sadness. We have wandered wearily through the temple of Nature, but it was a chamber in which there was no light ; we have watched all the seasons, yet they have been to us only as the beautiful garments of an unknown guest. All this has often made our heart ache, and destroyed the balance of our thoughts ; we have felt very lonely, and sometimes in our sorrow we have wished to die. This morning we glorify thee that Jesus Christ has satisfied all our hunger and thirst, and has given rest to eyes tired with long watching ; thine only begotten Son, who dwelt from unbeginning time in the bosom of his Father, has risen upon us as the dayspring from on high ; and our hearts are sufficed. We thank thee for his human form, because it brings him so near us ; and we thank thee for his great sorrows, because their recollection often lifts us above our own griefs. Truly thou didst in Jesus Christ give us an unspeakable gift ; we can sooner stretch a line upon the foundations of the earth, and comprehend the dust of the earth in a measure, than find out the length and breadth, the depth and height of thy love, which passeth understanding. Why didst thou so enrich us with all this love ? Surely we had destroyed our beauty and perverted all the comeliness of thine image, and all our dignity had been thrown down into the dust and covered with shameful dishonour ; yet thou didst come after us as if thy heart was troubled by our absence, and thou didst call us with a voice that was made tremulous by anxiety, so tender and overflowing was thy love. Feeling our own poverty and littleness, we have often wondered how thou couldst love us so much ; why didst thou not throw us into a pit of forgetfulness, and call around thee the unfallen children of light, and throne thyself above their adoring praises ? Surely thou hast purposed a great destiny for us, and in ages to come we shall know somewhat of the meaning of our amazing redemption : we confine our view within the dying day and are lost in troubled wonder ; but when we lay hold of our immortality in Jesus Christ, and think of the revelations which thou hast yet in tore for us, we are made strong and glad by a great hope. Amen.

Gen. iii. 17.

"Cursed is the ground for thy sake."

THE GROUND.

YOU do not suppose, and therefore I need not waste your time in answering the delusion, that Almighty God took *revenge* upon the ground because Adam, the first man, had broken the Divine law. Yet, at first reading, it is easy to see how that mistake might be made. Adam had broken the Divine revelation, and he was now in the presence of Almighty God for the purpose of receiving sentence. In the midst of that sentence occurs the remarkable words of the text, " Cursed is the ground for thy sake." Yet possibly there may be a tone of beneficence even in that denunciation. It was for man's advantage in many respects that the ground should be made hard to till and cultivate, and it is to that point that I wish to direct attention.

The ground is our first lesson-book. We must follow the law of the ground. I must get you away, as far I can, from manufactures, and science, and politics, and fix your attention upon the great law of the land. The land is the true wealth of the nation. Manufactures are a flash in the pan—they succeed, they fail, they change, they die ; they go abroad, they are unsteady, vagrant, almost unreckonable —rising or falling now and then—but the stability, the wealth, the greatness of the country is the land. Where agriculture is bad, manufactures cannot advance ; where farming is poor, the jeweller cannot live. Have you fully considered the moral meaning of this, or have you lived all your time in the city and have not known that there is a great place called the country, and that London would go down if the land went down ?

Not only is the land important in that political and economical sense, but—and this is the point to which we must

speedily come—the land is *a grand lesson-book.* Study the law
of land and agriculture, and let that be your first lesson in the
cultivation of your own life. If you have been taking your lessons
from the book of manufactures, I do not wonder at your being
sometimes ill-regulated and ill-behaved. If you have been making politics your model and standard, I do not wonder at your
being all twisted and gnarled and ill-conditioned wholly. You
should have lived on the *land* ; let us hasten to the green fields,
and teeming plains, and learn what we can of God's great law of
true and abiding progress.

A man does not cultivate the land to any great extent simply
by *waving his hand majestically over it.* It is a curious land ; you
would have thought that a man with six diamond rings upon his
fingers would have subdued the land and made it bring forth any·
thing he wished it to produce, by waving majestically several
diamonds across the astounded meadows. Yet that is exactly
how some persons wish to live : they do not want to give a *quid
pro quo;* they do not want to pay fair and square on the world's
counter for what they get ; they wish to throw up the window and
call Fortune, and say, " Fortune, obey me ; lay your gold here,
and go and get more and bring it also." There are certain very
grand persons who wish to live well and yet do nothing in return.
That is not the law of land ; that is not the first lesson that is
written in the great ground-book. The land says, " If you want
anything out of me you must work for it ; I answer labour, I respond to industry, I reply to the importunity of toil." That is the
great law of solid progress: ploughing, digging, harrowing, rolling,
watering, and then the sickle and the garner. You wanted to get
your living, you remember, without ever putting your coat off,
and the ground will not be tilled by men who go to it with their
coats on and look round, and wonder why they were called to
labour.

I have also observed that *the ground does not obey the dashing
and angry passion of any man.* You can go into your mill and
smash your looms, you can go into your laboratories and put out
your fires—but when you go into the fields how little you are !
The green field does not turn white, though you curse over it
till you foam again at the mouth. You cannot get usefully into a
passion with old Grandame Nature. You can spur a horse, you

can goad an ox, you can lash a dog—what can you do with the old mother earth ? Suppose now you should jump twenty feet into the air and come down again bang on the ground; what would happen ? Nothing to the earth ; if anything did happen it would happen to the foolish jumper.

This, then, is my first lesson-book. " If my horse, if my ox, if my dog, do not do as I want them to do," says the angry man, " I *make* them," and then with his blood boiling hot he goes out into the fields, and he can do *nothing* ! The ground says, "If you want to do anything with me you must do it with hopeful patienc :; I am a school in which men learn the meaning of patient industry, patient hopefulness. I never answer the anger of a fool or the passion of a demented man. I rest." We cannot compel nature to keep pace with our impatience ; man cannot hasten the wheel of the seasons ; man cannot drive nature out of its calm and solemn movement ; his own fields keep him at bay. He would like to get on faster, faster—it would please him to have three wheat harvests every year, it would delight him to have an orchard-stripping on the first day of every month. He makes his dog go out when he likes—his own trees put out their branches without him and mock his fury. Nature says, "I must have my long holiday"; nature says, "I must have my long, long sleep." Without recreation and rest, man's life would not be solidly and productively developed ; he may be lashed and scourged and over-driven and maddened, but broad, massive, enduring growth he never can realise unless he operates upon the law of steady slowness.

Such is the great lesson of nature. We sometimes think we could improve the arrangements of Providence in this matter of the ground. A man standing in his wheat-field is apt to feel that it would be an exceedingly admirable arrangement if he could have *another crop* of wheat within the year. He thinks it could be managed : he takes up the roots out of the earth and he says, " This will never do ; why, I have lost my year herein—now I will command the ground to bring forth another crop," and this agricultural Canute, having waved his hand over the fields, is answered with silence. That must be your law of progress. There is the very great temptation to hasten to be rich. I see a man in yonder corner, not half so able as I am, never had half the education I have had, and by a lucky swing of the hand he makes ten thousand pounds, and I am labouring at my mill, or at my counter, or in my field, and am getting very little—and very slowly. I look in the other corner and see exactly such another man, and he, too, by a lucky twist of the hand, makes ten thousand a-year; and I never make one, by long, patient, steady work. I know what I will do : I'll put off this old labourer's coat, and buy a new fine one, and go and join these men and do as they do, and I will have a hundred thousand pounds in a month, and horses and carriages and estates, and I will not go at this slow snail pace any longer—why should I ? I go— and I fail, as I deserve to do. Society never could be built upon the action of such men as have now been described. They may be doing nothing dishonourable, they may be acting in a very proper way, there are no laws that have not exceptions attached to them—I broadly acknowledge the honourableness of many exceptions to this law of land-like slowness of cultivation and growth, but the solid everlasting law of human life is labour, patience, expenditure, hopefulness, little to little, a step at a time, line upon line, and if you trifle with that law you will bring yourself into a state of intellectual unhealthiness, into a condition of moral exaggeration, and you will labour upon wrong principles, and reach, by rapid strides, unhappy conclusions.

Still there is a great temptation to *hasten* to be rich ; to be learned, to be great, in some way or other. We are impatient with processes; we like the conjuror; and yet, young men, young citizens of London, the law of progress is steadiness, getting up early in the morning, and going at it all day, *Nil Desperandum* on the banner, and " Excelsior " the burden of the song. 1 know you heard of that runaway boy from your town who went out, and by some happy stroke of fortune, as he called it, made a thousand pounds, and laughed at "the whole concern," and asked you how the " old fogies " were getting on at So-and-so. That was an exception : I do not know the value of it because there has not been time to test it, but the law, solemn, grand, sublime, Divine, is the law of agriculture, the plough, industry, patience : works *and* faith, as well as faith *and* works, and a contented hopefulness and belief that the harvest will be more plentiful than the seed-time. Thus I see God stooping and *writing with his finger upon the ground*, while we students stand before him in dumb amazement, wondering at the tracery of his finger, and when he erects himself and withdraws, behold the Bible he has written. "Behold the husbandman waiteth for the precious fruit of the earth, and hath long patience for it until he receive the early and latter rain." That is the first verse he has written for you in the dust. Another—still he speaks, still he writes, and this is the reading thereof. "Be not deceived; God is not mocked; for whatsoever a man soweth, that shall he also reap." Still he speaks and still he writes upon the verdant earth, "He which soweth sparingly shall reap also sparingly; and he which soweth bountifully shall reap also bountifully." And yet again he speaks and writes with that wondrous finger, "In the morning sow thy seed, and in the evening withhold not thine hand: for thou knowest not whether shall prosper, either this or that, or whether they both shall be alike good." See the earth inscribed with terms like these, and learn from the land how to live.

All these analogies and illustrations lead up to the great truth concerning *spiritual* cultivation, which I wish to urge upon my own mind and yours. Spiritual cultivation, like the culture of the land, *cannot be hastened.* I know that you have forcing pits and hothouses and frames made for the purpose of rapidly feeding the roots, and almost compelling the sun to do double duty upon their glass. But what are all these when gathered together compared with the hundreds and tens of hundreds of thousands of acres which make up the total area of the globe's cultivatable land? They are as nothing. It is as if a man should imagine that because he can have a warm bath in his own room, therefore it is possible to heat the Atlantic. You must not judge by little exceptions and by small experiments— you must seek out the central quantity and the abiding law, and that is a law of slow but steady succession: holiday, rest, sleep, patience, toil, well-directed industry. "Go to the ant, thou sluggard; consider her ways, and be wise."

So it is in spiritual cultivation—you cannot grow a character in a week. There are some long thin stalks that you can buy in a garden market for about a shilling a dozen, and you put up these, and say, "Do grow, if you please; do get up, and do broaden yourselves and make something like a garden about us," and the long thin stalks, spindle-shanks, look at you, and cannot be hastened, though you mock them with their leanness, and scourge them with your unruly tongue. Look at those grand old cedars and oaks and wide-spreading chestnuts. Why are they so noble? Because they are so old. They have been rocked by a hundred wintry nurses, blessed by a thousand summer visitants, and they express the result of the long processes. They have told their tale to fifty winters, caught the blessing of fifty summers, waved musically in the storm, guested the birds of the air, and all the while have been striking their roots deeper and deeper, farther and farther into the rich soil. So must it be with human character : you cannot extemporise moral greatness, it is a slow growth. Money cannot take the place of time : time is an element in the development and sublimising of character : time stands alone and cannot be compounded for by all the wealth in all the gold mines of creation.

This spiritual cultivation not only cannot be hastened, but sometimes it is *very hard.* As a general rule, indeed, it is very difficult ; it is not easy to grow in grace. Some of us live too near the smoke ever to be very great trees, or even very fruitful bushes. Circumstances are heavily against us ; we are not placed in favourable localities or under very gracious conditions. The house is small, the income is little, the children are many and noisy, the demands upon time and attention and patience are incessant, health is not very good and cheerful, the temperament is a little despondent and very susceptible to injurious influences, and how to grow in Christ Jesus under such circumstances as these, the Saviour himself only knows. Do not suppose, therefore, that I mock any of you, that I taunt you with your moral leanness and want of progress in your life that is in the Son of God. We do not all grow under the same sunny conditions ; how some of you grow at all is one of the practical mysteries of my life—under any circumstances I feel as if I could not grow at all. Be thankful to God, therefore, that the bruised reed is not broken, that though you are faint, still you are pursuing ; that though you are very weak in the limb and cannot run hard in this uphill race, your eye is fixed in the right quarter ; and the fixing and sparkling of your eye has a meaning which God's heart knows well.

Cheer thee, then ! Though growth is not so broad and obvious as thou wouldst like it to be, yet God is Judge : to whom little is given, from him shall little be expected. I do not look for such flowers in the poor man's little painted flower box, set upon his one-paned window-sill, as I look for in the great man's ample grounds in which is called into exercise the highest horticultural ability of the day. Yet—and, blessed be God, this is the supreme proof—yet nothing is lost that is meant in the way of moral growth and progress. Weary not in well-doing, for in due season ye shall reap if ye faint not. There are some things beyond your control. Shall I meet a farmer coming out of his well-tended fields with a few lean ears of corn as his only harvest, and mock him because he is not bringing in a thousand golden-headed sheaves ? I know the labour he has expended, I know the sleepless nights he has had—more or less foolishly it may have been, but still he passed them ; I know his labour and anxiety, and when he says to me, " This is all the result," do I encounter him with taunting and mockery ? God forbid ! So when I see some of you come out of your long moral labours, your many prayers and tears, your strong and urgent desires to be better men, and you say, " Look here, this is what we are, not worth looking at, so mean, so ill-favoured, so blighted "—am I the man, as Christ's minister, to laugh at you and mock you ? I ask about the labour you have expended, and God rewards the diligence, God has regard to the spirit, God knows what we mean ; he interprets the set and stress of the will, and if we would have built a temple for him, though we have not laid one stone upon another in its real erection, he takes the purpose of the honest heart as the execution of the industrious hand, and writes in his book that we have built temples to his name.

What is true in the land, and in attainments, is true, with infinite extension of meaning, in the spiritual realm. I want to preach like some dear old father in God, whose words are light, whose sentences are music, and I cannot until twenty more years have come and gone, and mellowed me into richer ripeness. I want to sing like some voice that makes the air melodious, and I cannot unless I practise hour after hour, every day, and obey the discipline of the severest and yet gentlest teachers. I want to be massive, noble in all truthfulness, and brilliant in all moral splendour, and I cannot be until long time has elapsed. The path of the just is not a flashing blaze that comes and goes, it is as the shining light, shining more and more unto the perfect day. Walk by the same rule, mind the same thing, persevere, go on, " never stand still, till the Master appear." Be this your purpose, and God will do the rest !

Gen. iv. 2.

"And Abel was a keeper of sheep."

EARLY FAMILY LIFE.

THIS chapter begins the family register of the world, and begins it, in truth, very awkwardly. Eve said that she had gotten a man from the Lord, but the man soon showed that the contrary supposition would have been sustained by a higher probability, for it would seem from Cain's spirit and conduct that the Lord had next to nothing to do with him. He took quietly, however, to his father's trade, and the three of them lived a dull, narrow life in some place now undiscoverable. A dull life, truly. The old people disgraced, the young man nothing to hear but how his father and mother had misbehaved themselves, and had been made to start the world with a skin a-piece and a rude knowledge of gardening. No newspaper, no telegraph, no politics, no theatres, no public-houses : why, some of you young men think your lives dull enough, but at any rate you can hear the noise, if you cannot join in the glee, and it is something after all to be able to hear a good loud noise : it scares the ghosts off and sets you wondering. Cain had nobody of his own age to speak to. He lived under the cloud of an unhappy memory, and day by day he got moodier and gloomier in temper.

When Abel was born his mother did not say *he* was from the Lord. She kept a silence full of meaning upon that point. Her experience of Cain's odd ways and fierce looks had led her to take Abel's coming very quietly, for if the one had led her such a life, what would two of them do ? So Abel came almost without a welcome, and Adam set him in due time to a new business, for no more gardeners were wanted just then. You know what became of Abel ; Cain killed him, as many elder sons are trying to kill their younger brothers to-day. Those who have been some time in possession do not like to be disturbed. Elder sons begrudge their wooden horses and their other toys to their baby brothers now-a-days, and pinch those baby brothers and grin at them unlovingly on the sly ; even in *your* nursery, my friend, though you think your little ones are angels. The late comers have a hard time often, for there is an unwritten law of primogeniture and an unwritten law of knuckles. Your Cain has bitten your Abel many a time when you were not looking, and has been grimly glad when the unlucky baby has had his fingers jammed in the nursery door.

Cain was not without a kind of religiousness, remember. He did go to the unroofed church sometimes, but he went so un-willingly, so slouchingly, so coldly, that it was no church to him he begrudged the few roots and fruits that he took, just as we be-grudge the weekly offering, and therefore God let him take them home, just as we would do if we could get secretly at the box. God takes nothing from our unwilling hand. He loves a cheerful giver ! He will take two mites, he will take a cup of cold water, he will take a box of ointment, if given gladly ; but none of your grudging, none of your dropping a penny as if it were a half-crown, none of your grunting, none of your porcupinishness ; all must be free, glad, honest, open, and joyous ; then the fire will come down and take back to heaven the gift of your love.

Abel was religious in the right way. He gave the best he had with an open heart, and the Lord said, " Of such is the kingdom of heaven." Now, observe, if you please, for it will help you through your whole life, that brothers are not necessarily akin. The greatest contrasts I have perhaps ever known have been between brothers. Yes, and they have been utter strangers to one another, have been these very brothers. And if you think of it, the thing is reasonable enough : the human family in all its bear-ings is *one*; human nature is not incoherent, but consolidated. We live in flats, and think that one flat has no connection with another ; that is our foolish and ruinous mistake. Your brother may be on the next continent; your mate-heart may be a stranger you have never seen. Cain and Abel were not akin.

Cain did things with his hand; Abel did them with his heart: Cain flung his gifts at you, and if you did not catch them so much the more pleased was he; Abel gave them with a hearty love, and was sorry he had not more to give. So Cain killed Abel, and will kill him to the end of the world, spite of all preachers and moralists, but now in a cunning enough way to escape the gaoler and the gibbet. But he will kill him! The man who lost the prize for which his essay was written will kill the man whose essay was accepted; he will sneer at him, and a sneer may be murder. The man who lost the election, being "defeated, not disgraced," will kill the man who got in; he will shrug a shoulder when his name is up, and a shrug may be homicide! You and I may have killed a good many people, and a good many people may have tried to kill us; they will take away our trade, they will say unkind things of us, they will close an eye or pucker a lip villainously, and then dry their mouths as those who have been drinking in secret. It is very horrible; it smells sulphurously; hell cannot be far away, and we are not to windward.

Some people are very curious to know what these sacrifices were, and grey-headed commentators, who ought to have known better, have spent no end of time in trying to gratify their idle curiosity. Some have thought that the virtue was in the thing taken, as if *that* could be! No; you must find out what the *heart* is, what the motive is, what the will is. "A broken and a contrite heart, O God, thou wilt not despise." It is for ever true that God abhors the sacrifice where not the heart is found. If you want to find out Cain's condition of heart you will find it after the service which he pretended to render; you know a man best *out* of church; the minister sees the best side of a man, the lawyer the worst, and the physician the real. If you want to know what a man's religious worship is worth, see him *out* of church. Cain killed his brother when church was over, and that is the exact measure of Cain's piety. And so, when you went home the other day you charged five shillings for a three-shilling article, and told the buyer it was too cheap: and that is exactly the value of your psalm-singing and sermon-hearing. You said you enjoyed the discourse exceedingly last Thursday; then you filled up the income-tax paper falsely: and you will be judged by the schedule, not by the sentiment. Do not trouble your heads about the details of the first sacrifice, but remember that what is required of us is that we do justice, love, mercy, and walk humbly with God. If thou doest well thou shall be accepted, and if not sin lieth at the door.

Cain killed Abel and then said he did not know where he was, and pettishly he asked, " Am I my brother's keeper ? " How sins go in clusters ! Murder, lying, selfishness, all found together in this incident. But blood makes itself heard ; you cannot wash out the deep stain. All human blood is precious ; there is not a drop too much of it in all the earth. It is a fountain that rises close by the throne of God. Slay a child, and the law of civilisation will seize you and kill you with a holy sword. " He that sheddeth man's blood by man shall his blood be shed." This is not a question of capital punishment in the vulgar sense of the term, but of capital punishment in its high and eternal necessity. Capital punishment, in our sense of the term, was not inflicted upon Cain, but in the fullest and deepest sense his life was forfeited to the inexorable and righteous law. Capital punishment is the doom of all sin. " The wages of sin is death." " In the day that thou eatest thereof thou shalt surely die." To do evil is to perish at the core.

As we proceed in the chapter we find that family life extends rapidly. What length of time elapses you see we cannot tell. The spaces may have been what some people like to call "geological periods." I fancy that the true explanation of all these difficulties about the rise of the human race from two people, and all these intermarriages, is to be found in the question of *time.* But I know nothing about it, and the people called " the commentators " know nothing about it ; the solid fact with which we have to deal is that the human race is *here,* and the account given of it in the Bible is the best account of it yet found in all the world. How wonderfully things begin to take shape in the following verses :—

"And Adah bare Jabal : he was the father of such as dwell in tents, and of such as have cattle. And his brother's name was Jubal : he was the father of all such as handle the harp and organ. And Zillah, she also bare Tubal-cain, an instructor of every artificer in brass and iron : and the sister of Tubal-cain was Naamah " (vv. 20-22).

Heretofore we have had rural and pastoral life, now we advance to manufacture and art. Man is awakening, and he demands more than he has yet had ; " it is the divinity that stirs within him." Jabal developed cattle and got men to live in tents, having a taste for architecture and order ; Jubal made musical instruments, as harps and organs ; Tubal-cain wrought in brass and iron. A grand thing it is for a man to see that his trade is from God ! The organ-builder is quite as much the creation of God as the sermon-builder. Your spinning and weaving and compounding, are all from heaven. "We are fellow-workers with God." The Divine meaning is that this earth and all belonging to it shall be developed to the highest possible point. And he who helps in that direction is called of heaven to the work. Build your organs for God ; keep your shops for God ; employ your men and your money for God : "whether ye eat or drink, or whatsoever ye do, do all to the glory of God."

Towards the end of the chapter Lamech seems to go out of his head.

"And Lamech said unto his wives, Adah and Zillah, Hear my voice ; ye wives of Lamech, hearken unto my speech : for I have slain a man to my wounding, and a young man to my hurt. If Cain shall be avenged seven-fold, truly Lamech seventy and sevenfold " (vv. 23, 24).

Thus Lamech seems to become the father of all such as are crazy. I cannot tell what he saith. Is it a riddle? Is it a mania? Does he think he has killed somebody? Or is it nothing but frenzy and incoherence? Truly Lamech has a large family to answer for. It is amazing how many incoherent people there are in the world. I believe it is a matter of fact that the most of men are lunatics. Not upon all points ; not openly and visibly ; not far enough gone to be confined in asylums ; but really insane on some vital questions. How else account for their lives ? How else explain the discrepancy between their creed and conduct ? How else give a reason for their going straight down to hell in the very face of the Cross and against the stress of the whole love of God ? "The whole head is sick," that is the terrible and sufficient answer !

Gen. iv. 13.

" And Cain said unto the Lord,.My punishment is greater than I can bear."

CAIN'S PUNISHMENT.

MY object is to show, so far as I may be able, some of the necessary *consequences* of sin, and to point out how those consequences prove the terribleness of wrong-doing. Sometimes we know a thing better by its consequences than by its essence. I think this is particularly the case with *sin.* It may require great intellectual power to see sin *as* sin, but the consequences of sin show themselves in glaring and appalling clearness to the dullest eyes. If, then, any man would really know the sinfulness of sin let him study its effects upon himself, and look at its consequences within the circle with which he is most familiar.

Have you ever noticed the effect of a wicked *thought* in its swift passage through the brain? I have—alas, too often!—in my own case. I have been in high intellectual health one moment, and in the next I have been thrown down as by an invisible bolt of fire; that invisible bolt was a wicked *thought*; an idea that flashed through the mind and was never known to any but God. I had suffered great loss. The brain was stunned, and for the moment it lost the fine delicate power of moving with ease through difficult questions and high speculations. Its most exquisite threads had lost their tension, and its bloom mouldered and perished. You cannot explain this fully to any one who has not felt it. But you who have felt loss of memory, a sensation of dizziness, and painful uncertainty in mental exercises; you who have turned giddy where once you stood like a rock, and have stammered where once you spoke with determined emphasis; *you* know what I mean by the sad effects of melancholy thought upon intellectual completeness and power; and in that desolating hour you may have said with infinite bitterness—" My punishment is more than I can bear."

But sin is moral rather than intellectual, and its moral consequences may be considered as more marked and terrible than the intellectual results. This is actually the case. Sin lures a man to his destruction. It eats out his soul piece by piece. If there is such a thing as a moral nerve it softens, crumples, wastes, kills it, and then it gets the whole man into its unholy and cruel dominion.

Take a lie, and trace what may be called its natural history. First of all, the man must lie to *himself*; note that fact carefully, if you please. In getting his own consent to the lie, the man told the lie to himself. In that moment he impoverished his vitality, and prepared himself to go the next step, and when he went the next step he became so weak that he could be driven to any length on the road of wickedness. Thus he exposed himself to a new attack—he came within the humbling and shattering influence of *fear*. "The righteous are bold as a lion"; but loss of righteousness is loss of boldness. Here, then, is an intolerable punishment. The scourge of *fear* is always lacerating the bad man. Beckon him, and his knees knock together by reason of false alarm. Turn suddenly upon him, and he feels a sword cutting through his very heart. He flees, "when no man pursueth," and a great shadow lies coldly across his merriest feast. This is punishment. It is a punishment that never ceases When the wicked man goes to rest his pillow is too hard for his throbbing head. If he fall into troubled slumber, an unexpected tap at his door will be to him as an earthquake, or as a call to sudden judgment. And he never gets the better of this. Indeed, he gets worse and worse, until his own shadow frightens him, and his own voice seems to be calling for his detection and punishment. His punishment is greater than he can bear; its reality is great, but its imagination is infinite! Hell, in its most terrible and revolting aspect, becomes simply the natural and proper end of sin. If we could think ourselves back into a state of innocence, it would probably be impossible to us to create, even imaginatively, the idea of hell. It would not come within the region or range of our thinking. It would be like something that required an *additional sense* to apprehend or lay hold of it. But let that innocence be lost—let the soul stray from its sacred sanctuary—let it lose its hold upon God—and instantly hell opens, and hell is felt to be the proper end of sin. The sinner creates his own hell.

Cain said, "My punishment is greater than I can bear." We sometimes say that punishment should be proportioned to sin. There is a sense in which that is most true and just. It is most true and just with regard to all punishment that comes from the outside. It is a law which must be obeyed by the parent, the magistrate, and every wronged or offended man. But this is by no means the limit of the question. *The punishment which a man inflicts upon himself* is infinitely severer than any punishment that can be inflicted upon him. "A wounded spirit who can bear?" You remember how you ill-treated that poor child now dead ; you saw the anguish of his soul, and he besought you and you would not hear ; and now a great distress is come upon you, and your bread is very bitter. Who is punishing you? Not the magistrate. Who then? *You are punishing yourself.* You cannot forgive yourself. The child touches you at every corner, speaks to you in every dream, moans in every cold wind, and lays its thin pale hand upon you in the hour of riot and excitement. You see that ill-used child everywhere ; a shadow on the fair horizon, a background to the face of every other child, a ghastly contrast to everything lovely and fair. Time cannot quench the fire. Events cannot throw into dim distance this tragic fact. It surrounds you, mocks you, defies you, and under its pressure you know the meaning of the words, which no mere grammarian can understand—"The wicked shall go away into EVERLASTING punishment."

All this will come the more vividly before us if we remember that a man who has done wrong has not only to *be* forgiven, he has to *forgive himself.* That is the insuperable difficulty. He feels that any external view of his sin, which even the acutest man can take, is altogether partial and incomplete ; and, consequently, that any forgiveness which such a man can offer is also imperfect and superficial. And even in relation to God the same difficulty arises, notwithstanding the completeness of his view as the necessity of his omniscience. To have grieved a Being so good, so holy, as God, is felt to be a crime that *ought not* to be forgiven, and that his mercy can only be extended at the expense of his righteousness. But to this we must return presently.

Have you ever watched the deteriorating effects of sin even upon the *personal appearance?* Take a youth of extreme beauty, and let him, little by little, be led into wicked practices ; in proportion as he is so led will the register of his descent be written upon his face, and upon his whole attitude and manner. Quite imperceptibly, I admit, but with awful exactness and depth. The eye, once so clear and so steady in its look, will be marked by suspicion, uncertainty, or timidity of movement; its glances will not be like sun rays darting through thick foliage, but rather like a dark lantern turned on skilfully to see what is happening here and there, but throwing no light on the man who holds it. And strange lines will be woven around the mouth; and the lips, so well-cut, so guileless and generous, will be tortured into ugliness and sensual enlargement; and the voice, once so sweet, so ringing, the very music of a character unstained and fearless, will contract some mocking tones, and give itself up to a rude laughter, partly deceitful and partly defiant. All this will not happen in one day. Herein is the subtlety of evil. If you do not see the youth for years you may be shocked when you miss the fine simplicity and noble bearing which you associated with his name. This is part of the man's punishment. It is the spot of leprosy on a forehead once so open and un-wrinkled, and it will grow and spread and deepen until there be no place fit for him but the silent and inhospitable wilderness.

This punishment, too, seems to get into a man's business and house. It lowers the high discipline which once ruled and ennobled them, and substitutes trickery and eye-service for the better law which once prevailed. Everywhere it touches and debases the sinner; to his very walk it imparts a swagger or a slouch, significant of debased character, and every relation of life it perverts, disennobles, and defiles.

Now a meditation of this kind might well drive us to despair, if there be nothing else to be said. Sin can only aggravate itself and relieve our torment by plunging into some still deeper excess. Where, then, is hope to be found? If there is any way of escape, let us have it pointed out so clearly that the wayfaring man, though a fool, need not err therein.

I have said that even God's forgiveness, strictly in itself, does not meet the case of a man being unable to forgive himself. That is so, philosophically, but, thank God, not evangelically. God's forgiveness, through Jesus Christ our Lord, is not *mere* forgiveness, however abundant and emphatic. It is not merely a royal or even paternal edict. It is an act incomplete in itself; it is merely introductory or preparatory, as the uprooting of weeds is preliminary to a better use of the soil. It is an *essential* act, for in the absence of pardon the soul is absolutely without the *life* that can lay hold of any of the higher blessings or gifts of God. To what, then, is forgiveness preparatory? To adoption, to communion with God, to absorption into the Divine nature, to the witness of the Holy Ghost. "The Spirit itself beareth witness with our spirits that we are the children of God." And if in moments of special trial "our heart condemn us, God is greater than our heart and knoweth all things." You will see, then, that if it was merely an act of forgiveness, it would be quite true that man would be unable to forgive himself; but it is "assurance," it is "sonship," it is joy of the Holy Ghost. "There is, therefore, now no condemnation, to them which are in Christ Jesus, who walk not after the flesh, but after the Spirit." "To be spiritually minded is life and peace." "Hereby know we that we dwell in him, and he in us, because he hath given us of his Spirit." "It is God that justifieth; who is he that condemneth?" Thus the soul is flooded with joy. Its daily song is of victory. It is stirred, and ruled, and gladdened by a mysterious and indestructible sense of triumph, for the grace of the blessed and infinite Christ fills the whole heart with sweet content and immortal hope.

Gen. v. 1.

" This is the book of the generations of Adam."

NOBODYISM.

THIS fifth chapter of the book of Genesis is the beginning of that long series of chapters in human history which are extremely uninteresting. What do we know about Seth, Enos, Cainan, Mahalaleel, and Jared? We know nothing and we care nothing, for they left no memorial behind them that shows their quality or excites our interest. You must have already noticed that this chapter is as true as any chapter in human history, especially as it shows so clearly, what we ourselves have found out, that most people are extremely uninteresting. They are names and nothing more. They are producers and consumers, tenants and tax-payers, and that is all; they are without wit, music, piquancy, enterprise, or keenness of sympathy. They listen to your best anecdotes and say 'm; they hear of Livingstone with a shudder; they suppose there must be a great noise at Niagara. Such people were Seth and Enos, Mahalaleel and Jared; respectable, quiet, plodding; said "good-night" to one another regularly, and remarked briefly upon the weather, and died. Just what many nowadays seem to do. Put down on paper everything that has passed between you and some people, and you will find how very little paper is needed. Now I want to show you that such people are often unjustly estimated, and to remind you that if all stars were of the same size the sky would look very odd, much like a vast chessboard with circles instead of squares. I want to remind you also that really the best part of human history is never written at all. Family life, patient service, quiet endurance, the training of children, the resistance of temptation, these things are never mentioned by the historian. The man who burns down an abbey or a minster is immortalised in history; the poor house-wife who makes a pound go as far as thirty shillings, and pinches herself that she may give her boy a quarter's more schooling, is not known even to have lived. Guy Fawkes is known all over the world, but your honest father, who has given you a good example and a good training, is hardly known six doors away from his own residence. If we remember these things we shall mitigate the contempt with which we are apt to speak of so-called nobodies. Because we admire brilliance we need not despise usefulness. When your little child is ill, he needs kindness more than genius, and it will be of small service to him if his mother is good at epigrams, but bad at wringing out a wet cloth for his burning brow. I am, then, quite willing to admit that Seth and Enos, Mahalaleel and Jared are not one-thousandth part so well known by name as the man in the moor, but I believe they did more real good than that famous character ever attempted.

You should remember, too, that a long flat road may be leading up to a great mountain. There are some very plain and uninteresting miles out of Geneva, but every one of them brings you nearer Mont Blanc. Now from Seth to Jared is a long run through quiet domestic scenery, through daily ploughing, daily milking, and daily gleaning; very quiet, very simple, no noise in the dull farmhouse louder than the clock tick (excuse the modern allusion), and no noise greater than the flap of wings in the high green trees. Oh, so dull that long road from Seth to Jared, but round the corner you find ENOCH, the Mont Blanc of his day! Many a child who never heard the name of Jared knows well the name of Enoch. So you do not know to what high hill your life may be quietly leading up. Even if you yourself are nobody your son may be a man of renown, or his son may be a valiant and mighty man. Three flat miles between Geneva and Chamounix said they would lie there no longer, so many travellers had called them dull and tame, so they went off in a huff, nobody knows where; but Mont Blanc himself bowed his crowned head and remonstrated, owning that but for them he himself would hardly have been known one mile away from home. So the three peevish miles came back again, proud to be a roadway to the monarch of hills. You know Enoch, but you know nothing of Jared; you know Moses well, but how many men amongst you can tell me his father's name?

It would seem that in Enoch we come to the first really good man, of any fame, in Biblical history. I do not except Abel. In fact what we know of Abel is next to nothing. Enoch reaches the point of renown in godliness; he walked with God three hundred years at least; his walk was on the high hills, so high that he simply stepped into the next world without troubling Death to go through his long dark process. "He was not, for God took——." As if he had walked so near that God opened the window and took him in; and we, too, might pass in as easily if we walked on the same sunny heights. But we are in valleys and pits, and God must needs send death to dig us out and send us to heaven by a longer road. Solemn indeed is the word, "Enoch walked with God"; it means so much; there was a serenity about the man unlike all other quietness; a tender light made his face shine, and in his voice there was a tone, rich, pensive, joyous, altogether wonderful in its combination of humility and triumph. To walk with God is to pray without ceasing; to walk with God is to be absolutely free from care and independent of human judgment; to walk with God is to be in heaven.

After Enoch we come to Methuselah. He, too, is well-known,

although for nothing but length of days apparently, yet as a matter of fact he ought to be known for something much more highly distinguished. It is wonderful how oddly and whimsically fame is gained : Methuselah is famed because he was the oldest man, and Samson because he was the strongest man ; another is known because he can walk upon a tight rope, and another because he can swim across a channel. If it were in my power to preach the most splendid sermon ever uttered by mortal lips not a newspaper in the world would take the slightest notice of it, but if I put up an umbrella in the pulpit or tore the pulpit Bible in two many a paragraph would report the eccentricity. A splendid sermon would be thought of as interesting only to the few, but an act of folly would be regarded as of universal interest. Thus it is (though it may not seem so) that things get into history. Any man living can have a world-wide notoriety to-morrow, can have his name telegraphed throughout the whole range of civilisation, and be the subject of editorial comment throughout Christendom. Shoot any member of the royal family, and see if this be not so. Everybody knows that Methuselah lived nine hundred and sixty-nine years, but nobody knows that but for you two orphan boys would never have had a chance in life. No preacher has a really world-wide name, known in slums and garrets, backwoods, steamboats, thoroughfares, and palaces, who did not in some way get it through " contemptible speech."

Now what is that other thing for which Methuselah ought to be better known than for his great age ? Tell me without looking at your Bibles. I give you a moment for recollection. Now tell me ; you cannot ! I knew you could not ! *He was the grandfather of Noah;* that is his glory, not his mere age ! You cannot tell what your boy may be, or his boy : so keep yourself up to the mark in all mental health and moral integrity lest you transmit a plague to posterity. It may be that Nature is only resting in you ; presently she will produce a man !

Methuselah was the father of Lamech, and Lamech was the father of Noah. Here we come once more upon the highlands of history and the air grows keener. Though Lamech had many sons and daughters, yet his hope glowed most brightly when he looked upon Noah. Truly "there is a spirit in man, and the inspiration of the Almighty giveth him understanding." A father

of such insight deserved a son of such renown. He did not know
the full meaning of his own words, and therein he was like the
rest of us; for oftentimes upon our small words God puts meanings which our hearts had never conceived, as out of one grain of
corn he brings a return of sixty-fold.

Precisely the same thing we have in this chapter we find in the
catalogue of the names of the early disciples of our Lord. We
know Peter and James and John. But how little as compared
with them do we know of Thomas and Bartholomew and Philip,
of Lebbæus, and Simon the Canaanite. Yet they were all
members of one company, and servants of the same Lord. We
speak of men of renown, forgetting that their renown is principally
derived from men who have no renown themselves ! Unknown
people make other people known. The hills rest upon the plain
ground. Besides, there is a bad repute as well as a fair fame :
Judas Iscariot is known as widely as the Apostle John ! Be not
envious of those who have high place and name ; could we know
them better perhaps we should find that they long for the quietness
of home and sigh for release from the noise and strain of popular
applause. Happily, too, we should remember that a deed may
be immortal, when the mere name of the doer may be lost in
uncertainty. Such deeds are mentioned in the Bible ; they are
told everywhere as imperishable memorials, though the names
of the doers have escaped the attention of the busiest watchers.

So closes this apparently uninteresting chapter. Let me say
that the hour will be dark in which we pine for things romantic
at the expense of a quiet and deep life. Christianity teaches us
that no child is to be despised, no work is to be considered mean,
and that suffering may have all the honour of service. Woe to
us when we can live only on stimulants ! When the house is
accounted dull, when only sensational books can be endured,
when music and drama and painted show are essential to our
happiness, life has gone down to a low ebb and death is at the
door. Let us do our quiet work as if we were preparing for
kings, and watch attentively at the door, for the next comer may
be the Lord himself

Gen. vi. 13.

" And God said unto Noah, The end of all flesh is come before me ; for the earth is filled with violence through them : and, behold, I will destroy them with the earth."

NOAH'S FLOOD.

THIS is exactly the tone of the creative chapters of the Bible. It is important to remember this, as showing that God's sovereignty has two distinct but consistent operations,—it creates, and it destroys, and the creature may not say, What doest thou ? It is important, too, to remember that no middle point is proposed between creation and destruction ; and as the one is taken literally, so the other must be taken in its plain and obvious meaning : when God " creates," he gives existence ; when God " destroys," he takes existence away. It is in this view that I regard the narrative upon the consideration of which we are now entering as singularly important—viz., as showing the Divine sovereignty in creation and destruction. Let us look at the narrative and see what we can of God's method, that we may see how he ripens and executes his severest purposes.

It is happily clear that God is moved by what we would call moral considerations, and not by arbitrary impulse, in his government of mankind. The man who does an action simply to please himself is said to act arbitrarily ; the action is not founded upon argument or reason, and is therefore arbitrary. In this case God gives his reasons, and discloses every step in the process of his pathetic and mournful argument. " God saw that the wickedness of man was great upon the earth, and that every imagination of the thoughts of his heart was only evil continually." That is the basis of action. God's purpose in creating man had been frustrated ; its frustration involved the ruin of man, as if by a suicidal act. God, therefore, seeing that ruin *must* come, acted judicially, as in the first instance he had acted creatively. The question would seem to have been simply this : " Shall sin be left to kill the human race slowly, as if inch by inch, without my asserting judicial rights, or shall I distinctly interpose, as I did in Eden, and bring judgment down upon iniquity ? " We ourselves would say, with all humility and reverence, that God was bound to take the second course, if he was to protect not only his own dignity, but the integrity of truth and righteousness. In this act we have on a large scale what in Eden we had on a small scale—a determination on the part of God to *destroy evil;* and by destroying evil I do not mean locking it up by itself in a moral prison, which shall be enlarged through ages and generations until it shall become the abode of countless millions of rebels, but its utter, final, everlasting extinction, so that at last the universe shall be "without spot or wrinkle, or any such thing"—the pure home of a pure creation.

But what is the meaning of there being no middle point between creation and destruction ? Does it mean that there is no effort on the part of God to save man ? It means nothing of the kind. God has never ceased to make this effort until he himself has proved the hopelessness of making it. In this very narrative the law of his working is most clearly defined : "My spirit shall not always strive with man." Many curious interpretations have been given of these words, but none, to my mind, so satisfactory as the one which is most obvious. It may be expressed thus : Man shall not die without remonstrance ; I will plead with him ; I will ply him with every consideration that can move his conscience and his heart; and not until hope is utterly extinguished will I release him from the importunity of my love. Thus, man is not coldly allowed to die : he is besought, importuned, urged; and by his own uncontrollable madness alone does he rush upon everlasting destruction.

In this chapter we see Divine forbearance exhausted. A very tender expression is here employed : "It grieved the Lord at his heart that he had made man on the earth." The apostle says, "Grieve not the Holy Spirit of God." By putting the two expressions together, we see the wonderful unity of the Bible history and of human nature in all ages. We raise many curious questions about Divine providence, but there is one which ought to arrest our attention, perhaps more gravely than any other—Why did God create a creature that had the power to grieve him ? It is because out of such power there comes the ability to worship and to serve God, and out of worship and service there comes a blessed progress in all purity and nobleness of life.

The Almighty is about to do here what some of us in our

imperfect wisdom have often wished to see done : we have supposed that if all notoriously bad people could be removed at a stroke from the world the kingdom of heaven would be at once established on the earth. The idea may be put roughly thus : Bring together all prisoners, all idlers, drunkards, thieves, liars, and every known form of criminal ; take them out into the middle of the Atlantic and sink them there, and at once society will be regenerated, and paradise will be regained. Now this is substantially the very course which the Almighty took in the days of Noah, with what results we know only too well. All our fine theories have been tested, and they come to nothing. The tree of manhood has been cut down to the very root, and it has been shown in every possible way that the root itself must be cured if the branches are to become strong and fruitful. If you were to-day to destroy all the world, with the single exception of one household, and that household the most pious and honourable that ever lived, in less than half a century we should see all the bad characteristics returning. Water cannot drown sin. Fire cannot burn out sin. Prisons cannot cure theft and cruelty. We must go deeper.

In the meantime it was well to try some rough experiments, merely for the sake of showing that they were not worth trying. If the Flood had not been tried there are some reformers amongst us who would have thought of that as a lucky idea, and wondered that it had never occurred to the Divine mind ! After all, it is a very elementary idea. It is the very first idea that would occur to a healthy mind : the world is a failure, man is a criminal and a fool, sin is rampant in the land ; very well ; that being the case, *drown the world.* There are persons who seriously ask, Do you think the Flood ever did occur ? and there are others who find shells on hill-tops and show them in proof of a universal deluge. O fools and slow of heart ! This Flood is occurring every day ; this judgment upon sin never ceases ; this protection of a righteous seed is an eternal fact ! How long shall we live in the mere letter and have only a history instead of a revelation,—a memorandum book instead of a living Father ? That there was a flood exactly as is described in the Bible I have not so much as a shadow of a doubt ; but even if I took it as an allegory, or a typical judgment given in parable, I should seize the account as one that is far more profoundly true than any mere fact could ever be. Look at it! God morally angry, righteousness asserted, sin judged, goodness preserved, evil destroyed,—it *is* true; it *must* be true; every honest heart demands that it be taken as true.

As we have a moral reason for the destruction of the earth, so we have a moral reason for the preservation of Noah. Observe this closely, so as to escape the idea that there is anything capricious or whimsical in the Divine government—"Noah was a just man and perfect in his generations, and Noah walked with God" (ver. 9). Of his great-grandfather, Enoch, the same testimony was borne,—" he walked with God." This man who so walked was spared. The judgments of God are not mere violences ; they keep their course by a law at once merciful and terrible : they spare the good, they overpass the house sprinkled with blood, they throw down no holy altar. How calmly those judgments come ! They seem indeed to come suddenly, but they really come up from eternity : slowly, surely, irresistibly ! It is something to be able to challenge the severest inquiry into the moral reason of this solemn transaction,—something to be able to say that, in all the severity of his judgments, God never mingles the righteous and the wicked in one indiscriminating punishment.

What a rain it was ! "All the fountains of the great deep were broken up, and the windows of heaven were opened, and th rain was upon the earth forty days and forty nights"; still the torrents came, and the great cataracts, so that men knew not the dry land from the sea ; "and the waters prevailed exceedingly upon the earth"; they rose to the high windows, and the billows dashed upon the drenched roofs like angry seas ; and men fled away to the mountains and watched the cruel pursuer from afar ; and still it rose, obliterating their footsteps, and rising quickly like one impelled by mighty anger to seek the prey ; the wolf, the lion, the leopard stood upon the crags, baying and roaring with fury that drove them mad, and high above the surging deep there screamed the affrighted eagle and the vulture, enraged by hunger : at last there was but one hill top left, and there the strongest and fiercest of the sons of men gathered, and there were heard prayers, and oaths, and curses, and cries that made the wild beasts quiet; and still the cold waters rose, the lightning at midnight showed the dreary waste on which no stars glittered, and amid thunders that shook the universe the last strong man plunged into the infinite gulf! "And all flesh died that moved upon the earth; all in whose nostrils was the breath of life, of all that was in the dry land, died." Oh, what a rain it was! What an outlook from the window of the ark! For many a long day no eye could venture to look out of that window; for who could bear to see the grey-haired man, and the fair woman, and the little child doomed to die! Who can steadfastly look upon the judgments of God, or bear the flash of his uplifted sword? "It is a fearful thing to fall into the hands of the living God."

"The waters prevailed upon the earth an hundred and fifty days." Then came the time of release. "God made a wind to pass over the earth, and the waters assuaged." At the end of forty days after, the tops of the mountains were seen; Noah opened the window of the ark and sent forth a raven; then he sent forth a dove, but the dove returned; a week after he sent out the dove again, and the dove returned in the evening with "an olive leaf pluckt off." In another week he sent forth the dove once more, and the dove came not again. And soon after the ark was broken up, and "Noah builded an altar unto the Lord, and the Lord smelled a sweet savour"; and thus a new beginning was made. We seem now to have a new Adam and a new Eve. How they will turn out remains to be seen. They have a great advantage over the original pair, for they have a solemn history behind them. They can never forget the surge that beat and dashed furiously against the ark; never can they forget that last lightning that flashed past the window, like an angel of destruction, and seemed to shake a sword threateningly in their own faces; never can these things be forgotten! Noah will do better than Adam, and make us grieve that the experiment of humanity was not begun with this noble and incorruptible man! We shall see.

MAKING, DESTROYING, AND SAVING MAN.

"And God said, Let us make man."—GEN. i. 26.
"And the Lord said, I will destroy man."—GEN. vi. 7.
"Will he reserve his anger for ever?"—JER. iii. 5.
"The Son of man is come to seek and to save that which was lost."—LUKE xix. 10.

IF you could bring together into one view all the words of God expressive of his purposes concerning man, you would be struck with the changefulness which seems to hold his mind in continual uncertainty. He will destroy, yet the blow never falls; he will listen to man no more, yet he speeds to him in the day of trouble and fear; he will make an utter end, yet he saves Noah from the flood, and plucks Lot as a brand from the fire; his arm is stretched out, yet it is withdrawn in tender pity. So changeful is he who changeth not, and so fickle he in whom there is no shadow of turning! We cannot but be interested in the study of so remarkable a fact, for surely there must be some explanation of changefulness in Omniscience and variation of feeling in the Inhabitant of eternity. You never read of God being disappointed with the sun, or grieved by the irregularity of the stars. He never darkens the morning light with a frown, nor does he ever complain of any other of the work of his hands than man, made in his own image and likeness! he does indeed say that he will destroy "both man and beast, and the creeping thing, and the fowls of the air," but it is wholly on account of man's sin; for, as everything was made for man, so when man falls all that was made for him and centred in him goes down in the great collapse. Why should there be blithe bird-music in the house of death? Why should the earth grow flowers when the chief beauty has lost its bloom? So all must die in man. When he falls he shakes down the house that was built for him. So we come again to the solemn but tender mystery of God's changefulness, and ask in wonder, yet in hope, whether there can be found any point at which are reconciled the Changeable and the Everlasting?

But let us be sure that we are not mistaken in the terms of the case. Is it true that there is any change in God? is not the apparent change in him the reflection of the real change that is in ourselves? I not only undertake to affirm that such is the case, but I go farther, and affirm that the very everlastingness of the Divine nature compels exactly such changes as are recorded in the Bible. If you say that man ought not to have been created as a changeable being, then you say in other words that man ought not to have been created at all. If you find fault with man's constitution, you find fault with God, and if you find fault with God I have no argument with you. I take man as he is, and I want to show that Divine love must manifest itself, either in complacency or anger, according to the conduct of mankind.

I must remind you that this principle is already in operation in those institutions which we value most, and that it is a principle on which we rely for the good order, the permanent security, and the progress of society.

This principle is in constant operation in family life. By the gracious necessities of nature the child is tenderly beloved. The whole household is made to give way to the child's weakness. The parents live their lives over again in the life of the child. For his sake hardship is undergone and difficulty is overcome. The tenderest care is not too dainty, the most persistent patience is not accounted a weariness. But sin comes: ingratitude, rebellion, defiance; family order is trampled on, family peace is violated; and in proportion as the parent is just, honourable, true, and loving, will he be grieved with great grief; he will not be petulant, irritable, or spiteful, but a solemn and bitter grief will weigh down his desolated heart. Then he may mourn the child's birth, and say, with breaking and most tearful voice, "It had been better that the child had not been born." Then still higher aggravation comes. Something is done which must be visited with anger, or the parent must lose all regard for truth and for the child himself. Now, all punishment for wrong-doing is a point on the line which terminates in death. Consider that well, if you please. It may, indeed, be so accepted as to lead to reformation and better life; but that does not alter the nature of punishment itself. Punishment simply and strictly as punishment is the beginning of death. Have you, then, changed in your parental love because you have punished your child? Certainly not. The change is not in you; it is in the child. If you had forborne to punish, then you would have lost your own moral vitality, and would have become a partaker in the very sin which you affected to deplore. If you are right-minded, you will feel that destruction is better than sinfulness; that sinfulness, as such, demands destruction; and if you knew the full scope of your own act you would know that the very first stripe given for sin is the beginning of death. But I remember the time when you caressed that child and fondled it as if it was your better life, you petted the child, you laid it on the softest down, you sang it your sweetest lullabies, you lived in its smiles; and now I see you, rod in hand, standing over the child in anger! Have you changed? Are you fickle, pitiless, tyrannical? You know you are not. It is love that expostulates; it is love that strikes. If that child were to blame you for your changefulness you would know what reply to make. Your answer would be strong in self-defence, because strong in justice and honour.

We have exactly the same thing in the larger family called *Society.* When a man is punished by society, it is not a proof that society is fickle in temper; it is rather a proof that society is so far conservative, and even everlasting in its substance, as to demand the punishment of every offender. Society is formed to protect and consolidate all that is good and useful in its own multitudinous elements, yet society will not hesitate to slay a man with the public sword, if marks of human blood are upon his hands. Is, then, society vengeful, malignant, or uneven in temper? On the contrary, it is the under-lying *Everlasting* which necessitates all those outward and temporary changes which are so often mistaken as signs of fickleness and uncertainty. What the Everlasting cannot tolerate is dishonour, tyranny, wrong, or impureness in any degree. Society offers rewards to-day and deals out punishments to-morrow. At noon, society may crown you as a benefactor; at midnight, society may drag you forth as a felon: the same society—not fickle or coy, but self-protecting and eternal in righteousness.

These side-lights may at least mitigate the gloom of the mystery with which we started. I want to make you feel that God's changefulness, so called, is not arbitrary, but moral; that is to say, he does not change merely for the sake of changing, but for reasons which arise out of that very Everlastingness which seems to be impaired! Not to be angry with sin is to connive at it ; to connive at sin is sinful ; to be sinful is to be no longer Divine. When God is angry it is a moral fire that is burning in him ; it is love in a glow of justice ; it is his protest on behalf of those who may yet be saved from sin.

See how it is God himself that saves man ! We trembled when he said he would destroy man, for we knew he had the power ; and now that he says he will save man we know that his power of offering terms of salvation is none the less. If man *can* be saved, God will save him ; but it is for the man himself to say whether he will be saved. "If any man open the door, I will come in to him." "Come unto me, all ye that labour and are heavy-laden, and I will give you rest." This is the voice that said, "I will destroy," and the two tones are morally harmonious. Looking at the sin, God must destroy ; looking at any possibility of recovery, God must save. "A bruised reed shall he not break, and smoking flax shall he not quench." Christ lives to save. He would no longer be Christ if human salvation were not his uppermost thought. His soul is in travail ; he yearns over us with pity more than all human pitifulness ; he draws near unto our cities and weeps over them. But he can slay ! He can smite with his strong arm ! His hand can lay hold on justice, and then solemn is the bitter end ! O, my soul, make thy peace with God through Christ. It is his love that burns into wrath. He does not want to slay thee ; he pities thee ; he loves thee ; his soul goes out after thee in great desires of love ; but if thou wilt not come to his Cross, his arm will be heavy upon thee !

How true, then, is it that there is an important sense in which God is to us exactly what we are to him ! "If any man love me, I will manifest myself to him." That is the great law of manifestation. Have I a clear vision of God ? Then am I looking steadily at him with a heart that longs to be pure. Can I not see him ? Then some secret sin may be holding a veil before my eyes. *I* have changed, not God. When I seek him he will be found of me ; but if I desire him not he will be a God afar off !

Gen. ix. 13.

" I do set my bow in the cloud, and it shall be for a token of a covenant between me and the earth."

THE NEW BEGINNING.

THIS second beginning was in many respects very different from the first : there is nothing here about a garden, or a forbidden tree, or a tempting serpent. So it would appear from the letter of the narrative ; yet, lo, as we go along the courses of the history, we find that they are every one here, only under different names, yet ending in precisely identical effects ! So much for variety in human history ! Believe me, there is no vital variety ; it is all superficial and apparent, not profound and real.

A beautiful sight was the altar which Noah built upon the reappearing earth. Beautiful to think that there was a Church before there was a house ! If you look at that first new building in the new world you will see it expand until it becomes a sanctuary wide as the earth, and all men are gathered in loving piety within its ample walls. Sweet was the savour that rose from earth to heaven ! And as the smoke curled upward to the approving sky the primeval blessing was repronounced ; the seasons were confirmed in their revolutions ; and all things seemed to begin again in unclouded hope. Was there, then, a new human nature, and did God succeed better in his second experiment than in his first ? No. The serpent is still here ! Listen : "The imagination of man's heart is evil from his youth." The first temptation was from without, the second was from *within.* This is the verdict of history. In the first account we read that man was made in the image and likeness of God ; and in the second we read that the imagination of his heart is evil from his youth. This, then, must be the accepted fact, and all Divine interpositions must be based upon it. The first thing we learn after this solemn declaration is that there is to be no more smiting of every living thing, plainly showing that mere destruction is a failure. I do not say that destruction is undeserved or unrighteous, but that it is, as a reformative arrangement, a failure as regards the salvation of survivors. We can see men slain for doing wrong, and can in a day or two after the event do the very things which cost them their lives ! It might be thought that one such flood as this would have kept the world in order for ever, whereas men now doubt whether there ever was such a flood, and repeat all the sins of which the age of Noah was guilty. You would think that to see a man hanged would put an end to ruffianism for ever; whereas, history goes to show that within the very shadow of the gallows men hatch the most detestable and alarming crimes. Set it down as a fact that punishment, though necessary even in its severest forms, can never regenerate the heart of man. From this point, then, we have to deal with a history, the fundamental fact of which is that all the actors are as bad as they can possibly be. " There is none righteous, no not one." " There is not a just man upon the earth that doeth good and sinneth not."

It is remarkable, however, that though God will not any more smite every living thing, he has surrounded human life with the most solemn sanctions : "And surely your blood of your lives [your life-blood] will I require; at the hand of every beast will I require it, and at the hand of man ; at the hand of every man's brother will I require the life of man." Under the old dispensation if an ox gored a man it was to be killed. The sovereignty of human life is with God, and secondarily with whomsoever he may appoint. This arrangement follows the account of the flood with remarkable propriety, because when human life has been destroyed on a large scale the value of it might seem to be worthless. Why quibble about the morality of killing one man when ten thousand have been swallowed up in a flood ? But God says in effect—Every human life is of great value; every man must set great store by his own life ; and every man must consider himself in a high degree responsible for the life of his brother,—"Of every man's brother will I require the life of man." Thus, too, he would seem to correct the notion which the destructiveness of this flood might seem to justify, viz., that he himself is careless as to the value and destiny of human life. His answer to this must be found in his Providence and his Redemption. If any man would know what value is set on man by his Maker let him study the life, the sacrifice, and the intercession of Jesus Christ.

You will probably ask whether capital punishment is not enjoined as the law of States in ver. 6 : " Whoso sheddeth man's blood by man shall his blood be shed, for in the image of God made he man." Wherever in civilised countries there is capital crime there must be capital punishment. But capital punishment may mean other and more than the signification usually attached to the expression. To shut a man up in life-long confinement is capital punishment. To imprison him for the whole term of his natural life is in reality to shed his blood. The mere manner of doing it is a trifle; the solemn and tragical fact is that the murderer is seized and held for ever by the strong and righteous arm of the law. *That* is capital punishment, and conscience and reason conspire to proclaim it *just.*

These solemn directions having been given about human life, a covenant, remarkable for beauty and tenderness, is established by the Almighty.

"And God spake unto Noah, and to his sons with him, saying, And I, behold, I establish my covenant with you, and with your seed after you; and with every living creature that is with you, of the fowl, of the cattle, and of every beast of the earth with you; from all that go out of the ark, to every beast of the earth. And I will establish my covenant with you; neither shall all flesh be cut off any more by the waters of a flood, neither shall there any more be a flood to destroy the earth.

"And God said, This is the token of the covenant which I make between me and you and every living creature that is with you, for perpetual generations: I do set my bow in the cloud, and it shall be for a token of a covenant between me and the earth. And it shall come to pass, when I bring a cloud over the earth, that the bow shall be seen in the cloud; and I will remember my covenant, which is between me and you and every living creature of all flesh; and the waters shall no more become a flood to destroy all flesh. And the bow shall be in the cloud; and I will look upon it, that I may remember the everlasting covenant between God and every living creature of all flesh that is upon the earth. And God said unto Noah, This is the token of the covenant, which I have established between me and all flesh that is upon the earth."

The covenant is that there shall not be any more a flood to destroy the earth, and the token of the covenant is the bow in the cloud. But was there not a rainbow before there was a flood? Of course there was. You do not suppose that the rainbow was made on purpose? There were rainbows, it may be, thousands of ages before man was created, certainly from the time that the sun and the rain first knew each other. But old forms may be put to new uses. Physical objects may be clothed with moral meanings. The stars in heaven and the sand by the seashore may come to be unto Abraham as a family register. One day common bread may be turned into sacramental food, and ordinary wine may become as the blood of atonement! The rainbow which was once nothing but a thing of evanescent beauty, created by the sun and the rain, henceforward became the token of a covenant and was sacred as a revelation from heaven. When you lived in a rich English county the song of the lark was nothing to you, it was so familiar; you had heard the dinning trill of a hundred larks in the morning air: but when you went out to the far-away colony, and for years did not hear the voice of a single home bird, you suddenly caught the note of a lark just brought to the land, and the tears of boyhood streamed down your cheeks as you listened to the little messenger from home. To hear it was like hearing a gospel. From that day the lark was to you as the token of a covenant!

In speaking to Noah, God did not then create the bow; he turned it into the sign of a holy bond. The fear is that we may have the bond and not the oath. We may see physical causes producing physical effects, and yet may see no moral significations passing through the common scenery of earth and sky. Cultivate the spirit of moral interpretation if you would be wise and restful: then the rainbow will keep away the flood; the fowls of the air will save you from anxiety; and the lilies of the field will give you an assurance of tender care. Why, everything is yours! The daisy you trod upon just now was telling you that if God so clothe the grass of the field he will much more clothe the child that bears his own image.

Very beautiful is this idea of God giving us something to look at, in order to keep our faith steady. He knows that we need pictures, and rests, and voices, and signs, and these he has well supplied. We might have forgotten the *word*, but we cannot fail to see the *bow*; every child sees it, and exclaims at the sight with glad surprise. If any one would tell the child the sweet meaning of the bow, it might move his soul to a still higher ecstacy! And so with all other things God has given us as signs and tokens: the sacred Book, the water of baptism, the bread and wine, the quiet Sabbath, the house of prayer;—all these have deeper meanings than are written in their names; search tor those meanings, keep them, and you will be rich.

And now, you say, all will be well. The spared family will be as a Church of God. Noah will walk before the Lord with a reverent heart, and, like his great-grandfather, Enoch, will go up to heaven as the morning dew goes up to the sun. Alas! it is not so. " Noah began to be an husbandman, and he planted a vineyard : and he drank of the wine, and was drunken." You cry " Shame," and go out and do exactly the same thing! You said that if you were spared in a certain affliction you would be a good man ever after : you were spared, and there is not a meaner soul on the earth at this moment. You said that if a certain calamity could be averted, you would walk before God with an honest heart · it was averted, and you have never prayed since! Then be careful not to blame Noah, for the severity which injures him slays us. Herein is God more merciful than man, for man would have said, " The bond is broken, and the bow is no longer a pledge "; yet God spared the drunkard, and kept the bow as a token in the cloud. Let us say that "his mercy endureth for ever." Let the house of Aaron say so, and the house that is our own, yea, let everything that hath breath, say, " his mercy endureth for ever."

Gen. x. 1-5.

" Now these are the generations of the sons of Noah, Shem, Ham, and Japheth : and unto them were sons born after the flood. The sons of Japheth ; Gomer, and Magog, and Madai, and Javan, and Tubal, and Meshech, and Tiras. And the sons of Gomer; Ashkenaz, and Riphath, and Togarmah. And the sons of Javan ; Elishah, and Tarshish, Kittim, and Dodanim. By these were the isles of the Gentiles divided in their lands ; every one after his tongue, after their families, in their nations."

THE FOUNTAINS OF HISTORY.

SHALL I be far wrong if I suppose that few of you have ever read the tenth chapter of Genesis right through ? Certainly, from a glance at the long, hard names, one would think that there is not much here for the edification of the reader, and that the best thing that can be done is to skip the chapter. Yet there are some home-words here, and hidden under rough husks are some germs, out of which perhaps we ourselves may have come!

In the fifth verse you find the word "GENTILES." Pause at that word. It may be like the writing outside a letter which is meant for your reading! There is also the word "ISLES." No Englishman can pass that word lightly over. He himself is an islander, the sea-fog dims his windows and the sea boom wakes the gruff bass of all his songs. Perhaps the Hebrew writer had his prophetic eye upon these very shores of ours, so sea-worn and bleak. There is also the word "FAMILIES." Surely we know that word well; we live at home; we have made poetry sing "The Old Arm-chair," "My Ain Fireside," and "The Children's Hour." The poorest Englishman tells you what "family" he belongs to, though he slept in the gutter last night, and pawned his coat for a shilling, which he spent in gin. So you see even here, in this chapter which seems to be all Hebrew and meant only for a Jew's eye, we pick out odd words that are plain good old English, the very freehold and charter of our own people.

Thus conciliated I think an Englishman might now stand at the point of view occupied by the writer of the tenth chapter of Genesis, from which he sees the going forth of the descendants of the sons of Noah, by whom "were the isles of the Gentiles divided in their lands, every one after his tongue, after their families, in their nations." A wonderful going forth, truly; having in it the germ of every civilisation, the outline of every tragedy, the promise of final redemption and glory. To us the chapter is full of difficult reading, because full of strange, hard names that mean nothing to our memory or our love. Who are Gomer and Magog, and who are Sabtah and Dedan? Is there any home-music in Ashkenaz, or is any heart-chord touched by Cush and Mizraim? Yet learned ethnologists have seen wonderful things in this tenth chapter of Genesis. They have seen the descendants of Gomer seeking for themselves a dwelling in the confines of Asia and Europe, making an irruption into Asia Minor, disappearing in Asia, and coming up long ages after in the Cimbri, and as the founders of the great Celtic race. From Javan they have seen arising, in wondrous beauty, chaste and strong, the whole Hellenic people. Tubal and Meshech have been followed into the Cappadocians and the Iberians; so that even in those few names we begin to see the peopling of Northern Europe, the land of Greece, and the region between the Euxine and the

Caspian. From Tiras will come the Thracian stock, and
collaterally the Goths and the Teutons; and the ethnologist
pauses at Ashkenaz, for in that root he thinks he finds the
Scandinavian and the Saxon. So if we say, standing beside this
great Hebrew cemetery, Can these dry bones live? the breath
of the Lord is blown upon them, and behold they start up and
claim even ourselves here and there as their own kindred,
according to the flesh. And as for God, "is HE the God of the
Jews only? is HE not also of the Gentiles? Yes, of the
Gentiles also."

A clear conception of the import of this marvellous chapter
should enlarge and correct our notions in so far as they have been
narrowed and perverted by our insular position. We should
recognise in all the nations of the earth one common human
nature. "God hath made of one blood all nations of men to
dwell on the face of the earth." This reflection is both humbling
and elevating. It is humbling to think that the cannibal is a
relative of ours; that the slave crouching in an African wood is
bone of our bone; and that the meanest scum of all the earth
started from the same foundation as ourselves! On the other
hand, it is elevating to think that all kings and mighty men,
all soldiers renowned in song, all heroes canonised in history, the
wise, the strong, the good, are our elder brothers and immortal
friends. If we limit our life to families, clans, and sects, we shall
miss the genius of human history, and all its ennobling influences.
Better join the common lot. Take it just as it is. Our ancestors
have been robbers and oppressors, deliverers and saviours, mean
and noble, cowardly and heroic; some hanged, some crowned,
some beggars, some kings; take it so, for the earth is one, and
humanity is one, and there is only one God over all blessed for
evermore!

If we take this idea aright we shall get a clear notion of what
are called home and foreign missions. What are foreign missions?
Where are they? I do not find the word in the Bible. Where
does home end; where does foreign begin? It is possible for a
man to immure himself so completely as practically to forget that
there is anybody beyond his own front gate; we soon grow
narrow, we soon become mean; it is easy for us to return to the
dust from whence we come. It is here that Christianity redeems

us; not from sin only, but from all narrowness, meanness, and littleness of conception; it puts great thoughts into our hearts and bold words into our mouths, and leads us out from our village prisons to behold and to care for all nations of mankind. On this ground alone Christianity is the best educator in the world. It will not allow the soul to be mean. It forces the heart to be noble and hopeful. It says, "Go and teach all nations"; "Go ye into all the world"; "Look not every man on his own things, but every man also on the things of others"; "Give and it shall be given unto you, good measure, pressed down, heaped up, and running over." It is something for a nation to have a voice so Divine ever stirring its will and mingling with its counsels. It is like a sea breeze blowing over a sickly land; like sunlight piercing the fogs of a long dark night. Truly we have here a standard by which we may judge ourselves. "If any man have not the Spirit of Christ, he is none of his." If we have narrow sympathies, mean ideas, paltry conceptions, we are not scholars in the school of Christ. Let us bring no reproach upon Christ by our exclusiveness. Let us beware of the bigotry of patriotism, as well as of the bigotry of religion. We are citizens of the world : we are more than the taxpayers of a parish.

A right view of this procession of the nations will show us something of the richness and graciousness of Christ's nature. What a man must he have been either in madness or in Divinity who supposed that there was something in himself which all these people needed ! The disciples asked what were five loaves amongst five thousand people, and truly we may magnify their amazement, as we ask, What is one man amongst all the nations of mankind ? Truly Christ is bold when he says to his Church, Go ye into all the world. Has he considered the difficulties of travelling? how hard a thing it is to go a thousand miles from home, up hill and over sea ? Has he considered the difficulties of language—one set of peoples writing from right to left, another from left to right, another knowing nothing about grammar and literature—one speaking nothing but monosyllables, another speaking hardly anything but polysyllables—one language a rhythmic stream, another something between a grunt and a growl ? Has he considered the expense of the undertaking ? Men cannot travel for nothing. Men cannot live upon nothing. Men cannot support their families upon nothing. Yet Christ said, Go ; go everywhere ; go at once, and, lo, I am with you alway, even unto the end of the world. Christ is undoubtedly to be credited with bold and daring conceptions. He had no material rewards for his messengers. He sent them away with the least possible allowance of personal comfort ; no portmanteaus, no wardrobes, no retinue ; he said, Go after all these people and tell them that I only am their Saviour and Lord. Never man spake like this man !

ON THE BUILDING OF BABEL.
Gen. xi.

COMPARING this account with our own method of life and art, it is clear that from the beginning of time men have been doing pretty much the same thing all the world over. The world's story is but short ; it is very much like a series of repetitions : the actors, indeed, have been innumerable, but the drama has always been contracted, and seldom profound. The actors have made noise enough, but when there has been a little break through the dust, we have observed that they have not always made equal progress. We have a short Bible, because we have a short life. We have a fragmentary Bible, because we have a fragmentary human story. We have a Bible that apparently contradicts itself, because we have a life full of discrepancies— because part of us is Divine and part of us earthly—because we have many chipped links, many unmatched and unmatchable patterns, which no skill can put into anything like decent unity. The world, too, is but a little world. Men jump together again and again as if they could not escape one another's presence, and as for thinking, strife of mind, intellectual projections and conceptions, originalities there are none ; *variations* many, but no *originalities*. We are still in the land of Shinar, plotting with one another, burning bricks, building cities and towers, and being thrown from depth to depth of confusion. We are shut up in a very small prison, and can see but little through the narrow grating of our separate cells. What can we do, then ? What is our calling ? It is to try to alter the *moral tone* of our work ; we must burn bricks, build cities, and erect towers in *the right spirit;*

and we must try to get to heaven, not as the builders of Babel did. If we get to heaven at all, it will never be through the dark and rickety staircases of our own invention. Let us, then, read the story of Babel together, and gather from it what we may.

"And the whole earth was of one language, and of one speech."

Unanimity is nothing, considered strictly in itself. It is of no value that we say, in excuse of this or that deed, "It was done unanimously." Men may do wrong things unanimously, as well as things that are right. We must distinguish between union and conspiracy; we must distinguish between identity and mere association for a given object. Twelve directors may be of one language and of one speech, but the meaning of their unity may be self-enrichment, at the expense of unsuspecting men, who have put their little all into their keeping and direction. It is nothing, therefore, to talk about unanimity in itself considered. We must, in all these things, put the moral question, "What is the unanimity about?"—"Is this unanimity moving in the right direction?" If it be in a wrong direction, then unanimity is an aggravation of sin; if it be in a right direction, then union is power, and one-heartedness is triumph. But it is possible that unanimity may be but another word for stagnation. There are words in our language which are greatly misunderstood—and unanimity is one of them; peace is another. When many persons say peace, what do they mean? A living, intelligent, active co-operation, where there is mutual concession, where there is courtesy on every hand, where there is independent conviction, and yet noble concert in life? Not at all. They say that a Church is unanimous, and a Church is at peace, when a correct interpreter would say it was the unanimity of the grave, the peace of death. So I put in a word here of caution and of explanation: "The whole earth was of one language, and of one speech"; here is a point of unanimity, and yet there is a *unanimous movement in a wrong direction.*

"And they said one to another, Go to, let us make brick, and burn them throughly; . . . and they said, Go to, let us build us a city and a tower, whose top may reach unto heaven."

There are times in life when lucky ideas strike men; when there is a kind of intellectual spring-tide in their nature, when men

rise and say, "I have got it! Go to, this is it!" And in the
bright hours when such ideas strike one, the temptation is to be a
little contemptuous in reference to dull men who are never visited
by conceptions, so bright and original as we deem them. A man
has been in great perplexity, month after month, and suddenly he
says, "Go to, the solution is now before me; I see my way right
out of this dark place"; and he heightens his tone, as the joy
swells in his heart. That is right. We could not do without intellectual birthdays; we could not always be carrying about a dead,
leaden brain, that never sees light or shouts victory. We like
these moments of inspiration to break in upon the dull monotony
of such a lifetime as ours. So it is perfectly right that men should
express their new conceptions—their new programme—and lay
out a bold policy in a clear and confident tone. But are all our
ideas so very bright? When we see our way to brick-making,
is it always in the right direction? When we set our mind upon
founding a city and building a tower the top of which shall rest
against the stars, *is it right?* You see that question of "right"
comes in again and again, and in proportion as a man wishes to
live a truly Divine life he will always say, before going to his
brick-making and his city-founding and his tower-building, "Now,
is this right?" Many of us could have built great towers, only we
knew that we should be building downwards if we had set our
hands to such work as has often tempted us. Do not let us look
coldly upon apparently unsuccessful men, and say, "*Look at us;
we* have built a great city and tower; and *you,* where are you?—
stretching in the dust and grovelling in nothing." They could
have built quite as large a tower as ours; they could have been
quite as far up in the clouds as we are, only we had perhaps less
conscience than they had. When we saw a way to burning
bricks, we *burned* them; and a way to establishing towers, we
founded them; and they, poor creatures, unsuccessful men,
began to *pray* about it, and to wonder if it was right, and to ask
casuistical questions, and to rack themselves upon conscience;
and so they have done no building! And yet they *may* have
built. Who can tell? All buildings are not made of brick; all
men do not require to lay hot brickfields, and burn clay, in order
to build. It may be found one day, when the final inspection
takes place, that the man who has built nothing *visible* has really

built a palace for the residence of God. It may be found, too, that some successful people have nothing but bricks—nothing but bricks, bricks, bricks! Then it will be seen who the true builders were. What I pause here to say is this : We may have bright ideas, we may have (to us) new conceptions; there are, to our thinking, original ways of doing things ; now and again cunning plans of overcoming difficulties strike us. Do I condemn this intellectual activity ? No; I simply say, Let your *intellect* and your *conscience* go together ; do not be onesided men ; do not be living altogether out of the head, be living out of your moral nature as well ; and if it be right, then build the tower with all industry and determination. Let it be strong and lofty, and God shall come down upon your work and glorify it, and claim it as his own.

"A tower, whose top may reach unto heaven."

Bold men,—men of vigorous mind, striking out something that is very definite, and about which there could be no mistake. We, too, are doing just what they did ; we are following the god *Ambition*—the restless god, Ambition, who never sleeps, never pauses, never gives his devotees vacation, but is always stirring them up to more and more furious desires. Do I condemn ambition ?—nothing of the kind. I praise ambition ; I say to every young man who may to-day accept me as his teacher, Be ambitious ; build loftily ; let your aspirations be confined only by the limits which God himself has set to human power and human capability ; *but*,—*but*,—that old question comes in again, Is it right ? *Is it right?* Our ambitions may be our temptations ; our ambitions may be stumbling-blocks over which we fall into outer darkness ; our ambitions may be the cups out of which we drink some deadly intoxicant, poisoning the mind and destroying the heart's life. Therefore, I pause again to ask, *Is it right?* Then, too, we pronounce some men ambitious, who are really not ambitious. All men do not understand the word *ambition*— ambition has been vulgarised, taken out altogether from its refined and beautiful associations, and debased into something that is intensely of the earth, earthy. I call men to *intellectual* ambition ; to *spiritual* ambition ; to the ambition which says, "I count not myself to have attained ; this one thing I do, I *press*." Alas ! there are ten thousand men in our city streets to-day who are

" pressing " ; but the question is, " Towards *what* do they press ? "
The apostle says, " I press towards the mark for the prize of my
high calling of God in Christ Jesus." That is better than saying,
" Let us build a tower whose top may reach unto heaven " ;
and yet it is true tower-building—it is palace-building. Men who
look at things only by their senses, who value things only
according to their market prices, may say, " These are castles in
the air " ; but I have a strong conviction that these castles in the
air are in many cases the only true and enduring castles. We
cannot *see* them, but what do we *see* anywhere but the shell of
things, or the little pedestal ? The great universe is beyond the
veil ; the great splendours are hidden from us ; the great realities
are things *not seen.* Do not let us, then, look from our lofty
scaffolding down upon praying people, and thinking people, and
spiritual people, and say they are not building. Our scaffolding
is a long way up. Take care lest the winds catch it, and spare
not ! Take care lest our elevation become our destruction !

"And the Lord came down to see the city and the tower, which the
children of men builded."

You believe in inspection, do you not ? You say that inspection
is of little worth, except it be conducted by competent power and
with strict impartiality of spirit ; and you are right in so thinking.
In the case before us, Almighty God himself came down to see
what the children of men were doing, and when he comes down
(a phrase which is used to accommodate himself to our methods of
expression), nothing can escape the penetration of his eye. He
looks at our day-books, ledgers, and other memorandum books,
to see how we are building the tower of our life ; he visits our
country residences and palatial buildings for the purpose of trying
their foundations ; he looks into all the building of our fortune,
that he may see whether our gains have been honestly secured.
Terrible is the day for the bad man on which Almighty God lays
his great hand—the hand in which the winds are hidden, the
great palm in which all the stars of the heaven are gathered—
upon the tower which is being built ; he will shake it, and, if the
foundation is bad, the whole superstructure will be thrown down
to the dust ! In passing through our city streets I observe that
the windows of many mercantile houses are left without defence,
except huge iron bars ; and it is easy to see that merchantmen

have left their letters and papers upon their desks that they might return to them on the following day and continue their business. Their places are vacant and silent, yet there is in them nothing less than the presence of God himself; and the Eye of Omniscience is passing over page after page and book after book ; thus God notes the whole process and tendency of men's lives. When men build their towers under the conviction that every stone of them will be tried by Divine power—when they build their cities, and erect their towers, and extend their properties, under the assurance that not one thing of all the things that their hands are doing will escape the test of God's Spirit— we may expect life to be built upon a true foundation, and according to a righteous plan. What we have to ponder is this most certain fact, that God will come down to see our work, and that there is no possibility of concealing from him any incorrectness of plan or any deficiency of service. For many a long day we may imagine ourselves secure from the supervision of Omnipotence ; but such imagination is an utter mistake, for there is nothing in our life that is not naked and open to the eyes of him with whom we have to do. Our little works and our great works alike ought to be conducted with an eye to the Divine judgment. The work that is internal, as well as the work that is external, should be conducted with that holy desire to do what is right, which alone is the guarantee that we are not living atheistic lives.

"Now nothing will be restrained from them which they have imagined to do."

Here we are brought face to face with the great question of the discipline of human imagination. Life that is lived entirely in the imagination is lived wastefully. We are not to condemn imagination, for most truly imagination is a Divine gift ; but it is a gift which is seldom, if ever, to be exercised alone. Our imagination must take counsel of our judgment, and our judgment must act in co-operation with our heart, so that there may be unanimity in all our faculties in carrying out the great objects of life. It is a terrible thing for any man to be given over to the unrestrained dominion of his fancy. Our imagination becomes intoxicated, and we are the victims of dreamings which may lead us into the wildest excesses, causing us to overlook all social claims and all Divine obligations, and to work only for our own aggrandisement and strength. Imagination never thinks; it only dreams. Imagination never reasons; it flies away, not knowing whither it is going. Imagination is never sober; it is always intoxicated with burning desire. I might challenge some of you to-day, to tell me whether you are not living lives of riotous imagination; dreaming of new plans of securing wealth, of novel projects for the defrauding of unsuspecting men, and whether in this awful excitement you are not forgetting the common duties of life. Men cannot always live upon the wings of their imagination; they must stand still, pause, think, reason, pray; and then, if their imagination can assist them to overcome difficulties, they are at liberty to follow all the will of their fancy. Let us take our starting-point from simple truth; let us hold deep and solemn consultation with the Spirit of Righteousness; let us know that our greatest power is little more than weakness; and then we shall walk without stumbling; and though our tower be not built very loftily, it will be built with a stability which God himself will never allow to be shaken.

"Go to, let us go down, and there confound their language, that they may not understand one another's speech."

This brings before us a hint of the unknown resources of God, in the matter of punishing those who disobey his will. Who could have thought of this method of scattering the builders of the city? God does not send a fire upon the builders; no terrible plague poisons the air; yet in an instant each workman is at a loss to understand the other, and each considers all the rest as but raving maniacs! Imagine the bewildering and painful scene! Men who have been working by each other's side, days and weeks, are instantly conscious of inability to understand one another's speech! New sounds, new accents, new words, but not a ray of intelligence in all! "It is a fearful thing to fall into the hand of the living God." God has innumerable ways of showing his displeasure at human folly and human crime. A man may be pursuing a course of prosperity, in which he is ignoring all that is moral and Divine, and men may be regarding him as the very model of success; yet, in an instant, Almighty God may blow upon his brain, and the unsuccessful man may sit down in a defeat which can never be reversed. God is not confined to one method of punishment. He touches a man's bones, and they melt! he breathes upon a man's brain, and henceforth he is not able to think. He comes in at night-time, and shakes the foundations of man's most trusted towers, and in the morning there is nought but a heap of ruins. He disorganises men's memories, and in an instant they confuse all the recollection of their lifetime. He touches man's tongue, and the fluent speaker becomes a stammerer. He breaks the staff in twain, and he who was relying upon it is thrown down in utter helplessness. We know but little of what God means when he says, "Heaven"; that word gives us but a dim hint of the infinite light, and blessedness, and triumph which are in reserve for the good. We have but a poor conception of what God means when he says, "Hell"; that word is but a flickering spark compared with the infinite distress, the endless ruin and torment which must befall every man who defies his Maker.

Speaking of this confusion of language, may I not be permitted to inquire whether even in our own English tongue there is not to-day very serious confusion? Do men really mean words to be accepted in their plain common-sense? Does not the acute man often tell his untrained client what he intends to do in language which has double meanings? Do we not sometimes utter the words that have one meaning to the world and another meaning to our own hearts? Yea does not always mean yea, nor does nay always mean nay; men sign papers with mental reservations; men utter words in their common meaning, and to themselves they interpret these words with secret significations. The same words do not mean the same thing under all circumstances, and as spoken by different speakers. When a poor man says "rich," he means one thing; when a millionaire says "rich," he means something very different. Let us consider that there is morality even in the use of language. Let no man consider himself at liberty to trifle with the meaning of words. Language is the medium of intercourse between man and man, and on the interpretation of words great results depend. It behoves us, therefore, who profess to be followers of Jesus Christ, so to speak as to leave ourselves without the painful reflection of having taken refuge in ambiguous expressions for the sake of saving ourselves from unpleasant results. It will be a sign that

God is really with us as a nation, when a pure language is restored unto us—when man can trust the word of man, and depend with entire confidence upon the honour of his neighbour.

What shall we carry away from this meditation? Man must work; but he may work in a wrong spirit and with a wrong intent. We may do the right thing in a wrong way. What we have to beware of is *atheistic* building! "He builds too low who builds beneath the skies." "Other foundation can no man lay than that is laid": "Jesus Christ himself being the chief corner-stone." The word of warning to every man is this, "Let every man take heed how he buildeth thereupon." A building may be noble in design, ample in magnitude, commodious and convenient in all its appointments, but the one great question relates to the foundation! Of what value is it that we build loftily and broadly, with an eye to all that is beautiful in proportion, and satisfactory in arrangement, if all the while we are building upon the sand? The fires will come, or the floods will descend, or the great winds will conspire to try our work, and though our work itself suffer loss, we shall be saved if we be resting upon the right foundation which God himself has laid. I have spoken especially of ambition. I have not dissuaded young men from being ambitious; I have rather sought to stimulate them to greater desires and more comprehensive plans. At the same time, I wish to caution them against ambition that is *atheistic.* You hear of men being the architects of their own fortunes; and there is a sense in which that expression conveys sentiments that are truly laudable. I wish, however, to alter the phraseology; henceforth let us consider God as the Architect of our fortunes, and ourselves but the builders working under his direction. Do not let us seek to be both architect and builder. "In all thy ways acknowledge God, and he will direct thy paths." We shall never be relieved from the discipline of work; the great trials of service will constantly be allotted to us; the one thing to be assured of is, that we are moving along the designs which God himself has set before us, and then, how stormy soever may be the days in which we labour, and how many soever the difficulties with which we have to contend, the building shall surely be completed, even to the putting on of the top-stone.

Do I immediately speak to any poor crushed man, whose tower during the recent commercial panics has been thrown down to the dust ? But a short time ago you had a good social position, you lived in comfort, if not in luxury, your name was a watchword of confidence among men of honour; but to-day you are surrounded by the ruins of your fortune, and your children are almost reduced to beggary. Let us speak about such matters with all tenderness, yet without shrinking from the moral aspects of life. How was your tower built ? Did you build it atheistically ? Did you live entirely in the realm of your imagination, losing all self-restraint, and plunging into the most riotous excesses of speculation ? If so, the explanation of the throwing down of your tower is not far to seek. On the other hand, if you were building honestly, and have been victimised by evil-minded men, it will one day be shown to you that the destruction of your tower has been ordered by Almighty God, and so sanctified as to bring into your heart a stronger faith, a tenderer love, and a more enduring patience. Do not say that all is lost simply because all is thrown down. The foundation abideth for ever; continue to build upon that, and be assured of the final reward. I do not know but that panics are sent of God himself, often directly, for the chastening and purification of man. Uninterrupted prosperity might prove itself to be the direst affliction which could befall society. Do we know what plagues might be engendered by the continuous shining of a cloudless sun ? The high winds which try men's buildings, and often throw them down, are sent for the cleansing of the air.

Do I speak to any who have but little standing-place in the world,—to men who have never built a city or a tower ? Let me say to such, " In my Father's house are many mansions "! We ourselves may not have built anything that deserves the name of a city or a tower, but Jesus Christ has gone away to prepare a place for us, and we who to-day are the children of want, having hardly where to lay our head, shall be called into a city of glory. The poor Christian has no reason to be discouraged so far as the great future is concerned; to-day there is little about him that men may call attractive; to-day he is the child of want, but insomuch as he is in Jesus Christ he holds a title to an inheritance incorruptible, undefiled, and that fadeth not away.

Let us now go out again into the world from hearing the word of the Lord; let us resume our building, and in doing so let us invoke the presence and the guidance of Infinite Wisdom through all the processes of our life. Our business is not to build quickly, but to build upon a right foundation and in a right spirit. Life is more than a mere competition as between man and man; it is not who can be done first, but who can work best; it is not who can rise highest in the shortest time, but who is working most patiently and lovingly in accordance with the designs of God.

Gen. xii.
ABRAM'S PILGRIMAGE.

IT may surprise you to find, unless you have paid long attention to the matter, how impossible it is to understand some actions unless you know the motive out of which they arose. You would suppose that if you knew any action you would know something that was self-contained and self-explanatory; something, in short, about which there could be no mystery. That, however, is a very serious mistake. That which is apparent is in reality the least part of anything which is not merely super-ficial and transitory. Whatever has any pith in it, any genuine life and force, is inspired and moved by hidden spiritual influences, over which even the actor himself has but partial control.

Take this expression—"*the Lord had said unto Abram.*" How? As a man would speak to a man? Audibly? What is this Divine voice to the sons of men? Suppose the answer should be, "the Lord came visibly before Abram, and spoke to him in plain Hebrew,"—what then? Many difficulties would arise at once, but no difficulties which faith could not overcome. Suppose the answer should be—"a spiritual revelation was made to Abram, no likeness was seen, no audible voice was heard, but his soul was made aware distinctly and certainly of the Divine purpose,"—what then? Substantially the results would

be the same, and it is with results we have to deal rather than
with processes. Mozart says in his letters that, whenever he saw
a grand mountain or a wonderful piece of scenery, it said to
him—"Turn me into music, play me on the organ"; and
Mendelssohn says in his letters to his sister, "This is how I
think of you to-day," or "This is what I have to say to you
to-day," and then follows a bar or two of music which she is
requested to play on the piano or the organ. So the mountain
spoke to Mozart, and the organ spoke to Fanny Hensel, and
why should we hesitate to say that the Lord spoke to Abram or
that he is speaking to ourselves? He spoke to Adam, Enoch,
Noah, Abram, Peter, Paul, John; has he ceased to speak unto the
children of men? We now say that we have a notion, an
impression, a conviction, or a feeling; and considering that our
life is so shallow and cloudy, perhaps it is best to speak thus
vaguely, but when we get right in soul we shall boldly say,
"The Lord calls me; the Lord tells me; the Lord sends me."
It will be more filial, more tender, more Christian.

Truly some things that we see in life require more than
ordinary influences to account for them, and this going out of
Abram from "Ur of the Chaldees" is one of them. According to
the account given in chap. xi., it would seem to have struck
Terah that it would be a good thing to go to the land of Canaan,
and that as soon as the idea struck him he and his family at
once started. But, on second thoughts, that is an account of the
movement which is extremely improbable. What did Terah
know about Canaan? He had no friends there. Nobody had
offered him a home there. The people who were there would
very likely give him a rough reception. How, then, did he come
to move in that direction? We have the answer in chap. xii., ver.
1: "*Now the Lord had said unto Abram, Get thee out of thy
country, and from thy kindred, and from thy father's house, unto a
land that I will show thee.*"

So, even a journey may be the outcome of an inspiration!
"There's a Divinity that shapes our ends, rough-hew them how
we will." I feel life to be most solemn when I think that inside
of it all there is a Spirit that lays out one day's work, that points
out when the road is on the left and when it is on the right, and
that tells one what words will best express one's thought. Thus

is God nigh at hand and not afar off. " The steps of a good man
are ordered by the Lord." And thus, too, are men misunderstood : they are called enthusiasts, and are said to be impulsive ;
they are not "safe" men : they are here to-day and gone to-
morrow, and no proper register of their life can be made. Of
course we are to distinguish between inspiration and delusion,
and not to think that every noise is thunder. We are not to call a
" maggot " a " revelation." What we are to do is this : we have
to live and move and have our being in God ; to expect his
coming, and long for it ; to be patient and watchful ; to keep our
heart according to his word ; and then we shall know his voice
from the voice of a stranger, for " the secret of the Lord is with
them that fear him." If *God* be our supreme consciousness he
will reveal his providence without cloud or doubtfulness. I think
it can be proved that the men who have done things apparently
against all reason have. often been acting in the most reasonable manner, and that inspiration has often been mistaken for
madness. I feel that all the while you are asking me to give
you tests by which you may know what inspiration is, you have
little or nothing to do with such tests,—you have to *be* right, and
then you will be sure to *do* right.

Possibly, Abram may have got more credit for this journey
than he really deserves. It is true that he knew not " whither
he went," and by so much this is what is called "a leap in the
dark " ; but Abram knew two things : (1) he knew at whose
bidding he was going, and (2) he knew what results were
promised to his faith. There is much more than a command in
the text ; there is a promise, beautiful as a plentiful vine in
autumn : " *I will make of thee a great nation, and I will bless thee,
and make thy name great ; and thou shalt be a blessing : and I will
bless them that bless thee, and curse him that curseth thee : and in
thee shall all families of the earth be blessed.*" The man who would
not go after that would have to justify his disobedience by very
strong reasons. We can only move some weights by very long
levers. To get a man to leave his " country, his kindred, and his
father's house," you must propose or apply some very strong
inducement. Now, it is worth while to take notice that from the
very beginning God has never given a merely arbitrary command :
he has never treated a *man* as a potter would treat a handful of

clay : the royal and mighty command has always ended in the tenderness of a gracious promise. God has never moved a man merely for the sake of moving him ; merely for the sake of showing his power : this we shall see in detail as we move through the wondrous pages, but I call attention to it now as strikingly illustrated in the case of Abram. Some of you yourselves may remember the words " Get thee out," who have forgotten the accumulated and glorious blessing. Let us be just unto the Lord, and remember that he treats us as his sons and not as irresponsible machines.

We need this exhortation the more, as it is incorrectly supposed that we are to act blindly and unreasoningly in the spiritual life. The precise contrary is the reality of the case. " No man hath left father or mother, houses or land, for my sake," says Christ, " but shall receive a hundredfold reward here and life everlasting beyond." If the command is " Believe on the Lord Jesus Christ," the promise is " Thou shalt be saved." If the Lord hath commanded men everywhere to repent, the promise is that he will " abundantly pardon." If the command is " Sell what thou hast," the promise is " Thou shalt have treasure in heaven." So, all through, from end to end, the good of the creature is the object of the Creator.

Does it follow, then, that God gives " the reason why " in the case of every command ? Certainly not. Probably he may give no reason at all, and where he does not give a reason he gives in reality the best reason of all. To give his reason would indeed be to propose discussion, but to give a promise is to show that the reason, though undisclosed, is all-sufficient, for in the case of the All-wise a promise is the harvest of which a reason would be but the bare seed. It is true, too, that we can understand a promise where we could not understand a reason : the reason is intellectual, metaphysical, or spiritual, too high or too recondite for our faculties ; but a promise is practical, positive, literal, and if we have faith in the speaker we know that if the promise be so good the command which precedes it must be founded upon a reason equally valid. In reality we have nothing to do with the reasons upon which God's commands are founded. If we meddle with hem we shall touch a fire that will burn us ! We are to walk by faith, not by sight. To have

faith iι. *God* is to comprehend all reasons in one act. I am not
to take God in the details of his several commandments, but in
the totality, the wholeness of his nature.

Away went Abram from Ur of the Chaldees (Ur of the people
of Chesed), and on his way he received a renewal of the promise.
Very beautiful was this! It showed that he was on the right
road, and that God's faithfulness followed him like an angel of
defence. It is so with ourselves on the journey to the better
Canaan, where the upper springs never dry, and the summer
lies like an infinite blessing over the whole land.

> "There shall be no more snow,
> No weary wandering feet."

O, fair Canaan! A land so near, did we but know it! Just over
the river, the stream, the faint dark rill; it was a river to our
youth, it is a stream to our manhood, it will be but a rill to the
faith of our old age! And as we move to it, step by step, what
words of love and hope are spoken to us by the Lord of the fair
land! How he helps us up the steps that are long and hard;
how he cheers us along the road that is flat and tedious; how
he throws a robe around us when the fierce winds blow upon us
in bitter cold!

Yet what are all God's promises when set against the heart that
is " deceitful above all things and desperately wicked "? When
Abram got into Egypt he got into trouble. Just before going
into the land he asked his wife to say she was his sister, lest he
should lose his own life! Thus we see how strong a man may
be—and how weak! Abram could trust a whole destiny to the
Lord, but not a particular circumstance in the process! We
must meddle a little with the Lord's plan. Just a little to show
what managers we are, and how neatly we can turn the corners
of life. And what foul finger-marks we leave upon God's work
when we touch it! I am not sure that we have met in all the
pages we have gone through with anything more humbling than
the rebuke given by Pharaoh to Abram, " *And Pharaoh called
Abram, and said, What is this that thou hast done unto me? why
didst thou not tell me that she was thy wife? Why saidst thou, She
is my sister? Now, therefore, behold thy wife, take her, and go thy
way.*" To be reproved by the heathen for telling lies! There

is a lesson here to us who are Christians. When men of the
world can justly blame men of the Church, how deep is the stain
of guilt which has fixed itself in the very substance of our
character :

And yet there is another lesson here which we need quite as
much : the lesson of Divine forbearance with human infirmity.
God did not cast off Abram, or send him back to Ur of the
Chaldees—a man disgraced and condemned. God forbid that I
should make any excuse for sin ; yet there are sins that come out
of weakness rather than out of love of sin for its own sake.
Abram's sin arose rather from weakness than depravity. A
great fear seized him. A sudden squall from the hills struck his
little boat sharply, and for the time being he foolishly took his
affairs into his own hands. " Let him that is without sin cast the
first stone" at Abram ! It was something after all, standing
between Babylonian and Egyptian idolatry—colossal and splendid
—to say, There is but one God and I put my faith in him ! It
was a new voice in the earth. It was the first note of Christian
civilisation. Now it is common to avow this creed, but it went
for something when a Chaldean shepherd declared it amidst
polytheistic and sumptuous idolatries. " Abraham believed God,
and it was counted to him for righteousness." Amid all the stars
that showered their glittering silver upon the Eastern night he
saw one larger and brighter than all others—"Your father
Abraham rejoiced to see my day, and he saw it and was glad."
Looking at Abram's sin, and trying, possibly, what we may get
out of it in excuse of our own, let us in justice remember that
if we copy the sin we ought to endeavour to copy the faith.
When we say Abram sinned, we ought also to say that Abram
was the friend of God ; and if we hide ourselves under the plea
of his weakness, we ought also to strive after the holiness and
sublimity of his faith.

Gen. xii. 1.

1. "Now the Lord had said unto Abram, Get thee out of thy country, and from thy kindred, and from thy father's house, unto a land that I will shew thee."

THE SAME—VARIED.

GOD'S claim upon the individual life is here asserted. God detaches men from early associations, from objects of special care and love, and makes them strangers in the earth. The family idea is sacred, but the Divine will is, so to speak, more sacred still ; when the God of the families of the earth calls men from their kindred and their father's house, all tributary laws must be swallowed up by the great stream of the Divine Fatherhood. These calls, so shattering in their social effect, and so painful in their bearing upon the individual heart, are necessary to shake men out of the secondary positions into which they would settle themselves. All earthly parentage is but a reflection of God's fatherly relation to mankind ; and if we have idolised and abused that which is merely secondary and typical, we need such calls as these to remind us that over all there reigns, in gracious majesty and tender righteousness, the Maker, the Sovereign, and the Redeemer of our lives.

In this call we see an outline of the great providential system under which we live. God comes into a family and breaks it up ; God sets the individual man upon a special course ; God shows the land in which we are to dwell. Up to this point there is harshness in the startling demand. Abram is to go out, not knowing whither ; and if he *did* know whither, still the fact that he was called to break up old and endeared associations is enough to fill him with sorrow and dismay. We must read further, if we would recover composure of faith in God's goodness. The first verse is authoritative ; but man cannot live a great life upon mere authority, even when the authority is known to be Divine. Men would starve on law. To law must be added grace, if the soul is to know all the joy and peace of life in God. Read the next verses, and say if there be in them one tone of severity.

2. And I will make of thee a great nation, and I will bless thee, and make thy name great ; and thou shalt be a blessing :

3. And I will bless them that bless thee, and curse him that curseth thee : and in thee shall all families of the earth be blessed.

Great lives are trained by great promises. The world has never been left without a great promise singing in its wondering and troubled heart—something to rely upon : something to appeal to when difficulty was extreme. God never calls men for the purpose of making them less than they are, except when they have been dishonouring themselves by sin. This may be taken as a law : God's calls are upward ; they are calls towards fuller life, purer light, and sweeter joy. Men do not know their full capacity, except in the service of God : his presence in the soul is a life-expanding and life-glorifying presence. This is the claim that we set up on behalf of true religion—the religion of Jesus Christ—that it exalts human nature, it enriches the soul, it increases the substance and worth of manhood. To confound obedience with slavery is to overlook the argument which is founded upon the nature of God ; to obey the little, the mean, the paltry is to be enslaved ; to enter the cage of custom or passion is to be subject to bondage ; but to accept the invitation of the Sun, and to poise ourselves in his gladdening presence is liberty and joy.

Look at this promise as throwing light upon the compensations of life. Abram is called to leave his country, his kindred, and his father's house, and, so far, there is nothing but loss. Had the call ended here, the lot of Abram might have been considered hard ; but when did God take anything from a man, without giving him manifold more in return ? Suppose that the return has not been made immediately manifest, what then ? Is to-day the limit of God's working time ? Has he no provinces beyond this little world ? Does the door of the grave open upon nothing but infinite darkness and eternal silence ? Yet, even confining the judgment within the hour of this life, it is true that God never touches the heart with a trial without intending to bring in upon it some grander gift, some tenderer benediction.

Look at this promise as showing the oneness of God with his people : " I will bless them that bless thee, and curse him that curseth thee." The good man is not alone. Touch him, and you touch God. Help him, and your help is taken as if it were rendered to God himself. This may give us an idea of the sublime life to which we are called—we live, and move, and have our being in God ; we are temples ; our life is an expression of Divine influence ; in our voice there is an undertone of Divinity.

Look at this promise, as showing the influence of the present over the future : "In thee shall all the families of the earth be blessed." This is a principle rather than an exception of true life. Every man should look upon himself as an instrument of possible blessing to the whole world. One family should be a blessing to all families within its influence. Of course, the true and full interpretation of the promise is to be found in the person and work of Jesus Christ, the Saviour and Brother of all who receive him by faith into their hearts ; yet there are great secondary and collateral meanings of the promise, which ought not to be held in contempt. We should not be looking for the least, but for the greatest interpretations of life—not to make our life as little and ineffective as possible, but to give it fulness, breadth, strength: to which the weary and the sorrowful may look with confidence and thankfulness. Christianity never reduces life to a minimum; it develops it, strengthens it in the direction of Jesus Christ's infinite perfectness and beauty.

4. So Abram departed, as the Lord had spoken unto him ; and Lot went with him : and Abram was seventy and five years old when he departed out of Haran.

5. And Abram took Sarai his wife, and Lot his brother's son, and all their substance that they had gathered, and the souls that they had gotten in Haran ; and they went forth to go into the land of Canaan ; and into the land of Canaan they came.

6. And Abram passed through the land unto the place of Sichem, unto the plain of Moreh. And the Canaanite was then in the land.

There will always be central figures in society : men of commanding life, around whom other persons settle into secondary positions. We cannot all be Abrams ; we cannot all have distinct names in the future. Yet, though we cannot have the greatness, we may have the goodness of Abram. But few men in any country touch the highest point of fame; thousands upon thousands, in all generations, come to honour and influence ; yet, in a few months after their death, their names cease to have any interest but for the smallest circles. This reflection ought not to discourage virtue. Peace of heart is better than mere renown. To be known in heaven is the best fame. To have a place in the **love of God** is to enjoy the true exaltation. In the company now journeying towards Canaan, there is one figure that gives unity and meaning to the whole group, yet there is not one in all the band, whose life, judged by the Divine standard, is unimportant.

The one man, Abram, holds the promise; all the other persons in the company hold it secondarily. All men do not receive the direct revelation and vision of God; they are followers, not leaders; echoes, not voices. Personal supremacy, to be beneficent and enduring, should be the result of Divine election. Abram was supreme because God had called him. The salvation of the soul is undoubtedly an individual act; the soul must think, repent, believe, resolve for itself. No man can repent or believe for another; yet, in the working out of Divine plans, one man must follow another, and be content to shine with reflected light. It is so in statesmanship, in literature, and in civilisation generally. Take Abram away from this group, and the group becomes ridiculous. One man is called to stand nearer God than another, and to interpret the purposes of God to the world. There is an empty defiance which proclaims itself in the well-known terms, "I don't pin my faith to any man's sleeve"; "I think for myself"; there is nothing but vanity in such lofty pretensions, made, indeed, the more mischievous by the grain of truth which barely saves them from the charge of insanity. As a matter of fact, we do pin our faith to each other's sleeve. Lot believes in Abram; the weak believe in the strong; we all follow our respective captains and leaders. Abram was the minister of God to all about him. Had his faith gone down, the whole company would have been disorganised; his followers were courageous in *his* courage, and hopeful in *his* hope. We think it a great honour to be set so high in the service of God; it is so, truly; yet it must be a burdensome responsibility, and often a pricking thorn, for those who follow can bring reproach and calumny to bear upon Abram and Moses and the chosen servants of God. There is a temptation for Lot to imagine himself as good as Abram, and in that imagining is the explanation of many of the petty torments which fall to the lot of men whom God has taken into his secret counsel.

The Abrams of society often have a difficult task. They cannot always explain themselves fully. Sometimes they cannot even vindicate themselves, nor can they account for circumstances which bear heavily against them. They live a separate life. They have secret intercourse with God. The translation of things heard in heaven is always difficult and often impossible.

7. And the Lord appeared unto Abram, and said, Unto thy seed will I give this land : and there builded he an altar unto the Lord, who appeared unto him.
8. And he removed from thence unto a mountain on the east of Beth-el, and pitched his tent, having Beth-el on the west, and Hai on the east : and there he builded an altar unto the Lord, and called upon the name of the Lord.
9. And Abram journeyed, going on still toward the south.

We shall be much comforted in this pilgrim-life if we think of God's relation to places, habitations, countries, and geographical positions. The wilderness and the garden are God's ; the fountain and the stream are directed in their course by the creating mind. Men are not here and there by haphazard. Cities are not founded by mere chance. Before the city there was a process of reasoning ; before the process of reasoning there was Divine suggestion—geography, as well as astronomy, is of God. " The earth is the Lord's." I would be where God wills ; with his blessing the desert shall be pleasant as the fruitful field ;— without it, the fruitful field shall mock the appetite which it tempts, and the river shall become as blood in my mouth.

Abram set up his altar along the line of his march. Blessed are they whose way is known by marks of worship. The altar is the highest seal of ownership. God will not lightly forsake his temples. This setting up of the altar shows that our spiritual life ought to be attested by outward sign and profession. Abram had the promise in his heart, yet he did not live a merely contemplative life ; he was not lost in religious musings and prophesyings—he built his altar and set up his testimony in the midst of his people, and made them sharers of a common worship.

10. And there was a famine in the land : and Abram went down into Egypt to sojourn there ; for the famine was grievous in the land.
11. And it came to pass, when he was come near to enter into Egypt, that he said unto Sarai his wife, Behold now, I know that thou art a fair woman to look upon :
12. Therefore it shall come to pass, when the Egyptians shall see thee, that they shall say, This is his wife : and they will kill me, but they will save thee alive.

13. Say, I pray thee, thou art my sister : that it may be well with me for thy sake ; and my soul shall live because of thee.

Showing what the best of men are when they betake themselves to their own devices. As the minister of God, Abram is great and noble ; as the "architect of his own fortune," he is cowardly, selfish, and false. I seek for no palliation of such conduct : it invites and deserves malediction and vengeance. In our own life we know what it is to have great faith and great unbelief. Abram went out at God's bidding, cheerfully encountering all the trials of pilgrimage in unknown places, yet he cannot trust God to take care of his wife. How little are the greatest men! If we are never stronger than our weakest point, we should take heed, lest in our proud sufficiency the dart strike us in the vulnerable spot. It is a bad thing to rack our brains for excuses on behalf of the Bible worthies when they fall ; if God did not excuse them, we need not stretch our cnarity into a covering for their sins. A lie was twice a lie in the mouth of a man like Abram. Where there was great grace there should have been great courage. We are not to qualify the disgrace by talking about spots on the sun ; we are to call poison "poison," and to learn by the failures of other men that our own life will be called to trials which will need higher strength than merely human power.

The last three verses of the chapter are these :—

18. And Pharaoh called Abram, and said, What is this that thou hast done unto me? Why didst thou not tell me that she was thy wife?
19. Why saidst thou, She is my sister? So I might have taken her to me to wife : now therefore behold thy wife, take her, and go thy way.
20. And Pharaoh commanded his men concerning him : and they sent him away, and his wife, and all that he had.

In this matter Pharaoh was a greater, a nobler man than Abram. Natural nobleness ought never to be underrated. Why begrudge to the heathen a nobleness which was as surely of God as our own Christian excellence? There are men to-day who make no profession of Christian faith : whose honour, straightforwardness, and generosity would put to shame many who claim a good standing in the Church. I make this statement without reservation ; yet it must be explained that it is not because of Christianity, but for the *want of it*, that professors are humbled before men of the world ; and it must be added, that men of natural elevation of temper and sentiment would attain a still intenser lustre by the possession of that life in Jesus Christ, without which all other life is either artificial or incomplete. Christianity does not equalise the character of all men, any more than the sun equalises the value of all trees. There are Christians who are barely saved from being devils, and if they are this *with* Christianity, what would they be *without* it ? Christianity is not to be judged by the lowest, but by the highest. We should not judge the repute of a medical hospital by the attainments of a student who has been scarcely a month within its walls ; it would be unfair to judge the master by the apprentice ; why, then, seize upon an immature professor of the Christian religion, and judge Christianity by his imperfect and tottering character ? We admire Pharaoh in the case before us ; we like the clear, steady tone in which he remonstrates with the culprit ; yet natural openness and honourableness of disposition must not be valued as a substitute for the renewed life which is wrought in men by God the Holy Ghost.

This incident shows that God calls men to special destinies, and that life is true and excellent in itself and in its influences only in so far as it is Divinely inspired and ruled. " Whosoever he be of you that forsaketh not all that he hath, he cannot be my disciple." The great demand is made upon *faith*. Life is to be *spiritual*; not made up of things that can be counted and valued, but of ideas, convictions, impulses, and decisions that are Divine and imperishable. The world of faith is large, and rich, and brilliant. Those who live in it dominate over all lower worlds. They have their peculiar sorrows, yet they are strong enough to say, " Our light affliction, which is but for a moment, worketh for us a far more exceeding and eternal weight of glory; while we look not at the things which are seen, but at the things which are not seen : for the things which are seen are temporal; but the things which are not seen are eternal." Have we received the call of God ? Has God left us without command or promise ? No ! Every man of us has heard the command to repent and believe the gospel, and our destiny depends upon the answer we return. We are called to honour, glory, and immortality in Christ Jesus ; let us awake and pursue our rugged but ever-upward way !

In view of this incident men may fitly ask themselves at whose call they are proceeding in life ? No man is at liberty to stray away at the bidding of his fancy, upsetting the order of civilisation and inflicting discomfort upon all who are connected with him merely to gratify a whimsical curiosity. Society is founded upon order. Permanence is a condition of healthy growth. On the other hand, where men are called of God to go forth, it should be theirs instantly and gladly to obey, how dark soever or stormy the night into which they move. Life is a discipline. Shrewd men say they want to know whither they are going before they set out on a journey ; but men of higher shrewdness, men of Christian faith, often go out into enterprise and difficulty without being able to see one step before them. The watchword of the noblest, truest souls is, "We walk by faith, not by sight"; faith has a wider dominion and a more splendid future. I call upon Christian young men to show *the practical strength of faith.* Don't pick your trembling steps across the stones pioneers have laid for you ; be your own pioneers, make your own ways, and show the originality and high daring of profound trust in God. I dare say you may be afraid of rashness—you are partly right, yet it is possible you may hardly know what rashness is. It is certain that the world is deeply indebted to its rash men, its first travellers, its leading spirits. Prudence (in its ordinary but most inadequate sense) has done very little for the world, except to tease and hinder many of its masters and sovereigns ; it would have kept back every mariner from the deep, and deterred every traveller from the desert—it would have put out the fires of science, and clipped the wings of poetry—it would have kept Abram at home, and found Moses a comfortable settlement in Egypt. Beware of imprudent prudence ; it will lull you to sleep, and bring you to a nameless and worthless end. Make heaven your aim !

> "Complain not that the way is long—
> What road is weary that leads there?
> But let the angel take thy hand,
> And lead thee up the misty stair,
> And there with beating heart await
> The op'ning of the golden gate."

Gen. xiii. 1.

And Abram went up out of Egypt, he, and his wife, and all that he had, and Lot with him into the south.

ABRAM AND LOT.

THIS is the first time, is it not, that a *rich* man is mentioned in the Bible. I do not remember that we have yet seen that great division of human society which is known by the names of "rich" and "poor." Now there is a rich man before us, and we shall see what rich men do when they are put to it. A wonderful thing it is, by the way, that some men should be rich and others poor they live on the same earth, they need the same comforts, yet one man seems to have everything and another to have nothing. Behind all this there must be a secret. It certainly looks like an unnatural state of things; yet we know that if all men had exactly the same to-day, in less than six months we should find ourselves very much where we are now.

In the text we learn that Abram was "very rich," and that Lot "had flocks, and herds, and tents." You will say, then, that this must have been a very happy company of travellers; they must be so, for they have come out at God's call, they are walking in God's way, and they have flocks and herds, and silver and gold, and every comfort that can be named. But even here a strife arose! "Their substance was great, so that they could not dwell together." Things got mixed. The cattle ran together so that sometimes the herdmen could not tell which was which; the count was always wrong at night; and the noise got louder and louder as the herdmen became fretful and suspicious. It was a quarrel in the kitchen, as we should say nowadays. The masters seemed to get along fairly well with each other, but the servants were at open war. Small credit to the masters, perhaps! They had everything nice; the lentil soup and the smoking kid were punctually set before them, and mayhap the wine-flagon was not wanting. But noise travels upward. It gets somehow from the kitchen into the parlour. It was so in this case. Abram heard of the vulgar quarrel and was the first to speak. He spake as became an elder and a millionaire: "Lot," said he "you,

must see to it that my peace be not broken ; you must lay the
lash on the backs of these rough men of yours and keep them in
check ; I will not stand any noise ; the lips that speak above a
whisper shall be shut by a strong hand ; you and your men
must all mind what you are at, or I will scourge you all to within
an inch of your lives." And when the lordly voice ceased there
was great fear amongst those who had heard its solemn thunder !
Now it so happens that the exact contrary of this is true.
Abram was older than Lot, and richer than Lot, and yet he took no
high airs upon him, but spoke with the meekness of great strength
and ripe wisdom. His words would make a beautiful motto
to-day for the kitchen, for the parlour, for the factory, for the
Church : " Let there be no strife, I pray thee, between me and
thee, and between my herdmen and thy herdmen ; for we be
brethren. Is not the whole land before thee ? separate thyself,
I pray thee, from me : if thou wilt take the left hand, then I
will go to the right ; or if thou depart to the right hand, then,
I will go to the left." And instantly Lot arose, and said : " No,
mine uncle, this shall never be ; I am the younger ; I am but a
follower ; without thee I cannot stand ; if we must part, the
choice shall be thine, and what thou dost leave I will take." A
beautiful speech for a young man to make : quiet and also great,
and full of tender pathos ; but, unhappily, never made by Lot !
This is what Lot really did ; listen : " And Lot lifted up his eyes,
and beheld all the plain of Jordan." And as Lot stole out alone
to take another look, he said to himself, " ' It is an ill wind that
blows nobody any good ' ; if these rattle-pated herdmen had not
come to high words this good luck never would have been mine."
And he looked round with the air of a rich lord, and hoped that
all quarrels would end as well.

Brave Abram ! we say as we read his words. He walked by
faith and not by sight. Certainly his foot slipped in Egypt, but
he is strong now, and he looks every inch a king as he stoops
before Lot. " Let this mind be in you, which was also in Christ
Jesus ; who, being in the form of God, thought it not robbery to be
equal with God : but made himself of no reputation." It is
beautiful to see strength stoop to weakness, but a very hard thing
for strength to do.

There is a clause in the story that has much meaning in it

which would be useful to us: "And the Canaanite and the Perizzite dwelled then in the land." No doubt their flocks helped to lessen the pasture which had already suffered from want of water, but I wonder whether we are not entitled to say that Abram did not want these strangers to hear any quarrelling amongst the Lord's people. As if he had said: "They are pagans; they are to be sent away from this land; they know not our God; but if we fight and bicker, and if we assail and devour one another, they must think evil of our religion, and they may secretly despise our God. Let us not shame our call and our destiny before the worshippers of idols." This is, at all events, a lesson which we may learn and put in force to-day. The world overhears the Church, and if we scold and fret, and throw hard words at one another, the world may mock us and say how mighty must their God be who cannot still the noise of their vanity and pride. My brethren, the Canaanite and the Perizzite are still in the land! The mocker has come across the threshold of the Church that he may find food for bitter mirth; his ear is set, if haply he can hear one note of discord which he will maliciously magnify into a great uproar. Let us give none occasion to the enemy to blaspheme. Let us forgive one another, if any man have a quarrel against any, and let mercy triumph over the letter of the law.

Now let us look for a moment at Lot's choice. The well-watered plain of Jordan is a great prize for any man, and Lot has made sure of it. His estate is large, and is favoured by the sun and the clouds. Is there, then, any drawback? Read: " But the men of Sodom were wicked and sinners before the Lord exceedingly." A great estate, but bad neighbours! Material glory, but moral shame! Noble landscapes, but mean men! But Lot did just what men are doing to-day. He made choice of a home, without making any inquiry as to the religious state of the neighbourhood. Men do not care how poor the Church is, if the farm be good. They will give up the most inspiring ministry in the world for ten feet more garden, or a paddock to feed an ass in. They will tell you that the house is roomy, the garden is large, the air is balmy, the district is genteel, and if you ask them what religious teaching they will have there, they tell you they really do not know, but must inquire! They will take

away six children into a moral desert for the sake of a garden to
play in: they will leave Paul or Apollos for six feet of green-
house! Others again fix their tent where they can get the best
food for the heart's life; and they sacrifice a summer-house that
they may now and again get a peep of heaven.

Abram will need some comfort now that Lot has gone. He
will want some one to speak to. He will be lonely and dull.
Many a strange talk they had at eventide as the great eastern
stars came trooping forth from their hiding, and shone like lamps
of silver on the crags and the green plains. Oh, the sight!
Every star a veiled sun, and the broad moon like the shield of
a king waiting peacefully for the fight, yet loathing war. And
the two men spoke softly. They lived in a holy church; every
wind a sweet hymn, every hill an altar set apart, every star a
flaming minister of God. But now Abram is left alone, and he
will need more than nature can give him; for nature becomes
monotonous, and at last a mockery and a pain. So the Lord
came to him and spoke to Abram in his mother-tongue: " Lift up
now thine eyes, and look from the place where thou art north-
ward, and southward, and eastward, and westward: for all the
land which thou seest, to thee will I give it, and to thy seed for
ever: and I will make thy seed as the dust of the earth: so that
if a man can number the dust of the earth, then shall thy seed also
be numbered. Arise, walk through the land in the length
of it and in the breadth of it; for I will give it unto thee." A
sweet word to speak to a dull heart, and a wonderful way of
making up loss to a man who has done a brave deed and said
good-bye to a friend he loved. God gives land. God gives
children. God sends our bread day by day. We think that he
looks at us only in church; we forget that he filleth our mouths
with good things, and makes our basket rich with all kinds of
store. Lot chose for himself. He took things into his own hands,
and put himself at the head of his own affairs. What became of
his management we shall see presently. He asked no blessing;
will the feast choke him? he sought no advice; will his wisdom
mock him and torment him bitterly? He snatched at good luck;
will he fall into a pit which he did not see? O, my soul, make
no model of this fool for thine own guidance. Perhaps his
honour is but for a moment. Commit thy way unto the Lord,

and choose nothing for thyself. In all thy ways acknowledge him, and. he will direct thy paths. O rest in the Lord, and wait patiently for him. Seek not high things for thyself, nor take thy life into thine own keeping. O, my soul, I charge thee, live in the secret of Christ's love. Walk in the way of the Lord · seek him always with eager heart, and whether the road be long or short, rugged or plain, it will lead thee into the city where the angels are, and the first-born and the loved ones who left thee long ago.

Gen. xiv.

1. And it came to pass in the days of Amraphel [the representative of Nimrod, the founder of the Babylonian empire] king of Shinar [Babel], Arioch king of Ellasar [the Larissa of the Greeks], Chedorlaomer king of Elam [the most powerful of the Asiatic princes], and Tidal king of nations [chief of several nomad tribes] ;

2. That these made war with Bera king of Sodom, and with Birsha king of Gomorrah, Shinab king of Admah. and Shemeber king of Zeboiim, and the king of Bela, which is Zoar.

3. All these were joined together in the vale of Siddim, which is the salt sea.

4. Twelve years they served Chedorlaomer, and in the thirteenth year they rebelled.

5. And in the fourteenth year came Chedorlaomer, and the kings that were with him, and smote the Rephaims [giants] in Ashteroth Karnaim [Ashteroth of the two horns], and the Zuzims [strong or mighty ones] in Ham, and the Emims in Shaveh Kiriathaim [the plains of the cities],

6. And the Horites [the inhabitants of caves] in their mount Seir, unto Elparan [the oak wood], which is by the wilderness.

7. And they returned, and came to En-mishpat [the well of judgment] which is Kadesh, and smote all the country of the Amalekites, and also the Amorites, that dwelt in Hazezon-tamar [the pruning of the palm, afterwards called Engedi, the fountain of the wild goat].

8. And there went out the king of Sodom, and the king of Gomorrah, and the king of Admah, and the king of Zeboiim, and the king of Bela (the same is Zoar) ; and they joined battle with them in the vale of Siddim ;

9. With Chedorlaomer the king of Elam, and with Tidal king of nations, and Amraphel king of Shinar, and Arioch king of Ellasar; four kings with five.

10. And the vale of Siddim was full of slimepits ; and the kings of Sodom and Gomorrah fled, and fell there ; and they that remained fled to the mountain.

11. And they took all the goods of Sodom and Gomorrah, and all their victuals, and went their way

12. And they took Lot, Abram's brother's son, who dwelt in Sodom, and his goods, and departed.

13. And there came one that had escaped, and told Abram the Hebrew; for he dwelt in the plain of Mamre the Amorite, brother of Eshcol, and brother of Aner : and these were confederate with Abram.

14. And when Abram heard that his brother was taken captive, he armed [or drew out, as a sword is drawn from its sheath] his trained servants, born in his own house, three hundred and eighteen, and pursued them unto Dan.

15. And he divided himself against them, he and his servants, by night, and smote them, and pursued them unto Hobah, which is on the left hand of Damascus.

16. And he brought back all the goods, and also brought again his brother Lot, and his goods, and the women also, and the people.

17. And the king of Sodom went out to meet him after his return from the slaughter of Chedorlaomer, and of the kings that were with him, at the valley of Shaveh, which is the king's dale.

18. And Melchizedek [supposed by some to be a title rather than a proper name, like Pharaoh or Cæsar] king of Salem [Jerome says it was not Jerusalem, but a city near Scythopolis] brought forth bread and wine : and he was the priest [this is the first time the word *priest* occurs in the Bible] of the most high God.

19. And he blessed him, and said, Blessed be Abram of the most high God, possessor of heaven and earth :

20. And blessed be the most high God, which hath delivered thine enemies into thy hand. And he [Abram] gave him [the priest] tithes of all.

21. And the king of Sodom said unto Abram, Give me the persons, and take the goods to thyself.

22. And Abram said to the king of Sodom, I have lift up mine hand [a solemn form of attestation in all nations] unto the Lord, the most high God [El-Elion, Jehovah], the possessor of heaven and earth,

23. That I will not take from a thread even to a shoelatchet, and that I will not take anything that is thine, lest thou shouldest say, I have made Abram rich :

24. Save only that which the young men [Abram's trained servants] have eaten, and the portion of the men which went with me, Aner, Eshcol, and Mamre ; let them take their portion.

BATTLE OF THE KINGS

WHEN Lot made choice of the well-watered plain, it does not seem to have occurred to him that it would be a likely place to excite the envy of king and men of war. Like his mother, and ours, he saw that the sight was pleasant to the eyes, and for that reason he put forth his hand and took all he could get. He soon found, however, that there were other people in the world besides himself, and that he could not keep the prize a secret. He would not leave it for Abram's enjoyment, and now we shall see if

he can keep it for his own. Kings were plentiful in that neighbourhood; some nine of them seemed to be within easy distance of
each other; and those nine kings divided themselves into fighting parties, four against five, and the four conquered the five,
driving the kings of Sodom and Gomorrah into the slimepits and
causing the others to flee to the mountains. Then, conqueror-
like, they took everything they could lay their hands upon, and
amongst the rest they " took Lot and his goods." But Lot had
made a good bargain, had he not ? The plain was well-watered,
and pasture was everywhere plentiful, and Lot was already a
king. It is always those things which we did not expect that
upset us ! One night Lot heard a noise and could not make out its
meaning; in the daylight, however, he saw that unbidden visitors
were not far off, and that their plan was not dictated by mutual
civility. They fought; the weak ones fell, the swift ones fled, the
thriving young Lot was walked off a prisoner of war, and uncon-
secrated mouths devoured his victuals and his wine. Think
of his reflections as he " lifted up his eyes " this time ! He was
looking round for his uncle ;—as you, young man, will one day be
looking round for your father—he complained that the grip was
too tight upon his arm, and his complaint was answered by a blow
that stunned him ; the wine he prized most was drunk without
a blessing, and the skins were thrown in his face that he might
smell the wine he should never drink. And Lot looked round for
his uncle ! His tent was torn up to make bandages, and his soft
mat was thrown upon a beast of burden. He complained again,
and the heathen laughed at his accent and told him to go back
beyond the Euphrates when he could steal away from their hand.
And they bade him speak again that they might have a heartier
laugh, and they mimicked this young man who had left his
mother to make his future in the west. And Lot looked round
for his uncle ! As I see him in that poor plight I feel 'hat some
bargains are not so good as they look, and that some young men
may set up for themselves a little too soon in business. Do not
go far out to sea in a cockle-shell. The young man should take
the old orator's advice to a young preacher : " Begin low; proceed
slow : rise higher ; take fire : wax warm ; sit down in a storm."
Lot got into the storm too soon, and in the battering rain and
roaring wind he looked round for his uncle !

The news of the fight was brought to Abram by "one that had escaped," and Abram armed his trained servants and set out to recover Lot. He did not sit in his tent and say, "He left me for his own pleasure, and now he must take the consequences of his selfishness : he thought he could do without me, now let him try." If Abram had said this there would have been a good deal of excuse for him. It would have been most human. We at all events could not have complained with any consistency, for this is exactly what we said when our friend offended us; but, to be sure, we are Christians, and Abram was only a Hebrew : and Hebrews are mean, greedy, crafty, villainous ! I find we must beware, though, lest the Jew beat us in noble behaviour ! He can be great ! He can forgive vile injuries ! How much greater should he be who has seen Christ slain and has named himself after the name of the Son of God ! How noble his temper, how forgiving his spirit, how hopeful his charity ! Charity ! Charity thinketh no evil; charity suffereth long, and is kind ; charity hopeth all things, believeth all things, endureth all things ; charity never faileth ! If we could reach this ideal it seems as if we might convert the world by charity alone !

Abram brought back Lot. What side-glances the younger shot at the elder, and how brave he thought his uncle ! It is in this way, that is by good deeds, by generous efforts, by high success in lawful daring, that men establish a natural kingship and become crowned without murmur or grudge. It is in this way, as in others, that Christ is King of kings and Lord of lords. He does good beyond all other men ; he brings the lost lambs home ; he sets the star of hope in the cloud of fear ; he stands at the door and knocks ! A beautiful picture is this of going after captive men and bringing them back to liberty. It is a New Testament picture. We are all taken captive by Satan at his will, and his hand is heavy upon us. Let us who know the joys of liberty go after that which is lost until we find it. Christ calls us to deliver the prey from the spoiler, and to save the lamb from the jaws of the lion. " Go ye into all the world and preach the Gospel to every creature." "He that winneth souls is wise." "They that turn many to righteousness shall shine as the stars for ever and ever."

And now wonderful things take place. The king of Sodom

goes out to meet Abram, and another king of mysterious name came forth with bread and wine, and with a priestly blessing on his lips. He is called Melchizedek, and Abram gives him a tenth of all. Some are anxious to know all about Melchizedek, but I prefer that the cloud of mystery should settle on his name. This wish to know everything in the letter is the curse of the human mind. Curiosity deposes reverence, and sight clamours against contented and holy faith. Oh, beautiful beyond most other scenes is this priest standing in the cloud, as if he had come up from eternity and was rather a voice than a man. And beautiful to think that his bread and wine had been brought from some high sacramental board, mayhap from the upper sanctuary where is the Lamb slain from eternity. I would not question this messenger. He is king and priest, perhaps he is but a shadow projected by One unseen! Leave the mystery. Do not pluck the stars from their places. By-and-by you will come to another Priest who will give you bread and wine and tell you the meaning of the symbols; by-and-by you will hear him called Melchizedek, and pronounced to be a Priest for ever. To other priests we have given tenths, to this Priest we must give all. Melchizedek is a mystery; Christ is a great light. Melchizedek appeared but for a moment; Christ abideth for ever. Melchizedek showed himself to one man; Christ fills the world with his presence.

After Melchizedek what could the king of Sodom do for Abram? The sight of some men transfigures us. We feel after being with them that we can never be mean again. Abram had seen Melchizedek, and the king of Sodom dwindled into a common man. Abram had eaten the holy sacrament, and after that all gifts were poor. Where the city was bad, the probability is that the king was bad too. Abram separated himself from the unclean thing. "Ye cannot drink the cup of the Lord and the cup of devils." "Ye cannot serve God and mammon." "The friendship of the world is enmity against God." Can a man rise from prayer to do evil? Can a man go from the Lord's table, and do the devil's work? The Church should never put itself under obligation to bad men. The people of God should build their own churches, support their own ministers, maintain the whole scale of their operations, without touching the tainted gold of Sodom, or the ill-gotten booty of Gomorrah.

Gen. xv. 1.

"After these things the word of the Lord came unto Abram in a vision, saying, Fear not, Abram : I am thy shield, and thy exceeding great reward."

ABRAM'S VISION.

AFTER Abram had slain the kings he might well feel uneasy as a stranger in a strange land, for how could he tell how many enemies might be stirred up and what reprisals might come upon him ? He was just in that state of exhaustion and bewilderment in which a word of comfort is especially precious There are times when we are not sure whether we have done right or not ; we may have been rash ; we may have sinned in our anger ; and we want a word from heaven to tell us that the deed was good and that our soul is safe.

It was in these circumstances that "*the word of the Lord came unto Abram.*" This is the first time that the expression, "the word of the Lord," occurs in the Bible. Afterwards it comes times without number ; but now it comes in all its fresh music. We have often read up to this point that "the Lord said" ; in this new expression it would seem as if the "Word" and the "Lord" were separated, or that the "Word" came separately, as if a messenger or a person. This is all the more likely from what follows : the Word came in a vision ; the Word spoke in its own name ; the Word answered the doubts and fears of Abram. What this "word of the Lord" may be, we are not supposed to know up to this point. We must mark the expression very carefully, and, perhaps, as we pass through the pages, light may be shed upon it. Hitherto the *Lord* has come to men—notably to Adam and to Noah ; now his *word* has come, and come in a vision !

"*Fear not, Abram : I am thy shield, and thy exceeding great reward*" : this is the first time that the word *shield* occurs in the Bible ; it means defence, guardianship invincible ! What is it that is a shield ? It is the *Word* of the Lord ! Is there, then, something of battle in human life, that such defences should be needful ? Does every man need a shield ? May we not go un-protected into the strife of the world ? The idea of a shield once having been suggested the ages have seized it as a prize and

wrought it into their speech as a tone musical above many.
Thus : "God is a shield unto them that put their trust in him";
"His truth shall be thy shield and buckler"; "With favour
wilt thou compass the righteous as with a shield"; "Thou art
my hiding-place and my shield"; "The Lord God is a sun and
shield"; "Behold, O God, our shield, and look upon the face
of thine anointed." The world will never let a word go out
that really touches its heart. There are words that will not
be allowed to die. They came into language as by right, and
they are welcomed as friends the very first time we hear them.
They are, too, nearly always short words, words that a child
can say and that the heart needs. Look at such short words as
—life, love, peace, rest, faith, hope, home! Words small as drops
of dew, yet holding the sun! And, wonderful in graciousness,
God himself and his dear Son take up these words and claim
them as their own. It is *God* that says "I am thy shield"; it is
not a low thought of man's; it is God's own sweet speech; and it
is *Christ* himself that says "I am the vine"; "I am the door";
"I am the true bread"; "I am the way, the truth, and the life";
"I am the light of the world." He who would speak to every
soul of man, through all time, must speak in figures and stoop to
pick up small words.

"*And Abram said, Lord God,*"—this is the first use of those
two words together. We have met them singly again and again,
and we have met them together in English often in the second
chapter, but in the Hebrew this is the first conjunction, the words
being *Adonai* Jehovah. The same combination occurs only twice
more in the whole of the five books of Moses, and these cases are
both in Deuteronomy. It is instructive to notice how great words
are used in great necessities : this sacred word "shield" is used
in the necessity of fear, and this holy word "Lord God" is used in
the necessity of doubt and wonder. Eloquence always comes out
of necessity. Abram felt that his own short life was too small to
hold all the riches that God was giving him. How could the
great Euphrates be confined within one man's garden-plot? How
could the stars be all crowded into one crown? God had given
Abram everything but a child, and therefore it seemed to him
that all this flow of God's love was running into a pool where it
could only stand still. And Abram told God his fear in plain

words. How true it is that we can say things in the dark that
we dare not say in the light! For a long time Abram wanted to
say this, but the light was too strong: he knew he would stammer
and blush in the daytime, so he hid the fear in his heart. But
now it is eventide! The shadows are about, and the stars are
coming! O sweet eventide, what words we have spoken in
its dewy quietness—words that would have been out of place in
the glare of open day! How the voice has become low, and the
heart has told what was deepest and tenderest, sending it out as
a dove that would find another soul to rest in! It was so that
Abram talked to God in the vision that came at star-time. He
said, " I have no child; all my goods are in the hands of a
steward, a true enough servant, but still not a son; what is to
become of all these tokens of thy love?" and whilst he was talking
the stars came out more and more, all of them—millions of
silvery eyes, throng upon throng, glowing over head, sparkling
over the distant hills, glittering in the east, throbbing like hearts
on the western horizon, the singing Pleiades, the mighty Arcturus
and his sons, Venus and Mars, and the Milky Way (names unknown then), there they were, angels talking in light, servants
watching the gate of the King's city. It was in that hour that the
Lord said to Abram, " Look up"; and Abram looked; and God
said, " Count them"; and Abram said, " My Lord, who can count
that host?" and the Lord said, "So shall thy seed be."

And now comes perhaps the greatest word yet spoken in
human history. I wish we could speak it in the right tone!
This is the word, " And Abram BELIEVED"! This is the first
time the word *believed* occurs in the Bible. How wonderful this
chapter is in the matter of first uses of words! It seems to be a
chapter of beginnings. *Believed,*—what a history opens in this
one word! The moment Abram believed, he was truly born
again. We may see here some of the great meanings of the
word. Paul says of Abram that " against hope he believed in
hope," and " that he staggered not at the promise of God through
unbelief." Here, then, we may study the word at the fountain
head. "Believed" means *supported, sustained, strengthened;* Abram
nourished and nurtured himself in God; Abram hid his life
and his future in this promise, as a child might hide or nestle
in a mother's breast. *That* is faith. He took the promise as a

fulfilment; the word was to him a *fact.* Thus he was called out of himself, out of his own trust, out of his own resources, and his life was fostered upon God,—he by-lived, lived-by, be-lieved, God! It was surely a perilous moment. Appearances were against the promise. Doubt might well have said, How can this thing be? But Abram "staggered not." God's love was set before him like an open door, and Abram went in and became a child at home. Henceforward the stars had new meanings to him, as, long before, the rainbow had to Noah. Abram drew himself upward by the stars. Every night they spoke to him of his posterity and his greatness. They were henceforward not stars only but promises, and oaths, and blessings. Thus dust is turned into flesh; bread into sacramental food; and stars become revelations and prophecies.

This act of believing in the Lord was accounted unto Abram for righteousness. From the first, God has always made much of faith. In no instance has it been treated as a mere matter of course, but rather as a precious thing that called for approbation and blessing. Faith was counted unto Abram for *character*; it added something positive to his being; he became more than merely harmless; he became noble, dignified, righteous. To believe, is not simply to assent; it is to take the thing *promised* as if it were actually *given*; and this action on the part of man is followed by an exactly corresponding action on the part of God, for he takes the faith as righteousness, the act of belief as an act of piety, a mental act as a positive heroism. What Abram did, we ourselves have to do. He rested on the word of God; he did not wait until the child was born, and then say, "*Now* I believe"; *that* would not have been faith, it would have been sight. It is thus that I must believe God : I must throw my whole soul upon him, and drive all doubt, all fear, from my heart, and take the promise as a fact. God asks me to do so; he says he will give me strength to do so; he says that without faith it is impossible to please him. Lord, increase my faith! See how large a life Abram entered into when he believed! He became a contemporary of all ages, a citizen and freeman of all cities the world over and time without end. Life without faith is an earth without a sky.

Then the covenant was made. Abram wished a ratification to

be given, and God gave it. Blood was shed, fire was enkindled, and words of strange import were spoken. The meaning of those words will appear as we become better acquainted with the his-tory. In our own life there is always some dream yet to be fulfilled. We have not come to the point which we feel sure has yet to be reached. Thus God lures us from year to year up the steep hills and along roads flat and cheerless. Presently we think the dream will come true—presently, in one moment more, to-morrow at latest; and so the years rise and fall, the hope abiding in the heart and singing with tender sweetness; then the end; the weary sickness, the farewell, the last breath, and the Dream that was to have shaped itself on earth welcomes us, as the Angel that guarded our life, into the fellowship of heaven. We call it Dream now; we shall call it Angel then!

Gen. xv. and xvi.

ABRAM'S DOMESTIC LIFE.

I TAKE these two chapters together, as completing one view of Abram's domestic life. It may be well to take notice that, up to this point, everything has gone on in regular order, with the exception of one great and solemn event. We have found just what we might have looked for : the growth of the population, the spreading out of families and tribes into distant places, a little invention, and the beginnings of discovery and progress. There has been nothing unnatural in the history. As we might have expected, domestic life has been carefully and vividly brought under notice. We have had family lists and registers in abundance, for, in truth, there was little else to talk about in those early days. The talk was of the children. To have the quiver full of such arrows was to be blessed of God in the most acceptable way; not to have children was to have great disappointment and distress. Abram had many children in promise, but not one in reality ; a joy which he himself could bear, but his wife did not accept the position with so glad a readiness. And out of this want of faith came grief, grief of her own making, but not wholly limited to herself. Want of faith always brings grief. It leads to meddle someness, and suspicion, and jealousy; and jealousy is a precipice over which men topple into the pit. Jealousy is as cruel as the grave. Its root is in suspicion. It suspects motives; it suspects actions; it suspects innocence itself: then it grows; it sees things that have no existence; it looks out under the eyebrows stealthily; it listens for unusual noises; it mistakes and misinterprets the ordinary signs and movements of life; and all the while it is killing the heart that nurses it. Have pity upon people that are afflicted with jealousy. They make you suffer, but they suffer more themselves. Oh, the dreams they have! The nightmare, terrible as hell, when the serpent rears itself at the bedside and shoots out its empoisoned fang, and coils its infinite length around their resting-place so that they cannot escape. It was so that Sarai dreamed by night, and in the daytime her heart was cruel towards Hagar. It all came from want of faith. She had no deep trust in God. And, observe, if it be not true for ever, that as the religious life goes down the evil powers set themselves up in awful mastery in the heart. O, my friend, keep fast hold of God, for when thy trust goes there is no more peace for thy poor life.

Sarai was so cruel that Hagar fled away from her. Sarai imagined that Hagar despised her. It was all fancy. How fancy tortures us! It turns the green branches of spring into serpents; it curdles and rots the milk of human kindness; it turns the child's sweet laugh into a mocking noise; it finds hell everywhere! Beware of thine imaginings, my friend, my brother, my sister—beware! One wrong turn, and there is nothing for thee but cloud and storm, and weary aching of heart.

The angel of the Lord sent Hagar back again, knowing that " what cannot be cured must be endured." Besides, submission itself, though so hard, may be so accepted as to become useful in the mellowing and strengthening of character. The angel did not say, " Fight it out and let the strong one win." He advised *submission,* and this is the first instance in which such advice is given in the Scriptures. It is a great Christian law, we know, but it is early to find it in Genesis! " Submit yourselves one to another for the Lord's sake," is a lesson which reads well in church ; but Hagar heard it not under a Gothic roof, half-chanted by surpliced priest, but "by a fountain of water in the wilderness, in the way to Shur,"—she the only hearer, the angel the priest of God! A good church, too, in which to learn the lesson of submission. I see Hagar taking a draught of the fountain, and trudging home again on weary feet ; going back to work among the sharp thorns, and to have words keen as stings thrown at her all the day long. A sorry fate, you say, to be pointed out by an angel! But wait. You do not know all. Who could bear all the ills of any one human life without having some help, some light, some hope ? A wonderful word was spoken to the woman —"I will multiply thy seed exceedingly, that it shall not be numbered for multitude." As if he had said—" If thou didst know thy destiny, thou wouldst think little of Sarai's mocking ; it is but a momentary pain ; bear it with the heroism of silent patience." And, truly, this same angel speaks to us all. He says, " If you walk in the way of the Lord you shall have blessing after sorrow, as the flowers bloom after the rain ; persecution you cannot escape, nor slander, nor cruel words ; but your light affliction, which is but for a moment, worketh out for you a far more exceeding and eternal weight of glory. One hour in heaven will banish every sad thought of earth ; submit, be patient, and return not evil for evil." Oh, listen to the angel ; it is God's angel ; it is God himself!

And now Hagar's days went with a new speed. Sarai mocked as before, but Hagar heard the angel's voice. The words of the angel became a kind of refrain in the melancholy music of her outer life : " I will multiply thy seed exceedingly ; the Lord hath heard thy affliction " ; these words never cease, and, under their influence, all taunts and sneers and bitter maledictions lost their effect. We, too, might have refrains still tenderer, the recurrence of which would refine and ennoble all coarse and cruel words. Thus : " Fear thou not, for I am with thee " ; " I will never leave thee nor forsake thee " ; " No weapon that is formed against thee shall prosper " ; " Weeping may endure for a night, but joy cometh in the morning." Ten thousand such promises are to be found in the Holy Word. Choose your own ; take the one that fits your woe best, and if you be in Christ fear not to use it when the bitter wind blows fiercely. Hagar left her house in overwhelming distress ; she went back to her sufferings with a new hope.

Our sufferings are so different when we take them at the Lord's
hand, and endure them because he tells us to do so. We cannot
triumph and rejoice in suffering merely on its own account. It
is impossible to like pain simply because it is pain. But take
the suffering at God's bidding; say, This is the cup of the Lord
and I must drink it for his sake; it is a burden chosen for me by
my Father in heaven; then you will sing with a new and
tenderer emphasis,

> "I can do all things, or can bear
> All suffering, if my Lord be there."

It was so with Hagar. She had heard the angel's voice; and
ever after, the words of scornful Sarai mingled with the flying
wind.

In the seventeenth chapter we read the renewal of the covenant
which the Almighty made with Abram, with a clear statement of
the terms upon which the covenant was based. Thirteen years
at least had come and gone since the promise was given the first
time. Thirteen years of waiting! Thirteen years of mortification
for Sarai! Thirteen years of discipline for Abram and Hagar and
Ishmael! They would have killed some of us : thirteen days
are to us eternity. The name Ab-ram which signifies "Exalted
father," now becomes Abraham, father of a multitude, and the
limited name Sarai (*my* princess) becomes Sarah, *princess*; the
limited becoming the unlimited. Mark how this renewal of the
covenant turns upon the consecration of *children.* Hitherto
we have to do with grown-up people, but now we are brought
face to face with little ones. We have hardly had a child at all
as yet in this long history. One wonders what notice God will
take of young life; will he say, "Suffer the little children to come
unto me," or will he shut them out of his view until they become
great men? Is a child beneath God's notice?

> "Is it much
> Too small a gem
> For his diadem
> Whose kingdom is made of such?"

Listen to the covenant : "he that is eight days old shall be
circumcised among you." What an oversight on the part of the
Lord not to observe that a child eight days old could not *under-*

stand what it was about! What a waste of piety to baptise an infant of days when it cannot understand what you are doing to it! It cries, poor thing; therefore, how ridiculous to baptise it! It plucks the preacher's gown, or chuckles and cooes in the preacher's arms; therefore how absurd to admit it into the covenant! For myself, let me say that when I baptise a child I baptise life,—human life,—life redeemed by the Son of God. The infant is something more than an infant, it is *humanity*; it is an heir of Christ's immortality. If there be any who can laugh at an infant and mock its weakness, they have no right to baptise and consecrate it, and give so mean a thing to God. God himself baptises only the great trees, does he ever baptise a daisy? He enriches Lebanon and Bashan with rain, but did he ever hang the dew of the morning upon the shrinking rose? Account for it as you please, God did appoint circumcision for the child eight days old! Christian baptism is founded upon this very covenant. Abraham was ninety-and-nine years old when he was circumcised, Ishmael his son was thirteen years old, and then came the infant men-children. So in heathen countries, the man is baptised, and the woman, and the child of days. We plead Divine precedent. Whatever objections stand against baptism stand against circumcision, and, therefore, stand against God. The child does not understand the alphabet, do not teach it; the child does not understand language, do not teach it; the child does not understand the Lord's Prayer, do not teach it. You say the child will understand by-and-by; exactly so; that answer is good; and by-and-by the child will understand that it was baptised in the name of the Father, and of the Son, and of the Holy Ghost, three persons in one God.

Beautiful, too, is Christian baptism when regarded as the expansion of the idea of circumcision. It well befits a tenderer law; circumcision was severe; baptism is gentle: circumcision was limited to men-children; baptism is administered to all: circumcision was established in one tribe, or family, or line of descent; baptism is the universal rite,—Go ye, therefore, and teach all nations, baptising them in the name of the Father, and of the Son, and of the Holy Ghost. So we go from law to grace; from Moses to the Lamb; from the mount that might be touched, and that burned with fire, to the quiet and holy Zion.

Gen. xviii.

ABRAHAM'S INTERCESSION FOR THE CITIES OF THE PLAIN.

THIS chapter gives two views of life as unlike each other as possible. The one is a quiet domestic scene, and the other a scene of terrible judgment. In the heat of the day Abraham was sitting in his tent under the shade of the trees, when three travellers came unexpectedly upon him. The account reads very curiously; for in the first verse we are told that "the Lord appeared unto Abraham as he sat in the tent door in the heat of the day," and in the second verse we read that "three men stood by Abraham"; then in the third verse instead of Abraham addressing his visitors in the plural number he spoke to them as if they were *one* only, saying : "My Lord, if now I have found favour in thy sight, pass not away, I pray thee, from thy servant." It was the Lord; it was three *men*! What contradictions we meet in the Bible! How could it be both the Lord and three men; how could there be one, yet three; three, yet one? Easily. The greater includes the less. Reality assumes many manifestations. Blessed is he who sees the Divine in the human, and the human in the Divine. Abraham would have had no difficulty with the Incarnation such as some moderns seem to have. He would have known the Lord at once when he saw Jesus; nay, verily, he *did* see the Christ; Jesus himself said so : "Your father Abraham rejoiced to see my day, and he saw it and was glad." That day was always visible to the eye that looked for it. Jesus has always been in the world, but the world as a whole knew him not; here and there some strong heart took hold of him and enjoyed the Gospel beforehand, and thus were the mysteries and the prophets of their day. In those three men at Abraham's tent door, I see the Lord Jesus Christ and two ministers of his, angels armed with the Lord's burning vengeance. How softly the way is smoothed to the end at which the three men were aiming! Thus: they came as ordinary travellers; they bathed their weary feet; they partook of the generous fare to which their host invited them; and in all other ways they seem to have done as other men would have done. Suddenly, however, they asked a question which might have startled Abraham : "They said unto him, Where is Sarah thy wife?" How did they know that Abraham had a wife, or how did they know her name? Are there eyes that can see into our tents? Can any one see through the roof of my house and tell all that is done in the quietest home? The question was not, Art thou married? but, Where is thy *wife*? and not that only, but, Where is *Sarah* thy wife? By-and-by you will hear the Lord say unto Moses, "I know thee by name"; farther on you will hear Jesus say to a publican and a sinner, "Zaccheus, make haste, and come down, for to-day I must abide at thy house"; and about the same time you will hear a man ask in a tone of surprise, "How knowest thou me?" If you put all these circumstances together you may reach the conclusion that in all the cases the Speaker was one and the same, and that his name is Wonderful!

Then, once more, Abraham was told that he should have a son. This was indeed weary work for Abraham, for it was quite thirteen years since the promise was first made to him, and now the son was to come next year. Sarah heard this in the tent door which was behind the speaker, and she laughed. Sarah did quite right to laugh if she lived within the range of mere facts. From any side of the *facts* of the case, the thing was ridiculous because impossible. Sarah denied that she laughed, and perhaps her denial was true ; she wished to say, "I did not laugh unbelievingly in any sense that meant disrespect to the Lord ; I did not laugh mockingly or profanely, but in an innocent way, thinking it out of the question that two such old folks should ever have a child." A question had been asked that had made Sarah serious : "Is anything too hard for the Lord?" When Sarah heard that question she wished to disown her laughter and to fall into the hands of the Lord. Abraham laughed, and Sarah laughed, and in their laughter there were blended joy, fear, hope, doubt : a right human laughter, yet it did not turn away the good purpose of God.

Then came a matter which in its immediate aspects was more solemn than any other. Thus softly have we been led up to it. The three men had strange work on hand, though they looked so quiet as they sat in the tent. Was the thing to be told to Abraham or not? Was he to kn w nothing until he heard noises and saw sights which might well lead him to think that the promise made to him of a son was a bitter mockery? When the whole sky was ablaze, and the air was pierced by beams of fire, and the earth trembled under a terrific blow, what was Abraham to think of the prophecies which had been spoken to his heart? The outward would contradict the inward, and there would be tumult in the good man's soul.

Yes; he would tell Abraham. Two of the travellers passed on towards Sodom. "But Abraham stood yet before the Lord," and he became a priest and an intercessor. Let us follow him in the noble course which he adopted when he was taken into the Lord's confidence.

1. *See how his moral nature is startled at the proposal.* "Wilt thou also destroy the righteous with the wicked?" "Shall not the Judge of all the earth do right?" There is a marked difference between the tone of Abraham and the tone of Noah. So far as we can learn from the record Noah did not put any such inquiries as those before the Flood, though, perhaps, they were in some measure rendered needless by the distinct separa tion of himself on account of his righteousness. Still, the inquiries are intensely interesting as showing how Divine judg- ments on a great scale strike a pious observer. Could such a thing be *right*? was Abraham's anxious question. A wonderful question, opening up a wonderful range of moral speculation! Remember from whom Abraham held moral nature, and you will see that this very question is itself a tribute to the righteousness of God. The question was an inspiration. And the course which God took in answering it shows that he has ever held it of the first consequence to secure the moral approbation of his creatures. In many things he has transcended their *reason*; in nearly all things he has baffled and even confounded and mocked their *speculations*; but in all instances he has been most careful not to excite con- troversy against himself in the human *conscience*. If it could once enter the mind of man that God has done *wrong*, that is to say has acted *unjustly*, man would be in a position to vindicate the most strenuous rebellion against his government. That God should tantalise our imagination, limit our influence, determine the measure of our days, and hold us completely under his dominion, are amongst the primary conditions of created life;

but *there must be no dissatisfaction in the conscience.* We must feel that how much soever our ideas are set aside, our *moral instincts* are respected. It is true, indeed, that we may come upon many things, even in moral government, which we can neither understand nor explain; but if where we *can* enter into God's purpose, and the method of its execution, we are enabled to see that *righteousness* is the habitation of God's throne, we are entitled to give our conscience rest in cases which are to our reason inscrutable. Let us be thankful that Abraham raised this question, and that it was raised so early in human history. Its importance is infinite.

2. *See how cautiously, yet how hopefully, Abraham's prayer enlarged itself.* From fifty to forty-five, to forty, to thirty, to twenty, to ten! A whole city would have been spared for the sake of ten righteous men. Here we see a great principle in the government of God. We are sparing others, or are being spared for their sakes. It may be your little child that is keeping the cloud of wrath from bursting upon your wicked house. Even now you may be getting the benefit of prayers your mother prayed long ago. The righteous man has to suffer many disadvantages on account of the presence of the wicked, whereas the wicked man receives nothing but advantages from the presence of the man who is good. Is there, then, injustice with God in this particular? In no wise. For there is not a just man upon earth that doeth good and sinneth not; and there is no man who is inherently and independently good : if you are *n w* good, you were once "dead in trespasses and sin," and *then* you were spared on account of the goodness of others. Besides, in proportion as any man is good is he willing to suffer disadvantage and loss rather than judgment should come upon the wicked. God himself suffers most. And if he is long-suffering and pitiful, who are we that we should speak of personal injury and distress? In this passage there are four great facts which should be borne in mind by Christian thinkers and teachers.

First : That God holds inquest upon the moral condition of cities. Second : That God is accessible to earnest human appeal. Third : That the few can serve the many. Fourth : That human prayer falls below Divine resources.

The Lord's people are the first to know the Lord's will. If we lived nearer heaven we should have earlier notice of God's purposes. "The secret of the Lord is with them that fear him; and he will show them his covenant." "Surely the Lord God will do nothing, but he revealeth his secret unto his servants the prophets." "Henceforth I call you not servants; for the servant knoweth not what his Lord doeth; but I have called you friends; for all things that I have heard of my Father I have made known unto you."

Gen. xix. 24, 25.

"Then the Lord rained upon Sodom and upon Gomorrah brimstone and fire from the Lord out of heaven; and he overthrew those cities, and all the plain, and all the inhabitants of the cities, and that which grew upon the ground."

THE DESTRUCTION OF SODOM.

THERE must have been some very strong justification for an act so terrible. This right of destruction may, I think, be fairly inquired into by human reason, and ought to be well studied as a fact that has been repeatedly realised in human history. Understand, if you please, that there is a Power above us which can utterly devour and consume our life. It is important to feel the whole force of this truth, especially as showing that life is not independent and irresponsible; and as showing that we hold it at the will of God, on certain distinct and intelligible conditions, the violation of which simply necessitates our utter destruction. I wish to point out this the more clearly because it might seem as if in giving life God has put it absolutely out of his own power to reclaim or withdraw it: having once given you life you are as immortal as he himself is, and you can defy him to interfere with his own work! The doctrine seems to me to involve a palpable absurdity, and hardly to escape the charge of blasphemy. Throughout the whole Bible, God has reserved to himself the right to take back whatever he has given, because all his gifts have been offered upon conditions about which there can be no mistake. He takes back the life of the body; he takes away the power of reason; he re-claims our physical strength ; by many a severity he asserts that the earth is his own and the fulness thereof; yet we are to suppose that he cannot put an end to our whole existence ; it has grieved him, mocked him, defied him, abandoned his sanctuary, violated his laws, slain his Son, quenched his Spirit, given the lie to his promises and heaped up the measure of its iniquity in his very face, but he cannot put an end to it! Not such is the doctrine I find in the Word of God. There the Lord is King; his power is infinite ; he *only* has the *right* to live; he *only* does live, and if *we* live it is because we abide in him, " as a branch abideth in the vine." I believe that the sovereignty of God is as absolute at the end as at the beginning; that " he can create, and he can destroy"; and that we live by his will alone. Furthermore, I can see the infinite reasonableness and justice of this sovereignty ; it subdues all things under the Lord's feet, and gives him an undivided throne.

In this case we have an instance of utter and everlasting destruction. We see here what is meant by " everlasting punishment," for we are told in the New Testament that "Sodom suffered the vengeance of eternal fire," that is of fire, which made an utter end of its existence and perfectly accomplished the purpose of God. The " fire " was " eternal," yet Sodom is not literally burning still; the smoke of its torment, being the smoke of an eternal fire, ascended up for ever and ever, yet no smoke now rises from the plain,—" eternal fire " does not involve the element of what we call " time " : it means thorough, absolute, complete, final : that which is done or given once for all.

As I look over those burning cities, and see the " smoke of the country go up as the smoke of a furnace "; as I see the sharp, keen tongues of flame piercing the gloomy cloud here and there, and catch a faint breath of the poisoned air, I ask myself, *Is this right?* Is God himself justified in sending this horrible desolation upon the earth ? If this were only an intellectual speculation I would not care to spend a moment upon its settlement. It is, however, an inquiry which proceeds from the *conscience,* and therefore its settlement is needful to give rest and satisfaction to the moral life that is in every one of us. To find out whether the judgment is right we must find out the moral conditions which called it forth. And first, it is important to observe that this judgment was preceded by an *inquiry* of the most unquestionable completeness and authority.   Hear this : "And the Lord said, Because the cry of Sodom and Gomorrah is great, and because their sin is very grievous ; I will go down now, and see whether they have done altogether according to the cry of it, which is come unto me ; and if not, I will know." You see, therefore, that we are only following the Lord's own example, in asking for information as to moral conditions.   It is, then, deeply satisfactory to know that the judgment was preceded by inquiry.

In the next place, the revelation made respecting the moral condition of Sodom is appalling and revolting, beyond the power of words to describe.   Let us put the case before ourselves in this way : Given a city that is full of corruption which may not be so much as named ; every home a den of unclean beasts ; every imagination debauched and drunk with iniquity ; every tongue an empoisoned instrument ; purity, love, honour, peace, forgotten or detested words ; judgment deposed, righteousness ' unished, th. sanctuary abandoned, the altar destroyed ; every child taught the tricks and speech of imps ; prizes offered for the discovery of some deeper depth of iniquity or new way of serving the devil ;— given such a city, to know what is best to be done with it ?   *Remonstrate* with it ?   Absurd !   *Threaten* it ?   Feeble ! What then ?   *Rain fire and brimstone upon it?*   Yes !   Conscience says Yes ;   Justice says Yes ;   concern for other cities says Yes ; nothing but fire will disinfect so foul an air, nothing but burning brimstone should succeed the cup of devils.   Just as we grasp the moral condition with which God had to deal do we see that fire alone could meet wickedness so wicked or insanity so mad.

This view is important not only historically as regards Sodom, but prospectively as regards a still greater judgment.   It would hardly be worth while to hold inquest upon a deed that took place innumerable years ago if that deed stood alone ; but it does not stand alone ; it is part of a great system of providence under which we ourselves live ; and it is an illustration of the working of the law by which we ourselves have to be judged.   Hence our interest in it.   This is no local tragedy.   The fire and brimstone are still in the power of God : not a spark has been lost : it is true to-day and for ever that "our God is a consuming fire"! A careful inquiry into the principles which determined the local and partial judgments of God will give us a clear view of the judgment which is to come upon the whole world. The principles are clearly these : We hold life as God's gift; we hold that gift upon certain conditions; we can choose good or we can choose evil; God loves us, cares for us, has given his Son to save us, and is watching us every moment; he wishes all men to be saved; he promises pardon to the penitent, and foretells the death of the impenitent sinner; by these principles he will judge us, and by these will the wicked go away into everlasting punishment, and the righteous into life eternal. The human conscience must answer, This is *right* ! Such a judgment gives us a sense of *rest.* With *such* a judgment to come, the presumption is that the Providence which leads up to it is as equitable and as sublime as itself. I call you, too, to witness that as God is to judge us, he also himself appeals to our judgment ! He asks us to consider his ways, and challenges us to tell what iniquity we have found in him. Hence in many parts of the Bible, notably in the Psalms, we have judgments pronounced by man upon the Lord, as if the Lord had placed himself at our bar and asked us to acquit or condemn his providence. He proceeds upon reasons. His principles are ascertainable, and such as can be judged ; hear what he says to Jerusalem—"Behold, this was the iniquity of thy sister Sodom, pride, fulness of bread, and abundance of idleness was in her and in her daughters, neither did she strengthen the hand of the poor and needy. And they were haughty, and committed abomination before me : therefore I took them away as I saw good." And in remembrance of all his ways, severe and gentle, the pouring out of the Flood and the visitation of Fire, the Psalmist says, "The Lord is gracious, and full of compassion ; slow to anger, and of great mercy"; "The Lord is good to all : and his tender mercies are over all his works"; "The Lord is righteous in all his ways, and holy in all his works." In heaven and earth the testimony is the same. "Just and true are thy ways, thou King of saints." "The Lord preserveth all them that call upon him, but all the wicked will he destroy." Wonderful is this, that God should allow us to judge his way ! He does not silence the Psalmist, nor does he reprove the acclaiming angels ; he will be judged by all who are honest in soul. And beautiful, too, is this, that notwithstanding the severity and awfulness of his judgments, the Lord is good to all, and his tender mercies are over all his works! It does not seem so at the time of the infliction of his judgments. With Sodom and Babylon, Egypt and Tyre, Nineveh and Jerusalem, before us, it does not seem so. But we must look at God's purpose and at great breadths of history, even from the beginning to the end of his ways, and as we see ravages repaired, verdure growing upon the slopes of the volcano, and the blade rising from the dead seed, we too shall say in many a song of thankfulness and joy, "The Lord is gracious, and full of compassion; slow to anger, and of great mercy." In the sum total of things we shall see that mercy has rejoiced against judgment, that righteousness and peace have kissed each other, and that all experience says with mighty voice, distinct and far-sounding, *God is Love.*

Returning to the narrative, Lot was saved from the burning, and in truth I cannot but wonder what he was saved for. Compared with the Sodomites he was indeed a man of "righteous soul." I will not question the goodness of his intentions or detract from the almost Divinity of his relative character; but he was a selfish man, little and mean in his notions, and fickle and timid in general bearing. Poor was the bargain he made when he chose the well-watered plain of Jordan! He did not see his mistake at the time. But as he took to his heels that hot morning when the lightning was astir, and as he was nearly choked with the sulphur that rolled in clouds around the skirts of Zoar, he began to think how foolish he had been and how true it is that "it is not all gold that glitters."

Gen. xx.

ABRAHAM AND ABIMELECH.

ABRAHAM went from Mamre to the south, and found a fertile country lying between two deserts, the desert of Kadesh and the desert of Shur. The earth is not all fertile, or we should think little of it; neither is it all desert, or we should be driven into despair. Abraham, the great man and prophet of the Lord, once more shows his littleness by giving way to a cowardly fear that strangely divided his heart with the noblest faith found in the ancient world. His fear in one direction was simply ridiculous and pitiful ; when he came amongst a powerful people he was always afraid that they would kill him in order to get possession of his wife : on the face of it the thing would seem to be incredible ; here is a man who left his kindred and his father's house, who braved the hardships of the wilderness, who arose and pursued kings and slew them, and delivered the prey from the hand of the mighty, tottering like a weak old coward when he thinks that he may be killed. He made a mean figure before Pharaoh, and he makes a meaner still before Abimelech. In one sense I am glad that Abraham made such a fool of himself, for had he been without flaw or blemish, perfect and invincible in faith, and complete in the sanctification of his character, he would have awed me by his supernatural respectability, and I should never have thought of him as an example or a pattern. From his own account he told a white lie by keeping back part of the truth.

The thing that is most remarkable in the whole story is that God should apparently have taken Abraham's part instead of humbling and punishing him in the sight of the heathen. To us the Almighty seems to have had just cause for contracting Abraham into Abram, and sending him back into his own country " a sadder but a wiser man." In discussing a subject so delicate we must awaken the attention of our whole mind and heart, for the loss of a word may be the loss of a truth

Observe, first of all, that if the Divine purpose is to be turned aside by the fault or blemish found in individual character, the Divine government of man is at an end, and human progress is an impossibility. Adam failed, so did Noah, so did Abraham, so did Lot. So clearly was it established as a sad and mournful truth that no individual man was perfect, that once and again God was moved to abolish the human race from the earth altogether. It was not Adam that sinned, or Noah, or Abraham ; it was *human nature* that sinned. There seems to be little advantage of one man over another in this or that particular, but the advantage even when real is only partial. Pharaoh seemed to be a better man than Abram, but he was not so in reality. Take them bulk for bulk, character for character, Pharaoh was not to be mentioned with Abram. Esau seemed to be a brave and noble son of the soul, and Jacob seemed to be a sneaking and vile schemer, with

the making of an assassin under his smooth skin; I admit this
fully, but the judgment is not to be fixed at any one point; you
must take the full stretch of time required by the Almighty in
working out his purposes, and then it will be seen that under all
appearances there was something undiscernible by the human
eye, which made every man chosen to leadership and renown in
the holy kingdom the best man that could have been chosen for
the purpose. You say that Abimelech was better than Abraham ;
now let me ask you what you know about Abimelech ? Nothing
but what is stated in this chapter. Very well. You are so far
right. You have seen Abimelech at his best and you have seen
Abraham at his worst, and then you have rushed to a conclusion !
This is not the right way to read history; certainly it is not the
right way to read the Bible. We are not to set act against act,
but life against life. If we were to set act against act, we should
reverse the most solemn verdicts of history, and disennoble some
of the very princes of human kind. You have seen a professing
Christian in a bad temper, and you have seen a man who made
no profession of Christianity unruffled and serene, and instantly
you question the sincerity of the professor and sing the praises of
the pagan. And you point to facts in justification. Now your
reasoning may be wrong, your facts may be illusory, and your
judgment may be most unjust and cruel. It is quite true that
you have seen the one man in a stormy passion, and the other
man without a flush of colour on his pale cheek, and it is quite
possible that in the particular case referred to the professor may
have been wrong and the pagan may have been right ; but take
them life for life, spirit for spirit, character for character, through
and through, and no man who is without Christ can compare for
true and lasting dignity of soul with the least in the kingdom of
heaven.

This principle may help us to come to larger and juster judgments of human character and human history. We must not
judge the universal by the local. When I think of the meanness
of Adam, the drunkenness of Noah, the selfishness of Lot, the
cowardice of Abraham, the cunning of Jacob, the sensuality of
David, and the inconstancy of Peter, my first wonder is that such
men should have a name in the Divine history at all. But therein
I show my folly not my wisdom, and I may show my impiety,

too, by my setting up my morality against the righteousness of God. It is easy for me to compare the flat and insipid respectability of some of my own acquaintance with the painful characteristics I have just named, and to depose the great historical characters in favour of my unimpeachable friends. But where would my unimpeachable friends have been *in the same circumstances ?* And what have they ever done to show that they would have stood where Adam fell, and that they would have been bold where Peter shrank and lied ?

This, then, is the point at which I find rest when I am disturbed by the evident and painful immorality of illustrious Bible characters, viz., human nature has never been perfect in all its qualities, energies, and services ; the perfection of human nature can be wrought out only by long-continued and severe probation ; in choosing instruments for the representation of his will and the execution of his purposes, God has always chosen men who were best fitted *on the whole* for such ministry, though in some particulars they have disastrously and pitiably failed. When I think I could have improved God's plan, the mistake is mine, because my vision is dim and I never can see more than a very limited section of any human character.

In the next place consider, knowing human nature as we do, how beneficial a thing it was to the great men themselves to be shown now and again that they were imperfect, and that they were only great and strong as they were good—as they were true to God. To be an illustrious leader, to have power and authority amongst men, always to be in high places, and to be absolutely without a fault of disposition, temper, or desire, is enough to tempt any man to think that he is more than a man ; and even to be without actual social fault, that can be pointed out and blamed, is not unlikely to give a man a false notion of the real state of his own nature. We may learn quite as much from our failures as from our successes. I have seen more truly what I am by my faults than by my graces, and never have I prayed with so glowing a fervour as when I have seen that there was but a step between me and death and that I had nearly taken it ! Speaking of faultless men I am reminded of Enoch. It is on record that " Enoch walked with God." I fear that these words may not be always fairly applied. Let me point out to you the difference between a contemplative and an active life. It is clear from the very form of expression that Enoch was of a retiring and meditative character. He loved the quiet nook in the hill. You find him away under the whispering trees, with eyes now fixed on the ground and presently lifted towards heaven in tender and expectant prayer. Let me ask you, What has Enoch done for the human race ? What dangers has he braved, what battles has he fought, what heroisms has he displayed ? Compare the position of Adam with the position of Enoch ! Compare the valour of Abraham with the peaceful disposition of Enoch ! This, I contend, is the just and honourable course of criticism. When men return from the far-away battle-field, I shall stand upon the shore and watch their debarkation. The artist who has drawn the pictures shall pass in cordial silence ; the literary correspondent, who has given graphic accounts of the bloody fray, shall have a friendly salute ; the ornamental soldier, who returns without scratch or stain, shall have a look of suspecting wonder ; but the grand old general who led the fight—who has come home with battered helmet and dinted shield, maimed, torn, half the man he was when he went out, whose old likeness we have to search for through scars and seams that tell of heroic suffering—when he steps forth, every war-mark shall make him dear to us, and, as his brave old limbs limp under him, we shall hail him as a patriot, a soldier, and a friend.

Do we, then, find any justification of our own evil-doing in these reflections ? I answer, not one tittle of justification. God forbid ! I am seeking to justify *God*, not to justify *man*. We are called to holiness, to honour, to purity, to nobleness : to all that is beautiful and resplendent in character. To this end Christ died ; to this end the Holy Spirit works ; to this end our whole being should move in one strenuous and hopeful effort. And yet in thought, or word, or deed ; by fear, or unbelief, or selfishness ; by suspicion, envy, jealousy, or uncharitableness, we may slip and even fall many times by the way. But if the root of the matter be in us ; if, under all our faults and sins we have that true faith which is the gift of God, and that deep love which lives through our inconstancy amounting sometimes to treason, and if we press and strive towards better things, we shall find in the last result that God's grace is greater than our sin, and that we shall b saved if only "so as by fire."

Gen. xxi. 14.

"And Abraham rose up early in the morning, and took bread, and a bottle of water, and gave it unto Hagar, putting it on her shoulder, and the child, and sent her away: and she departed, and wandered in the wilderness of Beer-sheba."

ISHMAEL.

THE first feeling we have in reading the story of Hagar and Ishmael is that they were both most cruelly used. If you were to read this story in the newspapers, as an incident happening in our own time, you would strongly condemn both Abraham and Sarah his wife. Hagar and Ishmael were cast forth out of the house of Abraham. Hagar received from Abraham " bread and a bottle of water," and she and her child " departed and wandered in the wilderness of Beersheba." They were sent away from comfort into destitution, and this, so far as we know, for no crime. Some offence may have been given to Sarah, an offence which Sarah visited with most excessive and unpardonable resentment, as it appears to us on the face of the story. The very reading of it makes us the eager partisans of Hagar. We instantly take sides with her in the hour of her injury and pain, and in her affliction we are afflicted with great distress. This woman was wronged, and in her suffering all other generations of women have been disennobled and outraged. It was indeed with no readiness of will that Abraham responded. " The thing was very grievous in Abraham's sight because of his son."

The first feeling is that a most cruel act has been done. The next feeling is that surely we do not know the *whole* case. It must be only the *outside* that we see. Behind all this there must be something we do not fully understand. Hagar would never go away so quietly of her own will. Ishmael, seventeen years old, would surely show some sign of discontent and rebellion. How is it that people go out to poverty, to loneliness, to all hardness of life, so *quietly*, so *dumbly*, with only great hot tears in their eyes, and no sharp word of reproach or revenge on their lips ? Had they gone away, Hagar and Ishmael, with violent upbraidings and threats hurled at the heads of those who banished them, the pathos would have been lost; the story would have been only a noisy brawl—a women's fight, in which the weakest got the

worst; that is all, nothing more! But what of this strange
quietness? Can the heart be hushed by voices which the ear
cannot hear? Can the poor fickle will, which so often mistakes
petulance for strength, be touched from infinite heights by a
tender and pitiful omnipotence which is working upon a sphere
so vast that anything we can now see of it is as a straight line?
When the first flush of anger dies away I begin to wonder
whether there may not be something behind, which when known
will explain everything, and add to this confused and riotous life
of ours a solemnity and a grandeur supernatural! Through this
incident, as through a door ajar, we may see a good deal of
human life on what may be called its tragical side. The *details*
are ancient and local, but the *meaning* is flowing around our life
to-day and should be understood by all who are seeking the great
principles rather than the passing accidents of human history.

1. As a mere matter of fact there are events in human life
which cannot but affect us with a sense of disorder in the government and administration of things, if indeed there be either
government or administration. One is taken, another left. One
moves upwards to wealth and honour, another is neither prosperous by day nor restful by night. Sarah is the centre of a home;
Hagar is a vagrant in the wilderness. Isaac is the idol of two
hearts; Ishmael has no father, and his mother's poor life throbs
between the points of disgrace and helplessness. Such is human
life as we ourselves know it. This is not fancy; it is fact. You
know it; you represent it; it is your own strange, perplexing,
immeasurable life. You may take one of two views of this state
of facts

(*a*) Life is a scramble; the strong man wins; the weak man
dies; Luck is the only god, Chance is the only law, Death the
only end. Suffering is the price paid by weakness for being
allowed to exist, and poverty is the penalty a man pays for being
conscientious. Society is the triumph of confusion. It is a giddy
whirl, and nobody can tell who will be down or who will be up
at the next turn of the wheel. The disorder of human life mocks
the order of material nature. Or thus:

(*b*) There must be a power mightier than man's, controlling
and shaping things. Looking at human history in great breadths
we see that even confusion itself is not lawless; it is a discord

in the solemn music; it is an eccentricity in the astronomic
movement; but it is caught up by the great laws, and wrought
into the general harmony; above all, beyond all, there is a benign
and holy power.   Now from my point of view it requires *less
faith* to believe this than to believe the other.   The man who
judges universal providence by solitary instances, is a man who
would prove to himself that the earth cannot be a globe so long
as there is a molehill upon its surface.   He denies that the
universal can affect the particular, and that the temporary can
be swallowed up by the eternal.

Prove that an action or an event begins and ends in itself, and
you establish a special law of judgment; but let it once be
allowed that actions and events are not self-contained; that they
have antecedents and consequents; that they are modified and
sometimes counteracted by unexplained and unexpected influences, and at once you introduce new laws and new standards
of judgment.   You have then an unknown and most subtle
element to deal with.   It may surprise you by new revelations
any moment.   It may make the desert blossom as the rose, or
it may turn the fair garden into barrenness.   You cannot measure
it by your reason; you cannot control it by your skill; you
cannot avert it by your adroitness.   It takes its own time, sometimes little, sometimes much.   It works in its own secret but
sure way.   It is silent, mighty, irresistible.

2. As a further matter of fact in human life, there are cases
marked by utter *despair*, for which it seems utterly impossible
that any deliverance can ever arise.   Hagar's is a case in point.
Her water was spent.   The hot sun was beating on her head.
Ishmael was faint with weakness.   There was no one to speak to.
No human friend answered the appealing voice.   Some of us may
have been in the same circumstances as to their effect upon the
soul.   When you were left a widow with six children—no fortune,
the water gone, the children crying for bread, the officer at the
door, you wished to die; you were subdued by a great fear.
But I ask you, in God's house, if there were not made to you
sudden revelations, or given to you unexpected promises that
brought light to the weary and hopeless heart?   How did friends
appear, how were doors opened, how did the boys get a little
schooling and get their first chance in life?   Are you the person

now to turn round and say that it all came by chance, or will you
not rather exclaim, "This is the Lord's doing; I was brought low
and he helped me"?

And what men God trains in the wilderness! It would seem
as if great destinies often had rough beginnings. "I will make
him a great nation," said the angel of God. We must go down to
go up. We must suffer if we would be *strong* with other than
a rude unmellowed power. Why this is human history repeated
in an individual example! Man's story had a rough opening.
Adam, in blighted Eden, was as Ishmael in the inhospitable
wilderness. God knows what we need, where we are, and when
to come for us. Compare your present self with your former
self, and say if God be not as gracious as he is mighty. If you
could take out of your character all the fine elements which have
come into it through sorrow, you would be turned into a crude
and selfish creature. Sorrow, rightly accepted, sorrow sanctified,
refines the gold of life; it raises the heart into noble elevation of
feeling; it enriches the memory with many helpful recollections;
it conquers and destroys the spirit of unbelieving and selfish fear.
My friends, God would make us very poor if he took from us the
results of sanctified sorrow.

3. You will bear me witness, as a further matter of fact, that
life is full of surprises and improbabilities, and that the proverb,
"Man's extremity is God's opportunity," is supported by innumerable instances. "God opened her eyes, and she saw a well
of water." She expected to die; and lo, she never was so sure of
life. Ishmael withered only at the top, not at the root, for out of
that root was to spring a great nation. These surprises not only
save life from monotony, they keep us, if rightly valued, lowly,
expectant, dependent. *They operate in two contrary ways*—lifting
up man, and casting him down.

4. As a matter of fact, the men who seem to be the most
prosperous have trials of a heavy and most disciplinary kind.
Early in the morning Abraham sent Hagar away; early on
another morning a heavier cloud gathered over his horizon, and a
keener pang tortured his heart. It seems as if great nations must
be built upon ruins—as if great prices must be paid for great
honours. Ishmael is to die of thirst; Isaac is to perish by the
knife—did ever brilliant destinies arise from such flickering

embers ? My friend, thou knowest not what thou shalt be, or thy children; life is very low with thee just now; it may be because immortality is so near!

I have not far to go for an evangelical application of this incident. It is in our *despair* that Christ brings his Gospel to us. It is when there is no well that he smites the rock. It is when the knife is lifted over our heart that he becomes a "Lamb" for us!

Gen. xxii. 2.

"Take now thy son, thine only son Isaac, whom thou lovest, and get thee into the land of Moriah ; and offer him there for a burnt offering upon one of the mountains which I will tell thee of."

THE OFFERING OF ISAAC.

IT must have seemed hardly possible to the patriarchs, and the elder Hebrews generally, that God could have made the heavy demands upon their trust and love which they were almost daily required to satisfy. In saying this I am judging primitive faith by modern religion : I am in fact judging Abraham by ourselves! Suppose that it should be borne in upon our mind, as the current phrase is, that we should do this or that great thing, requiring special self-denial and personal suffering, we should instantly reason that such a mental impression was the result of mental disorder or of physical derangement; the very last idea that would occur to us is that God meant to bereave and humble us until he had by suffering perfected the sanctification of our will. It is, therefore, the more startling to find Abraham, instantly, without fretful appeal or pathetic argument, going forth to a deed so terrible as the offering of his son, his only son Isaac, whom he loved. I propose to point out certain features of this severe trial, which closely resemble some of the operations of Divine Providence known to ourselves, and thus to confirm ancient and modern revelation, and so get some notion of the unity and completeness of human discipline and training. In a word, I want to show that the God of the Jew is the God of the Christian, and that the God of Abraham is, in the widest sense, "the God of the living."

1. The experience of Abraham and our own experience are strikingly coincident in the fact that we are often exposed to great trials *without any reason being assigned for their infliction.* Notice this in the case of Abraham. In the very midst of his domestic joy this desolating word falls. We do not read that Abraham had been committing sin, or that in any way he had been provoking the Most High to anger. From our point of view this trial is wholly without cause or reason, and the terms read like an edict of wanton and ruthless cruelty.

Such experiences are far from uncommon in our own day. We see human fortunes reversed without any apparent reason ; the innocent are impoverished and scourged ; men are paralysed in the very attitude and act of prayer ; honestly-gotten wealth is scattered beyond recovery ; the most useful workers in the Church are laid aside by sickness ; and they who would gladly be foremost in the fight are made to stand still because of pain and helplessness. No reason is given. No justification is offered. The fearful demand is made point-blank, and no compromise is possible. God sometimes insists upon a distinct Yes or No, and then to falter is to rebel.

In this part of the case it is not proper to say that all men have sinned, and that the universal fact is explanation enough of the particular instance. That suggestion would cover too much ground ; more, indeed, than is covered by the kind of providences now being considered. Universal depravity is of course the most mournful fact in human history, and, if followed in each instance with a trial as special as Abraham's, the reasoning would be sound. But we are looking at the case of men who stand nearest God, who love him most, and whom he himself most delights to honour, and we find that *they* are called upon to bear trials of unexampled and intolerable severity, without one word of explanation or argument. When such trials are accepted in a filial spirit, the triumph of faith is complete. Such faith is counted unto men for righteousness. It is not a faith that hesitates and falters and struggles ; it is a faith victorious in its way even infinite and omnipotent.

2. The experience of Abraham and our own are further coincident in the fact that even in our severest trials, in the very crisis and agony of our chastisement, *we have hope in the delivering*

mercy of God. This is strikingly shown twice in the story before us. "Abraham said unto his young men, Abide ye here with the ass, and I and the lad will go yonder and worship, and come again to you" (v. 5). Mark the promise to come again! It would be pitiful trifling with the solemn occasion to say that Abraham lied unto the young men. The man who could offer such a sacrifice was not the man to tell .ics to the on-lookers In the next instance, Abraham said to Isaac, "God will provide himself a lamb for a burnt offering" (v. 8), when he knew that Isaac was appointed to the altar! It is so often in human life that the inward contradicts the outward, and that the unseen controls that which is seen. Terrible as the storm may be, yet far away in some dim chamber of the heart is an angel singing softly of hope, and light, and rest. Sometimes it is a voice without words; a solemn sound that never comes within the narrow range of articulation; yet it is as a rock on which the soul builds. "We will come again," said Abraham, when the very earth was reeling under his feet! "God will provide himself a lamb," said he, when the appointed victim was walking at his side. All this is true to life, as we ourselves know it. We have said these very words. We have said things to dying friends which would not bear a strictly literal test of accuracy, yet which were true in larger interpretations than literal exactness could comprehend or contain. Sometimes we have spoken in the power of the spirit, when men have limited us by the poverty of the letter. It was so that Jesus Christ himself was often misunderstood. He gave infinite meanings to finite words, and so he was constantly being contradicted by students of the mere letter. He said he would "build the temple in three days"; he said that he was "before Abraham"; he said that the dead Lazarus was "asleep." Faith often substitutes a greater fact for a small one. The parable overruns the mere history. "You will get better," we say to the patient, when perhaps we mean that he will be healed with immortality; and when we meet him in heaven he will tell us that we were right when we said he would yet live. Sometimes we wist not what we say. Let us then be careful how we charge one another with false speech, for there is a fiction that is not untrue.

3. The experience of Abraham is coincident with our own in

the fact that we are often made to feel the uttermost bitterness of a trial *in its foretelling and anticipation.* Say whether you ever read anything so terrible as the second verse : "Take now thy *son*—thine *only* son Isaac—thine only son Isaac, whom thou *lovest* —and offer him for a burnt-offering"! The words must have dropped into Abraham's heart like molten lead. But not more hotly into his heart than some words have dropped into our own. Slowly has the finger of God moved over our most cherished treasures, marking them for ruin. They have not been spoken of in the gross, or hurriedly, as if with reluctance, but slowly, lingeringly, with a deliberation that aggravated the cruelty, until the steadiness of reason itself has been threatened. It was so with the regular and inexorable "calls" of the bankrupt bank in which you placed the savings of an industrious lifetime—it was so in the accursed chancery suit which remorselessly stripped you of everything ; and it was so in the shutting of door after door, until your last hope died, and you plunged into the black river of despair. A sudden reversal is nothing compared with the lingering death which some men have to die. They die upwards, inch by inch—the light brings them no hope, and spring brings no renewal of their withered strength. If we meditate on these things, and study their plain and solemn meaning, we shall see that we ourselves and Abraham have been afflicted with common sorrows.

4. The experience of Abraham and our own are coincident in the fact that *filial obedience on our part has ever been followed by special tokens of God's approval.* We have something more than mere Hebrew redundancy of language in the promise made to Abraham by the Almighty. Hear how that promise reads. It reads like a river full to overflow : " Because thou hast done this thing, and hast not withheld thy son, thine only son : that in blessing I will bless thee, and in multiplying I will multiply thy seed as the stars of the heaven, and as the sand which is upon the sea shore ; and thy seed shall possess the gate of his enemies; and in thy seed shall all the nations of the earth be blessed ; because thou hast obeyed my voice." I do not know of a more striking realisation of the promise, "I will open the windows of heaven, and pour you out a blessing that there shall not be room enough to receive it." I call upon you to witness whether you

yourselves have not, in appropriate degrees, realised this same overflowing and all-comforting blessing of God, in return for your filial obedience. Have you ever given money to the poor without repayment from the Lord? Have you ever given time to God's cause without the sun and the moon standing still until you had finished the fight, and made up for the loss? "Verily I say unto you, There is no man that hath left house, or brethren, or sisters, or father, or mother, or wife, or children, or lands, for my sake, and the gospel's, but he shall receive an hundredfold now in this time, houses and brethren, and sisters, and mothers, and children, and lands, with persecutions; and in the world to come eternal life." Exceeding great and precious are the promises of God! He is able to do exceeding abundantly above all that we ask or think!

Other points of coincidence as between the old experience and the new will occur on reading the text, such as (1) the unconscious aggravations of our suffering made by inquiries such as Isaac's (v. 7); (2) the wonderfulness of the escapes which are often made for us (v. 13) by Divine Providence; and (3) the sanctification of special places by sweet and holy memories of deliverance and unexpected joy (v. 14). But the supreme lesson which I would learn from this history is that Almighty God, in the just exercise of his sovereign and paternal authority, demands the complete subjugation of our will to his own. This is a hard lesson for man to learn. Man loves his own will. He thinks it best. He clings to it long. It is just here that the great battle must be fought. We are not called upon to give up one taste out of many; one pursuit out of many; one wish out of many; we are distinctly called upon to give up everything—to sink our will in God's; to be no longer our own; to sum up every prayer with "Nevertheless, not my will, but thine be done." That is pure religion before God and the Father. "Except a man deny himself, and take up his cross daily, he cannot be my disciple." If God wants your only child to be a poor missionary, when you mean him to be a rich merchant, let him be laid upon the altar if you love and honour God! If God strip your vines, and take away the one ewe lamb; if he bark your fig-tree, and cause the herd to die in the field—you are to say—"The Lord gave, and the Lord hath taken away, blessed be the name of the Lord." And never can we say this with the heart's full consent until we are crucified with Christ. We must say our greatest lesson after him. He speaks first, we speak second. He is the Master, we are the scholars. Lord, if thou wilt break the last link, break it; if thou wilt take away my last morsel of bread, take it; "though thou slay me, I will trust in thee."

Gen. xxiii.

THE BURIAL OF SARAH.

IT has been remarked as a singular circumstance that Sarah is the only woman whose age is mentioned in the Scriptures. At the time of her death her only son Isaac was thirty-seven years old, she herself being ninety at the time of his birth. We know little about Sarah, except that she was comely to look upon; somewhat severe towards Hagar her handmaid, and that she was the mother of Isaac! This seems quite little when mentioned in one sentence, but really it comes to a great deal in the full working out. Her good looks made travelling rather dangerous for Abraham; her conduct towards Hagar showed her temper and moral quality, and her motherhood of Isaac made her the mother of all believers (1 Peter iii. 6). How large an oak may come out of one acorn! As we are about to attend the burial of Sarah, we should reflect a little upon the lessons of her life before we leave the cave of the field of Machpelah, which is in Hebron in the land of Canaan.

Some of us have to live in a kind of reflected lustre and fame. We are next to nothing in ourselves, but our brother is famous, our uncle is influential; we have not seen the Queen ourselves, but we have seen a man who has seen her. Sarah was not much in herself, but she was the wife of Abraham. The window of your cottage is a very small one, but it looks out upon a park three thousand acres large. Some of us get our lustre at third or fourth hand, and of course it gets paler and paler as it comes along. John Stradwick kept a shop on Snow Hill; John Stradwick was the first deacon of one of the London Congregational churches; John Stradwick let a room or two above his shop, to lodgers; one of his lodgers was called John Bunyan; John Stradwick had a daughter and that daughter married Robert Bragge, and Robert Bragge was one of the pastors of this church! I like to think of one of my predecessors and his wife being with Bunyan in his last illness, and getting a grip of the tinker's hand now and then.

This is a long way to have fetched one's water, I admit; but when it is brought to me it is like water from the well of Bethlehem, and there is none like it! After all it is something to be in the tail of a kite if the kite be beautiful and a good flier. Even Boswell has become as one of the rings of Saturn. I should account it a fine thing if I could have an hour's talk with one of Shakespeare's servants, or spend a whole day with Luther's sexton. If I made right use of my time I should feel that I had been in high company and had touched the threshold of immortal fame. Now these are only the lower applications of a principle universal in its operation and influence, and which reaches its highest point in Christian fellowship. I can come to One in the touch of the hem of whose garment there is eternal virtue! Poor though we be and nameless, yet if we be in Christ Jesus, we come to an innumerable company of angels, to the general assembly and Church of the firstborn, and to the spirits of just men made perfect. Nothing in ourselves: we are yet kings and priests unto God! Our torch is lighted at the sun.

Some people have to wait a long time for their blessings. Sarah was ninety years old when Isaac was born. This thing itself is merely accidental, but the principle which is under it is living and beneficent. If we have the true life in our hearts, not one of us has yet seen his best days. Physically we may be on the wane; but spiritually we may win our greatest victories actually on the day of death. You have not yet got the best your brain can give. There is a finer wine in your heart than has yet been crushed out. Do not close the shutters, rather break out another window, for the light of the sun is yet plentiful. You may bring forth fruit in old age, and be fat and flourishing until the last. You have not got God's best. He keeps the good wine for by-and-by. I hear your sigh and your groan, and for every one of them you shall yet have a hymn or a loud psalm. Your great prayer shall be answered : the prayer that drags your heart out in passionate entreaty for the runaway boy, for the lost girl, for the healing of a wound in the spirit never spoken to mortal ear I Live in this hope, and this hope will keep you young. Sarah laughed at ninety, and made all her friends laugh in her late-come joy.

And now that Sarah is dead, Abraham came to mourn and to weep for her. But was not Abraham a man of faith ? Yes ; but he was a man of feeling too, and his piety did not make his heart hard. But was not Isaac his son alive ? Yes ; but a love ninety years old, and tested in many a sharp flame, was not to be given up lightly. It is a hard thing to part with those we have known longest and best. When such parting comes, " 'tis the survivor dies " ; memory is quickened into strange vividness ; the past life comes up and passes its days before the eyes in all their variety of colour and service. I hear Abraham talking to himself : " Oh, how sad is this loneliness ; how awful is the stillness of this silence ; I can talk to Isaac, but not as I did to his mother ; there are some eighty years of life that he knows nothing about ; Sarah and I wandered together, talked out our hearts to one another, planned and dreamed and suffered in one common experience, and there she lies a stranger amongst strangers, cold and silent for ever I" And Abraham wept I The man who slew the great kings, wept I The man whose name is to endure as long as the sun, wept I *Jesus* wept I Blessed will those of us be who have not to weep over neglect, harshness, bitterness ; over speeches that made the heart ache, over selfishness that hastened the very death we mourn I If you would have few tears by-and-by, be kind now ; if you would have a happy future, create a gracious present. Make your homes happy ; banish from the sacred enclosure of the family all meanness, hardness, suspicion, and unkindness ; that when the dark day comes, as come it will too soon, your deep and tender sorrow may not be mixed with the bitterness of self-reproach.

This is a sharp variety of experience for Abraham. In the last incident how brave he was, and what a kingliness dignified even the stoop of his sorrow as he went with Isaac to the altar I What is the difference between his case then and his case now ? It is the difference between *doing* God's will and *suffering* it. A

wonderful difference as we all know ! So long as we have something to do, something to call us from pensive meditation and set
us to hard strife, we bear up with hopeful courage ; but when the
strife ceases, and we are left alone with the wreck it has wrought,
we often express our emotion in tears which never came during
all the battle. Such an instance as this goes far towards proving
that Abraham's faith was as human as his sorrow. If we can
join him in grief, why not in faith ? If we thought him nearly
Divine on Moriah, we may see how human he is in Hebron. As
for ourselves, we can fight resolutely ; can we suffer patiently ?
We are heroes whilst the sound of the trumpet is maddening the
air ; what are we when laid up as wounded soldiers ? The patient,
uncomplaining sufferer, who for months or years has been waiting
for her Lord, without ever suggesting that his steps were tardy,
may have as strong a faith as Abraham had when he held the
knife over his son. All the world's faith is not historic. To-day
has its chronicles of trust and patience, and hope, quite as instructive and thrilling as those which are recorded in the Bible. It is
too early to read them through, or to comprehend all their sad,
yet glorious meaning ; but every syllable is accepted and honoured
of God. We often wish that we were as good as the holy men of
old ; it will be a poor thing, however, if we are not better than
the best man in any earlier dispensation. Among all that were
born of women there had not appeared a greater than John the
Baptist, yet the least in the kingdom of heaven was greater than
he. So may we be greater than Abraham, by reason of Jesus
Christ's promise that we should not only have life, but have it
" more abundantly." That some of the older generations might
have greater gifts is not denied ; but none of them had opportunities of having greater graces. They had special inspiration : we
have the general baptism of the Spirit ; they saw the unrisen
light, we see the sun in a cloudless zenith. My opinion is that
God never had better children upon the earth than he has at this
moment ; never was there such force of life, never such loyalty to
the kingdom of heaven. We do not, then, set forth Abraham as
a Divine model ; we call up his history to see its points common
with our own, to study the unchangeableness of God, and to take
an estimate of the development of human destiny.

Look at Abraham buying a grave ! True, he buys a field, and

a cave, and all the trees that were in the field, and in all the borders round about ; but, expand the list as we may, it was all for the sake of a place to bury his dead. The good man is forced into such commerce as well as the bad ; the best man of his age is here bargaining for burial ground. I need not remind a Christian congregation of the advantages which a good man enjoys under such circumstances. To him the place of Christian sepulchre is not a wilderness given over to the desolation of everlasting winter ; it is a garden, full of roots, that shall come up in infinite beauty in the summer that is yet to be. "Blessed be the God and Father of our Lord Jesus Christ, who hath abolished death, and hath brought life and immortality to light through the gospel." The law of mortality will operate until the close of this dispensation ; all lower life has been given over to death ; but death itself has been devoted by an unchangeable covenant to be destroyed by life. "The last enemy that shall be destroyed is death." Meanwhile we require graves. Our houses are overshadowed by a temporary destroyer ; we are smitten and impoverished by the angel of death. All this we know as a matter of fact ; in talking thus I trouble you with the tritest truisms ; but have we turned our knowledge to account ? Have we read the meaning of the shadow that lies along the whole path of life ? Have we so balanced our proportions as to give to each its honest due ? Have we not, on the contrary, forgotten our own mortality even in the very act of talking of other men's deaths ? What need there is then that we should see this transaction between Abraham and Ephron : listen to the words of the covenant, and ponder well that in return for four hundred shekels of silver Abraham gets a burying-place !

"From the stars of heaven, and the flowers of the earth,
From the pageant of power, and the voice of mirth,
From the mists of morn on the mountain's brow,
From childhood's song, and affection's vow,
From all save that o'er which the soul bears sway,
Breathes but one record,—Passing away ! "

The matter in which the children of Heth answered Abraham should attract the most appreciative notice : "Hear us, my lord : thou art a mighty prince among us : in the choice of our sepulchres bury thy dead ; none of us shall withhold from thee his sepulchre, but that thou mayest bury thy dead." How these incidental strokes of pathos attest the oneness of the human heart! Circumstances test the true quality of men. Irreverence in the presence of grief is an infallible sign of the deepest degeneracy: it marks the ultimate deterioration of the human heart. On the other hand, to be chastened by sorrow, to be moved into generous pity and helpfulness, is to show that there is still something in the man on which the kingdom of Jesus Christ may be built. Never despair of any man who is capable of generous impulses. Put no man down as incurably bad, who will share his one loaf with the hungry, or give shelter to a lost little one. Poor and crude may be his formal creed, very dim and pitifully inadequate his view of scholastic theology ; but there is a root in him which may be developed into much beauty and fruitfulness. For this reason, I cannot overlook the genial humanity and simple gracefulness of this act of the Hittites.

Man's final requirement of man is a grave. We may go down to the grave in one or two very different ways. Our grave may be respected, or it may be passed by as a dishonoured spot. We may live so as to be much missed, or we may live so as to leave the least possible vacancy. Whichever way it be, we should remember that there is no repentance in the grave, the dead man cannot obliterate the past.

Abraham mourned for Sarah. What then? Consecration to God's purposes does not eradicate our deep human love; say rather that it heightens, refines, sanctifies it! Every father is more a father in proportion as he loves and serves the great Father in heaven. We should be on our guard against any system of religion or philosophy that seeks to cool the fervour of natural and lawful love. It may be very majestic not to shed tears ; but it is most inhuman, most ungodly. We have heard of Abraham mourning, of David crying bitterly, of the Saviour allowing his feet to be washed with a sinner's tears, and of Jesus Christ weeping ; but who ever heard of the devil being broken down in pity or mournfulness? Christianity educates our humanity, not deadens it ; and when we are in tears it helps us to see through them nearly into heaven.

Gen. xxiv. 66.

"And the servant told Isaac all things that he had done."

REBEKAH: DOMESTIC LIFE.

INSTEAD of looking at the beautiful chapter before us as showing only how a wife was chosen for Isaac, look at it as a story full of family interest, and bright with many points of general human feeling. Of course the choice of a wife for Isaac is the one great fact in the chapter; but, without making its importance secondary, we may gather lessons about common household life which will touch a very large circle of sympathy and action.

The first figure is very touching: an old man, a wintry beard falling upon his breast, but a strange glow of fire in his eyes, which tells of life that winter cannot reach; a servant before him, God above him, and angels waiting! And the subject is the wedding of a son! Inconvenient jesting, or unseasonable laughter, there is none; there is a deep, solemn, hopeful joy; and even if there be a touch of melancholy about the picture, it is the sweet pensiveness without which rapture would be but a flippant and perishable delight.

We cannot but be deeply touched by the action of Abraham, "old, and well stricken in age." His eldest servant was a man who ruled over all that he had, and to this honest man Abraham said, "Thou shalt go unto my country, and to my kindred, and take a wife unto my son Isaac." A beautiful thing for a father to be interested in his son's wife! Not selfishly and meanly, not taking up an obstinate position and showing how ugly it is possible for an old man to be; but religiously, nobly, hopefully, with tender affection and genuine joy of heart. The good old Hebrews seemed to do all the ordinary work of life with such a broad and massive religiousness! They lived so thoroughly in the consciousness of all that was grand and prophetic in their history, that when they wanted to do any new thing they seemed to stop a great golden chariot by the road-side and to pick up the thing that was waiting there. See if this was not so in Abraham's case. Does he introduce the matter to his servant's attention in a light and gossiping way? Is he at all offhanded in his manner or tone? Far from it! Hear him: "The Lord God of heaven, which took me from my father's house, and from the land of my kindred, and which spake unto me, and that sware unto me, saying, Unto thy seed will I give this land; he shall send his angel before thee." How solemn the tone! The thing so well begun will surely be well done. We are apt to let our history slip away from us so fast, that, in facing the future, we have no inspiration of memory, no rock that took long in building, and never can be shaken down. It was so different with Abraham, Isaac, and Jacob! The first line and the last of their religious recollection were vivid in brilliance, and the very next thing they were going to do was taken up as a link belonging to a long golden chain, fashioned by the hand of God. The choice of a wife for Isaac was no casual incident; it was not something standing apart from the main line of his history, and something therefore which might be left to Isaac's unassisted thought and arrangement; it stood as a part of a promise; it was a clause in a solemn covenant; it was as sacred as prayer, and as joyous as a morning psalm. Why should we diminish our own sense of God's care in our life, by always regarding the patriarchal history as something never to be repeated—a miracle once for all, without counterpart in our life? God is *our* Father; our life is precious in his eyes; our family is part of the King's garden; and everything about us is dear to him. Get hold of that idea; store it in your hearts as a sacred faith, and you will know that the very hairs of your head are all numbered, and that the angels are with you as they were with Abraham.

The next picture disclosed in the scene is that of the angel and the servant. The angel went before and the servant followed after. And when he came unto Mesopotamia, unto the city of Nahor, the servant spake unto the Lord in prayer. Look at the preparation,—Abraham planning, the servant praying, the angel advancing, the camels kneeling down at the well, the presents all stored ready for distribution. It is like the preparation of a holy altar! This (if we were religious enough to give things their right names) is really what is happening in our own time. The angel of the Lord is still living, and he ministers variously and lovingly in human life. Of course we do not allude to him by name. We now talk of mental impressions, convictions, coincidences, inexplicable feelings, and divers impulses, but the angel we never name. This is a beautiful example of God's indirect way of working. Why does not the angel speak audibly to Rebekah ? Why should there be two servants, the winged one in the air, and the common one in charge of the camels ? It is by this double ministry that providences are confirmed ; the mental impression and the outward fact correspond ; the light of a new hope arises in the heart ; and at the same time the star appears to guide the way. All through life we see this principle of mediation, or double ministry, at work : in the conversion of men, in the determination of destiny, in things common, and in things unusual, —you find everywhere the invisible action of the Spirit, the imperfect action of human workers. You feel a strong impulse to do some good thing : it is the angel troubling with Divine energy the stagnation of your heart ; you are deeply impressed ; it is the finger of God writing his purpose on the soul. Look out, and you will find the opportunity and the service corresponding to your mental convictions or spiritual impulses : you will see, in fact, what you have dreamed in parable.

In this way you will see many curious coincidences in human life, things that are more easily explained upon religious than upon merely secular grounds. How you met certain persons, how they came to be at such a place at such a time, how you happened to drop a certain word or give a certain hint, why you should have gone just then and not at any other time ; these things, and a thousand others, will puzzle and bewilder you, on merely secular principles ; but if you believe in God, in his presence, care, and providence in human life, a great light will fall upon the whole outline of your history, and you will own with adoring wonder that God has been directing and stablishing you all your days. Life without a religious interpretation is a pitiful tragedy ; life with a religious interpretation may be a tortuous road ending in a quiet and blessed heaven.

Gen. xxv. 8.

"Then Abraham gave up the ghost, and died in a good old age, an old man, and full of years ; and was gathered to his people."

THE DEATH OF ABRAHAM.

NOW that he is gone we may be able to get a clear view of his whole character, and to see how one part looks in the light of another. It is almost impossible to be just to any living man who is doing a great work, because we see his imperfections, we are perhaps fretted by the manner in which he does it, and we are not quite sure that he may not even yet spoil it by a blunder or a crime. But when he has laid down his tools, and left his work for the last time, we may look quietly at the whole character, stretching clear through from youth to old age, and form a sound opinion of its quality and value.

Abraham is by far the greatest man we have met with in these studies, and his greatness is our difficulty, because we are apt to judge him by ourselves. That, indeed, is the difficulty of reading all the best biography ; we think what *we* should have done, and if the hero did not act just as we should have acted, it is very seldom that we give him credit. In some respects Abraham was the first great traveller in the world ; and his difficulty in travelling was the greater because he did not leave home to gratify any curiosity or whim of his own, but in obedience to a spiritual influence which bore him forward by a mighty impulse which he could hardly put into words. We should call a man who acts to-day as Abraham acted thousands of years ago, a fanatic ; we believe in a respectable and decorous Providence ; not in the God who drives us before the breath of a storm and makes us helpless under the spell of an irresistible inspiration. And we should doubt a man who acted like Abraham all the more because he did not get the very thing which he said God had promised to him before he left home. That would be fatal to any man's claim to having been directed of God nowadays. We judge the providence by the prize. If you *succeed*, then you have been Divinely guided ; if you *fail*, then you have either " not asked or else you have asked amiss." If you are invited from one church to another, as pastor, your wisdom in accepting the invitation

will be judged by the congregations you gather : if you fill the
pews and have to enlarge the building, people will say, "You
can have no doubt *now* that God sent you"; but if the hearers
be few and poor, the same people will tell you that you have
missed "your providential way." Judged by this standard of
miscalled success, Abraham's migration is the greatest blunder
in the pages of religious history. It was a failure. Canaan was
promised to him, and he never got a foot of it ! Surely, then, a
respectable and commercial piety may fairly call him a mistaken
man, an amiable enthusiast, a clairvoyant dreamer who mistook
a morning mist for a great estate. I wish, therefore, to learn
from Abraham's character the right way of judging Providence ;
to learn from a Jew how to be a Christian ! The rough and
ready way of stating this case is : Abraham went out from his
kindred and his father's house to get a land that God would show
him ; Abraham did not get that land, but actually " sojourned in
the land of promise as in a strange country," and was buried in
a grave which he had to buy ; it is clear, therefore, that he mistook a dream for a reality, a mirage for a landed property, and
he was punished for his selfish ambition. I fear that this notion
of God's providence is not unknown amongst ourselves ; that we
think nothing is heavenly but success ; and that it never enters
our minds that God's way may lie through the dreary region of
hunger and loss, pain and sorrow, weakness and death, and that
failure itself may be a sign of God's presence and care in our life.

Abraham's case shows that God may have fulfilled a promise
when he had apparently broken it ; and that God's promises are
not to be measured by the narrowness and poverty of the letter.
God promised Abraham and his seed a place or land called
Canaan, and yet Abraham and his seed never held the land ;
Abraham "sojourned in the land of promise, as in a strange
country, dwelling in the tabernacles with Isaac and Jacob, the
heirs with him of the same promise"; he had "none inheritance
in it, no, not so much as to set his foot on : yet God promised
that he would give it to him for a possession, and to his seed
after him, when as yet he had no child." Now, this brings us,
so to speak, into close quarters with God's providence, and
Abraham's character becomes a medium through which we
learn Divine lessons. *Abraham suffered for us.* It is beautiful

beyond expression to see how the true idea dawned upon the mind of the man of faith, that is to say, how he got from the letter to the spirit and saw God's meaning at last. When he came out of the land of the Chaldeans he had a very small notion of his future, but as he went on and on, from Charran, building his altar and pitching his tent, his eyes pierced beyond the little land of Canaan, and "he looked for a city which hath foundations, whose Builder and Maker is God." He could not have taken in the grandeur of that idea at first. It was too spiritual for him. He must have real land, real stones, real possessions of divers kinds, and by-and-by there would break upon his mind the higher light; these things would show their own worthlessness as mental supports and tonics, and he would let them slip out of his hands that he might become a citizen of "a better country, that is, an heavenly," "an inheritance incorruptible, and undefiled, and that fadeth not away," and the literal Canaan would cease to have a single charm for a man that had seen "the holy city, new Jerusalem, coming down from God out of heaven, prepared as a bride adorned for her husband." I beg you not to let this point slip, or you may "charge God foolishly": you may say, "God promises one thing and gives another, therefore he disappoints and distresses the believer of his promises,"—now, that is true as to the first part, and untrue as to the second, for it is in evidence in all the volumes of history and personal experience that God's way of fulfilling his promises always astonished with glad surprise the very persons who at first saw nothing but the letter, and grasped nothing but the common meaning of the word. God's promises are not broken, they are enlarged and glorified. The *receivers themselves* are satisfied, are overwhelmed with thankful amazement, and, instead of complaining that the letter has not been kept, they say, "He is able to do exceeding abundantly above all that we ask or think"; and so deep is this impression that they have said, and are saying every day, the things that are seen by the natural eyes are not worthy to be compared with the glories that shine on the eyes of the heart. Now this I hold to be the explanation of the difficulty arising from the supposed discrepancy between the promise and its fulfilment. It is fulfilled beyond all expectation. The answer is as a river which overflows the channel of the promise.

Your little boy is five years old : promise him that if he will learn such and such lessons he shall have the finest rocking-horse in the world when he is fifteen : I can easily imagine him seizing his lessons with great earnestness ; at five a rocking-horse seems the finest of prizes ; the child works, and reads, and learns (the figure of the rocking-horse still being before his imagination), but as five becomes seven, and seven grows into nine, and nine enlarges into twelve, and the mind strengthens and brightens by the very work which was to bring the prize, the rocking-horse goes down in value, until, at fifteen, the intelligent, well-trained, glad-hearted youth declines the very Canaan which he so eagerly started to win, and is almost insulted if you name to him the promised prize. Why does he decline it ? Because he has got something so much better : he has got information, culture, dis- cipline, habits of reading and observation, and these very things which he had no idea of getting when he started have actually wrought in him a proper contempt for the very prize that was promised.

So I see Abram starting from the land of the Chaldeans with a promise of getting another land. At first he thinks much about it. He wonders how long it is, and how wide, and how rich in wells and thick pastures, and many a long dream he has about the country far away ; travel tries him ; little disappointments trouble his daily life ; sorrow comes ; death overshadows him ; great judgments come down from heaven ; a solemnity grows upon his heart as he sees the seasons rise, flourish, and die, and life run its little round ; many a word God speaks to his heart ; he learns something of the greatness of manhood ; new possibilities disclose themselves ; unusual aspirations give a higher dignity to his prayers, and his soul almost unconsciously enters into new alliances and companionships, until at last he declares plainly, even in Canaan itself, that he seeks a country, a better country, a richer Canaan, an house not made with hands, eternal in the heavens. It is thus our manhood grows. "When I was a child, I thought as a child : but when I became a man, I put away childish things." I needed a *promise* suitable for a *child*; I sigh for a *fulfilment* worthy of a *man.*

When the young man started in business he probably set before his mind the idea of twenty years' service. a modest competence, and long years of leisure, a Canaan easily gained and easily held. As he went forward the very effort he was required to make evolved new opportunities, new habits, and new ambitions, until his first notion became ridiculous even to himself. Thus we are led on. First, that which is natural; afterward, that which is spiritual. To begin with we must have something to look at and to touch; by-and-by our better nature will be awakened, and spiritual meanings will be realised. "It doth not yet appear what we shall be" in spiritual elevation and desire; in our meaner selves we think that the earthly will be enough, but in our better moments we shall earnestly desire our house from heaven. The young lad whose pocket money is fourpence per month quite longs for the time when he will be called upon to pay the income-tax. He says he will be only too glad to pay the tax when he gets the income. In due time he obtains the income, but I listen in vain for any special gratification in the matter of the tax. The veteran servant who has received a gift of honour from his admirers, tells them that much as he values the silver and the gold, he prizes the love which gave them infinitely more. This is the same principle; it is the spiritual absorbing the material. The principle may be applied to heaven itself. The young Christian thinks of heaven as a magnificent collection of all the finest things he has ever heard of—of harps and trumpets, of gardens and fountains, of processions and banners, of crowns and thrones; as he grows in holy life he sees that something better must be meant; as he gets nearer and nearer the promised land he cares less and less for the magnificence which once satisfied him; and at the last he sees all the heaven he needs in being "for ever with the Lord."

These are beautiful words as showing one side of Abraham's character; "And his sons Isaac and Ishmael buried him in the cave of Machpelah." I am not aware that those names are thus united in any other transaction. Abraham never ceased to care for Ishmael, the son of the bondwoman, the wanderer; and Ishmael showed how he valued his father's care by thus uniting with Isaac in the last act of filial love. How true is it that sometimes relatives only meet one another at funerals! For years they may never speak to each other, but some cold, sad day they set out on a journey to one common grave. "Abraham

gave all that he had unto Isaac," yet Ishmael went to the funeral !
Isaac and Ishmael met over their father's dead body, and then
probably separated for ever.　Ishmael might have had hard feelings as he stood so near the bones of Sarah : thought of his mother
and of that day when she and he went forth into the wilderness.
Some recollections cut us very keenly, and even make us furious
with resentful anger.　It was surely not so with Ishmael.　The
wilderness had told well upon him.　He was not hardened by
hardship.　He was a giant and a true king, and his eye took in
wide sweeps of things, and thus helped his soul towards large and
noble judgments.

Abraham is our father, too, if we believe, for he is " the father
of the faithful."　If we blame him for aught of short-coming or
misdeed, we blame ourselves, for we are more to be reproached
than he.　Abraham lived in the twilight, we live in the full noon ;
Abraham stood alone, we are members of the general assembly
and Church of the first-born, with throngs of friends around us, and
blessed memories and inspirations.　Let us cultivate the pilgrim
spirit.　Let us " declare plainly that we seek a country."　Here
we have no continuing city, but we seek one to come.　Bind the
sandals, grasp the staff, tarry briefly everywhere, and though faint,
be evermore pursuing, content with nothing less than heaven.

Gen. xxvi. 17-33.

THE WELLS OF ISAAC.

IF you look at single verses of this chapter you might suppose
that Isaac was a very excellent man.　If you look at other
verses in the same chapter you will find that he was guilty of
express and abominable falsehood.　Is it not the same chapter
which records your life ?—mine ?　Our life is not one whole
chapter in a solid paragraph, to be read through as if it were but
one great sentence : our life-chapter is broken up into verses,
punctuated sometimes very strangely and surprisingly.　To pick
out a single verse from that chapter and say " That is the man "
might make us too good ; shall I add that to pick out another
kind of verse from the same chapter and to say " That is the man "
might perhaps hardly do justice to the roundness and the inner

most quality and meaning of our character ? Believe me we are
not quite so good as some little verse in our own life-chapter
would seem to imply, and you will believe me when I say that,
notwithstanding the blackness of some stinging verses—the
horrible blasphemy—we did not altogether mean it exactly as it
might be read by an elocution that was determined against us.
Blessed be Heaven ! it is not the business of any man to read my
life-chapter, nor my business to read any other man's life-chapter.
God will read all the writing—a wondrous Reader : skilled in all
the holy cunning of love which gets meanings and suggests
emphases, and reads up into accents quite out of the way of mere
scholarly reading and literary articulation. Jesus Christ has
given us an instance of his way of reading, and when he read the
chapter to the very people who were supposed to have dictated
it by their action, they said " Well, well." That will be so in
the last great reading. Comfort one another with these words.
Great meanings will come out of little actions, as great trees come
out of little bulbs. Spoken by the Lord, our life's speech will
expand into a noble eloquence, and throb with inexpressible meanings, and heaven will begin in the surprise with which we shall
listen to the testimony of him who is above our life. Never
exclude the other side of the picture. Let us be frank with ourselves. Some of our neglects may be turned into impeachments ;
some of our omissions may be charged upon us as high treason
against the law of love and trust and obligation. We do not
recognise them ; we have a way of over-leaping certain spaces
in the life, and of referring to some things in whispers ; but our
neglects may be the beginning of our hell. Suppose we are not
guilty of direct, overt, and nameable crimes,—we may be charged
with omissions—you ought to have done this beauteous deed of
charity ; you ought to have spoken that tender word of comfort ,
you ought to have visited such and such solitude and turned it into
sweet companionship. These are the things we make nothing of.
Because we are not guilty of murder, therefore we think we are
not guilty of heart-slaughter. God will read the life-chapter at
last, and in the reading of it he will divide the universe of
humanity into heaven and hell.

What a detestable man Isaac is when he tells lies to the king of the Philistines! Then he goes out well-hunting, as if he deserved to find water in the earth; and, secondly, calls the wells after the names which his father Abraham had given them. What contradictions we are!—telling lies to a living king, and sentimentally honouring a dead father. Mean man! has Isaac left any posterity upon the earth? Do we look upon him as an ancient character, or as a modern instance? We are doing the same thing ourselves in some form or way. What if in the very middle of our life there be just one great black lie, and lying outside two or three beautiful touches of sentiment—quite a skill in the drawing up of epitaphs, and quite a tearful and watery way of talking about old fathers and old associations? All these speeches make the lie the worse; when we see how little good we might be and might do, it aggravates the central evil of the life into overpowering and intolerable proportions. We never know how profane is the blasphemy until we catch ourselves in prayer. To think that the tongue blackened by that profanity could have also uttered that same prayer! Why, in the contrast is a new accusation and a fresh reproach. But let us follow Isaac in his well-digging. Man must have wells; man must go out of himself and pray to God in digging, if he will not pray in liturgy and uttered hymn and psalm in words. God lays his hand upon us at unexpected places: if we will not fall down upon our knees, we must still bend the proud back and dig in his earth in quest of water. At best we are dependants, seekers, always in quest of something which another hand alone can give us. Oh that men were wise! that in these true and inevitable providences we might see the beginning of inward and spiritual revelations, and that knowing the goodness of God in the gift of water and of bread, we might proceed to know that ineffable goodness which expressed itself in sacrificial and propitiatory blood. From the lower to the higher, I charge thee to go, or else thy reasoning is a base sophism and the beginning of an awful crime. Isaac's men are now in a little valley through which the summer torrent poured, and it is very dry, and they must seek water, and they dig and find the water of which they were in quest, and then the herdmen of the Philistines said, "The water is ours"; and Isaac called the well *Strife—Esek.* We have dug that well ourselves; you have dug it in your business. Do not suppose that men can find wells and be let alone. If Isaac's men had found nothing but dust, the men of Gerar would never have spoken to them. It is what you find that excites the surprise, the envy, the opposition of those who are not in sympathy with you. If you sometimes take that view of life, it may help you. If you had plunged your hand into the wild wind and plucked nothing out of it, your unkindest neighbour would not have spoken harshly about you ; he would have been rather pleased on the whole, and have treated himself to some new little luxury ; but when you bring back news of wells, and mines, and fruit-fields, and harvests plentiful and golden, and then have to enter into contest, do not look so much at the contention as at the prize : take the broader, brighter view of things, even the divine aspect of life's reality, and remember that all life is—after all, through all—a contest, a strife, a controversy, a sharp friction.

Isaac took the right course : he said, "Pass on and find another well." His men "digged another well," and the men of Gerar "strove for that also : and he called the name of it *Sitnah*"— *Hatred.* Who can bear two successes ? One might have been forgotten, but repetition is unpardonable. At first, mere strife, contradiction, contention of a worthy sort ; and then a settled frown, the awful disgust, the virulent detestation. To that pass may human feeling be driven ! Let us beware of it : it hinders prayer, it beclouds heaven, it dries up the beautiful well that springs in the middle of our own heart ; or it turns the crystal water rising from that human fountain into a kind of poison. Hatred and love cannot live in the same house. Hatred may seem to expend itself upon the outer object, but in reality it is hurting you more than it is hurting your victim ; it takes the angel out of you, it slays your very soul; it chokes the sweet song in your throat, and turns all the milk of human kindness into gall and bitterness. Hatred distorts the countenance into unbeautiful and hideous gnarls ; hatred takes out of the voice its frank trustfulness and sympathetic music ; hatred takes away the appetite, so that a man's bread becomes sour in his own mouth ; hatred gives the hand a wrong twist in writing letters of love and friendship, so that the readers can see between the lines indications of an unhappy and undivine condition of mind. Hatred does not expend itself upon the victim : it expends itself in the ruin of the soul of the man who hates. He who hates cannot pray; he who hates can offer no sacrifice upon God's altar that shall be accepted. If thou bring thy gift to the altar, and then rememberest that thou hatest thy brother and hast not forgiven him, or hast been unkind to him, run back, and when thou hast spoken the true and noble word to thy brother, return, and thy mouth shall be opened in prevailing prayer, and God will say Amen in the uptaking of thy sacrifice and placing it in heaven.

Isaac had a sweet nature, too : he was not turned sour by all this, as some of us might have been. The worst issue that these arrangements can produce is an issue of souring the mind of the sufferer, turning him away from social paths as a disappointed and wounded man. Brother, I would I could speak comfortingly to thee herein ! Surely, having dug two wells, and been driven away from both of them, there might be some excuse for a little pouting of the lip and hanging down of the head, and a groaning out of bitter words against men. Here I can but preach where I would gladly practise; but the right preaching would tell both you and me that, having been driven away from two wells, dug by our own industry, and secured, as we think, under God's blessing, by our own skill, we are not justified in complaining impiously; we ought to go straight on, and try to find another well. It is weary work. I do not like people to tell me in a jaunty and cheerful voice that I ought to carry my griefs and disappointments in an airy manner; I prefer the solemn tone that assures me that the grief is noted, is weighed, and is regarded as very serious ; but that, after all, the world is bigger than any part of it; the globe is larger than any section of its crust—the Lord reigneth, and perhaps I am only driven away from this place that I may find a larger; the disappointment which I now mourn may be the beginning of largess and fortune and benediction and heaven. I will up and go and dig again. Yes, that is the right preaching; and whoever alters his tone, the preacher must never alter his; whilst he stands in his pulpit, with God's book open before him, and the roof of the sanctuary over his head, he must speak the great word—ay, even though in speaking it he be pleading against himself, and convicting his practical life of a breach of every word he has spoken before the bar of God.

Our prayer must be right, whatever our life is; our speech must have in it the right tone and music, whatever our poor doing may be. It is our duty to lift up the life to the prayer, and the doing to the speech ; meantime, prayer to God and speech to man must be of the royalest kind, imperially pure, inexorable in righteousness, most tender in charity, most radiant in hopefulness.

The leade- being of sweet temper, the men went forward— " removed from thence and digged another well ; and for that the Philistines strove not." That is the way to wear out an enemy. Hatred does give in sometimes; black, hideous hatred, does sometimes exhaust itself. The Philistine herdmen strove no more, so Isaac said, " We will call this well *Rehoboth* "—*Room*, space to live in ; a place to stand upon. There is a place for every one of us, could we but find it; some have a long, long search in quest of the right place. Do not let us who stand in circumstances of comfort be the men to chide and sting such with reproaches; what have we that we have not received ? It is easy for men who are in great prosperity to sneer at poor strugglers, against whose faces every door is shut and locked and bolted; let us show our refinement by abstaining from vulgar criticism on the difficulties of other men ; let us show our gratitude by our sympathy, and let us prove our strength by the moderation of its exercise. The well you have found is God's gift : your beautiful home, your happy family, your prosperous business. You did not perhaps come to that estate of contentment and enjoyment all at once. Remember the first well you dug, and what a fight you had over it; the second, and how hatred turned you out of the place ; and, remembering your own difficulties, have pity upon the fruitless exertions of other men. That may be the beginning of piety ; to take a right view of such circumstances may be the dawn of prayer. I shall not despair of you if you have one kind, hopeful word for men who are still at the well of Strife, or at the fountain of Hatred.

After that another well was dug, and Isaac said, " We will call it *Sheba* "—an oath, a covenant : a settled and unchangeable blessing. So the course of life runs—Strife, Hatred, Room, striking of the hands in holy covenant. Happy is the consummation ; it is possible to us all under the providence of God. It is a surprising thing that we should have all this friction to pass through, if we look at some aspects of our character; but if we look at other aspects, it is surprising that we have so little discipline to encounter and to endure. Looking at certain aspects of our nature and position we say, "Is it not surprising that we should be called upon to endure all this?" Thus we mistake ourselves for ill-used men of piety. The right speech would be : "This comes of that lie I told the Philistines; God is hurting me now for that base falsehood; this is John the Baptist risen from the dead; this is God's ghost sent to make 'night hideous.' Thanks be unto God that the discipline is so little, so attempered, so adapted to my weakness. When I remember the great lie, the awful deed, the plucking of fruit from the interdicted tree, the treachery, and then think that I have only been driven from two wells, how good is God! I will join the house of Aaron, and say, His mercy endureth for ever." That is the view I would take of my own life-course, and therefore would exhort other men to follow the same method of judgment. We are not so deeply pious, so supremely holy, that God ought to spare us the prick of a pin, or the thrust of a thorn. Dwelling upon one side of our excellences, we might wonder that God should allow one touch of the goad to disturb us; then we are self-deceivers. I will reckon up the prayers I ought to have prayed but never spoke, the deeds I have done that I ought not to have accomplished; I will reckon up all neglects, all offences against God and man, all the weaknesses of my character; and, adding these up, the wonder is that God has not struck me through and through—not merely punctured me with a thorn here and there, but struck me with his seven lightnings, and utterly consumed me from the face of the earth. The trial has been severe, the disappointment has been acute; looked at from various standpoints we may have had too much to bear, but enclosing ourselves within the solemnity of God's holiness and our own deeds, we cannot but wonder that the men should have been men and not wolves that, springing from hidden places, might have devoured us because of our unrighteousness.

Then there is another and higher aspect. It is not necessary that a man's parents should have sinned that he should be born blind, nor is it necessary to find a crime in order to explain a suffering. This is the course of Jesus Christ himself. He came unto his own, and his own received him not; he came again, and he was despised and rejected of men ; he came again, and he is finding room ; he is coming again, and he will realise the oath that he shall have the heathen for his inheritance and the uttermost parts of the earth for a possession. He was made perfect through disappointment and cruelty and wrong, through injustice and suffering. Both sides of this question, therefore, must be carefully looked at, and each man must determine for himself in the secrecy of his own consciousness to which side he ought to look for comfort or for warning.

Speaking of wells, I like the word ; it is full of music, there is a plash in it as of the water which it represents. "With joy shall ye draw water out of the wells of salvation." "Whosoever drinketh of the water that I shall give him shall never thirst; but the water that I shall give him shall be in him a well of water springing up into everlasting life." O ye poor well-diggers, digging where there is no water, how long will ye turn your back upon the right way, and be as gods unto your little selves ? Why eat stones for bread ? Why dig where there is no stream to be found ? "Ho, every one that thirsteth, come ye to the waters, and he that hath no money." Whosoever will may come. We cannot explain these words : they are not to be treated exegetically, after the manner of analysis or vivisection ; but they cannot be uttered sympathetically without touching something in us that tells us we are not earth-born or time-imprisoned, but are made of God, and are meant for eternity.

Gen. xxvi. 34, 35.

"And Esau was forty years old when he took to wife Judith the daughter of Beeri the Hititte, and Bashemath the daughter of Elon the Hittite : which were a grief of mind unto Isaac and to Rebekah."

THE MARRIAGE OF ESAU.

THIS is not a personal matter, beginning and ending with Esau, Judith, Bashemath, Isaac and Rebekah : this is a little piece of the universal history—a line or two taken almost at random from the daily tragedy of social intercourse and experience. To think that a man's *age* is set down as an element in the moral reckoning of his life ! Esau was forty years old when he did this. A sin is aggravated, sometimes, by the age of the sinner. We excuse the young; we try to account for them; we assign a certain period of young life within which it seems to be —not right—but natural that certain seeds should be sown and that certain influences should come and go. If we can say regarding the accused one, " He was but eighteen "; " Certainly he was under twenty," we touch something in the human heart which answers the appeal on behalf of the young. We do not lower the standard of righteousness; we do not accommodate the terms of virtue so as to involve in any complacent manner or degree the actions of vice; yet far away back in the heart we say, " He was but a child, he will learn better; give him time, and all may yet come right." But Esau was forty years old when he did this. Some men learn nothing by age; they are only forty years old on the books of the registrar : they are no age at all in the books of wisdom. Forty years old ! Some men are patriarchs by that time, and other men have not begun to know that they are alive in a responsible state in society. Age is a variable term. You must find out the spiritual quality of a man before you can determine with moral precision what age he is, and almost the degree of responsibility that attaches to him. But do not excuse yourselves too easily. When you do the sin, think of the age; think of everything that can set forth the action in its most solemn and expressive meaning; think of the fine day, the insulted sunshine, the offended flowers, the summer blasphemed against; yea, if there is one thing you can think of that will show what the reality of the deed is, keep it steadily before the mind for the sake of its possibly restraining moral influence

Esau was forty years old when he took to wife Judith and Bashemath—and there the matter ended. No : matters do not end so. The next verse contains part of the consequence : " Which were a grief of mind unto Isaac and to Rebekah." You cannot shut up your sin within the four corners of your own life, or house, and say, " What matters it to anybody beyond ? " Sin has consequences. A motion made in the middle of the lake sends its palpitations to the shore. We do not think of this. You do not know sufficiently the effect of any unhappy, unwise,

or unrighteous thing you do. You did not see your mother put
her hand to her failing eyes to dry out the tears when she heard
that you had made that moral slip; when she met you the tears
had all gone, but there was a significant redness you might
have interpreted, if you had not already put out the eyes of your
own heart. Poor young fool! you have forgotten the old folks
at home; you are making the old man ill, you are doubling his
age, you are battering down his very last little pleasure ; and as
for your mother, you have taken a thousand lives out of her;
only a woman who is a mother could have survived the butchery.
Do not yield to the wicked sophism that what you do nobody
has anything to do with. We have a right to do with everything that is done. I have a right to stop any man who is cruelly
treating any beast upon the street that cannot defend itself. It
is my beast he strikes. We have the right of criticism in relation
to actions that touch the general human heart, that interfere with
the general moral temperature, and that involve the happiness
or unhappiness, perhaps, of countless generations. You cannot
do injury to yourself without in some way injuring the generation following. Actions are not solitary and uninfluential : they
have relations to other actions and to influences simply innumerable and incalculable. I passed to-day a poor ill-shapen thing
on the streets, and watched him as he hobbled his uneven way
down the road. Was he to blame for the misshapenness, the
deformity, the ungainliness ? What history was there in that
decrepitude !—a history stretching back twenty, fifty years and
more ; and there he—personally innocent thing—was carrying
the burden of life-long guilt on the part of his progenitors.
What a sacred thing is life ! What an unbuilt temple, so far as
hands are concerned. But how shapely, how visible, how
solemn to the eyes that can see it, and to the heart that can
respond to its inner meanings !

Thus should the preacher bring from every quarter, points,
circumstances, suggestions, facts, reflections, and possibilities
which can shape his argument into a powerful and tremendous
appeal which he shall lodge against the iniquity and the vileness
of his age.

A sin does not confine itself to one line of punishment. Esau
went against the law of his country and his people in marrying

Canaanitish women.   What was the punishment?   Endless,
ubiquitous, complete.   All heaven shuts itself against the violation
of heaven's law.   No star opens its door of light as if to guide
the evil-doer : every star, contrariwise, takes up arms for its
Creator, and denounces the doer of wrong.   Esau was, in the first
instance, alienated from his family.   His father and mother did
not want to see him as they used to do.   They were not going
openly to shut the door in his face, and say "You shall not come
within these doors any more."   The mother did not assume that
violent form, but assumed consequences far more pathetic and in
one sense far more terrible.   A grief of mind is far greater sorrow
than mere excitement of resentful temper.   The mother still
opened the door to the hunting son, but it did not go back with
the old swing ; the mother still looked upon that well-built, noble
form, but she wished that the interior of his nature had been in
this instance equal to the mould and fashion which nature had
bestowed upon his physical frame.   A wounded spirit who can
bear ?   This alienation is not a matter of arms, and revenge, and
bitter speeches, and reproaches, which ease the very heart that
launches them upon its object ; this was an instance of grief of
mind, sorrow of heart, a wounded spirit for which there is no
balm.

Esau committed an offence against organised society.   He took
the matter into his own hands, saying, " I know I am forbidden to
marry into Canaanitish families, but I will marry when I please,
where I please, how I please ; I am a man, and I will stand
upon my individual rights."   Take care how you accept that rea
soning !   What are individual rights ?   Who is the individual ?
Is it the solitary unit that bears the name of one individuality ? or
is it the social unit, the sum total, the great humanity ?   Tell me
one individual right.   Have I any right to blaspheme ? to assert
myself at the expense of the feelings of others ? to occupy more
space than is due to me ?   Have I a right to shut my eyes when
misery goes past my windows, that I may not see the bent and
tearful figure, or be moved by the spectacle of distress ?   Have I
a right to involve other people in my actions—to use their money,
to prostitute their influence, to trade upon their credit which has
never been given, to heap up riches to myself, without regarding
the cry of the poor and the helpless ?   There are no such rights.

Wrong can never be right; selfishness can never be right; the man whose policy is figured upon the surface of one world only can never be right. Right is a large term, a most comprehensive expression. Our actions should be weighed and measured as to their social influence upon those near at hand and those who have yet to come.

Esau was not only alienated from his family and a rebel against the laws of his organised society : Esau forfeited his hereditary rights. That is a point to which our attention may not have been sufficiently called. The law of his land was : To marry a Canaanitish woman is to lose your primogeniture. Where now your many tears for Esau, the fainting hunter, who was taken at a disadvantage by his supplanting brother? Esau supplanted himself. To marry thus was to drop out of the entail, to forfeit position, and to commit hereditary suicide. It was *then* that Esau sold his birthright. How we have felt for him as an injured man ! How often we have sentimentally said we prefer Esau to Jacob, the child of the mountains to the plain man dwelling in tents, the rough shaggy hunter to the hairless man who stayed at home ! It was too bad of Jacob to treat his brother so. Find out the roots and beginnings of things, and you will always discover that a man is his own supplanter : his own enemy. You will find far back—ten years ago, twenty, and more, yea, a quarter of a century—that a man did something which has been following him all the time. When the crises come that the public can look at, they pity him within the four corners of the visible crisis itself : they do not know how judgment has been tracking the man, watching him with pitiless, critical eye, waiting for its turn to come. We read over such little verses as these as though they were related to an ancient anecdote, and have really no immediate concern to the public of our own century. We come upon a second line, and say, "Poor Esau ! that was too bad !" Let us be just ! No man can injure you so much as you can injure yourself. If you have not injured yourself you may defy the world ; the world will come round to you in due time. Keep substantially right—that is, right in purpose, right in motive, right in the centre of the mind ; and slips and misadventures notwithstanding, God will have regard to the uppermost meaning of your life, and if you have been true to

him in the intent of your heart, the world cannot take your
birthright, cannot break your spiritual primogeniture. An awful
thing is this searching into the past. Long ago, in some unsuspected way, we sold our birthright. When we omitted, in
the first instance, our religious duty, the whole battle was lost;
when we shortened the prayer by two minutes, the birthright
was gone; when we haggled with the enemy, instead of smiting
him in the face with the lightning of God, our birthright passed
from us; when we first lost standing in our mother's heart we
slipped away from the hand of God. Verily, in such instances,
the mother and the God are very close to one another. When
the mother lets us go for moral reasons, I do not see how God
can help us. She has a firm grip upon us; she is inventive in
arguments on our behalf; she knows that we were not so much
sinners as sinned against; she says that if we had been in
another town we should not have misbehaved ourselves; she
says that if our lodgings had been more comfortable our morals
had been more complete; and, drying the very biggest, hottest
tear out of her eyes, she is quite sure that if we knew all about
it we should form a gentler judgment respecting the sin. When
she gives up her evangelical logic that has no logic in it, but only
one great outburst of motherly love, and says, "I cannot defend
him any more," I do not see that Omniscience can invent another
excuse. Many an Esau thinks himself an injured man, but
forgets that long ago he sowed the seed with his own hand which
he reaps to-day. There are not so many injured men, in the
sense of men who have been really maliciously used and un-
righteously wronged, as there might seem to be at the first blush
of things. Life is wonderfully complicated and intertangled : it
is not one thread or one straight line, but an infinite complexity,
and God only can disentangle it and set in order its component
and related parts. Long ago you broke a heart : do you suppose
that event will be without influence, if unrepented of, during the
remainder of your lifetime ? I believe in ghosts of that kind—
dropping poison into the wind ; swiftly changing the glasses—ay,
when we do but blink, the exchange is completed by a marvellous
magic. The air is full of ghosts. You refuse a benefit—your
bread shall choke you ! You treated a law as if you had a right
to trample it underfoot ; you set at defiance the God who ordained

it, and the men to whose trust it was committed—you cannot think to do such things and hear no more about them. "Be not deceived; God is not mocked: for whatsoever a man soweth, that shall he also reap." The law does not operate on one side only: it has its genial aspect and its happy outgoings. "Blessed are the merciful: for they shall obtain mercy." "With what measure ye mete, it shall be measured to you again." "Whosoever shall give to drink unto one of these little ones a cup of cold water only in the name of a disciple, verily I say unto you, he shall in no wise lose his reward" It is an impartial ordinance, a law with two sides moving with equalness of administration, of reward, and penalty, along all the lines of human life. Providence takes up our separate, and, apparently, unrelated acts, and makes a chain of them, and hangs it on the criminal in the sight of the universe; or Providence gathers up our separate and, apparently, unrelated acts, and finds heaven in them, saying to its own gracious heart, "Nothing but heaven can complete this process." "Come, ye blessed of my Father, inherit the kingdom prepared for you from the foundation of the world: for I was an hungred, and ye gave me meat: I was thirsty, and ye gave me drink: I was a stranger, and ye took me in: naked, and ye clothed me: I was sick, and ye visited me: I was in prison, and ye came unto me." When?— we do not know it: this is mistaken identity. "Verily I say unto you, Inasmuch as ye have done it unto one of the least of these my brethren, ye have done it unto me." So the law is no one-sided ministry: it is impartial; but from its hell there is no escape, and they who have endeavoured to obey the law will find that heaven is the prepared consummation for a life spent in the Spirit of the Lord. How awful, how dreadful is this place! this is none other than the house of God! The subject has been severe with me: it has cleft me in twain; but it is right; I was wrong when I pitied Esau sentimentally; I ought to have known the case before judging it, and as for the wounds and bruises we have suffered, they have a moral explanation.

Now, preacher, say some other word: we cannot break up thus, or we shall take out with us broken hearts. I will say this word —not my own: "If we confess our sins, he is faithful and just to forgive us our sins, and to cleanse us from all unrighteousness"

Can the blood of Christ act retrospectively, so as to take in all the black yesterdays? Every one of them. Is there any text that speaks upon this matter with a comprehensiveness all-inclusive? Yes. What is it? This is it: "The blood of Jesus Christ cleanseth us from all sin." "Behold the Lamb of God, which taketh away the sin of the world." Parting with that word, we part under fair skies and with the music of a benediction singing in our hearts.

Gen. xxvii.

THE DECEPTION OF ISAAC.

THE well-known story of the deception of Isaac has been so often misinterpreted, that it may be well to endeavour to get the key and meaning of the whole narrative. It has been made a puzzle to tender consciences and imperfect and uncertain minds—not an intellectual puzzle only, for mysteries of that kind are innumerable; but a moral difficulty, a great and most painful wonder as to how such things could be, if not actually sanctioned, yet tacitly permitted, by the Judge of all the earth, whose distinguishing characteristic it is, in the estimation of holy minds, that he will assuredly do right. Let us endeavour to master the case, and to see exactly what amount of difficulty there is about it, and to show that this difficulty seems to be a necessary quality and incident in the development of all human life. It is often forgotten that Jacob was divinely appointed to be the inheritor of the blessing. The omission from the calculation or thought of that one fact is likely to lead not only to mental perplexity but to moral confusion. You find the proof of the assertion in Genesis xxv. 23. The Lord said unto Rebekah, in view of the birth of her children, "The one people shall be stronger than the other people; and the elder shall serve the younger." The mystery, therefore, is Divine. The commentator cannot help us here; the light is too strong for his eyes. This is the mystery of to-day, in our own house, in our own consciousness, in the whole circle of our experience, observation, and knowledge. Read the solemn words again: "The one people shall be stronger than the other people   Is that only a forecast, or is it a sove-

reign appointment? **Is it an accident, or a** fiat? The mind
instantly says, Why should one people be stronger than any
other people? But there is the fact. Were there no Bible the
facts would still be there, plaguing the mind, challenging the
imagination, and tempting the moral nature. "And the elder
shall serve the younger." Why this inversion of all presumably
natural methods? But there is the fact. We might deny the
sovereignty in theory, but there it is in actual history—not the
history that stands centuries away from us, and by its very
distance in time becomes mythological; but the history of our
own little life and our own small household. We cannot explain
it. We see the mystery, and if we use it wrongly, it will but
add to the confusion of our life; if we accost it obeisantly, as we
might accost a visitant from the upper world, a tenderer solemnity
will cover our life, a holier influence will lift up our souls to a
bolder prayer. We shall do injustice to ourselves if we stumble
at such mysteries : in the meantime, when the day is nearly all
darkness, with just a glint of light here and there in the murky
gloom, we shall do well to stand still, wonder, and remit the case
to another occasion where we shall have more light and more
time. In all life there is a kind of groping after destiny—a dumb
consciousness that we are being called in this or that direction.
The voice says, "Samuel"! and we rise and go to our old friends
under the dream that they have called for us. Our old friends
were deep in sleep they knew not that a voice had fallen upon
our ears, even the voice from on high; so that they slept on in
peacefulness and in unconsciousness. A marvellous feeling is
this pressure towards a given direction. We may not want to go
in that special direction; but it seems to us as if we could not
resist the influence that is bearing us with gracious violence in
the line of a certain goal. We cannot calculate about it; we
cannot take paper and pen and ink, and set down and add up
reasons and bring them to the total of a logical conclusion. We
are in the Spirit, we are caught up by the Spirit in a moment,
in the twinkling of an eye : a trumpet has sounded and we are
up where the morning is born. We do not understand the
narrow and vulgar language of carnal reasoning and market-place
reckoning, and calculation and conjecture. This is a mystery we
must not omit from our view when we are looking out upon the

whole scheme of things; nor must we regard it as a mystery belonging to other people. It is the presence of God in our own soul. This operation of destiny is seen in animal life, even of the lowest kind. Animals are born to their destiny : the ram butts before his horns are visible; there is a scent in the nostril of the beast which stands to him in place of education and training; the eye is made for the kind of work it has to do in the day-time or in the night season. From the very earliest throb of life there is some intimation of destiny had we but keenness of mind enough to see it. So in morals—and there the mystery becomes a pain : it does seem as if some people were made to be bad. The commentator must here hold his peace; he can but feel the pressure of a great mystery and explain his feeling in imperfect terms. There is a difference of men in this respect. It is easier for some men to pray than for others to bow the knee in homage and look up to the heavens in expectation. We do not know what going to church costs some people in the way of pain and sacrifice of spirit. Others long for the church-day, the church bell, and the church door; they are filled with joy on Sabbath mornings because the sanctuary will be opened and music divine will make the very air glad; great revelations will be spoken by human tongues, and mighty prayers will make heaven's day brighter than the sun can make it; the whole time shall be a succession of festival hours, and the heart shall keep high jubilee, not knowing sin, or sorrow, or pain, or weakness, because of the absorption of the soul in God. What it costs another man even to stand up as if he were singing God's praises cannot be told. There is more devil in him than divinity; he does not want to pray; if you persuade him to church, you cannot tell what a conquest you have won. In all this we have no explanation. The Bible does not make these mysteries, it recognises them and treats them in the only possible, the only just and wise way.

We find also this groping after destiny along intellectual lines. You plan a course of life for your sons—say they are six in number—but you really are doing what you have no right to do. Your business is to find out the way in which the child should go : then train up the child in the way in which he should go, and when he is old he will not depart from it; there is something in destiny that confirms itself, something in consciousness and experience that says "This was the right way"; and the sunset shall be without a cloud. It is when parents seek to be the arbiters of their children's destiny that they set themselves up above God, and are therefore doomed to mortification and bitterness of soul. The Lord sends every life into this world for a point, a purpose, a destiny. Lord, what wilt thou have me to do? I will have no will but thine. What is the angel within me—painter, poet, merchant? Is mine to be a serving life, or a ruling one? Have I to give orders, or to obey them? Not my will, but thine be done. Then service is mastery, suffering is enjoyment, labour is rest.

Jacob was a destined man; Jacob was destined before he was born: what, then, was his error? Not in feeling, how mysteriously soever, the pressure of his destiny, but in *prematurely taking it into his own hands.* We must not force Providence. Is there not an appointed time to man upon the earth, in a much wider sense than in the sense of marking out the day of his death? Is there not a time for the rising of the sun and the going down of the same? Is there not a seed time in the year, as well as a harvest day? We are tempted to force Providence, thus to do the right thing in the wrong way, and at the wrong time. Right is not a question of a mere point; it gathers up into its mystery all the points of the case, so that it is not enough to be going in the right road; we must have come into that road through the right door, at the right hour, and by direct intervention and sanction of God.

It is tempting to natures like ours to help ourselves by trickery. We do like to meddle with God. Granted that the mother saw the religious aspect of this whole case, and knew the destiny of the boys, she had no right to force Divine Providence. "Isaac loved Esau because he did eat of his venison: but Rebekah loved Jacob." She knew not why. We cannot tell the genesis of our love; it is the mystery of being. What if she knew all the time, without being told in words—she could neither understand or explain—that Jacob would be the possessor of the first blessing? It is a difficult thing to have a secret entrusted to the soul, and yet not to tell that secret to others, or force its realisation by some little act of cunning and knavery. We may go to church at the wrong time, and in the wrong way, and in the wrong spirit. It is not enough to be in the sanctuary : we must be there in the spirit of the house ; then the roof will be heaven, and the walls rich as the jasper of the skies. A rough thinking says this or that is the right way, and that is enough ; a correct, profound thinking says, " It is not enough to be substantially right : not only must you have a destiny to realise; you must have also a process of destiny—a choice of equal value with destiny itself." Is not this an address to our innermost experience ? We will take things before the time. The vineyard is yours, every cluster of grapes is yours ; but do not touch one atom of fruit till the sun has wrought out his ripening ministry upon it. We may not touch even things that are our own until the right time comes. We know this in the field; we know it in many mercantile transactions ; but it seems impossible for us to carry up that knowledge into the highest religious applications. We cannot wait, because we are imperfect ; we cannot stand still, because we are impatient; and our impatience is but one phase of our ignorance.

There was an apparent justification of the action of Rebekah in the previous action of Esau already considered, namely : " Esau was forty years old when he took to wife Judith the daughter of Beeri the Hittite, and Bashemath the daughter of Elon the Hittite : which were a grief of mind unto Isaac and to Rebekah." The mystery of that act we have already considered, and it did seem to justify Rebekah in taking the administration of Providence partially into her own hands. We are not so pitiful of one another as God is pitiful of us. Rebekah would have Esau punished almost instantaneously because he had married out of the law. It is better to fall into the hands of God than into the hands of man. No doubt Esau had forfeited the primogeniture by this act of marrying the Canaanitish women ; no doubt he had become what the apostle centuries afterwards described as a "fornicator"; no doubt he had turned the stream of the blessing into wrong lineal channels; had there been no Divine sovereignty revealed even before that act he would by that act itself have forfeited his position in the family to which he belonged. How keen we are to make the faults of other people the reasons for excusing our own selfishness ! Was Rebekah moved by the consciousness of destiny, or was she excited by the spirit of revenge ? It is easy for us to mistake our revenge for religion. Some men *pray* out of spite ; some men preach Christ out of envy ; it is possible to build a church upon the devil's foundation, and to light an altar with the devil's fire. Whilst we have not spared Esau in our reading of his unlawful and unnatural marriages, we are bound now not to spare Rebekah in taking vengeance into her own hands. "Dearly beloved, avenge not yourselves, but rather give place unto wrath : for it is written, Vengeance is mine; I will repay, saith the Lord." But we like to handle judgment; the hand itches to bestow upon the evildoer some penalty or mark of discredit and degradation, on the plea that it is right to do so. What is right ? It is impossible for us to know in that sense what "right" is, because it covers a space the eye cannot take in, and involves relations which defy imagination. Right—it is God's word ; it is a word as large as God ; it is a word that involves the very being of God ; it is a term which shuts up God himself in a great necessity. What we have to do is to be patient, to be pitiful, to be kind one to another, tender-hearted, forgiving one another ; and when the pain is very keen—smarting like a sting of fire—and when the avenging weapon lies close at hand, and we feel that our arm has yet strength enough to inflict the deserved chastisement—it is then that we have to utter a prayer as from a cross : " Father, forgive them ; for they know not what they do " ! This is religion, the religion of Christ, the wine of the true heart and sacrament; this is the glorious Gospel of the blessed God. It is an awful thing to be a child of special destiny. It sets a man away from the common lines of things, and makes him the butt of every archer, the sport of every fool ; it brings upon him rapid judgments, sharp censures, biting criticisms ; he is unmanageable, impracticable, unintelligible ; he cannot be set in the straight line and current of things. Jacob was pre-eminently a destined child, a man with a special mark upon him : how he will come out of this we shall see ; but God will be King and Master, and right shall be done. What, then, is to be our attitude under the consciousness of destiny, and under the suggestion of tempting events ? Our attitude is to be one of perfect resignation. I do not mine own will ; the works that I do are not my works, they

are the works of him that sent me ; I am not creator but creature;
I am not musician but instrument—not my will, but God's will
be done. That being done, and being done in me and through
me, I am in heaven ; I am part of the great sum-total of things—
if not a pinnacle, yet a stone in the foundation ; if not a stone in
the front walls, yet a stone in the inner lining—part of the
temple, part of the holy building. God shall fix me where he
pleases; I will do nothing of myself; be my future kingly,
menial, triumphant, subservient, marked by a strength that
never tires, or by a weakness that can scarcely pronounce its
own name—it is nothing to me ; thy will, my God, be done. If
I can say this with the soul, night shall have no darkness, day no
cloud, death no sting, the grave no victory.

Gen. xxviii. 10-22.
THE DREAM OF JACOB.

ALTHOUGH Isaac lived sixty-three years after his deception,
the remainder of the book of Genesis is occupied mainly
with the history of Jacob and members of his family. It is
wonderful to mark how suddenly, and sometimes almost con-
temptuously, men are displaced in history, and especially how
some lives that opened in marvellousness pass away in commonplace or obscurity. So we cannot calculate the end from the
beginning; we cannot say, Given such a dawn and we shall
have such a sunset, in human life. God seems to govern to a
considerable degree by the element of surprise. Some suns we
never see but in their setting ; others are never seen after a
dazzling dawn, and others seem to shine all the day in cloudless
lustre. The disposal of human life is with the Lord. Whether
we rise or fall, whether we stand in the sun, like images to be
gazed upon by a universe, or perish in the dust under our feet,
the whole disposal of our life's lot and destiny is with the Lord.
If we could believe that, we should never be in dejected spirits,
we should never lose our strength through our want of faith.
Isaac was a passive, rather than an energetic character. He was
a despondent person. We thought he would have done otherwise ;
but that misjudgment upon our part is no discredit to Isaac. We

have forgotten that the Lord reigneth. Sometimes we have wondered how the Lord would remove certain characters from the panorama of history. Has he not performed many a miracle herein ? We have taxed our poor ingenuity to find methods by which certain men might disappear consistently with the harmony and music of things; and when we have failed, God has wrought out some miracle in providence which has astounded and yet completely satisfied us. We have seen the end and have been contented with it, as the soul is contented with a Divine revelation.

Now we begin with Jacob in earnest. He has, so far, escaped his brother's anger, which we thought to be just. Life is spared; but is the punishment evaded ? The supplanter has apparently succeeded, whereas he has but begun the discipline of purification and refinement ; he has gone at his mother's bidding ; but, instead of having escaped God, he has run more consciously and completely into his hands. Herein also is a mystery, black as a night cloud, and yet not without some wealth of stars in all its appalling gloom. Jacob had undertaken this journey on his mother's advice, with the narrow policy of allowing Esau's anger to subside. She was minimising Providence into a local incident ; she had undertaken too much. We cannot put our arms around the horizon ; we are under seven feet at the most. Rebekah little knew how large a door she was opening, when she bade her son good-bye. She opened the universe ! The supplanter has gone to meet Laban—he will meet the Lord before he meets Laban. God is waiting at the sleeping-place, and the revelation is already prepared. We require the darkness for the revelation of some things ; we do not see the stars whilst the sun is blinding us ; we speak flippantly of the day ; we forget the night.

How goes the great tale of inward experience and consciousness ? How beats the storm-music ?—or is it almost silence ? What is it ? Notice how large conceptions come in upon the man's mind. Here is, first of all, *larger space.* Jacob saw heaven. Enlargement of space has a wonderful influence upon mind and spirit of every degree and quality. Go abroad ; climb the hill, and leave your sorrow there. Take in the great revelation of space, and know that God's government is no local incident, or trifle which the human hand can take up and manage and dispose of. We perish in many an intellectual difficulty for want of room. Things are only big because they are near ; in themselves they are little if set up with the firmament domed above them, and numbered along with other things, which give proportion to all the elements which make up the circle of their influence. Why sayest thou, O Jacob, and speakest, O Israel, My way is hid from the Lord, and my judgment is passed over from my God? Lift up your eyes on high, and behold who hath created these things. You must bring your little flesh-wound against the mortal bruise of the universe ; you must set up your little, little cross against the infinite Cross of Christ. It is possible for a man to live so long in his own house, as to live downwards towards the point of extinction ; it is possible for a man to be so consumed with his own little business —for the greatest business of earth is but a noise and a spasm ; there is nothing in the most stupendous business that is worthy of more than one moment's consideration, though we are agitated lest we miss the final post—it is possible for a man so to live within his own business as to go down into narrowness of thought, despair of soul, utter littleness and vapidity and nothingness. Go into the field, pass over the ways of the seas, pray when the stars are all ablaze like altars that cannot be counted, and at which an infinite universe is offering its evening oblation ; take in more space, and many a difficulty which hampers and frets the mind will be thrown off, and manhood will take a bound forwards and upwards. Space is not emptiness ; space is a possible Church.

Enlarging space never goes alone ; it brings with it *enlarging life.* Jacob not only beheld heaven : he saw the angels coming down, going up—stirred by an urgent business. It is one thing to talk about the angels : it is another to see them. Blind bats ! we seldom see any angel ; mockers ! we are fond of laughing at others who think they do. Herein we need not be too literal. The music is possible of realisation without any debasement of the reason. The great, stimulating, solemn thought is this : that there is more than is visible to the naked and most wakeful eye. There ought to be : we have all friends lost enough to make a heaven. You can treat them in either of two ways : like dead dogs that leave no mark in the universe, no name in all creation's ample bound : or you can think of them as released persons, emancipated slaves singing songs, saints clothed in white raiment walking on hills of light, or flying or running on errands of mercy and love. Had there been no heaven of any kind without us, I repeat, we have lost enough of old companions to make a good strong heaven of. Let us not flippantly bid them good-bye, and think they have left nothing but a grave; amongst them are "The dead but sceptred monarchs who still rule our spirits from their urns." We must bear the reproach of believing in a heaven: we cannot consent to wither under the desolating negativism which deprives us of immortality.

Enlarging space brings enlarging life; enlarging life brings an *enlarging altar.* Jacob said, "Surely the Lord is in this place." We cannot enter into Jacob's meaning of that exclamation. He had been reared in the faith that God was to be worshipped in definite and specified localities. There were places at which Jacob would have been surprised if he had not seen manifestations of God. The point is, at the place where he did not expect anything he saw heaven; he saw some form or revelation of God. See how the greater truth dawns upon his opening mind, "Surely the Lord is in this place," and that is the very end of our spiritual education; to find God everywhere; never to open a rose-bud without finding God; never to see the days whitening the eastern sky without seeing the coming of the King's brightness; to feel that every place is praying ground; to renounce the idea of partial and official consecration, and stand in a universe every particle of which is blessed and consecrated by the presence of the infinite Creator. We have not yet attained this summit of education. We still draw a line between the Sabbath Day and the day that went before it; we have still a church and a market-place; still we vulgarly distribute the sum-total of things into Church and State. When God has wrought in us all the mystery of his grace, and reared us to the last fruition of wisdom possible below the skies, we shall know that there is no market-place, no State, no business, but one great Church; every speech holy and pure as prayer, every transaction a revelation of justice.

Immediately following these larger conceptions of things, we find a marvellous and instructive instance of the *absorbing power* of the *religious idea.* In Jacob's dream there was but one thought.

When we see God all other sights are extinguished. This is the beginning of conversion; this is essential to the reality of a new life. For a time the eye must be filled with a heavenly image; for a time the ear must be filled with a celestial message; a complete forgetfulness of everything past, and a new seizure and apprehension of the whole solemn future.

This is the very mystery and the very grace of regeneration. The mind is filled with God; all speech is resolved into one word —*God*, God, GOD. There will be reaction; there is menial work to be done, there are educative processes to be gone through and completed, and therefore the mind will throw off some measure of that complete absorption; but the influence of it will remain for ever. No man can go back from conversion; if he has gone back, he was never converted. When we forget some things, we forget or surrender the reason which makes us men. If we have been regarding regeneration as a mere emotion, a happy frame of mind, a time of gracious weeping, on account of vividly-remembered sin, I wonder not that we have gone back and walked no more with the sons of light. We mistook the occasion; we committed an error of judgment rather than a crime of will. When a man has once had his soul filled with God, he can never be a bad man again—slip he may a thousand times a day, but the seed of God abideth in him. From this sight Jacob begins a new life; he will often cheat and supplant, and scheme —that is in the man's queer blood—but he will die upwards, heavenwards. We must wait to see how he dies.

Wonderful is the effect of Divine communion. Take it in the case of Jacob. Jacob said he was *afraid*. We do not know the whole meaning of that word in such circumstances. Jacob said, "How dreadful is this place!" Circumstances are sometimes necessary to the definition of terms. What earthquakes shattered old policies and deceits we cannot tell; what idols of the heart were killed in that mighty awe we know not; what creeping things that defiled the soul were slain by the cold of that stony fear we cannot tell. "The fear of the Lord is the beginning of wisdom"—not the intellectual veneration which is sometimes mistaken for fear, but the moral obeisance of the whole man, feeling its littleness and seeing the infinite quality of God.

Jacob was also *humbled*. His expression is: "I knew it not

—I never suspected it; this is an enlargement of my imagination; this is a surprise of every faculty." We must be made to feel our ignorance before we can begin our knowledge. Jacob felt his smallness; Jacob cringed under the sharp bite of self-contempt. This is a necessary process in religious education. So long as there is one pulse of pride left, there is no conversion; so long as the right hand supposes it can do one good thing of itself apart from God, prayer is an impossibility; so long as the soul can say of the Ten Commandments "All these have I kept from my youth," it cannot enter the kingdom of heaven. It must have received a commandment that slays it with an utter and unsparing blow. The mighty must be brought down, the proud must be humbled, the supposedly wise must be uncrowned. "Ye must be born again."

What a beautiful moral sequence brings to a close the whole incident. "Jacob rose up early in the morning, and took the stone that he had put for his pillows, and set it up for a pillar, and poured oil upon the top of it. . . . And Jacob vowed a vow, saying, If God will . . . I will." The amended translation of Jacob's vow reads thus: "If Elohim will be with me, and will protect me on this journey that I go, and will give me bread to eat and clothing to wear, and if I come again in peace to my father's house, and Jehovah will be my Elohim, then this stone which I have set up as a pillar shall be Beth-Elohim; and of all that thou shalt give me I will surely pay thee tithes." We have all said so, and some of us have never fulfilled the vow. We rose up from the bed of sickness, and said, "Hence on, every pulse is God's, every breath a prayer." We have been delivered from danger, from poverty, from despair, and we have written our great vow, and have blasphemously forgotten every word of the covenant.

What has taken place in regard to the transaction with Esau? Everything; we are on the right course. First, be right with God. The time comes when there can be no amendment, no compromise, no arrangement with creditors, no compounding; no givings, takings, strange concessions, but when life becomes a religious agony and interview with God. Hence the two commands—which are one—" Thou shalt [first] love the Lord thy God; thou shalt [second] love thy neighbour as thyself." The second is impossible without the first. If you are at enmity with your fellow-creatures, you cannot settle it between you : both of you must first see God. Jacob saw him ; Esau beheld him ; and, when the men wept upon one another's neck, they realised, and manifested, and incarnated the love of God.

Gen. xxix.-xxxi.

IN THE SERVICE OF LABAN.

THE story occupied by Genesis xxix.-xxxi. represents one of the oft-recurring mysteries of human life. That is to say, in view of what has just taken place, that story seems to be an anti-climax, and is felt to be, in some serious sense, even a disappointment. It is almost impossible to bring the mind from the contemplations upon which it has just been fixed to read such an incident as that which spreads itself over these three chapters. When a man has seen angels, heaven, God : whatever he sees next must be poor and small, wanting in light and pale in colour. It is hardly just to some scenes to come to them from greater visions. By force of contrast they do not get the credit which is fairly due to their smaller dimensions and their simpler beauty. After all, in every sense, it is a long way from heaven to earth. We have first seen Jacob made solemn by a great fear, and ennobled by a surprising revelation ; now he has become as he was yesterday and the day before—one of ourselves. Yet this is the way through which we are divinely conducted all life through—sometimes on the mountain ; then swiftly driven down into lonely places; to-day in great rapture—almost in heaven —everything there but the body,—and to-morrow we shall be writing our names in the dust, eating the bread which stands for a moment between us and death, and be quite common men again. We tell of a great dream, saying what we have seen in the visions of the night, and presently we are sold off into Egyptian slavery; our faces burn when we commune with God upon the mountain-top, and presently we descend to be mocked by Aaron and Miriam ; now we are upon Tabor, the mount of transfiguration, where we would gladly build ; and behold presently we are sent down to heal the sorrow which is moaning at its base. It is so with Jacob now. After the fulness of light, the quiver of mysterious joy which is half fear, half hope, he must pick up the threads of life and work patiently like a drudge who has never been off the common way. This is so with us. The poetical balance of things would be disturbed when we read this history but for the confirmation of it which is supplied by our own daily experience ; we should say the contrast is too sudden, too violent ; only one hour has passed, and behold the great transformation has been wrought. As literary readers we would criticise the swiftness of the transition, and ask for more space, and a finer gradation of events ; but life is always contradicting criticism, for life will have its own strange way. God will not accept the pathways which we cut for his Providence ; he reigns, he is the One Sovereign ; there is no measure to be laid upon his scheme of things ; we must take its unfoldment as he sends it—always holding ourselves ready for gracious surprises, for new changes, for unexpected wonders and heavens. How wondrous the change here ! We, who have just been with Jacob in his dream, and have overheard his solemn words, now see him with staff in hand going on his journey, and coming into the land of the people of the east.

Jacob has left home as a *deceiver*—how will he be made to feel that ? In a very direct manner : Jacob himself will be deceived, as he had deceived his own father. There is no escape from that rule. Judgment cannot be avoided or evaded, eluded, bribed, or deprived of its terrific but righteous force and claim. Jacob goes out and is himself deceived : the only intelligible way by which he can be taught the wickedness of deceit. Yet how surprised we are when we are made the victims of our own policy. Jacob was amazed when he found that he had been deceived by his kinsfolk. His countenance was a picture ; his face was marked all over with signs of amazement that *he*, of all living creatures, should have been deceived. We do not like to be paid in our own coin ; it does not enter into our minds that we have to reap the produce which we have sown. Is it to be supposed that we can do just what we like, and hasten away from the consequences, or escape the penalty due to evil ? "Be sure your sin will find you out." What eyes it has ! what keenness of scent! what little need of rest or sleep! The sinner has but twelve hours in the day—judgment has twenty-four; it overtakes us in the dark. If we have been vainly thinking that we would sleep and the sin would sleep at the same time, we have miscalculated the operation of forces. Is not Jacob most human when he lifts up his pale, innocent face, and says, "What is this thou hast done unto me? did not I serve with thee for Rachel? wherefore then hast thou beguiled me?" How soon we forget our own selves. The mark of the supplanter was upon every feature of his face; he was a vagabond on the face of the earth; he had himself run away from the deception of his own father, and behold he says, "What is this thou hast done unto me?" Jacob turned into Daniel! The supplanter on the judicial seat! The beautiful innocence that never put on skins that his hands might be hairy asks Laban however it has come to pass that he, Jacob, of all guileless persons, should be deceived. We understand the mystery: it is part of our own daily life;—but how utterly surprising that any of *us* should be misled, that *we* should be robbed, that *we* should be unkindly treated. Is there not a cause? Can you rob others without in turn being robbed? Can you sow bad seed and reap good crops? Can you escape the solemn consequence of events which is now known amongst us and magnified under the holy name of Providence? Is there not a God that judgeth in the earth —a mysterious, unmeasurable, sometimes unnameable, Power that seizes us and says, "There is something due to you now"? Then comes the great stroke that almost severs us in twain; then the great blow that stuns us and lays us prostrate on the earth, or then the subtle craftiness that makes fools of us in the twilight, mocks us in the darkness, and leaves us helpless in the morning. We ask, What is this? Poor innocence, sweet guilelessness; how can it be that any Laban should have sunk to such a depth of wickedness as to practise an imposture upon *us*? How odd that *we* should have to suffer. How mysterious the ways of Providence. No: how mysterious the ways of *man* first. There is a mystery in us: that we, who were made to sing God's praise, and to hold converse with heaven in holy prayer, should have deceived the old, and the blind, and the helpless. *That* is the ineffable and eternal mystery. "Though hand join in hand, the wicked shall not be unpunished." "Whatsoever ye would that men should do to you, do ye even so to them." "With what judgment ye judge, ye shall be judged." "The Lord hath done unto me as I have done unto others." It is well; the balance of things is exquisitely kept. "Dearly beloved, avenge not yourselves, but rather give place unto wrath: for it is written, Vengeance is mine : I will repay, saith the Lord"—not to-day, or to-morrow, or here, or there according to your fixing and appointing: but God's word cannot be broken. Is this a shaft shot into the core of some hearts ? Is this an awful blow aimed at some self-righteousness? The Lord be blessed! There is a smiting that is followed by healing; there is a cry of contrition which may be followed by a hymn of praise.

Further pursuing the story, you will find that Jacob must be made to feel the strength and agony of natural instincts, and so enter into sympathy with his distressed father. The Lord will complete his educational work in Jacob ; the Lord will make him cry bitterly. We do not deceive our fathers for nothing. The Lord will not allow the old man's heart to be sawn asunder, as it were, by our cruelty, without making us feel some day what sorrow we have wrought. In the far-away land, Jacob speaks about "mine own place, and my country," saying, "Let me go back to them ; nor let me go alone : let me take with me my wives and my children." Thus God gets hold of us at a thousand points. God creates a great heart-hunger for the old country, the old homestead, the old folks we have left behind, the old associa- tions; and that hunger bites us, gives us mortal pain, and, through that hunger, we are sometimes led to pray. Jacob says, Let me take my wives and my children with me. He is begin- ning himself now to feel the mystery of the home-feeling. When he perpetrated the deed of supplanting, and accomplished the transfer of the blessing to himself, there was in the view of his selfishness but one man ; he seemed to have no one to consider but himself ; he could perform an evil deed and flee away without needing family counsel, or without rending family or paternal sensibility on his own part. Now the case is different : now Jacob has struck his social roots deep into the earth : now it is like taking up some well-planted tree to move him. Yet he says, "Let me go." God thus gets hold of us : he gets hold of us through our

little children, through our family interests, through our household
circle. We are nailed and bound down by uncontrollable instincts
and forces. Again and again these forces renew themselves. Why
does not Jacob go away alone? He cannot: there are some
murders which even Jacob cannot commit. How is it that even
men who can lie, deceive, cheat, rob, and do many wicked things,
always fall back from one particular crime which seems to
shock them and produce in their minds a feeling of unutterable
revulsion? This is the mystery of God. It is imaginatively hard
to break all the ten commandments at a stroke: who does not
leave just one that he cannot violate? and having left that one
which he himself cannot break, how the man wonders that any
other human creature can break that particular statute. He
prides himself that one is untouched, and has yet upon it the
bloom of its honour. In what various ways our hearts are
wrung. Could we see a map of all the ways by which men are
brought back again to God, we should be amazed at the intricacy,
and relations, and crossings of the innumerable lines ;—here they
coincide, there they sharply separate, again they seem to touch ;
across them run other lines in great surprises of movement, and
yet, by some mysterious action, all the lines converge upon the
abandoned house of the Father, the discarded altar of the Cross,
and all the various voices of life are one in the solemn pathos
of the confession and petition for pardon. This is the Lord's way.

As to the transactions between Jacob and Laban, they must
stand without explanation or defence. They amaze us. It would
seem impossible for some men to live other than a life of trickery,
scheming, and selfish policy. Did we not know it in ourselves, we
should resent it on the page of the biographer, or in the verses
of the poet. It is a mystery in the moral kingdom beyond all
other mysteries of a human kind that men can be perpetrating
deeds of evil, can be following policies of self-aggrandisement,
can be telling or acting lies, and yet all the time have a certain
broad line of religious feeling and aspiration drawing itself
through their divided and chaotic life. This is mystery. We
need not go into heaven to ask for wonders : we ourselves are
living problems; enigmas to which there is no present and
satisfactory reply. Jacob was still a swindler; Jacob still
divided his week into opportunities for promoting himself and

deceiving his mother's brother. Do not let us become special pleaders on Jacob's behalf. All I can say can be said under two divisions of thought. First, *God* spared Jacob : therefore I must not strike; God forbore him, had patience with him, saw something in him that no one else could see. Blessed be God! he is the same with us, or who could live one whole day upon the earth? Were he to mark one iniquity in a thousand, who could ever pray again? or lift up his head in hope? or feel upon his blanched face the warmth of the sun's bright smile? *God* sees in every Jacob more than Jacob sees in himself. Second : We may not really know the *whole* story. Who can tell all a man's life—every word, syllable, and tittle of it? We are all seen in phases, aspects, and partial manifestations, and the reports which are made of us partake very largely of the imperfection of the manifestations which we ourselves make to our fellow-creatures. We do not know all that Jacob did, or all that Laban did. We know in part; the part we do know we do not admire; but we must always fall back upon the circumstance that God spares, and therefore has a reason for the sparing. If the case were so narrow, and little, and puny, as we often make it—a criminal and a judge, a felony and destruction—why then the whole tragedy of life could be settled in a moment; but in the worst of us there is some faint sparkle of better things which God sees, —in the meanest of us there is a soul meant for heaven. Even the man who is basest, who has broken all the commandments, and has been almost sorry there were not more commandments to break,—has in him, in God's sight, some point on which, if not the Divine complacency, the Divine compassion may be fixed. His mercy endureth for ever ; his patience is greater than our transgression. Where sin aboundeth, grace doth much more abound—like a great billow of the sea rising, heightening, swelling into infiniteness of pathos. On these grounds, then, I rest, viz., the forbearance of God, therefore the possibility of features of a redeeming kind I do not see ; and, second, the incompleteness of my knowledge which, when completed, may enable me to judge otherwise. This will be the explanation of the rest of heaven ; this will be the mitigation of the judgment day—namely, that we shall then see things from God's own standpoint. We shall then see hell as God sees it ; we shall then know perfectly

according to the measure of our capacity; and whether the issue
be darkness outer and unspeakable, or light complete and ineffable, we shall say, " He hath done all things well."

How bold a book is the Bible. The Bible hides nothing of
shame; the Bible is not afraid of words which make the cheek
burn; the Bible conceals nothing of moral crippleness, infirmity,
or weakness, or evil. The Bible holds everything up in the light.
Recognise, at least, the fearless honesty of the book. This is not
a gallery of artistic figures; this is no gathering together of
dramatic characters—painted, arrayed, taught to perform their
part æsthetically, without fault and beyond criticism; these are
living men and women—when they pray, when they sin, when
they shout like a host of worshippers, and when they fall down
like a host of rebels, or flee like a host of cowards. The Bible
paints real characters. God says what is true about every one of
us. If there is shame in it, we must feel it : the wrong is ours,
not his. No other book could be so dauntless, could paint what
we call the defective side of human nature with so bold a hand
and yet claim to be the revelation of God. Things, however,
must always be looked at in their proper relation and in their
right perspective. You may bring some chapters of the Bible so
closely to your eyes as to be shocked by their revelations. You
say they are not to be read, they are not to be spoken of : they
are to be quickly hastened over. Or you yourself can rise by
the grace of God to such heroic righteousness as to be able to
look upon putrefaction, and blasphemy, and all wickedness, and
great hell itself, and name them all without a blush, or without a
shudder. Things are what they are in their right relation and
proper atmosphere.

So we return to our starting-point. Life is varied—sometimes
a dream all light, sometimes a vision of blue heavens; a great
cloudless day, or a night burning with innumerable stars—lamps
of an unseen sanctuary; sometimes a transfiguration, sometimes
a holy ecstasy, sometimes a vale of tears—a place of weeping, a
desert of sand, a sea all storm; sometimes extraordinary—all but
supernatural, without one trace of commonness or familiarity
upon it; and then servitude, sheep-tending, field-culture,—
monotony : rising in the morning, going the daily round, retiring at
night weary, eating the bread of industry, and sleeping the sleep

of honesty—a commonplace, dull, pendulum-life. So be it. It is not mine to choose my life : let me resign the disposal of the lot into the hand of God, saying, "Lord, if it be mine to dream on the way to Padan-aram, and to build a Bethel in unexpected places, blessed be thy name! Or if it be mine to be a common herdsman, a gatherer of sycamore fruit ; if it be mine to be a hewer of wood or a drawer of water, thy will be done ; if thou dost mean me to be a flying angel, thy will be done; if thou dost lay me upon a bed of suffering and say, 'By patience learn the mystery of my purpose,' thy will, my God, not mine be done." To say all this under such circumstances is to touch the very acme and sublimity of grace.

Gen. xxxvii. 19.

"And they said one to another, Behold, this dreamer cometh."

JOSEPH'S DREAM.

WE learn from this verse how prejudice shuts us up to one particular view of a man—the view which is most distasteful to us, and upon which we persuade ourselves, we can remark with the justice of injury and anger. Joseph was the child of his father's old age, the idol of the old man's heart, the light of the household,—and yet his brethren had got one view of him to which they could never close their eyes. He was nothing to them but a dreamer of unpalatable dreams, a seer of visions which more or less impaired their own dignity and clouded their own prospects. It is the same to-day. Envy never changes. Prejudice never modifies into a virtue. To-day we do not like the dreamers who have seen visions which involve us more or less in decay and inferiority. It is not easy to forgive a man who has dreamed an unpleasant dream concerning us. We cannot easily forgive a man who has founded an obnoxious institution. If a man has written a book which is distasteful to us, it is no matter, though he should do ten thousand acts which ought to excite our admiration and confirm our confidence ; we will go back and back upon the obnoxious publication, and whensoever that man's name is mentioned that book will always come up in

association with it. Is this right ? Ought we to be confined in
our view of human character to single points, and those points
always of a kind to excite unpleasant, indignant, perhaps vindictive, feelings ? The world's dreamers have never had an easy
lot. Do not let us imagine that Joseph was called to a very easy
and comfortable position when he was called to see the visions of
Providence in the time of his slumber. God speaks to men by
dream and by vision, by strange scene and unexpected sight,
and we who are prosaic groundlings are apt to imagine that those
men who live in transcendental regions, who are privileged
occasionally to see the invisible, have all the good fortune of life,
and we ourselves are but servants of dust and hirelings ill-paid.
No : the poets have their own pains, the dreamers have their
own peculiar sorrows. Men of double sight often have double
difficulties in life. Do not let us suppose that we are all true
dreamers. Let us distinguish between the nightmare of dyspepsia
and the dreams of inspiration. It is not because a man has had
a dream that he is to be hearkened unto. It is because the dream
is a Parable of Heaven that we ought to ask him to speak freely
and fully to us concerning his wondrous vision, that we may see
farther into the truth and beauty of God's way concerning man

"Come now therefore, and let us slay him, and cast him into some pit,
and we will say, Some evil beast hath devoured him : and we shall see
what will become of his dreams" (xxxvii. 20).

After this profound scheme no doubt there would follow a
chuckle of triumph. The thing was so lucky in its plan, in its
seasonableness, in its practicability ; it seemed to meet every
point of the case ; it made an end of the whole difficulty ; it
turned over a new leaf in the history of the family. Let us
understand that our plans are not good simply because they
happen to be easy. Let us understand that a policy is not
necessarily sound because it is necessarily final. In the case
before us we see both the power and weakness of men. Let us
slay,—there is the power ; and we will see what will become of
his dreams,—there is the weakness. You can slay the dreamer,
but you cannot touch the dream. You can poison the preacher,
but what power have you over his wonderful doctrine ? Can you
trace it ? Where are its footprints ? Ten or twelve men have
power to take one lad, seventeen years of age, to double him up,

and throw him, a dead carcase, into a pit. Wonderful power! What then? "And we will see what will become of his dreams." A word which perhaps was spoken in scorn or derision, or under a conviction that his dreams would go along with him. Still, underlying all the derision is the fact that, though the dreamer has been slain, the dream remains untouched. The principle applies very widely. You may disestablish an institution externally, politically, financially; but if the institution be founded upon truth, the Highest himself will establish her. If we suppose that by putting out our puny arms and clustering in eager crowds round the ark of God, we are the only defenders of the faith and conservers of the Church—then be it known unto us that our power is a limited ability, that God himself is the life, the strength, the defence, and the hope of his own kingdom. The principle, then, has a double application;—an application to those who would injure truth, and an application to those who would avail themselves of forbidden facilities to maintain the empire of God amongst men.

"And we will say, Some evil beast hath devoured him." It is convenient in life to have even a beast that you can lay the blame upon. Life would be to some of us very insipid if we could not blame somebody for every evil word we say, and every evil thing we do. "Some evil beast hath devoured him." We are unkind to beasts. No beast can be so bad as a bad man. There is no tiger in the forest that can be so savage as a pitiless mother. There is no wolf that ever came down upon a fold that can be so awful in passion, in malignity, and in evil deed, as a man who has lost self-control, and is carried away by his lawless passions.

"And Reuben said unto them, Shed no blood, but cast him into this pit that is in the wilderness, and lay no hand upon him : that he might rid him out of their hands, to deliver him to his father again" (xxxvii. 22).

We must not be harsh upon Reuben in this connection; although the Reubens of society are often difficult men to deal with. Instead of coming right to the front and speaking the decisive word, they avail themselves of some intermediate course, so that their very virtue becomes diluted into a kind of vice. When a man has not the courage of his convictions, his convictions may even become a temptation and a stumbling-block to society. Reuben's intention was good, and let all due credit be given to

every man who has a good intention : a merciful object in view.
No one of us has a word to say against such a man. But there
are times when everything depends upon tone, precision, definiteness, emphasis. I am not sure that Reuben could not have
turned the whole company. There are times when one man
can rule a thousand. A little one can put ten thousand to
flight. Why ? Because wickedness is weakness. There is more
craven-heartedness among bad men than ever you can find
among men who are soundly, livingly good. Is that a hard
message to some of you ? You know a very bold wicked
man. Well, so you do ; but that man is a coward. One day the
shaking of a feather will cause him to become pale, and to
tremble and turn round suspiciously, and timidly, as if every leaf
in the forest had an indictment against him, and all the elements
in the universe had conspired to destroy him.

Here is a call to us, most assuredly. We are placed in critical
circumstances. Sometimes eight or nine men upon a board of
directors have said that their plan will take this or that particular
course. We believe that the plan is corrupt ; we believe that it
is wicked ; displeasing to God, mischievous to man. What is our
duty under circumstances such as these ? To modify, to pare
away, to dilute sound principle and intense conviction, to speak
whisperingly, timidly, apologetically ? I think not. But to meet
the proposition with the definiteness of sound principle, and to be
in that minority which is in the long run omnipotent—the minority
of God. It is not easy to do this. Far be it from me to say
that if I had been in Reuben's place I should have taken a more
emphatic course. We are not called upon, in preaching God's
truth, to say what we should have done under such circumstances ;
but to put out that which is ideal, absolute, final, and then to
exhort one another, to endeavour, by God's tender, mighty grace,
to press towards its attainment.

"And they sat down to eat bread : and they lifted up their eyes and
looked, and, behold, a company of Ishmeelites came from Gilead with their
camels bearing spicery and balm and myrrh, going to carry it down to Egypt "
(xxxvii. 25).

There are times when circumstances seem to favour bad men.
Some of us are accustomed to teach that circumstances are the
voice of Divine Providence. There is a sense—a profound sense

in which that is perfectly true.   God speaks by combinations of
events, by the complications of history, by unexpected occurrences.
Most undoubtedly so.   We have marked this.   In many cases
we have seen their moral meaning, and have been attracted to
them as the cloudy pillar in the daytime and the fire by night.
At the same time there is another side to that doctrine.   Here in
the text we find circumstances evidently combining in favour of
the bad men who had agreed to part with their brother.   They
sat down to eat bread,—perfectly tranquil, social amongst themselves, a rough hospitality prevailing.   Just as they sat down to
enjoy themselves with their bread, they lifted up their eyes, and
at that very moment a company of Ishmaelites came from Gilead
with their camels.   What could be more providential ?   They
came in the very nick of time.   The brethren had not to go up
and down hawking their brother, knocking at door after door to
ask if anybody could take him off their hands ; but at the very
moment when the discussion was pending, and anxiety was at
white heat, circumstances so combined and converged as to point
out the way of Providence and the path of right.   Then we ought
to look at circumstances with a critical eye.   We ought first to
look at moral principles, and then at circumstances.   If the
morality is right, the eventuality may be taken as an element
worthy of consideration in the debate and strife of the hour.   But
if the principles at the very base are wrong, we are not to see
circumstances as Divine providences, but rather as casual ways
to the realisation of a nefarious intent.   Let us be still more
particular about this.   I do not deny that these Ishmaelites
came providentially at that identical moment.   I believe that the
Ishmaelites were sent by Almighty God at that very crisis, and
that they were intended by him to offer the solution of the
difficult problem.   But it is one thing for us to debase circumstances to our own use and convenience, and another to view
them from God's altitude and to accept them in God's spirit.

"And Judah said unto his brethren, What profit is it if we slay our
brother, and conceal his blood ?" (xxxvii. 26).

The very brightest and luckiest idea of all.   He touched human
nature to the very quick when he said, What profit is it ?   And
instantly they seemed to convict themselves of a kind of thick-

headedness, and said one to another, " Ah, to be sure; why, no profit at all. Here is an opportunity of selling him, and that will turn to the account of us all. Sell is as short a word as slay. Sell ! that will get clear of him. Let us sell. Sell ! we shall have no blood upon our hands. Then we shall, perhaps, have a couple of shekels a-piece, and throwing them up in the air an inch or so, and catching them again, hear their pleasant chink. This is the plan, to be sure. This is the way out of the difficulty. We are sorry we ever thought of shedding blood ; we shake ourselves from all such imputations. Let us sell the lad, and there will be an end of the difficulty." Selling does not always take a man out of difficulty. Bargain-making is not always satisfactory. There is a gain that is loss ; there is a loss that is gain. There is a separation that takes the hated object from our eyes, yet that object is an element in society and in life —working, penetrating, developing—and it will come back again upon us some day with greater power, with intensified poignancy ; and the man that was driven away from us a beggar and a slave may one day rise up in our path, terrible as an avenger, irresistible as a judgment of God. Well, his brethren were content. Men even say that they enjoy a very great peace, and therefore, if circumstances are tolerably favourable, they say that, on the whole, they feel in a good state of mind. Therefore they conclude that they have not been doing anything very wrong. Let us understand that vice may have a soporific effect upon the conscience and judgment ; that we may work ourselves into such a state of mind as to place ourselves under circumstances that are factitious, unsound in their moral bearing, however enjoyable may be their immediate influence upon the mind.

I am struck by this circumstance, in reading the account which is before me, namely, how possible it is to fall from a rough kind of vice, such as " Let us slay our brother,"·into a milder form of iniquity, such as " Let us sell our brother," and to think that we have now actually come into a state of virtue. That is to say, *selling* as contrasted with *slaying* seems so moderate and amiable a thing, as actually to amount to a kind of virtue. Am I understood upon this point ? We are not to compare one act with another and say, Comparatively speaking this act is good. Virtue is not a quantity to be compared. Virtue is a non-declinable

quantity. Comparing themselves thus they became wise. This
kind of comparison has given place to the proverb that there
is "honour among thieves." That is impossible. The thievish
man will have a thievish honour. It is true still, and will ever
remain true, that unless we can set our motives, purposes, intentions, in the full blaze of God's holiness, we shall become the
victims of phrases, and be deluded by appearances. We debase
circumstances into teachers of God's providences, which were
meant to be warnings, threatenings, and judgments. Against
comparative morality and comparative virtue, we are called upon
to protest. I know how easy it is, when some very startling
proposition has been before the mind, to accept a modified form
of the proposition, which in itself is morally corrupt; and yet
to imagine, by the very descent from the other point, that we
have come into a region of virtue. When men say, "Let us slay
our brother," there is a little shuddering in society. We don't
want to slay our brother. "Well, then," says an acute man,
"let us sell him." And, instantly, amiable Christian people say,
"Ay, ay, this is a very different thing; yes, let us sell him."
Observe, the morality is not changed, only the point in the scale
has been lowered. When God comes to judge he will not say,
Is this virtue and water? is this diluted vice? but, Is this
right? is this wrong? The standard of judgment will be the
holiness of God.

Now the brethren had to account for what they had done.
They had to make out a case, and case-making is a very difficult
business, where the morality is wrong. There is a good deal of
stuccoing and veneering, angling and patching, and stitching and
arranging to be done. We shall say some evil beast hath
devoured him, we will dip his coat in the blood of a goat and
say, Judge whether this be thy son's or no. Yes, men will
one day have to account for the things which make up their life.
"We will say,"—there is the point. Bad men have to argue
upon what they were going to say. Bad men could never afford
to be inconsistent and discrepant in their statements. Bad men
have to get together, and rub off corners, and rectify angles, and
agree upon methods of transition from this point to that point.
Twelve honest men have never to get together that they may

agree upon this statement and the next plan. They may go one after another and be judged alone, and each tell his own story. And when the twelve statements have been made, there will be little discrepancies, or points of inconsistency, yet all these admit of being wrought up into an impressive consistency, because the basis is true, and the intention of each witness is good. Forty or fifty bad men would never have written such a Bible as we have. It would have been a smoother Bible; there would not have been any apparent discrepancies and inconsistencies; it would have been an easy-flowing and consistent narrative. Observe, there is a consistency which is suspicious. There is a disagreement which is only the outcome of a healthy, loving, true, devout nature.

Gen. xxxix.

"And Joseph was brought down to Egypt; and Potiphar, an officer of Pharaoh, captain of the guard, an Egyptian, bought him of the hands of the Ishmeelites, which had brought him down thither" (ver. 1.).

JOSEPH'S CAPTIVITY.

UP to this time we hear next to nothing of what Joseph himself said or thought about the peculiar, the romantic, and the distressing circumstances under which he was placed. It occurs to me, however, to call attention to one observation of his, omitted in our last reading. You remember that Joseph had two remarkable dreams, in both of which his own prospective supremacy was broadly indicated. He dreamed that all other sheaves bowed down before his sheaf. He dreamed, also, that the sun and the moon and the eleven stars made obeisance to him; and yet, whilst these dreams were in his recollection, his father called to him and proposed that he should go to see whether it was well with his brethren and well with the flocks. When Jacob made this proposition, the prospectively great man, instantly, humbly, with filial simplicity and love, answered, "Here am I." There is a lesson, in this reply, to young men, who have dreams of future greatness,—who see sheaves falling down before their sheaf, and see the host of heaven making obeisance to them. Meanwhile, if you are children, obey your

parents in the Lord.   If you are servants, do the day's work, not
with the hireling's niggardliness, but with a servant's noble trust,
with self-expedniture, with an attention which commands confidence, and with a diligence that ought to merit reward.   It is
always a great pity when a man's' dreams destroy his strength
for practical work and his interest in the affairs that are round
about him.   No man can live healthily on dreams.   If the
dreamer be not superior to his dreams, in the meantime, then
he will become the victim of fancies ; he will be led about under
the enchantment of the most mocking delusions ; and he who
might, by humbly, patiently, and nobly waiting, have become a
great man, will subside into common-place, and leave no
recollection for which the world or his friends in particular will
thank him.

This is nearly all that we hear of Joseph's own speech.   Up to
this time he has been to a large extent silent.   In the verse
before us we hear nothing of his thoughts or of his speech.
How is this ?   The deepest things in life are never told.   When
men are in their greatest sorrows they are often also in the
deepest silence.   There are crises in life when we cannot speak,
—we are stunned, overwhelmed, dismayed.   We look almost
vacant to observers whose eyes are upon us.   They cannot
understand our speechlessness ; whilst they themselves are under
such great excitement, they wonder at our passivity.   There is
an excitement that is passive ; there is a passion that is latent ;
there is a vehemence of feeling which is often kept under
restraint.   Men misunderstand us because, in our sorest experiences, we do not exclaim aloud ; we do not protest against
the injury which is being inflicted upon us : we are led off in
silence, and we seem to justify those who injure us by want of
protest, and argument, and vehement denial of the justice which
is being accorded to us.   Learn that there is a sublimity of
silence.   There are two ways of enduring the wrongs of life.
An exclamatory, effusive, protesting style of endurance ; and a
silent, calm, dignified acceptance of trial, scourge, injury,
injustice, wrong.   The quiet man has suffering as well as the
stormy man ; and not always those who protest most loudly feel
most keenly the impression which the iron is making on their
souls.

"And the Lord was with Joseph, and he was a prosperous man; **and he was** in the house of his master the Egyptian" (xxxix. 2).

There are many ways in which the Lord is with a man. Not always by visible symbol; seldom by an external badge which we can see and read. God is with a man in the suggestion of thought; in the animation of high, noble, heavenly feeling; in the direction of his steps, in the inditement of his speech, enabling him to give the right love, the right answer at the right time under the right circumstances; giving him the schooling which he could never pay for; training him by methods and processes unknown in human schools, and not to be understood except by those who have passed under them. "If any man lack wisdom, let him ask of God." Ideas are the gifts of God, as well as wheat-fields, and vineyards, and other fruits of the earth. Suggestions in business, delivering thoughts in the time of extremity, silence when it is better than speech, speech when it will do more than silence. "This also cometh forth from the Lord of hosts, which is wonderful in counsel, and excellent in working." The Lord was with Joseph, and yet Joseph was under Potiphar. These are the contradictions and anomalies of life which ill-taught souls can never understand, and which become to them mysteries which torment their spirits and which distract their love. Undoubtedly this is an anomalous state of life: Joseph brought down to Egypt by his purchasers,—Joseph sold into the house of Potiphar,—bought and sold and exchanged like an article of merchandise. Yet, he was a prosperous man! Understand that there are difficulties which cannot impair prosperity, and that there is a prosperity which dominates over all external circumstances and vindicates its claim to be considered a Divine gift. Looking at this case through and through, one would say, it is hardly correct to assert that Joseph was a prosperous man, when he was to all intents and purposes in bondage, when he was the property of another, when not one hour of his time belonged to himself, when he was cut off from his father and from his brethren. Yet, it is distinctly stated that, notwithstanding these things, the Lord was with him and he was prosperous.

There must be a lesson here. When men live in their circumstances they never can be prosperous. When a man has to go out into his wheat-field to know whether there is going to be a good crop before he can really enjoy himself,—that man does not know what true joy is. When a man has to read out of a bank-book before he dare take one draught out of the goblet of happiness,—that man's thirst for joy will never be slaked. Man cannot live in wheat-fields, and bank-books, and things of the present world. If he cannot live within himself, in the very sanctuary and temple of God, then he is at the sport of every change of circumstance,—one shake of the telegraph wire may unsettle him, and the cloudy day may obscure his hopes, and darken what little soul he has left. If Joseph had lived in his external circumstances, he might have spent his days in tears and his nights in hopelessness; but, living a religious life, living with God, walking with God, identifying his very soul's life with God, then the dust had no sovereignty over him, external circumstances were under his feet. This is the solution of many of our difficulties. Given a man's relation to God, you have the key of his whole life. If that relation be disturbed, unequal, distracted, unsatisfactory, never bringing light and peace unto his heart and mind, then, whatsoever prosperity (so called) may attend his outward life, it is but a gilded coating which will be worn off by time, and which cannot stand the test of the greatest crises of life. Understand, then, how possible it is to be an exile, a slave: cut off from father, and mother, and home, and friendship, and yet to be a prosperous man. The man lies deeper than the slave. The Christian is, so to speak, higher than the man. He who has the bread of heaven to eat spends his life in the very banqueting-house of God.

"And his master saw that the Lord was with him, and that the Lord made all that he did to prosper in his hand" (xxxix. 3).

There is something about a religious man that is not to be found about any other man. Pagans can see whether God is with us. Heathens and idolatrous men have some notion of our religious position, our religious thinking, our religious relationships. Potiphar knew nothing about the true God, yet saw in this fair-faced youth something he had not seen before. Such is the mysterious working of the higher life in a man. How did Potiphar see that the Lord was with Joseph? Because Joseph made long religious speeches to him whenever he had a spare hour? It is not said so here. Because Joseph wrote out in illuminated characters a brilliant religious creed? hung it up in his chamber, or bound it round his forehead? It is not said so in the text. Potiphar saw that the Lord was with him because all that he did prospered. You can only get at some minds through external phenomena, through circumstances, through evidence that appeals to the senses. It was not through the deepest religious things that Potiphar came to understand that the Lord was with Joseph; but, reasoning from the outside to the interior, he came to the conclusion that, as a mysterious and unmingled prosperity attended everything this young man did, there was no solution for such a state of things but a religious one. This man is the Lord's servant, and the Lord's crown of approbation rests upon his honoured head. How far is it possible to be any man's servant, and yet to conceal from that man that we know the true God? A nice problem in casuistry! How long may a man be in the service of his employer, and his employer never have a conception that the man knows that there is so much as a God in the universe? Some of us have a very skilful way of concealing our religion. Perhaps you have been in the employment of your master seven years, and your master is surprised and startled to find that you are a member of a church, and that you take the Lord's Supper from time to time. Now, there ought to be ways of revealing the deepest life. We ought not to be all surface. There ought to be subtleties of expression, of movement, mysteries of conduct, which cannot be explained on any other ground than that we take our soul's law from the lips of the Eternal, and that we never do anything without first seeking the sanction and benediction of God. Oh, but some of us are exceedingly afraid of what we term "cant"! We can produce the evidences of our Christianity without saying a word. You cannot talk to some men without being the better, even for five minutes, in their company. It was said of one of our great English statesmen that you could not meet him under shelter during a rain-shower without being impressed with the fact that he was a remarkable man. We can understand that very well. There is influence in the expression of the countenance, in the glance of the eye, in the tone of the voice, in the little courtesies of life, in the small things which some men hold in contempt. Some men speak light. Some men bring with them the terribleness of judgment, when we are doing anything in their presence that is mean, sneaking, cowardly, or unworthy of manhood. We feel, when they get round about us, that they are like a flame—piercing, scorching at every point. Yet they never preach to us, they never lecture us, they never go over the points of their theology to us : still, it is as impossible to disbelieve their sincerity and nobility as it is to deny the shining of the sun at noonday.

Perhaps we ought to pause here to point out that prosperity of the kind to which Potiphar referred is not always granted to men in vindication of their Christian sincerity and filial relation to God. Sometimes our manner of bearing adversity is the seal of our sonship : our patience under failure, our magnanimity in the time of trial, our hopefulness and chastened cheerfulness when the east wind is blowing or the clouds are thick and threatening. This may testify that we have learned of God. It is enough, therefore, to lay down this doctrine broadly, thus : When a man loves the Lord, and his ways please the Lord, there will be some opportunity of showing the man is not all surface, but that he has a deep true Christian heart, that he is a child of God, a son of light.

"And it came to pass from the time that he had made him overseer in his house, and over all that he had, that the Lord blessed the Egyptian's house for Joseph's sake ; and the blessing of the Lord was upon all that he had in the house and in the field " (xxxix. 5).

One man blessed for the sake of another. Here is a great law, —here is a special lesson for many. A man looks at his property, and reasons that he must be good, and approved of God, otherwise he never could have so many blessings in his possession. It never enters the man's mind that he has every one of those blessings for the sake of another man. The master blessed because he has a good servant ! Would to God I could speak thunder-claps and lightnings to many thousands in our city and throughout all lands upon this very matter ! Here is a man for example, who never enters a place of worship. No, no,—not he. His wife is a member of the Church, and if ever she is five minutes late in on Sunday, his mighty lordship foams and fumes, and is not going to be put upon in this way, and have his household arrangements upset by these canting, fanatical, religious people. What shall I call him? The wretch owes every penny he has to his dishonoured praying wife. If that woman—the only angel in God's universe that cares for his soul—were to cease praying for him, God might rain fire and brimstone upon him and his dwelling-place. He does not know it. No! He is shrewd, cunning, wide-awake, has his eyes open, knows when the iron is hot, and when to strike it, and he is such a wonderful genius in business. A maniac—not knowing that it is his praying wife that saves him from ruin, meanwhile from hell!

Here is another man who thinks it manly to blaspheme, swear, and use profane language upon every opportunity, and to ridicule religion and religious people. And that man prospers! His fields are verdant in spring-time, his crops are rich and golden in autumn. If you speak a word to him about religion, he laughs at you, and intimates, in a not very roundabout manner, that you are a fool. And he owes all he has to a little invalid girl, who believes in God and prays to him, and connects the house with Heaven! God blesses one man for the sake of another. The husband is blessed because of the godliness of the wife. The parent is honoured because of the Christianity of the child. The strong man has prospered in his way because of the poor weak creature in his house, who is mighty in soul towards God and truth. Yet these are the elements and the facts which are so often overlooked, when men take stock and tell what they are worth. Ten men keep the brimstone-and-fire shower back. The righteous are the salt of the earth. The true, loving, and God-fearing are the light of the world. But for them, would God be patient with the world? What would it be to him, with his great power, to crush the little world, to pulverise and throw it away on the flying winds, and forget it? It is Paul that saves the vessel on the stormy sea. It is Joseph that blesses the house of Potiphar. It is the ten praying men that save the Sodoms of the earth from the lightning-showers of judgment.

And this is God's plan all through. There is one Man for whose sake all other men are blessed. This is the principle of mediation which runs through all the Divine government of man. "If any man sin, we have an Advocate with the Father." When we go to God with the story of our sin, and the cry of our penitence, we are heard, not for our own sake, but for the sake

of Jesus Christ. It is the same principle,—the principle of
interposition, the ministerial, mediatorial principle,—on which
he conducts his government of human society. Does any poor
guilty man want to talk to God? Here is the instruction for such
a man. It will be for Christ's sake that God will hear you. And
as long as Christ's name sanctifies and elevates your petitions you
may pray on. There is no prayer long that gushes from the heart,
and rises to God through the mediation of Christ.

After this Joseph had to encounter the great moral crisis of
his life. He has already passed over what I may term the social
crisis, the physical crisis. He has come out of that crisis calm,
strong, reliant upon God. And now the great temptation seizes
him,—is aimed at him, at least. Happily it cannot touch him.
What is his answer to the temptation? This. God! There is
no other true answer. When the tempter comes, when the en-
chantress stands there, what is the reply of the youth? God!
And he is more than conqueror. "How can I do this great
wickedness, and sin against God?" A man must go back upon
his religious principles when he is tempted; he must not try to
prove to the individual in question that it is inexpedient; he
must not quote the example of the man who has sinned before
him. He must take wing, and get away to God! And from the
height of God's throne he must answer the temptation, and, when
he does so, he will be more than conqueror. What are we, if we
have not struggled against evil,—if we have not proved our manhood, given to us of God, on the battle-field? You are tempted
to put forth your hand to steal; and ere you touch the forbidden
property, you thought of God and recoiled, and you are now the
stronger man for temptation overcome. There are temptations
in life—temptations at every turning of the street—temptations
in all the evolutions of daily circumstances—temptations that
come suddenly—temptations that come unexpectedly—temptations that come flatteringly. There is no true, all-conquering,
all-triumphant answer to the temptation of the devil but
this,—*God!* Be deep in your religion, have foundations that
are reliable, know your calling, and God will protect you when
the time of battle, and storm, and flood shall come. He will do
it, if so be we put our trust in him.

What is the cure for all that we have seen in the case of Joseph that is bad? For the envy of brothers, the malice of those who ought to be our saintly protectors from all evil-mindedness, from all worldly passion, from all selfishness, from all prejudice? What is the cure? The cure is crucifixion with the Son of God! Except we be crucified with Christ we shall have no hidden power. Except we know the fellowship of his sufferings we shall be foiled in the day of attack. There is one life that touches all other life beneficently, benignly, redeemingly,—that is the life of Jesus Christ. To those who need the exhortation, let me say :—Read that Life with an attention you have never bestowed upon it before, with special desire to know the meaning of that mysterious Life, and you will see that there is no point of human experience which it does not touch. Nothing has been forgotten, nothing overlooked. All sin, weakness, shame, fear, greatness, littleness—all man—has been comprehended within the scheme of that Life, and been redeemingly touched by the mighty power of the Son of God, who is also God the Son.

Gen. xxxix. 20.

"And Joseph's master took him, and put him into the prison, a place where the king's prisoners were bound : and he was there in the prison."

JOSEPH IN PRISON.

WE now know enough of the history of Joseph, to see that he had not done anything worthy of imprisonment and pain. Let us keep steadily in mind the fact that there are false accusations in human life. There is a tendency to believe charges against men, without patiently and carefully going into particulars, without making such moral inquest into them as ought alone to justify our belief in any charge that may be made against a human creature. We are prone to say, when an accusation is lodged against a man, "After all there must be something in it" We reason that it is impossible to get up a charge against a man without that charge having, at least, some foundation. We think it charitable to add, "That probably it is not quite so bad as it looks ; yet, after all, there must be *something* in it." Here is a case in which that doctrine does not hold true at all. There is nothing in this but infamy. May it not be so amongst ourselves, to-day? Has human nature changed? Are there not, to-day, tongues that lie, hearts that are inspired by spite? We are in danger, I think, of being very pathetic indeed over historical characters, and forgetting the claims of modern instances. There are people who will be exceedingly vehement in their pity for Joseph, who can say spiteful or unkind words about their neighbour who is labouring under an accusation quite as ground-less and quite as malicious as that which ended in the imprison-ment of Joseph. There are men who will preach eloquent sermons about the fall of the Apostle Peter, who will yet, in the most unchristian spirit, expel and anathematise brethren who have been overtaken in a fault. And the worst of it is, they are apt to think that they show their own righteousness by being very vehement against the shortcomings of other people.

Now, history is wasted upon us if we do but shed tears for the ill-used men of far-gone centuries. See how easy it is to do mischief! You insinuated against a certain man that there was something wrong in his case. You never can withdraw your insinuation. You lie against your fellow-creature, and then apologise. You cannot apologise for a lie! Your lie will go where your apology can never follow it. And men who heard both the lie and the apology will, with a cowardice that is un-pardonable, say, when occasion seems to warrant their doing so, that "they have heard that there was something or other about him, but they cannot tell exactly what it was." So mischief goes on from year to year, and a lie is, in the meantime, more powerful than the truth. It is always easier to do mischief than to do good. Let us, then, be careful about human reputation. The character is the man. It is better to believe all things, hope all things, endure all things, in the spirit of Christ's blessed charity, than to be very eager to point out even faults that do exist. There are men to-day who are suffering from accusations as false as the lie of Potiphar's wife. There are other men who have been sinned against by false accusations who have received withdrawments and apologies. But such, alas! is the state of so-called Christian charity, that, though we have a memory for the indictment, we have no recollection for what ought to have been a triumphant, all-inclusive, and all-delivering vindication. Terrible is the state of that man who has a good memory for insinuations, charges, innuendoes, and bad suggestions, but no recollection for things that are beautiful, and healing, and redeeming, and helpful. That man's destiny is to wither away.

"But the Lord was with Joseph, and showed him mercy, and gave him favour in the sight of the keeper of the prison" (xxxix. 21)

What a poor compensation! The man's character is taken away, and the Lord gives him favour in the sight of a jailer! There are honours in life which are aggravations. My name is blasted, my home is broken up, my whole life is withered right away down into the roots, and on either side there is a turnkey somewhere who says he has great confidence in me! Why not have vindicated the man before Potiphar? Why not have withered up the accuser who took away his dear fair name? That would have been compensation. If, when the woman's mouth had opened to tell the lie, God had locked her wicked jaw, that would have been vindication. Instead of that, Joseph has the wonderfully good luck of being thought well of by a jailer. This is the danger of our criticism. We mistake the process for the result. We rush at the semicolon as if it were a full stop. We judge God by the fraction, not by the integer. I am prepared to grant that if the whole scene had ended here—if this had really been the culminating point, the completion of the sad romance—the favour which Joseph received of his jailer would have been a mockery, and he might have thrown such favour back in the face of God, as a poor compensation for the injury which had gone like iron into his soul, for suffering which had destroyed his sleep, and turned his days into wintry nights.

The difficulty of the critic is to be patient. He is so anxious to make a point that he often ruins himself by his own sagacity. He jumps in upon the way of God with such impetuosity that he has to spend the remainder of his days in apologising for his rudeness, his want of patient saintly dignity in waiting until God himself said, "It is finished." Still, the point of the favour accorded to Joseph by the jailer ought not to be forgotten in making up our view of life, for this reason :—We shall redeem ourselves from much suffering, help ourselves towards a nobler, stronger, manlier endurance, by looking at the one bright point which remains in our life. Is there any life that has in it no speck of light? any day that has not in it one blue spot? What is the moral use and purpose of a glint of light and speck of blue? It is a reminder that there is still light; that the blue morning may come back again; and that God hath not—though the day be dark and cloudy and the wind be bitterly cold—forgotten to be gracious. Our honours may chafe us. We may reason from them that having so much, we ought to have more. What we require, when such impatience has reached us, is a devout, urgent desire that God will tame our impetuosity, and teach us the sweet mystery and the mighty power of child-like waiting.

"And it came to pass after these things, that the butler of the king of Egypt and his baker had offended their lord the king of Egypt. And Pharaoh was wroth against two of his officers, against the chief of the butlers, and against the chief of the bakers. And he put them in ward in the house of the captain of the guard, into the prison, the place where Joseph was bound" (xl. 1-3).

No man liveth unto himself. There is a little upset in the king's house, and, somehow or other, that will be linked with all these events that are happening a little way off. You run against a man in the dark; he remonstrates with you in a vexed tone, and, in that vexed tone, you hear the voice of your own long-lost brother. You go over the street without knowing what you have gone for, and you meet the destiny of your life. A child tells you its little dream, and that dream awakens a blessed memory which throws light upon some dark and frowning place in your life. Some people do not believe in dramas, not knowing that all life is an involved, ever-moving, ever-evolving drama. Life is a composition of forces. The chief butler gives Pharaoh the cup with a fly in it, and the chief baker spoils his baking. These things are to be added to some other things, and out of this combination there is to arise one of the most pathetic and beautiful incidents to be found in all the treasure-house of history. We do not know what is transpiring around us, and how we are to be linked on to collateral processes. There is a main line in our life; there are also little branch lines. You jostle against a man, and get into conversation with him, and learn from him

what you would have given gold for, had you known where it
was to be found. Everything in life has a meaning. Mistakes
have their meanings. Misunderstandings will often lead to the
h'ghest harmonies. No man can do without his fellow-men. It
is a very sad thing, indeed, that we have to be obliged, in any
sense, to a butler or a baker. But we cannot help it. It is no
good attempting to shake out of the sack the elements we do
not like. We cannot colonise ourselves in some fairy-land,
where we can have everything according to our pick and choice.
The labourer in the streets, the child in the gutter, the poor
suffering wretch in the garret,—all these, as well as kings and
priests, have to do with the grand up-making and mysterious
total of the thing we call human life. God is always coming down
to us through unlikely paths, meeting us unexpectedly, causing
bushes to flame and become temples of his presence. We go out
for our father's asses ; we may return crowned men. There are
some people who do not like religion because it is so mysterious,
not knowing that their own life is a constantly progressing
mystery. Whenever they would deliver themselves from the
presence of mystery, they must deliver themselves from their
very existence.

"And they dreamed a dream both of them, each man his dream in one
night, each man according to the interpretation of his dream, the butler and
the baker of the king of Egypt, which were bound in the prison " (xl. 5).

The chief butler told his dream to Joseph, and Joseph said unto
him, This is the interpretation of it. There are dreamers and
there are dream interpreters. There are men who live by their
ideas. Men who seem to be able to do nothing, and yet society
could not get on without them. You see fifty men building a
great house, and there is a man standing amongst them with his
hands idle, and a black coat on. You say the fifty men are building the house, and a lazy man is standing there with his hands in
his pockets, and your notion of political economy is that such men
ought to be put down. Put them down, and you will have no
more building. The man that is standing there, apparently
doing nothing, is the inspiration of the whole thing. Men in
the world—poor, poor men—who have nothing but ideas ! If
they were to sell bricks, they would eventually retire to detached
villas and tennis lawns. But, if they have nothing but ideas,

th.y retire into the workhouse. A man builds a bridge, and he is a great man; another man puts up a cathedral, and he, too, is a great man. I will not take away one iota from the just fame and honour of such men. We cannot do without them. We should be poor, if we had not such men amongst us. They are the glory of civilisation. But is it nothing to give a man an idea that shall change his life ? to tame the tiger-heart and make it gentle as a lamb's ? to put into man thoughts, and stir in him impulses, that shall heal him in his sorrows, chasten him in his joys, interpret to him the darkest problems of his life, and hold a light over his way when he passes into the wonderful dark Unknown ?

The preacher does not build stone cathedrals. But does he not build temples not made with hands ? He cannot say, "See in these mighty stoneworks what I have done"! But he may be able, through God's mighty grace, to say, "Look at that man : once he was the terror of his neighbourhood, the torment of his family, and now he is a strong, pure, kind man." Is that nothing ? Stoneworks will crumble ; time will eat up the pyramids. But this man, this soul, shall be a glorious unfading light when the world, and all the wondrous works upon it, shall be burned up. Be cheered, then, preacher of the gospel, teacher of the young, obscure one who can only work in the family, giving direction to young thought and young feeling, dropping into the opening heart seeds of Divine truth! Thou art doing a work which, though it cannot be valued by any human figures or by any arithmetic, is prized, and shall be rewarded, by God, who is not unrighteous to forget your work of faith and your labour of love.

Life is a dream, a riddle, a mystery, a difficult problem. But there is one Interpreter. What is his name ? Where can he be found ? His name is Jesus Christ, and he can be found wherever there is a heart that wants him. You have a dream—you cannot call it by any other name—about sin. You know there is something wrong somewhere. You cannot explain it ; you cannot set it down in order, proposition after proposition. It is as unsubstantial as a dream and impalpable as a vision. Yet it haunts you, and you want to know more about it. Christ is the Interpreter, and he alone can explain what sin is : show it in its reality,

and give the soul to feel how terrible a thing it is. You have
dreams about truth. Sometimes you see an image that you think
is the very angel of truth herself. Sometimes that angel comes
quite near you, and you are almost on the point of laying your
hand on the glittering vision. You cannot quite do so. It leaves
you, escapes you, mocks you ! Jesus Christ is the Interpreter of
that dream. He knows truth, he reveals truth, he sanctifies man
by truth, he enriches the human mind with truth, and he alone
has the truth. Why? Because he *is* the truth. It is one thing to
have a truth. It is then a possession, something to be pointed
out and described. It is another thing to *be* the truth. Christ
himself had not the truth in our poor sense of the term, for he
was the truth. He did not so much preach the gospel as *be* the
gospel. You are conscious of glimmerings of objects : dreamings
about better states of things. You have a moral nature that now
and again gives you hints about right and wrong, and truth and
falsehood. You have an imagination that will go out beyond the
present and the visible. Are you content to be tormented and
mocked by these dreamings, half visions, spectral revelations, and
tempting fancies ? Why not take them all up to the Son of God,
and say, " We have dreamed this ! We cannot make anything of
its harmonies,—anything truly beautiful. Yet we think it ought
to be made into something beautiful, because look what glittering
pieces there are here—what wondrous shapes, what marvellous
adaptations we think there are to be found amongst these
pieces." If you go up to him so, he, more readily than ever Joseph
or Daniel did, will show you the interpretation of the dream,
and will bless you with revelations of what is in yourself, as
well as what is in God.

You cannot get on without the interpreter of dreams, without
the man of thought, without the inspired teacher, without the profound interpreter of God. I know very well that when you get
among your day books and dust of various kinds, you are
apt to think you can do without ideas, imaginings, and dreams,
and mere thinking. But there are times in your life when you
begin to feel that without thought, idea, impulse, emotion, life
would be but a mockery, and death itself would be the welcomest
guest that ever crossed your threshold. Ho ! every one that
desires to know the highest thought, and the highest feeling in

the universe,—this can be found only in the book of God and in communion with the Holy Ghost.

"But think on me when it shall be well with thee, and shew kindness, I pray thee, unto me, and make mention of me unto Pharaoh, and bring me out of this house" (xl. 14).

The first touch of humanity we have seen in Joseph : human nature is in this little plea. He would have been far too great a man, if I had not seen this little trace of human nature coming out after all. I have wondered, as I have read along here, that he did not protest and resent, and vindicate himself, and otherwise come out as an injured man. He has been almost superhuman up to this point. Now the poor lad says, " The chain is very heavy, this yoke makes me chafe. I cannot bear this any longer." And he tells the butler, who has good luck before him, that he would like to be taken out of the dungeon. There are times when we want to find a god even in the butler ; times when our theism is too great for us, and we want to get hold of a man,— when our religion seems to us to be too aërial, afar off, and we would be glad to take hold of any staff that anybody could put into our poor trembling hands. This is natural, and I am not about to denounce Joseph, nor to reproach him, as though he had done some unnatural and unreasonable thing. I am glad of this revelation of his nature ; it brings me near to him. Though God will not substitute himself by a butler,—but will give Joseph two more years' imprisonment,—yet God will make it up to him somehow. He shall not want consolation. It was very human to seek to make a half-god of the butler to get out of that galling bondage. We shall see, in the course of our reading, whether God be not mightier than all creatures, and whether he cannot open a way to kingdoms and royalties, when we ourselves are striving only for some little, insignificant, and unworthy blessing.

After this the baker told his dream. He was a long-headed man. He waited to hear how the case would go with the butler, and when he heard all that the butler could know about his vision, he went and told his dream, and Joseph told him, "Within three days thou shalt be hanged." The interpreter of dreams must not always tell good news. The interpreter must not tell people's fortunes according to his own ideas. He must do as Joseph did. He must say, "Interpretations are with God. I am but the medium on which the Infinite Silence breaks into language. It is not in me to tell the meaning of the mystery. It is in God, and with God alone." This is a lesson for preachers of the gospel. It would be a joyous thing to say to every man, " You are right; you are on the road to glory; nothing can stand between you and heaven." That would be a very gracious thing to say. But if I fail to warn the ungodly man, to tell him that God is angry with the wicked every day, and yet that God has no pleasure in the death of the wicked,—that the Son of God has died for the sins of the world,— that there is no man too vile to be received and to be redeemed by the Great Sacrifice,—then shall I fail in my mission, and my word of joy for a moment shall be a mockery and a cruel thing, and your pale and reproachful countenance, on the last day turned upon me, would be an everlasting punishment. No, we must be faithful. There are interpretations that are favourable and helpful; there are interpretations that mean ruin, punishment, death.

May God make his servants faithful, that they may speak the cheering, the life-cheering word ; and that they may speak the terrible word with self-restraint and with heart-breaking pathos, that men may begin to feel that there is something in the message that ought to make the heart quake, and turn their minds to devout consideration. To every man's dream, and thinking and scheming about life there is an answer in One alone, and that One is Jesus Christ, son of Mary, Son of God, God the Son, Emmanuel, God with us ! He never refuses to have long, long talk, either by night or day, with the man who goes to him tremblingly, devoutly, penitently. Try if this be not so.

Gen. xli. 1.

"And it came to pass at the end of two full years, that Pharaoh dreamed; and, behold, he stood by the river."

PHARAOH'S DREAM.

SHOWING how soon men are led into mystery,—how thin, how flimsy is the veil which separates dust, and visibility, and ordinary things, from the spiritual, the invisible, and, in some senses, the terrible. There is mystery all around us, and ever and anon God gives us a peep into that mystery, that he may tame our impetuosity and call us to considerateness and devoutness. Pharaoh was a mighty man in his day, and yet a dream was too much for his power of interpretation. He had a dream, and it mocked him. He saw strange visions, and they said nothing to him which he could render into intelligible speech. Understand that just before us there is a power of mystery and concealment, a mockery and torment which can unsettle the strongest man amongst us,—can frighten us, and make poor, timorous, trembling creatures of the very sturdiest of us. This shows also the weakness of the greatest men. Pharaoh was king, but kings are not always interpreters. It would not do for one man to be every man. Men would forget themselves if they had at their girdles the keys of all locks. It is enough for some of us to dream, and to be puzzled by our dreams and visions. It would be too much for us if we were our own soothsayers, prognosticators, interpreters, and reconcilers. Every man needs the help of some other man.

Pharaoh is mighty, yet Pharaoh is puzzled by his own dreams. The prime minister for the time being is an influential man, but he might not be able to clean his own watch. The great general and warrior of the day has a renown peculiarly his own, but it might be inconvenient for him to get his own coals in. There is a meaning in these things. A man, though he be a king, wants an interpreter now and then to break into common speech the strange and terrible language which he has heard in the silence of the night-time. So the greatest, proudest man amongst us has, ever and anon, to call in the aid of some apparently little contemptible creature who has nothing but hands, or nothing but physical faculties. Let us learn from this our mutual interdependence, the Divine idea of unionism and reciprocity. We need one another. There is no man in the world, how brilliant soever his genius, how mighty soever his gifts, who does not need the humblest and the poorest creature to make up to him something that is wanting to complete the complement and sphere of his power.

"And it came to pass in the morning that his spirit was troubled " (xli. 8).

Showing us the discipline, the instructiveness, which may come out of the Unknown. If life were altogether a known quantity, we should forget ourselves. God recalls us, steadies us, gives us thoughtfulness, considerateness, by reminding us, now and again, that the greatest part of our being is an unknown quantity. Pharaoh was troubled. Why? Because some little rival had lifted his puny fist against his throne? He could have crushed such rivalry almost by a word. Why was the king of Egypt troubled? Because of an *unknown* factor; because of the elements he could not see all round about; because of something that glanced at him and then shut its eyes again swiftly; something that touched him on the shoulder and fled away. It is the same with us. God rules us often by the fear of the unknown. You saw a flash of light in your bedroom last night, after you had retired to rest, and that troubled you, shook you; you had to inquire of others in the morning to know what it was. Great man! poor insect! You thought you heard a voice, and yet there was nobody to be seen, and that chilled your marrow,—you drop your pen and run out into the busy streets, that you may retone your nerves. Ha! so it ever was with you. You could not rest because there was an unexpected glance of light in your room. You thought somebody touched you, and when you looked behind there was no one to be seen. You had a dream which shook your whole nervous system, agitated, disturbed you, made you unquiet and sad. Why? be a man! What was it? A shadow, an impalpability, a dream! You are a man, with your head upon your shoulders, your eyes in your head, with hands and feet, and completeness of physical constitution. Why should you be startled, chilled, afraid, by something that is mysterious, intangible, invisible? Be a man. But you cannot. There is God's power over you. He can frighten you by a dream; he can startle you, confound you, by an unexpected event or combination of events. This is the difficulty with some men. They cannot rest till they have done their very utmost to find out the meaning of a dream. They are disquieted until they find out whence came an unexpected shadow, whence issued an unexpected voice. They inquire; they give themselves no rest, until they have answered such difficulties with as great a measure of satisfaction as possible. Yet they care nothing for the subtle temptations that assail the heart, for allurements that seduce the spirit into evil, nor for the unholy thoughts that steal upon their minds and poison the fountain of their highest life. They care nothing for all the Great Unknown, the entrance to which is called "Death." Is this right? Is this reasonable? To be terrified by a vision of the night, and yet to have no care about the infinite, the invisible, the everlasting! Has God no meaning in the little frights with which he sometimes visits us? When he just touches us, as it were, with the finger-tip of mystery,—when he just seizes us for one moment by some sudden fear? Is it not a hint of the unsearchable riches of his mystery and the inexpressible fulness of his resources, whereby he can torment, trouble, slay men? Those who need this exhortation, if such there be, will have but a sorry answer to give to the last great trouble, the one all-inclusive, over-shadowing fear; because by the number of times you have trembled in the presence of unexpected events, by the experience you have had of disquieting dreams, God will charge upon you the capacity of understanding the hints and the monitions which he has given in all the cloud, and mystery, and wonder of your life.

"And he sent and called for all the magicians of Egypt, and all the wise men thereof; and Pharaoh told them his dream; but there was none that could interpret them unto Pharaoh " (xli. 8).

Showing how old schools of thought go out; how old tuitional functions are exhausted; how men who have served their day, after a clumsy and incomplete fashion, are dispossessed, put aside; and with such naturalness and beauty of adaptation of means to ends. God does not say to the magicians, soothsayers, and monthly prognosticators, "Now, your day is done, and you must retire from the field." He simply gives Pharaoh, king of

Egypt, a dream to which they have no answer. Thus the old
school drops out, and a new era of thinking, teaching, and interpretation is inaugurated. A man must not keep up old schoolisms,
when those isms are no longer the answers to the dreaming day
—the strange, novel, tormenting life of the current time. The
answers of the men referred to in this verse might have been
quite enough in other cases. Up to a given point they might
have been wise teachers. They had satisfied the Pharaohs of
Egypt from time to time. Yet God lets down a dream from
heaven, before which these men retire, themselves saying, " We
have no answer to it." This is how God trains the world. Old
answers will not do always to new dreams. Old forms will not
always do for new truths, or new aspects of truth, or new
inspirations of Divine wisdom. Herein ought we to learn
magnanimity, charity, noble-mindedness. I have a dream. Can
any man tell me what it is ? I have a sorrow at my heart. Can
any man tell me where there is balm for such wound ? My sin
torments me, reproaches me, makes demands upon me which I
cannot answer. Is there balm in Gilead ? Is there a physician
there ? There are times when we would give half our kingdom
for a *man*. A man of the right force of thought, the right capacity
of sympathy, the right tone of music—that wondrous, subtle,
penetrating tone, which finds the ear of the soul and charms the
spirit into rest and hope ! There are plenty of *men* ; but is there
a *man* ? Countless populations ; but is there a seer, a man who
holds upon his girdle the one key that can unlock the wards of
my difficulties and can open the lock of my life ? Now there is
a Man who professes to answer all questions, solve all problems,
dissipate all dreams, and give us a new start in life. You may
have heard his name ; you may have heard it so often that it has
ceased to be a name, and has become a mere sound—a wavelet
on the yielding air. It is a sweet name, and yet it is possible for
men to have heard it until they cease to hear it. The name is
this : Jesus Christ. Have you heard it before ? A thousand
times ! Yet there is not a name in the newspapers of to-day
which excites you less than that name. Such may be the
experience of some of you. It is a terrible thing to have out
lived Christ ; to have made Bethlehem, Gethsemane, Golgotha—
historic names, spectral shadows ! Yet I preach to-day thus :

no man's dream can be solved but by Christ; no man's greatest
dreams, Divinest dreams, visions of himself and of the future, can
be solved and interpreted but by the son of Mary, Son of God !

"Then spake the chief butler unto Pharaoh, saying, I do remember my
faults this day" (xli. 9).

Not his fault in respect of having forgotten Joseph, but his
fault in the matter for which he was sent to prison in company
with the chief baker. He makes a graceful speech concerning
his ill behaviour, and thus introduces to the notice of Pharaoh
Joseph, the Hebrew servant to the captain of the guard. The
speech of the butler is a speech to which every man ought to
give solemn heed : "I do remember my faults this day." Here
is the law of association. One thing suggests another, showing
how concatenated and intervolved are all the affairs of this life.
" I do remember my faults this day." There are days that go
back into our yesterdays and make them live again. There are
little circumstances that sound, as it were, the trump of resurrection
over all our past life, and summon buried things into personality
and impressiveness of position and aspect. So it shall be with
us all. There will come to us events, which will give recollection,
which shall recall the whole chain of our life. There *is* a way of
wrapping things up. Let us clearly understand that, lest any
evil-minded man should be discouraged, lest any man who has
an evil genius should be thrown into despair. Let us remind
him that there is a way of doing bad things, wrapping them up
with skilful fingers, and putting them away. That can be done.
You can easily scratch away a little mould and hide some fault
from the light, or some unholy word or mischievous deed, and
throw the mould over it again, and then take your staff in hand
and walk on. Do not think that your occupation, you bad
Othello, is gone ! The worst of it is, that some men think that
wrapping up a sin is equal to annihilation. They do a bad deed,
throw it behind them, look straight on, as if their looking straight
on had actually destroyed the deed. We shall come upon events
that shall be reminders, upon circumstances that shall turn us
round to face the past with all its variegations, its brightness and
its shadows, its purities and its corruptions. What an outlook
this is for some of us ! There are parts of our life we do not
like to think about. When we are suddenly reminded of them

we call, Wine! We turn aside a little to some one and say, Play something. There is a time coming when wine and music will have lost their power of enchantment, and we shall be turned right round—forced to look at the past! Oh, sirs! it is then that we shall have no little quibbling, wretched questions to put about Christ's Cross and Christ's atonement. When we see life from that point, and feel the bitterness and torment of sin, we shall then know that the Lamb of God never shed one drop too much of his blood, never suffered one pang too many for the sins of the world. We shall not be critics then, pedants then, little technical inquirers then. We shall feel that the Cross, and that alone, can go right into our life, with the answer to our difficulties, and the balm for our wound and sorrow.

"Then Pharaoh sent and called Joseph, and they brought him hastily out of the dungeon: and he shaved himself, and changed his raiment, and came in unto Pharaoh" (xli. 14).

There are great changes in life. Some of our lives amount to a succession of rapid changes; and it takes a man of some moral nerve and stamina to stand the violent alternations of fortune. Some men cannot bear promotion. It is dangerous to send little boats far out into the sea. Some men are clever, sharp, natty, precise, wonderfully well informed, newspaper-fed and fattened, and yet, if you were to increase their wages just a pound a week, they would lose their heads. That is a most marvellous thing, and yet nobody ever thought he would lose his head with such an increase of fortune. But it is a simple fact, that some men could not bear to step out of a dungeon into a palace: it would kill them. What helps a man to bear these changes of fortune, whether they be down or up? God,—he can give a man gracefulness of mien when he has to walk down, and God can give him enhanced princely dignity when he has to walk up; a right moral condition, a right state of heart, the power of putting a proper valuation upon prisons and palaces, gold and dross. Nothing but such moral rectitude can give a man security amidst all the changes of fortune or position in life. His information will not do it; his genius will not do it. Nothing will do it but a Divine state of heart. It is beautiful to talk to a man who has such a state of heart, when great changes and wonderful surprises come upon him,—when Pharaohs send for him in haste. It is always a good and stimulating thing to talk to a great man, a great nature, a man that has some completeness about him. It must be always a very ticklish, delicate, and unpleasant thing to talk to snobs, and shams, and well-tailored mushrooms; but a noble thing to talk to a noble man, who knows what prison life is, who knows what hardness of life is, and who has some notion of how to behave himself even when the greatest personages require his attendance. Few men could have borne this change. None of us can bear the great changes of life with calmness, fortitude, dignity, except we be rightly established in things that are Divine and everlasting. You will see that I cannot make too much of Joseph's princeliness of heart and mind when I read the sixteenth verse :—

"And Joseph answered Pharaoh, saying, It is not in me: God shall give Pharaoh an answer of peace " (xli. 16).

A reply that would give him foundation and solidity in the presence of any man. He who draws upon the well-head never has an empty vessel. He who knows himself to be the steward, instrument, medium of God, never has to retract his prophecies or to qualify his teaching. There is a lesson here for those of us who preach. When men ask us to tell the meaning of their life, the answer is not in us, it is in God. When men come to us with great problems, anxious questions, we are not called to put them down and to snub them, as if they had trespassed into forbidden provinces. Our answer is to Pharaoh or Cæsar, the poor man or the lone lost child,—The answer is not in me, the answer is in God. He who rests thus upon God will have new sermons, if I ⹂ have to preach every hour of the day. He will speak light; his words will be as the omnific fiat of God, "Let there be light," and man shall stand in a great blaze. Believe me, God has all answers. We have the lock, he has the key. We have the dream, he has the interpretation. What fools, therefore, some of us must be, going about from man to man, saying, "Can you tell me anything about this?" when God waits to be gracious, and bids us welcome to the unsearchable riches of his own wisdom and grace! "If any of you lack wisdom, let him ask of God, that giveth to all men liberally, and upbraideth not.'

"And Joseph said unto Pharaoh, The dream of Pharaoh is one: God hath shewed Pharaoh what he is about to do" (xli. 25).

God does sometimes give hints of his method among men. Not always are they complete hints; simply indications, outlines, shadows of things. The secret of the Lord is with them that fear him. But if we would fully entertain in our heart of hearts the Holy Ghost, I know not that we should not have more mastery over the future, keener insight into men, events, and purposes. Sure am I of this:—that no man loses anything in clearness of vision, microscopic penetrating insight into character, into history, into events, by living in God and serving God. What God is about to do! Now and then God comes down just to say, "You men are only tenants-at-will; you are not proprietors, you are not even leaseholders. Boast not yourselves of to-morrow!" We should get to think that the wheat-fields and the vineyards were all ours, if the Great Proprietor did not come down now and then and breathe upon them that they should wither away,— if he did not now and then withhold the dew, so that the roots of the earth cannot be nourished,—if, now and again, he did not send a plague through the air to proclaim to men that they hold things but for a moment, and ought to hold them in the spirit of stewardship. So Pharaoh, having had a dream from God, and interpretation from God through the medium of Joseph, was sharp enough to say, "Then if this be the case you are the man for chancellor." Christian people are thought to be very soft-headed people, not thought to have many business notions and business qualifications; great at singing hymns and going to church, but not much in the market-place or on the exchange. I will not reply to that further than to say that it is unworthy of a reply. As if God did not know more about money than we do,—and more about wheat-growing and wheat-storing than we do! as if God knew everything but how to get the morsel of bread for the meal that is due!

Believe ten thousand men when they say that they never knew what it was to have a clear mind, a far-sighted vision, until they knew God, knew Jesus Christ, not as their Creator only, but their Redeemer, their Sanctifier. Religion does not make business men, nor does it give man capacity, faculty. Religion will increase his capacity and refine his faculty. Religion—understanding by that term the religion of Jesus Christ, Son of God, who lived for us, died for us, and rose again for us—never diminishes the quantity of our manhood ; but increases it, refines it, and gives it unity, dignity, and effect.

So we have seen Joseph through what we may term the ill-fortunes. When we come to read about him again, we shall have to turn over a new leaf, on which there seems to be nothing but brightness. Let us, before turning over that new leaf, remind ourselves that there are trials which are *testing*, and other trials that are *punitive*. Many men are distressing themselves, when they think of their trials, by imagining that they must have done something wrong, or God never could have sent such afflictions to them personally or to their household. That is a mistake. There are trials that are simply tests, not punishments ; trials of faith and patience ; not rods sent to scourge men because they have been doing some particular evil thing. God's people are tried. "Whom the Lord loveth he chasteneth." The honour is not in the trial, it is in the spirit in which the trial is borne. Take the trial impatiently, with murmuring against God, and we shall be the worse for our trial, the poorer for our suffering. Take the trial as a veiled angel sent by our Father to say things to us which no other messenger could so suitably convey, then even the rod shall be precious to us, and the herald's utterances of God shall have music in them that shall comfort and revive and cheer the heart.

We all have our trials. Pharaoh and Pharaoh's butler and baker, king and subject, preacher and hearer,—every heart has its own bitterness, its own prison hours, its own times of darkness and sorrow and agony. But there is one healing for us all. Jesus knows, knows our frame, remembers that we are but dust ; knows what temptation is in its suddenness, its rapidity, its urgency, its ravenousness. He has promised to be with us when the lion comes, and the bear, and the fierce beast, and when the serpent tempts us, and our poor worn heart is failing for strength. To Christ, Son of the living God, Saviour of all men, let us crawl if we cannot fly ; and the mere turning of our tear-stained eyes towards the place of his dwelling shall be accepted, as if we had spread out the strongest wings, and out-stripped the eagle in our flight towards his presence! Oh, dear Son of God! hold thou us up, and we shall be safe! Hear the people when they say, Amen!

Gen. xli. 46.

"And Joseph was thirty years old when he stood before Pharaoh, king of Egypt."

JOSEPH'S ELEVATION.

JOSEPH was about seventeen years of age when he went out, at his father's request, to make inquiry concerning the well-being of his brethren. We find from the text that he was now thirty years old. Think of thirteen years being required for the fulfilment of a dream! The Lord counteth not time as men count it. He sitteth upon the circle of eternity. He seems to be always at leisure: though doing everything, to be doing nothing. A thousand years in his sight are but as yesterday, and all time is but as a watch in the night. But what about the effect of this long suspense upon the mind of the dreamer himself? It is hardly any comfort to us to know that God can afford to wait centuries and millenniums for the fulfilment of his purposes. There is another, there is a weaker side to this great question of the dreamer. Here is a young man exiled from his father's presence and the comforts of his home; labouring under the vilest imputations and the gravest suspicions; wasting, as it appears to us, thirteen prime years of his life. What about this waiting on the part of God, so far as Joseph is concerned? See, for example, how likely it was to discourage his faith in things spiritual. The youth had a dream, a vision, granted him as he believed of God; and yet through thirteen years his dream takes no shape, his vision is but a spectre of the memory—not a grand ruling fact of the life. Mark how his faith comes down accordingly. He reasons thus with himself: "Up to this time I have had faith in the God of my fathers. I have believed that dream and vision, strange token and wonderful signal, all meant something in the Divine providence and government of the world. I thought my own dream had a great meaning in it: but I waited

twelve months and nothing came of the dream; and twelve
months more, and my vision was as nothing; and another year,
and I have suffered nothing but ill-treatment,—and all this ill-
treatment has come to me through this very dream of mine.
Verily, it was but a vexatious nightmare ; or, if a vision of God,
it was sent to mock my ambition and to destroy my peace."

If the young man had run off into some such soliloquy as that,
he would be a very mighty man who could justly rebuke him for
taking that view of the affairs which constituted so large a portion
of his life. It is so with ourselves, my brethren. There are
many things which conspire to destroy our faith in the invisible,
the spiritual, the eternal. There are daily occurrences which
teach us that there is something higher than matter; yet there
are things occurring around us which are perpetually rebuking
our trust in the distant, the intangible, the spiritual, the Divine.
And who are we, that we should speak to men who for thirteen
years have been groaning under heavy burdens, and chide them,
as if all the while they ought to have been musical, bright with
Divine hope and beauty, and not sad and heavy-hearted, mournful
and pathetic in tone ?   We should look at such things seriously,
with consideration. It is a terrible thing for some men to believe
in God ! It takes the whole stress of their nature, and all the
help which can come of their personal history and their family
traditions, to bind them to the belief that, after all, though God
is taking a long time to fulfil their dream, yet he is working it
out, and in his own good hour he will show that not a moment
has been lost, that all the dozen years or more have been shaped
into a peculiar and bright benediction.

Then look at the inferential rectitude of his brethren. Joseph
might have turned in upon himself in some such way as this :
"Though my brethren dealt very harshly with me, yet they
had keener and truer insight into this business than I had.
They saw that I was the victim of a piece of foolish fanaticism.
I thought I was interpreting to them a dream of Heaven, a vision
of God. When I told my dream they mocked me ; they visited
me with what appeared to be evil treatment. But now that I
have had thirteen years of disappointment, vexatious delay, and
all the consequent embitterment of spirit, my brethren were right
after all. They might not have taken, perhaps, the very best

method of showing that they were right; yet now I forgive them,
because they were right on the main issue, and they were called
of God to chide my fanaticism, my imbecility and folly." Well,
there is a good deal of sound sense in that monologue. It does
appear as if the brethren were right and Joseph was wrong.
The brethren can turn to thirteen years' confirmation of their
view of Joseph's dream. They could say: "Where are his
dreams now? He had a vision of greatness. All the sheaves
in the field were to bow down to his sheaf, and all the stars were
to make obeisance to him as the central sun. Where are his
dreams now?" It is even so with ourselves. There are views
of life which I get that impress upon me this conclusion :—Bad
men are right after all. There are what are called "facts,"
which go dead against the good man's faith and the holy man's
prayer. There are men to-day who can tell you that they have
prayed and struggled and fought and endured, and for twelve
years nothing has come of their holy patient waiting upon God,—
nothing that is worthy of being set against the stress under which
they have suffered, the discipline that has pained them, the misunderstandings which have troubled and tormented their lives.
There have, indeed, been little flecks of light upon their daily
course; there have been little compliments and social courtesies;
but, putting all these things together, they are not worthy to be
named in comparison with the poignant anguish that their souls
have endured. Yet will not history be to us a tone without
language, a messenger without a message, a wasted thing, if we do
not learn from this incident that if we have waited twelve years,
yet, in the thirteenth, God may open the windows of heaven and
pour out upon us a blessing that there shall not be room to
contain? It is not easy to wait. It does not suit our incomplete
nature to tarry so long. But we fall back upon history, which
is God interpreted, and we find in that an assurance that when
the heart is right, the outward circumstances shall be shaped
and directed to our highest advantage.

Some men's dreams do take a long time to fulfil. The butler
and the baker's dreams were fulfilled in three days. But what
was there in their dreams? Everything depends upon the
vision we have had of God. If we have had a butler's dream we
shall have a butler's answer. If we have had such a dream as a

great nature only can dream, then God must have time to work
out his purposes. Joseph is not the only man who has suffered
for his dreams. God oftentimes punishes us by making dreamers
of us. Some men would be thankful to-day if they could close
nine-tenths of their sensibility,—if they could become leathern
or wooden, to a large extent. This power of feeling—of feeling
everything to be Divine, and to have a Divine meaning in it :
this power of seeing beyond the visible right into the unseen :
this power of dreaming and forecasting the future—brings with it
severe pains and terrible penalties. Here is a man who dreams
of the amelioration of his race. He will write a book, he will
found an institution, he will start certain courses of thinking, he
will seek to reverse the thought of his contemporaries and turn
it all into a directly opposite channel. He sees the result of all
this. He tells his dream, and men laugh at him. They say,
" It is just like him, you know. He is a very good sort of man,
but there is a great deal of fanaticism in him. He has always got
some new scheme, and some very beautiful vision floating before
him." And men who never dreamed—except it was that their
wretched little house was being broken into—feel called upon to
snub him with their contempt, and to avoid him as a man who is
too good or too clever for this poor common world. What are
we to make of history, if we do not get out of it this lesson ?—
that there are dreams which God gives, and there are dreams
which take a long time to fulfil. We do not make history—
we interpret it. God causes the facts to transpire, and he says
to us, " Be wise, be understanding : draw the right inferences
from these circumstances." But was it worth waiting thirteen
years for ? A good deal will depend upon the answer we
give to that inquiry. Is there nothing worth waiting thirteen
years for ? Some men require twenty-five years' hard, good
schooling before they are quite as they ought to be. Other
men may require only two days, and they are as sharp and
clear as any scholar need be. Others require thirteen years
on the treadmill, thirteen years' discipline and scourging,
thirteen years' weaning from old affections and old associations. Observe, God was now training a spoiled child, and
spoiled children cannot be drilled and put right in two
hours. Some of us have been spoiled in various ways. Some

with excess of goodness, and some with excess of harshness, it may be,—yet spoiled. Our nature has got a twist, or we have got ideas which require to be taken out of us; and only chastisement, suspicion, imprisonment, scourging, loss, hunger, affliction, and the very gate of death itself, can bring us to that measure of solidity and tenderness and refinement which God wants, in order to start us on the highest course of our manly service Was it worth waiting thirteen years for? Yes. All countries, according to the Biblical statement, came to Joseph for food, and all countries came into Egypt to Joseph to buy corn, because that the famine was sore in all lands. He was the feeder of the nations, the father, the preserver, the benefactor of innumerable multitudes! It seems to us to be an easy thing to step into that position. But we do not see the whole case; we do not see the temptations which beset it, the difficulties which combine to form that position; we do not know all the collateral bearings and issues. Let God be judge. He took thirteen years to make this man; and this man was the benefactor, and, under God, the saviour of nations. Why should not we endeavour to learn that lesson? We should like now to be second to Pharaoh. Some of us have the notion that we are tolerably ready, to-day, to receive all the homage which people can give us. That is our mistake. If we wait thirteen years, we shall be better; we shall be stronger and wiser, than we are now. The years are not wasted to souls that make a right use of them. Every year that goes by should lift a man up, give him enlargement of capacity, and tenderer sympathy, and sensitiveness of feeling. So Joseph waited thirteen years. But after he had waited, he went before Pharaoh, and was as Pharaoh to the people of Egypt.

"Now when Jacob saw that there was corn in Egypt, Jacob said unto his sons, Why do ye look one upon another?" (xlii. 1).

The old man was perfectly innocent: he had no evil tormenting associations with the word *Egypt.* If his sons had heard there was corn many a mile farther off than Egypt, surely these stalwart, active, energetic men would have been off before the old man chided them by this speech of his about waiting and looking upon one another. But, corn in Egypt! Some words are histories. Some words are sharper than drawn swords. Egypt was a keen double-edged weapon that went right into the very hearts of the men whom Jacob sought to stimulate. Jacob saw only the outward attitude. The sons appeared to be at their wits' end. Jacob thought his children were inactive—had no spring or energy in them; that they had faded away into ordinary people, instead of being the active, strong-limbed, energetic, and, as he thought, high-minded men of old. Men do not show all their life. Men have a secret existence, and their outward attitude is often but a deception. I have seen this same principle in operation in many stations of life. I have seen it in the Church. I have known men, whose interest in the sanctuary has begun to decline, who have been inattentive to the ministry, who have fallen off in their support of Christian institutions, and, when asked by the unsuspecting Jacobs, " Why is this ? " they have said " that they do not care so much for the minister as they used to do. There is not food for the soul; they want another kind of thing; and, therefore, until some change has taken place, they must withhold support from this and from that." So the minister has had to suffer : to suffer from unkind words, from chilling looks, from attitudes which could not be reported or printed, but which were hard to bear. And the poor minister has endeavoured in his study to work harder, and to get up the kind of food which such souls—souls !—could digest. He has toiled away, and in six months it has turned out that the wretch who criticised him and made him a scape-goat, was preparing for bankruptcy, and was edging his way out of the Church, that he might do it with respectability and without suspicion. Such a case is not uncommon. It may vary in its outward aspects and the way of putting it. But there are men that seek to get out of duties, and out of positions, by all kinds of excuses, who dare not open their hearts and say, " The reason is in myself. I am a bad man. I have been caught in the devil's snare; I am the victim of his horrible temptation and cruelty." It is the same, I am afraid, with many of you young men in the family circle. You want to throw off restraint. You want to alter this arrangement and that in the family ; and you speak of your health, your friends, or some change in your affections. You put altogether a false face and a bad gloss upon the affair, so that your unsuspecting father and mother may not know the reality,—the reality being that your heart is wrong, or your soul has poisoned itself. You want to be away, to do something that is truly diabolic, and which you would not like those who gave you birth and who have nourished you through life to see. Believe this, that not until the moral is right can the social be frank, fearless, happy. When men's hearts are right they will not have anything to hide. They may have committed errors of judgment, but these have been venial, trifling. But where there is no deep villainy of the heart, men can bear to tell their whole life, and show how it is that they are fearful concerning this, or despondent concerning something else.

This law of association is constantly operating amongst men. A word will bring up the memories of a life-time. You had only to say to ten great-boned men in the house of Jacob—and say it in a whisper—Egypt! and you would shake every man to the very centre and core of his being. If you could have met the oldest, strongest, sturdiest of them on a dark night, and said to him, Egypt! you would have struck him as with the lightning of God. Yes, it is a terrible thing to have done evil! It comes up again upon you from ten thousand points. It lays hold of you, and holds you in humiliating captivity, and defies you to be happy. That this may be so I think is tolerably clear from the twenty-first verse of the forty-second chapter. The men were before Joseph, after they had been cross-examined by him.—

"And they said one to another, We are verily guilty concerning our brother, in that we saw the anguish of his soul, when he besought us, and we would not hear; therefore, is this distress come upon us" (xlii. 21).

Many years after the event! Their recollection of that event was as clear as if it had transpired but yesterday. Learn the moral impotence of time. We say this evil deed was done fifty years ago. Fifty years may have some relation to the memory of the intellect, but it has no relation to the tormenting memory of the conscience. There is a moral memory. Conscience has a wondrously realising power,—taking things we have written in secret ink and holding them before the fire until every line becomes vivid, almost burning. Perhaps some of you know not yet the practical meaning of this. We did something twenty years ago. We say to ourselves, "Well, seeing that it was twenty years ago, it is not worth making any to-do about it; it is past, and it is a great pity to go twenty years back, raking up

things." So it is, in some respects, a great pity to bother ourselves about things other men did, twenty years ago. But what
about our own recollection, our own conscience, our own power
of accusation? A man says, "I forged that name twenty-five
years ago, and oh! every piece of paper I get hold of seems to
have the name upon it. I never dip the pen, but there is something in the pen that reminds me of what I did by candle light,
in almost darkness, when I had locked the door and assured myself nobody was there. Yet it comes upon me so graphically,—
my punishment is greater than I can bear!" Time cannot heal
our iniquities. Forgetfulness is not the cure for sin. Oblivious-
ness is not the redeemer of the world. How, then, can I get rid
of the torment and the evils of an accusing memory? The blood
of Jesus Christ cleanseth from all sin. " Let the wicked forsake
his way, and the unrighteous man his thoughts : and let him return
unto the Lord, and he will have mercy upon him ; and to our God,
for he will abundantly pardon." That is the kind of answer men
want, when they feel all their yesterdays conspiring to urge an
indictment against them as sinners before the living God. " If
we confess our sins, he is faithful and just to forgive us our sins,
and to cleanse us from all unrighteousness." Can I impress this
upon myself and upon you? Time cannot redeem us. Ten
thousand ages hence, a man's sin will confront him, scourge him,
and defy him to enjoy one moment's true rest. Who then can
destroy sin, break its power? Whose arms can get round it, lift
it up, and cast it into the depths of the sea? This is a Divine
work, God's work! It is not to be done by your ethical quacks
and your dreamy speculators. It is to be done only by the
mighty redeeming power of God the Son, Jesus Christ! This is
the gospel I have to preach to men. Fifty years will make no
difference in your crimes. Conscience makes us live continually
in the present ; and only the blood of Jesus Christ can wash out
the stains of evil deed and unholy memory.

" And Reuben answered them, saying, Spake I not unto you, saying, Do
not sin against the child ; and ye would not hear? therefore, behold, also
his blood is required " (xlii. 22).

Showing how bad men reproach one another, how little unity
there is in wickedness, what a very temporary thing is the supposed unanimity of bad men,—how bad men will one day turn

upon one another, and say "It was you!" Ha! such is the
unanimity of wicked conspirators! "My son, if sinners entice
thee, consent thou not"; they will turn against thee some day.
Though your swords be pointed against one man at the present
hour, and you may be unanimous in some wicked deed,—God's
great wheel is going round and round, and the hour cometh when
the men who urged thee to do the evil deed, and share with them
their unholy counsels, will seek thy heart, will accuse thee, will
charge thee with participation in their nefarious, hellish designs
and work. The way of transgressors is hard! Smooth for a
mile or two, and then hard, thorny—ravenous beasts there,
serpents lurking here. It is very difficult to get back when you
once start upon that way. I have known young men who have
said, "We want to go just a mile or two down this road, and
when we find it becomes rather intricate, we intend to turn
right round; and then, after all, you will see that we have only
been sowing a few wild oats, and just doing a few odd things,
and by-and-by we shall settle down into solid men." I am not
so sure about it. If a man goes into the evil way, and the great
Enemy of souls goes after him, he will blot out his footprints. So
when the man says, "I will now go back again; I can put my
feet where I put them before," he looks for his footprints, but
they have gone, and he cannot tell which is east, west, north,
south! Footprints gone; landmarks altered; the whole meta-
morphosed, and to him downward is upward. None so blind as
he, the eyes of whose soul have been put out!

All this, too, was in the hearing of Joseph. Joseph heard
them say that he was their brother. They used to call him
"dreamer." He heard them say "the child,"—tenderly. Once
they mocked him. He heard them speak in subdued, gentle tones.
He remembers the time when their harsh grating voices sent a
terror through his flesh and blood, and when he was sold off to
travelling merchantmen. It was worth waiting for to see further
into one another, after such experiences as these. He never
would have known his brethren, but for this terrible process.
Some disciplines open men's nature and show us just what they
are. "His blood is required," said Reuben. Certainly,—such
requirements made life worth having. There are pay days.

There are days when bills become due. There are times when business men are particularly busy, because the day has come on which certain things are due and must be attended to. And shall a paltry guinea be due to you or to me, and a man's blood never be due? Shall we be very conscientious about pounds, shillings, and pence, and forget the virtue we have despoiled, the honour we have insulted, the love we have trampled underfoot? God will judge us by our actions, and will charge upon us that we were conscientious in little things, in trivial relationships, and forgot that sometimes man's blood is due, and man's honour comes with a demand to be satisfied.

Gen. xlii. 24.

"And he turned himself about from them, and wept."

JOSEPH'S BRETHREN UNDER TRIAL.

JOSEPH had spoken roughly to his brethren, whom he knew, though they knew not him. He had declared unto them, by the life of Pharaoh, that they should not go forth from his presence, except their youngest brother came with them. Having heard Joseph's decision, they began to reproach one another. They said, "We are verily guilty concerning our brother, in that we saw the anguish of his soul, when he besought us, and we would not hear; therefore is this distress come upon us." And Reuben turned the whole thing upon them in a very pointed reproach. He said, "Spake I not unto you, saying, Do not sin against the child; and ye would not hear? therefore, behold, also his blood is required." Joseph understood their speech, though they did not understand the speech of Joseph, because he spake unto them through an interpreter. The interview having come to this point, Joseph turned himself about from his brethren and wept. Harsh experience need not destroy the finest sensibility, the tenderest feelings of the heart. Here is a man who has had twenty years' very painful, almost unendurable, treatment; and yet, at the end of that period, he is susceptible of the tenderest influences, responds emotionally, with tears, with unutterable yearning and tenderness of soul, in the presence of his brethren, and the mute appeal which was involved in that presence. There is something for us to learn here. Our harsh experiences often deaden our sensibility, work in us a sourness of heart and feeling which becomes misanthropic, selfish, resentful. We learn from the history before us that it is possible to be exiled from home, ill-treated by relatives and friends, thrown into the way of pain, sorrow, loss and desolation ; yet to come out of the whole process tender, sensitive, responsive to appeals which are made to our nature. Why, there are some men who cannot overget the very slightest offence. If they have not their own way in everything, they show their resentfulness in a thousand little ways,—they become peevish, censorious, distrustful, ungenial. You never meet them but they give you to understand that they have been insulted, offended, dishonoured. They have had to endure slight, or contempt, or neglect. How little, how unutterably paltry, such men appear in the presence of the man who, after twenty years of exile, solitude, evil treatment of all kinds, weeps when he sees his brethren,—keeps his heart through it all, —has not allowed himself to become soured or misanthropic ! He keeps a whole, tender, responsive heart through all the tumult, and trial, and agony, and bitter sorrow of thirteen years' vile captivity, and seven years of exaltation which might, by the very surprise it involved, and the very suddenness with which it came, have over-balanced the man's mind and given him false views of himself. If he was great, why should not we be great ? If he could·keep a whole heart through it all, why should we allow our moral nature to be frittered and dribbled away ? Why should we become less, instead of greater, notwithstanding the evils we have to endure, and the difficulties which press upon us on every side ? This is a great question, calling men to devout consideration, and to· a searching and complete review of their moral position.

After the lapse of many years, Joseph, on seeing his brethren, wept. Why, he might have been vengeful. It is easy for us glibly to read the words, " Joseph turned himself about and wept." But consider what the words *might* have been ! We oftentimes see results, not processes. We do not see how men have had to bind themselves down, crucify themselves—hands, feet, head, and side—and undergo death in the presence of God, before they could look society in the face with anything like benignity, and gentleness, and forgiveness. What the words might have been! Joseph, when he saw his brethren, might have said, " Now I have you! Once you put me into a pit,—I shall shake you over hell; once you sold me,—I will imprison you and torture you day and night; you smote me with whips, —I shall scourge you with scorpions! It shall be easier to go through a circle of fire than to escape my just and indignant vengeance to-day!" He might have said, " I shall operate upon the law : A tooth for a tooth, and an eye for an eye." That is the law of nature ; that is elementary morality. It is not vengeance, it is not resentment; it is alphabetic justice—justice at its lowest point—incipient righteousness. It is not two eyes for an eye, two teeth for a tooth ; but an eye for an eye, a tooth for a tooth a blow for a blow, a pit for a pit, selling for selling, and so on. A great many men are perfectly content with elementary morality and alphabetic justice. People do not educate themselves from this kind of righteousness into Christian nobility of disposition. It is not a question of education ; it is a question of sanctification. Few men can rise beyond mere justice. Many men find in mere justice all the moral satisfaction which their shallow natures require ; they cannot see that mercy is the very highest point in justice, and that, when a man stoops to forgive, he becomes a prince, and a king, and a crowned ruler in the house and kingdom of God. It requires all that God can do to teach men this : that there is something higher than the law of retaliation ; that forgiveness is better than resentment, and that to release men is oftentimes— if done from moral considerations and not from moral indifference —the highest form of Christian justice. But revenge is sweet! I am afraid that some of us like just a little revenge ; not that we would ourselves personally and directly inflict it ; but, if our enemies could, somehow or another, be tripped up, and tumble half-way at least into a pit, we should not feel that compunction, and sorrow, and distress of soul which, sentimentally, appears to be so very fine and beautiful. Nothing but God the Holy Ghost can train a man to this greatness of answering the memory of injury with tears, and accepting processes in which men only appear to have a part as if God, after all, had been over-ruling and directing the whole scheme.

"And Joseph turned himself about from them, and wept."
Afterwards he left their presence and went into his chamber and
wept. Think of the secret sorrows of men! The tears did not
flow in the presence of the ten men. The tears were shed in
secret. We do not know one another altogether, because there
is a private life. There are secret experiences. Some of us are
two men. Joseph was two men. He spake roughly unto his
brethren. He put it on ; he assumed roughness for the occasion.
But if you had seen him when he had got away into his secret
chamber, no woman ever shed hotter, bitterer tears than
streamed from that man's eyes. We do not know one another
altogether. We come to false conclusions about each other's
character and disposition. Many a time we say about men, "they
are very harsh, rough, abrupt"; not knowing that they have
other days when their very souls are dissolved within them ;
that they can suffer more in one hour than shallower natures
could endure in an eternity. Let us be hopeful about the
very worst of men. Some men cannot cry in public. Some
men are, unfortunately, afflicted with coarse, harsh voices, which
get for them a reputation for austerity, unkindliness, ungeniality.
Other men are gifted with fairness and openness of countenance,
gentleness and tunefulness of voice. When they curse and swear
it seems as though they were half praying, or just about to enter
into some religious exercise. When they speak, when they
smile, they get a reputation for being very amiable men, yet they
do not know what amiability is. They have no secret life. They
weep for reputation ; they make their tears an investment for a
paltry renown. We do not want all our history to be known.
We are content for men to read a little of what they see on the
outside, and they profoundly mistake that oftentimes. But the
secret history, the inner room of life, what we are and what we
do when we are alone, no man can ever tell,—the dearest, truest,
tenderest friend can never understand. Do not let us treat
Joseph's tears lightly. Under this feeling there are great moral
principles and moral impulses. The man might have been stern,
vengeful, resentful. Instead of that, he is tender as a forgiving
sister. When he looks he yearns, when he listens to their voices
all the gladness and none of the bitterness of his old home comes
back again on his soul.

" And he said unto his brethren, My money is restored ; and, lo, it is even in my sack : and their heart failed them, and they were afraid, saying one to another, What is this that God hath done unto us ? And it came to pass as they emptied their sacks, that, behold, every man's bundle of money was in his sack : and when both they and their father saw the bundles of money, they were afraid " (xlii. 28, 35).

What mistaken views we take about what is called the common-places of life ! Some of us are often discontented because of the insipidity of our existence. To-day so like yesterday, and to-morrow will be but a repetition of to-day. We are always wanting something to happen. We say, If anything would but occur to-day to stir the stagnant pool of our life ! We want to get out of old ruts and ordinary modes. Here are men to whom something had happened, and they were afraid ! We could not live sensationally. Men can bear shocks and sensations only now and then. In life there must be great breadths of common-place and ordinariness. We could not stand a shock every day. It is enough, now and then, to be stimulated and shaken out of what is common and usual, and what has come, by reason of its com-monness, to be under-valued and contemned.

They were afraid when they saw their money in their sacks. See the possibility of *mercies* being turned into judgments,—of the very goodness of God striking us in the heart,—of mercy itself smiting us as with the rod of wrath. How can this be so ? When the moral nature is wrong, when man's conscience tells him that he has no right to this or that privilege or enjoyment, when man is divided against himself, when he has justly written bitterness against his own memory and his own nature altogether, —then his very bread becomes bitter in his mouth, and the sun-light of God is a burning judgment upon his life. Naturally, one would have said that, when the men saw their money in the sacks, saw that it had been planned, that it was not an accidental thing, —being in one sack and not in another, but being in every man's sack,—when they saw order, regularity, scheme in the whole thing,—they might have said, " We are glad : we have been kindly and nobly treated by the men of Egypt ; we are thankful for their consideration." Yet, when they saw the money, they would not have been more surprised if a scorpion had erected itself out of a sack and aimed to strike them in the face. A time will come to bad men when even God's mercies will trouble them, when the light of the day will be a burden to their eyes, and when the softest music will be more unendurable than the most terrible thunder. Bad men have no right to mercies. Bad souls have no right to be in the pastures of God's richness of love and mercy and compassion. They feel themselves out of place, or they *will* do so. Altogether, sirs, it is a bad look-out for bad men! They cannot find rest anywhere. Put them in the very finest pastures you can find, and there will arise one day in their hearts this accusation : You have no right to be here; your place is in the sandy desert. Put them in the sandy desert, and the very wilderness will be filled with discontent and unrest until the bad men get out of it. Altogether the universe will not want them. God will turn his back upon them! There is no peace, saith my God, to the wicked.

See, further, how small things can upset man's enjoyment, man's pleasure and satisfaction in life. Here is a paltry handful of money in each man's sack, and because of the event there is no rest in the house of Israel that day. Life does not turn upon great events and sublime circumstances. Life, after all, has in it great breadths of repetition. One day is very much like another. It is upon little wheels that great things turn. We undervalue little things. The young man does not care to live to-day, because nothing great or sublime is occurring. He does not know that his very life is hung upon a little thread; that his breath is in his nostrils; that one element thrown into the air he breathes will destroy his animal existence, and that life is such a delicately constructed affair that little things will increase our joy a millionfold, or will utterly consume and destroy our pleasure. How, then, can I get mastery over this life ? I don't want to be it the mercy of these little things that occur every day. Is there no means by which I could have a sceptre of rulership and symbol of mastery ? Is there no way to the throne, seated on which, I could be calm amid tumult, rich amid loss, hopeful in the midst of disappointment, strong and restful when great things all about me are shaking and tottering to the fall ? Yes, there is a way. A way to independence, and mastery, and peace. What is that way ? It has a thousand names, but call it now—Fellowship with God through Jesus Christ our Lord. He who sits—through the mercy of the Most High—on the throne of God, sees all things from God's point of view. He does not grapple with mere details : is not lost amid a thousand mazy ways, but sees the processes of life in their scope, their unity, and their whole moral significance. " Great peace have they that love thy law." " O, rest in the Lord, and wait patiently for him." This alone can give a man steadiness, composure, child-like assurance, and saintly triumph amid breaking fortunes, vanishing enjoyments and comforts, and cause him to say, " Though he slay me, yet will I trust in him." When he hath brought his work to an end, I shall praise him for the mercy of his judgments, and for the gentleness of his rod.

"And Jacob their father said unto them, Me have ye bereaved of my children : Joseph is not, and Simeon is not, and ye will take Benjamin away : all these things are against me. And he said, My son shall not go down with you ; for his brother is dead, and he is left alone : if mischief befall him by the way in the which ye go, then shall ye bring down my gray hairs with sorrow to the grave " (xlii. 36, 38).

An old man, who does not know what he is talking about ! What does the oldest and best man amongst us know about life ? Jacob is writing a list of his grievances and misfortunes and distresses, and God's angels are looking down upon him and saying that the whole statement, though it is one of what men call facts, is a mistake from beginning to end. Think of a man writing his life, and of God's writing the same life in a parallel column ! Now old Israel is perfectly correct, so far as the story is known to himself. Jacob their father said, " Me have ye bereaved of my children." That is right. " Joseph is not." That is perfectly true, so far as Jacob is concerned, so far as his information extends. " And Simeon is not." That also is literally correct, so far as the absence of Simeon may be regarded. " And ye will take Benjamin away." Precisely so, that is the very thing they have in view. " All these things are against me." It is exactly the same with us to-day. Men do not know what they say when they use words. They do not know the full meaning of their own expressions. They will always snatch at first appearances and pronounce judgment upon incomplete processes. Every day I afflict myself with just the same rod. I know what a fool I am for doing so, and yet I shall do it again to-morrow. There comes into a man's heart a kind of grim

comfort when he has scourged himself well; when he knows all
the while that ten thousand errors are accusing him of a repetition
of his folly.

There are men who do not know their own family circumstances, yet they have undertaken to pronounce judgment upon
the Infinite! Some men are very familiar with the Infinite, and
have a wonderful notion of their power of managing God's concerns. We seem at home when we go from home. Here is an
old man saying, "Joseph is not, Simeon is not, Benjamin is to be
taken away. All these things are against me." Yet we who
have been in a similar position, though the circumstances have
been varied, have undertaken to pronounce judgment upon God's
way in the world, God's government, God's purposes. Why do
we not learn from our ignorance? Why do we not read the
book of our own folly, and learn that we know nothing, being
children of yesterday? We cannot rise to that great refinement
of learning, it would appear. Every day we repeat our follies.
It is but a man here and there who has a claim to a reputation
for religious wisdom.

How life depends upon single events! We may say, The old
man's life is bound up in the life of Benjamin. There are individuals without whom the world would be cold and poor to us
all. You may say, He is but one of ten thousand, let him go,—
she is but one of a million, why care so much for her? We live
in ones and twos. We cannot live in a countless population. We
live in an individual heart, a special individual, personal love and
trust. I cannot carry immensity! I can only carry a heartful of
love. There are men to-day who would not care to look at the
sun again if they lost that dear little child of theirs; men who
look at everything through the medium of an only daughter, or
an only son; who would not care for spring, and summer, and
golden autumn; for fortune, position, influence, or renown, if that
one ewe lamb were taken away. Life may be focalised to one
point of interest, impulse, desire, and purpose. A man's life may
be centred upon one individual existence.

Let us understand, however, that Jacob does not *begin* his
sorrow with the possible taking away of Benjamin. This is the
last sorrow of a series. That is how some of us are worn down
in soul, and heart, and hope. It is not because you have had

taken away one thing; but because that one thing happens to be the last of a series. The great hammer that fell on a block of marble and shivered it,—did that blow shiver it? No. It was blow upon blow, repercussion. No one stroke did it, though the last appeared to accomplish the purpose. Some of you have had many sorrows. You think you cannot bear the sorrow that is now looking at you through the dark, misty cloud. You are saying, "I should pray God to be spared that sorrow. I have had six troubles: I cannot bear the seventh." Not knowing that the seventh trouble is the last step into heaven! Is there no answer to this difficulty of human life that will give satisfaction to souls? There is one answer. There is a Comforter which liveth for ever. I would not teach—God forbid that I should ever so far lose my humanity as to teach; for a man can only teach well in proportion as he is a *man*—that we should be indifferent about children and friends, the hearts that we love. I do not want to grow into an independence of human regard, and human trust, and human love; I do not care to be lifted up into such a position of hazy, heartless sentimentality as to be able to let friend after friend die, and care nothing for the loss. That is not Christianity; that is a species of the lowest beasthood. There may be men who can see grave after grave opened, and friend after friend put in and covered away, and shed never a tear or feel never a pang of the heart. I would hope there are no such men. I do not teach that Christianity enables us to destroy our feeling, to crush our sensibility, and to be indifferent under the pressure of sorrow. But Christianity does enable us to see the whole of a case. Christianity comes to a man in his greatest losses, and troubles, and bereavements, and says to him, amid his tears, and regrets, and passionate bewailings, "Thou fool, that which thou sowest is not quickened except it die." Christianity teaches that death is but a variation of life; that the grave is not the full stop in the difficult literature of human existence; that when we put away from us the dearest and best things that belong to our hearts, God will bring them back again to us multiplied in strength, and beauty, and freshness.

Some of us require most varied and prolonged humiliation before we are prepared for the highest honours of our life. All these arrangements and tests on the part of Joseph tended towards the humiliation and the penitence of his brethren. He might instantly have said, "I am Joseph"! They could not have borne it. At once he might have said, "Brethren, I forgive you all." He might thus have done more harm than good. The men required to be tested. They had no right or title to any consideration that came before they were put to scrutiny and criticism. God has a long process with some of us. He has to take away the first-born child, and the last-born, and all between. He has to come in, time after time, and turn the cradle upside down. He has to wither our business, blight our fortunes, and smite us with sore disease. He has to foil our purposes, break up our schemes, turn our counsel back upon us, and confound us at every point, until we begin to say, What does all this *mean*? He has to make us afraid by day; he has to trouble us by night; he has to turn even his mercies into judgments, before he can bring us to say solemnly, with meaning, This must have some religious intent. What does God purpose by all this various discipline?

Gen. xliv. 1-5.

"And he commanded the steward of his house, saying, Fill the men's sacks with food, as much as they can carry, and put every man's money in his sack's mouth. And put my cup, the silver cup, in the sack's mouth of the youngest, and his corn money. And he did according to the word that Joseph had spoken. As soon as the morning was light, the men were sent away, they and their asses. And when they were gone out of the city, and not yet far off, Joseph said unto his steward, Up, follow after the men; and when thou dost overtake them, say unto them, Wherefore have ye rewarded evil for good? Is not this it in which my lord drinketh, and whereby indeed he divineth? ye have done evil in so doing."

JOSEPH'S REVELATION.

HOW wonderfully even *spoiled* children may be developed in those very faculties which are supposed to lie dormant under all the pampering and care-taking of exaggerated parental affection! You have observed, from time to time, how deep, yet how simple, how complete, yet apparently how easy, have been all the plans and schemes which Joseph devised to meet the exigencies of his trying course. Think of him as the *spoiled* boy with whom we began. The rough wind was not to beat upon him; he was never to get his feet wet; any little thing that his father could do for him was to be done; he was to be coddled, and protected, and saved from every little annoyance; and if there was an extra drop of sweetness for any member of the family it found its way into Joseph's cup. You say, after reading all this, "What kind of a man will he make? Why, if there were any germ in him of manhood at the beginning, it must have been worn out and wasted by such excessive pampering, such ill-spent care and attention, as Jacob's." Yet he comes out of it all sagacious as a statesman, with a wonderful breadth and solidity and substance of character, upsetting all the calculations and notions of people who say that if you take too much care of a boy, pamper a life to excess, you are actually doing more harm than good. Now, let us be clear about that, because there is a particle of truth in that theory. I pause here, if haply my printed words—I dare not say my spoken message—should reach any spoilt child, any over-pampered life. There is no reason why you should not, after all, be a man! Your father's fondling and your mother's caresses need not kill the vigour that God gave you. You may come out of it all a strong and tender, wise and efficient servant of the public. It has been said, too, by those people who observe the ways of men, that oftentimes those who have been most carefully brought up can, when occasion requires, rough it with the best grace, and can do things which excite everybody's wonder. We say, concerning certain boys who have had nothing but confectionery to eat ever since they were born, that have always been kept out of dangerous places, "Depend upon it, when the wind turns into the east, when there is a flood or a fire, when there is some sudden and terrible adversity in their lives, they will be unprepared for such a visitation." And it has turned out that the spoilt child has sometimes been the best man. He has stooped with a grace which has excited the wonder of everybody; he has shown how possible it is, under the covering of decoration and excess of attention, to be cultivating the best strength, and preparing for the wettest day. Some of us, who never had two halfpennies to make a noise with, when we have got into a little prosperity, and then a little adversity has come sharply and suddenly round upon us,—why, we have grunted and complained, and been pettish and snappish, as though we had been nursed in the very lap of heaven and never set our feet on anything coarser than gold. Oh, be men! Do have a life that domineers over circumstances; that takes the bitterest cups, or the exile's solitude, or the slave's lash, and that says, "After all, I am God's child, and I will live for that dear Father."

"And Judah said, What shall we say unto my lord? what shall we speak? or how shall we clear ourselves? God hath found out the iniquity of thy servants: behold, we are my lord's servants, both we, and he also with whom the cup is found" (xliv. 16).

Contrast that speech with the scene at the pit's mouth. Can you recall the former scene? They put the boy into the pit, sit down and eat bread, see a party of merchantmen in the distance, suddenly resolve on selling him; and they exchange their brother —body, soul, and spirit—for a handful of shekels, and never say good-bye to the child. But, now, "What shall we say unto my lord?" Judah came near and said, "Oh, my lord." "My lord asked his servants." "And we said unto my lord." Yet once again Judah said, "My lord." It is the same Joseph, it is the same Judah. Such are the alterations which occur in man's life! One great difficulty which some of us feel, is the difficulty of punishing a body of men. It is comparatively easy to punish one man. But it is next to an impossibility to punish a committee. The Church can injure its one poor minister; but what can the minister do in the way of bringing punishment—not vindictive punishment, but righteous retaliation—upon an immoral, corrupt Church, that will do things in its corporate capacity which every individual member would shrink from in horror and disgust?

Joseph has had his task set in this business,—so to work that he can bring the rod down upon the *whole* lot. How is it that we lose our consciences when we join bodies of men? How is it that our moral nature becomes diluted the moment we consent to act upon a committee? How comes it, that the honest man, when he joins a Church, may be persuaded to hold up his hand in confirmation of a resolution which is based on corrupt morals? Yet this may be done. There is in England to-day many a man smarting from resolutions passed by corporate bodies, and yet not one of the members of these corrupt bodies will come forward and say, "I took my full share of that resolution, and I accept the responsibility connected with it." One hands over the responsibility to another. One man says "he would not have voted for it, just as it stands, but he thought it might have saved something worse." Another says that he "didn't fully understand it: it was made in such a hurry, and passed in such a tumult." And so they go on! But they are breaking one man's heart all the time. God's righteous curse rest upon such foul conspiracy! These are not passionate words. If I have spoken fire, it is because there was fuel enough to light.

So they called him, My lord! my lord—my lord! You cannot redeem your character by paying compliments after the deed is done. No man can redeem himself by too late courtesies. There are civilities which are right in their season, beautiful when well-timed. But they may come at a time which aggravates the old memory and tears open the old sore. This was so long in coming! Let us add up the years, and see how long Joseph was in hearing such words. He was seventeen when he went out first to seek his brethren; he was thirty when he stood before Pharaoh. Thirteen years we have up to this point. Then there were seven years of plenty, during which time Joseph never heard from his brethren. At the end of the seven years, making twenty in all, his brethren began to come before him. So it required something like twenty years to bring about the scene which is now before us. Some interpretations are a long time on the road. Some men have long to nurse their hopes, and to cheer themselves up, thinking that after all God will come. Twenty years is a period which takes the strength out of a man, sucks the very sap out of his power, unless he have meat to eat that the world knoweth not of, unless he knows the way to the well-head and can refresh himself with the springing water. So long in coming, but it came at last! This is it, sirs. The bad man's day is a wasting day. Every moment is a moment ticked off,—it is one fewer. But the good man's day is an augmenting quantity,—knows no diminution. Whilst it wastes, it grows; every passing hour brings the day nearer; and the day of the good man has no sunset. Judah continued to speak with marvellous eloquence and pathos, pleading for the release of Benjamin and making wonderful use of the old man and the grey hairs.   In the thirty-second and thirty-third verses he said :—

"For thy servant became surety for the lad unto my father, saying, If I bring him not unto thee, then I shall bear the blame to my father for ever. Now, therefore, I pray thee, let thy servant abide instead of the lad a bondman to my lord ; and let the lad go up with his brethren " (xliv. 32, 33).

Showing the possibility of being so very careful about one member of the family and caring nothing about another.   Here is Judah pleading for Benjamin as if he were his own child ; yet this same Judah took part in selling another brother.   So many of us are only good in little bits !   We have points of excellence. People say about us, "After all, there are some points about him that are tolerably good."   But what is that ?   We don't want to be good in points, we want to be good altogether !   Not to love for such reasons as Judah suggested even, in this eloquent and pathetic appeal ; but to be good for goodness' own sake. Not to save some man's grey hairs ; but to honour God's law, and thus to be most profoundly and universally gentle and pathetic.

Then there is a great fallacy underlying all such pleading as Judah's ; at all events, a possible fallacy.   We try to compensate for our evil deeds to some people, by being extra-kind to others. Brethren, it cannot be done !   You used your poor friend very ill, twenty years ago, and the memory of it has come upon you again and again.   You have reproached yourself, and cursed yourself, for your unkindness, neglect, misapprehension, cruelty ; and, in order to appease yourself, to make atonement to yourself, you have been very kind to some other friend.   But you cannot touch the dead one !   all your efforts towards helping Benjamin have had in them some hope of doing something at least towards making up for your cruelty to Joseph.   But these efforts have been unavailing.   Whilst your friend is with you, love that friend.   It is but a short grey day we are together.   There ought not to be time for strife, and debate, and harshness, and bitterness.   The hand is already laid on the rope that shall ring the knell !   And when the eyes once close in the last sleep they do not open again.   It is all over !   Then come pangs, scorpions, poisonings, piercings !   We would give all the world to have another hour —one more short hour—with the dear, dear dead one! But it may not be. Whatever we may do to survivors and relatives, we do not touch the great and terrible blemish of our past life.

Now I have this question to ask : Is there any means by which I can touch the whole of my life? There is not. "Why," you say, "that is the language of despair." So it is, for you, believe me ; and if the despair is settled upon your soul, then you are so far prepared for the gospel, which is this : *You* can find no means of touching all your yesterdays, all your past life ; but *God* has found such means. "The blood of Jesus Christ, Son of God, cleanseth from all sin." When we get into the mystery of his Cross, we see how every sin can be met. Believe me, it can be met only by all the mystery of that infinite, unspeakable love. So why should we be endeavouring to reach the past, when we have enough to do to-day? Why should we seek to hold a lifetime, when we cannot keep ourselves right for one hour? What then? I rest on Christ, and go up to his dear Cross, and say, "If I perish, I will perish here, where no man ever yet did perish." May God torment our consciences, raise us to the highest point of self-accusation, remind us of all our neglects, all our harshness, and all our cruelty, till we feel ourselves surrounded by scorpions, by messengers of judgment, and by terrible forces of all kinds : until there be extorted from our hearts the cry, "God be merciful to me a sinner!" Then there shall come out of the Cross a glory which will cast the night of the soul away.

Judah having concluded his speech, we read in the next chapter that Joseph could not refrain himself before all those that stood by him. The room was cleared. Joseph wept aloud, and said unto his brethren, "I am Joseph!" Joseph, and yet more than Joseph. We shall not be the same men twenty years hence that we are to-day. The old name—yet there may be a new nature. The old identity—yet there may be enlarged capacity, refined sensibilities, Diviner tastes, holier tendencies. I am Joseph! It is as if the great far-spreading umbrageous oak said, "I am the acorn"! or the great tree said, "I am the little mustard-seed"! Literally it was Joseph ; yet in a higher sense it was not Joseph : but Joseph increased, educated, drilled, magnified, put into his right position. You have no right to treat the man of twenty years ago as if twenty years had not elapsed. I don't know men whom I knew twenty years ago! I know their names; but they may be—if I have not seen them during the time, and if they have been reading, thinking, praying, growing—entirely different men. You must not judge them externally, but according to their intellectual, moral, and spiritual qualities. To treat a man whom you knew twenty years ago as if he were the same man is equal to handing him, in the strength and power of his years, the toys with which he amused his infancy. Let us destroy our identity, in so far as that identity is associated with incompleteness of strength, shallowness of nature, poverty of information, deficiency of wisdom; so that men may talk to us and not know us, and our most familiar acquaintance of twenty years ago may require to be introduced to us to-day as if he had never heard our name.

But the point on which I wish to fasten your attention most particularly is this: that in human life there are days of *revelation*, when people get to know the meaning of what they have been looking at, notwithstanding the appearances which were before their eyes. We shall see men as we never saw them before. The child will see his old despised mother some day as he never saw her. And you, young man, who have attained the patriarchal age of nineteen, and who smile at your old father when he quotes some trite maxim and wants to read a chapter out of what he calls the Holy Bible, will one day see him as you have never seen him yet. The angel of God that is in him will shine out upon you, and you will see whose counsel you have despised and whose tenderness you have contemned. We only see one another now and then. Sometimes the revelation is quick as a glance, impossible to detain as a flash of lightning. Sometimes the revelation comes in a tone of unusual pathos, and when we hear that tone for the first time we say, "We never knew the man before. Till we heard him express himself in that manner, we thought him rough, and coarse, wanting in self-control, and delicacy, and pathos; but that one tone! Why, no man could have uttered it but one who has often been closeted with God, and who has drunk deeply into Christ's own cup of sorrow."

Joseph made a more eloquent speech than Judah had done. He

said to his brethren in the course of his address : "So, now, it was not you that sent me hither, but God." The great man is always ready to find an excuse for the injury that is done him, if he possibly can find one! This grand doctrine is in the text : that all our little fightings, and scratchings, and barterings, and misunderstandings : all our tea-table criticisms of one another, and magazine articles in mutual depreciation : all our little schemes to trip one another up, and to snip a little off each other's robe, all these things are after all secondary and tributary. "The Lord reigneth, let the earth rejoice."

"Moreover he kissed all his brethren, and wept upon them : and after that his brethren talked with him" (xlv. 15).

A day of reconciliation! A family made one. Brethren coming together again after long separation. It is a beautiful picture. Why should it not be completed, where it needs completion, in our own day amongst ourselves? Ministers sometimes have misunderstandings and say unkind things about one another—and exile one another from love and confidence for years. Is there never to be a day of reconciliation and Christian forgetfulness of wrong, even where positive wrong has been done? Families and households often get awry. The younger brother differs with his elder brother,—sisters fall out. One wants more than belongs to him ; another is knocked to the wall because he is weak; and there come into the heart bitterness and alienation, and often brothers and sisters have scarce a kind word to say of one another. Is it always to be so? Do not merely make it up, do not patch it up, do not cover it up,—go right down to the base. You will never be made one, until you meet at the Cross and hear Christ say, "Whosoever shall do the will of my Father which is in heaven, the same is my brother, and sister, and mother." It is in Christ's sorrow that we are to forget our woes ; in Christ's sacrifice we find the answer to our sin ; in Christ's union with the Father we are to find all true and lasting reconciliation. But who is to begin? That is the wonderful question that is often asked us. Who is to begin? One would imagine that there were some very nice people about who only wanted somebody to tell them who was to begin. They want to be reconciled, only they don't know *who* is to begin. I can tell you. *You* are! But I am the eldest,—

yes, and *therefore* ought to begin. But I am the youngest. Then why should the youngest be obstinate? Who are you that you should not go and throw yourself down at your brother's feet and say, "I have done you wrong, pardon me"? Who is to begin? You! Which? Both! When? Now! Oh, beware of the morality which says, "I am looking for the opportunity, and if things should so get together——" Sir, death may be upon you before you reason out your wretched casuistry; the injured or the injurer may be in the grave before you get to the end of your long melancholy process of self-laudation and anti-Christian logic.

Gen. xlvii.-xlix.
THE LAST DAYS OF JACOB.

WE have seen Jacob a runaway, a stranger, a hireling, and a prince having power with God. His deceptions, his dreams, his prayers, his visions, are now closing; and the sunset is not without gorgeousness and solemnity. Every sunset should make us pray or sing; it should not pass without leaving some sacred impression upon the mind. The dying sun should be a teacher of some lesson, and mystery, and grace of providence. We shall now see Jacob as we have never seen him before. Who can tell but in the splendours of the sunset we shall see some points and qualities which have been heretofore concealed? Some men do seem to live most in their dying; we see more of them in the last mysterious hour than we have seen in a life-time; more goodness, more feeling after God, more poignant and vehement desire for things heavenly and eternal. How is this to be accounted for? Base hypocrisy is not the explanation. We may be too ready to find in hypocrisy the explanation of death-bed experiences. Is there not a more excellent way,—a finer, deeper, truer answer to the enigma of that sacred and most tragical moment? Who can tell what sights are beaming on the soul, what new courage is being breathed into the heart, timid through many a weary year? Who can tell what the dying see? *We* have yet to die! Even Christ was revealed by the Cross. We had not known Christ without the crucifixion. The agony came into his prayer when the trouble came into his soul.

The history is a simple one, yet with wondrous perspective. Seventeen years did Israel dwell in the land of Egypt, in the country of Goshen, and when he was a hundred and forty and seven years old, the time drew nigh that Israel must die. Who can fight the army of the Years? Those silent soldiers never lose a war. They fire no base cannon, they use no vulgar steel, they strike with invisible but irresistible hands. Noisy force loses something by its very noise. The silent years bury the tumultuous throng. We have all to be taken down. The strongest tower amongst us, heaven-reaching in its altitude, must be taken down—a stone at a time, or shaken with one rude shock to the level ground :—man must die. Israel had then but one favour to ask. So it comes to us all. We who have spent a life-time in petitioning for assistance have at the last but one request to make. "Take me," said one of England's brightest wits in his dying moments, "to the window that I may feel the morning air." "Light, more light," said another man greater still, expressing some wondrous necessity best left as a mystery. "Bury me not, I pray thee, in Egypt," said dying Jacob to his son Joseph, "but bury me in the burying-place of my fathers." What other heaven had the Old Testament man? The grave-yard was a kind of comfort to him. He must be buried in a given place marked off and sacredly guarded. He had not lived up into that universal humanity which says—All places are consecrated, and every point is equally near heaven with every other point, if so be God dig the grave and watch it. By-and-by we shall hear another speech in the tone of Divine revelation ; by-and-by we shall get rid of these localities, and limitations, and prisons, for the Lion of the tribe of Judah will open up some wider space of thought, and contemplation, and service. With Joseph's oath dying Jacob was satisfied.

Now we come upon family scenes. Joseph will have his two sons Manasseh and Ephraim blessed, and for so sweet an office Israel strengthened himself and sat upon the bed. What hints of life's mystery are there! The courteous old gentleman strengthened himself when he heard that princely Joseph was coming with his sons. How we can whip ourselves up to one other effort! How we can just blow the smouldering embers into a little flash and flame—one last sparkle! the effort of

desperation. Now the old man will tell his life-story over
We wonder how he will *begin,* and where. It is a delicate
matter to be autobiographical. Jacob is about to look backwards,
and to relate the story of his own earthly career. Where will he
begin? There are some graves we dare not rip open. What will
he tell Joseph about his own early life? To the last he is a
kind of inspired schemer; to the last he knows where to draw
boundary lines, how to make introductions and exceptions. He
will tell about the old blind Isaac? No. He will say how he
ran away from Esau whom he had supplanted? No. What
will he say then by way of beginning? He will begin at the
second birth. That is where we, too, are called to begin. Do not
celebrate the old natural fleshly birthday—that was in reality
death-day. Jacob will begin where he himself truly began to be,
"God Almighty appeared unto me at Luz in the land of Canaan,
and blessed me." What a subtle narrator! What a gift in
history! Not a word about the old homestead and old doings;
but beginning with regeneration, when he threw off the old man
and started up—though with some rudeness of outline needing
infinite discipline—into a brighter, larger self. This is a mystery
in Providence as revealing itself in the consciousness of the
redeemed and sanctified soul. We should be in perpetual despair
if we went back to our very earliest doings, and bound ourselves
within the prison of our merely fleshly and earthly memories.
Each of us has had a Luz in his way. Surely every soul calling
itself in any degree right with God, or right in its desires at least
towards God, has had a vision-place and a vision-hour,—a place
so sacred that other places were forgotten in its memory : an hour
so bright that all earlier hours absorbed their paler rays in its
ineffable effulgence. Now are we the sons of God. We began
our true life when God began his life within the soul. So this
well-skilled autobiographer will say nothing about other times.
God himself has promised never to mention them to us. He
says,—Come, now, and we will gather up the sins as into one
great stone, and plunge it into the infinite depths, and the billows
shall keep it concealed for ever. We must not drag back the
memory to days of murder, dissipation, blasphemy, and all
wickedness. We begin our life where God began the life of the
soul. Now, being free at the beginning, Jacob is eloquent. After

getting over some sentences how the soul can flow away in easy copious speech! He told how Rachel died in the land of Canaan when yet there was but a little way to come unto Ephrath, and how he buried her in the way and set a pillar upon her grave which he meant to stand evermore, thinking that all ages must weep over the woman whose soul departed as she travailed in birth with Benoni. Heedless ages! The pillars of the dead have no sanctity in their cold eyes, yet it does us good to think that many will cry about the spots which mark our own heartbreak. Surely every man must cry where we cried; surely our tears have consecrated some places; surely no fool can laugh where our soul nearly died.

Now a scene occurs which must have had the effect of a moral resurrection upon dying Jacob. Joseph set his sons in the order of their ages. He was so far a technicalist and a pedant that he would keep up the well-known law of succession by primogeniture. But Jacob guided his hands wittingly and crossed them so as to violate that sacred law. Joseph was displeased and said "Not so, my father, but otherwise"; and Jacob said "I know it, my son, I know it; but this is right." Who can tell what passions surged through his own soul at that moment? What is this duplication of one's life? What is this sudden enbodiment of shadows standing up and confronting us in a silence more terrible than accusatory speech, our other-selves, strange shadow-memories, actions which we could explain but may not: benedictions which express a philosophy which we dare not reveal in terms? A wonderful life is the human life—yea, a life within a life, a sanctuary having impenetrable places in it. Others may see some deeds or shadows of deeds upon the window as they pass by, but only the man himself knows what is written in the innermost places of the silent soul.

Israel is now in a mood of benediction. We need but to begin some things in order to proceed quite rapidly and lavishly. So Jacob will now bless his own sons. We must read the benedictions as a whole. Months might be spent in the detailed analysis and criticism of the blessings, but even that detailed examination would leave us in almost total ignorance of the real scope and value of those benedictions as revelations of the quality of the mind and heart of the man who pronounced them. What a mind was Jacob's, as shown in the various blessings pronounced upon his children ! How discriminating those now closing eyes ! How they glitter with criticism ! How keen—penetrating, even to the finest lines of distinction ! Surely what we see in those eyes is a gleam of the very soul. This is no joint salutation or valediction ; this is no greeting and farewell mixed up in one confused utterance. This is criticism. This is the beginning of a career of mental development which is the pride of human education and culture. How affectionate too ! In nearly every line there is some accent of affection peculiar to itself. And how prophetic ! The ages are all revealed to the calm vision and sacred gaze of this man who is more in heaven than upon earth. But this prophecy is no phantasy. We have accustomed ourselves now to a definition of prophecy which enables us in some degree to understand this way of allotment and benediction. Prophecy is based on character. We have already defined prophecy as *moral prescience.* Retaining the definition, we see in this instance one of its finest and clearest illustrations. This is no fancy painting. It is the power of the soul in its last efforts to see what crops will come out of this seed and of that ; it is a man standing upon fields charged with seed, the quality of which he well knows, forecasting the harvest. Moral prophecy is vindicated by moral law. There was no property to divide. There was something better than property to give. What a will is this ! It has about it all the force of a man being his own distributer—not only writing a will like a testator, which is of no force until after the testator's death, but already enriching his sons with an inheritance better than measurable lands. What have you to leave to your children ? to your friends ? You could leave an inheritance incorruptible, undefiled and that fadeth not away,—bright memories of love, recollections of sacred sympathy, prayers that lifted the life into new hope, forgiveness that abolished the distinction between earth and heaven, and made pardoned souls feel as if they had seen their Father in heaven ; great will : eternal substance.

How Jacob's conscience burned up in that sacred hour ! He remembered the evil of his sons. He reminded Reuben of what he had done ; he recalled the deed of shame, never to be spoken aloud by human tongue, wrought by Simeon and Levi in the land of

Hamor the Hivite; and because their anger was fierce and their
wrath was cruel, he divided them in Jacob and scattered them
in Israel. " The evil that men do lives after them." Simeon and
Levi had forgotten what they did in their sister's case. Jacob had
not. In such a malediction there are great meanings, even so far
as Jacob is concerned. Jacob knew the cost of sin. Jacob knew
that no man can of himself shake off his sin and become a free
man in the universe. The sin follows him with swift fate, opens
its mouth like a wolf and shows its cruel teeth. No man can forgive sin. Who but God can wrestle with it ? We fly from it,
try to forget it; but up it leaps again, a foe that pursues unto the
death, unless some Mighty One shall come to deal with it when
there is no eye to pity and no arm to help. But presently Jacob
will come to a name that will change his tone. How some faces
brighten us! How the incoming of some men makes us young
again ! Jacob we have never seen until he comes to pronounce
his blessing upon Joseph.

"Joseph is a fruitful bough, even a fruitful bough by a well; whose
branches run over the wall : the archers have sorely grieved him, and shot
at him, and hated him : but his bow abode in strength, and the arms of his
hands were made strong by the hands of the mighty God of Jacob ; (from
thence is the shepherd, the stone of Israel :) even by the God of thy father,
who shall help thee ; and by the Almighty, who shall bless thee with
blessings of heaven above, blessings of the deep that lieth under, blessings of
the breasts, and of the womb : the blessings of thy father have prevailed
above the blessings of my progenitors unto the utmost bound of the everlasting hills : they shall be on the head of Joseph, and on the crown of the head
of him that was separate from his brethren " (xlix. 22-26).

We read this as a speech of words : it came from the original
speaker like a sacrifice of blood. What a marvellous poem !
How judgment blazes in it in certain directions ! " The archers
have sorely grieved him, and shot at him, and hated him. They
have hamstrung this noblest of the offspring of Israel. Did the
" old man eloquent " look round upon the brethren as he said this :
" and blessings shall be upon the crown of the head of him that
was separate from his brethren " ? What sharp darts fell upon
the consciences of the listeners ! There are benedictions that
are judgments. We encourage some men at the expense of the
destruction of others. Words have atmosphere, perspective,
relations that do not instantly appear upon the surface of the

speech. The singing of a hymn may be a judgment to some who hear it; a kind word may awaken burning memories in many consciences. We cannot tell what we say. We cannot follow the whole vibration which follows the utterance of our speech.

Now let Israel die. Bury the old man where he would like to be buried. Wherever such a man is buried, now that God has wrought the evil out of him, sweet flowers must grow;—Eden must begin.

Gen. xlv. 9-11.

"Haste ye, and go up to my father, and say unto him, Thus saith thy son Joseph, God hath made me lord of all Egypt: come down unto me, tarry not: and thou shalt dwell in the land of Goshen, and thou shalt be near unto me, thou, and thy children, and thy children's children, and thy flocks, and thy herds, and all that thou hast. And there will I nourish thee; for yet there are five years of famine; lest thou, and thy household, and all that thou hast, come to poverty."

JOSEPH'S DEATH.

JOSEPH was still a *son*, though lord of all Egypt. He had still an affectionate heart, though pomp and circumstance conspired to give him great eminence and wonderful power in the whole land of his enforced adoption. A man should never forget his father. Twenty years afterwards and more, Joseph's heart yearned after his father with all a child's clinging trustfulness and unsophisticated trembling pathos. A man should always be a boy when his father is at hand. Did I say always? Alas! I am compelled to add that there are circumstances under which fathers cease to be fathers. There may arise such combinations of circumstances as shall dispossess a man of his fatherhood, that shall turn him into a stranger and an alien. It is well, therefore, for us, whether fathers or children, clearly to understand this matter. Nothing but moral considerations should ever separate a father and his child. Not because the father is poor should the child disown him or treat his name lightly; not because he is destitute of learning should a child affect to contemn his parent. But when the father is morally corrupt,—when all the rain, and sunshine, and dew, and living breeze of a child's long-continued patient love have been lost upon him,—then there may come a time of final separation, when the child says, "I have no father." What is animal parentage, after all? You say you are a man's father: but what is the meaning of that? If that fatherhood is but fleshly, it is not parentage in any deep, tender, lasting sense of the term. It may be a relationship that can hardly be helped,—an external temporary relationship; there is no kinship enduring that is not moral. It is when souls are akin that fatherhood and sonship, brotherhood and sisterhood, are established. It may come to be the same thing with the son. There are fathers who have been compelled to shut the door on their own sons, and did not do so lightly; it was not for the first offence,—it was not until every hope had been disappointed, every godly desire had been repulsed and mortified, and all the volume and passion of human love had been repelled and scorned and blasphemed. Blessed are they who would for ever keep all family relationships, all tender kindreds, fresh, blooming, bright! If they would do so they must live in Christ,—their centre must be fixed upon the eternal love of the One Father. Then they will never outgrow their affections; they will be young for ever, responsive to the voice of love, always sensitive, tender, good.

A very beautiful speech is this which Joseph makes concerning his father. "Say unto him, God hath made me lord of all Egypt; therefore the bond between us is cut. Say to him, I disown my relationship to a shepherd: a man living in the bush, keeping flocks and herds, and wandering about from place to place. Say I am lord of all Egypt, and to come within the circle of my influence is to be blinded and dazzled by my glory." What a chivalrous, filial, beautiful speech! But, fortunately, we have put that speech into Joseph's mouth. Yet how well it would come after the introduction, "Say unto him, I am lord over all Egypt." But that is not the message. You would say, you who had not read it, but only heard it, "It sounded very like that." So it did, but it was perfectly different from that. The speech reads: "Thus saith thy son Joseph, God hath made me lord of all Egypt." It is the word *God* that saves the speech, that makes it musical, that gives it high tone and noble bearing, profound and gentle meaning. If Joseph had said, "Tell my father I am lord over all Egypt," I should have expected a different ending to the speech. But when a man's greatness—whatever it be, political, social, or religious—is all traced to God, out of that one consideration will come wisdom, and nobleness, and pathos. Always depend upon a man who finds in God the Redeemer of his soul, the Elevator of his circumstances. Religion never made a man haughty ; Christianity never made a man unendurable. There have been many great men,—self-conceited, dangerous to go near, self-important,—always standing upon what they call their dignity ; but they did not know what it was to live in God and to live for Christ, and to exert their influence from the elevation of the Cross. My young friend on the way to eminence, having a sceptre of wide influence just in view, seeing thy way clear to ten thousand a year and many accessories to thy greatness and stability, know this : that thy throne will have but a tottering foundation if it rest anywhere but upon the omnipotence and all-graciousness of God.

The next point arises in connection with Jacob's receipt of the intelligence :—

"And they went up out of Egypt, and came into the land of Canaan unto Jacob their father, and told him, saying, Joseph is yet alive, and he is governor over all the land of Egypt. And Jacob's heart fainted, for he believed them not. And they told him all the words of Joseph, which he had said unto them : and when he saw the wagons which Joseph had sent to carry him, the spirit of Jacob their father revived : and Israel said, It is enough ; Joseph my son is yet alive : I will go and see him before I die " (xlv. 25-28).

Observe, in the first instance, the old man's heart fainted, for the news was to him too good to be true. There is in life an element which is continually upsetting probabilities,—thus calling men up from lethargy, from that flatness, staleness, and unprofitableness of existence which would necessarily predominate if there was nothing strange, sensational, and romantic in our human relationships and in the events by which we are surrounded. Now and then we require to be startled a little. Men do us good who rouse us. The preacher who makes me shake does me good,—who gives me a new view of truth, who rouses me out of my indifference, who gives me to feel that as yet I know next to nothing. So in daily life, things that are common sometimes flame up before us into new significance. and old ruts seem sometimes to have new spikes of grass and new roots coming out of them. These things call us away from apathies that would benumb and deaden the soul. But we cannot always live in the wonderful. It is there that so many persons get wrong. You cannot live upon champagne ; you cannot live upon luxuries ; you cannot live healthily upon sensation. You must have something substantial, real, deep, vital,—something that touches the profoundest experience of your life, the inmost consciousness of your spirit, and that follows you through all the engagements of the day. You must have the practical, as well as the imaginative ; you must have the substantial, as well as the poetical. I believe in the airy dream ; I believe also in the solid rock. I like to look on the far-flashing cross that surmounts the great pile ; but let me remember that yonder cross never would have blazed in the rising or setting sun if there were not somewhere the great strong foundation upon which it is rested.

So though the news was too romantic for Jacob, though it caused him to fall into a swoon, yet the old man, who always had an eye for the practical, looked up, saw the waggons, and his heart revived. We must have waggons as well as poems. It is a sad and vulgar thing ; but we must have the substantial, the tangible, and the appreciable, as well as the metaphysical, the transcendental, the mystical, the bewildering, and the grand. It is even so in the religious life. The long prayer must be succeeded by the noble deed. The bold theological statement must be flanked and buttressed, or otherwise supported by un-challengeable morality. What if a man says he believes in God and his deeds be ungodly ? what does his belief in God do for him ? What if a man says "I have faith," and have no works ? What if a man preach the gospel and be not *himself* the gospel ?

The brethren had good news for their father. But beyond the good news there must be something else to bring it near to his appreciation. You require to meet men according to their circumstances. God must himself become man before he can touch us and get his mighty redeeming hold upon us ; for we know not the infinite except as it be accommodated to us through the medium of Christ's dear personality, except as it be focalised in the one redeeming life. What did Jacob say when power of speech returned to him ? " It is enough ; Joseph is yet alive.' What did his brethren say about his being in Egypt ? They said he was *governor* over all the land of Egypt. Joseph sent word that he was *lord* over all the land. Jacob said, "He is alive!" A man cannot live upon lords, and governors, and fine eminent personages, in their merely official capacity. There are times when we strip away all ribbons, and flowers, and decorations, and other trumperies, and go right into the life and heart of things. Why, if they had said to Jacob, "Joseph is yet alive: we found him lying in the hedgeside, just alive, with hardly anything to cover him,—a poor, lonely, forlorn wanderer"! would that have made any difference to Israel? Would he not just as much have yearned for his child? Let us hope he would. There are times, I repeat, when we want to know about the life rather than the condition. A man's life consisteth not in the abundance of the things which he possesseth.

Whatever Israel's feelings might have been concerning Joseph, had the statement of the circumstances been other, let me preach this glorious gospel : God does not ask whether we be lords, potentates, or governors; but whether we have turned our poor dying eyes towards our abandoned home. The moment he hears —and he always listens—the soul say, "I will arise and go to my Father," he comes to meet us, to anticipate the statement of our sin and penitence, and to clothe us with his unsearchable riches. Men cannot believe that. It is at that point that souls are ruined by the million. They want to send word to him that they are lords over the land and governors over their circumstances; that they can maintain themselves pretty well, after all; but, if he likes to meet them on an independent basis, they will hold an interview with Almighty God. He will not accept that challenge. He does not know us when our heads are lifted up in that insanity. It is when we are nothing and have nothing, and *know* it, and turn our poor disappointed, shattered hearts towards his dwelling-place, towards the Cross of Christ, that he meets us with the infinite fulness of his pardon, and all the assurance of his willingness to save.

Then the third point brings up the meeting between Joseph and his father :—

"And Joseph made ready his chariot, and went up to meet Israel his father, to Goshen, and presented himself unto him ; and he fell on his neck, and wept on his neck a good while. And Israel said unto Joseph, Now let me die, since I have seen thy face, because thou art yet alive" (xlvi. 29, 30).

A beautiful combination of official duty and filial piety! The whole land of Egypt is suffering from famine. Joseph is the controller and the administrator of the resources of the land. He does not abandon his position and go away to Canaan; but he gets the chariot out, and he must go part of the road. "I know I am father to Pharaoh and all his great people. I shall not be away long; I shall soon be back again to my duties. I must go a little way to meet the old man from home." Yes, I do not care what our duties are, we can add a little pathos to them if we like; whatever be our lot, we can add a little sentiment to our life. And what is life without sentiment? What are the flowers without an occasional sprinkling of dew? It may be a grand thing to sit on a high stool and wait till the old man comes upstairs. But it is an infinitely grander thing, a "lordlier chivalry," to come off the stool and go away to meet him a mile or two on the road. Your home will be a better home—I do not care how poor the cot—if you have a little sentiment in you, a little tenderness and nice feeling. These are things that sweeten life. I do not want a man to wait until there is an earthquake in order that he may call and say, How do you do? I do not want a man to do earthquakes for me. Sometimes I want a chair handed, and a door opened, and a kind pressure of the hand, and a gentle word. And as for the earthquakes, why—wait until they come!

What a beautiful picture of reunion is this! "He fell on his neck, and wept on his neck a good while." See them there! The old man not speaking, because he cannot speak,—speaking most because saying nothing. Joseph not speaking for some time. Only weeping upon one another! Then Jacob, not wanting the thing to be spoiled, says, "Now the next thing, the next thing, Joseph, must be heaven! Whatever comes after this will be an anti-climax. Now let me die!" It was as old Simeon spake when he saw the Child of God, "Now let thy servant depart in peace." We do now and again in life come to points we do not want to leave. We say, "Lord, let us build here." But the Lord says, No, not here, because there is a lunatic at the foot of the hill; and you must not build and put yourself into nice places, and settle down, until you have seen whether you cannot heal the lunacy that is in the world below.

I cannot look upon those two men together without feeling that moral gulfs may be bridged. Joseph was no prodigal son. But, as I see Joseph and his father resting on each other, and weeping out their joy, I cannot but think of that other and grander meeting, when a man who has been twenty years away from God, or fifty years away from all that is true and beautiful in moral life, finds his way back! He does not go in a chariot or walk uprightly, but crawls on his bare hands and knees; and God meets him, lifts him up, and when the man begins to tell " how poor and—" God hushes him with a great burst of forgiving love! It seems as if God will never allow us to finish the statement of our penitence. It is enough for him that we begin the story, punctuating it with sobs and tears. He causes the remainder of the statement to go down in the ocean of his love, in the infinitude of his mercy! Is there to be any home-going to-day? Is any man going to say, " I will arise and go to my Father"? Go! He calleth thee,—poor old pilgrim, grey-headed, burdened, sinful, self-abhorring! Go! And thou shalt come out no more for ever!

The fourth point arises in connection with Jacob's introduction to Pharaoh :—

"And Joseph brought in Jacob his father, and set him before Pharaoh: and Jacob blessed Pharaoh. And Pharaoh said unto Jacob, How old art thou? And Jacob said unto Pharaoh, The days of the years of my pilgrimage are an hundred and thirty years: few and evil have the days of the years of my life been, and have not attained unto the days of the years of the life of my fathers in the days of their pilgrimage" (xlvii. 7-9).

It is very tender, pathetic, and instructive to hear an old man sum up his life. How did Jacob sum up his earthly course? He said it was a " pilgrimage." He had been going from place to place, hardly ever resting, always on the move, scarcely ever taking off his sandals, scarcely laying down his staff. Life is a pilgrimage to us. We are strangers here ; we have no continuing city here. Jacob also said that the days of the years of his life had been few ! Think of a man over a hundred years of age saying that his days had been few ! They are few when looked back upon. They seem so to run into one another as to make but a moment. You look a hundred years ahead, and you cannot endure the thought of existing under present circumstances, so long a time. Yet, if you could go to the end of the century and look back upon the vanished days, you would say they had been few. Jacob said that not only the days had been few but evil. We get to see the brokenness of life, its incompleteness, its fragmentariness, when we get through it. But when it is all over, and the old man looks back, he says, "Evil have been my days. If not morally evil altogether, if here and there there are signs of holiness and trust in God,—yet, looked at as a whole, my life has been a poor structure; my days have been evil; I have been wanting in effective work. There is not one word of self-praise I can claim, when I look back on the days of my pilgrimage."

Now we come to the last scene of all—to the close of this strange eventful history. "Joseph died, and all his brethren, and all that generation." Joseph died! Then after all, he was but mortal, like ourselves! It is important to remember this, lest we should let any of the great lessons slip away under the delusion that Joseph was more than man. We have seen fidelity so constant, heroism so enduring, magnanimity so—I had almost said—Divine, that we are apt to think there must have been something more than human about this man. No. He was mortal, like ourselves. His days were consumed, as are our days; little by little his life ebbed out ; and he was found, as we shall be found, dead. So, then, if he was but mortal, why cannot we be as great in our degree ? If he was only a man, why cannot we emulate his virtues, so far as our circumstances will enable us to do so ? We' cannot all be equally heroic and sublime. We can all be, by the grace of God, equally holy, patient, and trustful in our labour.

Joseph died ! Thus the best, wisest, and most useful men are withdrawn from their ministry ! This is always a mystery in life : that the good man should be taken away in the very prime of his usefulness ; that the eloquent tongue should be smitten with death ; that a kind father should be withdrawn from his family circle ; and that wretches who never have had a noble thought, who do not know what it is to have a brave, heavenly impulse, should seem to have a tenacity of life that is unconquerable ; that drunken men and hard-hearted individuals should live on and on,—while the good, the true, the wise, the beautiful, and the tender, are snapped off in the midst of their days and translated to higher climes. The old proverb says, "Whom the gods love die young." Sirs! There is another side to this life, otherwise these things would be inexplicable,—would be chief of the mysteries of God's ways. We must wait, therefore, until we see the circle completed before we sit in judgment upon God.

Joseph died! Then the world can get on without its greatest and best men. This is very humiliating to some persons. Here is, for example, a man who has never been absent from his business for twenty years. You ask him to take a day's holiday, go to a church-opening, or to a religious festival. He says, " My dear sir! Why, the very idea! The place would go to rack and ruin if I was away four-and-twenty hours." It comes to pass that God sends a most grievous disease upon the man,—imprisons him in the darkened chamber for six months. When he gets up at the end of six months, he finds the business has gone on pretty much as well as if he had been wearing out his body and soul for it all the time. Very humiliating to go and find things getting on without us! Who are we? The preacher may die, but the truth will be preached still. The minister perishes,—the ministry is immortal. This ought to teach us, therefore, that we are not so important, after all ; that our business is to work all the little hour that we have ; and to remember that God can do quite as well without us as with us, and that he puts an honour upon us in asking us to touch the very lowest work in any province of the infinite empire of his truth and light.

When few die we can name them one by one,—count them on our fingers. "Joseph died." Some deaths are national events. Some deaths are of world-wide importance. "And all his brethren." There we begin to lose individuality. Death is coming upon us now quicker. We have no time to go through them,—Judah, Simeon, Reuben, and so forth. " All his brethren, and all that generation." Death is mowing them down! You have no time to read their names and pick each out individually. Such is death! Crushing up one generation in one grasp ; mowing down the next with one swing of the scythe. We cannot all, therefore, be equally conspicuous ; each cannot have his name written in history as having died. Some of us will be classed in dozens. "All his brethren," and no name left! Others of us will not even be known as families and households. We die as parts of a generation,—a great crowd, an innumerable body! What of it ? The thing is not to leave a name behind us—a mere name. It is to leave behind influences that hearts will feel, memories that will be cherished at home, and that will be blessed by those whom we have served and helped in life. Die! The time will come when men will laugh at death. We shall one day get such a view of the universe, that we shall look down upon death, and say, " O death, where is thy sting ? " How so? Jesus Christ abolished death. If we believe in him, death will no longer be to us a spectre, a ghost, an ugly guest in the house, sucking out our blood and darkening our future. It will then become a swinging door,—and, as it swings, we shall pass in to light, to music, to rest. Death will always be a frightful thing to the man who has no Saviour. Death must be more or less a terror to every man who is not in Christ. He may have lived himself into that measure of beasthood that will not confess terror. I never knew of a felled ox, saying, "Death is very terrible." So there are some men who have lived themselves down so beastward and devilward that they hardly know death from life. But to a man who has any consciousness of right and wrong, any moral sensitiveness, if he have not God in the house, death must be an unwelcome thing to him, a dark and terrible interlocutor. But the man who is in Christ, his life is above the reach of death. When the body crumbles and falls down, to get up no more in this state of things, the soul is a guest in Heaven. A guest ? Nay,—he is a child at Home!

"HANDFULS OF PURPOSE," FOR ALL GLEANERS.

I. *"Ye shall be as gods."*—GEN.
iii. 5.
Tempted to an *upward* fall !
Another instance of *forcing*
destiny.
Man *was* meant to be some-
thing better.
Man must not *know* evil by
creating it.
Men drink that they may be
happy.
Men lie that they may *succeed*.
Beware of temptations to *up-
ward falls*.

II. *"God took him."*—GEN. v. 24.
What God is *always* doing.
What God has a *right* to do.
Various roads to the end.
Every death a *Divine* act.
God knows when the fruit is
ripe.
Times and ways are *fixed*.
The *fact* of sovereignty proves
the theory.

III. *"The place of the altar, which
he made there at the first."*
GEN. xiii. 4.
Returning to *first faiths*.
Returning from *iniquity*.
Returning from *scepticism*.
Returning from *indifference*.
Experience teaches what life
needs

God *awaits* our return (Isa. lv.).
The *Divine* side is right.

IV. *"And his sons Isaac and
Ishmael buried him."*—GEN.
xxv. 9.
Meeting only at *funerals*.
The *separations* of life.
The value of *special* occurrences.
Sometimes *joyous* occasions.
Should always meet in *sorrow*.
Opportunity is a phase of *Pro-
vidence*.
We *might* have met but did not !

V. *"I have learned by experience."*
GEN. xxx. 27.
The *true* teacher.
The *universal* monitor.
The *indisputable* evidence.
Experience of *sin,—pardon,—
peace*.
Character thus becomes argu-
ment.
Let *sin* be subjected to this test.
The Christian triumphant *here*.
Many can answer by *experience*
who cannot answer by *con
troversy*.

VI. *"And Laban called it Jegar-
Sahadutha, but Jacob called it
Galeed."*—GEN. xxxi. 47.
Both these words mean the
same thing.

Just what people are doing now.
Different names for the very
same thing!
The difficulty is always in
words.
There is less difference in the
Church than is often supposed.
Evolution and *Providence* may
often be used identically.
Environment and *Circumstances*
are one and the same, in
many uses.
Each man is at liberty to speak
in the language he knows
best.

VII. "*The sun rose upon him.*"
Gen. xxxii. 31.
After an experience of *darkness.*
After a night of *prayer.*
The morning tells what the
night has been.
Blessed are they who can *bear*
the sunlight.
Men may prefer darkness.
The sun *will* rise,—on *what*
shall he rise?

VIII. "*And Esau said, I have
enough, my brother.*"—Gen.
xxxiii. 9.
The first man who ever said so.
What even non-spiritual men
may say.
Should not Christians say more?
Property should be a *heart-store.*
"Enough" can never be true
of *spiritual* blessings.
The evils of avaricious grasping.
We must not be avaricious, even
on the plea that it is for *others.*

Christianity should be proved
by contentment.
Examples of Christ and Paul.

IX. "*Gad, a troop shall overcome
him : but he shall overcome at
the 'ast.*"—Gen. xlix. 19.
Intermediate failures and final
triumphs.
Do not judge until "the last."
Men who are overcome should
be *encouraged.*
Apply this to beginners in
business—in Christian life—
in the reformation of bad
habits.
Apply this to spiritual *doubt.*
Do not too readily describe
men as infidels. Even un-
believers may at *last* believe.
Hope for your *children.*

X. "*And when Joseph's brethren
saw that their father was dead,
they said, Joseph will peradventure hate us, and will certainly
requite us all the evil which we
did unto him.*"—Gen. l. 15.
The memory of *conscience.*
The powerlessness of mere
time.
The difficulty of self-forgive-
ness.
The difficulty of crediting others
with magnanimity.
They measured Joseph by
themselves.
Joseph's true greatness (v. 19,
20).
Was he not worthy of the
great blessing?

THE PANORAMA OF GENESIS.

ALL books of action, as distinguished from books of thought, admit of being viewed in what may be termed a panoramic way; that is to say, the whole may be so seen as to express the purpose of the book without being distracted by the endless detail; the difference between a panoramic view and a critico-historical view being in some degree the difference between a terrestrial globe and a set of topographical maps. In the latter, a market place may be quite an important feature; in the former, it is utterly without recognition. Such a book as Genesis may be thrown into a panoramic form, so as to impress the memory and affect the heart as no mere detail can ever do. Suppose the whole book to have been read through at once without pause or distraction, what would be the mental condition of the reader? The mind would, for the moment, be stunned by the infinite action. Rest—there has been none. The action has been as the swell and rush of great seas, and the varied noise has blended in its boom, tempests of wind, roars of thunder, and cruel floods. Never book spake like this book. What is the vision? How lies the land of wonder? Son of man, what seest thou? Form rises out of shapelessness ; beasts wander over the earth ; birds fly in the wide firmament ; a man is made, and then a sweet, fair woman, who seems to be himself idealised ; a garden—a home all blossoms, a church of leaves, through which, as the soft wind parts them, one can see God. Two men—a murderer, one of them ; more men ; cities ; interchanges, inventions ; then dreams, pilgrimages, new outlooks, and covenants which tell that falsehood is possible. Amid all the rush there is a strange quietness ; there are men who stay at home to make fields fruitful, and keep the flocks from harm ; quiet women, who know every change in the face of the sky, and the temper of every wind that hides its fury in a moan. Yes, sweet scenes on the uplands, in the valleys, and on the edge of the wilderness— homes where peace lives, and prayer opens the upper gate ; and homes of another sort, where jealousy rises before daybreak, where discontent makes every feast a disappointment, and where revenge whets its weapon in secret. So lies the wonderland—so breaks the morning on the awakening earth.

The mind can keep no steady line in the contemplation of this book of wonders. This "beginning" of creation is the burial of ages. The punctuation of the first chapter of Genesis is a punctuation of centuries; say every comma represents ten thousand of our little years, every semicolon a myriad ages, every period a practical eternity. If we had a right sense of *duration*, we should read the Book of Genesis more intelligently. We are the victims of the clocks we have made. We think we have made the "day" as well as the clock, and by our clock we measure God's "evening" and God's "morning." We need, too, to correct our ideas of space as well as our conceptions of time. About space we know nothing. Quantity is a term we cannot define. In the highest imagining Time is impossible, and Space is also impossible, except in relation to other duration and quantity, towards which the relation is only possible, not actual; for whilst an hour may have a relation to a millennium, a millennium can have no relation to an eternity. So we cannot read the first of Genesis at all, excepting in some mumbling manner which leaves out all the music. We should read better, if we had no vexing clock ticking its impertinences in ears that should be filled with the boom of eternity. As for space, let the firmament rebuke us. There is room enough in that roof to make Venus but a diamond and Jupiter a sparkle of amber. Up there, the burning worlds are mere glints of pale fire; there the constellations take up no room; there the created universe is less than nothing beside the majesty of the uncreated God. We must not play the critic in this chapter, for we can neither measure its distance nor handle its materials. Be it history, be it allegory, be it fact in a dream, or a poem framed in fact, we cannot grasp it; we want more light, more time, more space.

So the heavens and the earth are formed, and the host of them set in temporary order. We see, at least, the outline of a universe. What is the universe? Is it but a mighty aggregation of mud, without living relations, and high purposes, and methods full of wisdom and beneficence? Is its movement a hap-chance whirl which will bring itself to a stop by its own madness, and the star-dancers drop out of rank through sheer giddiness and exhaustion ? What is the universe ? To me, at present, it is a boundless school, a house of God, a magnificent exemplification of unity, order, harmony, and balance of cause and effect. Its order is sensitive ; let but a pin or loop in all the mechanism get out of place, and creation would shudder as if in pain. Behold the blessed, peaceful, unity—no atom out of course, no dew-drop in excess, no shaft of light too luminous, no grass-blade omitted from the great audit, not a sparrow falling without record, the very hairs of our head all numbered ! What harmony of movement ! What infinite intersection, without rush or noise, collision, or confusion ! Star glittering to star as if in cipher of light ; thunder and sea utter the same sad melody ; night and day but phases of the same majestic Presence. That is the universe outlined in this chapter of Eternity.

Son of man, what seest thou ? The vision is now full of mystery. Men are building pillars, and writing strange words upon them ; Noah builds an altar on the drenched earth ; Abram piles an altar in the plain of Moreh, in the face of the hostile Canaanite ; Jacob sets up a pillar near the foot of the dream-ladder—fires are burning, and the Lord is smelling a sweet savour as of an acceptable sacrifice. Yet, amidst all the memorial pillars and altar fires, a marvellous work of deception and varied wickedness never ceases. Men turn from the altar to tell new lies. Men offer the sacrifice with one hand and rob their neighbour with the other. Floods, fires, devastations, all express the righteousness of God and the wickedness of man ; yet the Lord will not give up the sinner, and the sinner will not wholly turn away from heaven the expectations which are prayers. The scene is full of confusion. If men would always pray, or if men would always curse, we should have the rest of consistency. But they will not. Cain murders Abel, yet in some way asks the protection of God. Jacob robs Esau, and asks for a blessing. Quite a wonderful thing is this. Is there inconsistency in God ? Is he not inconsistent when he permits the wicked man to live ? Does he not cease to be God when he ceases to slay the unholy ? Nay, did he not uncrown himself when he made a being to whom sin was possible ? Did not God himself begin the infinite rebellion ?

Thus, so soon, do great questions bring great troubles, and solemn wonders darken into heavy afflictions. A great moral tragedy here sets in. We must not attempt to catch this torrent in the tank of our ignorant wisdom. Let it rush on in its overwhelming fury, and, when it settles into a quiet river, we may ask some questions. Turn to some quieter scene, and say what are those black lines that run through the pages of Genesis ? These are the early funerals of the race—Sarah buried in the field of Ephron, in the cave of the field of Machpelah ; Rachel buried in the way to Ephrath ; Abraham laid to rest by the side of Sarah, in the land of Heth ; Jacob going on his last journey, to join Abraham, and Sarah, Isaac, and Rebekah, and Leah. So long ago did men die ! So soon were graves dug in the earth, and empty places left in the household ! Ever since, the funeral march has never ceased. Well-trodden is the road that runs to the grave ; a hard path ; solid as lead ; without a flower in all its weary miles—the road that every human foot must tread. Poor burials they were, too, in that far-away time. Mere burials, solemn farewells ! Yet nothing of dignity is wanting, nothing of noble pomp, nothing of ceremonial reverence. But where is the resurrection trumpet ? Where the speech of immortality? Where the oath of reunion ? Where the flower that cannot fade ? Ah me ; these are not in Genesis. Grim death is there ; separation is there ; good-bye is there ; but if we would see Immortality we must see him of whom Moses and the prophets did write. " I am the resurrection and the life. He that believeth in me shall never die." "Death is swallowed up in victory." But the mid-day of this triumph must be waited for.

We spoke of black lines a moment since. Is there not a cause ? What is sin ? Is it a wart upon the hand that may be eaten off with sharp acid, or a stain upon the heart not to be touched but by the blood of Christ ? Is it a mere mistake, a mischance, a knot or twist in life's string, which any child may untie or straighten ? Is it a little grit on the smooth wheel, which tissue paper well used will remove, or chemist's oil dissolve and cleanse ? What is sin ? A stumble, but not a fall ? A skin-wound, but not a fatal mischief of the heart ? A discord that sets off the harmony, or a thunderbolt that crashes the organ into splinters, and leaves it without shape or tone ? "Fools make a mock at sin." Fools look upon it as a variety of sport. If an enemy can twist the circles of the universe, reverse the order of the seasons, cause the sun to stagger at mid-day, and the moon to totter from the throne of night, that enemy would be sin, and there are fools who would mock the hideous disorder. Who could bear to see the blue heavens churned into foam by the plunging orbs that have been their eternal crown? Fools. What is the universe? Is it an infinite stretch of insensibility? An infinite heartlessness? An infinite vacuity? Then, truly, we may mock its misfortunes and find our laughter in the ghastliness of its ruins. To me the universe is other than this. It is my Father's house; it is a sanctuary; the very life of God runs through it and makes it glad. It is not God, indeed, but an expression of his wisdom and power, his preliminary disclosure and incarnation—the light is his garment, and as for the wings of the wind he walketh upon them. My God is not an infinite Intellect; he is an infinite Heart as well. He feels, he sympathises, he suffers; he is glad in the pureness of our joy; he mourns in the bitterness of our grief. I cannot explain this. But what is there that man can explain? Not the throb of his own heart, not the uplifting of his own hand, not the origin and outgoing of his own thought. For God's fullest answer to sin we must wait further revelation than we have in Genesis. Meanwhile, even there an altar burns: even there blood begins to mean some moral mystery.

So we close this Unbeginning Beginning, or, rather, open this Gate of Wonders. The very name *Genesis* would seem to be inspired. "This beginning of miracles" did the Spirit of God. Other titles may be left to what we call Authorship; *this* is the creation of God. "Beginning" is a word which pledges no date, excludes no sane imagining—a definition without boundaries—not an earth, divided between the gardener and the sexton, but a Sky, a Heaven, an Eternity.

"HERE ENDETH THE FIRST LESSON."

PREACHING THROUGH THE BIBLE

BY
JOSEPH PARKER

VOL. 2

EXODUS

Originally printed
under the title,
The People's Bible

CONTENTS.

"HANDFULS OF PURPOSE"—

THE SECOND BOOK OF MOSES.

A CONTINUOUS perusal of the book of Exodus from end to end leaves upon my mind the impression that there is in it the protoplasm of the whole action of God in the complete sphere of human history; in other words, I have not met with any phase of Divine revelation or ministry which is not to be traced in at least a dawning outline in this second book of Moses. Emphasis is to be laid upon the continuousness of the reading, for it is quite conceivable that a casual glance would discover a ruggedness amounting almost to chaos in the distribution of the infinite materials ; a ruggedness not to be subdued, and smoothed into the general music, but by a mood of soul at once ardent and devout. Take, first of all, the personal revelation of God, the abruptest of all the miracles, and yet the most suppressed ; a flame in a wilderness, barred in and made intense by branches that the wind might have broken,—and a Name as mysteriously human as the bush is mysteriously equal to the solemn occasion ; then another Name not human at all, in its first impression on the mind, a Verb whose conjugation cannot go beyond a line, an I AM that doubles back upon itself and waits with mysterious patience to " become flesh and dwell among us." Meanwhile it will leap like a spirit into the Shepherd-wanderer and find in him a rude and temporary incarnation. But the first name is the human one, and truly most unexpected and startling when we consider its import. " I am the God of ———." Given such a beginning to find what the

end will be ? Where does the Speaker begin his
historical Godhood ? Surely Adam and Eve will be
recovered from their unaccountable obscurity, and in the
bloom of Edenic beauty will be to Moses an almost rival
revelation,—or Abel who died at the altar,—or Enoch who
never tasted death,—or Noah who began the new world :
all these surmises, so obvious because so natural, are contradicted by the fact. Abraham is the head of the new race;
the larger Adam ; the living Faith. God did nòt date
himself so far back in history as to bewilder the solitary
and overpowered inquirer, but placed himself within
domestic associations and in living relation to names that
made the very earth and sky of the lone man's little
world. Thus was God quite near to Moses, yet in a
moment he withdrew into Eternity and spoke as the I
AM, without angel, or child, or spirit, to break his awful
solitude. For what purpose is he so revealed ? That
he may bring to pass the most terrific collision yet
known in human history. A battle is being arranged
within the sanctuary of the burning bush. Egypt is the
pride of the world, and her power is to be broken. No
doubt her arm is mighty, but the bones of that mean
strength shall be melted like wax by the fire that spares
the frail bush. Chariot against chariot shall dash in war ;
the lightning of heaven against the iron of Egypt, so
now we shall see whether the Lord's thunder or Pharaoh's
noise conceals the heavier bolt. And why this trial of
arms ? Will the Lord set himself in array of battle
against a candle which a breath might extinguish ? For
one reason only,—viz., that he may deliver and redeem
and sanctify a people,—that his strength may make a
way for his love,—that the education of the world may
be moved one battle-field nearer the temple of wisdom.
If God fought for victory he need never fight ; he fights
that he may teach ; he lengthens the day of battle that
he may enlarge all human conceptions of his purpose and
sway with infinite persuasion every human will in the
direction of holiness and truth The details of the

mortal contest must be separately studied. How it ended may be known from the song and the dance, the passionate refrain and the clanging timbrel, the harmonious shout and the ordered rapture, which in all their ecstasy but dimly typify the apocalyptic music whose storm shall welcome the completion of the purposes of God. To the Revelation, the Battle, the Song, many an addition must be made if Exodus is as complete as it has just been supposed to be. A little wandering and chiding, a miracle or two, and then comes the first magnificent addition, the LAW! The moral universe begins to take shape. Instincts, habitudes, wordless motions, aspirations which cannot fall immediately into fit speech, now undergo crystallisation and stand out in many a strange figure as might stand the world to the opened eyes of a man born blind. A greater battle than the fight with Pharaoh began with the giving of the Law, —a subtler contest,—a strife between darkness and light. The law vindicates its own Divine origin, so exceeding broad is the commandment, so infinitely exquisite the infusions of Mercy, a mere flush of warm colour on the neutral grey of the steel statute, a tint, rather than a stain, of blood-like hue, as if an Atonement were not far away, yet the time of its agony not fully come. The Law will not have any man smitten with impunity, the pregnant woman shall be sacred from all injury, the eye of the slave shall be paid for with liberty, no man shall wantonly feed his beast in another man's field, no stranger shall be vexed or oppressed, no widow or fatherless child shall be afflicted, the ass or the ox of the enemy shall not be permitted to go astray, the innocent and the righteous were not to be slain,—a pathos so profound brings tears of joy to the reader's eyes, and so tenderly is the heart moved that when Israel cries in battle music—" the Lord is a man of war," we answer in a thankful hymn,—" his tender mercies are over all his works." So Israel was not taken out of Egypt merely to humble the oppressor, or destroy the tyrant. The purpose vindicates the

means. The river must be turned into blood, frogs and
lice and flies must be sent, boils and blains, and hails
in blackest tempests of ice must not be spared ; in themselves they would be but a display of dramatic violence,
but in the purpose they were intended to express they
were servants of righteousness and liberty and education. By such means, initially, were the evil effects of
four centuries of servitude to be overcome ;—the violence
is the love, in adapted action. The same process is
repeated in every age, with change of accidents it may
be, but the purpose is unchangeable.

Revelation, Battle, Song, and Law. What more is
needed ? God himself will answer, so our invention need
not disquiet itself. Perhaps the answer may be so
expressed as to be its own proof of origin. This is the
answer :—" Let them make me a sanctuary, that I may
dwell among them." This comes after the compassionate
parts of the law with tender grace. All the way God
seems to have been coming nearer as the law softened in
its tone almost into gospel. At the beginning of the
law no man was permitted to come near ; if so much as
a beast touched the mountain it was to be stoned or
thrust through with a dart ; and so terrible was the sight
that Moses said, "I exceedingly fear and quake"; and now
God says, as if his heart ached with some agony of desire,
" Let them make me a sanctuary, that I may dwell
among them." The movement is thus evermore from
law to grace, from distance to nearness, from the throne
to the Cross. In no rhetorical sense, or sense needed to
make up halting rhythm, but in a solid and historical
way exact enough in its throb for science itself, yet
sublime enough in its symbolism to throw prophecy into
despair. Beginning with fire, with smoke as the smoke
of a furnace, with a trumpet sounding long and waxing
louder and louder, who could have foretold that the
Majesty thus accompanied would desire to dwell with the
sons of men ? But this is the effect of all true law. At
the one end it cleaves asunder, at the other it enlarges

itself into new relations and looks wistfully over happier possibilities. The course of literal law is always self-vexatious. Why is the letter impotent? Because man himself is not a letter. Man is a spirit and can be ruled by spirit only. Not the Law, but the Law-giver can satisfy the soul that burns in the bush of the body. The rod smites and hurts, but not until it blossoms does it fulfil even the purpose of law. So now the meaning of the burning bush begins to dawn : it meant that God wished to " dwell " with men, to set his tabernacle side by side with human habitations, and to be accounted Father by all generations. Sinai was too high, the cloud too thick, the lightning too awful, so a house must be built, and the very building of it should be to the builders a spiritual education,—a most gracious condescension, and on the one side of it a mystery profoundly adapted to human nature by permitting man to build the house whilst forbidding him to fashion the God. In view of these spiritual and transcendent revelations, all other questions drop into secondary interest. We care but little at this lustrous point whether Philitrion built the pyramids, or Rameses the oppressor of Israel was the best or worst of Theban kings ; in view of Sinai the avenue of sphinxes sinks into contempt, and " the petrifactions of the sunbeam " look small beside the unhewn towers of the rock : not only Egyptian history but the history of Israel also assumes new valuations : it is now quite matter of secondary interest to trace the march from Succoth to Etham, from Etham to the encampment between Migdol and the pastures of Pi-hahiroth over against Baal-zephon, and on to the point made memorable by the passage of the Red Sea, whether in the north by Magdôlon or in the south under the shadow of Jebel Attâka. The mind is in no temper for such holiday investigations, for the Lord God has himself proposed to " dwell " with men. It is of small import at this critical moment to know that the Song of Moses is marked by the usual " parallelism of clauses," and that

from a critical point of view the triplet stanzas interrupt
the regular cadence with unusual frequency, for we are
about to witness the setting up of the very presence-
chamber of Jehovah.

The character of the book of Exodus seems to change
immediately upon the announcement of the Divine purpose. Although still in the wilderness we are imaginatively amongst the treasures of Memphis, and Zoan, and
Heliopolis, and Rameses, with abundance of blue, and
purple, and scarlet, and fine twined linen, and with such
wealth of metal as to be able to make the very hooks of
gold and the sockets of silver. The Temple of the Sun
is to be extinguished by a new glory, and the consecrated calf of Ra is to give place to sacrifice charged with
sublimest meanings. Is there not a subtle and suggestive
harmony between what Israel had seen in Egypt and
what it was about to see in the wilderness? The gods
of Egypt had been well housed, could Israel suppose that
the God of heaven would dwell in a mean habitation?
For spiritual realisations men have to be long and almost
severely prepared,—a wilderness requires a contrast. So
this tabernacle is no fancy work. The sequence in which
it follows is as severely logical as the point towards
which it tends is ineffably spiritual. A strange thing is
thus wrought in the earth. Invention is not invited, or
any form of natural cleverness ; the inspired house like the
inspired Book employs but willing hands to carry out the
labour, the Builder and Maker is God. He builds all
houses—all lives—all books—that rest on the true Foundation : at first the sacred house was outlined in cloud far
up the hill ; but was not the universe itself thus outlined
" from everlasting, from the beginning, or ever the earth
was, before the heavens were prepared, or a compass had
been set on the face of the deep,"—was it not all wrought
in mystic but palpable cloud ? Did not the cloud revolve
at his touch, and wheel in gyrations infinite, and cast out
sparks that held in their heat the astronomic pomp that
glows like a tabernacle in the wilderness of space? What

is all that upper glory, but blue and purple and scarlet, with an atmosphere for a vail, and a lamp fed eternally with consecrated oil? He that built all things is God. If he built them out of a cloud, the greater is the miracle; if he elaborated them from a molecule, he is even vaster in power than our imagination had dreamed. The nebulous tabernacle may be a hint of the nebulous universe. The most wonderful of God's visible creations are still wrought out in cloud; what landscapes, cities, temples, forests, minarets of snow, and palaces fit for heavenly kings, are to be found in the clouds, let them say who have watched the sky with the patience of love.

The meaning of all this had a mysterious relation to the shedding of blood! We come upon this revelation with a shock. The sequence is shattered by a tremendous blow. Up to this point we have been conscious of more than human refinement, and in a moment we burn with shame as if we had done some deed forbidden. So long as we were working with acacia wood, and pure gold, and blue and purple and scarlet and fine twined linen, and stones precious as sardius and topaz, ligure and jasper, we were content, for a certain elevation moved us to nobler consciousness : but suddenly, even whilst we gaze with religious delight upon the ephod, the breast-plate, and the mitre of Aaron, the blood of a young bullock flows by the door of the tabernacle of the congregation, and whilst the flesh of the bullock is being burned as a sin-offering without the camp, two rams without blemish are slain, and the blood of the second is put upon the tip of the right ear of Aaron, and upon the tip of the right ear of his sons, and upon the thumb of their right hand, and upon the great toe of their right foot, and their garments are sprinkled, and the altar is bathed with the red stream ; thus in a moment we who had touched with reverence the Urim and the Thummim, and the robe of the ephod blue as heaven's fairest summer, must watch " the fat that covereth the inwards, and the caul that is above the liver, and the two kidneys, and the

fat that is upon them," burn upon an altar whose horns
dripped with the bullock's blood. The revulsion is infinite
For the explanation we must wait. Nevermore shall
we get rid of blood. There was a mystery about its being
sprinkled on the door-posts in Egypt—a mystery about
the paschal lamb—that mystery will now follow us to
the end, and re-appear in a heavenly anthem. It may
be that the blood will become the true refinement, and
that what we once accounted precious shall be less than
nothing when compared with its infinite value

GENERAL NOTES ON THE BOOK OF EXODUS.

I N order to understand almost any book it is necessary to read it right through at once, without entering minutely into its detailed portions, or asking any special questions regarding its local structure. Dean Stanley was accustomed to say that he read a great work of fiction first for the story, secondly for the thought, and thirdly for the style—that is to say, he perused the work three distinct times, these being the distinct objects which he had in view in the respective perusals. It will be well, therefore, for the reader to begin Exodus and go steadily through it, with a view of getting a general conception of the outline of the history. After that he may sit down to a critical perusal of the exact purposes of the writer in each section of the work ; but he will find this second perusal very much aided by the general conception derived from the first complete reading.

The best books upon the structure of Exodus that I have seen, are essays by Canon Cook, in the "Speaker's Commentary," and by Canon Rawlinson, in the "Old Testament Commentary for English Readers." If to these two essays we add Dean Stanley's "History of the Jewish Church," with special reference to the period of the exodus, we shall have a good notion of what the ripest scholars have to say regarding this section of Holy Scripture. It has been pointed out by one of those writers that the Book of Exodus consists of two distinct portions. Canon Cook shows that the first portion extends from chapter i. to chapter xix. inclusive, and that it gives a detailed account of the circumstances under which the deliverance of the Israelites was accomplished. The second part includes chapters xx.–xl., and describes the giving of the law and the institutions which completed the organisation of the people as "a kingdom of priests and a holy nation." The Canon points out a very distinct difference in the styles of the two portions, but contends that their mutual bearings and interdependencies are evident, so much so as to leave no doubt as to the substantial unity of the book. The word "Exodus" means "departure," "outgoing," or "setting forth." It is perhaps needless to say that Exodus is the Latin word which represents the Hebrew title, and that " Exodus " was adopted by Jerome in his translation of the Bible. Canon Rawlinson has pointed out that although the outgoing of the Israelites from Egypt is one of the principal matters treated of in the Book of Exodus, yet it was not the sole, nor even the main purpose of the writer to give an account of that remarkable passage of history. According to the Canon, the purpose of the author was a wider and grander one, being theocratic rather than historic. It was, in the words of Keil, "to give an account of the first stage in the fulfilment of the promises made by God to the patriarchs, with reference to the growth of the children of Israel," by tracing their development from a family into a tribe, and from a tribe into a nation. It has been strikingly shown that Genesis left Israel in Egypt a family or "house" (Gen. l. 22); Exodus leaves them a nation of about two millions of souls organised under chiefs (Exod. xviii. 21–24), with a settled form of worship, a priesthood, a code of laws and a judicature. It finds them still a family (ch. i. 1–6); it leaves them the people of God (ch. xxx. 3–13). By the entrance of the "glory of the Lord " into the tabernacle (ch. xl. 34) the theocracy is completed—God locally dwells with his people as their Ruler, Director, and Guide. The nation receives its head and becomes a "kingdom" (ch. xix. 6). It is still nomadic — it has no settled country — but it is an organised whole.

Canon Cook says that the first seven verses are introductory to the whole book. In accordance with the almost invariable custom of the writer, there is first a brief recapitulation of preceding events, and then a statement of the actual condition of affairs. The narrative begins with the eighth verse of the first chapter. The second division, from chapter iii.–vi., opens after an interval of some forty years, but from this point the narrative is almost critically minute in its statement of facts. Chapter vi. 2–27 forms a distinct portion, in which Moses is instructed to explain the bearings of the Divine name upon the relations

of God to the people : his mission to the Israelites and Pharaoh
is renewed, Aaron being formally appointed as his coadjutor.
It is essential to understand this portion thoroughly, as it is
structurally in its right place, and has a distinct bearing on preceding and succeeding sections. "In chapter vi. 28 to the end
of chapter xi. the narrative," says Canon Cook, "makes a fresh
start." The next section (ch. xii. 1–42) gives an account of the
institution of the Passover and the departure of the Israelites
from Rameses. This section, though closely connected with the
preceding one, is evidently intended to be read as a separate
lesson, and, according to the Canon's theory, may possibly have
been re-written or revised fo that purpose towards the close
of the life of Moses. The narrative begins again at chapter
xiii. 17, giving the history of the march of the Israelites towards
the Red Sea, the passage across it, and the destruction of
Pharaoh's hosts. Then comes the song of Moses, which does
not interrupt the history. In the third month after the exodus,
Israel came to the Wilderness of Sinai and camped before the
Mount ; and in chapters xix.–xx. we read of the promulgation of
the law. The remainder of the book gives the directions received by Moses touching the tabernacle and its appurtenances,
and the institution of the Aaronic priesthood.

Referring to the fact that the credibility of Exodus is assailed
on two principal grounds—viz., first, the miraculous character
of a large portion of the narrative, and secondly, the exaggeration
which is thought to be apparent in the numbers, Canon Rawlinson says : " It is observable (1) that the miracles were needed ;
(2) that they were peculiarly suitable and appropriate to the
circumstances ; and (3) that they were of such a nature that it
was impossible for eye-witnesses to be deceived with regard
to them." The Canon is very distinct and emphatic in his view
of the reality of the circumstances recorded in Exodus. There
is no mistake about such language as the following :—" Either
the plagues of Egypt happened, or they did not. Either the
Red Sea was *divided*, or it was not. Either the pillar of fire and
of the cloud guided the movements of the hosts for forty years,
or there was no such thing. Either there was manna each
morning round about the camp, or there was none. The facts
were too plain, too simple, too obvious to sense for there to be

any doubt about them. The record is either a true account, or a tissue of lies. We cannot imagine the writer an eye-witness, and reject the main features of his story, without looking on him as an impudent impostor. No 'enthusiasm,' no 'poetic temperament,' could account for such a record if the exodus was accomplished without miracles. The writer either relates the truth, or was guilty of conscious dishonesty." This is the only sound view, as it appears to me, to take of such circumstances. We must have no evasion, or verbal refining, or skilful doubling, but a distinct acceptance or rejection of the substantial body of the text. The Canon's remarks upon the numerical difficulties are such as he is entitled to make : —" It is to be borne in mind in the first place that numbers are peculiarly liable to corruption in ancient works, from the fact that they were not fully expressed, but written in a sort of cipher. It is quite possible that the numbers in our present copies of Exodus are in excess, and express the ideas of a reviser, such as Ezra, rather than those of the original author. The million of full age who quitted Egypt *may have been* one hundred thousand, or sixty thousand, instead of six hundred thousand, and the migration one of four hundred thousand or two hundred thousand souls, instead of two million. But, on the whole, judicious criticism inclines to uphold the numbers of the existing text. Alarm would not have been felt by the Egyptian kings until the people had *greatly* multiplied, and become formidable from a military point of view, which they could not have been until the fully grown men numbered some hundreds of thousands. For the population of Egypt was probably from seven to eight millions, and the military class, at a far less flourishing time than that at the exodus, was reckoned at about four hundred thousand. Nor could Canaan well have been conquered by an emigrant body which did not amount to some millions, since the country was well peopled at the time, and its occupants were brave and warlike. The difficulty of subsistence for two millions of persons in the desert is entirely met by the continuous miracle of the manna, and that of sufficient pasture for their numerous flocks and herds by the far greater fertility of the Sinaitic peninsula in ancient than in modern times, of which abundant indications have been observed by recent travellers. Ewald, Kalisch, Kurtz, and Keil, accept the numbers of the present text of Exodus, and believe the migration to have been successfully accomplished by a body of about two millions of persons."

Canon Cook makes some suggestive remarks regarding the particular times at which some of the plagues appeared. He calculates that two full months elapsed between the first and second interview of Moses with the king, and that during that time the people were dispersed throughout Egypt, subjected to severe suffering, and impelled to exertions of a kind differing altogether from their ordinary habits, whether as herdsmen or bondsmen, and he rightly suggests that this was the first and a most important step in their training for a migratory life in the desert. Canon Cook fixes the end of June at the beginning of the rise of the annual inundation of the Nile, as the time when the first series of plagues began. Three months, he adds, appear to have intervened between this and the next plague. The plague of frogs is fixed as coinciding in time with the greatest extension of the inundation in September. The plague of frogs assailed native worship in one of its oldest and strangest forms. An ancient vignette represents the father of Rameses II. offering two vases of wine to a frog enshrined in a small chapel, with the legend, "The sovereign lady of both worlds." It is then pointed out that the third plague differed from the preceding in the important point that no previous warning was given. It is thought to have followed soon after the plague of frogs, namely, early in October. The second series of plagues—viz., swarms of poisonous insects—began probably soon after the subsidence of the inundation, which was a season of great importance to Egypt, because from that season to the following June the land is uncovered, cultivation begins, and a great festival marks the period for ploughing. The cattle plague is thought to have broken out in December, or at the latest in January, and is pointed out as thoroughly Egyptian both in season and in character. Next came the plague of boils, which appears to have lasted about three months. Speaking of the next plague, Canon Cook says the hail-storms followed, just when they now occur in Egypt, from the middle of February to the early weeks of March. This plague drew from Pharaoh the first confession of guilt. The plague of locusts occurred towards the end of March. The Egyptians had now given way, and only the stubbornness of the king's will remained to be overcome.

One or two remarks respecting the account of the tabernacle may be profitably quoted from Canon Cook :—" In form, structure, and materials, the tabernacle belongs altogether to the wilderness. The wood used in the structure is found there in abundance. It appears not to have been used by the Israelites in Palestine ; when the temple was built it was replaced by cedar. The whole was a tent, not a fixed structure, such as would naturally have been set up, and in point of fact was very soon set up, in Palestine ; where wooden doors and probably a surrounding wall existed under the judges of Israel. The skins and other native materials belong equally to the locality. One material which entered largely into the construction, the skin of the tachasch, was in all probability derived from the Red Sea. The metals, bronze, silver, and gold, were those which the Israelites knew and doubtless brought with them from Egypt. The names of many of the materials and implements which they used, and the furniture and accessories of the tabernacle, the dress and ornaments of the priests, are shown to have been Egyptian. It is also certain that the arts required for the construction of the tabernacle, and for all its accessories, were precisely those for which the Egyptians had been remarkable for ages, and such as artisans who had lived under the influence of Egyptian civilisation would naturally have learned. The rich embroidery of the hangings, the carving of the cherubic forms, the ornamentation of the capitals, the naturalistic character of the embellishments, were all things with which the Israelites had been familiar in Egypt, but which, for ages after their settlement in Palestine—in which the traces of Canaanitish culture had been destroyed, as savouring of idolatry, and where the people were carefully separated from the contagious influences of other nations on a par with Egypt—must have died out, if not from their remembrance, yet from all practical application." Further on the Canon continues :—" The peculiar way in which the history of the erection of the tabernacle is recorded suggests another argument, which has not hitherto received due attention. Two separate accounts are given. In the first, Moses relates the instructions which he received, in the second, he describes the accomplishment of the work. Nothing would be less in accordance with the natural order of a history written at a later period than this double account. It has been represented as an argument for a double authorship, as though two sets of documents had been carelessly or surreptitiously adopted by a compiler. It is, however, fully accounted for by the obvious hypothesis that each part of the narrative was written at the time and on the occasion to which it immediately refers. When Moses received these instructions, he wrote a full account of them for the information of the people. . . When, again, Moses had executed his task, it was equally appropriate, and doubtless also in accordance with the habits of a people keen and jealous in the management of their affairs, and at no time free from tendencies to suspicion, that he should give a formal account of every detail in its execution ; a proof to such as might call for proof that all their precious offerings had been devoted to the purpose, and what was of far more importance, that the Divine instructions had been completely and literally obeyed. It is a curious fact that in the two accounts the order of the narrative is systematically reversed. In the instructions given to Moses, and recorded for the information of the people, the most important objects stand first. The ark, the mercy-seat, the cherubs, the table of shewbread, the golden candlestick, the whole series of symbolic forms by which the national mind was framed to comprehend the character of the Divine revelation, are presented at once to the worshippers. Then come instructions for the tabernacle, its equipment and accessories ; and when all else is completed, the dress and ornaments of the officiating priests. But when the work of Bezaleel and his assistants is described, the structure of the tabernacle comes first, as it naturally would do when the ark was commenced ; the place was first prepared, and then the ark and all the sacred vessels, according to all that the Lord commanded Moses."

I have only to recommend the critical reader to peruse the essays to which I have referred, and the commentaries which they introduce, as presenting all that the ripest learning can furnish as to the purely archæological and critical matter of this wonderful book. My object has been to discover the modern uses to which the whole teaching of the history can be put. From time to time it will appear in the following discourses that where difficulties have arisen to my mind as to matters of merely Oriental or local significance, I have inquired into the moral purpose of the writer, and having satisfied myself as to his exact spiritual design, I have fixed attention upon that in order that I might throw into proper perspective and proportion things which, from their very nature, could only be local and transient.

EXODUS.

Exodus i. 22.

"And Pharaoh charged all his people, saying, Every son that is born ye shall cast into the river, and every daughter ye shall save alive."

MOSES ON THE NILE.

A VERY easy plan, was it not? Whom you fear, *destroy;* that is a brief and easy creed, surely? This was turning the river to good account. It was a ready-made grave. Pharaoh did not charge the people to cut the sod, and lay the murdered children in the ground; the sight would have been unpleasant, the reminders would have been too numerous; he said, Throw the intruders into the river: there will be but a splash, a few bubbles on the surface, and the whole thing will be over! The river will carry no marks; will tell no stories; will sustain no tomb-stones; it will roll on as if its waters had never been divided by the hand of the murderer. All bad kings have feared the rise of manhood. If Pharaoh has been afraid of children, there must be something in children worthy of the attention of those who seek to turn life into good directions. The boy who is the terror of a king may become valiant for the truth. Never neglect young life: it is the seed of the future; it is the hope of the world. Nothing better than murder occurred to the mind of this short-sighted king. He never thought of culture, of kindness, of social and political development; his one idea of power was the shallow and vulgar idea of *oppression.*

"And the king of Egypt spake to the Hebrew midwives" (i. 15).

So the king could not carry out his own command. A king can give an order, but he requires the help of other people to carry it into effect. Think of the proud Pharaoh having to take two humble midwives into his confidence! The plan of murder is not so easy a plan after all. There are persons to be consulted who may turn round upon us, and on some ground deny our authority. From the king we had a right to expect protection, security, and encouragement; yet the water of the fountain was poisoned, and the worm of destruction was gnawing the very roots of power. What if the midwives set themselves against Pharaoh? Two humble women may be more than a match for the great king of Egypt. No influence, how obscure soever, is to be treated with contempt. A child may baffle a king. A kitten has been known to alarm a bear. A fly once choked a pope. What if a midwife should turn to confusion the sanguinary counsels of a cowardly king?

"But the midwives feared God, and did not as the king of Egypt commanded them, but saved the men-children alive" (i. 17).

They who fear God are superior to all other fear. When our notion of authority terminates upon the visible and temporary, we become the victims of fickle circumstances; when that notion rises to the unseen and eternal, we enjoy rest amid the tumult of all that is merely outward and therefore perishing. Take history through and through, and it will be found that the men and women who have most devoutly and honestly feared God, have done most to defend and save the countries in which they lived. They have made little noise; they have got up no open-air demonstrations; they have done little or nothing in the way of banners and trumpets, and have had no skill in getting up torch-light meetings; but their influence has silently penetrated the national life, and secured for the land the loving and mighty care of God. Where the spiritual life is profound and real, the social and political influence is correspondingly vital and beneficent. All the great workers in society are not at the front. A hidden work is continually going on; the people in the shade are strengthening the social foundation. There is another history beside that which is written in the columns of the daily newspaper. Every country has heroes and heroines uncanonised. Let this be spoken for the encouragement of many whose names are not known far beyond the threshold of their own homes.

"Therefore God dealt well with the midwives. . . . And it came to pass, because the midwives feared God, that he made them houses" (i. 20, 21).

They who serve God serve a good Master. Was God indifferent to the character and claims of the midwives who bore practical testimony for him in the time of a nation's trial? His eye was upon them for good, and his hand was stretched out day and night for their defence. They learned still more deeply that there was another King beside Pharaoh ; and in the realisation of his presence Pharaoh dwindled into a secondary power, whose breath was in his nostrils, and whose commands were the ebullitions of moral insanity. No honest man or woman can do a work for God without receiving a great reward. God made houses for the midwives! He will make houses for all who live in his fear. There are but few who have courage to set themselves against a king's commandment; but verily those who assert the authority of God as supreme shall be delivered from the cruelty of those who have no pity. There are times when nations are called upon to say, No, even to their sovereigns. Such times are not to be sought for with a pertinacious self-assertion, whose object is to make itself very conspicuous and important; but when they do occur, conscience is to assert itself with a dignity too calm to be impatient, and too righteous to be deceived.

How will these commands and purposes be received in practical life? This inquiry will be answered as we proceed to the second chapter.

"And there went a man of the house of Levi, and took to wife a daughter of Levi" (ii. 1).

There is nothing extraordinary in this statement. From the beginning men and women have married and have been given in marriage. It is therefore but an ordinary event which is described in this verse. Yet we know that the man of Levi and the daughter of Levi were the father and mother of one whose name was to become associated with that *of the Lamb!* May not Renown have Obscurity for a pedestal? Do not the pyramids themselves rest on sand? What are the great rocks but consolidated mud? We talk of our ancestry, and are proud of those who have gone before us. There is a sense in which this is perfectly justifiable, and not only so, but most laudable ; let us remember, however, that if we go back far enough, we land, if not in a common obscurity, yet in a common moral dishonour.

Parents may be nameless, yet their children may rise to imperishable renown. The world is a great deal indebted to its obscure families. Many a giant has been reared in a humble habitation. Many who have served God, and been a terror to the Wicked One, have come forth from unknown hiding-places. I would dart this beam of light into the hearts of some who imagine that they are making little or no contribution to the progress of society. Be honest in your sphere,—be faithful to your children, and even out of your life there may go forth an indirect influence without which the most sounding reputation is empty and worthless.

"And when she could not longer hide him, [that is, the child that was born to her,] she took for him an ark of bulrushes, and daubed it with slime and with pitch, and put the child therein; and she laid it in the flags by the river's brink" (ii. 3).

The first going from home of any child always marks a period of special interest in the family. What a going was this! When some of you went from home, how you were cared for! How your family gathered round you to speak a kind farewell! What a box-filling, and portmanteau-strapping, what a fluttering of careful, anxious love there was! What has become of you? Were you suffocated with kindness? were you slain by the hand of a too anxious love? Truly, some men who have had the roughest and coldest beginning have, under the blessing of God, turned out to be the bravest, the strongest, the noblest of men! I believe in rough beginnings: we have less to fear from hardship than from luxury. Some children are confectioned to death. What with coddling, bandaging, nursing, and petting, the very sap of their life is drained away. There is indeed another side to this question of beginnings. I have known some children who have hardly ever been allowed to go out lest they should wet their feet, who have been spared all drudgery, who have had every wish and whim gratified, whose parents have suddenly come to social ruin, and yet these very children have, under their altered circumstances, developed a force of character, an enduring patience, and a lofty self-control never to have been expected from their dainty training. But a man is not necessarily a great man because he has had a rough beginning. Many may have been laid on the river Nile, whose names would have done no honour to history. Accept your rough beginning in a proper spirit; be not overcome by the force of merely external circumstances; wait, hope, work, pray, and you will yet see the path which leads into light, and honour, and peace. The mother of Moses laid the ark in the flags by the river's brink. Ay, but before doing so she laid it on the heart of God! She could not have laid it so courageously upon the Nile, if she had not first devoutly laid it upon the care and love of God. We are often surprised at the outward calmness of men who are called upon to do unpleasant and most trying deeds; but could we have seen them in secret we should have known the moral preparation which they underwent before coming out to be seen of men. Be right in the sanctuary, if you would be right in the market-place. Be steadfast in prayer, if you would be calm in affliction. Start your race from the throne of God itself, if you would run well, and win the prize.

"And his sister stood afar off, to wit what would be done to him" (ii. 4).

Society needs watchers as well as workers. Had we been passing the spot at which the sister of Moses took up her position of observation, we might have condemned her as an idler standing there and doing nothing! We should be careful of our condemnation, seeing how little we know of the reality of any case. In doing *nothing*, the girl was in reality doing *everything*. If she had done more, she would have done less. There is a silent ministry as well as a ministry of thunder. Mark the cunning of love! The watcher stood *afar off*. Had she stood quite close at hand, she would have defeated the very object of her watching. She was to do her work without the slightest appearance of doing it. Truly there is a great art in love, and in all good ministry. There are wise master-builders, and also builders who are very foolish. Sometimes we must look without staring; we must speak without making a noise; we must be artful without dissimulation, and hide under the calmest exterior the most urgent and tumultuous emotion.

"And the daughter of Pharaoh came down to wash herself at the river; and her maidens walked along by the river's side; and when she saw the ark among the flags, she sent her maid to fetch it. And when she had opened it, she saw the child: and, behold, the babe wept. And she had compassion on him, and said, This is one of the Hebrews' children" (ii. 5, 6).

"One touch of nature makes the whole world kin." When the child cried, the heart of the daughter of Pharaoh was moved, as simple and beautiful a piece of human nature as is to be found anywhere. How poor would the world be without its helpless ones! Little children by their very weakness make strong men stronger. By the wickedness of the wicked, the righteousness of the righteous is called forth in some of its most impressive and winsome forms. Looking at the daughter of Pharaoh from a distance, she appears to be haughty, self-involved, and self-satisfied; but, stooping near that little ark, she becomes a woman, having in her the instinct of motherliness itself! We should all be fathers and mothers to the orphan, the lost, and the desolate. The government of humanity is so ordered that even the most distressing circumstances are made to contribute to the happy development of our best impulses and energies. No man can be permanently unhappy who looks into the cradles of the poor and lonely, as Pharaoh's daughter looked into this ark of bulrushes. Go by the river's side, where the poor lost child is, and be a father and a mother to him if you would have happiness in the very core of your heart! Even a king's daughter is the richer and gladder for this stoop of love. Some have been trying to reach too high for their enjoyments; the blooming fruit has been beyond their stature; they have therefore turned away with pining and discontent, not knowing that if they had bent themselves to the ground they would have found the happiness in the dust, which they attempted in vain to pluck from inaccessible heights.

"Then said his sister to Pharaoh's daughter, Shall I go and call to thee a nurse of the Hebrew women, that she may nurse the child for thee?" (ii. 7).

The watcher came without making a noise. Who ever heard the light come over the hills? Who ever heard the violet growing? The watcher, too, spoke to the king's daughter without introduction or ceremony! Are there not times in life when we are superior to all formalities? Are there not sorrows which enable us to overcome the petty difficulties of etiquette? Earnestness will always find ways for its own expression. The child might well have pleaded timidity; fear of the greatness of Pharaoh's daughter, or shamefacedness in the presence of the great and noble; under ordinary circumstances she would

undoubtedly have done so ; but the life of her brother was at
risk, the command of her mother was in her heart, and her own
pity yearned over the lonely one : under the compulsion of such
considerations as these, the watcher urged her way to the side of
Pharaoh's daughter, and made this proposition of love. False
excuses are only possible where there is lack of earnestness. If
we really cared for lost children, we should find ways of speaking
for them in high quarters. There is a boldness which is consistent with the purest modesty, and there is a timidity which
thinly disguises the most abject cowardice.

"And Pharaoh's daughter said to her, Go. And the maid went and
called the child's mother. And Pharaoh's daughter said unto her, Take this
child away, and nurse it for me, and I will give thee thy wages" (ii. 8, 9).

All done in a moment, as it were ! Such are the rapid changes
in lives which are intended to express some great meaning and
purpose of God. They are cast down, but not destroyed ; persecuted, but not forsaken ! From the action of Pharaoh's daughter
we learn that first thoughts are, where generous impulses are
concerned, the only thoughts worth trusting. Sometimes we
reason that second thoughts are best ; in a certain class of cases
this reasoning may be substantially correct, but, where the heart
is moved to do some noble and heroic thing, the first thought
should be accepted as an inspiration from God, and carried out
without self-consultation or social fear. Those who are accustomed to seek contribution or service for the cause of God, of
course know well what it is to encounter the imprudent prudence
which says, " I must think about it." Where the work is good,
don't think about it; *do* it, and then think. When a person goes
to a place of business, and turns an article over and over, and
looks at it with hesitation, and finally says, " I will call again,"
the master of the establishment says in his heart, " Never ! " If
Pharaoh's daughter had *considered* the subject, the probability
is that Moses would have been left on the Nile or under it ; but
she accepted her motherly love as a Divine guide, and saved
the life of the child.

" And the woman took the child, and nursed it " (ii. 9).

What her self-control in that hour of maddening excitement
cost, no tongue can tell. She took the child as a stranger might

have taken it, and yet her heart was bursting with the very passion of delight. Had she given way for one instant, her agitation might have revealed the plot. Everything depended upon her calmness. But love can do anything! The great question underlying all service is a question not so much of the intellect as of the heart. We should spoil fewer things if our love was deeper. We should finish our tasks more completely if we entered upon them under the inspiration of perfect love. The mother consented to become a *hireling,*—to take wages for nursing her own child! Love can thus *deny* itself, and take up its sweet cross. How little did Pharaoh's daughter know what she was doing! Does any one really know what work he is doing in all its scope and meaning? The simplest occasion of our lives may be turned to an account which it never entered into our hearts to imagine. Who can tell where the influence of a gentle smile may end? We know not the good that may be done by the echo as well as by the voice. There is a joyful bridegroom throwing his dole into the little crowd of laughing eager boys. One of those boys is specially anxious to secure his full share of all that is thrown : he has snatched a penny, but in a moment it has been dashed out of his hand by a competitor : see how anger flushes his face, and with what determination he strikes the successful boy : he is a savage, he is unfit to have his liberty in the public streets, his temper is uncontrollable, his covetousness is shocking : he wins the poor prize, and hastens away ; watch him : with his hard-earned penny he buys a solitary orange, and with quick feet he finds his way up a rickety staircase into a barely-furnished garret ; he gives his orange to his poor dying sister, and the juice assuages her burning thirst. When we saw the fight, we called the boy a *beast;* but we knew not what we said !

We call the early life of Moses a miracle. There is a sense of course in which that is literally true. But is there not a sense in which every human life has in it the miraculous element? We are too fond of bringing down everything to the level of commonplace, and are becoming almost blind to the presence of elements and forces in life which ought to impress us with a distinct consciousness of a power higher than our own. Why this worship of commonplace ?　Why this singular delight in all things that are supposed to be level and square, and wanting in startling emphasis ?　I would rather speak thus with myself :— My life too is a miracle ; it was put away upon a river and might have been lost in the troubled water ; kind eyes watched the little vessel in which the life was hidden ; other persons gathered around it and felt interested in its fortunes ; it was drawn away from the stream of danger and for a time hidden within the security of love and comfort and guidance.　It has also had to contend with opposition and difficulty, seen and unseen ; it has been threatened on every side.　Temptations and allurements have been held out to it, and it has been with infinite difficulty that it has been reared through all the atmosphere intended to oppress and to poison it.　I could shut out all these considerations if I pleased, and regard my life within its merely animal boundaries, and find in it nothing whatever to excite religious wonder or religious thankfulness ; but this is not the right view. To do so would be to inflict injustice upon the Providence which has made my life a daily wonder to myself.　I will think of God's tender care, of the continual mercy which has been round about me, and of the blessed influences which have strengthened and ennobled every good purpose of my heart ; and I, too, will stand side by side with Moses when he sings the wonders of the hand Divine.　The miracle is not always in the external incident ; it may be hidden in the core of things and may slowly disclose itself to the eyes of religious reverence and inquiry.　O that men were wise : that they would consider their beginning as well as their latter end, and learn to trace the hand of Heaven even in those comparative trifles which are supposed to lie within the scope and determination of time.

" And the child grew, and she brought him unto Pharaoh's daughter, and he became her son."

MOSES IN MIDIAN.

THERE seems to be a considerable gap between the ninth verse and the tenth. We parted with Moses when he was three months old, and we know nothing more of him until he became the son of Pharaoh's daughter. We wish to know something of his home training. We would fain pry into the mother's methods of dealing with such a child. What truths did she inculcate upon him? How did she explain the condition of the children of Israel to her son? Did she seek to prejudice his sympathies? Whilst he was being nurtured upon Pharaoh's bread, did she instil into him teaching that would upset Pharaoh's throne? Upon all these points we are left uninformed, though our interest is excited to the highest pitch. We like to know something of the home training of the men who have written the most famous chapters in history. There is a special pleasure in watching the growth of the sapling. The boyhood of the giant must be unlike the boyhood of ordinary men. We would see the giant in his teens, and watch him eagerly in the daily accretion of his strength. In this instance we are disappointed. Moses was trained in secret, and no tittle of his mother's ministry is put on record. Is it true, however, that we have no means of learning the principles upon which Moses was trained? Are we so totally in the dark as we have supposed ourselves to be? Let us from the history of the man gather what we can concerning the tuition of the child.

"And it came to pass in those days, when Moses was grown, that he went out unto his brethren, and looked on their burdens: and he spied an Egyptian smiting an Hebrew, one of his brethren" (ii. 11).

A good deal of his mother's training is visible in this verse.

Moses was the son of Pharaoh's daughter, yet he claimed the
Hebrews as his brethren. The signature written in blood was
not to be washed out by all the waters of the Nile. Nature
asserted herself under circumstances which might have attempered the severity of her demands. Moses was not ashamed
to recognise the Hebrews as his brethren. He himself had had
a day of wondrous luck so called ; he might have sunned himself
in the beams of his radiant fortunes, and left his brethren to do
as they could ; he might, indeed, in self-excuse, and in order to
quiet the monitions of any little unsophisticated nature which his
seductive circumstances had left within him, have actually taken
part against the Hebrews, and made his censures the bitterer by
the fact of his alienated kinship. It was not so that Moses acted.
And is no credit to be given to Jochebed, his mother, for this fine
fraternal chivalry ? Is it not the *mother* who is speaking in the
boy when he calls the Hebrews his brethren ? Observe, too,
Moses looked upon the *burdens* of the Hebrews. Alas ! some of
us can go up and down society, and never see the *burdens* which
our brethren are called to bear. It is something in a world like
this to have an eye for the burdens of other men. We look upon
difficulties without sympathy, we regard the burden-bearer as
fulfilling but an ordinary vocation ; Moses looked upon burdens
as having *moral significance,* and so regarding them his deepest
sympathies were drawn towards the oppressed. "Bear ye one
another's burdens." A friendly recognition of the fact that a man
is bearing a burden may itself help to lessen the load. It ought
to have been something to the Hebrews to know that a man had
risen amongst them who looked upon their burdens. Such a
looking might be the beginning of a new state of affairs. There
are some looks which have in them reform, revolution, and
regeneration ! Is there no trace of the *mother* of Moses in all
this ? Would he have known what a " burden " was, but for the
explanations of his mother ? Would not the Hebrew have been
to him but a beast of labour, had not his mother revealed to his
young eyes the *man* that lay silently within the *slave?*

" And he looked this way and that way, and when he saw that there was
no man, he slew the Egyptian, and hid him in the sand " (ii. 12).

This is one of the first recorded acts of the meekest of men !
Do not let us be hard upon him. The impulse was right. There

must be men in society who can strike, and who need to strike but once. Let it be understood that this, after all, was but the lowest form of heroism,—it was a *boy's* resentment,—it was a youth's untempered chivalry. One can imagine a boy reading this story, and feeling himself called upon to strike everybody who is doing something which displeases him. There is a raw heroism ; an animal courage ; a rude, barbaric idea of righteousness. We applaud Moses, but it is his impulse rather than his method which is approved. Every man should burn with indignation when he sees oppression. In this instance it must be clearly understood that the case was one of oppressive strength as against down-trodden weakness. This was not a fight between one man and another ; the Egyptian and the Hebrew were not fairly pitted in battle : the Egyptian was smiting the Hebrew,— the Hebrew in all probability bending over his labour, doing the best in his power, and yet suffering the lash of the tyrant It was under such circumstances as these that Moses struck in the cause of human justice. Was there nothing of his mother in that fine impulse ? Are we now as ignorant of his home training as we supposed ourselves to be a moment ago ? In this fiery protest against wrong, in this blow of ungoverned temper against a hoary and pitiless despotism, see somewhat of the tender sympathy that was in Jochebed embodied in a form natural to the impetuosity of youth. Little did Moses know what he did when he smote the nameless Egyptian. In smiting that one man, in reality he struck Pharaoh himself, and every succeeding tyrant !

"And when he went out the second day, behold, two men of the Hebrews strove together : and he said to him that did the wrong, Wherefore smitest thou thy fellow ? " (ii. 13).

In the first instance we might have thought that in taking part with the Hebrew against the Egyptian, Moses was but yielding to a clannish feeling. It was race against race, not right against wrong. In the second instance, however, that conclusion is shown to be incorrect. We now come to a strife between two Hebrews, both of whom were suffering under the same galling bondage. How did the youthful Moses deport himself under such circumstances ? Did he take part with the strong against the weak ? Did he even take part with the weak against the strong ? Distinctly the case was not one determined by the mere disparity of

the combatants. To the mind of Moses the question was altogether a *moral* one. When he spoke, he addressed the man who
did the *wrong;* that man might have been either the weaker or
the stronger. The one question with Moses turned upon injustice
and dishonourableness. Do we not here once more see traces
of his mother's training? yet we thought that the home life of
Moses was a life unrecorded! Read the mother in the boy;
discover the home training in the public life. Men's behaviour
is but the outcome of the nurture they have received at home.
Moses did not say, You are both Hebrews, and therefore you may
fight out your own quarrel : nor did he say, The controversies of
other men are nothing to me ; they who began the quarrel must
end it. Moses saw that the conditions of life had a moral basis ;
in every quarrel as between right and wrong he had a share,
because every honourable-minded man is a trustee of social justice
and common fair play. We have nothing to do with the petty
quarrels which fret society, but we certainly have to do with
every controversy, social, imperial, or international, which violates
human right, and impairs the claims of Divine honour. We
must all fight for the right : we feel safer by so much as we
know that there are amongst us men who will not be silent in
the presence of wrong, and will lift up a testimony in the name
of righteousness, though there be none to cheer them with one
word of encouragement.

"And he said, Who made thee a prince and a judge over us? intendest
thou to kill me, as thou killedst the Egyptian? And Moses feared, and said,
Surely this thing is known " (ii. 14).

So it is evermore ! Even his own brethren did not understand
Moses. Though only yesterday he had killed an Egyptian, yet
to-day he is snapped at and abused as if he had been an enemy
rather than a friend. But when did a man's own brethren ever
fully understand and appreciate him? Jesus "came unto his
own, and his own eceived him not." A man's foes are often
those of his own household. One would have supposed that
upon seeing Moses both the Hebrews would have forgotten their
own quarrel, and hailed him with expressions of gratitude and
trust. The heroic interposition of yesterday ought not to have
been so soon forgotten. Forgotten? Nay, it was surely remembered, but that which might have been considered an honour was

held over the head of Moses as a sword of vengeance. Men are often discouraged in attempting to serve their brethren ; generally speaking, it is a thankless task. Good offices are resented, kind words are perverted, and the valiant man is hunted to death.

"But Moses fled from the face of Pharaoh, and dwelt in the land of Midian : and he sat down by a well. Now the priest of Midian had seven daughters : and they came and drew water, and filled the troughs to water their father's flock. And the shepherds came and drove them away : but Moses stood up and helped them, and watered their flock " (ii. 15–17).

We find Moses in early life upon the river's brink,—now we find him sitting alone by a well. It will be quite easy to interpret the feelings which govern him as he sits in a strange land. Let us overhear him : "Never so long as I live will I interfe e in another quarrel : I have had experience of two interpositions, and my heart is sad. When men are fighting again, I shall let them finish as they please ; not one word will I say either on the one side or the other : from this day forth I shut my eyes in the presence of wrong, and hold my peace when righteousness is going to the wall." What a wonderful speech to be delivered by such a man ! He has fully made up his mind too ! Nevermore can he be tempted to go with the weak against the strong ! Watch him as he looks about, not knowing which way to turn. He hears sounds in the near distance. Presently he notices seven women coming to the well, and presently, too, he observes shepherds driving them away. Gloriously the late rough heroism reasserts itself ! He had promised nevermore to interfere ; but the moment that he sees another act of oppression, his mother's training makes itself felt, and he springs to his feet to resist a cowardly tyranny. The wretches, who for many a day had driven the women from the well, had never heard a *man* speak to them before ! The voice quite startled them, and they fell back unable to confront the face of an honest and determined man. So may all bad resolutions perish ! We *must* interfere. The cause of righteousness is entrusted to us, and woe be to us if we take counsel with ourselves to save our own quiet at the expense of justice and honour !

Exodus iii. 1.

Now Moses kept the flock of Jethro his father-in-law, the priest of Midian: and he led the flock ¦to the backside of the desert, and came to the mountain of God, even to Horeb."

MOSES AT HOREB.

SO ends the romance of the young hero! We have often seen brilliant beginnings turn to cloudy endings. A man has come out very sensationally for a day or two, and then has subsided into commonplace and obscurity. But what would Moses have been had he pursued the line upon which he so vigorously commenced? Suppose that from day to day he had gone abroad smiting men, where would the story of his life have ended? It was but a poor way, after all, of attacking the moral confusion of society. It is not much in the way of reform and progress that any man can do with his mere fist. On the whole, therefore, we are glad that a pause has come in the destructive though chivalrous career of this young smiter. It was not amiss, perhaps, for him to knock down one or two men, and to frighten away from the well a number of cowardly shepherds; but as a life course it was morally shallow and politically self-defeating. We must have something more fundamental than we have yet seen, or Moses will be provoking reprisals which no individual arm can resist. It is then not a subsidence into commonplace that we find in this verse; it is going into the severest and most useful of schools—the school of loneliness, meditation, self-measurement, and fellowship with God. Fiery natures must be attempered by exile and desertion. They must be taught that the end of merely manual or military reform is unsatisfactory. Men can be held by the throat only so long as they are unable to take revenge; but they may be held by the heart evermore. All true reforms and all beneficent masteries are essentially *moral*. We must

exchange rough and romantic chivalry for the deep, calm, vital
revelation which emancipates and purifies the spiritual nature
of mankind. This is no anti-climax in the history of Moses !
Moses has been looking upon the outside of things; now he
must be trained to estimate *spiritual* forces and values.

"And the angel of the Lord appeared unto him in a flame of fire out of the
midst of a bush : and he looked, and, behold, the bush burned with fire, and
the bush was not consumed " (iii. 2).

A beautiful conjunction of the natural and supernatural. A
bush burned into a sanctuary! Though the heavens cannot
contain the Great One, yet he hides himself under every flower,
and makes the broken heart of man his chosen dwelling-place.
So great, yet so condescending; infinite in glory, yet infinite in
gentleness. Wherever we are, there are gates through nature
into the Divine. Every bush will teach the reverent student
something of God. The lilies are teachers, so are the stars, so
are all things great and small in this wondrous museum, the
universe! In this case it was not the whole mountain that
burned with fire ; such a spectacle we should have considered
worthy of the majesty of God ; it was only the *bush* that burned :
so condescendingly does God accommodate himself to the weakness of man. The whole mountain burning would have dismayed
the lonely shepherd ; he who might have been ove whelmed by
a blazing mountain was attracted by a burning bush.

"And Moses said, I will now turn aside, and see this great sight, why the
bush is not burnt. And when the Lord saw that he turned aside to see,
God called unto him out of the midst of the bush, and said, Moses, Moses.
And he said, Here am I " (iii. 3, 4).

Many a man has been led through the gate of curiosity into the
sanctuary of reverence. Moses purposed but to see a wonderful
sight in nature, little dreaming that he was standing as it were
face to face with God. Blessed are they who have an eye for the
startling, the sublime, and the beautiful in nature, for they shall
see many sights which will fill them with glad amazement.
Every sight of God is a " great sight "; the sights become little
to us because we view them without feeling or holy expectation.
It was when the Lord saw that Moses *turned aside to see* that he
called unto him and mentioned him by name. This is indeed a

great law. If men would turn aside to see, God would surely
speak to them. But we do not do this. We pass by all the
great sights of nature with comparative indifference, certainly,
as a general rule, without reverence. The sea wants to speak to
us, but we listen not to its sounding voice; the stars are calling
to us, but we shut them out; the seasons come round to tell their
tale, but we are pre-occupied with trifling engagements. We
must bring so much with us if we would put ourselves into
healthful communion with nature : we must bring the seeing eye,
the hearing ear, and the understanding heart : we must, at all
events, be disposed to see and hear, and God will honour the
disposition with more than expected blessing.

"And he said, Draw not nigh hither : put off thy shoes from off thy feet,
for the place whereon thou standest is holy ground. Moreover he said,
I am the God of thy father, the God of Abraham, the God of Isaac, and the
God of Jacob. And Moses hid his face; for he was afraid to look upon
God " (iii. 5, 6).

Curiosity must not become familiarity. The difference between
the creature and the Creator must always be infinite. Is not *all*
ground holy ? Is not God everywhere ? Certainly so ; yet it
hath pleased God to mark special lines and special places as
peculiarly holy. We are not to treat all places alike. Every
successful appeal to man's reverence redeems him from vulgarity.
When a man loses his sense of religious awe, he has exhausted
the supreme fountain of spiritual joy. He then measures everything by himself : he is to himself as God, and from the point of
self-idolatry he will speedily sink to the point of self-despair. It
is only the *good* man who can be satisfied from himself, and this
is only because goodness has its very root in God.

In what a tender manner God reveals himself to the lonely
shepherd ! He does not say, I am the God of majesty, of eternity,
whose habitation is unapproachable, and whose power is infinite.
He says, " I am the God of thy father." Could any designation
have been more tender ? Was it not precisely the best way to
arrest the attention and conciliate the confidence of Moses ? " I
am the God of thy father,"—the God of thy home, the God of thy
fireside, the God around whose name cluster the tenderest and
purest associations of life. Who can stoop so condescendingly as
God ? Again and again in this conference with Moses, God

declared himself to be the God of Abraham, the God of Isaac, and the God of Jacob. He is thus the God of generations, the God of individuals, and also the God of the whole human family. There is something inexpressibly beautiful in the idea that God is the God of the father, and of the son, and of all their descendants; thus the one God makes humanity into one family; we live in different zones, and acknowledge the sovereignty of different political kings, yet all nations are one, in so far as they worship and serve the same living God.

"Now therefore, behold, the cry of the children of Israel is come unto me: and I have also seen the oppression wherewith the Egyptians oppress them. Come now therefore, and I will send thee unto Pharaoh, that thou mayest bring forth my people the children of Israel out of Egypt" (iii. 9, 10).

In the eighth verse God says, "I am come down to deliver them out of the hand of the Egyptians," and in the tenth verse he says, "I will send thee unto Pharaoh, that thou mayest bring forth my people." Is there not a discrepancy here? If God himself came down to do a work, why did he not go and do it personally? One word from him would surely have done more for the cause which he had espoused than all the words which the most gifted of his creatures could have used. Looking at this episode as standing entirely alone, it does undoubtedly appear most remarkable that God did not personally execute what he had personally conceived. The thinking was his, so was the love; all the spiritual side of the case belonged exclusively to God; yet he calls a shepherd, a lonely and unfriended man, to work out with painful elaboration, and through a series of most bewildering and discouraging disappointments, the purpose which it seems he himself might have accomplished by a word. We find, however, that the instance is by no means an isolated one. Throughout the whole scheme of the Divine government of the human family, we find the principle of *mediation.* God speaks to man through man: he did so throughout the history of the Old Testament, and he does so to-day in the gospel of his Son. Undoubtedly this is most mysterious. To our imperfect understanding, it would seem that the direct personal revelation of his presence and glory would instantly secure the results which are so desirable, and yet so doubtful. It is here that Faith must lead, because Reason cannot see the advantages which—to ourselves as men, when employed as ministers of God to each other, to our intellectual progress, and to our moral nature—are obvious and inestimable. God educates and glorifies us by making us his servants. We learn the highest wisdom and the highest music by repronouncing the words which we have received from the lips of God. Moreover, this principle of individual selection in the matter of all great ministries is in keeping with the principle which embodies in a single germ the greatest forests. It is enough that God gives the one acorn; man must plant it and develop its productiveness. It is enough that God gives the one idea; man must receive it into the good soil of his love and hope, and encourage it to tell all the mystery of its purpose. So God calls to himself, in holy solitude, one man, and puts into the heart of that man his own gracious purpose, and commissions him to expound this purpose to his fellow-men. God never works from the many to the one; he works from one to the many.

"And Moses said unto God, Who am I, that I should go unto Pharaoh, and that I should bring forth the children of Israel out of Egypt?" (iii. 11).

No wonder that he so inquired. The message seemed to be so much greater than the messenger. Moses herein disclosed the right spirit in which the communications of Heaven are to be received. It is under such circumstances that weakness is strength. When a man can set himself in imagination upon an equality with God, and receive the messages of God as if they were but common words, he is no longer fit to be a minister of light and hope to nations groaning in sorrow, and perishing under oppression. If Moses had not seen the greatness of the proposed ministry, he would not have felt his own inability to discharge it. The idea was too much for him. The proposition blinded him like a sudden and intolerable light. Men are the better for this humiliation of their self-esteem. Moses was fully equal to the humble duty which he had undertaken under Jethro his father-in-law, but to go forth as the emancipator of an oppressed nation seemed to overweigh and mock his powers. He works best who magnifies his office. Preachers, teachers, emancipators, and all ministers of good, should see their work to be infinitely greater than themselves, if they would work at the highest point of energy.

Let a man suppose his work to be easy, to be beneath him, to be unworthy of his talents, and he will work flippantly, without taxing his strength or making any drain upon the life of his heart. He will not be a worker; at best he will be but a fussy idler in the great field overgrown with the weeds and tares sown by the power of evil.

"And he said, Certainly I will be with thee" (iii. 12).

God thus puts himself apparently into a secondary position. Moses is to stand at the front, and, so far as publicity is concerned, to incur the whole responsibility of the proposed movement. It was easy for Moses to say that he was prompted of God to make certain representations to Israel and Pharaoh, but how were they to be convinced that Moses was servant and not master? This is the difficulty of all the highest service of life, namely, that the spiritual is *invisible,* and yet omnipotent; public attention is fixed upon the human agent, and professions of spiritual inspiration and impulse are treated with distrust, if not with contempt, by the most of mankind. It is the *invisible* Christ who is with the Church. Were he present manifestly, it is supposed that greater results would accrue from Christian service; but the supposition must be mistaken, inasmuch as he to whom such service is infinitely dearer than it ever can be to ourselves has determined the manner of Christian evangelisation. What, then, is the great duty and privilege of the Church? *It is to realise the presence and influence of the Invisible.* The Church is actually to *see* the *Unseen.* There is another vision beside the vision of the body; faith itself is sight; and where faith is complete, there is a consciousness of God's presence throughout our life and service which amounts to a distinct vision of God's personal presence and government.

This incident has brought very closely before me the mystery of what may be termed the Spirit of Destiny. Moses has been, as it were, audibly and visibly called to service and invested with authority. A keen pleasure would seem to attach to experiences of that kind. Surely it was a blessed thing to speak face to face with God, and to go straight away from the communing to do the work which had been prescribed. The directness of the interview, the absence of all second causes and instrumentalities has about it a solemnity which profoundly affects the heart. But is my destiny less Divine because it has been revealed to me under conditions which seem to separate widely between the Creator and the creature ? Has God only one method of working in revealing to a man what that man's work in life is intended to be ? We do not always see the fountain ; sometimes we have to be content to drink at the stream. The danger is lest we imagine the stream created itself, forgetting in our irreligion and folly that the stream is impossible apart from the fountain. A man is sometimes awakened to his destiny by his fellow-men. In other cases a man's destiny seems to be determined by what he calls his circumstances or his environment. But why this wide and circuitous way of putting the case to the mind ? We do not depose God by mistaking the origin of our action ; we do but show the poorness of our own judgment, or the want of justice which impoverishes our lives of their best qualities. Every man should put to himself the question—What is my destiny ? What does God mean me to be and to do in the world ? This inquiry should shape itself into a tender and continual prayer which will not cease its intercession until a gracious answer gives assurance to the heart that the will of Heaven has been made clear. It is a most pitiful thing that a man should read of Moses being Divinely called to certain service, and forget that he himself is also a subject of the Divine government. If God called any one man to special work, we are entitled to reason upon the basis of that fact that God has a special work for every man to do. It is in our power to turn such miracles into gracious commonplaces by seeking for their repetition in our own lives. It is impossible that God has called us into existence without having some purpose for us to work at within the limit of time. To be here at all is to be in possession of a destiny. It is, indeed, an awful power with which we are endowed, that we can shut our eyes to destiny which is beckoning us to duty, and can, indeed, so pervert and misinterpret circumstances as to press them into a justification of self-will and apostasy. To know that my life may be called to a unique vocation excites me with very tender and anxious emotion. What if I have mistaken the Divine will ? What if I am pursuing the wrong road ? What if I have been judging by appearances and neglecting the teaching of reality ?

Has self-interest determined my action? Has self-indulgence wrought its unholy spell upon my energies and affections? Have I been earnestly listening to hear the voice which teaches men the way of duty and the path of sacrifice? Spirit of the Living God, reveal my destiny to me, though it mean pain and loss, continual discipline of fear, or the blessed experience of daily joy. If I may but know thy purpose, sucn knowledge shall itself be inspiration and defence.

Exodus iii. 13, 14.

And Moses said unto God, Behold, when I come unto the children of Israel, and shall say unto them, The God of your fathers hath sent me unto you; and they shall say to me, What is his name? what shall I say unto them? And God said unto Moses, I AM THAT I AM: and he said, Thus shalt thou say unto the children of Israel, I AM hath sent me unto you."

MOSES EXCUSES HIMSELF.

THE wisdom of Moses is seen in the nature of the inquiry which he proposed. He was resolved not to go a warfare at his own charges. Every man should know upon *whose* business he is going in life. Who is sending me? is an inquiry which a man should put to himself before venturing upon any course that is doubtful, hazardous, or experimental. Moses wished to be able to identify the *personal* authority of his mission. It was not enough to have a message, he must also know the name of the Author. There are some doctrines which are independent of personality; there are others which depend upon personality for their authority and beneficence. Amongst the latter are all religious doctrines and appeals. The Giver is greater than the gift. The Speaker is greater than the speech. To know the Speaker is to have deep insight into the meaning of the words spoken. The answer returned to Moses was the sublimest reply ever made to reverent inquiry. God announces himself as Personal, Independent, Self-existent. There is no word to qualify or limit his personality—it is, so to speak, pure *being*—it is infinite life—it is the fountain out of which all other lives start on their little course. Mark the comprehensiveness of the name. It relates not only to being, but to *character*, to self-completeness; it is the ONE life which can live without dependence and without society. The element of sublimity must be found in religion; the measure of the sublimity is the measure of the condescension. A man proceeding to his work under the influence of such a revelation as was granted to Moses must be superior to hardship and triumphant in the presence of difficulty. A man's inspiration should always be in excess of the duty which is imposed upon him. The inspired man descends upon his work and conducts his service with an overplus of power ; but he whose inspiration falls below his duty toils fretfully and unsuccessfully, and eventually becomes the prey of the spirit of the hireling. It is here that the Christian worker actually triumphs in his labour, and rejoices even in persecution and tribulation : God the Holy Ghost is in him, and so the whole tone of his life is infinitely superior to the influences which seek to distract his attention and baffle his energy. In the absence of God the Holy Ghost, Christian service becomes a toil, and ends in failure and mortification : but under the influence of the life-giving and light-giving Spirit of God, sorrow itself is turned into joy.

Notwithstanding this revelation, Moses was unable to overcome his infirmity ; he still doubted, as well indeed he might, in the presence of such a vocation as had probably never been addressed to man. Let us listen to his excuses, and we shall see how unbecoming it would be on our part to sneer at a man upon whom the Divine burden pressed so heavily. Moses himself was not disobedient unto the heavenly vision, nor did he doubt the authority with which he had been charged ; but a difficulty presented itself from the other side. Moses thus puts the case :

"And Moses answered and said, But, behold, they will not believe me nor hearken unto my voice: for they will say, The Lord hath not appeared unto thee " (iv. 1).

Human distrust is a difficulty which every preacher, teacher, and holy labourer has to encounter. All great movements are carried by consent of parties. God himself cannot re-establish moral order without the concurrence of the powers that have rebelled against his rule. Moses had difficulty to fear on the side of Israel, as well as on the side of Pharaoh. His message was to be addressed, in the first instance, to the children of Israel. The tidings of their proposed deliverance might be too much for their faith. They had been the sufferers of so many terrors and disappointments,—they had been so long buried in the darkness of despair,— that the gospel of emancipation might appear to them to be but a mocking dream. What if they should hear the message of Moses, and treat it in a spirit of unbelief? The suggestion of Moses was not at all unreasonable. He will work none the less effectively for putting these preliminary inquiries, provided he does not carry them to the point of excess. So long as they come out of a humble and reverent spirit, God will answer them with gracious patience; but should they become degraded into mere excuses, or discover a cowardly spirit, the patience of God will become a flame of judgment. After all, the spiritual labourer has less to do with the unbelief of his hearers than with the instruction and authority of God. We have to ascertain what God the Lord would have us say, and then to speak it simply, distinctly, and lovingly, whether men will hear or whether they will forbear. The preacher must prepare himself for having doubts cast upon his authority; and he must take care that his answer to such doubts is as complete as the authority itself. God alone can give the true answer to human doubt. We are not to encounter scepticism with merely ingenious replies and clever arguments, but in the power and grace of the living God.

Moses, having being furnished with signs by which to convince the children of Israel that he was the messenger of God sent to redeem them from the oppression of Egypt, might be supposed to be fully qualified for his mission. Surely, there is now an end of inquiry and debate upon his part. Not so, however; Moses fell back upon his own unworthiness.

"And Moses said unto the Lord, O my Lord, I am not eloquent, neither heretofore, nor since thou hast spoken unto thy servant: but I am slow of speech, and of a slow tongue. And the Lord said unto him, Who hath made man's mouth? or who maketh the dumb, or deaf, or the seeing, or the blind? have not I the Lord? Now therefore go, and I will be with thy mouth, and teach thee what thou shalt say" (iv. 10-12).

Moses has now descended from the high level of the argument, and narrowed the case into one of mere human personality. He has forgotten the promise, "Certainly I will be with thee." The moment we get away from Divine promise and forget great principles, we narrow all controversy and degrade all service. Self-consciousness is the ruin of all vocations. Let a man look into himself, and measure his work by himself, and the movement of his life will be downward and exhaustive. Let him look away from himself to the Inspirer of his life, and the Divine reward of his labours, and he will not so much as see the difficulties which may stand ever so thickly in his way. Think of Moses turning his great mission into a question which involved his own eloquence ! All such reasoning admits of being turned round upon the speaker as a charge of foolish if not of profane vanity. See how the argument stands : " I am not eloquent, and therefore this mission cannot succeed in my hands," is equivalent to saying, " I am an eloquent man, and, therefore, this undertaking must be crowned with signal success." The work had nothing whatever to do with the eloquence or ineloquence of Moses. It was not to be measured or determined by his personal gifts : the moment, therefore, that he turned to his individual talents, he lost sight of the great end which he was called instrumentally to accomplish. How sublime is the rebuke of God ! Cannot the Maker of man's mouth touch with eloquence the lips which he has fashioned ? What is human eloquence but the expression of Divine music ? Pedantic rhetoricians may fashion rules of their own for the refinement of human speech, but he who waits diligently upon God, and whose purpose is to know the will of God that he may speak it to men, will be entrusted with an eloquence rhythmic as the sea, and startling as the thunder. Rhetoric is the gift of God. Eloquence is not a merely human attainment. The secret of convincing and persuasive speech is put into the hearts of those who forget themselves in their homage to God and truth. Moreover, God condescended so far to the weakness of Moses as to find for him a coadjutor in his mission to the children of Israel and to the king of Egypt. Aaron could speak well. Moses was a thinker; Aaron was a speaker. Aaron was to be to Moses instead of a mouth, and Moses was to be to Aaron instead of God. Thus one man has to be the complement of another. No one man has all gifts and graces. The ablest and best of us cannot do without our brother. There is to be a division of labour in the great work of conquering the world for God. The thinker works ; so does the speaker, so does the writer. We are a chain ; not merely isolated links; we belong to one another, and only by fraternal and zealous co-operation can we secure the great results possible to faith and labour. Some men are fruitful of suggestion. They have wondrous powers of indication : but there their special power ends. Other men have great gifts of *expression* ; they can put thoughts

into the best words; they have the power of music; they can
charm, fascinate, and persuade.   Such men are not to undervalue
one another; they are to co-operate as fellow-labourers in the
kingdom of God.

Here we leave the region of the miraculous and come into
relations with which we are painfully familiar.   Man excusing
himself from duty is a familiar picture.   It is not a picture
indeed; it is a personal experience.   How inventive we are in
finding excuses for not doing the will of God!   How falsely
modest we can become! depreciating ourselves, and putting ourselves before God in a light in which we could never consent to
be put before society by the criticism of others.   Is not this
a revelation of the human heart to itself?   We only want to
walk in paths that are made beautiful with flowers, and to
wander by streams that lull us by their own tranquillity.   Nerve,
and pluck, and force we seem to have lost.   In place of the inventiveness of love we have the inventiveness of reluctance or
distaste.   It should be our supreme delight to find reasons for
co-operating with God, and to fortify ourselves by such interpretations of circumstances as will plainly show us that we are in the
right battle, fighting on the right side, and wielding the right
weapon.   The possibility of self-deception is one of the most
solemn of all subjects.   I cannot question the sincerity of Moses
in enumerating and massing all the difficulties of his side of the
case.   He meant every word that he said.   It is not enough
to be sincere; we must have intelligence and conscience enlightened and enlarged.   Mistakes are made about this matter
of sincerity; the thing forgotten being that sincerity is nothing in
itself, everything depending upon the motive by which it is
actuated and the object towards which it is directed.   The Church
is to-day afflicted with the spirit of self-excusing:—it cannot
give, because of the depression of the times; it cannot go upon its
mighty errands, because of its dainty delicateness; it cannot
engage in active beneficence, because its charity should begin at
home; it cannot enter into ardent controversy, because it prefers
the comfort of inaction.   Churches should not tell lies to themselves.   The first great thing to be done is for a man to be
faithful to his own heart, to look himself boldly in the face, and
speak the clear truth emphatically to his own consciousness.

Exodus iv. 21.

"And the Lord said unto Moses, When thou goest to return unto Egypt, see that thou do all those wonders before Pharaoh which I have put in thine hand : but I will harden his heart, that he shall not let the people go."

MOSES BEFORE PHARAOH.

THERE are of course many difficulties, by us insoluble, in connection with the sovereignty of God. This must be distinctly recognised, and no man must expect to have all mysteries dwarfed to the measure of his own understanding. The greatest of all mysteries is God himself, yet we are not therefore to doubt his existence, or to deny his loving providence. The mere fact of any question being mysterious does not in any way affect its truthfulness. There are mysteries which are *against* reason, and there are mysteries which are *above* reason. It is in full view of these principles that we discuss this difficult subject.

Looking at human history generally in relation to Divine sovereignty, three things are clear :—

First : *That all nations are not equally honoured.* This difference amongst the nations, let it not be considered trite to say, is not made by the Bible, or by any system of theology ; it is simply a matter of fact, whatever may be our views respecting either God or the Bible. One nation is highly civilised, another is in the lowest condition of barbarism ; yet all the nations are under the government of the same gracious God. Every day the sun sees some nations worshipping the true Spirit, and others bowing down before idols ; yet all people, let it be repeated, are under the government of the same Creator. This is pointed out as a mere matter of fact, and as presenting the gravest possible difficulties, whatever may be the theological or philosophical theory by which we regulate our observation of human affairs.

Second : *That all individuals are not equally endowed.* We are

all men, and yet no two men are alike. In every history you
find the great man and the little man. The poetic dreamer and
the prosaic clown ; the daring adventurer and the self-regarding
coward ; the child of genius and the creature of darkness ; yet
all claim to be men, and all may theoretically acknowledge the
same God and Redeemer. These are facts with which we have
to deal whether we open the Bible or not, whether we acknowledge a system of Divine Providence or not, whether we are
atheists or saints.

Third : *That Divine judgment is regulated by Divine allotment.*
Here we open the Bible, in which we find that to whom much is
given, from him shall much be required, and that it shall be more
tolerable for Tyre and Sidon in the day of judgment than for
nations which have enjoyed a fuller revelation of Divine purpose
and requirements. The heathen are a law unto themselves.
Five talents are expected to produce more than two. The
Divine plan of judgment therefore is not arbitrary, but moral.
If we lose hold of this principle, we shall see confusion where we
might see the order of righteousness. First of all, and last of all,
it must be our settled and unalterable conviction that *God must
do right,* or he is no longer God. Everything must perish which
opposes this law. We are not, however, to look at incomplete
cases, and regard them as final criteria by which to test the
wisdom and righteousness of the Almighty. In many cases we
shall have to repress our impatience, and calmly to wait until
fuller light is granted.

So much for general principles ; let us now look at the
particular instance before us, and in doing so we must at the
outset clearly mark the limits of the ground which it occupies.
The children of Israel were under the sovereign control of the
king of Egypt. In some sense he had property in them. They
were his bondsmen, delivered into his hands, and subject to his
government. His relation to them was distinctly that of a
political ruler ; not based upon theological antipathies. He did
not maltreat the Israelites because of their religious opinions.
Pharaoh was a king, and it was strictly in his royal capacity that
he dealt with the question of Israelitish bondage. Suddenly, to
himself, Moses and Aaron proposed in the name of the Lord God
of Israel that Pharaoh should let the people go to held a religious

feast in the wilderness. Pharaoh was of course startled. As a pagan he did not acknowledge the name or government of the God of Israel. A political petition was addressed to him, and he dealt with it on political grounds. It was not a spiritual question which was proposed to Pharaoh. It was not a question which involved his own personal salvation, or his own relation to the great future; it was purely, simply, and exclusively a political question. It was, therefore, within this sphere that the Divine action was taken, and that action is fitly described as a hardening of Pharaoh's heart. We do not attempt to modify the words, or in any sense to gloss them over; we accept them in their plain and obvious signification. The question now arises, what the meaning of that hardening was, and what useful results accrued from a process which appears to us to be so mysterious. We have already laid down the fundamental and eternal principle that God must do right, and that, consequently, however mysterious may be the processes through which he moves, his purpose is infinitely just. The hardening of Pharaoh's heart, as involving the development of a merely political scheme, may amount in effect to no more than this,—" I will delay the process; this request shall not be granted at once; and I prolong the process in order that I may bring out lessons for Pharaoh himself, for the children of Israel, and for mankind at large : were Pharaoh to let the children of Israel escape from him at once, the result would be mischievous to themselves; therefore, in mercy, not in anger, I will harden Pharaoh's heart." This is eminently reasonable, and has been found to be so in our own experience. When men have snapped at their blessings, and instantly secured all their purposes, they have undervalued the advantages which have been thus realised. There is a hardening that is really merciful. "God cursed the ground for man's sake." Instead of the word *cursed*, insert the word *hardened*, and you will see what is meant by a hardening process taking place at the suggestion of a merciful disposition. God hardened the ground for man's sake ; God hardened Pharaoh's heart for the sake of all parties involved : by delaying the result, he urged and exemplified lessons which could not have been successfully inculcated in any other way.

So far, the question is not a moral one, except in the degree in which *all* questions have more or less of a moral bearing. It has been supposed by some that in the case of this exercise of Divine sovereignty, the sum total of Pharaoh's wickedness was increased. This, however, was by no means the case. There is the greatest possible difference between wickedness being focalised, and wickedness being increased. Let us then assume that it was altogether a moral question, and show that the sovereignty of God did in no wise add to the iniquity of Pharaoh. It is possible for a man to become virtuous in one direction, that he may concentrate his wickedness in another. Here, for example, is a man who has been notoriously indolent, intemperate, or otherwise evil-disposed ;—by some means that man becomes energetic, self-controlled, and apparently attentive to some discipline which has a good moral effect upon him ; looked at outwardly, it is evident that a beneficial transformation has taken place upon him. What, however, is the reality of the case ? The man has actually put himself under discipline, that he may prepare for a prize-fight ! He has made his very virtues contribute to the purposes of his vice. Instead of his wickedness being distributed over large spaces of his life, it is gathered up and expressed in one definite act. Even, therefore, were we to suppose that the hardening of the heart of Pharaoh involved moral consequences, it would by no means follow that the sum total of his wickedness was thereby increased. It would only show that wickedness in its intensity ; it would focalise the scattered energies of the bad man, and show their fierceness in one supreme act.

As the history proceeds, we see that the political situation enlarges itself into a spiritual problem. Pharaoh sees the wonders of the Lord, and feels the terribleness of his scourge Under the influence of fear, he makes a *promise* unto Moses and Aaron that if the Lord will withdraw his hand, he will let Israel go. Thus the question becomes *moral* as well as political. Pharaoh makes a promise, and therefore implicates his honour and his conscience. It is to be observed, too, that the promise was made in connection with a special request for religious supplication on the part of Moses. Thus Pharaoh said, " Entreat the Lord, that he may take away the frogs from me, and from my people ; and I will let the people go, that they may do sacrifice unto the Lord." Thus the ground is entirely changed. By some means or other the moral nature of Pharaoh has been touched, and the consequence is a pledge on his part to permit Israel to do sacrifice. But was Pharaoh faithful to his word? Was he not in reality trying to turn the moral into the political, and so to get out of an honourable pledge by an unworthy strategy? It would appear that this was really the case, for " when Pharaoh saw that there was respite, he hardened his heart, and hearkened not unto them ; " " And Pharaoh sent, and called for Moses and Aaron, and said unto them, I have sinned this time : the Lord is righteous, and I and my people are wicked. Entreat the Lord (for it is enough) that there be no more mighty thunderings and hail ; and I will let you go, and ye shall stay no longer." Did Pharaoh fulfil his promise? No! " When Pharaoh saw that the rain and the hail and the thunders were ceased, he sinned yet more, and hardened his heart, he and his servants." Thus it is clear that Pharaoh hardened his own heart, and whatever may be the mystery of Divine sovereignty in this matter, Pharaoh himself is distinctly charged with the responsibility of his own obstinacy. There was undoubtedly a Divine action in the process ; but that Divine action did not involve the spiritual destiny of Pharaoh

Applying these lessons to ourselves as sinners, I have now to teach that Jesus Christ tasted death for every man, and that whosoever will may avail himself of the blessings secured by the mediation of the Saviour. If any man excuses himself on the ground that God has hardened his heart, that man is trusting to an excuse in the most solemn affairs of his being which he would not for a moment tolerate in the region of his family life or commercial relations. We must not be sensible in ordinary affairs and insane in higher concerns. Were a servant to tell her mistress that she is fated to be unclean in her habits, that mistress would instantly and justly treat her with angry contempt. Were a clerk to tell a banker that he was fated to come late every morning, and go away early every afternoon, the statement would be received as a proof of selfishness or insanity. Were a travelling companion to tell you to make no attempt to be in time for the steamboat or the train, because if you were fated to catch it there would be no fear of your losing it, you would treat his suggestion as it deserved to be treated. Yet men who can act in a common-sense manner in all such little affairs, sometimes profess that they will not make any attempt in a religious direction, because they believe in the doctrine of predestination or fatalism. Wicked and slothful servants, they shall be condemned out of their own mouth! "Come unto me, all ye that labour and are heavy-laden, and I will give you rest." "Whosoever will, let him come." "Him that cometh to me, I will in no wise cast out." "How often would I have gathered you, as a hen doth gather her brood under her wings, and ye would not!" In presence of such statements as these, it must be the very consummation of blasphemy to turn round upon God and say, "I wanted to be saved, but thou didst harden my heart and condemn me to hell."

NOTE.

The taskmasters were Egyptian bailiffs or general managers; the officers were Hebrews, and had each the charge of a certain number, of whom, and their work, they had to keep account (hence called *Shoterim* or *Writers*). When recently in Egypt, I saw this very system still in operation on a road which the Viceroy was constructing. A Turkish officer superintended so much of the road; under him was an Arab, generally a sheikh of an adjoining village, whose duty it was to mark out to his people what they had to do, and to keep strict account how it was done; and under him was a miscellaneous company of men, girls, and boys, working in a state of semi-nudity, under the discipline of the stick. The stick served a double purpose: laid along the road, it marked out how much was to be done within a given time; laid on the backs of the unfortunate *fellaheen*, it painfully reminded them, that, whether able for it or not, their full tale of task-work must be completed.

A European who has not been in the country can hardly imagine the extent to which the stick is used in Egypt. The natives seem almost to glory in it as an ancient and venerable institution. "The Moslems have a proverb that 'the stick came down from heaven a blessing from Allah.' . . . . . To 'eat stick,' as a sound thrashing is technically termed, is submitted to with a degree of *sang froid* quite astonishing to European nations, and is not at all degrading in the eyes of the Egyptian."—W. L. ALEXANDER, D.D.

Exodus vii. 3.

"And I will harden Pharaoh's heart."

THE HARDENING OF PHARAOH'S HEART.

WE have already remarked upon the hardening of Pharaoh's heart; let us now look at some of the broader aspects of that supposed mystery. We must never consent to have God charged with injustice. Stand at what distance he may from our reason, he must never separate himself from our conscience. If God could first harden a man's heart, and then punish the man because his heart was hard, he would act a part which the sense of justice would instantly and indignantly condemn ; therefore, he *could not* act that part. Whenever there is on the one hand a verbal difficulty, and on the other hand a moral difficulty, the verbal difficulty must give way. It is a rule of interpretation we must fearlessly apply. Let me re-state it. If ever there should be a battle between language and the instinct or sense of justice, the language must go down ; the Judge of all the earth must be held to do right. The key of the whole difficulty is in the very first chapter of the Book of Exodus; in the eighth verse of that chapter we read : "Now there arose up a new king over Egypt, which knew not Joseph." That is the beginning of the mischief. That is the explanation of all the hardening of heart. What is the full translation or paraphrase of that verse ? It is this : Now there arose a new king, who knew not the history of his own country ; a Pharaoh who remembered not that Egypt had been saved by one of the very Israelites who had become to him objects of fear ; a king guilty either of ignorance or of ingratitude ; for if he knew the history of his own country and acted in this way he was ungrateful, and therefore hardened his own heart ; and if he did not know the history of his own country, he was. ignorant of the one thing which every king ought to know, and therefore he was unfit to be king. The explanation of all that follows is in this ignorant or ungrateful Pharaoh, not in the wisdom or grace of the providence of God. Whether this particular Pharaoh came immediately after Joseph, or five centuries after him is of no consequence, since we are dealing with a moral progeny—a bad hereditary—and not with a merely physical descent. The point to be kept steadily in view is that Pharaoh had hardened his own heart in the first instance, had forgotten or ignored the history of his country, and was ruling his whole course by obduracy and selfishness. That is the Pharaoh with whom God had to deal. Not some young and pliable Pharaoh, who was willing to be either right or wrong, as anybody might be pleased to lead him ; an immature and inexperienced Pharaoh, who was simply looking round for a policy, and might as easily have been led upwards as led downwards—a very gentle, genial, beautiful soul; but a man who had made up his mind to forget the saviour of his country, and to bend every consideration to the impulse of a narrow and cruel policy. In this criticism Pharaoh must be to us something more than an Egyptian term. We must know the man before we can even partially understand the providence. What is the material with which God has to deal ? That is the vital inquiry. God may be reverently represented as speaking thus :—This man, having hardened his heart, has shown clearly the specialty of his moral and mental constitution ; he must be made, therefore, to see what hardness of heart really means ; for his own sake, I will treat him as he has treated himself, and through him I will show the ages that to harden the heart is the most terrible of all crimes, is indeed the beginning and pledge of the unpardonable sin, and can only be punished by the destruction of the body and soul in hell. There is no other way of dealing with the world. Men supply the conditions with which Providence has to work.

The case now begins to lift itself out of the narrow limits of a historical puzzle and to assume the grandeur of an illustration of Divine methods and purposes ; in other words, it is no longer an instance of the sovereignty of force, but an example of the sovereignty of love, and though the example is unavoidably costly in its individual suffering it is infinitely precious as an eternal doctrine. God is to us what we are to God. He begins where we begin. One might imagine that the Lord treated Pharaoh arbitrarily, that is to say, did just what he pleased with that particular man or class of man. Nothing can be further from the truth. There is nothing arbitrary in the eternal government. It is begun with justice, in the whole process justice, in the whole issue justice. What other elements may come in will appear as the case is evolved and consummated. The Lord hardened the hearts of the Israelites just as certainly as he hardened the heart of Pharaon, and in the very same way and for the very same reason. Do not imagine that God has some partiality for one man at the expense of another. God deals with each man according to each man's peculiarity of constitution and purpose. See how the Lord treated the Israelites : "So I gave them up unto their own hearts' lust : and they walked in their own counsels." The marginal reading is still more vivid : "I gave them up unto the hardness of their hearts." That is to say, the Divine Teacher must at certain points say, in effect : You have made your determination, you must work it out ; no reasoning, even on my part, would dissuade you ; you must for yourselves, in bitterness and agony of experience, see what this condition of mind really means—"So I gave them up unto their own hearts' lust : and they walked in their own counsels "—not as an act of sovereignty, arbitrariness, and determination that could not be set aside because of the Divinity of its origin ; but I, the Living God, was for their sakes necessitated to let them see what a certain course of conduct must logically and morally end in. The Apostle puts the same truth in very striking language : "They received not the love of the truth, that they might be saved. And for this cause God shall send them strong delusion, that they should believe a lie." "My Spirit shall not always strive with man,"— I will, at a certain point, stand back and let you see what you are really at ; doctrine would be lost upon you ; exposition, appeal, would be abortive ; I am necessitated, therefore, though the Living God and Father, to let you have your own way, that you may really see that it was an angel that was stopping you, it was mercy that would have prevented your downward rush.

This is the secret of all Biblical providence, and rule, and education. From the very beginning, the first man started up with a disobedient heart. For some reason or other, he said he would pursue a policy of disobedience. The Lord allowed him to do so, and the result was death. He was told that death would be the result, but the telling had no effect upon him : he said, " I will try." If our narrow suggestion of reasoning, and persuading, and pleading, were correct and profound in its moral conception, and absolute in its philosophical wisdom, Adam would not have incurred God's prediction, but instantly have fallen back from the tree forbidden, and on no account would have touched it ; but philosophy is lost, appeal is a voice in the air that brings back no great heart-cry of allegiance and consent. Every man must touch hell for himself. Another man started life upon a different policy. He said he would rule by violence ; nothing should stand in his way ; resistance on the part of others, or aggravation on the side of others, would simply elicit from him an answer of violence and destruction. Said he, in effect, " I will not reason, I will smite ; I will not pray, I will destroy." The Lord said in effect : " It must be so ; you must see the result of this violence ; that disposition never can be got out of you but by exhaustion ; argument would be lost on a fiery spirit like yours ; it would be in vain to interpose gentle persuasion or entreating prayer between a nature like yours and the end which it contemplates. Take your own course, and the end of violence is to be Cain for ever, to be branded externally, to be a lesson to the ages that violence only slays itself, and is a wickedness, a crime, in a universe of order." Another man arose, who said he abhorred violence. Issues which the soul wished were accomplished must be secured by other and wiser and deeper means. Said he, " I will try deception, I will tell falsehoods, I will answer inquiries lyingly ; there shall be no noise, no tumult, no sign of violence or passion; but I will answer with mental reservations, I will play a false part, and thus pass smoothly through life." The man was of a false heart. He did not *tell* lies : he *was* a lie. The Lord had but one alternative. Though he be omnipotent in strength, he is limited when he deals with the creatures which he has made in his own image. So said he, in effect, " If it must be so, it must be so ; your policy you have adopted— attempt it." The man attempted it, and was laid in the dust a dead, blighted victim of his own sin. The universe will not have the liar in it. It may find room for his body to rot in, but it will not suffer him to live. All through and through history, there-

fore, the same thing is again and again demonstrated. We cannot account for personal constitution, for singularities of mind; in
this profound problem there are metaphysics not to be penetrated
by human reason, and the expositor, how careful and anxious
soever he may be, can only begin where the facts themselves
begin. What lies beyond his ken also lies beyond his criticism.
The solemn and awful fact is, that every man has a constitution
of his own, a peculiarity and specialty which makes him an
individual and separates him from all other men, giving him
an accent and a signature incommunicably his own, and that
God deals with every man according to the conditions which
the man himself supplies.

But a narrow criticism would tempt us to say that mercy will
prevail where hardening will utterly want success; gentleness,
tears, compassion—they will succeed. If God had, to speak
figuratively, fallen upon the neck of Pharaoh, and wept over him,
and persuaded him with gentle words, Pharaoh would have been
a different man. That criticism is profanity; that criticism is
historically false: hear the Apostolic argument: "For he [God]
saith to Moses, I will have mercy on whom I will have mercy,
and I will have compassion on whom I will have compassion.
So then it is not of him that willeth, nor of him that runneth, but
of God that sheweth mercy. For the Scripture saith unto Pharaoh,
Even for this same purpose have I raised thee up, that I might
shew my power in thee, and that my name might be declared
throughout all the earth. Therefore hath he mercy on whom he
will have mercy, and whom he will he hardeneth,"—perfectly easy
words, if taken from the right point of view, and constructed in
harmony with the broad method of Divine providence, even as
that method is known amongst ourselves. The Lord has in this
way, which is the only way, shown that the exercise of mercy is
as useless as the process of hardening. We have foolishly
imagined that mercy has succeeded, and hardening has failed:
whereas all history shows us, and all experience confirms the
verdict of history, that mercy is utterly useless. We ourselves
are living examples that all God's tears cannot soften the obduracy
of our heart. This interpretation clears away all difficulty from
this Pauline passage, enabling us to read it in this way: God has,
in the exercise of his sovereign wisdom, tried different methods

with different minds. In some instances he has demonstrated the inevitable issue of hardness of heart; in other instances he has shown the utter uselessness of mere mercy; he has had mercy on whom he would have mercy, and whom he would he has hardened, or on them tried a hardening process; in other words, he has let both of them work out the bent of their own mind, fulfil their own line of constitution, and see what it ends in, and the consequence is this : letting men have their own way has failed, pitying their weaknesses has failed, terror has accomplished nothing, and mere mercy has only wrung its own tender heart; the rod and the tears have both failed. Let us wait before we come to the final conclusion. We are now in the midst of a process and must not force the issue by impatience.

So then it is unrighteous to blame God for showing men what hardness of heart really means, as if by adopting a contrary course he could have saved them; for he has again and again, in his providence, shown that his goodness has been no more effectual than his sovereignty. This is the other side of the great problem. We pitied Pharaoh, saying, " If the Lord would but try the effect of mercy upon him, Pharaoh would be pliant.'' The Lord says : " No ; I know Pharaoh better than you do; but to show you what mercy will do or will not do, I will try it upon other men." And we have stood by, and seen God cry rivers of tears, we have seen him thrill with compassion ; we have seen him make himself pliable in the hands of his own children, as if they might do with him what they pleased ; and they have in reply to his mercy smitten him in the face.

The seventy-eighth Psalm is an elaborate historical argument establishing this very point, and is the more striking that it deals with the very people whom Pharaoh refused to liberate. The whole case is thus focalised for us; we see the double action at one view. If you want to see what hardening can do, look at Pharaoh ; if you want to see what mercy can do, look at Israel ; in both instances you see utter failure. God had compassion on whom he would have compassion, and on whom he would he tried the giving up of men to the hardness of their own hearts, and in both cases the issue was disappointment and grief on the part of God. So our little na row theory that mercy would have succeeded has been contradicted by the unanimous verdict of

the ages. Can language be tenderer than that of the Psalmist?
"Marvellous things did he in the sight of their fathers in the
land of Egypt, in the field of Zoan. He divided the sea, and
caused them to pass through ; and he made the waters to stand
as an heap. In the daytime also he led them with a cloud, and
all the night with a light of fire. He clave the rocks in the
wilderness, and gave them drink as out of the great depths. He
brought streams also out of the rock, and caused waters to run
down like rivers." What is the upshot? They all prayed, they
all loved God, they all responded to the magic of mercy? "And
they sinned yet more against him by provoking the Most High in
the wilderness." "But he, being full of compassion"—this is
the very theory you wanted to have tried—"forgave their
iniquity, and destroyed them not : yea, many a time turned he
his anger away, and did not stir up all his wrath. For he
remembered that they were but flesh ; a wind that passeth away,
and cometh not again." How did they answer him? By love?
by allegiance? by covenants of loyalty? Read the history :
"How oft did they provoke him in the wilderness, and grieve
him in the desert ! Yea, they turned back and tempted God, and
limited the Holy One of Israel. They remembered not his hand :
nor the day when he delivered them from the enemy." There
mercy stands back, and says, "I have failed." Seeing that both
severity and mercy have failed, what was to be done with the
race? Says God : "I have had compassion on these; I have
hardened the hearts of these—or, in other words, have allowed
them to see what the hardening of their own hearts really
means; I have thus created a great human history, and the
result is failure, failure. The law has failed, sentiment has
failed, the sword I put back as a failure, my tears I dry as a
failure—what is to be done?" Now comes the sublimity of
the evangelical philosophy, the glory of the gospel as it is known
in the Cross of our Lord Jesus Christ. Righteousness and
mercy must meet together, justice and pity must hold their
interview ; God must be just, and yet must himself find means
by which he can be the Justifier of the ungodly. This reconciliation has been effected. We, as evangelical thinkers, believe
in the Cross of our Lord Jesus Christ, and if that fail there
remaineth no more sacrifice for sins.

Exodus xi. 1.

"And the Lord said unto Moses, Yet will I bring one plague more upon Pharaoh, and upon Egypt; afterwards he will let you go hence : when he shall let you go, he shall surely thrust you out hence altogether."

THE PLAGUES OF EGYPT.

THE river was turned into blood, frogs came up upon the land of Egypt abundantly, and lice and flies; beasts were destroyed, locusts covered the whole land ; darkness that might be felt filled the earth, and in one awful night the firstborn died,—"from the firstborn of Pharaoh that sitteth upon his throne, even unto the firstborn of the maidservant that is behind the mill ; and all the firstborn of beasts." And in that night of agony there "was a great cry throughout all the land of Egypt, such as there was none like it, nor shall be like any more." Some things can only be done once ; some things do not permit repetition. The magicians of Egypt could do, apparently at least, or in some measure, what Moses and Aaron did in the way of miracles : they were skilled men, abundantly clever in conjuring and all manner of dexterity. The Lord seemed to take delight in developing their power so far as it would go : but there came a time when it broke down. Do not suppose that the whole race can be run by any competitor of God. For a mile you might outrun the wind, but the wind will conquer you : for a mile you might run faster than the lightning locomotive, but only for a little time. There came a day, we read, when "the magicians could not stand before Moses because of the boils ; for the boil was upon the magicians, and upon all the Egyptians." When the sting was in themselves they felt themselves to be but men.

Let us look at these plagues from Pharaoh's side and from the Divine side, and learn the modern and immediate uses of these tremendous judgments.

There is a period in life when we can only see sin in the
light of its punishments, that, indeed, is not to see sin at all, but
that is the chronic sophism with which all high spiritual teaching
has to contend, and to contend almost impotently, because of the
deceitfulness of the heart. When we are in the right mind we
shall not need to see hell in order to know what sin really is :
we shall know it afar off, before it has shaped itself into overt
evil behaviour. We should hate it as a spiritual possibility, if
no stain had ever been made upon the snow of the universe. We
should be so quick of spiritual imagination as to know what the
sin would be—not a measurable taint to be reckoned up and
named in plain inches. We should feel so sympathetically with
the spirit and holiness of God as to see how one, so-called, little
lie would darken creation and put out the very lamps of heaven
and make it impossible for God to live. How far from that state
are we ? We have become so familiar with sin as to have
broken it up into the plural number, and now we speak of sin as
sins, and, once having given way to the pluralising of the word,
we have missed all its gravity and all its terribleness. To speak
in the plural number is to bring sin within the region of
statistics. We now classify sin, distributing it into schedules
and publishing what is done in separate lines ; and thus we come
to construct a comparative morality. When we see the punishment of sin, we think we see what sin itself really is. We must
rid the mind of that most mischievous misconception. We do
not see sin from any penalty that has yet fallen upon it. When
Adam died, we did not see what Adam had really done. He had
made the universe impossible ; he had taken away for ever the
happiness of God ; he had made heaven an impossibility—unless
there could be found in the Divine nature itself some answer
profound enough, beneficent enough, to undo in some mysterious
and wordless way the tremendous and infinite catastrophe.
No wonder we take light and frivolous views of human conduct,
when we have turned sin into *sins*, because that is the first step
of a process which means a comparison of one sin with another :
the weighing of one sin against another, and the distribution of
sins into venial and mortal. These are the clevernesses of men,
the refinements of human deceit,—not permissions which have
been granted by any charter Divine,—thus to trifle with law and

consequence. Many would be struck by the plague who would not be impressed by the hardness of heart which it was intended to chasten,—hence you will hear more criticism about the miracle of the plague, than about the infinitely greater miracle of human obduracy. We miss the point: we wonder about the river turned into blood, and wonder not about the heart turned into stone.

Immediately following this line of remark comes the solemn doctrine that suffering is often mistaken for penitence. The two things go inseparably together. When we think of punishment instead of thinking of sin, we are very likely to think that suffering is the equivalent of contrition. We say "the poor man seemed to be suffering intensely." So he may have been; but there may have been no contrition in his heart. It was a physical or mechanical suffering, not a moral pain; a spiritual agony, a revulsion of the soul against the terribleness of sin. Such ideas, perhaps, never occurred to the offender, but when the darkness turns creation into night, when he goes out for water, and is forced to drink blood, when he cannot put down his foot because of the abundance of the insects which cover the ground, then he begins to whimper, and to cry, and to say that things are going hard with him; and when we see him with bent head and eyes all tears, we say pensively "the poor creature did seem to be suffering so much." So he was; but the suffering was in the wrong place. He cried out because of fear; he cried because he was a coward,—not because he was a sinner. A man has done something in society which he ought not to have done: he is brought before the judge and condemned to imprisonment and servitude. The circumstances being wholly unfamiliar, the man is cowed by them,—the days are long, the nights are burdens, the whole time is charged with intensest suffering; so the man breaks down and is sorry for what he has done. That is a mistake. No man can be made sorry by punishment, except in the narrowest and most trifling degree. We do not begin to be sorry until we feel that one false word, one wrong deed, has spoiled the universe, and grieved the Spirit of the living God, no matter what the weight is upon our heads, or the laceration upon our backs—no matter how we are overwhelmed by mere suffering. We must distinguish between the coward and the sinner, the sinner that cries out and the soul that would repeat the offence if the punishment could be escaped. Until we get down to these vital lines we never can begin our first lesson in gospel theology. How easy it is to mistake mercy for weakness ! This was Pharaoh's mistake. The moment the Lord lifted his heavy hand from the Egyptian king, Pharaoh began to forget his oath, and vow, and promise, and to harden his heart,—saying, in effect, " He can do no more ; the God of the Israelites has exhausted himself; now that he has removed his hand he has confessed his weakness rather than demonstrated his pity." We are committing the same mistake every day : whilst the plague is in the house we are ready to do anything to get rid of it ! we will say prayers morning, noon and night, and send for the holy man who has been anointed as God's minister, and will read nothing but solid and most impressive books, listen to no frivolous conversation, and touch nothing that could dissipate or enfeeble the mind. How long will the plague be removed before the elasticity will return to the man and the old self reassert its sovereignty ? Not a day need pass. We begin to feel that the worst is past : we say it is darkest before it is dawn, " hope springs eternal in the human breast " ; and so easily do we fall back into the old swing between self-indulgence and nominal homage to God. We think we have felt all the Lord can do, and we say, " His sword is no longer ; it cannot reach us now that we have removed away this little distance from its range ; now and here we may do what we please, and judgment cannot fall upon us." Thus we play old Pharaoh's part day by day. He is a mirror in which we may see ourselves. There is nothing mysterious in this part of the solemn reading. However we may endeavour to escape from the line when it becomes supernatural or romantic, we are brought swiftly and surely back to it when we see these repetitions of obduracy and these renewed challenges of Divine anger and judgment.

How wonderful, too, does self-interest extinguish the sense of justice ! Pharaoh will not let Israel go. He is turning away so much property, he is giving up so many opportunities of enhancing his royal dignity, or his imperial wealth. He will let them go ; then he will not ; he will relax his grasp a little ; then he will tighten it, and make it doubly sure. What is it that is in the man, thus making him halt, hesitate, and balance him-self as between duty and not duty ? It is the fiend that still reigns in human thought—its name is Self-interest, or Self-consideration—that will make any man, king or peasant, a thief; in fact, wherever it exists it is of necessity thievish. Self-interest never considers another man's rights. It rises early in the morn-ing to outwit that other man; when he turns round it will encroach upon his rights if it can. It will bend in the attitude of homage and prayer, and all the time be using that posture for the promotion of its own purposes. This illustration need not take us back to ancient Egypt. We know it, we represent it, we attest it by every oath possible to earnestness. We assure ourselves of the evil sovereignty of this principle of self-interest. It is in every one of us; it cannot be got out of us here and now. Whether it must be burned out of us by fire, drained out of us by blood, are questions we may ask : but it will never be argued away. Eloquence will spend its persuasion in vain upon it, and music will lull it to that kind of sleep which will but recruit its strength.

Looking at the Divine side of these plagues we notice the variety of the Divine resources. What we have here are mere examples of what might have been. God has but to look, and the miracle is done. His chariots are twenty thousand. He can touch us at countless points. The same variety is seen to-day. We are afflicted in innumerable ways. Every man has his own peculiar plague. There may be a common likeness amongst the plagues, but every man has his own accent of sorrow, his own particular point where things beat upon him as a blow might beat with cruel repercussion upon a wound. Why throw all these plagues away from us, as teachers and counsellors, because in their little narrowness they are said to have occurred thousands of years ago ? They are occurring to-day ; they are occurring in our houses, or in the secrecy of our hearts. Many a man is drinking blood when he seems to be drinking water. Many a man has countless plagues of frogs, or lice, or flies, within his soul, stinging him, annoying him, hampering him; keeping him back from the way which he would pursue. Horrible times his soul has by itself,—nights of darkness that may be felt ; losses compared with which the loss of the firstborn is but a gain. If we dwell upon the mere letter, we shall begin to ask questions of curiosity, and wonder how this could be, or that could be; but, looking at the broad solemnity of the case, human life is now attesting the variety of the Divine justice, the infinity of the penalties of God.

We here see how necessary it was for God to reveal the heart to itself. That is one of the mysteries of the Incarnation of the Son of God. Men would never have known that they could have murdered God, if Christ had not been born into the world. Prophets they killed by the score. Angelic men of radiant face and eloquent tongue they had banished without compunction; and last of all, God said "I will send my Son." The treatment of the Son of God revealed the human heart to itself. We do not know what we are unless we look at what is done, not by ourselves only, but by the sum-total of humanity. But who can preach with discrimination severe and just enough on this appalling theme? No man can separate himself from the race and claim to be a little whiter in morality than some other man. That is self-interest again; that is the self-element asserting itself over the generic and total quantity called human nature. When a man committed murder, you committed it. There is a narrow sense in which that is not true, but if you could see yourself in all the possibilities of yourself, you would see that you committed the awful crime. It is necessary that we should shudder at it: it is even necessary that we should punish it; but in doing so we should not forget to ask ourselves the solemn question: were we in the same circumstances, what should we have done? We are not made of different clay, of different sorts of flesh and blood: "God hath made of one blood, all nations of men." That being the case, there is but one heart, one human nature, and in the profoundest conception of this mystery we must look to what has been done by the whole race, if we would know what it is possible to the purest and whitest soul amongst us to do. Be afraid of any criticism that would withdraw you from these broader contemplations, and fix your attention strongly upon little moralities, and cherished virtues, which you set up in protest against being numbered with the totality of mankind.

Here we see the uselessness of punishment. If punishment could have saved the world, Christ need never have come. The

world had been drowned, and yet it came up with a bolder hand
to repeat its boldest iniquities. Cities had been burned, yet the
sulphur had hardly emitted its last fume before the sinner
returned to play the devil again. We speak of the reality of
these plagues, the reality of the Divine judgments; we begin
to wonder whether such and such things did really happen.
What do you mean by *really*? What, is reality? It would be
impossible for me to believe that the plagues ever took place
in Egypt after this fashion and on this scale, if I had not a witness
in my own heart and life that it was quite possible for them so
to be manifested and realised. What a man sees in delirium
tremens *is* real. It is the only reality. The sober, cool mind
could never see these things; it is only the mind in a given
condition of wreck and debasement that can grasp these awful
realities. When the suffering man sees the curtain removed and
grim death looking at him, it *is* real. Tell him that it is some
phantom of the brain; reason with him about it, and he tells you
he saw it, and your reasoning is like sprinkling water upon
Etna or Vesuvius, when the mountain is ablaze. When the
delirious brain sees the whole bed become a nest of intertangled
serpents with gleaming eyes and darting fangs and approaching
cruelty, it *is* real. Nothing ever can upon earth be so real.
After that, facts become dramatic incidents, and things that can be
touched, seen with the bodily eyes, are but theatrical commonplaces. We see with the inner eyes; we see with the soul's
vision. In some moments God connects us with the eternities,
and if we shrink back from them, he is the false teacher who tells
us that our experiences are not real. The man who speaks so
is a narrow teacher; he is limited within arbitrary lines; he does
not touch the agony and the Divinity of things.

So, allowing all that may be called romantic, supernatural, to
fall off from this story of the plagues, there remains all that God
wanted to remain—three things :—first, the assertion of the
Divine right in life. God cannot be turned out of his own
creation : he must assert his claim, and urge it, and redeem
it. The second thing that remains is the incontestable fact of
human opposition to Divine voices. Divine voices call to right,
to purity, to nobleness, to love, to brotherhood ; and every day we
resist these voices, and assert rebellious claims. The third thing

that remains is the inevitable issue. We cannot fight God and
win. "It is hard for thee to kick against the pricks." Why
smite with feeble fist the infinite granite of the infinite strength ?
who will lose ? The certain result will be the overthrow of the
sinner : the drowning of every Pharaoh who hardens himself
against the Divine will and voice. Stripped, therefore, of everything of the nature of romance—if you will import that word into
criticism so solemn—there remains the threefold fact that God
has rights amongst us; that man resists those rights; that the
battle comes, and the battle ends in but one way—"The Lord
reigneth." ·

Now that I come to think of it, have not all these plagues
followed my own obstinacy and hardness of heart in relation to
things Divine ? We speak of the plagues of Egypt as though
they began and ended in that distant land, and we regard them
now as part of an exciting historical romance. I will think
otherwise of them. The local incident and the local colour may
be dispensed with, but the supreme fact in my own consciousness
is that God always follows my obstinacy with plagues. The
plagues he can indeed vary, because his understanding is infinite
and his resources are without bound. What is the meaning of
the sleeplessness which has turned night into a longer day ?
What is the true interpretation of the diseases which have
enfeebled my bodily strength ? What is the meaning of the
graves which I have dug one after another for the burial of
wife, and child, and friend ? What is the interpretation of every
loss which has befallen my possessions ? It is easy to call all
these things by ordinary names and reckon them as part of the
common lot of man, and so miss all their meaning and all their
sacred pith. It is better for my soul's health that I should regard
all these circumstances as having a distinct religious application.
I need not amaze my judgment or bewilder my conscience by
inventing new romantic names or starting new casuistical difficulties. It will sober and elevate me to regard all the visitations
which have caused my life its keenest pains as ministries originated and directed by Heaven's beneficent wisdom. By consideration of the case in suitable temper I am able to drive away the
plague which has been a burden to my life. Even now I may

pray unto the Lord, and seek deliverance from the dangers which threaten my life on every hand. Dangers are rightly used when they move us to bolder prayer; losses are turned into gains when they lift our lives in an upward direction; disease is the beginning of health when it leads the sufferer to the Father's house. Pharaoh had his plagues, many and awful; and every life has its penal or chastening visitations which for the present are full of agony and bitterness, but which may be so used as to become the beginning of new liberties and brighter joys.

NOTE.

"We remained two months at Khartoum. During this time we were subjected to intense heat and constant dust-storms, attended with a general plague of boils. Verily, the plagues of Egypt remain to this day in the Soudan. On the 26th June (1865) we had the most extraordinary dust-storm that had ever been seen by the inhabitants. I was sitting in the courtyard of my agent's house at about half-past four p.m.; there was no wind, and the sun was as bright as usual in this cloudless sky, when suddenly a gloom was cast over all,—a dull yellow glare pervaded the atmosphere. Knowing that this effect portended a dust-storm, and that the present calm would be followed by a hurricane of wind, I rose to go home, intending to secure the shutters. Hardly had I risen when I saw approaching, from the south-west apparently, a solid range of immense brown mountains, high in air. So rapid was the passage of this extraordinary phenomenon, that in a few minutes we were in actual pitchy darkness. At first there was no wind, and the peculiar calm gave an oppressive character to the event. We were in a 'darkness that might be felt.' Suddenly the wind arrived, but not with the violence that I had expected There were two persons with me,—Michael Latfalla, my agent, and Monsieur Lombrosio. So intense was the darkness, that we tried to distinguish our hands placed close before our eyes; not even an outline could be seen. This lasted for upwards of twenty minutes: it then rapidly passed away, and the sun shone as before; but we had *felt* the darkness that Moses had inflicted upon the Egyptians."—SIR S. BAKER.

Exodus xii. 1-20.

The section from verse 1 to 28 is independent of the previous narrative, and is probably part of the law rather than of the history. It was not delivered at once, but is in all likelihood a gathering up of instructions given at different times. Up to verse 20 the section might form part of the book of Leviticus. Let us read the chapter thus :—

1. And the Lord spake unto Moses and Aaron in the land of Egypt, saying,

2. This month (the Hebrews had formerly begun the year at or near the autumnal equinox. The Egyptians began the year in June ; the Babylonians at the vernal equinox) shall be unto you the beginning of months : it shall be the first month of the year to you.

3. Speak ye unto all the congregation of Israel, saying, In the tenth day of this month (thus allowing ample time for the examination of the animal) they shall take to them every man a lamb (all Israelites are supposed to possess a lamb, or to be able to purchase one), according to the house of their fathers (rather, for the house of their fathers), a lamb for an house ;

4. And if the household be too little for the lamb, let him and his neighbour next unto his house take it according to the number of the souls ; every man according to his eating shall make your count for the lamb (ten was the least number regarded as sufficient ; twenty not considered too many).

5. Your lamb shall be without blemish (the teaching of natural piety); a male of the first year (that is, not above a year old) ; ye shall take it out from the sheep, or from the goats :

6. And ye shall keep it up (separate it from the flock and have it in special custody for four days) until the fourteenth day of the same month (the day of the full moon) ; and the whole assembly of the congregation of Israel shall kill it in the evening.

7. And they shall take of the blood, and strike it (with a bunch of hyssop, a plant supposed to have purifying properties) on the two side posts and on the upper door post (the latticed window above the door) of the houses, wherein they shall eat it.

8. And they shall eat the flesh in that night, roast with fire, and unleavened bread ; and with bitter herbs (signifying the putting away of all defilement and corruption) they shall eat it.

9. Eat not of it raw, nor sodden at all with water, but roast with fire ; his head with his legs, and with the purtenance (inside) thereof.

10. And ye shall let nothing of it remain until the morning (thus avoiding both profanation and superstition) ; and that which remaineth of it until the morning ye shall burn with fire.

11. And thus shall ye eat it; with your loins girded, your shoes on your feet, and your staff in your hand; and ye shall eat it in haste: it is the Lord's passover (the word is here used for the first time).

12. For I will pass through the land of Egypt this night, and will smite all the firstborn in the land of Egypt, both man and beast; and against all the gods of Egypt, I will execute judgment: I am the Lord (*Jehovah*).

13. And the blood shall be to you for a token (a token to me on your behalf) upon the houses where ye are: and when I see the blood, I will pass over you, and the plague shall not be upon you to destroy you, when I smite the land of Egypt.

14. And this day shall be unto you for a memorial; and ye shall keep it a feast to the Lord throughout your generations; ye shall keep it a feast by an ordinance for ever (the Passover is continued in the Eucharist).

15. Seven days shall ye eat unleavened bread; even the first day ye shall put away leaven out of your houses (leaven was typical of corruption): for whosoever eateth leavened bread from the first day until the seventh day, that soul shall be cut off from Israel.

16. And in the first day there shall be an holy convocation (a general gathering of the people to the door of the sanctuary for sacrifice, worship, and perhaps instruction), and in the seventh day there shall be an holy convocation to you; no manner of work shall be done in them, save that which every man must eat, that only may be done of you.

17. And ye shall observe the feast of unleavened bread; for in this self-same day have I brought your armies out of the land of Egypt: therefore shall ye observe this day in your generations by an ordinance for ever.

18. In the first month, on the fourteenth day of the month at even (the even on which the fourteenth day closed), ye shall eat unleavened bread, until the one and twentieth day of the month at even.

19. Seven days shall there be no leaven found in your houses: for whosoever eateth that which is leavened, even that soul shall be cut off from the congregation of Israel, whether he be a stranger (a foreigner in blood), or born in the land (of Canaan).

20. Ye shall eat nothing leavened; in all your habitations shall ye eat unleavened bread.

THE PRESERVATION OF THE ISRAELITES.

DURING the plague of hail,—when the hail smote throughout all the land of Egypt all that was in the field, both man and beast, when the fire ran along upon the ground and the hail was so grievous that there had been none like it in all the land of Egypt since it became a nation,—" Only in the land of Goshen, where the children of Israel were, was there no hail "—"The Lord doth put a difference between the Egyptians and Israel." After the plague of hail came the plague of darkness. It was a darkness that might be felt. "There was a thick darkness in all

the land of Egypt three days," during which period the people
"saw not one another, neither rose any from his place." In the
midst of this darkness "all the children of Israel had light in
their dwellings"—"The Lord doth put a difference between the
Egyptians and Israel." After the plague of darkness came a
still more terrible midnight, the midnight in which the firstborn
of Egypt were destroyed. But in view of that infinite darkness
the Lord changed the beginning of the year. He changes the
beginnings of time now. He will not have your history
reckoned from your fleshly birthday, but from the day when
you were born again. On the tenth day of the new year every
man in Israel took a lamb, "a lamb for an house,"—a lamb
without blemish, either a sheep or a goat. So a touch of grace
is in this technical regulation. On the fourteenth day—four days
having elapsed, during which the lamb would be examined to see
if there were spot or blemish in his flesh—the lamb was killed in
the evening, and each family took of the blood and struck it on
the two side posts and on the upper doorpost of the houses
wherein the lamb was eaten. The sign was blood : the blood
was a token upon the houses,—"and when I see the blood I will
pass over you, and the plague shall not be upon you to destroy
you, when I smite the land of Egypt." So in hail there was
dryness; in darkness there was light; in destruction there was
preservation—"The Lord doth put a difference between the
Egyptians and Israel." To explain the detail is not in human
power, but to me the detail is a small mystery compared with the
greater problem that these trifling acts of mitigation still left the
people themselves in the cruel bondage of Egypt. They were
dry in the midst of the hail, but they were not the less in
bondage; they had lights in their houses, but their houses
themselves were prisons; they were not killed in sudden judgment—the very suddenness of which is mercy;—but they died
the slow and sevenfold death of studied cruelty. If I had read all
this in an ancient book written by an author unknown, I should
have been staggered by its romance, and strongly disposed towards
unbelief. But it is not written in an ancient book; it is not a
romance by an anonymous author; it is not a weird poem
written by a poet who plucked his feather from the pinion of a
flying eagle and madly dipped it in some sea of sulphur. It is a

picture of our own life; it is stiff prose, hard as facts, true to the lines which give definiteness to every day. We may give up every one of the descriptive words and leave in its splendid integrity the internal doctrine. The fear is that the critic should never get beyond the door of the words, simply because he is a critic only within a narrow compass. The great and solemn question to be put by every reader is this :—What is the purpose of the description ? What is the moral truth which the description is intended to picture and convey ? Having seized the spiritual teaching, all that is external and decorative may be traced to national habits of expression—perhaps to Oriental exaggeration. Our business does not end with the language, but with the inner truth which that language was intended vividly to represent. In the light of this canon of interpretation let me repeat that this whole incident, turning upon the differences which it represents between men, is part of our own history, and the whole drama is passing before our own eyes,—yes, through the very centre of our own houses and dwelling-places. See if this be not so.

Is it an experience quite unknown that the most terrific and overwhelming flood should be kept back from some part of our life and hope ? Is it a universal deluge ? The flood was very tempestuous; it seemed to break upon the poor life from every point; but now that we have had time to look at the whole case, what is the reality ? Was nothing left untouched ? Was there not some little ark sailing quietly on the great water ? Is there any man who can say, " The flood utterly destroyed me ; nothing was left,—no token of mercy, no sign of the Divine providence, no expression of heavenly care; the ruin was total, absolute, overwhelming and irreparable " ? Can we not say,—" The ruin was very great, but, thank God, the sweet child was left : in Goshen's land we had that gracious comfort " ? Or can we not say,—" Amidst it all our health was wonderfully preserved " ? or " Reason never staggered " ? or " In the midst of all there was a strange peace, deeper than any measured sea in the very centre of the heart " ? Can we not say,—" In the midst of all there was a sanctuary, there was a stairway leading straight up into the heavens " ? Once discover that fact, and see how natural it is to express it in poetic form. Cold prose is not fit for this holy service. We will speak of it rapturously, poetically : with exaggeration to the man who does not understand the experience. We will say that a chamber was found for us in the steeps of the mountain whilst the valleys were engulphed by the roaring flood. We will say that in the sunlit cloud of heaven we rested whilst the thunder-rains flashed and foamed far under our uplifted feet; and in our rapture we may feel as if heaven itself had warmly curtained us whilst the earth was drowned in seas of rain. The imagery is not the point; the mere verbal expression has next to nothing to do with the reality of the case,—except that it must ever be an effort to express the inexpressible. Our boldest metaphors, our fiercest eloquence must be but a dim symbol indicative of the infinite, the unutterable, the profound and eternal. The temptation is to wrestle with the words, to raise a controversy where no battle is needed, and where battle indeed is wholly out of place. The one inquiry which should urge itself upon the mind is :—What is the reality? What is it that occasions the poetry? Why this use of brilliant colour? —and we shall find in reply to that inquiry that the reason is that God, though terrible in judgment, has yet given us dryness in the midst of the storm, a quiet resting-place amid the tumult of the seas ; a hiding chamber, a sanctuary stronger than rock, amidst all the transient and mutable—all that could be upset and filled with the spirit of ruin.

Then again is it an experience quite unknown that, amidst darkest darkness, there has yet remained to Christian hearts some ray of tender light—a lustrous edging of a cloud vast as the span of heaven? The experience is familiar; we can all testify to it,— that in the very blackest night we have at least supposed we could see some star battling its way to us as if bearing messages of hope. Who has been stripped utterly? What Job is there who has been so impoverished as to have taken away from his soul the desire to pray? That being left, all is left,—a clear, dry way up to the throne, and nothing is lost. In the consciousness that full and bold access can be had to the Father poverty is wealth ; loss is gain ; weakness is immortal strength. Never have I met a man that has not had upon him some little token that God had not absolutely forsaken him :—some of his old friends were living : his memory was unusually quick in bringing up incidents

of the gone time which warmed him like prophecies : stress and
agony had forced to his lips some new and surprising eloquence
of prayer. In some cases the sufferer has said,—"I would not
have been without that affliction, now that I see the whole case ,
before I was afflicted I went astray ; I have seen in darkness
what I never could see in the common daylight ; I bless God for
the night, for if the sun had always glared upon me I had not
known that 'the floor of heaven is thick inlaid with patines
of bright gold.'" Once let the mind seize that fact, and
instantly there will be a light in the habitations above the
brightness of the sun,—a glory humbling the pomp of summer,
a splendour which angels might wish to see,—a miracle wrought
in light. Then the heart will invent words. The heart is not
to be silenced by the taunt of exaggeration. The mean man who
never felt the throb of a noble passion shall not be invested with
power to put down the rapture of souls that are aflame with
thankfulness. There is a danger in this, however. There are
some men who never warm. They are not children of the sun,—
no music can thrill them, no colour can bring tears to their eyes,
—a sunset is upon them a wasted miracle. The boldness of the
Bible is seen in that it is never afraid to put the case in exactly
opposite light and with exactly opposite bearing. Sometimes
all the advantage is upon the side of the ungodly. The Psalmist
was not afraid to say respecting those who made themselves
their own gods,—"They are not in trouble as other men ; neither
are they plagued like other men. Therefore pride compasseth
them about as a chain ; violence covereth them as a garment."

So the Bible does not shrink from changing the ground entirely
and representing the exactly reverse picture of that which is
presented in the Book of Exodus in relation to the children of
Israel. How is this ?—because the Book is true,—true at the
core, true in its purpose and meaning,—bearing upon it all the
colours of all the ages through which it has passed ; but the
root is the same, drawing its nutriment and its force from the
very heart of the Divine power.

As to the sprinkled blood, have we no feeling of its relation
and sublimity ? Do we part company with the historian here,
saying we have no corresponding experience ? We do touch the

historic spirit in the matter of protection from the overwhelming flood, and of having some gleam of light in the midst of surrounding darkness ; but when the lamb is provided a language is spoken which has no interpretation to our souls,—here we fall out of the music, having no answering harmony in our own experience.

Was not a Lamb slain for us also ? Here silence is better than speech. We worship him who by his own blood entered once into the holy place, having obtained eternal redemption for us. We are redeemed not with corruptible things as silver and gold, but with the precious blood of the Lamb slain from before the foundation of the world. He was brought as a lamb to the slaughter ; he hath redeemed us to God by his own blood. Why here we seem to have still larger confirmatory experience. This is our hope in the day of judgment. Not that we have been moral, clever, free from public charge ; but that the sprinkled blood is upon the poorest of our forfeited lives. When the angels shall come to execute the Divine judgment what is our hope ? That we were not so immoral as some other man ? If that is all, there is no blood in the mean, frivolous speech. That we have kept ourselves from the cognisance of the magistrate and the penalty of the national law ? By such protestations and felicitations we may but aggravate the guilt which is at once our burden and our curse. What then is our hope ? The Lamb— the Lamb slain—the Lamb of the precious blood. Can we explain it ? Thank God, no. We cannot explain the sin,—how then can we explain the remedy ? We feel it, and we know it by feeling. The highest knowledge comes to us not along the narrow way of the intellect, but through the broad thoroughfares of the responsive and sympathetic heart. We keep ourselves outside the sanctuary because we will only have the intellect satisfied with all its vain questionings, and curious analyses and propositions, whereas it is the heart that must enter. The intellect as a clever, boastful, self-idolatrous faculty must be left outside, and only the heart come within the sanctuary of the Divine forgiveness and the Divine complacency,—the broken heart, the contrite heart, the heart that has no speech in self-defence, but that yields itself into the hands of the loving Saviour to be treated by his grace, not daring to encounter his judgment.

We are not ashamed of this word *blood*. We are not to be driven away from it because some minds have debased the term, having taken out of it all its highest symbolism and noblest suggestion. We speak not of blood merely as it is commonly understood, but of blood as the life, the love, the heart,—the whole quality of Deity—a mystery in words having no answer in speech. Is the blood upon the house of my life ? Is the blood upon the doorpost of my dwelling-place ? Have I put up against the Divine judgment some hand of self-protection ? Verily, it will be swallowed up in the great visitation. In that time nothing will stand but the blood which God himself has chosen as a token and a memorial. " The blood of Jesus Christ, God's Son, cleanseth from all sin." There is a fountain opened in the house of David for sin and for uncleanness. Do not attempt to bar iron window, to close iron door, to protect yourself against the judgments of God. All we can do will be overwhelmed in the Divine visitation. We must allow God to find his own answer to his own judgments.

> " My faith looks up to thee,
> Thou Lamb of Calvary !
> Saviour Divine ! "

That is the attitude which God will respect. A looking in any other direction will be regarded as an aggravation of our offence ; but a hopeful, tender, trustful looking towards the Cross will keep back the thunder, and God will spare us when he makes inquisition for blood.

Exodus xiii. 13.

"And every firstling of an ass thou shalt redeem with a lamb ; and if thou wilt not redeem it, then thou shalt break his neck."

THE REDEMPTION OF THE ASS.

ACCORDING to the ritual the ass was reckoned among the unclean animals. On that account, if it was to be continued in service it must be redeemed—that is to say, its uncleanness must be recognised, and recognised through the usual medium, namely, of sacrifice. Israel had no horses. Unless we keep this fact in mind, many a passage in the Old Testament will be wholly unintelligible. Horses were for the rich, the mighty, and the proud ; horses were symbols of strength, independence, majesty. Remembering this, we shall see the meaning of a line in the song of triumph : "The horse and his rider hath he thrown into the sea." That has but little meaning to us. We are accustomed to the sight of horses, and to the use of them ; but Israel had been in long servitude—Israel might use the ass, but in the land from which Israel had come only the proud Egyptian could enjoy the advantage of a horse. "Some trust in horses, some in chariots, but our trust," said they who had no horses, "is in the God of heaven." The ass was hated in many ancient lands. It was given over to contempt. One nation of antiquity hesitated, in organising an instrumental band, whether to allow the admission of the trumpet, because the sound of the trumpet reminded the people of the bray of the hated ass. Without these historical circumstances in remembrance we cannot understand the Scriptures ; we shall wonder because of our ignorance, and be surprised at exclusions and inclusions which knowledge would amply and satisfactorily explain.*

---

* Speaking of the Scriptural history of the ass, Dean Stanley has given the following summary in his "History of the Jewish Church ": "With he-asses and she-asses Abraham returned from Egypt; with the ass Abraham went up

The subject thus comes near to us with pressing spiritual meaning. God has made provision for the redemption of the vilest, " Rejoice greatly, oh daughter of Zion ; shout, oh daughter of Jerusalem : behold thy King cometh unto thee : he is just and having salvation ; lowly, and riding upon an ass, and upon a colt the foal of an ass." The abhorred may be set amongst the beloved ; that which is farthest away may be brought nearest to the centre ; the first shall be last and the last shall be first, and let no man glory in his strength or in his wisdom : let him that glorieth glory in the Lord. The Lord will classify his creatures ; we make some initial distributions, but the classification is a heavenly act, and we shall in the long run, after innumerable

---

with Isaac to the sacrifice ; on asses Joseph's brethren came thither ; on an ass Moses sat his wife and his sons on his return from Arabia to Egypt ; an old man seated on an ass was the likeness of him, which, according to Gentile traditions, his countrymen delighted to honour. On white asses, or mules, through the whole period of the early history till their first contact with foreign nations in the reign of Solomon, their princes rode in state ; the prophecy fulfilled in the close of their history was that their King should come riding on an ass, and a colt the foal of an ass. It was the long-continued mark of their ancient pastoral simple condition. The rival horse came into Palestine slowly and unlawfully, and was always spoken of as the sign of the pride and power of Egypt ; in the funeral procession of Jacob the chariots and horses of Egypt are specially contrasted with the asses of the sons of Israel ; they who in later times put their trust in Egypt founded that trust in her chariots and horses. But we know not only the Israelite, but Egyptian feeling also. Whilst on the Theban monuments the war-horse is always at hand, the ass, in their minds, was regarded as the exclusive, the contemned, symbol of the nomadic race who had left them. On asses they were described as flying from Egypt ; asses, it was believed, had guided them through the desert ; in the Holy of Holies (to such a pitch of exaggeration was the story carried), the mysterious object of Jewish worship was held to be an ass's head ; and so generally was this persuasion communicated to the heathen world, that when a new Jewish sect, as it was thought, arose under the name of Christian, the favourite theme of reproach and of caricature was that they worshipped in like manner an ass, the son of an ass even on the Cross itself. So long and far were the effects visible of this primitive diversity between the civilised kingdom of the Pharaohs and the pastoral tribe of the land of Goshen ; so innocent was the occasion of this long-standing calumny—a calumny not of generations' or of centuries', but of millenniums' growth, before it was dispelled ; perhaps the most curious of all the many like slanders and fables invented in the course of ecclesiastical history by the bitterness of national or theological hatred."—"The Jewish Church," vol. i., pp. 81-83.

experiments, find ourselves shaping things after the pattern which was shown to man in the mount. What becomes of the favourite argument that all things are the good creatures of God in view of the distributions which God himself has made? He has said to man again and again : Thou shalt not eat this animal. Why not? Are not all animals the good gifts of God? By this shallow plea we excuse the indulgence of our passions and seek to sanctify the profanation of our appetite. Who made the living things? They were made by the God who fashioned all life ; yet he has surrounded some with sanctitudes that may not be violated. He has given others to be food for the hunger of men. Within the law there is another law, and above it there is a higher law still, and no cheap rendering or shallow interpretation of apparent facts can be admitted for a moment near the altar which sanctifies the universe. It requires a long time to teach some men that the very lowest may be turned into the highest, and the uncleanest may be set amongst those who are clothed in the purity of snow. Said one such man : "God hath showed me"—his eyes were even then glazed with semi-unbelief—"that I should not call any man common or unclean." It takes God to show that revelation to us. It has become a commonplace because all things have become commonplaces, but in its inner meaning it is a revelation charged with the very glory of the Shekinah.

God having thus laid down the method of redemption—the scheme by which inequalities can be levelled up and uses made of things temporarily forbidden—proceeds to show that behind this mercy there burns a law. "And if thou wilt not"—what then? We are not left to mere disobedience. God has not so constituted things that we can obey or disobey, and no consequence will follow. All things beat upon one another in sacred and vital pulsation. It is not given to any of us to obey without recompense, or to disobey without loss. The law is : "If thou wilt not redeem it, then thou shalt break his neck." The unredeemed ass shall not live. Looked at within narrow boundaries, the circumstance seems to be trivial, but to the eye of wisdom— the gaze that has in it the look of other worlds—there is a symbolic interpretation which is verifying itself every day in our experience. God cannot be out-witted. We have gone into his presence with half a gift, saying it was all. We have called the fraction an integer. What has been the consequence?—death. We may be dead whilst we live. We have mistaken the limit of the individual. We have thought that in the body is the death, and because the bones were still in joint and the locomotion was not interrupted we have supposed that we lived. The man within fell down dead when we told the lie—the real man, the Divinely-imaged man, the man meant for immortality in heaven. "Within," said Jesus Christ to some, "ye are rottenness." By skill, by wealth, by study, we have been enabled to clothe ourselves with purple and fine linen; but the purple smells rank; through the fine linen there comes an odour which tells of internal death. So foolish are we and ignorant that we suppose that concealment amounts to a complete reversal of the law inexorable. We cannot defeat God. We are cunning tricksters; we have a wonderful faculty of altering figures and forging names and putting in false returns and schedules and bribing auditors whom we hire out of our own family, and who wish us to be auditors in return, that we may conspire in a common felony. But God cannot be defeated. His word is looking at us all the time and throttling us; that is the literal rendering of the passage. All things are naked and *throttled* by the word with which we have to do—the eyes burning us, the hands grasping us; and because we have thrown dust into our own vision, and do not see the reality of things, we call the Biblical appeal an ancient cry and the modern preaching an obsolete claim. Oh that men were wise, that they understood these things! We have temporarily deceived God. We have many an ass in our fields that we have not redeemed; we have reserved the price of the lamb; we have kept back and have not restored unto God that which is right, and we say: Behold, he knows it not. We mourn over our losses and difficulties in the house, and in the field, and in the market-place: we say, "There is an epidemic in the stable, there is a blight in the pasture, there is a cold in the air, before which warm life cannot stand." It is all true—it all comes out of the unredeemed property. Is there not a cause? There is always a moral explanation. They are shallow philanthropists who seek to stop the judgment of God by cheap breakfasts for the poor. God will not have his broken laws tinkered and soldered in that fashion. Judgment must begin at the house of God, and we must deal with the realities of the case. "It is a fearful thing to fall into the hands of the living God."

What a comprehensive aspect of redemption is presented by this incident! Who can tell where redemption ends? Who dare say that the dogs die and are never heard of or known any more? Who has entitled us to assert that every living thing will not live again, and live for ever? We do not know what life is. We may take it lawfully and consume it, but we have not therefore destroyed it. Why did God make all these little winged things that flutter in the sunbeam—all these busy tiny creatures that toil night and day in the fecundant earth? Why did he fill the water with life and the forests with the throb and tread of mighty beasts? It cannot be merely to please himself, as a child might invent new toys to please a momentary fancy. Life is a greater mystery than any explanation has yet wholly covered. The only word that begins to touch it is the word *Redemption.* We cannot tell how large redemption is, but we may judge somewhat of its amplitude by another word akin to it and preparatory to it, and that is the word *Providence.* God thus enables us to judge in some degree one thing by another, one scheme by another. Redemption would have overwhelmed us; we should have called it a supernatural word, or a term lying a long way from the common reach of our thinking and experience. So we begin with the word *Providence*—that under-word, that younger term that does the housework of the universe; busy, kindly, thoughtful, hospitable word, that makes things ready for us, cares for all our life, busies itself about us, and that says to us, "The very hairs of your head are all numbered." A student of Providence cannot, therefore, be so much surprised at the vastness of redemption as he who has not made that study. The providence has been so minute that we cannot wonder the redemption should exceed it in its critical care for the weal of life.

The giving of such a law is specially interesting as suggesting certain inferences as to the Law-giver. This is an apparently trivial enactment. There is nothing trivial in the dispensations of God. He who makes trifles anywhere will make a trifle of himself, of his business, and of his destiny. Little things are made

important in the Scriptures; little things are made important
by all wise men in the relations of life. This is also an
apparently out-of-the-way incident. Out of the way! What
way? Out of our way, possibly; but what is our way?—a little
path leading nowhere: a road we have made with which to
please ourselves to go up and down upon, and suppose to be
the universe. The way! Who knoweth the way of the Lord?
His way is in the great waters; he walketh upon the winds, and
the clouds are the dust of his feet. Out of the way! Even the
universe is too narrow a path for his progress. Even the heaven
and heaven of heavens cannot contain him. There is nothing
out of the way to God. Show me some life that God never
fashioned, or that never came within his purpose when he
started the mystery of the kingdom of life, and that may be
out of the way.

Then comes the cumulative argument, which Jesus Christ
himself often employed. "If a beast—much more a man."
Speaking of the flowers of the field and the fowls of the air,
Jesus Christ said, "Are ye not much better than they?" And
again he asks, "How much better is a man than a sheep?" He
said, "If ye, being evil," give certain good things, "how much
more will your heavenly Father," who is perfect, do things
gracious and beneficent? May the ass be redeemed, and the
unclean beast brought into a right status before God—and has no
arrangement been made for the redemption of man?

Under what a system we live! We think the old laws and
statutes have been abolished. Not one of them. We suppose
the book of Exodus to be full of ancient precepts. If so, I have
not found any of the precepts. They must be wise enough to
take me into their school who can show me one obsolete line in
all the Bible that relates to the education and the discipline, the
training and the completion of human life. The words may have
been changed, but every statute is still here. We are still in a
network, and live in a cage of service. If we have come into a
larger liberty, it is only because we have come into a larger cage.
Is God less watchful of human life than of the lives of beasts?
Even if many of the little narrow laws have been done away, it
is only in the sense of their having been displaced by the greater

law. The invitation issuing from all these considerations is an invitation of love—"Come unto me, all ye that labour and are heavy-laden, and I will give you rest. Take my yoke upon you, and learn of me; for I am meek and lowly in heart : and ye shall find rest unto your souls. For my yoke is easy, and my burden is light." How is the yoke easy? Because the increased strength has been so cultured and enlarged as not to feel the chafing which was once intolerable. How is the burden light? Because the back is stronger to bear it. The burden of law remains eternally the same, but the inspiration of grace, the nutriment and the comfort of internal edification, enables men to carry the burden as if it were a feather, and to run all the days of life with an untiring energy. God shows his grandeur by his love—

> "God, in the person of his Son,
> Hath all his mightiest works outdone."

They reason narrowly and superficially who suppose that there is no law under love—its guarantee and its glory. God has not changed. Love is the blossom of law; love is the liberty of law. The whole law is fulfilled in love. The law seems to say in every page of human history : Do not stop me here; I am moving on to a culmination; let us meet in the orchard in blossom time, in the field in earing time, and then we shall know the meaning of all this supposedly hard, stern, sterile law which has been training the human family to the higher realisations and exemplifications of tenderest, Divinest love. "I will rest in the Lord, and wait patiently for him."

All the way along where I have been permitted to accompany him he has never forgotten one thing, even according to the history imperfectly written, because written by human hands. I cannot charge God with one deed of negligence. He would need to be of a dull mind with hardly any vision at all who would shrink from undertaking to prove that all human history, as related in the Scriptures, proves the watchfulness, the tenderness, and the love of our Father in heaven. But he is not to be trifled with. Do not suppose we can come and go as we like ; now in a high mood, now in a low one ; now obey, now disobey ; now be up among the angels, then among the exiles and rebels. God is watchful on every side ; he keeps a register. In the twenty-fifth chapter of the Gospel by Matthew he startled men by saying what he knew about them. God is not unrighteous to forget your work of faith and labour of love. Can any man stand up and say that he redeemed the ass, and yet God broke his neck? —he fulfilled the law, yet God inflicted the penalty?—he was good, and God was unkind? No such man rises to the challenge of the universe.

NOTE.

The law of Moses declared the firstborn, if a boy, to be sacred to God, and required him to be redeemed from the priest. The modern Jews maintain, "if the firstborn of an Israelite be a son, the father is bound to redeem him, from the thirtieth day forward. If he redeem him before that time, it is not accounted a redemption. If he omit it after that, he is guilty of neglecting an affirmative precept. On the thirty-first day the father sends for a priest and places his little son on a table, saying, 'My wife, who is an Israelitess, has brought me a firstborn, but the law assigns him to thee.' The priest asks, 'Dost thou therefore surrender him to me?' The father answers in the affirmative. The priest then inquires which he would rather have, his firstborn, or the five shekels required for his redemption. The father replies, he prefers his son, and charging the priest to accept the money, pronounces a form of benediction. The father then produces the value of five shekels, and the priest asks the mother if she had been delivered of any other child, or miscarried. If she answers no, the priest takes the money, lays it on the head of the child, and says, 'This son being a firstborn, the blessed God hath commanded us to redeem him, as it is said, "And those that are to be redeemed from a month old thou shalt redeem them, according to thine estimation, for the money of five shekels, after the shekel of the sanctuary, which is twenty gerahs" (Num. xviii. 16). Whilst thou wast in thy mother's womb thou wast in the power of thy Father who is in heaven, and in the power of thy parents; but now thou art in my power, for I am a priest. But thy father and mother are desirous to redeem thee, for thou art a sanctified firstborn, as it is written, "And the Lord spake unto Moses, saying, Sanctify unto me all the firstborn, whatsoever openeth the womb among the children of Israel, both of man and of beast: it is mine"' (Exod. xiii. 2). He then turns to the father, and says, 'I have received these five shekels from thee, for the redemption of this thy son; and, behold, he is therewith redeemed, according to the law of Moses and Israel.'" This ceremony is followed by feasting. When the father dies before the thirty-first day, the mother is not bound to redeem her son, but a piece of parchment or small plate of silver is suspended on the child's neck, with a Hebrew inscription, signifying a *firstborn son not redeemed*, or a *son of a priest.—Biblical Antiquities.*

PRAYER.

ALMIGHTY GOD, who is sufficient to obey the call which thou hast addressed to the human soul? We wonder at thy patience. When we grow in wisdom we grow in anger, for ignorance then becomes so hateful to us. What must our ignorance be to the all-wisdom of God? Blessed be thy name; it is all-wisdom, and therefore the more patient. It is better to fall into the hands of God than into the hands of men. We have fallen below the miracle; yea, we have said there are no miracles now; and therein we have spoken the lying truth. We look at the letter, but see nothing of its flush and colour of fire; there is no God in it, either of Abraham, Isaac, or Jacob, or our own forefathers in the flesh. It is now become a letter amongst many, and might be numbered, and volumed, and forgotten. It is not the bush that burns with fire, that fastens the wondering shepherd to the road, or makes him turn aside, not from duty, but towards worship. We think we have read thy book. We are only content with it as we can move about in it here and there. How canst thou live with fools? How canst thou spare the Church that has no blood-mark upon it—a great hypocrisy? Sometimes thou dost show us thy patience most vividly, and that is when we ourselves see that we are undeserving. Blessed be thy name; thy patience is longer than our obstinacy, and the goodness of the Lord will yet conquer us, and thou shalt, long ages after this, which arithmetic cannot number, have some around thee who can look upon God and not die. Thy way is wonderful; the sea is shallow compared with the depths of thy wisdom, and the firmament a low height which a child can touch, compared with the infinite ascension and majesty of thy thought. God be merciful unto us. We were born yesterday, and in our pride and folly we think we are living to-day, not knowing that we are only beginning to be. Spare us! Pity us! Take to thyself the greater glory in our preservation, and not the readier glory of our destruction; take thy glory by-and-by in the patience which has ripened into success, and not in the destruction which has burned like an angry judgment against creatures of a day. We bless thee for thy Word—great mighty Word, more terrible than fire, sharper than a sword, softer than dew, more beautiful than all colour, with a whisper in it that never can be imitated; a still small voice: now of reason, now of expostulation, now of encouragement, but hiding in itself all the waves, and thunders, and winds that went before it—the very suppression of almightiness. All things are naked and prostrate to the eyes of that Word with which we have to do. It lays a grip upon us like the grip of a wrestler, and throws us to the ground, and binds us there in servitude that cannot be resisted. Blessed be God for his Word; it is a lamp, a light, a trumpet, a music, a song, a friend; it is everything that can cheer, satisfy, and delight, and content the soul without one touch of satiety; and all this we know in Christ thy Son, Blessed One, Second in the Trinity, yet God over all; Alpha, Omega, shining in the star of morning, gleaming in the star of eventide, burning in the noonday sun, filling all things with the glory of his presence. May he fill our hearts with his Cross, with the spirit of sacrifice, with an agony like his own; without him we could not bear it, but with him we can turn sorrow into joy, and a crown of thorns into a crown of blessedness. Pity us whenever we have to carry great weights with unequal strength. Make our bed for us when we cannot make it for ourselves. Touch the bread when it is coming down to the last cut of the loaf, and behold we shall have more at the end than we had to begin with. As for our enemies, we cannot see them because thou art so near; thou wilt deal with them. Destroy them not, we pray thee, but turn them into friends. The Lord comfort the sick. Speak to hearts that have been impoverished and desolated lately, in which a great grave has been dug, and the lovedest of all lives has been taken. God help us, sustain us. The days are but a handful when they are all reckoned, but they are linked on to God's eternity. Amen.

Exodus xiii.

THE DROWNING OF PHARAOH.

"WHAT, still talking about miracles? We thought that faith in miracles had been given up long ago by intelligent men." Some such expression as this would not be unnatural from certain quarters. The answer is that "intelligent men" are just beginning to believe in miracles. They are nearly always the last men to come round to great conceptions and noble spiritual realisations. But even "intelligent men" are stirring themselves with somewhat of reluctance in the direction which we should term spiritual and evangelical. All the greatest books that are being written to-day, upon what would once have been called the hostile side, force upon their readers the consciousness of a hunger which nothing in time or space can satisfy—a voracity of the soul. We may be more or less sated after having read arguments upon which we have been nourished for a life-time, but we are pinched with gnawing and agonising hunger after perusing the pages which were intended to tell us all that can be told. Did the miracles as here reported actually occur? Why not? You can only be puzzled by a miracle when you are puzzled by a God. If your conception of God were like mine,

no miracle that ever was reported could touch the region of impossibility. No wonder men are troubled, even to perplexity
and sore distress of heart, by so-called miracles, when they have
not acquainted themselves deeply with the power and spirit and
purpose of God. The study is begun at the wrong point. To
me it is easier to believe that the miracles occurred than that
they could not have occurred. The difficulty from my point of
view is wholly on the other side. Whether they did historically
occur or not is not the immediate question. To me, I repeat, it
is easier, with my conception of God, to believe that the miracles
could have occurred than that it was impossible for them to occur.
Everything turns upon our conception of the Worker of the
miracles. We do not begin at the miracle itself. We begin with
the Teacher, the Worker, the realised Jehovah, or the incarnate
Logos. Having first entered into fellowship, we next pass into
faith. Knowing by the penetration and sympathy of love what
the spirit of the Worker is, we have no difficulty. We pass with
him into all his action, and when the action is mightiest our rest
is deepest, because the proportion between the Worker and the
work impresses the mind with a sense of infinite harmony. The
greater the miracle the easier to believe in it. The greatest miracle
must be infinitely less than the Worker who accomplished it. If
ever faith falters it must be because the miracle is too small.
The great miracle challenges our best self like the trumpet of
resurrection; as the miracle increases in volume and grandeur,
in pomp and nobleness, something within us hitherto unknown
rises and claims kinship with the Worker of that stupendous
wonder. This was curiously illustrated in the life of Jesus Christ.
When the people fell into unbelief it was because the miracle
was of what may be termed a commonplace character,—that is
to say, some possible explanation of jugglery might in some
degree account for it. To open the eyes of the blind might be
some trick of magic; but the man himself stood up and said,—
"Since the world began was it not heard that any man opened
the eyes of one that was born blind." He seized the true
emphasis and meaning of the action. To open the eyes of the blind
might be accounted for by some species of cleverness or legerdemain; but, says the man : "I was *born* blind; I believe this
miracle, not because it 's little but because it is great." Thus man

is made to know subtly and profoundly that he was created in
the image and likeness of God, and when God is, so to say, most
God, man realises his human grandeur as he can realise it under
no other circumstances. To heal the bruised or broken joint
might be some successful trick in occult surgery ; there might be
pretence about it. We allow a miracle of that kind to pass under
our review without being deeply moved by it,—it comes not up
to the level of our truest grandeur ; but when a dead man is
raised—one who has been four days in the grave—when he
comes forth, a new feeling seizes the mind, and because the
miracle enlarges and ennobles itself, we rise with corresponding
and harmonious dignity of conception and sympathy. It is only,
therefore, where the miracle is supposedly little or imitable, or
commonplace, that faith hardly cares to stoop to take up a trifle so
insignificant. The soul of man being really roused, and burning
through and through with a celestial fire, asks for infinite
miracles,—asks for God. Grow in grace, and you will take up
all the minor miracles as very little things, and yearn in sweet
and ardent prayer for the greatest of all miracles—the conscious
presence of the Living God.

But there is another mode of treatment which we have not in
these pastoral studies hesitated to adopt, which will enable us to
seize the supernatural element with a firmer hand.

Let us in the first instance always inquire into the moral
doctrine of these unusual events : asking what is the underlying
truth, what the spiritual and moral meaning the narration of
the exciting incidents is intended to convey to us. Having discovered the intent of the writer we shall have no difficulty about
the romantic or amazing incidents. This is what we do with a
parable, and a parable is a miracle in imagination. The great
miracle has about it the touch and the mystery of the marvellous.
It is not an off-hand thought. It is reason at its best; or, to
speak figuratively, it is reason on wings,—no longer walking on
the narrow earth but flying in the unmeasured heaven. We do
not force a parable into literal meanings at every point ; we ask,
What is its central intent or meaning ? and having seized that we
treat all the outward and literal as decorative, suggestive, or
merely incidentally helpful ; but we do not risk the truth because
of the peculiarity of the medium of its conveyance.

"And the Lord went before them by day in a pillar of a cloud, to lead them the way; and by night in a pillar of fire, to give them light; to go by day and night:

"He took not away the pillar of the cloud by day, nor the pillar of fire by night, from before the people" (xiii. 21, 22).

What is the great doctrine of that expression?

This :—The consciousness of the Divine presence is in proportion to the circumstances in which we are placed. In other words, our circumstances determine our consciousness of the Divine nearness. Sometimes life is all day—almost a summer day with great spans of blue sky overhead, and where the clouds gather they gather in beautiful whiteness, as of purity akin to the holiness of the inner and upper cities of the universe. *Then* what do we want with fiery displays of God?—they would be out of keeping, out of reason and out of proportion. There are days that are themselves so bright, so hospitable, so long ending, and so poetic in all their breezes, and suggestions, and ministries that we seem not to want any dogmatic teaching about the personality and nearness of God. All beauty represents him. Any more emphatic demonstration would be out of harmony with the splendid serenity of the occasion. Then there are periods in life all night, all darkness, all storm or weariness. We cannot say where the door of liberty is, nor dare we step out lest we fall over a precipice; all is dark, all is trouble; friends are as absent as if they were dead, and all the sanctuaries to which we have hitherto resorted are concealed by the infinite darkness. What do we want then? A bird to sing to us? That would be helpful. A little tiny voice to break the troubled silence? That would not be amiss. But what do we really want? A column of fire, a pillar of glory, an emphatic incarnation and vision of Providence; and the soul gets both these manifestations of God according to the circumstances under which the soul is living. Take it, therefore, simply as an analogy, and then it is a rational analogy; it is true to every man's experience. And if the pillar of cloud and fire should drop off, there will remain the eternal truth, that according to the soul's circumstances is the Divine revelation of itself. Where the visible is enough why add more? A man should not want much theology of a formal sort on a bright summer day. Some little tuft of cloud will represent the

Infinite. Some almost invisible wing in the air—more a thought than a thing—hardly to be identified by the bodily eye, will symbolise the all-embracing power and the all-brooding love. Then at night we want what is called dogmatic teaching, broad emphasis, piercing declaration, vividness that cannot be mistaken, God almost within the clasping of the poor arms, God almost in sight of the eyes of the body. Thus God deals with us. This is true to our history. The mere cloud may go, the pillar of fire may be accepted as figurative ; but the eternal truth that God comes to us in different ways under different circumstances— now as a cloud, now as a fire, now as a judgment, now as without mercy, now a roaring tempest, now a still small voice,— is a truth that remains whatever havoc may be wrought amid the mere figurativeness by which that truth is symbolised.

Then the cloud went behind the Israelites and separated between the camp of the chosen people and the camp of the Egyptians. That is occurring every day. Our circumstances have different readings from different points of view. It is possible for a life to be so lived that the enemy shall be afraid of it. The enemy shall say, " I do not understand this people ; there is a mystery about them, say what you please, criticise them night and day with all possible sharpness and severity ; there is a magic ring around them ; there are circumstances attendant upon them which are the more perplexing in that they sometimes seem to be disasters : now we say, ' Everything is against them,' and presently the very things we thought to be against them turn out rather to the furtherance of their purposes." This is a mystery ; and thus the Divine Providence turns a different view upon the Church and the world, the son and the alien, the family and the rebel-camp. So long, therefore, as these central truths can be attested and positively verified, why should we fritter away a splendid occasion by a petty criticism of mere figure, and robe, and parabolic symbol and representation ? Thus, take it from the literal side, take it from the imaginative and parabolical, my faith has no difficulty whatever with the miracles, except when they are small. It rises to their majesty. The greater they are the more will every Nicodemus be compelled even at night time to steal out and say to the Worker, " Rabbi, we know that thou art a teacher come from God : for no man can do these miracles that thou doest, except God be with him." Mark how Nicodemus fixed upon the *quality* of the miracles—the miracles that separated themselves from the magician's wonders of heathen or cultivated lands.

"And they said unto Moses, Because there were no graves in Egypt, hast thou taken us away to die in the wilderness? wherefore hast thou dealt thus with us, to carry us forth out of Egypt? Is not this the word that we did tell thee in Egypt, saying, Let us alone, that we may serve the Egyptians? For it had been better for us to serve the Egyptians, than that we should die in the wilderness" (xiv. 11, 12).

That is a miracle in very deed! That is the marvel that astounds the reason, the heart, the imagination, and the conscience. That is the miracle which grieves Heaven. "Hear, O heavens, and give ear, O earth : for the Lord hath spoken, I have nourished and brought up children, and they have rebelled against me." That is the upsetting of the law of continuity. That is the violation of things permanent. That is an ugly and wicked twist in the movement of the law which you call "the persistence of force." After all they had seen,—after all the miracles of love, and grace, and deliverance, and comfort,—after all they had known of the government of God,—they turned round with so base a falseness and smote, as with darts seven times whetted, the heart of Moses their leader. That is the impossible miracle. How mean we are and paltry in our judgment and in thinking that the dividing of a sea or the breaking up of a firmament is the impossible thing, when every day we are working in our own degree and region moral miracles that make the breaking up and reconstruction of the universe mere child's fancy and child's play. Why do we not fix our attention upon moral incongruities,—violations of moral law, rebellion against natural instinct? He who smites his father or his mother violates every law of nature with a more forceful and violent hand than the God who interferes or intervenes in his own infinite machine—the universe—to do what pleaseth him for the good of his creatures. We like little intellectual puzzles ;—we flee away because "conscience makes cowards of us all," from the violations of moral law of which we are guilty. We love to speak of "continuity,"—it costs us nothing ; it does not wring the conscience, it does not set up a bar of judgment in the life ; it has a bold resonance which we can utter without moral expense or agony ;

therefore we play upon it; it delights our intellectual vanity. When we come to ourselves we shall know that we have sinned against Heaven and against ourselves and are no more worthy to be called children. In the sublime agony we shall forget all physical miracles in the stupendous wonder that we have grieved the Father's heart.

"And the children of Israel went into the midst of the sea upon the dry ground : and the waters were a wall unto them on their right hand, and on their left " (xiv. 22).

Did they really do this ? Why not ? Suppose we set aside the miraculous incident for a moment and ask : What does the writer mean to convey by this high imagining? He means to convey this lesson, namely, that a way was found where a way was supposed to be impossible. Is that his meaning ? Yes. If that is so, the doctrine is verifying and illustrating itself every day in the history of every man. This then is the true miracle : —that when our poor life has been driven up to a point from which there seemed to be no escape, God has shown an opening in the rock, or a way through the deep ; and we who expected to perish because the way was ended have been enabled to enter upon larger liberties. Who will swear to that ? I will. Ten thousand times ten thousand witnesses will avouch it. There will be no halting in that oath ; and if you represent to us these deliverances as the breaking up of mountains, the dividing of seas, the cleaving in twain of deep and rapid-flowing rivers, we will say, " Pile up the parables, stir your imagination to some nobler figurativeness, for you can never by symbol, or dream, or romantic art, represent the whole truth which we have realised as to the delivering, protecting, preserving, redeeming providence of God."

Instead, therefore, of joining the unbelievers who waste life in trying to show that Almightiness cannot be Almighty, I prefei to begin the study from the other end and to say,—" Even if this be a figure, it is a happy one, for I have been in circumstances just of this very kind : the enemy behind me, the foe almost with his hand upon my weary back, and no way out of the difficulty has presented itself, and yet suddenly my extremity became God's opportunity, and at a bound I was beyond the reach of the destroyer." We want personal testimony about matters of this kind. We want such incidents proved by modern consciousness and present-day facts. That can be done,—and is being done. When the Church rises as one man and repeats the challenge of the psalmist—" Come and hear, all ye that fear God, and I will declare what he hath done for my soul "—the critic will first have to prove us false in our character and in our spirit before he can prove us false in our theology and our worship. Do not find fault with the manner in which the truth itself is presented. To find fault with the mere manner of conveying the truth is foolish, is unjust. We should seek the truth, realise it, own it, and abide by it.

Leaving the merely miraculous line, these incidents show us human life in a state of panic and distress.

" When Pharaoh drew nigh, the children of Israel lifted up their eyes, and, behold, the Egyptians marched after them ; and they were sore afraid : and the children of Israel cried out unto the Lord " (xiv. 10).

How soon we are driven into a panic ! In the very midst of our prayers we are startled into atheism. A sudden fear shoots through the soul, sometimes in the very act of intercession, and petrifies the holy aspiration, so that we rise from the altar worse than when we bended down before its sacred stones. The incidents show us human nature in a spirit of rebellion and ingratitude. " And they said unto Moses, Because there were no graves in Egypt, hast thou taken us away to die in the wilderness ? " How we are like staves that break in the hands of those who use them ! There is but a step between the truest friendship and the bitterest enmity. The brother who adores you to-day will hate you to-morrow, if you cross his will or stain his pride. Here is human life in a condition of utter helplessness.

" Fear ye not, stand still, and see the salvation of the Lord " (xiv. 13).

These are noble times—times when we have to be everything by being nothing ; days when our poor arms have to fall down at our sides unable to do the very simplest thing in the way of self-deliverance or self-extrication from difficulty. This three-fold condition was the state of the world prior to the birth of Christ. The world was in a state of panic and distress ; the spirit of rebellion and ingratitude urged itself against the heavens, it had exhausted every possible means of self-deliverance and self-progress, and could go no further. It had begun a circular movement, and in its helpless rotation was dying of monotony. Suddenly there was a voice heard :—"Glory to God in the highest, and on earth peace, good-will toward men." History took a new turn from that day. Account for it as you please—again resent the miraculous and supernatural element,—there is the fact, that to-day men will do more for Jesus Christ than for any other leader. The men who know him best love him most, and have entered most profoundly into his spirit. Paul was not a weak man,—Paul could take hold of an argument by both hands and weigh it, measure it, test it; Paul was a man who is proved by his mere style of writing and of speech to have been a man of great intellectual capacity as well as of fine moral quality,—a philosopher, a reasoner, a critic,—a man of most penetrating intellect and of ample judgment ; and he, having approached this great miracle from the hostile side, left it at last, when he was old, bruised, stripped, almost dead, saying—" I have fought a good fight, I have finished my course, I have kept the faith : henceforth there is laid up for me a crown of righteousness, which the Lord, the righteous Judge, shall give me at that day : and not to me only, but unto all them also that love his appearing." It was a philosopher who said, "God forbid that I should glory, save in the cross of our Lord Jesus Christ." It was a critic who said, "I am crucified with Christ." It was an aristocrat of the highest Pharisaic blood who gathered together all pedigrees and genealogies and prides of families and said, " I do count them but dung, that I may win Christ." The Man who made such an impression on such a mind was himself a greater miracle than any wonder or sign which he performed before the imagination, the curiosity, or the unbelief of his contemporaries. Now unto him that loved us, and washed us from our sins in his own blood, unto him be glory and dominion and all majesty day without end. Amen.

OLD ENEMIES PURSUING.

SOME resemblances between the condition of the children of
Israel in Egypt, in their flight from the tyranny of Pharaoh,
and the condition of man in sin and his escape from the tyranny
of the devil are obviously suggested. The state of Israel in
Egypt was one of the severest depression. At every point the
Israelites were overborne; their manhood was insulted; they
had no rights, privileges or claims. Their time was not their
own. If ever they looked up complainingly into the face of the
taskmaster, their answer was another stroke of the lash. The
light of their best nature was put out, and they were treated
simply as beasts of burden. The political condition of Israel in
Egypt in these particulars very fitly resembles the spiritual condition of man in a state of sin. However loud may be his boasting, he is a slave; however much he may think he has liberty
which he can enjoy as he pleases, he can only go the length of a
chain. Sin is slavery; sin is continual oppression. No man
who has tasted of the bitterness of sin will contradict the statement, that a state of sin is a state of exhausted manhood. All
that is noble, true, pure, and beautiful has been expelled from
the nature; and there is nothing left behind but great gaps,
blanks and voids, which the world cannot fill, and what hopes
remain are only turned to the bitterness of disappointment and
mortification. The enemy of Israel was powerful. Pharaoh had
everything at his command; a nod was law; the lifting of a
finger was equal to the extension of a sceptre; whenever Israel
threatened to become rebellious he could bring forces to bear
upon the rising that could soon crush it. He was powerful, they
were weak; he was on the throne, they were under his feet—

and Pharaoh's feet were heavy! The spiritual condition of mankind in a state of sin is precisely the same. The enemy of man is powerful. When he is described by earthly figures, those figures themselves are terrible. He is a roaring lion going about seeking whom he may devour; he is a prince; he is the prince of the power of the air; he has all but unlimited resources; his hand is heavy and cruel, his arm is long, and we have no power to break it; he is subtle; he comes to us in a thousand ways we do not dream of; he comes to us along the streaming of music; he looks at us through the beauty of pictures; he meets us on the highway, smiles himself into our confidence, entangles us in many peculiar combinations. And when we say, "Now we shall be free," he says, "*Will* you?" No man who has lived deeply, who understands life, who has seen below the outside of things, but knows that sin gets a daily increasing power over him. The habit which to-day we can snap because it is but half-formed, will, in the course of a few weeks, become so strong as to mock all our strength. The young man says that he knows when to turn back. He may be perfectly sincere in saying that he has that good knowledge,—but is his power equal to his information? He says, "I will go down this way a certain distance; I will drink so much worldly pleasure; I shall sit so long at the devil's table; I shall just peep in behind the curtain which conceals hell; and then I will come back again after I have formed some idea of the reality of things in that direction." His purpose is very good; he fully intends to do what he says, but the footprints which he made on the road are rubbed out, and he has not gone down the road a mile before he loses all his bearings; he knows not which is east, west, north, south; going back and going forward are the same thing; he is locked up in the most terrible of jails—the prison of darkness! I point out these things with this care, not to wound or shock anyone's sensibilities or tastes, but to show who it is that has the sinner under his foot, and whose hand it is that strikes at everything good, and true, and beautiful in human nature. The enemy of man is powerful.

Israel *escaped* from the hand of Pharaoh. By a strong and mighty deliverance Israel was brought out from Egypt. The Israelites had gone along the road of promise and liberty so far, but they turned round to look back, and behold, the Egyptians were after them! The Israelites had said, "Now we have escaped at last"; and behold the breath of the destroyer was breathed upon their necks! That is precisely the case with redeemed and liberated man in a spiritual sense. Upon this point I would speak with a good deal of remonstrance in one direction and hopefulness in another. With a good deal of remonstrance thus :

Here is a man who professes to have been redeemed from sin, and who has taken upon himself the Christian profession, and there is one who is watching him at a little distance who is expecting that the man will instantly step out of Egypt right into Canaan ; and because the man is weak and worn, and less than half himself, some cruel word is used when he stumbles or falters a little! Is that right? Is that decent? Look at the man's condition, as typified by the circumstances. Israel in Egypt bowed down,—the hand of cruel tyranny upon his neck,—the lash of cruel oppression cutting his back to the bone. He has only been liberated a day. Do you expect him to stand erect, as if he had been a man for half a century ? This is precisely what so many persons do in interpreting moral character and spiritual profession. Let me suppose that, at the age of forty, you have been saved from your sin ; you have lifted up your face towards the light ; you have taken the solemn pledge in the name and strength of God to be good and to do good. But your forty years' history is behind you,— forty years of moral exhaustion, forty years of spiritual tyranny ; and because you cannot step right out of Egypt into Paradise you will find some persons who will mock you, and will say, " Ha, ha! Is this your piety ? I thought you had become a Christian now. Is *this* your Christianity ?" The mocker is never wanting in the good man's path. Those who have the cruel gift of taunting are never wanting to mock men who would live well, who would go in the right direction, and hold their worn faces and their streaming eyes towards the light of God.

I would speak hopefully. I would remind you that you cannot expect to escape from all your old associations in a moment. I would speak hopefully, because I know some of you have been distressed by the uprising of forces in your heart which you thought had been settled and quenched for ever. A man cannot throw off his old past as he can throw off an old garment; he cannot strip himself and throw the old slave into the fire, and say, " Now I will begin at this point, and never have any connection with the past." Old slaveries, old tyrannies, old recollections, and habits, and companionships, will assert themselves in one way or another. It is more than a *step* from hell to heaven. You are now a professor of Christianity. Let me suppose you are sincere in your profession. You are ardent in your pursuit of Christian knowledge, you omit no opportunity of improving your spiritual faculties, you pray, you search the Scriptures, you attend helpful ministries; and yet you say, just when you think you are becoming safe and can take a little rest, and enjoy somewhat of the beauty and prospect of the scene,—just then the old devil, that you had supposed to be dead, turns over in your heart! It is not unnatural, it is not some strange thing that has happened to you. It is a long way from evil to goodness, from darkness to light, from the depths of sin to the highest attainments of grace! There will be many a struggle, many a reappearance of your old self; your old self will become a thousand ghosts, and they will frighten you. It is so with us all. We think now, after this lesson or that prayer, or some well-accepted appointments of God, that at last we have attained, and are something like already perfect; and suddenly an unexpected event occurs, and, to our own surprise, we find that, notwithstanding our hope of rest, we are in some respects as weak and as bad as ever we were—I am. I am no separated priest; but a man, a fellow-sufferer. I know this, and my heart cries over it bitterly; because it seems as though one never could be at rest, and never could say that we are complete and beyond the region of fear. In some directions we are so happy, so buoyant, so full of glad expectancy, and softened and chastened by the most hallowed influences, and yet in a moment we slip right down, back again into the old Egypt, where our condemnation was written in the dust, and the air was filled with the voice of our torment.

And there are persons who mock us! When a Christian man makes any slip at all, you know how bitter is the taunt that is levelled against him, as though he ought to have stepped clear out of Egypt right up to the throne of God,—as though there had been no wilderness, and no Red Sea, and no long wandering, and no daily severe discipline. Let us be gentle with one another. We were in Egypt but yesterday, and the enemy will not let us go easily. The devil does not say, "You are going, are you? Yes; well, good-bye." No, no. Just as a man is going into heaven he makes a dash at the skirts of his garments; he fights battles in the chamber of death; he troubles the last hours of the saint, and it is not until heaven's door shuts upon the redeemed man that the devil gives up the pursuit with a sob of disappointment, and falls back to be the severer with those who are yet upon the earth!

There was an omnipotent and gracious Redeemer in the case of Israel; so there is in the case of redeemed men. We are not saved by sheer power. Power in itself considered is a terror; it is something very awful and unapproachable. But power in the hands of mercy becomes redemption. The Redeemer of Israel was not only powerful but gracious. The Israelites upon this occasion were sore afraid, they lifted up their eyes and they cried unto the Lord. They were weak; they had no strength left in them; and as for weapons of war, what had they? or if they had them, how could they use them with any successful effect when they had been so long trampled upon and unmanned and disquieted? There they were; and Egypt, mighty in her pride and cruel in her wrath, was upon their track. Egypt never knew the mystery of mercy. What was to be done then? The word reads so sweetly, the word is this: "Stand still, and see the salvation of the Lord." Precisely the gospel that was adapted to their weak condition. If the command had been, "Rouse you; fight!" it would have been like asking dead men to fight those who were in the very bloom and pride of their strength. But the command is, "Stand still." The adaptation of God's message to our condition is so perfect, so gracious, so sufficient. When we are weak and cannot fight he says, "Stand still, and I will fight for you." When we have our energies in all their completeness, he says, "Rise! fight!" He meets us according to the condition that we are in. The Lord shall fight for you and ye shall hold your peace.

The Egyptians were to be seen that day for the last time-
"The Egyptians whom ye have seen to-day, ye shall see them

again no more for ever." How so? "Because the Lord will fight for you." When God shuts his hand he crushes Egypt. There will be no stir, or tumult, or great ado; the lifting up of his hand is destruction; the outlook of his eye annihilation; the breath of his nostrils is a wind that carries with it desolation and death, when he is so pleased. Here a little mistake was made by the great leader of Israel. I am so thankful when men like Moses stumble, because their stumbling gives inferior men hope and heart. Moses began to make it too much a question of prayer; he began to talk to the Lord as if it were a great case of grief and despondency, as if all difficulties had culminated in one terrific crisis. The Lord said unto him, " Moses, do not pray at all." He told them to do just as they were doing when they saw the Egyptians coming after them, namely, to go on.

Consider the circumstances. Israel was going on. Israel turned round and saw the Egyptians; and Israel was full of weakness, and trembling, and despair; and Moses spake unto the Lord. And the Lord said unto Moses, " Go on as if this thing had not happened; do not take it into your calculations at all; leave the Egyptians in my hands; there is a time to pray, but not now; only lift up thy rod, and stretch thy hand over the sea, and divide it, and behold I will get me honour upon Pharaoh and upon all his host, upon his chariots, and upon his horsemen." " All !" with holy, mighty scorn, he named them, and they seemed to perish whilst he enumerated them ! Mighty in their degree, but when compared with Jehovah but so many insects fluttering in the air—a breath being able to destroy them.

Then occurred this beautiful incident. The angel of the Lord, which went before the camp of Israel all the journey long up to this hour, removed and went behind them. The angel of the Lord could do as he pleased. God is not the victim of law. God is the *Lawgiver*. Life is above law. For ages he has been yonder, in the front; when it pleaseth him he can turn round and be at the rear of things. He has a right to every chamber in his own house; he built it; he has the key of every room, he can enter when he pleases. On this occasion it pleased him to reverse the order of things, and from the van he came to the rear. So beautiful are his adaptations ! He said to Israel, in effect and substance, "Are the Egyptians behind thee, O Israel? Then I will come behind thee." " But the Egyptians are so very near to us, Lord ! " "I can come between you and them, how near soever they be; I made all spaces, and have them all under my control, and though the Egyptians were just upon thy neck I could come in between you,—I will go behind." And Israel sang a song unto the Lord : " Thou hast beset us behind and before, and laid thine hand upon us." There are men who tell us that God must move in this direction and must move in that ; they have been looking into affairs, they have been adding things up, and they have been drawing their conclusions, and the conclusion of the thing is this—that we are prisoners in the great jail of law. I am not. I am a prisoner of God's love ; I am shut up in the great sanctuary of his heart. I believe he is greater than aught he has made ; that the Lawgiver is greater than the law, and that he who established the universe has the key of its secret in his own heart. I teach this gracious truth because I have lived it ; I have known its completeness, its excellence, and its redeeming power. God can be at one point to-day and at another to-morrow. He can be before them in this case, behind them in that ; he determines all things by a sovereignty we cannot control. His sovereignty is his grace, at its highest point. The supremacy of love is the sovereignty of God. I will trust myself with the Most High, I will cast myself solely upon him, I will call him my Father and my King !

We are, then, in the wilderness ; we have had long and bitter experience of sin, and that experience has made us very weak , we have been under a most powerful and oppressive enemy ; he has never spared us, he has been severe with us ; he has taken away from us all that made life strong and desirable and useful, and we have been redeemed by a gracious and omnipotent Redeemer ; and still the great enemy has pursued us, as though he never, never would give us up whilst there seemed, even to himself, to his infernal hope, the slightest possible chance of recapturing us, and locking us up in his great prison-house. This is our condition ; we are still in the wilderness ; old associations still remind us of their existence, evil memories still trouble our recollection, ghosts and spectres of the past come to terrify us, even when we sit down at the board of Sacrament, and when we repeat the oath of Christian love at the Cross. But our

Redeemer is sufficient; he says to us in the time of despair, " I will come behind thee." When we are just giving up, and asking, " Who is sufficient for these things?" he says to us, in his own sweet voice, " My grace is sufficient for thee; thy shoes shall be iron and brass, and as thy days so shall thy strength be; no weapon that is formed against thee shall prosper. Hast thou not known, hast thou not heard, hath it not been told thee from the beginning, that the Lord, the Creator of the ends of the earth, fainteth not, neither is weary?" " He giveth power to the faint; and to them that have no might he increaseth strength. Even the youths shall faint and be weary, and the young men shall utterly fall; but they that wait upon the Lord shall renew their strength; they shall mount up with wings as eagles; they shall run and not be weary; and they shall walk, and not faint." They shall be troubled on every side, but not distressed; cast down, but not destroyed; persecuted, but still there shall be room enough left for the triumphing of the grace of God. Sirs, your redemption is not of your own skill, energy, or wit. " O Israel, thou hast destroyed thyself; but in me is thine help." When there was no eye to pity and no arm to save, his own eye pitied, and his own arm brought salvation. And I am persuaded that he who hath begun this good work will continue it even unto the end.

Let us hope in this. Are you persecuting anybody? Are you pursuing any one who has escaped the clutches of your evil influence? Know this, that if their hearts be set on God, you cannot get at them. " Cannot get at them?" No. " But they are now within sight." But God could blind you, if you were within an inch of them. " Not get at them? Why, I can almost touch them now." Yes, you can *almost* do it, but your " almost " is to God as wide as infinitude. Are you pursued? Do you say you cannot get away from old influences, companions, associations, and conditions? Not all at once, but little by little. If you be in God and love his truth, the pursuit of the enemy will bring salvation nearer to you; if you cast your heart's poor weakness and distrust entirely upon his keeping,—then, nor mountain nor sea shall keep the pilgrim back from the Canaan of God !

Exodus xiv. 31; xix. 7; xxxvi. 5.

REDEEMING POINTS.

IN the book of Exodus we have an account of the character of the people delivered by the power of Jehovah and guided and directed by the statesmanship of Moses. Sometimes in reading the history we think there never were such rebellious and stiff-necked people in all human history. Moses is often angry with them; the Lord himself often burns with indignation against them; sometimes, as cool and impartial readers, we feel the spirit of anger rising within us as we contemplate the selfishness, the waywardness, and the impracticableness of the children of Israel. We feel that they were altogether undeserving the grace, the compassion, the patient love which marked the Divine administration of their affairs. The spirit of impatience rises within us and we say, "Why does not God bury this stiff-necked and hard-hearted race in the wilderness and trouble himself no longer about people who receive his mercies without gratitude, and who seeing his hand mistake it for a shadow or for some common figure? Why does the great heart weary itself with a race not worth saving?" Sometimes the Lord does come nigh to the act of utter destruction : and it seems as if justice were about to be consummated and every instinct within us to be satisfied by the vindication of a power always defied and a beneficence never understood.

Give yourselves a little time to discover if you can the redeeming points even in so ungracious and so unlovable a history. It will indeed be a religious exercise, full of the spirit of edification and comfort, to seek some little sparkles of gold in this infinite mass of worthlessness. It will be quite worth a Sabbath day's journey to find two little grains of wheat in all this wilderness of chaff. Surely this is the very spirit of compassion and love, this is the very poetry and music of God's administration, that he is

always looking for the redeeming points in every human character.
Allowing that the mass of the history is against the people : still
there cannot be any escape from that conclusion.   If it were a
question of putting vice into one scale and virtue into the other,
and a mere rough exercise in avoirdupois-weighing, the Israelites
could not stand for one moment.   To find out the secret of patience,
to begin to see how it is that God spares any man, surely is a
religious quest in the pursuit of which we may expect to find, and
almost to see face to face, the Father, Son, and Holy Ghost.
Moses, having come from the Divine presence :

"called for the elders of the people, and laid before their faces all these
words which the Lord commanded him.   And all the people answered
together, and said, All that the Lord hath spoken we will do" (xix. 7, 8).

That was an outburst of religious emotion ; that exclamation
showed that the heart was not all dead through and through.
That one sentence might be remembered amidst many a hurricane
of opposition and many a tumult of ungrateful and irrational
rebellion.   We understand this emotion perfectly.   There have
been times in our most callous lives when we have caught ourselves singing some great psalm of adoration, some sweet hymn
holding in it the spirit of testimony and pledge and holy oath.
It would seem as if God set down one such moment as a great
period in our lives—as if under the pressure of his infinite mercy
he magnified the one declaration which took but a moment to utter
into a testimony filling up the space of half a lifetime.   It is long
before God can forget some prayers.   Does it not seem as if the
Lord rather rested upon certain sweet words of love we spoke to
him even long ago, than as if he had taken a reproach out of our
mouth at the moment and fastened his judgment upon the severe
and ungrateful word ?   Is it not within the Almighty love to beat
out some little piece of gold into a covering for a long life ?   It is
not his delight to remember sins or to speak about the iniquities
which have grieved his heart, or to dig graves in the wilderness
for the rebellious who have misunderstood his purpose and his
government.   "His mercy endureth for ever," and if we have
ever spoken one true prayer to heaven, it rings, and resounds,
and vibrates, and throbs again like music he will never willingly
silence   It would seem as if one little prayer might quench the

memory of ten thousand blasphemies. "And all the people answered together, and said, All that the Lord hath spoken we will do." Here you find a religious responsiveness which ought to mark the history of the Church and the history of the individual as well.

"The people feared the Lord, and believed the Lord, and his servant Moses" (xiv. 31).

Every good thing is set down. The Lord is not unrighteous to forget your work of faith. We wonder sometimes in our ignorance whether any little sign of good that has been in the heart is not written most legibly in heaven; and all things unlovely, undivine, so written that none but God can decipher the evil record. It would be like our Father to write our moral virtues in great lustrous characters and all the story of our sin and shame so that no angel could read a word of it. This is the way of love. How much we talk about the little deed of kindness when we want to save some character from fatal judgment, from social separation, and from all the penalties of evil behaviour! There is no monotony in the recital; love invents new phrases, new distributions of emphasis, wondrous variations of music, and so keeps on telling the little tale of the flower that was given, of the smile that was indicative of pleasure, of the hand that was put out in fellowship and pledge of amity. Again and again the story so short is made into quite a long narrative by the imagination of love, by the marvellous language which is committed to the custody of the heart. It is God's way. If we give him a cup of cold water, he will tell all the angels about it; if we lend him one poorest thing he seems to need, he will write it so that the record can be read from one end of the earth to the other; if we give him some testimony of love,—say one little box of spikenard,—he will have the story of the oblation told wheresoever his gospel is preached. Yes, he will tell about the gift when he will hide the sin; he will have all his preachers relate the story of the penitence in such glowing terms that the sin shall fall into invisible perspective. God is looking for good; God is looking for excellences, not for faults. Could we but show him one little point of excellence, it should go far to redeem from needful and righteous judgment and penalty a lifetime of evil-doing.

"The people bring much more than enough for the service of the work"
(xxxvi. 5)

There is a redeeming point. The spirit of willingness is in the
people. They have a good season now; they are in their best
moods at this time; they are most generous; they come forward
in their very best force and look quite godly in their daily
devotion and service to the tabernacle. Surely in the worst
character there are some little faint lines of good! Why do we not
imitate God and make the most of these? We are so prone to
the other kind of criticism : it seems to be in our very heart of
hearts to find fault; to point out defections; to write down a whole
record and catalogue of infirmities and mishaps, and to hold up
the writing as a proof of our own respectability. God never
does so; he is righteous on the one side and on the other; he
never connives at sin; he never compromises with evil; he
never fails to discriminate between good and bad, light and darkness, the right hand and the left; but when he does come upon
some little streak of excellence, some faint mark of a better life
he seems to multiply it by his own holiness, and to be filled with
a new joy because of pearls of virtue which he has found in a
rebellious race. Character is not a simple line beginning at
one point and ending at another, drawn by the pencil of a child
and measurable by the eye of every observer. Character is a
mystery; we must not attempt to judge character. "Judge not,
that ye be not judged." "Blessed are the merciful : for they
shall obtain mercy." The Pharisees dragged up those whom
they found doing wrong, but their doing so was never sanctioned
by the Master; in all their attempts at judgment they were
judged; whenever they displayed their virtue he burnt up the
rag and left them to carry the cinders away. This should lead
us to much seriousness in estimating character, and should keep
us from uncharitableness; but at the same time it should
encourage our own souls in the pursuit and quest of things
heavenly. We do not know the meaning of all we feel and do.
Let me suppose that some man is not regarded by others as
religious and spiritual; let it be my business as a Christian shepherd to find out some point in that character upon which I can
found an argument and base an appeal. I may find it sometimes
in one great hot tear; the man would not have allowed me to see

that tear on any account if he could have helped it, but I did see it, and having seen it I have hope of his soul. He is not damned yet. I may notice it in a half-intention to write to the wronged ones at home. The young man has taken up his pen and begun to address the old parents whose hearts he has withered. When I observe him in the act of dipping his pen, I say, "He was dead and is alive again"; and though he should lay down the pen without writing the letter of penitence, I have hope in him : he may yet write it and make the confession and seek the absolution of hearts that are dying to forgive him. Do not tell me of the spendthrift's course, do not heap up the accusation—any hireling can be bribed to make out the black catalogue ; be it ours to see the first heavenward motion, to hear the first Godward sigh, and to make the most of these signs of return and submission. Good and bad do live together in every character. I never met a human creature that was all bad : I have been surprised rather to see in the most unexpected places beautiful little flowers never planted by the hand of man. All flowers are not found in gardens, hedged and walled in, and cultured at so much a day ; many a flower we see was never planted by the human gardener. In every nation, he that feareth God and worketh righteousness is accepted of Heaven. At the risk of incurring the unkind judgment of some in that I may be ministering to your vanity— how they mistake the case who reason so !—I will venture to say that in every one, however unrecognised by the constables of the Church or by the priests of the altar, there are signs that they are not forsaken of God.

Now comes the thought for which I have no language adequate in copiousness or fit in delicateness. It would seem as if the little good outweighed the evil. God does not decide by majorities. There is not a more vulgar standard of right and wrong than so-called majorities ; it is an evil form of judgment wholly— useful for temporary purposes, but of no use whatever in moral judgment. The majority in a man's own heart is overwhelming. If each action were a vote, and if hands were held up for evil, a forest of ten thousand might instantly spring up ; and then if we called for the vote expressive of religious desire, there might be one trembling hand half extended. Who counts ?—God. What says he ? How rules he from his throne ? It will be like him to say, "Inasmuch as ye have done it unto one of the least of these my brethren, ye have done it unto me." If he could find out in our life that we once dropped on one knee, and began a prayer, there is no telling what may be done by his love in multiplying the act into an eternal obeisance and regarding the unfinished prayer as an eternal supplication. This is how the judgment will go. God has not forsaken us. To open his book with any desire to find in it reading for the soul is a proof that we are not abandoned of our Father; to go into the sanctuary even with some trouble of mind or reluctance of will—to be there is a sign that we are not yet cast out into the darkness infinite.

Yet even here the stern lesson stands straight up and demands to be heard—namely :—If any man can be satisfied with the little that he has, he has not the little on which he bases his satisfaction. It is not our business to magnify the little; we do well to fix our mind for long stretches of time upon the evil, and the wrong, and the foul, and the base. It is not for us to seek self-satisfaction; our place is in the dust; our cry should be "Unclean! unprofitable!"—a cry for mercy. It is God's place to find anything in us on which he can base hope for our future, or found a claim for the still further surrender of our hostile but still human hearts.

Exodus xv. 1-21.

1. Then sang Moses and the children of Israel this song unto the Lord, and spake, saying, I will sing unto the Lord, for he hath triumphed gloriously : the horse and his rider hath he thrown into the sea.

2. The Lord is my strength and song, and he is become my salvation : he is my God, and I will prepare him an habitation ; my father's God, and I will exalt him.

3. The Lord is a man of war : the Lord is his name.

4. Pharaoh's chariots and his host hath he cast into the sea : his chosen captains also are drowned in the Red sea.

5. The depths have covered them : they sank into the bottom as a stone.

6. Thy right hand, O Lord, is become glorious in power : thy right hand, O Lord, hath dashed in pieces the enemy.

7. And in the greatness of thine excellency thou hast overthrown them that rose up against thee : thou sentest forth thy wrath, which consumed them as stubble.

8. And with the blast of thy nostrils the waters were gathered together the floods stood upright as an heap, and the depths were congealed in the heart of the sea.

9. The enemy said, I will pursue, I will overtake, I will divide the spoil ; my lust shall be satisfied upon them ; I will draw my sword, my hand shall destroy them.

10. Thou didst blow with thy wind, the sea covered them : they sank as lead in the mighty waters.

11. Who is like unto thee O Lord, among the gods? who is like thee, glorious in holiness, fearful in praises, doing wonders?

12. Thou stretchedst out thy right hand, the earth swallowed them.

13. Thou in thy mercy hast led forth the people which thou hast redeemed : thou hast guided them in thy strength unto thy holy habitation.

14. The people shall hear, and be afraid : sorrow shall take hold on the inhabitants of Palestina.

15. Then the dukes of Edom shall be amazed ; the mighty men of Moab, trembling shall take hold upon them ; all the inhabitants of Canaan shall melt away.

16. Fear and dread shall fall upon them ; by the greatness of thine arm they shall be as still as a stone ; till thy people pass over, O Lord, till the people pass over, which thou hast purchased.

17. Thou shalt bring them in, and plant them in the mountain of thine inheritance, in the place, O Lord, which thou hast made for thee to dwell in ; in the Sanctuary, O Lord, which thy hands have established.

18. The Lord shall reign for ever and ever.

19. For the horse of Pharaoh went in with his chariots and with his horsemen into the sea, and the Lord brought again the waters of the sea upon them; but the children of Israel went on dry land in the midst of the sea.

20. And Miriam the prophetess, the sister of Aaron, took a timbrel in her hand; and all the women went out after her with timbrels and with dances.

21. And Miriam answered them, Sing ye to the Lord, for he hath triumphed gloriously; the horse and his rider hath he thrown into the sea.

THE SONG OF DELIVERANCE.

THE spirit of this song is above verbal criticism. This is the first composition of the sort which has come under our notice, and therefore it occasions the greater surprise and delight. We are not just to the song when we go back upon it from a perusal of Isaiah. We put the song into a wrong time-setting, and therefore miss the music of the occasion. Yet even to go back upon it from a perusal of " Paradise Lost " no whit of its magnificence is surrendered. It is not, I assert, a fair treatment of the song, to go back upon it from all the poetic experience and culture of many generations and centuries. In the interpretation of Holy Scripture time is an instrument, or a medium, or a standard, which ought never to be neglected. Who is conscious of an intellectual fall from the perusal of Milton to the perusal of this song of Moses? He sings well for the first time. It is a marvellous song to have been startled out of his very soul, as it were, without notice. Verily, he must have been as much surprised as we by its magnificence, by its height that knows no dizziness, and by its audacity that loses nothing of the tenderest veneration. Milton staggers under the stars of poetry which he has enkindled, but Moses treads the nobler orbs of a sublimer fancy under his feet. Milton cringes under an effort; he is exhausted; when he has done he sighs and pines for rest, and puts out a blind man's hand for something to lean upon. He must have time to recruit and re-tempt the muse into eloquence so high. Moses speaks his native tongue; the singing of Moses is as the breathing of a man who is in his native air, and who is not conscious of speaking more like a god than the creature of a day. But what is the poem or song, when we do not go back

upon it from Milton, but advance to it through the strife and
hatred, the sin and the danger, of the preceding pages? *That*
is the right line of approach. It is manifestly unfair to judge
earlier poetry by later standards. Who would think it just to
judge the first mechanical contrivances by present mechanical
inventions? Would it be fair to the very first locomotive that
was ever made to compare it with the locomotives of to-day,
that seem to challenge the wind and the lightning? Every man
would protest against such comparison and criticism. The fair-
minded man would protest that the right way to judge of any
contrivance or invention, would be to come up to it along the
line of its development, and to judge it by its own day and its
own atmosphere. That is right. But when you compare earlier
poetry with later, and say the old is better, how do you account
for that? "There is a spirit in man, and the inspiration of the
Almighty giveth him understanding." Moses could not amend
the song. Is there a genius now living who could paint this
lily? Point out one weak line in all the mighty pæan; change
one figure for a better. Where this is the case and considering
the times and circumstances, do we not feel as if approaching the
beginning of an argument for the profoundest view of Biblical
inspiration? We have sometimes tried to amend one of Christ's
parables, and nowhere could we replace one word by a better.
Authors wish to go back upon their works, to retouch them; they
issue new editions, "revised and corrected." Who can correct
this Song? Who can enlarge its scope, ennoble its courage, or
refine its piety?

We feel ourselves under the influence of the highest ministry
that has yet touched us in all these ancient pages. Our critical
faculty is rebuked. Religious feeling has found sweet music to
express its eloquence, and now we are carried away by the sacred
storm. The heart will not permit grammatical analysis. The
people are aflame with thankfulness, and their gratitude roars
and swells like an infinite tempest, or if for a moment it falls
into a lull, it is only to allow the refrain of the women with
timbrels to be answered by the thrilling soprano of Miriam, for
she answered the women, saying, "Sing ye to the Lord, for he
hath triumphed gloriously : the horse and his rider hath he
thrown into the sea." Then with the clang of timbrels and the

tumult of the solemn dance Israel expressed thankfulness to the delivering God. The Church has now no great days of song —whole days spent in praise, with a tumultuous harmony of trumpet and cornet, flute and clarionet, bassoon and sharp fife : men and women pouring their hearts' emotions forth in broad song shot through and through with the silver threads of children's brighter praise. The Church now objects to timbrels. To that objecting Church I do not belong. That objecting Church I disavow. We are making atheists in multitudes. We have turned the trumpet into an atheist, and the drum, and the flute, and the whole organ. We have shut them up for wicked enjoyment. Every Sabbath morning the city or town should vibrate with the crash of instruments religiously played. We must rid ourselves of the bigots who are impoverishing Christ's Church, who are loading the Church with the burden of their cold respectability. We pay too heavy a price for the keeping of such men amongst us. The Church is now adjusting opinions, bandying controversial words, branding small heretics, and passing impotent resolutions ; the timbrel is silent, the trumpet is dumb, the drum throbs no longer, the song is a paid trick in gymnastics, not a psalm bound for heaven. We have killed music in the Church. Who would not have music all day ? It would refine us, it would ennoble us, it would show us the littleness and meanness of verbal criticism and paltry opinion, and fill the soul with Divinest breath. Why this atheistic silence ? Are there no deliverances now ? Is God no longer our God, and our fathers' God ? The great slave orator, Frederick Douglas, is reported to have said in a mournful speech, on a dark day for his race : " The white man is against us, governments are against us, the spirit of the times is against us ; I see no hope for the coloured race ; I am full of sadness." Having concluded this melancholy utterance, a poor, little, decrepit, coloured woman rose in the audience, and said, " Frederick, is God dead ? " In a moment the whole spirit of the man was changed. He had forgotten the principal thing—speaking about white people, and governments, and spirit of the times, and forgetting the only thing worth remembering. Why this atheistic silence ? Those who believe in God should not be afraid of his praise on a scale and after a method which will make people wonder and tremble, and for a time flee away. Music is better than argument. You can always answer a statement—it is difficult to reply to a song.

We must be careful to distinguish between true praise and mere rhapsody. The song of Moses is simply history set to music. Through the whole song there is a line of what may be termed historical logic. Are these flowers? Underneath the soil in which they grow are infinite rocks of solid, positive fact and experience. Those who sang the song witnessed the events which they set to music. I protest against music ever being set to frivolous and worthless words. That is profanation. Such music is made into mere rhapsody; it is turned into sound without sense; it is a voice and nothing more. The music should owe all its nobility to the thought which it expresses. Persons who know not whereof they affirm have sometimes foolishly said that the words are nothing—it is the music that is everything. As well say the tree is nothing—the blossom is all. The words are the necessity of the music. The thought is so ardent, tender, noble, celestial, that it asks for the vehicle of a universal language for its exposition, and not for the loan of a dialect that is provincial or local. Even where there are no words to express—where the music is purely instrumental—the thought should be the majesty of the execution. We do not need words to tell us what music is in certain relations. Without the use of a single word we can easily tell the difference between the jingle meant for a clown's dance, and the passion which expresses the fury of war or the agony of grief. So you can have thought without words—a noble expression without the use of syllables that can be criticised. But whether you have words in the ordinary sense of the term, or thought without words, the music is but the expression of the soul's moods, purposes, vows, prayers, and as such it can be distinguished even by those who have had no critical musical culture. We know the cry of earnestness from the whimper of frivolity. We need not hear a word, and yet we can say, "That is a cry of pain, and that is a song of folly." Music is the eloquence which flies. If, then, our music is poor, it is because our piety is poor. Where the heart is right it will insist upon having the song, the dance, the festivity, the banner of gold written with God's name in the centre of it. Poor piety will mean poor singing ; small religious conceptions will mean narrow services scampered through with all possible haste, so much so that decency itself may be violated. A glowing piety—a noble thought of God—then where will be the dumb tongue, the vacant face, the eye without accent or fire ? Realise the deliverance, and you cannot keep back the song ; exclude the providence, and silence will be easy.

The spirit which would degrade poetry into prose is a more destructive spirit than is sometimes imagined. Whoever would turn poetry into prose would destroy all beauty. There are some who boast of being prosaic. Let us not interfere with the fool's feast ! Those who would take out of life its poetry, colour, fire, enthusiasm, would silence all bells, put out all light, extinguish all joy, cut down all flowers, terminate the children's party when the children are in the very agony of the rapture. They are bad men. I know no crime that lies beyond their doing, if they could perform it without detection. The spirit that would make prose in life, at the expense of life's too little poetry, is the enemy of love. It is an evil spirit. It values the house more than the home. Its treasure is laid up where moth and dust doth corrupt, and where thieves break through and steal. It is a Pharisee who has no kiss for the celestial guest. It is a destroyer who would take the lily-work from the top of the pillar. It is an enemy that would take away the garden from the tomb. At first it does not appear to be so, but by appearances we must not finally and conclusively judge. Have faith in any man who stoops to pick a wayside flower for the flower's sake— because of the colour that is in it, the suggestions with which its odour is charged, and the symbolism which writes its mystery in the heart of the modest plant. The house is not wholly deserted of God that has its little sprig of Christmas holly in it. The heart that thought of the holly may have a great deal of badness in it, but there is one little point that ought to be watched, encouraged, enlarged.

Music should not be occasional. Music should express the life. We cannot always be singing great triumph-songs ; but music will come down to minor keys, to whispered confidences, to almost silent ministries. There are soft-toned little hymns that can be sung even when there is a coffin in the house. Who would argue

at the grave? yet who would not try, though vainly because of
the weakness of the flesh, to sing there in memory of disease
exchanged for health, time enlarged into eternity, corruption
clothed with immortality?

We, too, have a sea to cross. We are pursued; the enemy is
not far behind any one of us. The Lord has promised to bring
us to a city of rest, and, lie between us and our covennated land
what may, it shall be passed. That is the speech of faith. We,
too, shall sing, "I heard the voice of many angels round about
the throne and the beasts and the elders: and the number of
them was ten thousand times ten thousand, and thousands of
thousands: saying with a loud voice, Worthy is the Lamb that
was slain to receive power, and riches, and wisdom, and strength,
and honour, and glory, and blessing. And every creature which
is in heaven, and on the earth, and under the earth, and such as
are in the sea, and all that are in them, heard I saying, Blessing,
and honour, and glory, and power, be unto him that sitteth upon
the throne, and unto the Lamb for ever and ever." We, too,
shall sing; the dumb shall break into praise, the cry will be,
"O death, where is thy sting? O grave, where is thy victory?"
"All the angels stood round about the throne, saying, Amen:
Blessing, and glory, and wisdom, and thanksgiving, and honour,
and power, and might, be unto our God for ever and ever. Amen."
It shall not always be grim silence with us. We shall learn
the song of Moses and the Lamb. Then all argument will have
ceased; controversy will have fought out its little wordy fight and
have forgotten its bitterness and clamour, and all heaven shall be
full of song. They shall sing who enter that city the song of
Moses and of the Lamb. But we begin it upon earth. There is
no magic in death; there is no evangelising power in the grave,
whither we haste. The song begins now, because it immediately
follows the deliverances and benedictions of Providence. It may
be a hoarse song, uttered very poorly, in the judgment of musical
canons and according to pedantic and scholastic standards; but
it shows that the soul is alive, and would sing if it could; and
God knows what our poor throats and lips would do were we
equal to the passions of the soul, and therefore he accepts the
broken hymn, the poorly-uttered psalm of adoration, as if it were
uttered with thunder, and held in it all the majesty of heaven.

Exodus xv. 23-25.

"And when they came to Marah, they could not drink of the waters of Marah, for they were bitter: therefore the name of it was called Marah. And the people murmured against Moses, saying, What shall we drink? And he cried unto the Lord; and the Lord shewed him a tree, which when he had cast into the waters, the waters were made sweet."

MOSES AT MARAH.

THE children of Israel had just concluded their song of thankfulness for deliverance from the hand of Pharaoh and his hosts. A very wonderful song too had they sung. It might have had the thunder for an accompaniment, so solemn was it and so majestic. It rises and falls like the great billows of the sea. Now it roars by reason of its mightiness, and presently it subsides into a tone of tremulous pathos. The children of Israel had been made "more than conquerors"; they had not simply conquered by the expenditure of every energy as is sometimes done in hotly contested fields,—they had actually stood still, and in their standing had seen the salvation of God. Their references to Pharaoh and his hosts were made in a tone of derisive victory. "Pharaoh's chariots and his host hath he cast into the sea: his chosen captains also are drowned in the Red Sea." "Thou didst blow with thy wind, the sea covered them: they sank as lead in the mighty waters." "Sing ye to the Lord, for he hath triumphed gloriously: the horse and his rider hath he thrown into the sea," —thrown, as a child might throw a pebble into the deep! After singing such a song, Israel will never again know the meaning of doubt or fear. The singing of such a song marks an epoch in the history of life. In the presence of difficulty Israel will remember this hour of holy triumphing, and under the inspiration of such a recollection will surmount every obstacle. Is not this a reasonable supposition? Will not the greatest event in life rule all secondary events, and determine all subordinate considerations?

Surely, if this hour could be forgotten, the fear of death might return upon those who have already conquered the grave. Alas! we soon find how much difference there is between singing a hymn and living a life. The people had not gone more than three days into the wilderness of Shur when they showed the fickleness of the most intensely religious passion, and the inconstancy of the profoundest religious homage.

1. "They could not drink of the waters of Marah, for they were bitter,"—*so the greatest triumphs of life may be succeeded by the most vexatious inconveniences.* God had divided the Red Sea for his people, yet he suffered them to go into places where there was no water to drink! For their sakes he had destroyed Pharaoh and his hosts, yea, his chariots and his chosen captains, yet he allowed them to suffer the pain of thirst! It is specially to be observed that the children of Israel were actually in the right way when they found themselves exposed to this inconvenience. Could we have learned that the people had strayed but one yard from the appointed path, we should have found in that fact an explanation of this trial. We should have exclaimed as men who have suddenly discovered the key of a great difficulty —"See what comes of disobedience to the Divine voice! If the people had walked in the way marked out for them by the Almighty, their bread and their water would have been sure, but now that they have taken the course into their own hands, they come to bitter streams which they cannot drink!" The contrary, however, is the fact of the case. The people marched along the very road which God intended them to occupy, and in that very march they came upon waters that were bitter. Is it not often so in our own life? We have been delivered from some great trial, some overwhelming affliction which brought us to the very gates of death, some perplexity which bewildered our minds and baffled our energies, and then we have lifted up our hearts in adoring songs to the Deliverer of our lives, and have vowed to live the rest of our days in the assured comfort arising from the merciful interposition and gracious defence of God; yet we have hardly gone three days' march into the future before we have come upon wells which have aggravated the thirst we expected them to allay. Compared with the great deliverance, the trial itself may

seem to be trifling, yet it becomes an intolerable distress. Suffer
not the tempter to suggest that the trial has befallen you because
of disobedience. History has again and again shown us that the
field of duty has been the field of danger, and that the way which
has conducted directly from earth to heaven has been beset by
temptations and difficulties too great for human strength. You
may be right, even when the heaviest trial is oppressing you.
You may be losing your property, your health may be sinking,
your prospects may be clouded, and your friends may be
leaving you one by one, yet in the midst of such disasters your
heart may be steadfast in faithfulness to God. If, however, we
are able to trace our trial to some outward or inward sin, then
indeed it well becometh us to bow down before the God of heaven
and to utter the cry of penitence at the Cross of Jesus Christ, if
haply we may be forgiven.

2. "The people murmured against Moses,"—*so the greatest
services of life are soon forgotten.* Instead of saying to Moses,
"Thou art our leader, and we will trust thee ; we remember thy
services in the past, and we believe thee to be under the inspiration of God," the children of Israel turned round upon Moses and
openly treated him as incapable, if not treacherous. Where was
their recollection of the overthrow of Pharaoh ? Where was the
memory of the thunderous and triumphant song which they sang
when the sea covered the chariots and horsemen of the tyrant
king ? The people murmured and whimpered like disappointed
children, instead of bearing their trial with the fortitude of men
and the hope of saints. So soon do we forget the great services
which have been rendered by our leaders. Moses was the
statesman of Israel, yet see how he was treated when he came
upon difficulties over which he had no personal control ! It is so
that we deal with our own patriots : they think for us, they
scheme for us, they involve themselves in the most exhausting
labour on our account; so long as they repeat our sentiments,
and give effect to our wishes, we laud them and write their
names upon the bright banner, but let them turn round and utter
a conviction with which we cannot sympathise, or propose a
scheme with which we are but ill-fitted to grapple, so comprehensive is its scope and so numerous its details, and in a moment

we strike them in the face and trample their reputation in the
dust. We do the same with our preachers. We want our
preachers to be but echoes. So long as they will say from the
pulpit the things which we have been saying with cuckoo-like
regularity for many years, we call them excellent preachers, and
pay them their paltry dole with as much enthusiasm as small
natures can feel; but if they attempt to lead us into unwonted
tracks, if they do but suggest in the most remote and delicate
manner that possibly there are some truths which we have not
yet mastered, the probability is we shall in an hour forget the
pastoral solicitude and the ministerial zeal of years, and treat as
enemies the men who have been our wisest and gentlest friends.

3. "And Moses cried unto the Lord!"—*so magnanimous
prayer is better than official resignation.* Think what Moses might
have said under the circumstances! With what indignation he
might have answered the murmuring mob! "Am I God that I
can create wells in the desert? Are we not moving under the
express command of Heaven, and has not God some purpose in
leading us this way? Do I drink at a secret well of pure water,
and leave you to be poisoned by waters that are diseased!
Avaunt, ye unreasoning and ungrateful reptiles, and learn the
elements of civility and the first principles of morality." Instead
of speaking so, what did Moses do? *He cried unto the Lord!*
All great leaderships should be intensely religious, or they will
assuredly fail in the *patience* without which no strength can be
complete. The question was not between Moses and Israel, it
was between Moses and the Almighty One, revealed by the
gracious names of the God of Abraham, and the God of Isaac, and
the God of Jacob; hence to that Almighty One Moses directed
his appeal. Did the chief relations of life subsist wholly between
the human parties involved, there might be a ready way of
escaping from difficulty and vexation; such however is not the
fact; the relation of parent and child, or of pastor and church, or
of strong and weak, is not a relation complete in itself,—it has a
religious basis, and it involves religious responsibility. What
then are men to do when they are assailed by murmuring and
distrust from those who are under their care? They are not to
take the high and mighty plan of standing on their so-called

d'gnity, nor are they at liberty to enter the chariot of their own proud indignation, that they may pass away into quieter realms ; they must take the case to him who is Lord and Master, and must wait the indication of his will.   I cannot think of the patience of Moses, or of any man or woman who has ever been concerned in the best training of life, without seeing in such patience a faint emblem of that higher patience which is embodied in the life and ministry of the Saviour of mankind !   Were he not patient with us beyond all that we know of human forbearance and hope, he would surely consume us from the face of the earth, and so silence for ever the voice of our petulant and unreasoning complaint ; but he cares for us, he yearns over us ; when we strive most vehemently against him, when we smite his back and pluck the hair from his cheek, he inquires with agony of wounded love, " How shall I give thee up ? "

> 'Kindled his relentings are ;
> Me he still delights to spare ;
> Cries—How shall I give thee up ?
> Lets the lifted thunder drop."

Parents, instead of resigning the oversight of your children, pray for them !   Pastors, instead of resigning your official positions, pray for those who despitefully use you !   All who in anywise seek to defend the weak, or lead the blind or teach the ignorant, instead of being driven off by every unreasonable murmuring, renew your patience by waiting upon God !

4. "And the Lord shewed him a tree,"—*so where there is a bane in life, there is also an antidote.*   The water was bitter, but there was a tree of healing at hand !   Things are never so bad in reality as they often appear to be.   Undoubtedly there are bitter experiences, but quite as undoubtedly there are remedies precisely adapted to these experiences.   The tree was not created in order to meet the case : it was actually standing there at the time of the complaint.   The cure is often much nearer us than our irrational distrust will allow us to suppose.   Remember that the tree was not discovered by Moses himself : it was specially pointed out by the Lord.   God is the Teacher of true methods of healing the body, as well as the only source of spiritual salvation. We may divide the spheres amidst which we live, and may for

the sake of convenience call one Agriculture, another Medicine, another Architecture, and others by distinguishing names, but, regarded profoundly and truly, human life is still under a Theocracy.   Theology contains all that is true in art and in science, as well as the doctrines which apply to our highest capabilities and aspirations.   An ancient saint looking upon the ploughman and upon the sower, and observing how they prepared the earth to bring forth and bud, that there might be bread for the world, exclaimed, " This also cometh forth from the Lord of hosts, which is wonderful in counsel, and excellent in working."   The true physician is inspired of Heaven ; so is the true poet; so is the true painter ; so also is the true preacher.   We must not narrow theology until it becomes a sectarian science ; we must insist that within its expansiveness are to be found all things and all hopes which minister to the strength and exalt the destiny of human life.

Hast thou come, my friend, in thy wilderness way, to the place of bitter waters ?   Canst thou not drink of the stream, even though thy thirst be burning and thy strength be wasted ? Know thou, there is a tree the leaves of which are for the healing of the nations !   A tree ?   Truly so ; but a tree as yet without a leaf,—a tree bare as the frosts and the winds of winter can make it,—the great, grim, dear, sad, wondrous Cross of the Son of God !   Some have sought to touch the wells of life with other trees, but have only aggravated the disease which they sought to cure.   By the grace of Heaven others have been enabled to apply the Cross to the bitter wells of their sin and grief, and behold the waters have become clear as the crystal river which flows fast by the throne of God !

Exodus xvi.

1. And they took their journey from Elim, and all the congregation of the children of Israel came unto the wilderness of Sin (exactly one month after the departure from Egypt), which is between Elim and Sinai, on the fifteenth day of the second month after their departing out of the land of Egypt.

2. And the whole congregation of the children of Israel murmured (this is the third murmuring) against Moses and Aaron in the wilderness :

3. And the children of Israel said unto them, Would to God (Heb. omits the word *God*) we had died by the hand of the Lord (perhaps an allusion to the last of the plagues) in the land of Egypt, when we sat by the flesh pots, and when we did eat bread to the full (a compliment to Egypt); for ye have brought us forth into this wilderness, to kill this whole assembly with hunger.

4. Then said the Lord unto Moses, Behold, I will rain bread from heaven for you; and the people shall go out and gather a certain rate every day (a day's meal for a day), that I may prove them (what God did in Eden) whether they will walk in my law, or no.

5. And it shall come to pass, that on the sixth day (in Egypt the week of seven days was at this time unknown) they shall prepare that which they bring in ; and it shall be twice as much as they gather daily.

6. And Moses and Aaron said unto all the children of Israel, At even, then ye shall know that the Lord hath brought you out from the land of Egypt :

7. And in the morning, then ye shall see the glory of the Lord ; for that he heareth your murmurings against the Lord : and what are we, that ye murmur against us ?

8. And Moses said, This shall be, when the Lord shall give you in the evening flesh to eat, and in the morning bread to the full; for that the Lord heareth your murmurings which ye murmur against him : and what are we ? your murmurings are not against us, but against the Lord.

9. And Moses spake unto Aaron, Say unto all the congregation of the children of Israel, Come near before the Lord : for he hath heard your murmurings.

10. And it came to pass, as Aaron spake unto the whole congregation of the children of Israel, that they looked toward the wilderness, and, behold, the glory of the Lord appeared in the cloud (the pillar of the cloud is meant).

11. And the Lord spake unto Moses, saying,

12. I have heard the murmurings of the children of Israel : speak unto

them, saying, At even ye shall eat flesh, and in the morning ye shall be filled with bread; and ye shall know that I am the Lord your God.

13. And it came to pass, that at even the quails came up (the common quail is very abundant in the east), and covered the camp: and in the morning the dew lay round about the host (literally, there was a lying of dew).

14. And when the dew that lay was gone up (drawn by the heat of the sun), behold, upon the face of the wilderness there lay a small round thing, as small as the hoar frost on the ground.

15. And when the children of Israel saw it, they said one to another, It is manna (what is this?); for they wist not what it was. And Moses said unto them, This is the bread which the Lord hath given you to eat (and which they did eat for forty years).

16. This is the thing which the Lord hath commanded, Gather of it every man according to his eating, an omer (about three pints English) for every man (for every head), according to the number of your persons; take ye every man for them which are in his tents.

17. And the children of Israel did so, and gathered, some more, some less.

18. And when they did mete it with an omer (publicly measured in the camp), he that gathered much had nothing over, and he that gathered little had no lack; they gathered every man according to his eating.

19. And Moses said, Let no man leave of it till the morning.

20. Notwithstanding they hearkened not unto Moses; but some of them left of it until the morning, and it bred worms, and stank: and Moses was wroth with them.

21. And they gathered it every morning, every man according to his eating: and when the sun waxed hot, it melted.

22. And it came to pass, that on the sixth day they gathered twice as much bread, two omers for one man: and all the rulers of the congregation came and told Moses (who had either not made known the law, or the rulers had forgotten it).

23. And he said unto them, This is that which the Lord hath said, To-morrow is the rest of the holy sabbath unto the Lord (not *the* rest. The absence of the article intimates that it is a new thing that is announced): bake that which ye will bake to-day, and seethe that ye will seethe; and that which remaineth over lay up for you to be kept until the morning.

24. And they laid it up till the morning, as Moses bade: and it did not stink, neither was there any worm therein.

25. And Moses said, Eat that to-day; for to-day is a sabbath unto the Lord: to-day ye shall not find it in the field.

26. Six days ye shall gather it; but on the seventh day, which is the sabbath, in it there shall be none.

27. And it came to pass, that there went out some of the people on the seventh day for to gather, and they found none.

28. And the Lord said unto Moses, How long refuse ye to keep my commandments and my laws?

29. See, for that the Lord hath given you the sabbath, therefore he giveth you on the sixth day the bread of two days; abide ye every man in his place, let no man go out of his place on the seventh day.

30. So the people rested on the seventh day.

31. And the house of Israel called the name thereof manna : and it was like coriander seed, white (a small round grain, of a whitish or yellowish grey) ; and the taste of it was like wafers made with honey.

32. And Moses said, This is the thing which the Lord commandeth, Fill an omer of it to be kept for your generations ; that they may see the bread wherewith I have fed you in the wilderness, when I brought you forth from the land of Egypt.

33. And Moses said unto Aaron, Take a pot, and put an omer full of manna therein, and lay it up before the Lord, to be kept for your generations.

34. As the Lord commanded Moses, so Aaron laid it up before the Testimony to be kept.

35. And the children of Israel did eat manna forty years, until they came to a land inhabited ; they did eat manna, until they came unto the borders of the land of Canaan.

36. Now an omer is the tenth part of an ephah.

MANNA IN THE WILDERNESS.

ALWAYS remember that these are the people who had just been singing. Whatever they did they seemed to do with a will. We thrilled under their song : we called it sublime, religiously impressive, and morally full of the spirit of education and comfort. The song has hardly died away from their lips when they begin to murmur. They first murmured at Marah because the waters were bitter, and now they murmur in the wilderness because food is scanty. There are many people who sing with great expression and fervour when everything is going just as they want it to go. Their song is full of emptiness ; it is a vain speech and a profanation of music. There are many such living and have lived in all ages. We know how their business is going by the way in which they accost us. They have no souls. Always remember, further, that just one month had elapsed since the departure from Egypt. The poet makes a point of the two little months that had elapsed between two circumstances which were apparently incongruous and irreconcilable. He cries the more bitterly when he says,—"But two months— two little months!" Here that act, so startling, marked by cruelty and by baseness of design, is completely out-done : for there was but one month—one little month between the mighty deliverance and the atheistic murmuring. It is difficult to have a solid piety—really four-square, permanent in its dignity, independent of all circumstances, except so far as its immediate being is concerned,—a piety founded upon a rock lifting up its turrets and pinnacles to the sky, defying all wind, and thunder, and tumult of the elements. Until we realise such a piety as that, our education is immature and incomplete.

Observe how the most astounding miracles go for nothing. Then the miracles were nothing to those who observed them. They were applauded at the time, they sent a little thrill through those who looked upon them with eyes more or less vacant and meaningless; but as to solid result, educational virtue and excellence, the miracles might as well not have been wrought at all. It was the same in the days of Jesus Christ. All his miracles went for nothing amongst many of the people who observed them. A miracle is a wonder, and a wonder cannot be permanent. Wonders soon drop into commonplaces, and that which astounded at first lulls at last,—yea, that which excited a kind of groping faith may by repetition soon come to excite doubt and scepticism and fear. What wonder, then, if the miracles having thus gone down in importance and value, the most splendid personal services followed in their wake? This is a necessary logic; this is a sequence that cannot be broken. He who goes down on the Divine or upward side of his nature must go down on the human and social side in the same proportion; when faith in miracles goes, faith in all that is noblest in brotherhood will follow it. A kind of socialism will be trumped up, a species of commonwealth will be attempted, men will try to make up for their non-religion by their surplus philanthropy; but the adequate truths being absent the attempt will end in spasm, and impotence, and uselessness. We owe more to the religious element than we suppose. Religion is not confined to the region of contemplation, speculation, metaphysical inquiry, secret and ineffective worship. It comes down into all the lines of life; it lifts up common speech into uncommon eloquence; it raises out of the stones children unto Abraham; it turns the common supper-bread into a symbol of the Lord's body. Do not let us imagine, then, that we can dismiss faith in the miracles, faith in inspiration, faith in the Bible,—and yet retain society in all its deepest meaning and tenderest ministries and noblest uses. When the altar falls, the home is no longer safe.

Observe what an effect long servitude had produced upon the children of Israel. Was there ever a meaner cry than this :— "Would to God we had died by the hand of the Lord in the land of Egypt, when we sat by the flesh pots, and when we did eat bread to the full"? That is not manly. How is such *un*manliness of whining and whimpering to be accounted for ? By long subjugation; by days and months and years and generations of servitude. The man can be driven out of the man ; the man can be debased into almost a beast of burden. He can forget his yesterdays, his heaven-pointing book, his prayer, and all the upward look that made him almost an angel. Servitude has done this in every country ; and we cannot expect people who have been for generations in bondage to stand up and claim intellectual equality with men who have been living under the sun of freedom century after century. The .criticism would be unfair. Were this a merely historical matter, it would be of comparatively little consequence; but it is a spiritual matter. The eternal form of the lesson is this :— that servitude to sin takes the pith out of manhood. A man cannot be both a bad man and a strong man. The law—unwritten, if you please —of heaven, of the eternities is against this anomaly. Repeat the sin, and you drop into a deeper baseness; renew your loyalty to the devil, and your power of resisting him goes down with every new act of obeisance. So the time comes when the strong man becomes himself in abject servility to the foe. He who once could say No with all the roundness and emphasis of the thunder, can now only whisper his consent to the temptations of the devil. Virtue grows stronger and stronger. He that hath clean hands becomes a mightier man every day ; at the last he is a giant, as in the midst he was a hero

What do the people do ? They rest in second causes. The people saw no further than Moses and Aaron : they complained against their leaders; they murmured against the Divinely-appointed princes of Israel. What is the all-healing method of looking at things ?—looking at the whole, or taking a comprehensive view. This is the difficulty of all time. It is the supreme trial of many men. Who can see a whole horizon ? Who has a pivotal mind that can turn round and see all that there is to be

seen? We suffer from our very intensity of mind,—that is to
say, from our power of fixing the attention upon one point only
and not taking the whole circle and the whole balance of the
Divine economy. What a difference there is amongst men in this
respect! How needful it is to get rid of the sophism that one
man is equal to another, or is upon a level with another, or is
to be accounted only as one by any other. We need correction
upon the matter of personality. Moses was more than a person
in the narrow and familiar sense of that term. So are all the
prophets and leaders of the Church, so are all the seers and
mighty men of God in every age. Luther was not one; Wesley
was not one—simply a man, a figure, a unit. There are personalities that are compendiums; there are individualities that are
full of nations and empires and fatherhoods of glory. There are
Abrahams who have in them a multitude no more to be counted
than is the sand upon the sea-shore. So when we talk about
"personal following" we talk about that which needs definition.
Who is the person? Is he the father of a multitude, the prince
of nationalities? Is he fruitful of thought, having ideas on which
ages may feed? So we say "Take him for all in all," or, to use
a commoner form of expression, "Looking at him all round."
But in many cases there is no "all for all" to take: there is no
"all round" to survey. In such instances, we cannot talk about
persons and personalities and individual followings, for following
there will be little or none. It is the man who is himself a
Multitude that takes the nations with him. Moses, therefore, is
not to be noted in the census of the wilderness as one but as
a whole nation.

So far the children of Israel were right: they complained
against the right man—if it were proper to complain against
him at all. What we need is the complete view, the all-including
view,—the Apostolic view, lifted up to which the greatest man
born of woman has said, " All things work together for good to
them that love God." We sometimes miss the sublime boldness
of that speech by omitting to reflect that the man who spoke it
had a mind that could stretch itself by sacred imagination and
tender sympathy over all the things of which the Divine economy
is compounded. God is the real object of murmuring. Moses put
this point very clearly :—" Your murmurings are not against us,

but against the Lord." The people did not mean that, perhaps ;
but we cannot be measured by our own reckoning when we come
into the sphere religious and moral. We are always doing things
we do not mean to do, and sometimes we do things of which we
are wholly ignorant ; and when we are sharply reminded of what
the real meaning óf our action is, we stand back in affront and
express the language of surprise, and assume an attitude of
unbelief. But we need the great teachers of the Bible, the
men of penetration of every age, to show us what an action
is. The man of science tells us that when we lift a hand we
send a motion to the stars. Having heard that statement we
account it grand, because it is the statement of one of the exact
sciences. When another man of science says that every breath
you draw affects the general level of the Atlantic, we say,
"How amazing are the discoveries of science !" When the
moral seer tells us that our whining is not against man but
against God, we call him a " fanatic " ! The ways of man are not
equal. He who is amazed, because he is given to understand that
the lifting of his hand sends a shudder to the stars, listens with
unbelief to the statement that a lie grieves the Spirit of God,—a
sin of any name wounds the peace of Heaven.

God knows how far he himself is responsible for our circumstances, and up to that degree he is faithful. He will find a
solution of all difficulties how tangled and obstinate soever. This
is a case in point :—The people had not taken themselves into
the wilderness : God had taken them there, and he will see them
out of it. So we say about honourable men when they undertake to lead us, and certain circumstances transpire which are of
the nature of difficulty and hindrance. They say, in the spirit
of honour,—" We are accountable for this ; our strength is yours
until this battle is fought ; you did not bring yourselves in here,
and out of it we will see you, health permitting, life being
spared." So the Lord will not leave us in wildernesses into
which he himself has brought us. If we ourselves have gone
into the desert without his permission or consent, we may be
allowed to die there, and to remain without a grave in the sand in
which we vainly thought to find a heaven : but if we have obeyed
the Divine voice, and gone in the providential way, whatever
there is on the road—Marah, or place of sand, or great river, or

greater sea—God will find a way through all. Wherefore comfort one another with these words.

See how wonderfully God asserts law in the very midst of the most compassionate mercy :—I will give you bread in the wilder-ness, but on the sixth day you shall gather a double quantity; the Sabbath must be kept. How marvellous are the compassions of God ! and how marvellous the law of God ! We are not given over to wantonness and licence, gathering just as much as we please and every day of the week. God will have his time respected. If you gather more than he wants you to gather, it will rot,—it will offend your nostrils by its pestilent odour, and you will be glad to get rid of it. If you go out on the Sunday to see if you cannot do something that you did on Saturday, God will attend to the penal side of the act; you are building a house of smoke, and you can never live to enjoy it. Life is law—mercy; work-day—rest-day ; labour—prayer ; on the earth—in heaven. Blessed is the man whose life is thus balanced.

"Verily, verily, I say unto you, Moses gave you not that bread from heaven ; but my Father giveth you the true bread from heaven. For the bread of God is he which cometh down from heaven, and giveth life unto the world. Then said they unto him, Lord, evermore give us this bread." A noble prayer ! Made for every age, capable of being uttered by every tongue. " He that believeth on me hath everlasting life. I am that bread of life. Your fathers did eat manna in the wilderness, and are dead. This is the bread which cometh down from heaven, that a man may eat thereof, and not die. I am the living bread which came down from heaven: if any man eat of this bread, he shall live for ever: and the bread that I will give is my flesh, which I will give for the life of the world. This is that bread which came down from heaven : not as your fathers did eat manna, and are dead : he that eateth of this bread shall live for ever." So there is an evangelical use of the ancient incident. Thus old history is turned into new uses, and all the days of the past are regarded as parables which have been teaching some higher truth than was at first observed within the corners of the narrow facts.

God is repeating this manna miracle every day. All food comes from above. You mistake, if you think you find your food otherwhere than from heaven. No sky, then no wheat; no cloud overhead, then no garden round about; no firmanent, then no earth; no rain, no beauty; no fragrance of flowers, no summer feast. What are we eating? On what is our life being supported? We ought to ascertain this, and be very clear and distinct about it. At what table are we sitting? a table of our own spreading, or of God's? "Ho, every one that thirsteth, come ye to the waters, and he that hath no money; come ye, buy, and eat; yea, come, buy wine and milk without money and without price. Wherefore do ye spend money for that which is not bread? and your labour for that which satisfieth not? hearken diligently unto me, and eat ye that which is good, and let your soul delight itself in fatness." These are the invitations that make the Bible the most hospitable of all books. The Bible will have us eat and drink abundantly at God's banquet board. What is our reply? Shall we eat bread for the body and have no sustenance for the mind? Shall we feed the flesh and starve the soul? Are we—men of boasted wisdom and education—the men to strengthen the bones and make as iron the sinews, and attend to all the wants of the flesh, and to let the soul, the spirit, the inner guest die for want of light and air, and nutriment? Count him a murderer who kills his soul.

Exodus xvi. 3.

"Would to God we had died by the hand of the Lord in the land of Egypt, when we sat by the flesh pots, and when we did eat bread to the full; for ye have brought us forth into this wilderness, to kill this whole assembly with hunger."

MOSES IN THE WILDERNESS OF SIN.

PEOPLE may be strong and hopeful at the beginning of a project, and most effusively and devoutly thankful at its close, but the difficulty is to go manfully through the *process*. Israel was in the desert, and never were spoiled children more peevish, suspicious, and altogether ill-behaved. If they could have stepped out of Egypt into Canaan at once, probably they would have been as pious as most of us; but there was the weary interval, the inhospitable wilderness! It is so in our life. Accept it as a solemn and instructive fact that life is a *process*. It is more than a beginning and an ending: more than a cradle and a grave. The *child* may be good, and the *old man* may be tranquil, but what of the petulant, self-willed, and prayerless *being* between these extremes?

The history leads us to dwell on *Processes*. See how far the historical teaching represents our own experience.

First. *Processes try men's temper.* See how the temper of Israel was tried in the wilderness ! No bread, no water, no rest ! How do processes try men's temper? (1) They are often *tedious*; (2) they are often *uncontrollable*; (3) they often seem to be made worse by the *incompetency of others.*

We must not drive life. Nature is not to be whipped and spurred by impatient riders. God's administration is calm. The wheels of his chariot are not bespattered by the mud of blustering and reckless haste. On the other hand, we are not to find in this reflection an excuse for the indolence and incapacity of *men.* There are stones which we can roll away. There are turbid little streams which we can bridge. There are gates which weaker men than Samson can carry away. There is the profoundest difference between the indolence of men and the eternal calm of God. "Whatsoever thy hand findeth to do, do it with thy might." " I must work while it is called day."

Second. *The trials of processes are to be met not all at once, but a day at a time.* "I will rain bread from heaven for you ; and the people shall go out and gather a certain rate every day, that I may prove them, whether they will walk in my law, or no." See the law by which the manna was given. There was not a large store sent down. Daily hunger was met by daily bread. We are not allowed to live two days at once. In the parable the pendulum was told that it had to give but one tick at a time. The heart beats in the same way. Upon how little sleep it lives !

This daily display of Divine care teaches (1) that *physical* as well as spiritual gifts are God's ; (2) that one of God's gifts is the *pledge of another.* "Not as the world giveth, give I unto you." Why am I to be easy about *to-morrow?* Because God is good *to-day !* "He is the same yesterday, and to-day, and for ever.

Third. *Processes show the different dispositions of men.* Not their tempers only, but the deeper realities and aspects of their character. They were told not to leave any of the manna until the morning of the following day, but some of them *did* leave it. You cannot convince some men, nor can you bind them by authority, nor can you bring them under a common discipline. No. Provision must be made for madmen. Every society out of heaven is probably disturbed by some kind of eccentricity. Though the people were told in the distinctest manner that there would be no manna on the seventh day, yet they went out to gather it just as if they had never been warned ! Such men are the vexation of the world. They plague every community of which they are a portion. You tell them that tickets cannot be had after a certain day, but they give you the lie, as far as they can, by coming for them two days after. There are such wise men everywhere, but happily they are now and then effectually checked and humbled. What a humiliation awaits them in the long run !

The history, at this point, urges the most direct application of its truths upon our spiritual nature. (1) We have the *means of life* at our disposal : the manna lies at our tent-door ! (2) We are distinctly assured that such means are given *under law :* there is a *set time* for the duration of the opportunity : the night cometh ! Some men will set themselves against God in these matters. They will persistently work contrariwise. They will defy the law : they will challenge the sword : they will tell you that the night has no darkness for them, and that when God has shut the door the key of their importunity will open it ! Beware of such men. They will fail you at last ; and when you smite them with your reproaches, you can add no pain to the torment of their damnation.

Fourth. *All the processes of life should be hallowed by religious exercises.* There was a Sabbath even in the wilderness. The Sabbath is amongst the very oldest institutions. God rested on the seventh day, and blessed it. Before the law was given from Sinai God gave the Sabbath to Israel. Man *must* have rest, and all true rest is associated with religious ideas and aspirations. The animal rest is but typical : the *soul* must have its hours of quietness ; the spirit must pause in the presence of God to recover its strength.

(1) The Sabbath is more than a mere *law;* it is an expression of *mercy.* (2) No man *ever loses anything* by keeping the Sabbath : " The Lord giveth you on the sixth day the bread of two days." (3) *He* is the *loser* who has no day of rest.

Fifth. *Processes should leave some tender and hope-inspiring memories behind them.* " Fill an omer of it to be kept for your generations ; that they may see the bread wherewith I have fed you in the wilderness, when I brought you forth from the land of Egypt." The way to enrich life is to keep a retentive memory in the heart. Look over a period of twenty years, and see the all-covering and ever-shining mercy of God ! How many special providences have you observed ? How many narrow escapes have you experienced ? How many difficulties have you surmounted ? How often have you found a pool in unexpected places ? We should lay up some memory of the Divine triumphs which have gladdened our lives, and fall back upon it for inspiration and courage in the dark and cloudy day. Go into your yesterdays to find God ! Search for him in the paths along which you have come, and if you dare, under the teaching of your own memories, deny his goodness, then betake yourselves to the infamous luxury of distrust and reproach !

Sixth. *The process will end.* Though the wheels move slowly, yet will they reach the goal ! You are not the men you were twenty years ago ! The most of the desert-road is now *behind* some of you. Your future on earth is narrowing itself to a point. How is it with your souls ? Your *feet* are sore with the long journey ; are your *wings* ready for flight into the kingdom of the crystal river and the unsetting sun ?

NOTE ON MANNA.

"It may have been derived from the *manna rains* known in various countries. There is an edible lichen which sometimes falls in showers several inches deep, the wind having blown it from the spots where it grew, and carried it onwards. In 1824 and in 1828, it fell in Persia and Asiatic Turkey in great quantities. In 1829, during the war between Persia and Russia, there was a great famine at Oroomiah, south-west of the Caspian Sea. One day, during a violent wind, the surface of the country was covered with what the people called 'bread from heaven,' which fell in thick showers. Sheep fed on it greedily, and the people who had never seen it before, induced by this, gathered it, and having reduced it to flour, made bread of it, which they found palatable and nourishing. In some places it lay on the ground five or six inches deep. In the spring of 1841, an amazing quantity of this substance fell in the same region, covering the ground, here and there, to the depth of from three to four inches. Many of the particles were as large as hail-stones. It was grey, and sweet to the taste, and made excellent bread. In 1846, a great manna rain, which occurred at Jenischehr, during a famine, attracted great notice. It lasted several days, and pieces as large as a hazel-nut fell in quantities. When ground and baked it made as good bread, in the opinion of the people, as that from grain. In 1846 another rain of manna occurred in the government of Wilna, and formed a layer upon the ground, three or four inches deep. It was of a greyish-white colour, rather hard, irregular in form, without smell, and insipid. Pallas, the Russian naturalist, observed it on the arid mountains and limestone tracts of the Great Desert of Tartary. In 1828, Parroth brought some from Mount Ararat, and it proved to be a lichen known as *Parmelia Esculenta,* which grows on chalky and stony soil, like that of the Kirghese Steppes of Central Asia. Eversmann described several kinds of it, last century, as found east of the Caspian, and widely spread over Persia and Middle Asia. It is round, and at times as large as a walnut, varying from that to the size of a pin's head, and does not fix itself in the soil in which it grows, but lies free and loose, drinking in nourishment from the surface, and easily carried off by the wind, which sweeps it away in vast quantities in the storms of spring, and thus causes the 'manna rains' in the districts over which the wind travels."
—*Geikie's " Hours with the Bible."*

Exodus xvii.

1. And all the congregation of the children of Israel journeyed from the wilderness of Sin, after their journeys, according to the commandment of the Lord, and pitched in Rephidim : and there was no water for the people to drink.

2. Wherefore the people did chide with Moses, and said, Give us water that we may drink. And Moses said unto them, Why chide ye with me ? wherefore do ye tempt the Lord ?

3. And the people thirsted there for water; and the people murmured against Moses, and said, Wherefore is this that thou hast brought us up but of Egypt, to kill us and our children and our cattle with thirst ?

4. And Moses cried unto the Lord, saying, What shall I do unto this people ? they be almost ready to stone me (tumultuary, not legal stoning).

5. And the Lord said unto Moses, Go on before the people, and take with thee of the elders of Israel ; and thy rod, wherewith thou smotest the river, take in thine hand, and go.

6. Behold, I will stand before thee there upon the rock in Horeb (some particular rock in the Horeb range) ; and thou shalt smite the rock, and there shall come water out of it, that the people may drink. And Moses did so in the sight of the elders of Israel.

7. And he called the name of the place Massah (trial or temptation), and Meribah (chiding or quarrel), because of the chiding of the children of Israel, and because they tempted the Lord, saying, Is the Lord among us, or not ?

8. Then came Amalek (the first formal mention as a nation), and fought with Israel in Rephidim.

9. And Moses said unto Joshua (the first mention of Joshua, the tenth in descent from Joseph, probably forty-five years old), Choose us out men, and go out, fight with Amalek : to-morrow I will stand on the top of the hill with the rod of God in mine hand.

10. So Joshua did as Moses had said to him, and fought with Amalek ; and Moses (upwards of eighty), Aaron (eighty-three), and Hur (the grandfather of Bezaleel, and not much younger than Moses or Aaron) went up to the top of the hill.

11. And it came to pass, when Moses held up his hand, that Israel prevailed : and when he let down his hand, Amalek prevailed.

12. But Moses' hands were heavy ; and they took a stone (only an eyewitness would have noted this), and put it under him, and he sat thereon and Aaron and Hur stayed up his hands, the one on the one side, and the other on the other side and his hands were steady until the going down of the sun.

13. And Joshua discomfited Amalek and his people with the edge of the sword.

14. And the Lord said unto Moses, Write this for a memorial in a book, and rehearse it in the ears of Joshua: for I will utterly put out the remembrance of Amalek from under heaven (done finally and completely in the reign of Hezekiah, see 1 Chron. iv. 43).

15. And Moses built an altar, and called the name of it Jehovah-nissi (Jehovah, my banner).

16. For he said, Because the Lord hath sworn that the Lord will have war with Amalek from generation to generation (because the hand of Amalek is against the throne of God, therefore the Lord hath war with Amalek from generation to generation).

REPHIDIM: ANCIENT AND MODERN.

CHAPTERS like this enable us to see how far the race has advanced in a moral direction. How far have we travelled from Rephidim? This is more than a question in geography: it is a profound inquiry in morals. We are too apt to dismiss as ancient history terms which we consider to be merely local. The terms themselves may be strictly local and hardly worth remembering; but they may be associated with qualities, influences and ministries, which constitute an eternal presence in human life. The New Testament did not hesitate to make use of the history of the Old, and we are called upon in this matter to follow the example of Christ and to imitate that of the Apostles. They told us the meaning of the things which happened aforetime; and every teacher who would maintain a profound influence upon any age must see to it that he does not allow the unity of the ages to be broken, but rather insist upon their continuousness, their solidarity, and their unanimous meaning. The ages are one. If we ask how far have we advanced in a mechanical direction, it will be difficult to establish any link of union between our country to-day and five hundred years ago. Verily, we have travelled from ourselves innumerable thousands of miles in all matters of a merely mechanical nature. Our ancestors would not know us in these particulars. All things have been created anew. It would be impossible for us to go back upon the olden days. We should scorn their narrowness, wonder at their poverty, and hold in more or less gracious contempt the slowness, and the weariness, and the dull monotony of the old times of our forefathers. We rejoice in this progress; we mark it in a way that cannot be easily mistaken, and say that civilisation has expanded its influence and consolidated its empire. So be it. How far have we advanced in a literary direction? Again the progress has been almost immeasurable. In words, in pureness of literature, in daring boldness of conception, in loftiness of speculation, in splendour and vividness of diction and representation, we seem to have advanced almost incalculably from many of the old standards. So be it. In this respect there is in very deed what may be termed ancient history. We have almost a new English. We have been so complete in our criticism and progress as to have almost established a new alphabet of things. We rejoice in this, and call it progress, and boast of it with honest and legitimate triumph. But the preacher's question is : How far have we advanced *morally*, spiritually, and in all the higher ranges and Diviner outlooks of our being? Here we seem to be still at Rephidim. Geographers say they cannot find out the exact locality. Verily, there need be no difficulty about the exact locality—it is just where we are. We carry the locality with us. Let men who like to search the sand, and turn over the stones, and compare ancient and modern geography, bewilder themselves in seeking for square feet and precise positions; we interpret the event by a broader law, and have no difficulty whatever in affirming that we carry Rephidim with us, and this day, four—five thousand years away in time from the place, we are standing in the very foot-prints of old Israel, and doing in all their broader meanings exactly the actions which old Israel performed. Unless we seize this idea of the Scriptures we shall separate ourselves very far indeed from their truest and deepest meanings. We must not allow little boundaries, and local names, and occult Hebraisms and Chaldaisms to come between us and the great unity of the human race. We must overleap these, or crush our way through them, and claim association with the central and abiding line which marks the development of human history and Divine purpose.

Why be so emphatic about our being at Rephidim? Because, first of all, I said that the people at Rephidim were tormented by a continual consciousness of necessity. How far have we got from necessity? Not one inch. Necessity has followed us all the time. It is awake in the morning before we open our eyes, and the last thing we see, before we close our vision in sleep, is the grim image of necessity. The people wanted bread a day or two ago—now they are consumed with thirst, and are chiding Moses and murmuring bitterly against him because of the want of water. If that is so, verily we are still at Rephidim. Every life knows the bite of necessity ; every man represents the great void of need ; every soul cries out in pain because there is wanting some completing favour, some culminating and all-contenting benediction. Here it is bread ; there it is water ; but everywhere a famine—a hungrier famine than the wolf's cry for food in many a case,—a famine of the soul, a spiritual destitution, a consciousness of a void which time cannot satisfy or space content. Why did they not find themselves water ? Why did they not supply their own necessity ? This is the mystery of human life : that we are not self-complete, but are debtors to nature. We must put out our hand and receive from another that which we daily need. Poor creatures !—yet so august in greatness. We are indebted to one another. We find a leader when we are in pain, sorrow and deep necessity. In the great round of daily occurrences we pay but small heed to him—he is there, or will soon be present, or where he is we hardly know and do not specially care ; but let us become surrounded by danger, let us become conscious of some new necessity, let a sudden pain strike our life and torment our happiness, and up goes the cry, Where is Moses? Where is the leader? Where the priest who can pray ? Where the man who is a host in himself? These are the hours in which we discover just what we are and just what we can do. Strange that men who cannot support the body without help have in some infatuated cases supposed that they could nurture the soul without assistance. God will have hold of us somewhere. If we do not give him the opportunity of laying hold of our consenting minds, and burning, loyal, devoutest love, he will get hold of our fleshly necessities, and we shall cry to him, whom we spiritually deny, when our tongue is athirst for water and our life is perishing for want of bread. Pray we must—a prayer of agony and hopefulness. Prayer in its deepest meaning—not in its formality, or as a matter of attitude, and posture, and mechanical expression—is a necessity of life, an instinct of the soul, and an aspiration that separates us from the base and makes us men

We must advance from the lower to the higher. We have it before us as a certain and indisputable fact that for the support of the body we need external help : we need the whole ministry of kind and gracious nature. What wonder if in the education, and culture, and strengthening of the soul we need all heaven, with its infinite Trinity of Father, Son, and Holy Ghost ? Were we pressed to affirm that necessity it would be in strict consonance with all the other wants that follow and devour our wasting life.

Why be so emphatic about our still being at Rephidim ? Because at Rephidim help was found in unexpected places and given in unexpected ways: "Thou shalt smite the rock, and there shall come water out of it, that the people may drink." Is that ancient history ? It may be ancient, but it is very new—quite modern, young as the morning, present as our immediate consciousness and experience. We are always helped by unexpected people, in unexpected ways, and at unexpected places. God would appear to delight in baffling the ingenuity that would forecast the future with too exclusive a minuteness. God will not allow us to trifle with his prerogatives. He will find water where we should find none. The rock is not an inhospitable stone ; it is a congealed fountain. Human necessity and Divine grace meet in sweet consent. Have no fear then. I know that there is a rock immediately ahead of me ; but God can melt it into a river. I know that there is a Red Sea just in front of me ; but God can divide it and let me pass as through an iron gate. I am aware that Jordan's water is rolling just a few paces ahead, and I may have to go so near it as to touch it ; but the moment the foot of faith splashes in the waters of danger they must give way, for faith can never fail. Lord, increase our faith.

In the great encounters of life, either the spiritual or the material must give way, and God has never been stopped by that which is material and physical. Say that it is a work of imagination if you please, but as such it is done with infinite skill—a skill so infinite as to be more than human. God is never represented as being worsted, baffled, by any of the material which is built up into the house which we call his universe. "If ye have faith as a grain of mustard seed, ye shall say unto this mountain, Remove hence to yonder place ; and it shall remove; and nothing shall be impossible unto you." We die when our faith dies. Our power is not a power of genius, but an almightiness of belief. Nature is always equal to our physical necessities. God has put everything into nature which that other nature, called human, requires for its bodily sustentation. All food is in the kind earth. All medicine is in the garden. All healing is in the air which is blowing around us like a Divine benediction. The water is sometimes kept in the rock, and the bread is sometimes locked up in the cloud and allowed to drop down upon us like a very small coriander seed which we gather with wonder, and eat with an inquiry, saying, What is it ? All help is near, if you did but understand it :—" there standeth One among you, whom ye know not; he it is." The unknown is sitting next to you. The tree you need for the cure of the bitter pool is bending over the very water that needs to be healed. We realise the nearness of food, the nearness of music, the nearness of the living air, the nearness of those elements which are essential to the upbuilding and maturity of our lower nature,— why do we not realise the nearness of the redeeming God—the immediate presence of him who says—" Behold, I stand at the door, and knock : if any man hear my voice, and open the door, I will come in"? In all other things we glory in the nearness of the remedy, in the close proximity of what we need : yet, when we come into spiritual inquiries, the soul says—" Why standest thou afar off, O God?" and the inquiry is rebuked by the infinitely tender gospel—"I am a God near at hand," saith the Lord, "and not a God afar off." A wonderful rock !—I cannot explain it ; but rocks and more than rocks ; rivers and more than water—the Lord hath turned every Nile into saving blood, every rock into living water, and he has interpreted the parable of nature into the great and saving gospel of love. Do you ask the meaning of the rock ? The Apostle Paul shall give it :—" I would not that ye should be ignorant, how that all our fathers were under the cloud, and all passed through the sea ; and were all baptised unto Moses in the cloud and in the sea; and did all eat the same spiritual meat ; and did all drink the same spiritual drink : for they drank of that spiritual Rock that followed them : and that Rock was Christ." Be it mine to belong to the school that sees great things in little ones, that sees the moulding hand of God in the dew-drop as well as in the infinite constellations which seem to crowd the very amplitude of infinity. The very hairs of your head are all numbered; and as for so-called small things, take heed that ye despise not one of these little ones; it were better for that man that a millstone were hanged about his neck, and that he were drowned in the depths of the sea, than that he should dispossess or offend one of God's little ones. Look for great meanings. See in the dust the possibility of children being raised up unto Abraham. See in the temple stones possible voices of praise, if the natural worshippers should suddenly become dumb; and see in every rock not stone only, but an unhewn stairway up to the Jerusalem which is lighted by the Lamb.

> "Rock of Ages cleft for me,
> Let me hide myself in thee."

Why be so emphatic about still being at Rephidim? Because peevish tempers were corrected by great duties in that ancient locality. So the providence of God continues to work in us. The children of Israel were peevishly sighing and crying for the old Egyptian life, longing for the fleshpots of Egypt, desiring to be back again where they had food enough, because even Egyptian slave-drivers were wise enough not to starve their beasts of burden. So Israel fell into fretfulness, and whining, and dissatisfaction, and rebellion. What did God do? He sent Amalek upon Israel. That is the function of war among the nations. It is no use reasoning with peevishness. It is time wasted to try to expostulate with any man who is in a whining mood of soul, displeased because of his bread, discontented because of the scarcity of water, making no allowance for the undulations of life,—reasoning, remonstrance, expostulation would be lost. What must be done? An enemy must be raised up to smite him with the sword. Then he will come into a new mood of mind, forget his littleness, and, springing forward to a realisation of his true power, he will lose in service the discontent which he contracted in unbelief.

What we want to-day is persecution. We do not want eloquence, criticism,—new learning, some new invention in theological confectionery that shall tempt appetites that have been sated ; we want war—persecution—the enemy at the gate. Then we should begin to forgive one another, to pray for one another, to come more closely together at the altar and more near in that consent of soul which is blessed with insight into spiritual mysteries. We have lost in losing the enemy. The sting of Smithfield fire would correct our theology a good deal ; the old gibbet would take the fretfulness out of our tone ; the great earthquake rocking our cities would make us forget our animosities and unite us in bolder intercession. This is the meaning of your commercial depressions, of your mercantile losses, of your great and small afflictions in the family. This is the meaning of the little coffin in the upper chamber, of the father's dead body being carried out to the churchyard. This the meaning of all the gloom, and cloud, and battle, and contest. We have been too peevish, wandering, discontented. We have been in need of knowing the true tragedy of life and of being whipped out of our peddling criticism, out of our mean and contemptible conceptions of God and his universe ; and if we accept the Divine discipline in the right spirit, when that discipline has exhausted itself, each man will say for himself, " It was good for me that I was afflicted ; before I was afflicted I went astray." " No chastening for the present seemeth to be joyous, but grievous : nevertheless afterward it yieldeth the peaceable fruit of righteousness unto them which are exercised thereby." " My brethren, count it all joy when ye fall into divers temptations ; knowing this, that the trying of your faith worketh patience." When God sends the Amalekite upon you, it is that the enemy may teach what the friend has failed to convey.

A most beautiful picture :—the old men up the hill praying, Moses, and Aaron, and Hur—a man almost as mysterious in history as Melchisedek himself,—all the three men more than eighty years of age, away supplicating Heaven ; the young men fighting as young men always should be, and the Lord watching. Now the Amalekite prevails—now Israel. How goes the fight ? Watch the leader's arms. They are up ; then the banner is Israel's that floats with triumph in the hot air ;—the poor arms have fallen down, and Amalek springs towards the temporary victory It is a great parable ; it is a most tender idyl. This scene is full of present mystery and present grace. Mock the suppliants if you will ; but they are men who are engaged in the upper regions of the battle. They are not cowards who have fled from the fight, they are heroes who are standing at its front and have undertaken the responsibility of its success. Young men, go forth to the war. I am ashamed of the young man who stays at home and sates himself with debasing luxury, when there are great wars to be fought, great positions to be taken, mighty fortresses of evil to be overthrown. Awake ! awake ! put on thy strength, oh redeemed life, and carry the Lord's banner away to the front and set it up in sign of victory.

Wondrous is one little line in the history :—"And thy rod, wherewith thou smotest the river, take in thine hand, and go," and afterward Moses, having spoken to Joshua, said, " I will stand on the top of the hill with the rod of God in mine hand." Never forget the old rod, the old book, the old truth ;—the sword that cut off the head of Goliath—" Give me that," said David, " there is none like it." Thus God hides inspiration in things of apparently little value, and touches the imagination and the faith by books, ministries, churches, altars, which we thought had passed away into desuetude, perhaps oblivion. Your first prayer may help you to-day. The faith of your youth may be the only thing to win the battle which now challenges your strength. One little hour with the old, old book may be all you need to obtain the sufficiency of light which will drive away the cloud of mystery and bring in the heaven of explanation. Of ancient Rephidim we know nothing : the geographers and discoverers are still searching for it ; but the modern Rephidim of conscious necessity, of finding help in unexpected places, of having peevish tempers corrected by great duties,—that Rephidim is our present environment. May we answer the call of God when challenged to battle with a heroism that cannot cringe and with a faith that can only satisfy itself with prayer.

Exodus xviii.

1. When Jethro, the priest of Midian, Moses' father in law (his relation by marriage, a term of very wide application), heard of all that God had done for Moses, and for Israel his people, and that the Lord had brought Israel out of Egypt (the supreme fact);

2. Then Jethro, Moses' father in law, took Zipporah, Moses' wife, after he had sent her back (after her dismissal by Moses),

3. And her two sons; of which the name of the one was Gershom; for he said, I have been an alien in a strange land:

4. And the name of the other was Eliezer; for the God of my father, said he, was mine help, and delivered me from the sword of Pharaoh:

5. And Jethro, Moses' father in law, came with his sons and his wife unto Moses into the wilderness, where he encamped at the mount of God (used in a broad sense of the whole mountain region):

6. And he said unto Moses, I thy father in law Jethro am come unto thee, and thy wife, and her two sons with her.

7. And Moses went out to meet his father in law, and did obeisance (Oriental etiquette, not implying the superiority of Jethro), and kissed him (common form of salutation in the East); and they asked each other of their welfare (said to each other, Peace be with you); and they came into the tent.

8. And Moses told his father in law all that the Lord had done unto Pharaoh and to the Egyptians for Israel's sake, and all the travail that had come upon them by the way, and how the Lord delivered them.

9. And Jethro rejoiced for all the goodness which the Lord had done to Israel, whom he had delivered out of the hand of the Egyptians.

10. And Jethro said, Blessed be the Lord, who hath delivered you out of the hand of the Egyptians, and out of the hand of Pharaoh, who hath delivered the people from under the hand of the Egyptians.

11. Now I know that the Lord is greater than all gods: for in the thing wherein they dealt proudly he was above them.

12. And Jethro, Moses' father in law, took a burnt offering and sacrifices for God: and Aaron came, and all the elders of Israel, to eat bread with Moses' father in law before God (and thus acknowledged his priesthood, as Abraham had acknowledged the priesthood of Melchisedek).

13. And it came to pass on the morrow, that Moses sat to judge the people (ability to judge was thought to indicate fitness for kingship): and the people stood by Moses from the morning unto the evening.

14. And when Moses' father in law saw all that he did to the people, he said, What is this thing that thou doest to the people? why sittest thou thyself alone (this word is emphatic), and all the people stand by thee from morning unto even ?

15. And Moses said unto his father in law, Because the people come unto me to inquire of God :

16. When they have a matter, they come unto me; and I judge between one and another, and I do make them know the statutes of God, and his laws.

17. And Moses' father in law said unto him. The thing that thou doest is not good.

18. Thou wilt surely wear away, both thou, and this people that is with thee: for this thing is too heavy for thee; thou art not able to perform it thyself alone.

19. Hearken now unto my voice, I will give thee counsel, and God shall be with thee (May God be with thee, a prayer rather than a promise) : Be thou for the people to God-ward, that thou mayest bring the causes unto God (do the highest work) :

20. And thou shalt teach them ordinances and laws, and shalt shew them the way wherein they must walk, and the work that they must do.

21. Moreover thou shalt provide out of all the people able men (Jethro himself had his subordinates), such as fear God, men of truth, hating covetousness (a comprehensive description of "able men"); and place such over them, to be rulers of thousands, and rulers of hundreds, rulers of fifties, and rulers of tens (organisation on the decimal system) :

22. And let them judge the people at all seasons : and it shall be, that every great matter they shall bring unto thee, but every small matter they shall judge : so shall it be easier for thyself, and they shall bear the burden with thee.

23. If thou shalt do this thing, and God command thee so, then thou shalt be able to endure, and all this people shall also go to their place in peace.

24. So Moses hearkened to the voice of his father in law, and did all that he had said.

25. And Moses chose able men out of all Israel, and made them heads over the people, rulers of thousands, rulers of hundreds, rulers of fifties, and rulers of tens.

26. And they judged the people at all seasons : the hard causes they brought unto Moses, but every small matter they judged themselves.

27. And Moses let his father in law depart; and he went his way into his own land.

JETHRO'S COUNSEL TO MOSES.

THE work which Moses attempted in his own strength strongly indicated the character of the man. He undertook to settle the dispute between the Egyptian and the Hebrew, and he did settle it by the destruction of the former. He interposed between the Hebrews who were striving one with another, and would have determined the contest without consultation with any man. He asked no help when he saw the shepherds ill-treating the daughters of Jethro ; he took counsel with himself alone, and delivered the maidens from their oppressors. In the case before us we see precisely the same characteristics : Moses was the sovereign of Israel, and as such administered all matters, great and small. He did not foresee the results of the service in which he was so laboriously engaged. It was an older head than his own that saw the consequences of toil so uninterrupted and exhausting. For the time being Moses was borne up by the excitement of the situation, or by his love of the work; but Jethro foresaw that an increase of this kind of exacting labour would wear out the strongest and boldest man in all the hosts of Israel. The worker does not always see the bearing or the issues of the ministry in which he is engaged. Excitement suspends the judicial faculty. The warrior in the midst of the battle is not in a position to judge so completely and certainly as the spectator who observes the scene from a distance. It ought to be the part of a wise and generous friendship to point out to men when they are working too much, and wasting in exaggeration energies which might be beneficently exercised through a longer period of time. Some men live intensely,—their lives are short, but the measure of their service is complete ; they do not pause, they have no Sabbath days : with an unwise prodigality they expend their whole force within a brief hour. Such men are not always just to society. A rich man has no right to give so profusely as to cut off the occasion of liberality in others. The strong man ought not to be at liberty to do so much work with his own hands as to render the labour of others unnecessary.

It was upon this principle that Jethro proceeded in the case of Moses. The great leader of Israel, though leading a life of laborious self-sacrifice, was actually falling below the requirements of social justice. He seemed to be acting on the conviction that he only could manage, arrange, and otherwise successfully administer all the affairs of the people. It never occurred to him that he was allowing the talent of others to lie idle. Talent requires to be evoked. It is true indeed that genius asserts itself, and clears for itself space and prominence equal to its measure of supremacy ; on the other hand, it is equally true that much sound ability may become dormant, simply because the leaders of society do not call it into responsible exercise. The counsel which Moses received from Jethro inspired Israel with new life. From the moment that it was acted upon, talent rose to the occasion : energy was accounted of some value, and men who had probably been sulking in the background came to be recognised and honoured as wise statesmen and cordial allies. There is more talent in society than we suspect. It needs the sunshine of wise encouragement in order to develop it. There is a lesson in this suggestion for all who lead the lives of men. Specially, perhaps, there is a lesson to pastors of churches. It is a poor church in which there is not more talent than has yet been developed. When Saul saw any strong man and any valiant man, he took him to himself. This is the law of sure progress and massive consolidation in church life. Let us keep our eyes open for men of capacity and good-will, and the more we watch the more shall our vigilance be rewarded. We should try men by imposing responsibilities upon them. There is range enough in church organisation for the trial and strengthening of every gift. Better be a door-keeper in the house of God than a sluggard, and infinitely better sweep the church floor than lounge upon the pew-top, and find fault with the sweeping of other people. Every man in the Church ought to be doing something. If the pattern be taken from the case described in the context, there need be no fear of rivalry or tumult. The arrangement indicated by Jethro was based upon the severest discipline. The position of Moses was supreme and undisputed ; every great case was to be referred to his well-tried judgment, and in all cases of contention his voice was to determine the counsels of the camp. There must be a ruling mind in the Church, and all impertinence and other self-exaggeration must be content to bow submissively to the master-will. Very possibly there may be danger in sudden development of mental activity and social influence ; but it must be remembered, on the other hand, that there is infinitely deadlier peril in allowing spiritual energy and emotion to fall into disuse. In the former case we may have momentary impertinence, conceit, and coxcombry ; but in the latter we shall have paralysis and distortion more revolting than death itself.

Jethro counselled Moses " to be for the people God-ward, that he might bring the causes unto God." The highest of all vocations is the spiritual. It is greater to pray than to rule. Moses was to set himself at the highest end of the individual, political, and religious life of Israel, and to occupy the position of intercessor. He was to be the living link between the people and their God. Is not this the proper calling of the preacher ? He is not to be a mere politician in the Church, he is not to enter into the detail of organisation with the scrupulous care of a conscientious hireling : he is deeply and lovingly to study the truth as it is in Jesus, that he may be prepared to enrich the minds and stimulate the graces of those who hear him. He is to live so closely with God, that his voice shall be to them as the voice of no other man, a voice from the better world, calling the heart to worship, to trust, and to hope, and through the medium of devotion to prepare men for all the engagements of common life. The preacher is to live apart from the people, in order that he may in spiritual sympathy live the more truly with them. He is not to stand afar off as an unsympathetic priest, but to live in the secret places of the Most High, that he may from time to time most correctly repronounce the will of God to all who wait upon his ministry. When preachers live thus, the pulpit will reclaim its ancient power, and fill all rivalry with confusion and shame. Let the people themselves manage all subordinate affairs ; call up all the business talent that is in the Church, and honour all its successful and well-meant experiments ; give every man to feel that he has an obligation to answer. When you have done this, go yourself, O man of God, to the temple of the Living One, and acquaint yourself deeply with the wisdom and grace of God, that you may be as an angel from heaven when you come to speak the word of life to men who are worn by the anxieties and weakened by the temptations of a cruel world.

Many a man inquires, half in petulance and half in self-justification, " What more can I possibly do than I am already doing?" Let the case of Moses be the answer. The question in his case was not whether he was doing enough, but whether he was not doing too much in one special direction. Some of the talent that is given to business might be more profitably given to devotion. Rule less, and pray more. Spare time from the business meeting that you may have leisure for communion with God. Some persons apparently suppose that time is lost which is not spent

in the excitement of social activity. Understand that silence may
be better than speech, that prayer is the best preparation for
service; and that the duties of magistracy may well be displaced
by the higher duties of spiritual devotion. Moses was, undoubtedly, to all human appearance, a much busier man when
he did all the business of Israel himself than when he called
lieutenants to his assistance; but what was subtracted from his
activity was added to the wealth of his heart, and though he
made less noise, he exerted a wider influence. Is there not a
lesson for the people in the position which Moses occupied at the
suggestion of Jethro? Is it nothing to society to have intercessors? Is it nothing that the chief minds of the age should be
engaged in the study of truth for the benefit of others? It ought
to be the supreme joy of our social life that there are men of
capacity, of earnestness, and of high spiritual penetration and
sympathy, who devote their whole energy to the stimulus and
culture of our best powers. The ministry of any country should
be the fountain of its power. Ministers are to study the
character of God, to acquaint themselves with all the secrets of
truth, and to comprehend as far as possible the necessity and
desire of the human heart, and the result of their endeavours
will express itself in a luminous and tender ministry. This is
work enough for any man. He who is faithful to this vocation
will find that he has no energy to spare for the trifles of a
moment, or even for the subordinate questions of serious public
life. The time which a minister spends in secrecy may enable
him most successfully to teach the deep things of God. It is
not enough that he be prepared with matter, he must have time
and opportunity to enter into the *spirit* of his work. His
knowledge may be wide and correct, but whatever is wanting
in the reality and sensitiveness of his sympathy will be so much
subtracted from his spiritual wisdom and strength.

Exodus xix. 1-13.

1. In the third month, when the children of Israel were gone forth out of the land of Egypt, the same day came they into the wilderness of Sinai (about eighteen miles).

2. For they were departed from Rephidim, and were come to the desert of Sinai, and had pitched in the wilderness; and there Israel camped before the mount.

3. And Moses went up unto God (ascended Sinai), and the Lord called unto him out of the mountain (while he was yet a great way off), saying, Thus shalt thou say to the house of Jacob, and tell the children of Israel:

4. Ye have seen what I did unto the Egyptians, and how I bare you on eagles' wings ("As an eagle stirreth up her nest, fluttereth over her young, spreadeth abroad her wings, taketh them, beareth them upon her wings"), and brought you unto myself (out of Egypt and its corrupting influences).

5. Now therefore, if ye will obey my voice indeed, and keep my covenant, then ye shall be a peculiar treasure (some valuable possession which the owner has got by his own exertions) unto me above all people: for all the earth is mine:

6. And ye shall be unto me a kingdom of priests, and an holy nation. These are the words which thou shalt speak unto the children of Israel.

7. And Moses came and called for the elders (the usual channel of communication) of the people, and laid before their faces (a curious piece of literalism) all these words which the Lord commanded him.

8. And all the people answered together, and said, All that the Lord hath spoken we will do. And Moses returned (reported) the words of the people unto the Lord.

9. And the Lord said unto Moses, Lo, I come unto thee in a thick cloud (in the denseness of a cloud) that the people may hear when I speak with thee, and believe thee for ever. And Moses told the words of the people unto the Lord.

10. And the Lord said unto Moses, Go unto the people, and sanctify them (an outward purification symbolic of inward fitness) to day and to morrow, and let them wash their clothes (the Levitical law requires the washing of clothes on many occasions),

11. And be ready against the third day: for the third day the Lord will come down in the sight of all the people upon mount Sinai.

12. And thou shalt set bounds unto the people round about, saying, Take heed to yourselves, that ye go not up into the mount, or touch the border of it: whosoever toucheth the mount shall be surely put to death:

13. There shall not an hand touch it, but he shall surely be stoned, or shot through; whether it be beast or man, it shall not live: when the trumpet soundeth long, they shall come up to the mount.

THE RESULTS OF OBEDIENCE.

ISRAEL having gone from Rephidim, came to the desert of
Sinai, and there Moses, having gone up the mountain, received
from God a distinct message, "If ye will obey my voice, ye shall
be a peculiar treasure unto me." This is a tabernacle without
form ; this is a sanctuary not made with hands. If we can seize
the meaning of this passage we shall have in our hands one of the
key-paragraphs of the whole history. Let us try to classify the
thoughts which grow as in a garden planted by the Lord himself;
a garden whose hedges are far away ; for he whose mercy
endureth for ever makes no small gardens ; he would, indeed,
have no desert land.

Here is a Gospel originating in heaven. Moses is not the leading speaker. No desire has been expressed by the people that
any such arrangement as this should be completed. The movement is always from above. The rains that water the earth, that
make it bring forth and bud, are clouds far above our heads
and far beyond our influence. The great thoughts all come down
tipped with a light above the brightness of the sun. If any man
lack wisdom he is to ask of God. It is not a plant that is grown
in the clay ; it is a flower that blossoms and blooms in the eternal
paradise. Keep this steadily in mind in the perusal of the sacred
record, that no great thought ever came from the human side.
Man has had but to reply; the infinite appeals of judgment and
of grace have come out of the hidden heavens. We are, therefore, debtors to grace. We have nothing that is worth having
that is of our own invention or manufacture. All eternal thought
and all eternal feeling, being wise, pure, and beneficent, can be
traced to him who giveth all good and perfectness. This is the
foundation thought.

Now comes a Divine method which attests the heavenliness of
its origin, having about it all the mystery of the infinite and
unspeakable. God says : "If ye will obey my voice indeed, and
keep my covenant." Can he not make them do so ? There is no
compulsion in worship, or in morals, or in true spiritual obedience.
A child can turn his back upon God and treat the Almighty with
sullenness. The tiniest knee can stiffen itself, and decline to bow

before the heavens. In its bodily relation, it can be crushed, broken, destroyed; but representing the mind, the heart, the will, God cannot bend that obstinate iron. So God begins by seeking consent. Man has to be a party to this marvellous covenant. If we sing, it is because our love is so burning that we cannot keep back the music; if we obey, it is because our hearts consent to the statute which demands obedience. Has God, then, given any detailed laws up to this time which he means the people to accept? No. Here is the wondrousness of the method, the laws —using that word in the plural number—have yet to come. Mark the Divine wisdom—the wondrous reach of the Divine thought. To have come with ten words, or a thousand lines of statute and precept would have excited argument and discontent, criticism, and possible rebellion. Not a word was said about the detail. God will not light the mountain until the sacrifice is prepared; the smoke, and the fire, and the trumpet will come by-and-by. What is first wanted? The spirit, not the act, of obedience. Everything turns upon that distinction. God asks broadly and comprehensively for obedience. He must have a spirit in tune with the music of his own purpose, and then, as to the separate melodies that must be played, they will fall into their right place, and will assume new relations and new value, because of the spirit of obedience which has been enkindled and sanctified in the human heart. That is the Divine philosophy— not to come with two tables of stone, and to invite detailed criticism and wordy controversy, but to face the creature, as it were, and to say, "Wilt thou obey thy Creator in very deed?" The creature answers gladly, "I will." After that you may have as many tables of stone as the occasion requires, or as human development may call for in the ages of education yet to dawn upon an advancing race.

Mark the wondrousness of the Divine providence, and the Divine method : First, the spirit of obedience is created; then the separate words, or individual and singular laws, are uttered to a prepared heart. Probably it could be proved that a great deal of our conscious disobedience has arisen from our looking at the law we have to obey, rather than preparing the heart to obey the whole counsel of God. You have no right to look at the laws, until you have promised obedience, and pledged with an oath of the heart that you will be true to the Divine proposals. Men first disqualify themselves for judgment, and then proceed to criticism; they say, "What are the Commandments?" That is not a permissible inquiry. We are not dealing with plurals and details, with daily discipline and momentary demands; we are dealing with the soul of things, with the spirit of man, with the mood and temper of the heart. Granted that all is right in this direction, then turn to the laws, and you will take them up as a very little thing, understanding the sweet music of him who came to "fulfil the law." "My yoke is easy, and my burden is light," —a most heavy yoke and a burden grievous beyond all other weight, if we come to it without a prepared spirit; but having filled the heart with preparedness, and filled the mouth with a song of adoration and a hymn of loyalty, then let the tables of stone come to us: the stones shall have no hardness, and the law shall no longer be arbitrary, but part of the happy music and sacred necessity which characterise the whole order and intent of God.

Here is the explanation of the Divine preferences which have distressed so many hearts under the cruel name of sovereignty and election. There need be no torture in using those words. If we feel distressed by them, it is because we have come upon them along the wrong path. They are beautiful and noble words when set in their places according to the Divine intent. "Then ye shall be a peculiar treasure unto me above all people." Is that partiality in any exclusive sense? Not at all; it is really meant to be *inclusive.* God elects *humanity.* "And ye shall be unto me a kingdom." In what sense? In the ordinary sense— namely, a great aggregate of subjects ruled by one arbitrary and despotic king? In no such sense. The literal meaning is, ye shall *all* be kings. Now you see the meaning of that great name, "King of kings"—not king of an individual monarch here and there, as in Britain, or Russia, or China, but of all believers. All obedient souls are lifted up unto kinghood. We are royal equals if we obey Heaven's will, and God is King of kings,—King of all. We are a royal generation. All this language is typical. Beautiful is the historical line when seized and wisely applied. Let **us attempt such seizure and application.** The firstborn were chosen, and the firstborn were to be priests. In what sense are the firstborn chosen? Not as relegating the afterborn to positions subordinate and inferior; but in the sense of being their pledge and seal. God has the eldest son, and therefore—that is the sacred logic—he has all the other children. Then the laws regarding the priesthood underwent a change, and the family of Aaron was called. We proceed from an individual, namely, the firstborn, to a family, namely, the Aaronic stock. But why were they chosen? That all the children of Aaron might also be priests, in the truly spiritual and eternal sense, though not in official and formal name and status. Then the family was deposed and a tribe is chosen—the tribe of Levi. Mark how the history accumulates and grows up into a prophecy and an argument! First the individual, then the family, then the tribe, then the Son of man,—absorbing all the past, gathering up into its true and official meaning all priesthood, all intercession. There is one Advocate with the Father, the Man Christ Jesus.

A new light thus begins to dawn upon the cloud. There is nothing arbitrary in the movement of God when we can penetrate its infinite philosophy. Will God have the first-fruits of the harvest field? He claims all such. Why will he claim the first-fruits? That in having the first-fruits he might have all the field. He will not take the whole wheat acreage of the world into his heavens and devour our poor loaf of bread; but he will take the first ear of corn that we can find in all the fields, and, having taken that, he says: "In giving me this you have given me all." He is not to be charged with arbitrariness and severity because he takes one little ear of corn, or one poor little sheep, and says, "This is mine." He is to be charged with a nobler grace than our fancy had dreamed, for he takes a visit to the poor prisoner as a visit paid to himself, bread given to the poor as bread given to the Triune God. The lifting up of one sheaf of wheat and waving it before him is not the result of an arbitrary sovereignty, but is sign, symbol, and type that we have given him all—that "the earth is the Lord's, and the fulness thereof." The Lord said to the man whom he constituted the new head of the race: "In thee shall all the families of the earth be blessed." Think of that noble inclusion when you speak of elective sovereignty and reprobating judgment.

This also throws light upon the vexed question of inspiration. We ask, "Why were some inspired?" You say Moses and David, Isaiah and Daniel, and John and Paul—they were inspired that we might all be inspired. They are the firstborn; they are the leaders and prototypes. Because Paul was inspired, it does not follow that the Holy Ghost is withheld from us. The Spirit is the abiding Comforter; he is the possession of the whole redeemed and regenerated Church. He will never leave us. Know ye not that ye are the temples of the Holy Ghost? Do not dwarf the mighty argument by asking shallow questions about the relative degrees of inspiration. We cannot discuss an inquiry which lies beyond the evidence at our command. Enough it is to know that the Holy Ghost is Christ's gift to the whole believing Church. "If ye then, being evil, know how to give good gifts unto your children: how much more shall your heavenly Father give the Holy Spirit to them that ask him!" So the whole idea of priestism is destroyed, and the whole conception of arbitrary and despotic sovereignty goes down, and must be branded as an unspeakable blasphemy. We are all kings and priests unto God and the Father; we are all royal, chosen, elect, precious. This conception alone fits the character of him who is symbolised by the firmament, and who gives good things to the unthankful and to the evil, as well as to the grateful and the good.

Here is God's conception of "an holy nation." A holy nation in the Divine view is an obedient nation, a nation living in the spirit of obedience. Let the spirit of obedience be right, and the letter of obedience will soon become right also. First must come the spirit, then the literal obedience. So in all things. Our Christian character in its integrity and massiveness is destroyed by our foolish attention in the wrong place to detailed precepts and instances. It is notably so in the matter of Christian liberality. There are but few who understand the philosophy of joyous consecration in this department. What is wanting? The total gift. If it were a question of detail as to whether this or that sum should be given, or the whole appeal be shirked, then a series of vexations would torment the conscience and the judgment. There is no such law. We give the all, and therefore it becomes quite easy to give the little particular. But until we have given the all we cannot give the other. It may be extorted from our hands by a complaining conscience, but it is no acceptable oblation on the altar of the Church. It is notably so in the matter of time. How do we come to give one day in seven to Christ's worship? We do so, when we do it at all properly, because we have first given all the seven days. It is easy to give one in particular when we have consecrated the whole. The one day is the wheat-sheaf taken up from the harvest of time, and God says, receiving it, " You have given me all the days in giving me this, the queen-liest of the seven." This is the meaning of still being under the law and not under grace, namely, that we are striving to do little things, and separate laws, and keep particular commandments with which we have no business, until the soul is adjusted by the meridian of the eternal sovereignty, and the whole spirit goes out only anxious to obey.

Read the commandments in the light of this explanation, and how easy they are. " *Thou shalt have no other gods before me.*" The soul is amazed—as if the conception of having any other God could have dawned upon such glowing love. " *Honour thy father and thy mother.*" The spirit springs up, and says, " Nothing can be easier, more delightful, or in accord with my wish." " *Thou shalt not steal.*" The heart is, as it were, momentarily and subtly affronted—as if such a commandment could be needed, where the sacrifice of the body is so complete. Was the human obedience first pledged? So was the Divine promise. The way of the Lord is equal. Did he who asked for the obedience lay down the ground of his claim? He did, saying, " Ye have seen what I did unto the Egyptians, and how I bare you on eagles' wings, and brought you unto myself." First the history, then the obedience, then the promise, then the detailed law; and the detailed law coming after the promise becomes an easy burden, and a yoke so light as to be like a necklet of jewels.

THE COMMANDMENTS.

WE cannot get rid of Sinai in human education. If we persuade ourselves by some false reasoning that the things recorded in these chapters did not literally happen, we are playing the fool with ourselves. God could only come to us at the first by the letter. He touches us by infinite accommodations of his own nature and by a gracious study of our own. This is the plague of the imperfect reason, that it will quibble about the incident, the wrappage, and decoration of things. It seems to be unable to penetrate to inmost thoughts, essences, qualities, and meanings. Sinai is in every life. Let us part with as much as we can of the merely external, and still there remains the fact that in our lives are lightnings, and thunderings, and great trumpetings of power, as well as solemn claims and urgent appeals to every quality and force in our nature. Who has not been in stony places in the carrying out of his education,—great, black, inhospitable localities, well called *wildernesses;* wild and howling deserts; mountains of stone; embodiments of difficulty; types of arduous discipline and inexorable demand? Why play the fool? Why miss the wine of God's grace and wisdom by asking narrow or foolish questions about the vessel which contains it, when within the whole mystery of life there stands the barren mountain—the inhospitable sand stretches mile on mile on every hand and nothing speaks to us in all the terrific scene but law, claim, and obligation—the tremendous demand of an unyielding creditor, who has come to arrest and imprison us until the uttermost farthing be paid? Our spiritual experience makes the letter quite small. There are still those who are asking questions about the local Sinai, the narrow and comparatively trivial incident, and are missing all the poetry of the occasion, not hearing the Divine and solemn voice, and not an wering the sublime demand for more perfect purification, completer refinement, and profounder obedience. Why not start our inquiries from the other side ?—What is this voice of law ? What is this standard of discipline which forces itself upon our moral attention ? What is this claim that is pressed upon us by every variety of expression which follows us, now affrontingly, now pleading, according to the moral phase which we exhibit towards it ? Did we begin our inquiry at that end, and so come along the line of revelation, Sinai, the local mountain, and the desert, and all trumpetings, thunderings, lightnings, tempests, all upheavals, and earthquakes, and terrible scenes, would fall into their right proportion and relation, and the one sovereign thought would be, —Lord, what wilt thou have me to do ?

Instead of looking at the commandments one by one, and thus running the risk of missing their whole meaning, let us look at the commandments in their totality and call them One Commandment with many different phases, and aspects, and bearings upon human life.

What is the teaching of that great law pronounced from heaven ? Is there any grace in it ? Is there any touch of love ? Is there any trembling of pathos ? Is it all hard iron ? Is it all tremendous exaction, pitiless, tyrannous claim ? Have we always read the commandments aright ? and have we been just to their innermost meaning when we have characterised them as hard ? I think not. What do these commandments urge upon us ?— *A right view of God.* That is the first injunction. We are called to right theology—not of a formal and technical, but of a moral and spiritual kind. The great movement of the heart must first of all be God-ward. We cannot work until the soul is brought into the right mood and proper quality by a full perception of the sovereignty and righteous claim and tender grace of God. We cannot break in upon the commandments where we please, and obey the law in parts and parcels. There is a temptation to think we can do so. We are sometimes tempted to think that we can keep the eighth commandment, but not the fifth; the fourth, but not the ninth; the tenth, but not the first, and so on. That is impossible. To keep one commandment is to keep all; to offend in one commandment is to break all. This may not seem to be so on the surface; but a complete analysis of the occasion and circumstances will result in the finding that the commandments are one law, complete, indivisible, only set forth in points and aspects for the convenience of learners, and as an accommodation to the infirmity or incompleteness of children. First of all, then, we are called to a right view of God. We cannot move one step in a right direction until something like this view has been realised. Every succeeding commandment will be dumb to us, if we have not entered into the mystery of the first. What is God to us? What are his claims upon us? What is there in us that responds to his presence, and that, so to say, reveals him before he comes with any obvious manifestation of his personality upon us? Are we akin? Are we his children? Is there any sound in the ear or the heart which, being interpreted, means,—" In the beginning God made man in his own image and likeness"? That is our first study. We shall be mere moralists if we begin at the second commandment. That is so-called legalism and morality, —the pedantry which snaps off the commandments from the great central stem and treats them as separate particles, as isolated possibilities of virtue. We must come from the Divine point, from the spiritual communion of the soul with God, and then the commandments will come upon our souls as appeals to our power, and as sweet necessities, not as arbitrary impositions and tyrannies.

What next have we in this consolidated commandment? Having a right view of God, we have a right view, in the next place, of *labour.* God condescends to take notice of our working ways, of our allotments and appointments of a temporal kind. The voice of mercy is in this injunction regarding labour. In effect, God says to us, "You must not always toil; your heads must not be bent down in continual proneness to the earth; you may labour six days, but the seventh part of your time should be devoted to spiritual communion, to the culture of the upper and better nature, to the promotion of your higher and nobler education." This is the gracious law; but, say, is this law without tears? Is this commandment without grace? Is there no mercy here? Is there not a subtle allusion to an earlier charter in which God made man to commune with himself? If you are doomed to seven days' work, it is against God's mind. If any have to work seven days for the mouthful of bread they need, it is the doing of an enemy; it is not the claim of God. I ask you to praise him for this defence of feeble human nature and this plea for a higher human education. Do not fritter away the blessing by technical inquiry and pedantic analysis of meaning. The sublime, infinite purpose is this : that man is more than a labourer; he is a worshipper ; he is a kinsman of God; he has belongings in the sky. A religion that thus comes to me and takes me away from my toil, and bids me rest awhile and think of the larger quantities, and the more ample time, and the heavenly kingdoms, is a religion I cannot afford to do without. It is a religion of grace; it is a religion which knows my necessities, pities my infirmities, spares my wasting strength. The Sabbath, in its spiritual aspect and meaning, is one of the strongest defences of the inspiration of the Bible and the Divinity of the religion which it reveals. It is man's day and God's day ; more thoroughly man's day because completely God's day. It is their united time,—time of fellowship, hour of communion, opportunity for deeper reading, larger prayer, and Diviner consecration.

Having a right view of God and a right view of labour, we have also a right view of *physiology*. The Bible takes care of man's body. Thou shalt not waste it ; thou shalt not poison it ; thou shalt not degrade the inner nature by a prostitution of the outer constitution. "Thou shalt not commit adultery." A commandment which so speaks to us is associated with a religion that is no merely spiritual phantasy. This is a practical monitor. It enters every room, remains in the house night and day, tarries as a guest seven days a week, goes out with us to the market-place, takes care of our bodily ablution and cleansing, and regards the sanctity of the body with a Divine care. Who are they that tell us that the Bible religion is a superstition, an affair of fancy, something having in it bright points here and there, and to be treated with proportionate respect ? The Bible searches us, tries us, and finds if there is any wicked way in us, and is as careful about the body in its degree as about the soul in its higher plane, because nobler quantity. No man ill-treats his body with the permission of the Bible ; no soul quenches its thirst at forbidden wells with the sanction of the Book which we believe to be God's. The Bible would keep society sweet, would watch over our life with ineffable tenderness, would have us right in tone, wholesome, good at every point. A book so graciously exacting, charged with so Divine a spirit of discipline, is a book which will survive every assault made upon it, and return to the confidence of man after many an act of apostacy and ingratitude on his part.

A right view of God, a right view of labour, a right view of physiology, and then a right view of *society.* Not only is God interested in the individual man, he is also interested in the social, imperial, national world—humanity. What says he?— "Thou shalt not kill,"—however hot thy blood, thou shalt not kill; however apparently just thine anger, restrain thyself, lift not the hand to strike, have no weapon in thy fist,—"Thou shalt not kill." Woe betide society when it holds human life lightly, when it regards human existence as a mere trifle in an infinite aggregate of circumstances and events! Blessed be that society which numbers the hairs of its children, in which a sparrow is not lost without knowledge, and in which a gracious economy will gather up the fragments that nothing be lost! This is Christian society which will not allow one chair to be vacant. Seeing that vacant chair, Christian solicitude becomes akin to Divine agony; a parental yearning makes the heart sore because one little child is absent, one wanderer is not at home, one man is missing.

"Thou shalt not steal." It is not enough to be less than a murderer, we must be honest,—not superficially honest, not having hands merely untainted with overt crime, and theft, and felony; but thoroughly honest, sweet in the soul, really, superbly, almost Divinely honest in thought, in speech, in feeling, and in all the relations of life. Where is there an honest man, except in the common and superficial sense of a man who is not a thief? Honesty is not a negative virtue; honesty is a positive excellence. It renders to every man his due; it steals no man's reputation; it trifles with the property of no heart; it is more anxious to give than to take away. "Thou shalt not covet." We are becoming more spiritual still. "Thou shalt not kill,"—to that we assented readily; "Thou shalt not steal,"—to that we also assented with large concession; "Thou shalt not covet,"—who knows when he covets? We can covet in secret; we can covet, and never speak about the covetousness. Desire need not commit itself to audible terms. We can desire what another man has and yet can look the embodiment of innocence. The law is now becoming sharper, keener, more like a two-edged sword piercing to the dividing asunder of the joints and marrow. We cannot keep company with this law in its inner and deeper meanings without finding that its intention is to divide us asunder, and search us, and try us, and never leave us until we become like the Law-giver himself. Can we wonder that Jesus Christ said he had not come to destroy but to fulfil?—that is, to interpret the law and give it its fullest and deepest meaning. When asked what the law was, he said, ' All the law is fulfilled in one word—love." But we read the commandments and found no love in them,—because we misread every tone in the ancient and solemn music. You could not have the commandment but for the love which makes it law. Outwardly it looks iron-like, stern, rigorous, exacting, pitiless; but within its heart is large as the heart of God.

Mark the elevation of the commandments,—of what god are they unworthy? Their Divinity must have impressed us. Point out one weak word; lay the critical finger upon one line that is wanting in intellectual dignity or in moral splendour. By the nature of the laws themselves their inspiration may be vindicated. A bold task it was for any mere poet or dreamer to attempt to invent a commandment which would be worthy of God; but the task was realised. Great opening lines have been expressed in the very finest terms, in the most delicate and exquisite exactions and compulsions. Nowhere does this Decalogue fray away into pointlessness, vagueness, intellectual meanness, moral declension. From first to last the level is one, and the level is worthy of God. To find fault with the commandments is to injure ourselves; to trifle with the commandments is to jeopardise society. They are not repeated formally in the New Testament, but they are fulfilled in that holy covenant. We are now in Christ Jesus, if we are living up to Gospel privileges and opportunities; and, being in him, we breathe the commandments, rather than execute them as with arduous effort. They become part of our very life; they belong to us as the fragrance belongs to the odorous flower. They are no longer burdens grievous to be borne. We love them because we have experienced their love. Away with moral legerdemain ! Away with the gymnastics which attempt to climb to heaven by their own moral cleverness ! We must go the right road, from God to man, from the law to the neighbour, from the heavenly image to the social obligation; and if the Church would, in the spirit of Christ, without one taint of legalism or servility, keep the commandments, we should have a right view of God, a right view of labour, a right view of the body, and a right view of society. The life would be consolidated upon love and law, and lifting itself up with infinite strength, would be crowned with beauty, and on the top of the pillar would be lilywork; RIGHTEOUSNESS and GRACE would form one noble, sublime, everlasting figure.

NOTE.

"The promulgation of the law, including the construction of the tabernacle, occupied nearly twelve months—from Whitsuntide to Whitsuntide—as we should say. Throughout this period the people were encamped in the wide plain at the foot of the 'Mount of God.' The whole region seems to be called 'Horeb'; the *mount* is called 'Sinai.' Travellers seem now disposed to identify it with an isolated mountain which rises so abruptly from the great plain at its foot, that its northern cliff might be said to be touched by one standing in the plain. The northern peak is called Ras-Susâfeh; the southern, Jebel-Mûsa. It rises to a height of 2,000 feet above the plain, and about 7,000 above the sea level."—*Bible Educator.*

"A spacious plain (Er Rahah) confronts a precipitous cliff 2,000 feet in height, which forms the north-western boundary of that great mountain block called Jebel-Mûsa, which tradition and the opinion of travellers and authors of eminence alike point to as the mountain of the law. The plain is of a level character—as flat as the palm (*rahah*) of the open hand. It is large enough, if needs be, to encamp all the hosts of the Israelites. There are fully 400 acres of the plain proper, exactly facing the mount, with a wide lateral valley, which extends right and left from the base of the cliffs. Besides this, there is a considerable further open space extending north-westward from the watershed or crest of the plain, but still in sight of the mount—the very spot, it may be, to which the trembling Israelites 'removed and stood afar off' when they feared to come nigh by reason of the cloud and thick darkness."—CAPTAIN PALMER.

Exodus xxi., xxii.

MINOR LEGISLATION.

WE have just heard the ten words. They deafened us For a time we could not sufficiently discriminate between the accompaniments and the words themselves, for they were all blended in a most majestic and solemn music. Immediately following the ten words we find the almost endless details relating to human conduct and society which fill these chapters. The details are called "judgments," and they were spoken by the Lord whose voice was heard in the great thunders of Sinai. It is the same Lord; but how different is the voice! What a quiet tone pervades the utterance of the judgments! Was it really so quiet? or quiet only by contrast? What voice would not seem to be quietness itself after the reverberations of the thunder that shook the mount of God? In the one case, we have what we may term a very agony of legislation; in the second, a tranquil conversation or a private instruction. The figure which suggests itself instantly to the mind upon reading the twentieth chapter of Exodus and those chapters immediately following, is the figure of a torrent succeeded by a river. In the commandments we have a cataract rushing with infinite force; in the judgments we have that same cataract softened and quieted down into deep fluent water. If in the commandments, distinctively so called, we see the Sovereignty and Majesty of God, in the judgments we see the Fatherhood and gentleness of the Lord. In the commandments he stands far away from us, and drops upon the staggering earth syllables of lightning that make men afraid, —hence the people said unto Moses, "Speak thou with us, and we will hear; but let not God speak with us lest we die."

Some voices need to be accommodated to the hearing that is infirm. The great thunder cannot be borne seven days a week.

To hear it now and again is a sacred and memorable event; but we were not made—so frail are we—constantly to be addressed by thunder and tempest. As if God had heard the request, he gave Moses the instruction which fills these two chapters. The tone of this minor legislation, if it may be so called, is full of Divine care for Divine work. The provisions of this code relate specifically to *life*. They are, as it were, commandments which God addresses to himself and which he then remits to the people. He will take care of everything he has made; nothing escapes his attention. He did not make the eye for nothing, or the ear as an exercise of his power for the gratification of his vanity. Every hair of the head is claimed by him who made it. "If a man smite the eye of his servant, or the eye of his maid, that it perish; he shall let him go free for his eye's sake." We can trust this legislator,—he cares for the serving man, for the serving woman. What price does he put upon the smitten and perished eye? Liberty! In truth, he values his creatures highly. Not one day's rest, not one week's remission from labour, not one year's holiday; but—liberty! "And if he smite out his manservant's tooth, or his maidservant's tooth, he shall let him go free for his tooth's sake." What a singular balance! In the one scale a tooth, wickedly struck out, cruelly injured; in the other scale—liberty! Surely, the injured man has in some sense the best of it. Yet only in a local and narrow way: for truly interpreted, nothing can compare in value with anything the Lord God has made. The Maker charges highly for all his works. You must not trifle with your own eye, with your own tooth, with your own fingers,—they are God's. "Know ye not that your body is the temple of the Holy Ghost?" Are you still under the narrow baptism that teaches that a man's eye is his own, or his tooth, or his hand, or his ear? Into what baptism have you been baptised? Not into the baptism of Christ, if you are trusting to these base sophisms. "Whether we live, we live unto the Lord; and whether we die, we die unto the Lord." We have nothing that we have not received. We are not our own; we are bought with a price; therefore glorify God in your body, which is Christ's. Whilst men are careless about the body, they cannot be careful about the soul. You cannot be careful about one part of God's work and careless

about another. A great argument sets in here. We must watch
its majestic construction and prepare for its gracious and solemn
application. In these two chapters everything goes down before
manhood. The master has a writing by which he claims some
property in the servant, but that covenant goes down before the
manhood of the person who is held in temporary servitude. Man
first, institutions next. "The Sabbath was made for man, and
not man for the Sabbath." Nothing you can build up around man
is so precious as the man himself. This is the central truth of
Divine revelation. In fact this explains everything which makes
up the mystery and the singular characteristic of the Bible.
Philosophers endeavour to render in some brief and memorable
formula the result of all investigations,—here is one which will
serve our purpose in the meantime. The value which God sets
upon man is the key-thought of the Scriptures. He begins now
with some solicitude about the eye, and the tooth, and the limb,
—by-and-by, who can tell what he will say? These are but
alphabetic signs,—symbols, suggestions,—who knows what literature he will work out of these few initial signs? We must
watch critically and religiously the outgoing and whole issue of
these, comparatively speaking, insignificant and trivial beginnings.
There is nothing trivial in heaven. All little laws are ruled by
laws greater than themselves. This also is a principle in the
Biblical philosophy,—if we neglect it we shall come speedily and
hopelessly into great moral confusion. You may be narrowly
right and broadly wrong. You may be operating by a little and
temporary law at the expense of an eternal and irreversible
statute or judgment Divine. Said the tempter to Christ, "All
these things will I give thee, if thou wilt fall down and worship
me." It is right to have the "things"; there is nothing whatsoever wrong in the temporary proprietorship of the things of earth
and time. The law quoted—"All these things will I give thee"
—is right enough within given limits. What is the greater law
that over-reaches this,—swallows it up? That greater law is,—
"Thou shalt not tempt the Lord thy God." All gifts, all
possessions, all rights, interests, institutions, expedients, understandings, covenants, must be held in obedience to that sovereign
and all-absorbing law.

The Divine care of the *body* is the beginning of a still wider and grander care. In the Old Testament the Lord could only begin with the body; any other speech would have been out of time, and, being out of season, would not have been understood. Its utterance would have created a perplexing mystery in the mind of man, and therefore would have led to all manner of misconception and misadventure. So the Lord begins by promising men *land,* and if the term *land* is not enough, he adds, the land is "flowing with milk and honey." The ancient man heard these words and understood them. Had he been promised a new realm of thought, a new imagination, a higher universe of dreams, he would not have understood the appeal. God promised his ancient ones *length of days,*—the only promise of the kind they could have understood. The world was not then prepared for the great word *Immortality,—Eternal Life.* So the Lord must begin according to the infancy of his pupils. They were but children; they would be pleased with milk and honey, and broad lands, long—long life. That was not the Divine meaning. The Lord could only rest for a moment in such a tabernacle as that. He never puts up a tabernacle without meaning a temple; he never offers land without meaning heaven, or length of days without meaning immortality. Blessed are they who have the inner eyes to see, in the little covenant written with ink, the beginning of a greater covenant which cannot be written, for no sea could hold ink enough nor would the firmament be broad enough to write the amazing stipulation.

If we could read these judgments regarding the body and society aright, we should feel that the Legislator must go farther into spiritual regions and into the most profoundly solemn religious issues. Reading along this line, given in these chapters, we become prepared for further communication. There is a spirit in man, and that spirit says we cannot rest in such judgments as these; we feel that these judgments must of necessity be but beginnings. The *Atonement* is in the very protoplasm of things; the Cross is in creation. We have too sharply and narrowly cut things into pieces as if they were not related to one another. Hear, oh Israel! the Lord our God is one Lord, and the law is one, and creation is one, and the ox, and the ass, and the bird, and the dog, and the wolf, and the worm,—all these are parts of an infinite quantity. The Atonement is not an after-thought, an arrangement which the infinite Mind made to meet a temporary necessity. This is the meaning of "foreknowledge," and "predestination," and "election," and all the words which to some minds have been so grim and terrible. The very first thing that God did contains in suggestion and possibility everything he can ever do. Could we seize that thought we should be at rest! God can do but one thing. Had we the eyes to see and the ears to hear things innermost and eternal, we should know that God's *first* word was also his *last.* "I am Alpha and Omega." When God said, "Let there be light," he said all he has ever said or can ever say! The rest is detail; the rest is explanation given to infantile and backward minds. Constituted as we are, we require bulk as well as quality. God must not be too concise for our dense minds : he must put his word into a thousand shapes and utter it in a thousand tones before some of us can begin to understand that he has actually spoken at all. How lost we have become in the bulk,—in the quantitive department of revelation, not knowing that when God said, in the first chapter of Genesis, "Let there be light," he had no more to say. Everything is in light. It chases the darkness, it shows things as they are, it develops capacities and completes actions and uses; it is the revealer, it is as the Spirit of God amongst us. Men love darkness rather than light because their deeds are evil. When light comes and the darkness flees away, we shall be in God's bright heaven.

There is an undoubted law of *evolution* in what may be called the Bible view of Providence. Find out that God cares for any one thing he has made, and all the rest of his Fatherhood is involved in that one act. Such is the argument of Jesus Christ ; he said : "God cares for oxen." That involves the whole evolution of the Fatherhood. Said Christ: "Not a sparrow falleth to the ground without your Father,"—if so the Atonement is there ; the whole mystery of the Cross is in that vigilance of God. Said the Saviour : "The very hairs of your head are all numbered,"—if so, the Atonement is the culmination of that elementary principle,—care, ministry on the part of God. Grand is the view of evolution from a scientific point. It is a noble and majestic thought. Say that God created molecule or germ, requiring the most powerful microscope which man can construct o detect ; or say that it is too minute to be brought within the power of any microscope yet constructed; say that out of that all the rest came by persistence of force—by what law you please—it fills the mind with a nobler wonder, it constrains from the enlightened soul a higher yet profounder adoration. You but increase the mystery of the Godhead and the majesty of his government.

It is so with the great question of Providence, law, and care for man. Given, that God cares for the least thing he ever made—that he asks for it, claims it—and you have in that assumption all the sphering out of ministries of care, and watchfulness, and love; yea, in God's claiming any leaf of the forest he ever made, any insect of the air he ever created, or brought into being by processes we cannot describe—having assumed that, you have involved in that assumption Atonement, Providence, Resurrection—all the mysteries of the gospel. God does not stop at points. The Lord's system of things is not incoherent and unrelated. The mystery is beyond all words. Yet when we say—"God over all, blessed for evermore," we use a form of expression which relieves the heart which is burdened with holy gratitude. Man is puzzled by details yet man will persist in plunging into the very middle of the Bible as if he could read it in that way. Man seems but in rare instances to have the power of setting himself right back at a proper point of view and seeing the movement of God, so far as the human family is concerned, in its totality.

So we read the commandments one by one, and ask if we have obeyed this or that. We have just seen men priding themselves upon pet virtues and upon special commandments which have never been violated; we have endeavoured to expose that sophism. The commandments are one; if we have broken one, we have broken all. Thus condensed may all things be, yet out of that condensation may all things rise as universes out of molecules, constellations out of quantities too small for microscopic recognition. This is the abbreviation of the judgment; this is bringing things back to the single point by which everything must be criticised and determined. We cannot be profound scholars in this book if we are reading it verse by verse, if we are building our life upon chapters and verses. The very breaking up of the Bible into this form is only for preliminary and infantile purposes. The Bible is one,—a line, a flash of light, a tone, a spirit;

it is not to be quoted in the last result; it is to be breathed; it is
to be lived. Oppose the Bible! They do so who do not know it.
Revelation is the indestructible fact, could we but come into the
sanctuary of things and weigh them with the golden balances of
the Divine appointment. Follow not those who, having found
isolated texts or curious discrepancies, suppose that they are in a
position to assail the citadel of revelation and overthrow the
temple of faith,—blind leaders of the blind! "they will fall into
the ditch"!

How bold a book is the Bible! What other book cares thus
for man? God always looks after his child. He will have such
arrangements made as never to allow the supreme value of man
as a Divine creation to be ignored. Given that sublime conviction and acknowledgment, then you may have your temporary
arrangements of high — low, employer—employed, master —
servant, and the like. But all these little laws, necessary for a
society in a process of education, must submit themselves for
periodical criticism and judgment to the supreme law. One is
your Master, One is your Judge. What book, let us ask again
and again, cares so much for man as the Bible does?—Not one.
Keep it in your families,—it will keep the father in his place, and
the child in his place, and give a blessing to each. Keep it in
your politics,—it will teach men to do unto others as they would
have others to do unto them. Keep it in your business,—it will
burn your false measuring rod and destroy your unequal balances,
and be just to persons on both sides of the commercial counter.
Hold up the Bible; read it in the right tone; distribute the
emphases with the inspiration wrought in the soul by the Holy
Ghost; let the Bible itself in its own language, in its own way,
in its own spirit, be heard, circulated, understood; and even yet
we may rescue it from the hands of the conjuror, tear it away
from the hands of the priest, and make it God's own word to
God's own children.

Exodus xxi.-xxiii.

BYE-LAWS

AMONGST these bye-laws there are some sayings which may be considered hard, and on reading them we may ask in almost plaintive and despairing tones, " Who is sufficient for these things ?" There are also ome out-of-the-way responsibilities, which only Divine wisdom and justice could in the then state of society have imposed. We must not permit ourselves to lose the religious philosophy and the religious benficence of the Mosaic legislation by going back upon it with our Christian instincts and culture. We must forget all we have ever learned in the Christian school, and think ourselves back into the comparative barbarism of the age. Then we shall see a light above the brightness of the sun, and feel round about us an influence which cannot be satisfactorily explained without taking into account the possibility of supernatural existence and Divine sovereignty. We shall lose the whole meaning of ancient writings, so far as their religious philosophy is concerned, if we compare them to their disadvantage with Christian standards and the advanced civilisation of the day in which we live. Critically examined, fibre by fibre as it were, this is not crude legislation ; there is nothing rough and ready in this distribution of offices, duties, and obligations. This legislation is, on the contrary, highly spiritual in its assumptions, and full of sublime tribute to the nature which is addressed. The dignity of law pre-supposes the dignity of man. Little laws for little creatures, great laws for great beings—that is the philosophy of the Bible system. Looked at, therefore, narrowly and critically, we shall find that, however crude in appearance may be some of these bye-laws, the substance under them, and of which they may be said to be the mere phenomena, is a holy quantity, a Divine substratum, nothing less than God, the Eternal Creator and Sovereign.

Without attempting to go through all the bye-laws, we can touch them here and there with sufficient distinctness and sympathy to understand the whole scheme of which some parts are here quoted.

"And if men strive together, and one smite another with a stone, or with his fist, and he die not, but keepeth his bed : if he rise again, and walk abroad upon his staff, then shall he that smote him be quit : only he shall pay for the loss of his time, and shall cause him to be thoroughly healed " (xxi. 18, 19).

Are our little personal strifes noted in heaven ? The answer is : Yes, every one of them. But *can* men strive together ? Properly looked at, that would seem to be the harder question of the two. Coming suddenly upon a line of this kind, we should exclaim, in surprise, " The assumption is impossible. We must begin our criticism of a statement of this kind by rejecting its probability, and, that being done, there is no case left. How can men strive together ? Men are brothers, men are rational creatures, men recognise one another's rights, and interests, and welfare ; society is not a competition, but a fraternal and sacred emulation ; therefore, the assumption that men can strive together is a false one, and, the foundation being false, the whole edifice totters down." That would be fine theory, that would be sweet poetry, it might almost be thrown into rhyme, but there are the facts staring us in the face. What are those facts ? That all life is a strife, that every man in some way or degree, or at some time, begrudges the room which every other man takes up. The tragedy of Cain and Abel has never ceased, and can never cease until we become children of the Second Adam. Great degrees of modification may, of course, take effect. The vulgarity of smiting may be left to those who are in a low state of life—who are, in fact, in barbarous conditions ; but they who smite with the fist are not the cruellest of men. There is a refined smiting—a daily, bitter, malignant opposition ; there is a process of mutual undermining, or outreaching, or outrunning, in the very spirit of which is found the purpose of murder. But mark how beneficence enters into the arrangement here laid down. Not only is the man who smote his brother to pay for the loss of his brother's time ; that would be a mere cash transaction. There are men ready enough to buy themselves out of any obligation ;

a handful of gold is nothing. Their language is, "Take it, and let us be free." That would be poor legislation in some cases, though heavy enough in others. To some men money has no meaning; they have outlived all its influences; they are so rich that they can bribe and pay, and secure silence or liberty by a mere outputting of the hand. But the beneficence is in the next clause, "and shall cause him to be thoroughly healed." The man must be made as good as he was before, therefore he must be inquired about; he must be taken an interest in; he must become a quantity in the life of the man who injured him, and, however impatient the man who inflicted the injury may become under such chafing, the impatience itself may be turned to good account. Some men can be taught philanthropy by only such rough and urgent schoolmasters.

"If an ox gore a man or a woman, that they die: then the ox shall be surely stoned, and his flesh shall not be eaten; but the owner of the ox shall be quit. But if the ox were wont to push with his horn in time past, and it hath been testified to his owner, and he hath not kept him in, but that he hath killed a man or a woman; the ox shall be stoned, and his owner also shall be put to death" (xxi. 28, 29).

In the one case provision is made against what we term an accident, and accidents are treated within their own narrow limits; but from accident we pass to purpose. The ox was "wont to push with his horn in time past,"—the ox was known to the owner to be an unmanageable ox; notice had been given to the owner of the temper of the ox; the ox, in short, had won for itself a bad character and reputation. If the owner allowed such an ox to go where danger and injury were possible, the owner was not released on the plea that an accident had occurred: he was held guilty of manslaughter. Is that ox still living? Yes. Is it possible that there are men to day who have oxen "wont to push with their horns," and who have killed ten thousand men, and are yet permitted to live and carry on this work of devastation? Do not fritter away the meaning of the injunction by fixing on the literal term, *ox.* The meaning is not to be confined within any one definition; the great solemn meaning is this: If your trade, occupation, method of life, is inflicting injury anywhere, and you have been made aware of it, you are responsible for the injury that has been done, and you cannot throw off that responsibility. It was not the ox that did it, it was the owner of the ox. Guilt comes home to man. How stands the case? Each must answer for himself. The case applies to ministers of the Gospel, and teachers of every kind of doctrine. If a man preach any doctrine that poisons the life of the hearer, that degrades his best ambition, that narrows and diminishes his life's quantity, that fills him with discontent, peevishness, distrust, and jealousy; and if that preacher has been made aware of the effects of his doctrine, he is responsible for all the heart-ache, for all the up-breaking of life, for all the poisoning of health, and, at the last, hell will be too good a lot for so huge a murderer. The same applies to all men who lecture upon platforms, or who issue vicious books or other literature from the press. Whoever is guilty of the propagation of ideas that injure life, that impair its majesty, and that crush its best endeavours, is a murderer, and he must be held liable for the consequences of his deed. I fix the charge thus particularly upon those who are in the spiritual and intellectual function, that I may the more broadly and pungently suggest the lesson to every man in every other sphere and line of life that he may apply the doctrine to himself. This is the Divine doctrine: it is the rational doctrine, it is the right doctrine. There is nothing so supernatural about this as to cause us to resent it on the ground of its being supermundane, too lofty for us to realise. Reason is satisfied; conscience says "Amen"; the just heart rises up and says, "The judgment is true and righteous; let it stand." But what a revolution would be created in all teaching, in all commerce, in all social relations, if this one bye-law, respecting the "ox wont to push with his horn," were carried out this day!

"If a man shall steal an ox, or a sheep, and kill it, or sell it; he shall restore five oxen for an ox, and four sheep for a sheep" (xxii. 1).

That is the only way of getting at a thief. You cannot reason with him. He dismissed his reason before he committed his felony. He had first to strangle his reason; he committed murder in the sanctuary of his soul before he committed theft in the fields of his neighbour. What then is to be done with him? He must be made to feel the folly of theft; he must be made to feel that theft is a bad investment; he must be made to feel that he has played the fool even in the excess of his cleverness. The thief would be made to know what dishonesty is, when for the one ox he must pay five in its place. He could have evaded an argument; he could have doubled upon a covenant, and have quibbled about the ambiguity of its terms; but he could not shuffle out of this four-square arithmetical arrangement. Five oxen for an ox, four sheep for a sheep; and by the time the thief had played at that game two or three days, he would have put on the garb, at least, of an honest man !

"If fire break out, and catch in thorns, so that the stacks of corn, or the standing corn, or the field, be consumed therewith; he that kindled the fire shall surely make restitution" (xxii. 6).

This is right. The Bible really builds upon granite bases; there is nothing merely fanciful in this legislation. This is sound common-sense, and common-sense in the long run wins the esteem and confidence of the world. No man may trifle with bread. Bad enough to burn down any kind of property; but to consume stacks of corn is to commit murder with both hands; to light the standing corn when it waves in the fields is to thrust a knife, not into one heart, but into the very life of society. How can restitution be made? It cannot be made. You cannot replace corn; money bears no relation to corn; corn is not an arithmetical quantity. Destroyed bread is destroyed life. Who destroys bread? He who makes poison of it; he who turns it into a drink that takes away the reason and deposes the conscience of men. He who holds back the bread-stuff until the time of famine that he may increase his own riches by an enhanced market value is not a political economist, unless, under such circumstances, a political economist is a heartless murderer. And if it is wicked to set fire to corn, is it a light or frivolous matter to set fire to convictions, faiths—the bread-stuff of the soul? Is he guiltless who takes away the bread of life, the bread sent down from heaven? Is he a pardonable incendiary who burns down the altar which was a stairway to the light, or reduces to ashes the Church which was a refuge in the day of storm?

"If thou meet thine enemy's ox or his ass going astray, thou shalt surely bring it back to him again. If thou see the ass of him that hateth thee lying under his burden, and wouldest forbear to help him, thou shalt surely help with him " (xxiii. 4, 5).

Man never imposed that law. That is not a trick of human
wisdom. It is too profound, too exacting, too full of implications
of the noblest kind to have been invented by human nature.
Who would not take vengeance upon his enemy's ox? Who
would not hamstring the bullock? Who would not be pleased
to see his enemy's ox going astray, running furiously mayhap
along the wrong road? Who would not felicitate himself on
such an occurrence, and think with cruel gladness about his
enemy's disappointment and loss? But the other picture is more
vivid still: "If thou see the ass of him that hateth thee lying
under his burden." The enemy himself would be present
personally or representatively, because the ass is not unburdened
but burdened; he is, therefore, upon an appointed road and
journey. Who would not rather taunt his enemy with the petty
disaster and tell him to send for his friends to help him, and not
to his hated and hating ones? "Who is sufficient for these
things?"

But this is Judaism? It is *humanism.* But this old law is
abolished? No, never can be abolished. It is one of the very
laws which Jesus Christ came to "fulfil." Who can do it? To
help the cause of a friend would be a pleasure, but to lift up the
burden from the back of the ass of an enemy tears us in pieces:
tests our quality. Nor can we do it in a mere law-keeping spirit.
We know that to keep this law we must be above the law; grace
must have begun its redeeming and inspiring ministry in our
hearts before we can keep this law in the perfectness of its
meaning. We have all opportunities of doing honour to this
law. Our enemies need help to day. The man who spoke
basely about us may need bread at our hand at this moment;
his trade is in a bad way, though a good trade in itself. We
could bring custom to his hand, and help him out of his
embarrassments. If we hesitate to do so we must no longer
bear the Christian name. Do release Jesus Christ from the responsibility involved in such reluctance, or in such disobedience.
First let *him* go! We cannot love Christ and hate an enemy.

But is not sentiment now supplanting law? Have we not
left the marble halls of justice, and entered a chamber decked
with coverings of tapestry? Certainly not. Read on:—

"Neither shalt thou countenance a poor man in his cause" (xxiii. 3).

There is no mere sentiment in that.   The meaning is : A man is not to be excused because he is poor.   The effect of the law is, that a man is not to be treated with mere pity on the ground of his poverty ; the judge is not to say—"If you had been a rich man you would have been punished, but being a poor man we take pity upon you."   When a man stands before the law, he stands neither rich nor poor ; he stands as one who appeals to the law of right ; he is there as a criminal : let him prove his innocence. So the Bible is not softly sentimental.   It has not one law for the great, and another for the small, one ordinance for the rich, and another for the poor ; it is exceeding broad, it is impartial, it has in it the elements and the guarantees of complete security.

And is it all law—hard, iron, pitiless law ?   Is all life reduced to a schedule of regulations—an infinite placard of times, seasons, appointments of a merely hireling kind, so much equivalent for so much labour ?   Read on :—

"Three times thou shalt keep a feast unto me in the year.   Thou shalt keep the feast of unleavened bread (thou shalt eat unleavened bread seven days, as I commanded thee, in the time appointed of the month Abib; for in it thou camest out from Egypt : and none shall appear before me empty) : and the feast of harvest, the firstfruits of thy labours, which thou hast sown in thy field : and the feast of ingathering, which is in the end of the year, when thou hast gathered in thy labours out of the field " (xxiii. 14-16).

There is to be feasting as well as law-keeping ; there is to be a recognition of the Lawgiver as well as a continual attempt to obey the letter of the law.   There was to be a feast of *memory*— the liberation from Egypt—there was to be a feast of *firstfruits,* and there was to be a feast of *ingathering.*   When men put the sickle into the wheatfield there was to be a feast unto the Lord. Fifty days were supposed to elapse between the putting in of the sickle and the full ingathering of the harvest.   At the end of the fifty days, there was to be a feast of ingathering, a looking up into heaven, a recognition of the Divine and supernatural element in life.   They whose faces had been towards the earth, and whose hands had been put out in daily labour, were to look up to heaven and stretch out the hands to the skies, and to say by attitude and by voice, " We are not the hirelings of men : we are the servants of the living God." We need these festivals; we need the holy day; we are better for touching one another in Christian companionship and worship. We ought to be the more righteous, the more lofty, for spending one hour in the house consecrated to Jehovah's praise. We cannot keep the law in all the fulness of Christian obedience until we have been with Christ, and learned of him. It is not our enemy's ox that is in distress, but our enemy himself. We are not called upon to study the mere framework of regulated society, and to attend to enactments and stipulations which will keep that society in skeleton-outline together; we have not come into a political society, but into a Christian brotherhood. We are not to be kept back from smiting only—that we have outlived long ago—but we have to come into the spirit of forgiveness, largest pardon, multiplied, heaped up, forgiveness and pardon—yea, here we may resort to all tautology of expression, if in the infinite redundance of our speech we do but give some feeble hint of the passion of love that has been created in our hearts by the Spirit of the Cross of Christ.

Thus the law was given by Moses, but grace and truth came by Jesus Christ, and Christ came not to abolish the law, even about ox, and ass, and theft, and burning of standing corn, but to fulfil it, to glorify it, to carry it up to higher meaning, and thus to consolidate the New Society—his Church—and make it infinitely precious and secure.

We look with some curiosity upon all these endless laws and exactions, and think ourselves well quit of a mechanism so detailed and vexatious. Herein we rejoice before the time. We are not quit of one of them. Is not our life also set in a marvellous network of law? If all the laws which are continually operating upon us and impoverishing us by their taxation could be set down in a book, we should marvel with exceeding astonishment at the mechanism under which our own boasted liberty is breathing. We call ourselves free, and rejoice that all the exactions of the past are done away, and that now it lies very much with our own will to say when life's work shall begin and end and of what it shall exactly consist. We enjoy no such liberty. We cannot put our foot down upon any point of the

earth that is not throbbing with the energy of law. Not a hand
can be put out that is not entangled in the meshes of never-
ceasing ordinances of life and nature. Cause and effect proceed
eternally. The seedtime and the harvest are still linked by
bonds that cannot be sundered. The evil-doer finds a thorn in
his pillow every night. The oppressor is made to feel that he
himself is under domination. Every morning has its duty, every
night its sacrifice; the whole year round is but one unceasing
opportunity for self-expenditure and self-control. Our liberty
consists in our being able to do all the law requires with a
steadier hand and a loftier purpose. The law itself is not sus-
ponded. Not one moment less of time does God demand; not one
penny less of gold, not one thought less of spiritual consecration
and intensity of mind; only by the grace of our Lord Jesus Christ
we have come to such complete devotion of soul that what aforetime was grievous is now pleasant, and what at the beginning
was almost impossible has now become the chief delight of life.
Never suppose that law has been lessened in its force or in its
details; the effort is wholly on the other side, that we ourselves
have been blessed with greater power and have been brought
into sweet consent with the Divine purpose.

Exodus xxii., xxiii.

NEGATIVE COMMANDMENTS.

WE cannot read the book of Exodus without being struck by the number of things which we are not to do. These detailed and emphatic prohibitions we may regard under the name of negative commandments. We are not left to ourselves in any instance to determine a case of doubt; from beginning to end the Divine voice is clear, and direct, and final in its tone. These negative commandments are interesting upon every ground; but perhaps especially so as revealing human nature to itself. When we hear a command to do, or not to do, we hear in that command a voice which startles us into a new consciousness of our own nature and quality. To be told not to do certain things is now considered equivalent to a kind of affront —assuming it possible that we could do such things as are thus forbidden. We are annoyed, we are excited in a hostile way, at the very thought of it being supposed that we could have done these things which a high legislation attempts elaborately and penally to forbid. We must, however, think ourselves back to the time of day at which all these negative and positive commandments were given. We do not find them in the New Testament, because it is there assumed that we have attained that moral sensitiveness and that spiritual responsiveness which render it entirely unnecessary that we, with many centuries of civilisation culminating in our experience and history, should be forbidden to do certain things.

Take some instances, and use them especially as showing what human nature is apart from Divine direction and continual and gracious supervision.

Who, for example, would imagine that such a commandment as this could be given to any people who profess to know anything about the true God?

"Thou shalt neither vex a stranger nor oppress him" (xxii. 21).

Is it possible to vex a stranger ? Does not the very fact of his being a stranger entitle him to generous hospitality ? to a kind construction of his mistakes ? Ought we not to be ready to turn his ignorance into wisdom and his inexperience to certainty of knowledge ? Yet is it not true that man can vex a brother man who is a stranger and oppress him ? Is it not done every day ? Is it not one of the tricks by which we live ? Do we not pride ourselves upon being too quick for the stranger, or knowing more than he knows ? and do we not turn our knowledge to our own advantage and to his personal loss ? Why, in this command from Heaven, we have the beginning of the great Gospel of Christ. To God there are no strangers. And to ourselves there would have been no strangers had we been faithful to God. Why all this strangeness ? Simply because we have become estranged from the Father of us all. The strangeness began between man and God, not between man and man, and not until we are right with God can we be right with one another. We may make arrangements for momentary convenience ; we may consult public sentiment and study the bearing and influence of public doubts in relation to one another ; but we cannot be as one heart, and one soul, until we are one with God through Jesus Christ his Son. You cannot permanently tinker the world ; there is no rent in it that can be filled up with material at man's command. The disease is desperate, vital, and only God, the Physician that is in Gilead, can find the healing for the disease infinite and unspeakable. But the command is a looking-glass. A man looking into it may see himself, see what he would do under given circumstances. The assumptions of the text are impeachments ; put those impeachments into words, and how stands the great accusation ? Thus : you would vex a stranger if you could ; you would oppress a stranger if you could do so with impunity. You perhaps think you would not, but the deepest reading of human nature gives this as a result of the study of the human constitution that none can be so savage as man ; there is not a beast in the field or in the forest that can equal man in cruelty. We talk about savage beasts and cruel and fierce creatures made to devour one another ; but there is no cruelty so terrible, so unsparing, so pitiless, as the cruelty of the human heart. That is the accusation ; we must leave the proof to human consciousness and to human history. We understand how men revolt from the suggestion, and how they cover up their passions by paying compliments to own their tenderness and sensibility; but the mischief is—the subtle and tremendous mischief is—that our very tenderness may be a calculation, our very tears may be shed as an investment for our own benefit. "The heart is deceitful above all things, and desperately wicked."

Akin to this commandment there is another. The tender words are these :—

"Ye shall not afflict any widow, or fatherless child " (xxii. 22).

This is the Gospel of Christ in the book of Exodus. This is God the Father. There is a majestic solemnity in his voice that is full of ineffable tenderness. This is the Father of all. Would men afflict the widow, or the fatherless child? The answer must be frank and direct, and that answer will be in the affirmative. Who speaks for the widow?—God; and the orphan?—God. Then be cheerful, take heart again; the Orator who speaks for you is God. There are no fatherless children in the deepest sense of that term. As for the fathers we have had after the flesh, they themselves were children, as were their fathers and all their ancestors. There is only one Father. Let us take hold of hands and make a great ring round the family centre and say—holding each tremulously, lusty manhood, thriving childhood—timidly and lispingly,—"Our Father which art in heaven." Given the time when men shall say so with a sound heart, with an undivided mind, with a loyal and constant affection, and then find the angel who can tell where earth ends and heaven begins. Wondrous it is—yea, more and more so—that there should be found any friendless people, poor lonely destitute people, who do not love the Bible. Find me in it one text that does not warn the rich man to take care, for he is standing upon a very slippery place, and when he does slip he plunges a long way down. Find one text in all the glowing volume that rebukes the poor, that is hard with the struggling, that smites the penitent man in the face, that forbids a little child to trouble the Jehovah of the universe. Weakness, poverty, helplessness, homelessness, disease, pain, hunger, thirst—these are thy clients, thou Servant of us all.

Changing the place altogether, you will find another commandment of a tone somewhat startling and surprising.

"Thou shalt not revile the gods . . . of thy people " (xxii. 28).

This is a passage difficult to understand and impossible fully to explain. In other places, we find idols broken, temples erected to forbidden names thrown down, as by great thunders, and lightnings, and strong winds blowing contempt from eternity upon the petty creations of the debased religious imagination. Yet consistently with all this there is to be no reviling of gods. This is a subtle lesson. Mock no man's religion—point out the inadequacy of it, show the vanity of the small idolatrous form, remark with pungency, if you please, upon its grotesqueness and its helplessness; but confine your remarks to the visible thing. That can be treated in this way with obvious reasonableness; but the religious instinct lies deeper than you have yet realised if you have been confining your attention to the mere forms of idol worship. The religion is beyond the idol,—above it, below it, away from it. The idol itself is a mere symbol to typify the inexpressible infinite. You do not convert men by mocking their convictions, by reviling them on account of their mistakes. Do what you please with the opprobrious idol—lift it up to prove how little it is in weight; set it down to show how helpless it is in your hand; throw it over to show that it cannot defend itself; but you have not treated the whole case in its entire scope and reality by thus treating the merely visible form of a religious conviction. Men may be mistaken in their convictions of a religious kind; show them the truth; live the truth; illustrate the possibility of living perfect, lofty, noble lives; create a religious wonder in the observer of your life as to the range of motive by which your conduct is mellowed and impelled; so live that you cannot be accounted for, except on the basis that you are living, moving, and having your being in God. Thus, and not by fluent mockery will men be drawn from their own mistakes to partake of the convictions which are as rational as they are beneficent. There is no poor suppliant crying to idols and praying to the empty and mocking wind that does not prove by that very act the mysterious, the Divine origin of the heart that can thus make such egregious mistakes. They are the mistakes of a Divine creation : they are not the petty mistakes of human ignorance. In the plunge of idolatry there is the apostacy of one almost God. It is a rush into a darkness from which any

mere beast would flee in terror. Do not mock conviction; do
not revile mistakenness of apprehension. Do what you please
with the mere idol and with the transient ceremony; be even
angry with these,—yea, destructively angry,—but find out in
them an instinct, an emotion, a mystery to which you must address
yourselves, not in the language of taunt, but in the language of
sympathy, with a burning desire to redeem from prostitution an
instinct which makes humanity.

"Thou shalt not follow a multitude to do evil" (xxiii. 2).

Can a multitude do evil? One soul may stray, but can a whole
multitude go away from the light and make itself houses in forbidden places? Can the majority be wrong? There is a sense
in which the majority is at this moment against Christ. I would
not count it so; rather would I see Christ in many disguises;
but I should know it to be the very Christ, whatever the disguise
which concealed the dignity. Christ has been with men when men
did not know it; their eyes have been holden that they should
not see him; he has revealed himself to men under many
concealments of a strange kind. There is more Christ in the
world than we possibly may suppose. God is infinite; God fills
all space, and yet takes up no room; God mingles with thinking,
civilisation, action, and yet the human factors in all the mysterious action may be unaware of the Divine presence and
impulse; but there has been an unveiling, a sudden revelation of
the reality of the case. We are waiting for that millennial disclosure. What if some day God shall look right in the face of
the very people who have been doubting or denying any relation to
him, and should thus convince them that all the time they have
had nothing that they have not received from himself? and what
if they should also be surprised by the recollection of a warmth
of the heart, a glow of the soul, they had never felt before, and
should find in that fire the presence of the God of Abraham, and
Isaac, and Jacob? God may be working in you without your
knowing his name, or without your being at present able to trace
the Divine action, as distinctly separate from human thinking. We
are waiting for the day of revelation, the morning of surprise, when
we shall stand before God, saying, "Lo! thou wast with us and we
knew it not. How solemn is every place which thou hast made!"
But when the multitude does evil, we are not to follow it; we

must stand still and protest against the evil ; in other words, we must see the evil and not the multitude. Always put the emphasis upon the right word, in order to encourage yourself in good action and in straightforward conduct. The emphasis is not altogether upon the word *multitude*, it is upon the word *evil;* and we ought to ask God to be enabled so to pronounce the word *evil* as to feel revolt from everything which it implies and suggests.

Looking at these negative commandments, are we not surprised at the wonderful knowledge of human nature which they reveal ? We cannot get away from them ; we cannot plant ourselves right in front of them and say, "This is a misinterpretation of human nature." We cannot return the dreadful look of the eyes that shine out of this revelation ; we feel that we are in the hands of a Legislator who knows us altogether, and who speaks to us not according to transient and accidental phases of human nature but in the totality of our being. This is the strength of the Bible, this is the vindication of the commandments : that they root themselves in our constitution, that they know us, and that we can only escape their pressure by telling lies to our own souls. Herein is the inspiration of the Book. Its portraiture of man is a portraiture without a blemish or a flaw. He who drew man so completely in every lineament of his image, in every emotion and sensibility of his nature, must have made the man whose portrait he has delineated.

These commandments also show the true relation of God to the human race. He is the Ruler. He enjoins, he forbids ; he never comes with apology from the skies, or palliation of sternness, but with the majesty of right. Yet there is one little word in the midst of all these commandments full of sweetest gospel— a word that might have been found in one of the four Evangelists and that might have formed the text of every sermon preached by Apostolic wisdom and eloquence. The sentence you find in the twenty-second chapter and the twenty-seventh verse : "For I am gracious "—a word we cannot do without. We cannot explain it, yet we feel that it fills all space in human necessity and consciousness which no other word can fill. This is the defence of the commandments : that they are not arbitrary expressions of mere sovereignty of will and position in the universe, but that they, though commandments, are expressions of grace, mercy, pity, love. The very Spirit of the Cross is in the commandment. Sinai is but one phase of Calvary.

We try to evade many of these commandments on the plea that they were not addressed to us. It is a hollow plea; it is in fact a lie. We turn away from the commandments, saying, with an explanatory gesture, that we are not Jews. We are, if we are in Christ; if we have any love for Christ; if we feel that we must follow in some fashion the way and method of the Son of God. The Christian is a Jew *plus.* Christianity is the fruition of Judaism. The blood of the One Priest that abideth for ever and hath an unchangeable priesthood gathers up in its redness all the meaner blood which typified and prophesied its shedding. As well may the oak say "I am not an acorn" as Christianity say "I am not Judaism." We cannot have the two Testaments torn asunder as though they had no relation one to the other. The New Testament would have been impossible but for the Old Testament. The song uttered in heaven is the song of Moses and the Lamb. "The law came by Moses, but grace and truth came by Jesus Christ." Yet Jesus Christ said, "Think not that I am come to destroy the law, or the prophets : I am not come to destroy, but to fulfil." If he did not recite these negative commandments, it was because he came to put within us a Spirit, a Paraclete, that should abide for ever, whose presence was a law, whose operation in the soul was a daily instruction in righteousness and wisdom, in love and pureness, in which he may stand above the commandments and treat them as an obsolete letter—who has entered into the Spirit of Christ, and who is breathing in his daily life the obedience to which earlier men had to struggle through many an effort, and in struggling towards which they effected many a mournful failure. God never tells us to trust our moral instinct ; God never assumed that the child could find its own way through a universe which it had darkened by its sin. He wrote down every line, made it complete ; he wrote a detailed and complete specification of duty, service, action, and worship ; if any of us have outlived the mere letter and need it no more, praised be God for a spiritual education which has delivered us from the bondage of the letter and led us into a nobler bondage of the heart, a sweet servitude of the soul, a glorious slavery, a glorious liberty .

Exodus xxiii. 20-33.

20. Behold, I send an Angel before thee, to keep thee in the way, and to bring thee into the place which I have prepared.

21. Beware of him, and obey his voice, provoke him not; for he will not pardon your transgressions: for my name is in him.

22. But if thou shalt indeed obey his voice, and do all that I speak; then I will be an enemy unto thine enemies, and an adversary unto thine adversaries.

23. For mine Angel shall go before thee, and bring thee in unto the Amorites and the Hittites, and the Perizzites, and the Canaanites, and the Hivites, and the Jebusites : and I will cut them off.

24. Thou shalt not bow down to their gods, nor serve them, nor do after their works: but thou shalt utterly overthrow them, and quite break down their images.

25. And ye shall serve the Lord your God, and he shall bless thy bread, and thy water: and I will take sickness away from the midst of thee.

26. There shall nothing cast their young, nor be barren, in thy land : the number of thy days I will fulfil.

27. I will send my fear before thee, and will destroy all the people to whom thou shalt come, and I will make all thine enemies turn their backs unto thee.

28. And I will send hornets before thee, which shall drive out the Hivite, the Canaanite, and the Hittite, from before thee.

29. I will not drive them out from before thee in one year; lest the land become desolate, and the beast of the field multiply against thee.

30. By little and little I will drive them out from before thee, until thou be increased and inherit the land.

31. And I will set thy bounds from the Red sea even unto the sea of the Philistines, and from the desert unto the river: for I will deliver the inhabitants of the land into your hand; and thou shalt drive them out before thee.

32. Thou shalt make no covenant with them nor with their gods.

33. They shall not dwell in thy land, lest they make thee sin against me: for if thou serve their gods, it will surely be a snare unto thee.

THE ANGEL IN LIFE.

LAWS without angels would turn life into weary drudgery. Life has never been left without ome touch of the Divine presence and love. From the very first this has been characteristic of our history. When our first parents were cast out of the garden, the Lord said, "The seed of the woman shall bruise the head of the serpent." That was a prophecy, bright as an angel, comforting as a gospel, spoken from heaven. The difficulty is that we will interfere with the personality of the Angel; we will concern ourselves about his figure and name. Instead of accepting the ministry, and answering a great and solemn appeal addressed to our noblest faculties, we ask the little questions of prying and often profane curiosity. It would seem to be our nature to spoil everything. We take the instrument to pieces to find the music, instead of yielding ourselves to the call of its blast, to the elevation of its inspiring gladness, and to the infinite tenderness of its benediction. We are cursed with the spirit of vain curiosity. We expend ourselves in the asking of little questions, instead of plunging into God's great sea of grace, and love, and comfort, and waiting patiently for revelations which may address themselves to the curiosity which is premature, and to the prying which now can get no great answers. The solemn—the grand, fact is, that in our life there is an Angel, a spirit, a presence; a ministry without definite name and altogether without measurableness; a gracious ministry, a most tender and comforting service, always operating upon our life's necessity and our heart's pain. Let us rest in that conviction for a moment or two until we see how we can establish it by references to facts, experiences, consciousness against which there can be no witness. We prove some assumptions by the facts which flow from them. We can only establish the existence of some substances by grouping together the phenomena which they present. Into the substances themselves philosophy cannot penetrate; but philosophy can gather together the appearances, sometimes all the elements and effects which are grouped under the name of phenomena, and can reason from these groupings that there must be underneath some unknown, some unknowable substance which expresses itself in these superficial and visible appearances. So our assumption that there is an Angel ahead of us, a radiant light in advance, a heavenly presence in our whole life, may be established by references which appeal not to imagination only but to experience; and if we can establish such events we shall have also to establish the sublime doctrine that in the midst of humanity there is a light of Divinity, and at the

head of all the truly upward advancing host of men goes the
Angel appointed of God.

See how our life is redeemed from baseness by the assumption
that an Angel is leading it. Who can believe that an Angel has
been appointed to conduct a life which must end in the grave?
The anticlimax is shocking; the suggestion is charged with the
very spirit of profanity. We could not allow it in poetry; we
should resent it in history; we should despise it in all dramatic
compilations and representations. You must not yoke a steed of
any blood in too small and mean a chariot; you degrade some
horses of repute by sending them to do certain base and unworthy
service. Is it not so with men also? Are there not men whose
names are so lofty, so illustrious, that we could never consent to
their doing certain actions too vulgar and low to be worthy of
their brilliant repute? Does not the law admit of the highest
and widest application? If an Angel is leading us, is he leading
us to the grave? Surely it would not need an Angel to conduct
us to that poor destiny! We could wander thither ourselves;
the blind could lead us, and they that have no intelligence could
plunge us into that dark pit. And we *feel* that we are not being
led to the grave. It is possible that some of us may have so lived
that the grave would be too good a destiny for us; but I speak of
those who have tasted of the sweetness of true life, who have
risen above the dreary round of mere existence, and who have
tasted in ever so small a degree of the wine of immortality,—
men who have felt throbs of infinite life, hearts that have been
conscious of pulsings never started by human ingenuity, and such
men shrink from the suggestion that all this life, so full of sacred
possibility and gracious experience, should terminate in the gloom
of the grave. Who says that life was not meant for the grave?
The Angel. Whose ministry is a daily pledge against annihilation? The Angel's. What is it within us that detests the grave,
that turns away from it with aversion, that will not be sent into so
lone and mean a prison? It is "the Divinity that stirs within us."

Then again, who could ask an Angel to be a guest in a heart
given up to evil thoughts and purposes? Given the consciousness that an Angel is leading us, and instantly a series of pre-
parations must be set up corresponding with the quality and title
of the leading Angel of our pilgrimage. We prepare for some

guests. According to the quality of the guest is the range and
costliness of our preparation. Whom our love expects our love
provides for. When we are longing for the coming one, saying,
" The presence will make the house the sweeter and the brighter,
and the speech will fill our life with new poetry and new hope.
Oh, why tarry the chariot wheels ? " then we make adequate—
that is to say, proportionate—preparation. The touch of love is
dainty, the invention of love is fertile, the expenditure of love is
without a grudge or a murmur,—another touch must be given to
the most delicate arrangement ; some addition must be made to
the most plentiful accommodation ; love must run over the
programme just once more to see that every line is worthily
written. Then the front door must be opened widely, and the
arms, and the heart, and the whole being to receive the guest of
love. And that is so in the higher regions. If an Angel is going
to lead me, the Angel must have a chamber in my heart prepared
worthy of myself. Chamber !—nay, the whole heart must be the
guest-room ; he must occupy every corner of it, and I must array
it with robes of purity and brightness that he may feel himself at
home, even though he may have come from heaven to do some
service for my poor life. Any appeal that so works upon every
kind of faculty, upon imagination, conscience, will, force, must be
an appeal that will do the life good. It calls us to perfectness, to
preparedness, to a nobility corresponding in some degree with
the nobility of the guest whom we entertain. If you please, you
can fill your heart-house with mean occupants. There are evil
visitants that will sit down in unprepared hearts and eat up your
life a mouthful at a time. It lies within your power—not within
your right—to make your heart-chamber the gathering place of
evil things, evil thoughts, evil presences ; but any conviction
that would lead in that direction proves its own baseness, lies
beyond the circle of argument, and is not to be treated seriously
by earnest men. Now it is the distinguishing characteristic of
Bible-teaching that it wants clean hearts, large hearts, ample
entertainment, noble thoughts, sweet patience, complete sacrifice,
having in it the pledge of final and eternal resurrection. Any
book offering such suggestions of Angel presences, radiant
leaderships, Divine associations, proves its own goodness, and
its own inexpressible value.

Suppose, however, that in our obstinacy and narrowness of mind we hesitate to accept the suggestion of a living Angel, we lose nothing of all the gracious meaning of the text by substituting other terms. We have to grow up to the apprehension of Angel-hood ; but the stages of growth can be marked by common terms, and so the growth can be proved to be possible. Many a life has in it a memory playing the part of an Angel, a recollection full of tenderness, a reminiscence that lures the life forward little by little up steep places and through lone and dark valleys. Some might call such a memory an Angel. Why not ? It discharges the offices of a blessed minister, it redeems life from despair, it fills life with gracious encouragement, it nourishes life in times of destitution and dejection. Now whilst some minds may be unable to accept the transcendental suggestion of Angel ministry, it is a poor mind—hardly to be reasoned with—that cannot conceive the idea that a memory, a recollection, a vow, an oath, may play an inspiring part in human education, and may save men from evil deeds in the time of tremendous temptation. We all have memories of that blessed kind. We know the vow we spoke, the oath we took, the pledge we gave, the word that passed from us and became solemn by sanctions that could not be remitted except at the expense of the soul's integrity. Yet we have killed many an Angel. What slaughter we have left behind us ! Stains redder than blood show the awful track our lives have made. Mark Antony pointed out the various rents in the robe of the murdered Cæsar, and identified each rent with the name of the cruel smiter. So we could do with the robe of our own lives. See where the dewy pureness of young prayer lies mangled ; see where the holiest oath of obedience lies with a gashed throat which can never be healed ; see where purposes chaste as mountain snow lie murdered and forgotten ; see where words of honour plighted at last interviews in whispers softened by tears lie crushed, contemned and mocked,—gather up all the images, the facts, and the proofs, which memory will accumulate, and, as you look upon the hideous heap, regard it as God's Angel, unheeded, degraded, murdered ! Thus we do not escape the pressure of the argument by refusing to accept the supernatural term *angel;* we do not elude the critical judgment by endeavour-ing to run away from appearances which are charged with such high titles as Spirit, Angel, Divine minister. We have to answer appeals formed in terms of our own creation. Our common speech itself gathers up into an expression of judgment, and if we imagine that we have never seen an Angel or resented his ministry, we have to account for it that our memory, our vow, our plighted word, our testimonies spoken to the dying, have been forgotten, neglected, abandoned, disavowed; and when we have answered a lower appeal we may be prepared to reply to the challenge which sounds upon us with a more terrific thunder from higher places.

The Divine presence in life, by whatever name we may distinguish it, is pledged to two effects, supposing our spirit and our conduct to be right. God undertakes our cause as against our enemies. Would we could leave our enemies in his hands! I do not now speak altogether of merely human enemies—because where there is enmity between man and man, though it never can be justified, yet it admits of such modification in the system of words as to throw responsibility upon both sides—but I speak of other enemies,—the enmity expressed by evil desire, by the pressure of temptation, by all the array against the soul's health and weal of the principalities of the power of the air, the princes of darkness, the spirits of evil. Send the Angel to fight the Angel; let the Angel of Light fight the Angel of Darkness. We have no weapon of our own invention and manufacture fine enough to strike the subtle presence; but God is our Guardian. Are not his angels "ministering spirits, sent forth to minister for them who shall be the heirs of salvation"? Sometimes we in our own human personality have not to fight, we have to stand still and see the salvation of God,—to stand back in God's eternity and say, "The battle is not mine, but thine; I cannot fight these dark ones; I cannot strike these presences, for they elude all weapons at my disposal : undertake for me and I will stand hands down waiting to see the outworking of thy redemption." If we had more faith we should have fewer enemies; if we had more trust in God we should have less anxiety about our foes. We must not encounter the serpent alone; we must not attempt to find answers in the ingenuity of our own minds to the plaguing challenges and temptations of the evil one. The enemies arrayed against us are not those of flesh and blood, or we might in some degree meet them, elude them, disappoint them,—we fight "not against flesh and blood, but against principalities, against powers, against the rulers of the darkness of this world,"—what have we to oppose to these? The Angel—God's Angel, the white-robed one,—and he by his holiness shall overthrow all evil, for it lies with the Lord to chase the darkness and with holiness to put down all iniquity.

The second effect to which the Divine presence in our life is pledged is that we shall be blessed with the contentment which is riches. God said he would take sickness away from the midst of his people: "There shall nothing cast their young, nor be barren, in thy land: the number of thy days I will fulfil." We must not be too literal, or here we shall miss the meaning. As we have been in danger of misinterpreting the term *angel,* we are equally in danger of misinterpreting the term *sickness,* or *poverty,* or the general word *circumstances.* We know nothing about these terms in the fulness of their meaning. We do but live an approximate life; we see hints and beginnings, not fruitions and completions. What will God do for us then?—He will give us a contented spirit. What does a contented spirit do for a man? It turns his poverty into wealth, his sickness into energy, his loss into gain; it gives him to feel that a man's life consisteth not in the abundance of the things which he possesseth, but is a life hidden in the mystery of God's own being. Thus we have mysteries amongst us which the common or carnal mind cannot understand. Man asking God's blessing upon what appears to be unblest poverty,—men saying it is enough when we can discover next to nothing in the hand uplifted in recognition of Divine goodness. Thus we hear voices coming from the bed of affliction that have in them the subdued tones of absolute triumph; thus the sick-chamber is turned into the church of the house, and if we would recover from dejection, and repining, and sorrow, we must go to the bedside of affliction and learn there how wondrous is the ministry of God's Angel, how perfecting and ennobling the influence of God's grace.

The "hornets," spoken of in verse 28, must be taken figuratively. The Egyptian made as a symbol of princely quality and princely power the wasp and the bee. These were Egyptian symbols.

Remembering the history of his people, going back to the period of their Egyptian bondage, seeing upon Egyptian banner, and fresco, and all manner of things royal, the image of the wasp and the bee, God said,—I will send hornets before thee that can do more than these painted things can possibly do : I will destroy by a power that cannot be controlled : I will kill armies by hornets, I will dissolve hosts by winds that are charged with elements that life cannot withstand; I will be thy friend. God does not fight with one weapon ; God's method cannot be predicted. The wind is his, and the pestilence, and the tempest, and many things that we cannot name or control, and they are all pledged to work in favour of the cause of righteousness and the white banner of truth.

Thus our hearts may claim a great and solid comfort. We are not going through the wilderness *alone.* As Christians we believe in the guardianship of Christ. Our prayer is " Jesus, still lead on." Angel of the Covenant, let us feel assured of thy continued presence. Guide us with thine eye. The road is long, hard, and often inhospitable, but it is measured every inch, and no man could lengthen it. It is good for us to be sometimes in the wilderness ; there we long for rest, there we sigh for companionship, there we mourn for one sight of flowers and one trill of birds carolling in the sunny air. The wilderness tames our passion, chastens our ambition, modifies our vanity : we can do nothing in sand ; we cannot cool the fierce air ; we cannot melt the rocks into streams of water. In the city man becomes boastful, there men outrun one another and get richer than their brethren ; they spread themselves like green bay-trees ; and fester in the noisomeness of unblest success ; but in the waste of the wilderness, in the dead flats of affliction, in the monotony of sorrow, they learn how frail they are, how helpless, how dependent upon Angel ministries. Bless God for the wilderness ; thank God for the long nights ; be thankful that you have been in the school of poverty and have undergone the searching and testing of much discipline. Take the right view of your trials. You are nearer heaven for the graves you have dug if you have accepted bereavements in the right spirit ; you are wiser for the losses you have bravely borne, you are nobler for all the sacrifices you have willingly completed. Sanctified affliction is an Angel that never misses the gate of heaven.

HORNETS AND ANGELS.

"And I will send hornets before thee."—Exodus xxiii. 28.
"And I will send an angel before thee."—Exodus xxxiii. 2.

GOD brake the ships of Tarshish with an east wind, a puff of breath. He told the east wind to seize their masts and torment them to their destruction. Dagon was thrown down upon his face, though he was locked up with the ark, and no hand was near him ; yea, he was utterly broken to pieces so that he was not a god at all. How was this ? The chariots of God are twenty thousand. Can you remember twenty thousand names ? Can you venture to say, "This is, and this is not, one of the twenty thousand" ? It is a fearful thing to fall into the hands of the living God. A great wind battered the Armada of Spain in a critical moment in English history. Thus God has more resources than those which are merely human. We gather ourselves together as if we were all his belongings, as if he depended upon us alone, and we talk, and resolve, and organise, and go forth, as if the Lord had nothing else to depend upon. Mayhap that is partly right. A man may do more if he thinks that everything depends upon himself; but he should cheer himself, and bring great encouragement into his soul, by remembering the number of God's chariots ; they are twenty thousand. The stars in their courses fought against Sisera, and the stones of the field were covenanted to help those that feared the Lord. Nature helps, nature hinders, nature is God's other self, and his chariots are twenty thousand strong. The Lord God is a sun and shield, he is a spear and buckler, he is a pavilion and a sanctuary. The lightnings gather themselves round him, and say, "Here we are"; his ministers are the frog and the fly, the hornet and the locust; the fiery flying serpent and the hidden viper, the child, the angel, poverty and plenty, are his servants ; yea, all things praise the Lord by their sympathy and help, so much so that if we were to hold our tongues, the universe would not be silent. "I tell you that if these were to hold their peace, the very stones would cry out, for God is able of these stones to raise up children unto Abraham." He shall never want a minister to stand before his face. If so be thou art a minister, boast not thyself of thy ministry, for a hornet may take thy place, a frog may dispossess thee, and there may be none to find out thy footsteps. Be thankful, hopeful, energetic, glad; but boast not, for boasting hastens death.

The one thought that is to inspire us is that God has many ways of helping his people, likely and unlikely, but they are ways of his own choosing, and therefore they will end in success. Hornets and angels,—Are not the ministers of God both visible and invisible? The flying hornet you can see, but who can trace the angel in the air? Can you see the angel? He is there, notwithstanding your inability to descry him. You see the hornet. Ah! we are all quicker in seeing the hornet than in seeing the angel. Fie on us, shame on shame, till we be burnt with blushes. Can you see the angel? You cannot always tell what forces and ministries are fighting either for you or against you. We do not know the meaning of nature. She is a parable we have not fully read or understood; an eternal lesson, God's perpetual illustration of himself. Oh that we had eyes to see and hearts to understand; for the library is always open, and the writing is always done by an angel's hand.

A man says, "A curse on this hornet, this winged, stinging insect, only a large bee, only an exaggerated wasp—a curse on the thing. I dare not open my window, for it may fly in; I dare not go out, for it hovers near my door and may smite me with its cruel sting. It never sleeps, it seems ever to fill the sultry air." He does not know what he is talking about: he thinks it is an insect; he says: "Why did God make such a creature?"—ah, why? He calls it insect; when he has been longer at school he may call it minister of God, and servant of the Most High. He is fretted by its unceasing and energetic buzz; by-and-by he will hear music in it, a sad and terrible music. That hornet is sent of God to drive you out: it will not die; you have been doing wrong and it has come to punish you. That hornet is death, or loss, or pain, or bitterness of soul. That hornet is not a mere

insect ; it means judgment, penalty, retribution, death. I wish
people would see the great meaning of things and not the little
trifling suggestions.

I will tell you what to do with the hornet. Hear me—bad
man, hear me : I have a gospel for thee. Outrun it : thou hast
two legs, two leaden feet—outrun the hornet. "I cannot." Then
that will not do. Close your hand upon it. "I dare not." No,
you dare not. Then that will not do. Bribe it : coat your
window-sill with sugar, inches thick, and it will glut itself to
death. "Aye, I will try that." Ah, it grows by what it feeds
on. It is a stronger hornet for the sugar. It took your bribes
and strengthened itself against you. I will tell you what to do :
compromise with it, propose terms, negotiate, send a third party.
"Oh bitter irony, oh mocking man," say you ?—Yes, I mean to
mock, for who can outrun the chariots of God ? No, sir, no :
stop, turn round, fall down, confess, pray ; cry mightily to God to
take the hornet back. That is the true gospel : hear it, and thou
shalt live.

Then on the other hand there is a kind angel that can be nearly
seen, and that can be almost heard, and that can be all but felt.
Thank God for the things that are *nearly*, that are *all but*, that are
just about to begin to be. Thank Heaven this verb of life is
not all shut up in the indicative mood. Wondrous conjugation
—indicative, potential, subjunctive, infinitive—how the verb
grows ; how the little "I am," a child's first mouthful, grows into
the immeasurable eternity. Think of this kind angel, who is all
but seen, who is so near as to be almost felt. You catch an
aroma which he must have shaken from his wings. Bless God
for these occasional hints, and touches, and blessings as we go on.
The angel of the Lord encampeth round about them that fear
him. Are they not all ministering spirits, sent forth to minister
for them who shall be heirs of salvation ?

Then remember the hornet will fight for you as well as against
you. If you are in the right way, the hornet is your friend. It
will pursue your enemies, it will bring them to reflection, it will
drive them to repentance, it will force them to prayer. That
hornet never dies. My God, my Father, follow not my enemies
with the hornet, if gentler means will bring them to their senses ;
but bring them to their senses, even if it take the hornet to do it.

Hornets and angels—are not the agencies of God both humble and illustrious? See the contrast, the flying insect and the flying angel, yet they are both the messengers of Heaven. Suppose them to meet one another in the summer air—what a talk they might have! Saith the hornet, "Why does he send me when he has servants like you who can do his work so much better than I, poor winged insect, charged indeed with a sting, can do?" Saith the angel, "Why am I not employed in studying the deeper problems of the universe, when little mean insects like this could go about the work of visitation, and penalty, and judgment?" Then they catch the Divinity of the purpose, they realise their election in God, and they say, "He doeth as it pleaseth him in the armies of heaven and among the children of men. There is no meanness in doing his work. His household is infinite and his servants are many—away, sting the enemy, bless the friend, let the decree of punishment be confirmed, and let the gospel of benediction be proclaimed." So away they go, hornet and angel, to carry out the will of just but clement Heaven. Beware : the angels of God and the hornets are both his servants.

Hornets and angels—are not God's agencies material and immaterial? Of matter and of spirit doth he not make his ministers? The hornet is of the earth, the angel is of the skies ; the hornet is from below, the angel is from above. There are no barren spaces in God's universe. All that great sky, on which you have never driven your small vehicles—beginning in your little baby's cart, and ending in your last hearse-ride to the gaping tomb—all that blue ground, what is it but an armoury in which he stores his resources? All things are his ; all things are mine it I be in him : if I am in Christ all things are mine : death, life, angels, principalities, powers, past, present, future—all, for I am Christ's and Christ is God's. Oh, hide thee in the broken heart of Christ, shelter thee in his wounded side : do not be living in thy little mean propositions, and small theories, and miserable dogmas, and noisy controversies—hide thee in the bleeding side of the wounded Lamb of God. Then all things that fought for him will fight for me, and if I do not fight, but stand still and suffer, draw no sword for me : thinkest thou not that I could pray to my Father, and he would give me more than twelve

legions of angels to defend me wherein I am right, and am hidden
in his Son Jesus Christ ?

Has there been a hornet in your estate lately ? I wonder
what it meant. Why cannot you kill that hornet ? It comes by
every post. You dare not open that letter—there is a hornet in
it. It comes by many a telegram. You dare not open the third
telegram you get to-morrow—there is a hornet in it. When life
is sharpened into a pain, when loss swiftly succeeds loss, when
the rich showers fall everywhere except on our own garden, when
every flower withers, when the first-born sickens and the eyes
are filled with mist, when the strong hands tremble—men should
bethink themselves : the hornet of the Lord is then piercing the
very air with its sting, puncturing our life and giving it great
agony. Do not call it insect ; call it God—do not call it misfortune
—let the atheist use up that same inheritance ; it is not misfortune,
it is—Providence. Oh, the hornet stings me, frets me, plagues
me ; will not let me have a holiday, knows when I am going out,
flies faster than the lightning express, waits for me at the sea-
shore, goes with me over the sea.—Beast ?—no : God, law, righteousness, mercy, didst thou but know it. It is sent to pain thee
into prayer, for thou hast sinned away thy visitation day, and
now it is God's turn. Lord, teach us the meaning of these
hornets ; they are hard to bear. We dare hardly turn over any
leaf for fear a hornet should spring up and sting us : our life is
now one daily fear—teach us the meaning of this, and by prayer
may we find the remedy.

Has there been an angel in your estate lately ? I say it with
shame that we are much quicker in seeing the hornet than in
seeing the angel ; our cry is readier than our hymn, our fear is
more emphatic than our love. Is the angel in your estate ? Do
you say you do not know ? Then I will find him for you. Be
still awhile. Are the children all well ? "Yes." Flowers
budding, singing-birds returning, the rain over and gone ? "Yes;
but the garden is much less than it used to be." A few flowers
in the window ? "Just a little box full, about eighteen inches
long." Still, you have them ? "Yes." Bread enough ?
"Plenty." A few friends ? "Few, but good." The angel is in

your lot. Give these things their highest meanings. There are plenty of people outside who would drag down life and make it smaller and smaller in its meanings. I would be sent of God to widen speech till it takes in all that it can of God's purpose and God's life. Poetry will have faith; faith itself is the poetry of reason; carry it up to its highest uses, and make your life as large and luminous as you can.

There are some people who are afraid of giving too great meanings to the events of life. There they get miserably wrong. When the ruddy morning comes, do not be afraid to call it the awakening angel. There are people near you who will call it fantasy; those people are lean, bony, shrivelled, dessicated, mean; and when they tell you that this is fantasy, and that is poetry, they speak out of themselves: they have no gospel to deliver. If thou dost meet a man on the high-road who takes up a flower and says, " Sir, this flower is a child of the sun," make friend of him rather than of the man who takes it up and says, "Ah, poor thing," and throws it over the fence. When spring spreads her green carpet and makes the warm air live with wordless songs, do not be afraid to call it God's angel. There be little, narrow, pence-table men who say, " It is spring, and there is rent day in spring, and there is hope of good trade in spring, and spring is one of four seasons of the year, and spring begins on the sixth and ends on the twentieth, and spring . . . . is nothing more."

"A primrose on the river's brink,
A yellow primrose is to him,
And it is nothing more,"——

quoth William Wordsworth in one of his poems. So happily did he hit the fool who does not see the angel in the flower. Get you books teachers, preachers who greaten things, who raise up children unto God out of the stones. The world needs such apostles and interpreters, or we should get very low indeed. The great expectation will bring the great reality; the great name will be as a bush with the great fact glowing in it like a revelation. Look you for the angels, for the angels prepare with all the generous hospitality of your love, and the angels will come and make your house their sanctuary, and show you the Eternal Presence

So God rules his world. "I will send hornets before thee, and they will drive out the Hivite and all the nations that set themselves against thee. I will not send angels to fight the Hivites : let the hornets do it. And I will send an angel before thee, and he will find thee a resting-place, space for the sanctuary, and he will give thee peace." Great God! rule us still; spare the hornets, we cannot bear them, but send the hornets, if nothing else will bring us home.

"I will send," saith the first text, "I will send," saith the second. Then do not *you* be sending anything; sit still; I am afraid of your sending things. "I will send hornets,"—then do not you be sending your nasty, bitter, cantankerous letters, keep your hands off post-cards, do not write anonymous slanders on sheets of paper you borrow from other people. "I will send," then do not interfere with God's movements. He knows when to send, how to send, how many to send, where to send—let him do it. "Dearly beloved, avenge not yourselves, but rather give place unto wrath, for it is written, Vengeance is mine, I will repay, saith the Lord." No weapon that is formed against thee shall prosper. I have seen the wicked in great power, and spreading himself like a green bay-tree. Yet he passed away, and, lo, he was not : yea, I sought him, but he could not be found. I have seen the great gourd of the wicked arching over his blasphemous head—lo, in the morning it was not. Why? For God prepared a worm—a worm, and the worm cankered the root of the gourd, and it withered away. Send angels if you can—live as if you would send ten thousand angels, sweet blessings, tender gospels, messages of the heart. You live in that direction, and some day God will pick you up in one of his chariots and drive you to the very camp of your enemies and show you unto them as their true friend. I will stand in God ; I will rest in God.

Let the hornet do its work ; let the angel fulfil his ministry. God's people cannot be permanently injured ; and as for God's Church, it shall be set up on foundations broad and immovable, and all its glowing pinnacles shall pierce the clouds, **and God's will shall be done on earth as it is done in heaven.**

MOSES IN THE MOUNT.

THIS account would seem to be supernatural and miraculous. What is supernatural? What is miraculous? We are fond of using these great words, but it is one thing to employ them and another rightly to measure and apply their meaning. What is miraculous to one man is commonplace to another. We should not be astounded by the miracles if we had correlative faith. The surprise of the disciples at the miracles did not throw any doubt upon the miracles themselves, but showed only too plainly the want of faith on the part of the observers. "How is it," said the Master, "that ye have no faith?" If we had faith there would be no miracles in the present narrow conception of that term; all our course would be lifted to a new level. Our wonder is the measure of our ignorance; our scepticism expresses the lack in our hearts of that wondrous power of interpretation and assimilation which is known by the name of *faith*. What is supernatural? and to whom is it supernatural? What is the standard? By what scales do you weigh things? We do not all stand upon one mental level. We must, therefore, go into individuality of heart, mind, attribute, and general condition, before we can understand the particular uses of so marvellous a term. What is supernatural to one man would seem to be the natural climate of another man's soul. When we read the large words of advanced philosophy,—when these words are brought under the attention of a great variety of persons, to some they will appear to be almost supernatural. They are so odd, so wholly unknown; they bear upon their faces lineaments not strange only but almost repellent; their image awakens no recognition in the consciousness of the reader; they are words that might be dismissed without the consciousness of loss. But to another kind of reader the words are friends, the longest of them is short, the

most out-of-the-way term is a well-known companion in many a
long day and night's study. So when we come upon incidents in
the Scriptures which appear to be uncommon to a degree involving what is generally known as the supernatural and the miraculous,
we ought to find out the quality of the reader before we determine
the quality of that which is read. All men do not read the Bible
with the same eyes. Some men can read the Bible through at
one perusal : they eat and drink abundantly at God's table, and
the festival never sates the appetite, but rather whets it and makes
it long for further revelation and satisfaction. Other men cannot
read the Bible at all. The very first verse is a gate they cannot
open : they are puzzled, bewildered, discouraged : in them is no
answering spirit; when the Bible and they meet, a process of
indignation seems to be instantly set up. Beware, therefore, of
the indiscriminate and lavish use of such terms as *supernatural,
miraculous, transcendental,* and fall back upon the mystery of your
own constitution as explaining a good many of the difficulties
which rise like mountains in your way. If ye had faith as a grain
of mustard-seed, ye would say to these mountains " Begone ! "
and they would vanish, like mist in the dissolving sun. But we
must, in the spirit of decency and justice, protest against a man
bringing his no-faith as the standard and measure of Divine revelation. The more spiritual we are, the less we shall be affrighted
by the supernatural ; the more carnal we are—loving the dust
and living in it—the more we shall be alarmed by what is termed
the miraculous element in the Bible. Sometimes by our criticism
we rebuke ourselves—it may be unconsciously, but not the less
severely. It is the reader who has fallen from the upper level ;
the Divine revelation has never lost its line. Suppose we regard
this marvellous incident as setting forth the possibility and
blessedness of rapturous communion with God, we lose nothing
of the moral grandeur and scenic majesty of the occasion. Even
as a historical record it may only transcend reason as poetry
transcends arithmetic. If you take away the poetry of
life, you take away the vowels from the alphabet. What is
left when you have taken away the few from the many, the
speakers from the dumb ? You have a cluster of consonants,
but no language. The consonants are dumb, the consonants
cannot utter a tone, the consonants wait until the vowels

breathe into them the breath of life. It is the same with the
Bible and the spiritual element. It is no Bible when the supernatural element, so called, is removed. Take out the spiritual,
and the Bible is but a framework of consonants; insert the
spiritual, and the Bible becomes a revelation. Many of us are
waiting for the vowels. We feel as if we had something to say,
but could only set the lips in a certain attitude, but utter no
articulate speech. We have much because the consonants are
more in number than the vowels. We have thought that bulk
was wealth; we have said that it is more important to have
many than to have few. Therein we have made a foolish speech.
We must have both consonants and vowels if we are to have
language, song, true music. So the spiritual or miraculous element
plays the part of the vowels in this wondrous Book of God.

But Moses was called to *solitary* vision and communion of a
spiritual kind. So he was. We need not stumble at that. "Aaron,
Nadab, and Abihu, and seventy of the elders" were not called
to the same summit as Moses. Quite true. This is happening
every day. The peaks of the mountain are less populated than
the base. We must not deny the mountain because we have
never climbed it. More persons have admired the Matterhorn
than have stood upon its pinnacles. It is always the one man
who sees first, hears most clearly, and is gifted with special
utterance. It is so in all departments and ranges of life. Each
of us has some prince who leads our thought—ay, and who gives
speech to our heart's dumb desire. The hireling waits for the
clock; the poet longs for the dawn. Dawn!—what language is
that? Not a hireling's. Say "bell," say "clock," "hour," and
you speak the hireling's measurable terms. But what is the
"dawn"? Who made that sweet, liquid, tender word, without
one line of hardness in it, requiring a woman's softness of heart
and speech to utter it as it ought to be spoken? Many a man has
risen in the morning who has never seen the dawn. Others have
gone up into the dawn, and have seen much and pledged the soul
in many a holy oath and covenant before coming down into the
market-place to do life's rough day's work. The prophet is
always alone. You cannot pluralise him. When he is near
you, he is not one of you. The prophet is always—mad. When
a man is solitary in scientific investigation, when he is far ahead

of "Aaron, Nadab, and Abihu, and seventy of the elders," we
call him a philosopher; when the daring traveller goes out
alone over sea and land and finds a river, a hill, a village, a
colony, that no man of his country or speech ever saw before, we
call him a discoverer;—when a man ascends the hills of
religious contemplation and communion and is shut up with God
forty days and forty nights, not knowing the pain of hunger or
the silence of solitude, we call him an enthusiast, a fanatic, a
dreamer. Thus we distribute our tinsel honours! There will
be a better judgment some day,—the first shall be last and the
last shall be first. He will be most philosopher who has prayed
most, most a discoverer who has brought to bear upon the
inspired record the keenest insight and quickest sympathy; he
shall be a prince who has had power with God. We must not
judge the acquisitions of others by the meanness of our own
spiritual results. Do not blame Moses for the rapture,—let us
blame ourselves for the want of it.

We need not stumble even at the tenth verse, which reads
thus: "And they saw the God of Israel: and there was under
his feet as it were a paved work of a sapphire stone, and as it
were the body of heaven in his clearness." The soul has eyes.
There are hours not related to the clock; there are birthdays
for which the calendar provides no line of registry. How natural
is this endeavour to make the conception plain by a visible
picture, and how visible pictures are lifted up to new meanings
and clothed with new solemnities by such sacred uses. There
have been times, even in our cold experience, when nature has
had to be called in to help the expression of the soul's delight.
We too have made comparisons; we too have been inventors of
parables, sometimes roughly outlined, but still having jewels in
their meaning, even "sapphire stones" and the "body of heaven."
We have compared our supreme love to a company of horses in
Pharaoh's chariot; we have chosen the apple-tree amongst the
trees of the wood, and have said that best images our soul's one
Love, and he in his turn looking round has seen a lily among the
thorns and said, "That sweet lily represents my chosen one."
Every heart has its own image, or parable, or symbol, by which
it sets forth to itself the best aspect of its supreme delight. When
we want to represent God, and our view of him, how naturally

we turn to the heavens. No earthly object will suffice. There
burns in us a sacred contempt for all things measurable. We
want all the broad brilliance of noonday, all the tender glory of
the midnight, all the pomp of the summer sky. There is
verily a natural religion ; it is a poor deity that can be set forth
in clay, and iron, and carved stone. Find any race that has lifted
up its religious conceptions so as to require for their imaging
all heaven, and surely you have found a race that may at any
moment alight upon the true God. What Ezekiel saw was as
the appearance of the likeness of a throne. John said that the
face he saw was like a jasper and a sardine stone, and the rainbow
which gave tenderness to the throne was in sight like unto an
emerald. When Jesus was transfigured, his face did shine as the
sun, and his raiment was white as the light. Do not take these
as equivalents, but as hints,—some idea of the majesty which
must have beamed upon the eyes of worship as they gazed with
religious awe upon sights for which there is no language. It
does us good to be wrought into passions which transcend all
adequate speech,—yes, it does the soul good to pray itself into
silence. We may have clear vision of God to such an extent as
to have every word taken away from our use and be left dumb in
the eloquence of silence.

Nor need we stumble at the twelfth verse, where the law is promised and where the written commandments were given. When
we are most religious we are most inclined to proclaim the law.
It is a poor rapture that does not come down upon legislation
with a new force, a firmer grip, and a deeper conception of its
moral solemnity. Know whether you have been with God upon
the mount by knowing how much law you have brought back
with you ; and when you would read the law, read it after you
have been long days and nights with the Lawgiver. Then there
will be no harshness in the tone, nothing terrific, repellent,
unsympathetic, but the laws, the commandments, the stern words
will be uttered with a suppressed power equal to tenderness,
with an awe equivalent to an interpretation, with a quiet solemnity that will have in it none of the sophism or violence of
threatening. The commandments have not been rightly read :
they have been pronounced in a judicial tone. How much better
to speak them in tender whispers. Thou *shalt not* have any God

before the true Jehovah,—I have seen him. Thou shalt *honour* thy father and thy mother, for God is *both,* and I have been a long time with the Father and have studied and felt his motherliness. Thou *shalt not* steal. Thou *shalt not* commit adultery. Thou *shalt not* kill. All these things grieve him, are opposed to him excite not the petty anger of vindictiveness but the ineffable grief of wounded holiness. Thou *shalt* not—thou *must* not. In the name of righteousness, holiness, tenderness, beauty, harmony, music, truth, *do not* on the one hand, and *do* on the other.

Moses was absorbed in holy vision. The visible is not always the most real—may we say that the visible is sometimes not real at all? We must be in certain mental moods before we can understand that speech. People speak about believing their eyes. I know not of less credible witnesses than our eyes! Discredit them and distrust them at once. You will be duped by many a sophism if you trust to your eye for sight. The eyes are within—faculties spiritual, themselves unseen but always seeing. We ourselves have been so transported with sacred rapture or have been so absorbed in deep thought as not to have known where we were, by what circumstances we were environed. Speak of environment!—it has a thousand times been burst asunder or transcended by consciousness for which there is no adequate name. These give us hints of the sublime future of disembodiment. We shall be clothed upon with our house from heaven. The leaden flesh that keeps us tethered to one place shall go back to the dust whence it came, and the spirit-winged fire shall go back to the God who gave it. We shall not always be slaves, or prisoners, bound to particular places and fastened down by particular chains.

These absorptions, raptures, supernatural communions, if you so please to term them, give us hints of jubilee, festival, immortality. Do not dissipate their meaning by a superficial criticism of the letter, but magnify and glorify their meaning by giving to them all the sympathy and adoration of the spirit. From the level of every life there is a way up to the mount of God.

Exodus xxv. 21:

"Thou shalt put the mercy seat above upon the ark; and in the ark thou shalt put the testimony that I shall give thee."

THE ARK OF THE TESTIMONY:
THE TRANSIENT SYMBOL OF AN ETERNAL TRUTH.

THIS twenty-fifth chapter supplies minute information as to the construction and contents of the ark. The children of Israel had but recently received the formal law through the ministry of Moses. Up to this time they had worshipped under the open sky, and all the host of heaven had seen the manner of their life. In this chapter it is proposed to have an enclosure, a tabernacle, a place screened and roofed, how unsubstantially soever, which was to be known distinctively as the house of God. This proposition was, indeed, the commandment of God himself: "And the Lord spake unto Moses, saying, Speak unto the children of Israel that they bring me an offering: of every man that giveth it willingly with his heart, ye shall take my offering, and let them make me a sanctuary that I may dwell among them."

But was not this a movement towards limitation, instead of a progress outward and onward towards wider spaces, even towards infinitude itself? How if the Divine message had read thus: "Speak unto the children of Israel that I am about to enlarge the sphere within which their life has heretofore been confined; they shall now see the higher and larger stars, and an ampler horizon shall gladden and satisfy their vision"? Instead of this, God proposes the erection of a small house, by which he would seem to shut out all the beauty and most of the light. For the moment, at least, we are disappointed; expansion, not contraction, would have seemed more like the way of God. But think awhile, lest we mistake proportions and meanings which lie out of sight. What we call Infinitude—the quality which overflows and confounds our imagination—must contract itself, so to speak, if we are to get sight of it; and in this sense the building of the small house, called the Tabernacle, was not a movement towards limitation, but towards concentration, and intensity, and tender nearness. A man may have all the earth round about him, and yet have nowhere to lay his head; plenty of space, but no home; a universe, but no Sanctuary; infinitude to roam through, but no Father to speak to, and no Heart to rest in. All great love has to make boundaries for itself; to put itself into little homely acts, and to use words which simple souls can understand. The mother who would die to save her child has to put her great love into a picture, a toy, a babble better than all eloquence. The great ALL must break itself up into the available *Some.* It was but small consolation to the petulant man in the parable to be told, " All that I have is thine "; he wanted some of it to be going on with,—" a kid, that I might make merry with my friends." So, even in our common life, we get hints of things that are going on above.

This tabernacle was built for the reception of the ark. A wonderful tabernacle it was, as one glance at the specification will show—" Gold, silver, brass, blue, and purple, and scarlet, and fine linen; goats' hair and rams' skins dyed red; oil for the light; spices for anointing oil, and for sweet incense; tables overlaid with pure gold, dishes, spoons, covers, all of pure gold." So God's house was no poor hut run up in an hour or two; but so delicate in its richness and beauty as to be more a thought than a thing. It was no creation of human fancy. Moses was no more left to settle the plan and the furniture than Noah was left to settle the colours of the rainbow. There was not a ring, a knob, a loop, a socket, a coupling, or a pin, which God did not specifically design. It was the same when he made the larger house which we call Nature: there was none with him when he laid the foundations of the earth, and when he made a tabernacle for the sun he was alone. It is wonderful, indeed, how little there is of man's own doing anywhere. He has undoubtedly hammered a few things into shape, and brought together a few walls and roofs which he calls cities; but he borrows the foundation from God, and the rivers are not his own, nor is the light cther than a visitor sent from God. It is pitiful to see man's work exactly as it is; pitiful to see the shortness of his ladders and what trouble he has to set them up; and it sometimes makes one cry bitterly to watch him falling off the very summit of his victories into the dust out of which he came. He cannot bind the unicorn with his hand in the furrow, nor doth the eagle mount up at his command. He is a servant. Let him know his place and keep it. Take your counsel from God, and ever listen for the voice which says—" And look that thou make it after the pattern which was showed thee in the mount,"—the mount of Suggestion, where we may see in forecast, in gilded and wreathen clouds, what God would have us build for his glory and our own comfort.

As God made a tabernacle for the sun, so he made a tabernacle for the ark, out of which streams a light above the brightness of the sun. The ark of the covenant was a box or chest, say fifty-four inches long, thirty inches broad, and thirty inches high. This box, made of choice wood, was overlaid with pure gold. The lid which covered the box was called the Mercy Seat. Observe that particularly. Over the lid, or mercy seat, were two golden cherubs, one at either end, facing each other and covering it with their expanded wings. God promised to meet Moses at the mercy seat : " There will I meet with thee, and I will commune with thee from above the mercy seat, from between the two cherubims which are upon the ark of the testimony,"—a promise which explains the words of the Psalmist, " Thou that dwellest between the cherubims, shine forth "; a tender reference to the olden time, a memory of childhood, full of pathetic meaning and tender retrospect. Within the box were placed the two tables of stone on which the ten commandments were written by the finger of God : " I will write on the tables the words that were written in the first tables which thou brakest, and thou shalt put them in the ark." Thus furnished, the ark was deposited in the inner place, in the holy of holies ; indeed, in the first Book of Chronicles, the holy of holies is called "the house of the mercy seat." So much, then, as a help towards an outward view of the ark of the testimony. A box ; a box made of choice wood and covered with pure gold ; a box set away in a holy and well-guarded place ;—plain enough, so far, yet around this box there shall gather meanings deep as the springs of life, and histories full of uproar, and tragedy, and progress ; and in the end the ark of wood shall be lost, but the Law and the Mercy which it enshrined or symbolised shall be felt to be in a still holier place and in a more enduring sanctuary. Thus, the corruptible shall put on incorruption. "And the temple of God was opened in heaven, and there was seen in his temple the ark of his testament." What we call History—the shallow and insecure vessel which holds the dregs, but allows the aroma to escape—says that the ark was destroyed when the Babylonians set fire to the temple, and declares as a certainty that the ark was not contained in the second temple. Perhaps not. We need not be curious about the merely material ark. It descended, in idea and purpose, out of heaven from God, and it was seen amid " lightnings, and voices, and thunderings, and an earthquake, and great hail," in the temple not made with hands, —uncontaminated by the earth which it had blessed, and unchanged in meaning by all the mutations and dangers of its eventful history.

The ark may be taken as symbolical of the Divine presence, or the Divine plan in human life. It was a visible form of an invisible power. Again and again in private and public history we come upon a peculiar and almost unthinkable *Something* which focalises and rules all minor administrations ; a subtle something, which makes superstition tremble, and constrains religion to pray ; now a hand upon the wall, now as the spell of a dream, a benediction of heavenly sweetness, a judgment pure and terrible as fire ;—Something which analysis cannot exhaust, and which scepticism cannot deny. In the ark, for example, you find *law*. See, too, the peculiar place occupied by law : the ark is in the tabernacle ; not only in the tabernacle, but in the most sacred part of that sacred place ; not only in the holiest part of the holy house, but actually in the *midst* of the ark is found the immutable law of God. Thus we have law at the very centre and heart of things ! Not an occasional flash, but a steady, ever-abiding, all-controlling force. Under all surfaces, far below all coverlets woven and arranged by skill of man, deeper than all foam, and tumult, and revolution, is to be found righteous and inexorable law ! Some call it fate ; some, " a divinity that shapes our ends"; some, "God over all, blessed for evermore." But there it is! Creation is held fast together at all points by the grip of law. Not a pebble slips off the edge of the world; not a bird wanders away to another star, though it be the nearest light; no drop of dew trickles into forbidden places; and as for men, in their maddest ambitions they do but strike the bars of their prison, and awake by their frantic impotence the remonstrance, "Why do the heathen rage, and the people imagine a vain thing?" Sometimes, indeed, the excellency of the wicked has mounted to the heavens and his head has reached unto the clouds; yet out of this hidden ark there has come a voice of doom—"Though they dig into hell, thence shall mine hand take them; though they climb up to heaven, thence will I bring them down." Nor is this a boast which cannot be tested. All history confirms it. To deny the operation of this mysterious and sovereign law is to take away the key without which history is an impenetrable and confounding enigma. Human history is the visible side of Divine revelation. You have *law* at the centre; and you must obey that law in all material things, even though you resist or despise its spiritual demands. You may have an atheistic character, but you shall not have an atheistic wall; though the bricks and the stones be banded with iron and cemented with molten lead, yet will they be thrown down if you mock the law which holds up the older masonry of the universe. In this matter, as in all others, peace can only come by righteousness. That which is at the heart of things is *right:* not something fickle, eccentric, tantalising; but *law,* RIGHTEOUSNESS, GOD!

But, happily, the ark represents something more than law; and every reflective man will acknowledge that in the system within which we live, there is a mystery for which some gentler name than law must be found. The lid of the ark was the seat of mercy. It signified propitiation, favour, mediation, ground and medium of communion with God. Study that tender symbol a moment, if you please. Law, in coming up from the centre, comes through the lid or covering of mercy; it is, so to speak, attempered, or it would come like a sword, or a fire, or a judgment terrible in righteousness. On the other hand, starting the movement from the outside, in our appeal to law we go through

the medium of mercy. We do not, dare not, challenge the law
in its own name or on its own merits. "By the deeds of the law
shall no flesh living be justified." Our approach is through
mercy, and our daily prayer is, "God be merciful to me a
sinner." It is most instructive to mark how a life founded as
ours is on law, is continually proving the presence of something
other and sweeter than law; and it is humiliating to find how
easily we exaggerate that tenderer quality, so as to delude ourselves into the belief that law is secondary and impotent. See
how law is made almost gracious. Take, as an illustration, the
law of hunger,—how terrible, how urgent, how inexorable is that
law ; how soon it assails the life with consuming fire ! Yet God
has made our food more than a mere satisfaction of hunger : he
has provided things savoury and dainty in pasture and vineyard,
so that hunger brings with it enjoyment and even religious
gladness. That which would burn us with unquenchable fire, is
attempered, and softened, and turned into an occasion and process
of enjoyment. Yet how true it is that this very attempering and
softening of law brings with it temptation and peril ! Hence,
appetite conquers reason, and the tender mercy of God becomes
an occasion of licentiousness and aggravated sin. Take any law
of your own nature ; see how severe and terrible it is in itself ;
observe how it is graded and modified, so as to become, not
tolerable merely, but enjoyable in its operation; and then say
whether we have not every one of us made the goodness of God
an excuse for trespass and indulgence.

Thus, then, the ark is symbolical of something we ourselves
have known in life, apart from specific religious teaching,—something of law, and something of mercy; a power of condemnation,
and a power of recovery and healing ; a severity very terrible,
and a goodness that yearns over our life and offers us redemption.
Whether we accept the Biblical names and interpretations of these
forces, or laws, or phenomena, there they are, as broad and vivid
facts in our daily life ; and no sophistry of reasoning, or perver-
sion of fancy, can get rid of their solemn and pathetic operations.
The severe winter and the gentle summer ; the stormy wind and
the still small voice; the bitter pool and the tree which sweetens
it ; the dark fear and the sunny hope ; the herb that stings and
the herb that heals,—these things, known to our senses, strewn

all over our life as lessons we ought to learn, show us that this
ark, even if only a creation of fancy, symbolises with startling
clearness the reality, the grandeur, and the sweetness of life as
we know it.   This, indeed, is the peculiar glory of the Bible,
namely, its marvellous forecast of things that have turned out to
be, and its felicitous representations of the times that were to
come upon the world.   He would be a churl only, and an unjust
man, who would deny at least this literary tribute to the dreamers
and seers of the Bible.

In noticing a few remarkable points in the history of the ark,
we shall be more careful about the spiritual teaching than about
the mere chronology of that history, and thus we shall secure
closer continuity of doctrine and illustration.   As our song is to
be of mercy and judgment, it will be grateful to us first to see
how the mercy of the Lord was revealed amongst his people.
Thus :—" And the Israelites departed from the mount of the
Lord three days' journey : and the ark of the covenant of the
Lord went before them in the three days' journey, to search out
a resting-place for them. . . . And it came to pass when the ark
set forward that Moses said, Rise up, Lord, and let thine enemies
be scattered ; and let them that hate thee flee before thee : and
when it rested he said, Return, O Lord, unto the many thousands
of Israel."   And again, though Moses died, yet the ark remained
a symbol of mercy in the days of Joshua :—" The officers commanded the people, saying, When ye see the ark of the covenant
of the Lord your God, then ye shall remove from your place and
go after it ; yet there shall be a space between you and it, about
two thousand cubits by measure ; come not near unto it, that ye
may know the way by which ye must go ; for ye have not passed
this way heretofore."
Thus the law of human movement is turned into a tender and
minute direction by God's condescension.   Unquestionably there
is a law of movement.   We *must* go forward.   How ?   Into
darkness ?   Into danger ?   Into thickening mysteries that bring
with them sevenfold darkness, and trouble that makes the soul
afraid ?   No ; we are offered guidance, defence, and rest !   " The
steps of a good man are ordered by the Lord " ; " Thine ears
shall hear a word behind thee, saying, This is the way."   The

journey was only three days long, yet it must not be taken without the foregoing ark. The people had not gone a certain road before, and therefore they must be accompanied by the sacred symbol of the Divine presence. A flood was ahead of them ("for Jordan overfloweth all his banks all the time of harvest"), and therefore the mercy of the Lord must prevent and defend and mightily save his chosen ; so "the waters of Jordan were cut off before the ark of the covenant of the Lord." A wonderful hint this of the place of what is called Providence, in nature. The ark clears a space for itself everywhere. Strange roads become as familiar scenes, and threatening waters are dried up in the channels they have proudly overflowed. Why should we doubt the mere letter when the spirit of such miracles is attested by evidence so accessible and incontrovertible ? Christian missions alone furnish a history radiant with this self-same miracle. Foreign lands have become sweet homes under the benediction of the sacred ark, and hearts that overflowed with contempt and rage have opened themselves in wondrous submission and love to welcome the Lord and his hosts. The same miracle has turned our own life into a marvel and a joy, times without number. Have we not been called to unknown places, and thrown into combinations which have baffled us by their intricacy, and forced into roads which seem to end in darkness ? What of the days when we were poor and friendless ? What of the first gate ajar that tempted our feet into new pastures ? What of the first great sorrow that threatened to swallow us up and to destroy our life as with a flood ? Did we not then hear a voice which said, "Ye have not passed this way heretofore" ? In proportion as we have been in difficulty and distress, in peril and loneliness, and have seen the delivering hand of God, do we read the record of these old miracles as a familiar language,—not the less real and spiritually *true* because of figures and symbols which to the unsympathetic mind are mere creations of poetry. We ourselves have seen visions, and have felt raptures, which poetry alone could hope to express even in dim and imperfect outline. So much for what has been already known. Ahead of us rolls the overflowing river. "What wilt thou do in the swellings of Jordan ?" Arise, O Lord, thou and the ark of thy strength, and the waters that I fear shall flee away, and the floods of Jordan shall be as heaps on either side of thy redeemed and rejoicing servant.

At this point of the history we touch the ark of the covenant with sympathy deep and tender. We ourselves have seen, felt, known, and handled this ark of God. Now and again we have in impious venturesomeness gone forward without it; and what has come of our self-confidence? The imaginary rocks have been as bogs under our feet, and our best devices have lured us into peril. The river has not parted before us, nor has a way been found for us in the desert. On the other hand, we have awaited the rising of the ark; and have followed as it led; and what has been the result? Progress, safety, rest; mountains have been thrown down, and fierce countenances have softened into friendliness and welcomes; we have entered upon a way where no lion lay in wait, nor any ravenous beast could be found,—the way of the Lord's redeemed upward without steepness, with heaven shining at its end. Well may we say, therefore, that the ark has not been lost: "In the temple of God is the ark of his testament." The wood and the gold have perished, but mercy and judgment still rule us from the heavens. "Lightnings, and voices, and thunderings, and an earthquake, and great hail," still have their place in this earthly life; but in God's temple is seen the "ark of his testament."

As we have thus seen the goodness of the Lord, we may now behold also his severity, as shown here and there in the history of the ark.

(1) Remember the account of the fall of Jericho, and how usual it is to represent the overthrow of the city as almost due (such is the popular impression) to the blast of "seven trumpets of rams' horns." Out of this circumstance has come much teaching about the possible success of improbable instruments and agencies, as if it were only necessary to have a ram's horn in order to do great wonders in the wars of the Lord. The ark of the testimony was at the taking of Jericho, and *must* be at the taking of every stronghold. "And Joshua the son of Nun called the priests, and said unto them, Take up the ark of the covenant, and let seven priests bear seven trumpets of rams' horns before the ark of the Lord." "And the ark of the covenant of the Lord followed the priests." "And the rearward came after the ark."

"So the ark of the Lord compassed the city." It was not the tramp of priests, or the blast of rude horns, but the ark of the Lord, that brought down the strong wall. It is not our officialism, our music, or our noise, but the name of Christ—the true ark of the covenant—that must bring down the pride of heathenism and all the ramparts of ungodliness. "My grace is sufficient for thee : for my strength is made perfect in weakness." "Be still, and know that I am God : I will be exalted among the heathen, I will be exalted in the earth."

(2) Recall a second instance. Israel went out against the Philistines to battle, and pitched beside Ebenezer; and the Philistines pitched in Aphek ; and Israel was smitten before the Philistines, and they slew of the army in the field about four thousand men. In dismay, Israel sent to Shiloh for the ark of the covenant, saying, "When it cometh among us, it may save us out of the hand of our enemies." So the ark was brought ; and when the ark of the covenant of the Lord came into the camp, all Israel shouted with a great shout, so that the earth rang again. And the Philistines were afraid, and said, "God is come into the camp." But the Philistines conquered Israel, and there fell of Israel thirty thousand footmen. And the ark itself fell into the hand of the enemy ; and the Philistines took the ark of God, and brought it from Ebenezer unto Ashdod, and set it in the house of Dagon their god. Israel sent for the ark in extremity, as many a man sends for God in the hour of fear and mortal distress ; but the ark would not become the mere convenience of capricious and disheartened men. If we stopped here, mistaking, as hurried readers are apt to do, a semicolon for a period, we should say that the ark was worsted, and that Dagon had triumphed over Jehovah. But, lo, the strong god of Philistia was found in the early morning "fallen upon his face to the earth before the ark of the Lord" ! It was but an accident, mayhap, so Dagon must be lifted up and set in his place again ; but the second morning found Dagon in still sadder plight, for his head and both the palms of his hands were cut off upon the threshold, and only the stump of Dagon was left to him. Many warriors have taken Christ captive; but he has troubled them until they have cried with the Philistines, "What shall we do with the ark of the Lord ? Tell us wherewith we shall send it

to his place." Some victories are the profoundest defeats which any cause can sustain. When Christ and Dagon are brought into close quarters, it is Dagon that dies ! A man of Benjamin rent his clothes when the ark was taken ; when Eli heard that the ark had been borne away, he fell backward and died; and the wife of Phinehas called her son Ichabod, saying, "The glory is departed from Israel, for the ark of God is taken !" Such is our shortsightedness in looking upon the ways of the Lord. Unchristian men do not know what to make of Christ, even when they suppose themselves to have taken him prisoner in some fierce war of words. They seize him as their prey ; they condemn him to exile or death; yet there is something about his name that troubles them, and there is a fire in his words which gives them pain. " It is a fearful thing to fall into the hands of the living God," said the falling Dagon. " God is a consuming fire," say all they who intrude upon his throne. How to get rid of Christ—the living Ark—was the urgent question of his enemies ! They besought him that he would depart out of their coasts. " Away with him ! crucify him !" was the indignant cry. He was slain, yet he is found in heaven ; as the symbolic ark was burned by Nebuchadnezzar, yet seen in the temple of God. In the kingdom of God, Destruction is an accident, Ascension is a law. Weep not for the ark, weep for yourselves. " Behold, the Lord rideth upon a swift cloud, and shall come into Egypt ; and the idols of Egypt shall be moved at his presence, and the heart of Egypt shall melt in the midst of it." " Bel boweth down, Nebo stoopeth ; they stoop, they bow down together," for the hand of the Lord is heavy upon them.

(3) A third instance will confirm what has been said about the severity of God. At the bidding of the priests and the diviners, the Philistines sent away the ark, upon a new cart, drawn by two milch kine on which there had come no yoke, and by the side of the ark they put jewels of gold as a trespass offering. Even then the Philistines were not sure whether it was "a chance that happened" to them, or a judgment direct from Heaven. They set a test that they might know this, and the test showed that God had been amongst them of a truth. When the ark came to Bethshemesh, the people were reaping their wheat harvest in the valley, and when they saw the ark they rejoiced with exceeding

joy. But, alas, the men of Bethshemesh looked into the ark of
the Lord ; and the anger of the Lord was kindled against them,
and he slew of them a great multitude. Is the Lord ever
patient with our foolish curiosity ? Can any man *see* God and
live ? It is precisely here that so many men are slain to-day.
We go too near the sun, and we are blinded by the glory we
would analyse. God will not submit himself to our examina-
tions ; hence we find thousands of dead critics where there ought
to have been a living Church countless as the stars in number !
Let there be a space between us and the ark—"about two
thousand cubits by measure"—for "God is greatly to be feared
in the assembly of the saints, and to be had in reverence of all
them that are about him."

(4) An incident not remotely related to this scene at Bethshemesh occurred when, at the instance of David, all Israel went
up to Kirjath-jearim, which belonged to Judah, "to bring up
thence the ark of God the Lord." The bringing up of the ark
was again the occasion of great joy. The people had not
inquired at it in the days of Saul. David's proposition, therefore, revived an ancient and precious memory, and gathered, as
by the call of a battle-trumpet, "all Israel, from Shihor of Egypt
even unto the entering of Hemath." As the ark was borne away,
"David and all Israel played before God with all their might,
and with singing, and with harps, and with psalteries, and with
timbrels, and with cymbals, and with trumpets." At one point
of the journey the oxen stumbled, and to save the ark from
apparent danger, Uzza put forth his hand to keep it in its place.
But the anger of the Lord was kindled against Uzza, and he
smote him, and there he died before God. Will man attempt to
eke out the failing strength of Omnipotence? Doth it become us
to watch the stars lest they fall, or to open the clouds at dawn
lest the sun should miss his way ? Shall we appoint ourselves
the special guardians of the truth, and surround it with our
defences, lest God should have no foothold on his own earth ?
God is not to be worshipped with men's hands, as though he
needed anything,—"I will take no bullock out of thy house, nor
he-goats out of thy folds ; for every beast of the forest is mine
and the cattle upon a thousand hills." "If I were hungry, I
would not tell thee : for the world is mine, and the fulness

thereof." We have written books, and endowed communities, and passed Acts of Parliament, to keep steady the ark of God. Can we wonder that there are so many dead men, who have a name, indeed, to live, but in reality are plucked up by the roots? Sympathy without meddlesomeness, reverence without self-exaggeration, willingness to help without obtrusion of service,— Lord, with this spirit baptize us every one in the pitifulness of thy great mercy!

Coming to still more closely practical applications. Here and there in the course of the study we have indicated one or two modern bearings of the subject, which admit of obvious amplification. Let us look at one or two others.

The Israelites had a *visible* symbol of the Divine presence so long as they retained the ark in their midst. It was something to look at,—something for the heart to stay itself upon in the time of fear and trouble. But look at our own case. Are we not left without a centre that can be seen, and without a locality sanctified above all other places? We are truly in a great wilderness, but to what shrine can we point men when they mock our faith, and foretell a disastrous end to our pilgrimage? Sometimes, indeed, we find our hearts in a mood of intense longing for the days that are gone; they live backward through the many and cloudy yesterdays until they come upon the exciting times when God spake, as it were, face to face with his loved ones; when the guiding pillar went before the host day and night; when the ark was the signal of movement and the pledge of security; when the "fourth like unto the Son of man" walked in the burning fiery furnace with the faithful, and when the Son of God took little children in his arms and blessed them. To have lived then! To have had the eye filled with his beauty and the ear satisfied with the music of his sweet voice! To have touched the hem of his garment, to have stood within his shadow, to have plucked and kept for ever some poor flower of the meadow pressed by his feet,—to have seen *something* that was his! So yearns the heart in tender wish and sad regret. And to the world we seem to have nothing. The rain is not ours, for it falleth on the just and on the unjust; the sun is not ours, for it shineth on the evil and on the good. We look into the great

voids of space, but no image makes us glad. And there is no
rod in our hand with which we can make scoffers afraid because
of the wonders of the Lord. Have we not, then, fallen on mean
times,—all poetry dead and gone, all music hushed for ever?
To such questionings the Scriptures give a distinct reply. They
tell us that ours are the brightest and noblest of all the days of
time! "If the ministration of death, written and engraven in
stones, was glorious, which glory was to be done away, how
shall not the ministration of the Spirit be rather glorious? For
if that which was done away was glorious, much more that which
remaineth is glorious." But the natural man seeth not this glory,
neither can he know it, for it is spiritually discerned. "And it
shall come to pass, when ye be multiplied and increased in the
land, in those days, saith the Lord, they shall say no more, The
ark of the covenant of the Lord: neither shall it come to mind;
neither shall they remember it; neither shall they visit it;
neither shall that be done any more." Herein is that saying
true, "The hour cometh, and now is, when ye shall neither in
this mountain, nor yet at Jerusalem, worship the Father." The
local has become the universal, and all things are inscribed—
"Holy unto the Lord."

That law and mercy are still at the heart of things is a
truth which is acknowledged in some form even by others
than Christian believers; but by Christian believers it ought
to be ardently and gratefully maintained as at once the glory
and the security of life.

We know that there is law,—a law of *continuity,* for all things
remain from one generation to another,—the stars do not burn
themselves out with all their shining, nor is the sea dried up by
the fire of the sun; a law of *development,* for life changes, im-
proves, and matures itself, subtly but certainly; a law of *trespass,*
for who can take fire into his bosom and not be burned, or trifle
with poison and save his life? We know that there is law
round about us, and high above us. What is it that causes
ambition to break its billows into harmless foam upon the eternal
rocks of Truth and Right? What is it that drives the diviners
mad when they seek to misread the writing or forge the signature
of God? What is it that throws down the half-built tower,

whose summits were to have reached the stars? We are shut in, watched, ruled; and yet we see no Hand moving amongst our affairs. We make our plans, and our programmes read like music; but lo, we never enter the City that lured us, or get near the Tree whose fruit was to have made us wise. Wickedness swells with rage, and comes against the righteous in the fury of its strength; and lo, it staggers, and moans, and dies. The winds blow high and the clouds shut out the light, yet no star is lost, nor is any planet-ship wrecked in the wild storm. If we should fear that some loss may have happened in that upper sea, all the stars quiet us with the words, "Do thyself no harm, we are all here." There must be some meaning in all this,—in this infinite order, this calm profound which underlies the storm, this vengeance that consumes, this life that cannot die! What is the secret? Can any man name the spell, so baleful yet so gentle? Do not mock us with a word that we shall instantly feel to be hollow and untrue. Speak to us a word that shall, at all events, have a sound of reality in it,—mysterious as if it came up from Eternity, sympathetic as if it issued from a Heart of love. "But the temple of God was opened in heaven, and THERE WAS SEEN IN HIS TEMPLE THE ARK OF HIS TESTAMENT."

We know that there is mercy;—mercy in the very "process of the suns," for time turns many a bitter pain into a hallowed recollection, and wounds thought to be incurable have been staunched and healed,—mercy in the gifts of nature, for in bread there is sweetness, and the meadow and the garden are full of pleasantness,—mercy in social life, for sympathy puts our misery to sleep, and friendship revives our drooping strength,—mercy in returning slumber, and mercy in the peacefulness of our awaking;—minor mercies, all of them, leading, star-like, to a larger love,—leading to Bethlehem, to Gethsemane, to Golgotha, and there merging their secondary rays in the ineffable light, the infinite glory out of which they came. "It is of the Lord's mercies that we are not consumed." "According to his mercy hath he saved us." There are times in our life when the memory of sin is so vivid, and its burden so grievous, that one cry only can express our necessity and our pain, our self-helplessness and our hope—"God be merciful to me a sinner";

" Have mercy upon me, O Lord, according to thy lovingkindness, according unto the multitude of thy tender mercies blot out my transgressions." It is at such times that we feel the power of words like these, " The blood of Jesus Christ cleanseth from all sin"; " There is a fountain opened in the house of David for sin and for uncleanness." All the other mercies that have been softening and beautifying our life, say to us in pleading tones, " If *we* have thus quieted your fears, and set a lamp for you in the time of darkness; if *we* have found for you unexpected help, and surprised you with unlooked-for gladness, how much more shall the blood of Christ, who, through the eternal Spirit, offered himself without spot to God, purge your conscience from dead works to serve the living God:" If you would see Mercy written in largest letters, " Behold the Lamb of God that taketh away the sin of the world"; if you would see Mercy in its sublimest attitude, look upon the uplifted dying Son of God ; if you would hear Mercy's sweetest, gentlest tone, hear it as Jesus says, "Him that cometh unto me, I will in no wise cast out." What is the meaning of all the mercy which comes down upon our weary life ? Is it a transient shower ? Are the influences that quicken and bless us merely fugitive and accidental ? Was the Cross the culmination of a rude tragedy ? What does Mercy mean ? Is it a mere sentiment? Is it a momentary suspension of discipline ? Or is it Law in its highest mood ? Is it Righteousness weeping ? Is it Majesty bowing down from the heavens that it may find the lost ? Hear the answer which alone satisfies the judgment and the heart—" The temple of God was opened in heaven, and THERE WAS SEEN IN HIS TEMPLE THE ARK OF HIS TESTAMENT."

And yet we are not left without a visible sign of God's presence. So long as we have the Bible we have the Ark of the Covenant. The most terrible yet the most gentle of all books is the Bible ! Law is in it, and Mercy. It plagues the house, or blesses it, as the house of Obed-edom was blessed when he received the ark of the Lord into his dwelling. It throws down the Dagon of false worship, of dishonest trade, of false appearances. Yet how it overflows with mercy, and promise, and hope ! It is like a river the streams whereof make glad the city of God. It is quiet as a green pasture in the summer noon. It is as a gentle rain on the tender herb, and as showers of blessing on the fainting field. Yet what a sword it is, and how like a fire it burns! Let the bad man look into it for a text with which to sanctify his meanness or falsehood, and it will scorch him with intolerable heat! Let the penitent look into it that he may know how to return unto the Lord, and it will glow with welcomes and benedictions! Let a man fall upon it, and he will be broken ; let it fall upon a man, and it will grind him to powder! Verily this book is the Ark of the Testimony. The Babylonian may burn the book, but he cannot destroy the Revelation. The infidel may take the book in some controversial war, but it will trouble him until it be released and sent away in honour. Like the Son of man, it is here, yet it is in heaven. It fears not them that kill the body. Fire will not consume it, nor will the sea hold it in prison. Its name is Wonderful, and the government is on its shoulder. "The temple of God was opened in heaven, and in his temple was seen the ark of his testament."

Exodus xxv -xxvii.

The two chief objects within the Court were the Brazen Altar and the Tabernacle. Sacrificial worship was old, but the local Sanctuary was quite new. The Tabernacle is most frequently called the Tabernacle of the Congregation. A better rendering is supposed to be, "The Tent of Meeting." The Tabernacle was also called "The Tent of the Testimony," in allusion to the fact that it was the depositary of the Tables of the Law. The highest meaning of the structure was expressed by the Ark, which symbolised the constant presence of Jehovah. *The Speaker's Commentary* says: "We may regard the sacred contents of the Tabernacle as figuring what was peculiar to the Covenant of which Moses was the Mediator, the closer union of God with Israel, and their consequent election as 'a kingdom of priests, an holy nation': while the Brazen Altar in the Court not only bore witness for the old sacrificial worship by which the Patriarchs had drawn nigh to God, but formed an essential part of the Sanctuary, signifying by its now more fully developed system of sacrifices in connection with the Tabernacle those ideas of Sin and Atonement which were first distinctly brought out by the revelation of the Law and the sanctification of the nation." In the Ark there was no image or symbol of God. The Ark of the Covenant was never carried in a ceremonial procession. In all important particulars it differed from Egyptian shrines. When the Tabernacle was pitched the Ark was kept in solemn darkness. The staves were to remain always in the rings, whether the Ark was in motion or at rest, that there might never at any time be a necessity for touching the Ark itself or even the rings (2 Sam. vi. 6, 7). "The cherubims were not to be detached images, made separately and then fastened to the mercy seat, but to be formed out of the same mass of gold with the mercy seat, and so to be part and parcel of it." The Holy of Holies was a square of fifteen feet, and the Holy place an oblong thirty feet by fifteen. So far as known, "horns" were peculiar to Israelite altars.

THE TABERNACLE.

THE specification for the building of the tabernacle purports to be Divinely dictated. We can form some idea of the validity of such a claim, for we have the test of creation by which to try it. We can soon find out discrepancies, and say whether this is God's work or an artificer's. A revelation which bounds itself by the narrow limits of an architect's instruction admits of very close inquiry. Creation is too vast for criticism, but a tabernacle invites it. Let us, then, see how the case stands,— whether God is equal to himself, whether the God of the opening chapters of Genesis is the God of the mount upon which, according to this claim, the tabernacle was Divinely outlined in expressive cloud. Note, at the very outset, that the account of making the tabernacle occupies far more space than the history of the creation of the heavens and the earth. We soon read through what is given of the history of creation, but how long we have had to travel through this region of architectural cloud. It seemed as if the story would never end. This is a remarkable corroboration of the authenticity of both accounts. A long account of creation would have been impossible, presuming the creation to be the embodiment and form of the Divine word executed without human assistance. That account could not have been long. When there is nothing, so to say, between God's word and God's deed, there is no history that can be recorded. The history must write itself in the infinite unfoldment of those germs, or of that germ with which creation began. A short account of the tabernacle would have been impossible, presuming that all the skins, colours, spices, rings, staves, figures, dishes, spoons, bowls, candlesticks, knobs, flowers, lamps, snuffers, and curtains, were Divinely described ; that every tache, loop, hook, tenon, and socket was on a Divine plan, and that human ingenuity had nothing whatever to do with a structure which in its exquisite fashioning was more a thought than a thing. So far, the God of Genesis is the God of Exodus : a subtle and massive harmony unites the accounts, and a common signature authenticates the marvellous relation. When God said, "Let there be light," he spake, and it was done. There is no history to write, the light is its own history. Men are reading it still, and still the reading comes in larger letters, in more luminous illustration. When God prescribed lamps for the tabernacle he had to detail the form of the candlesticks, and to prescribe pure olive oil, that the lamp might always burn. You require more space in which to relate the making of a lamp than in which to tell of the creation of the light ; you spend more time in instructing a little child than in giving commands to an army. God challenged Job along this very line. Said he, "Where wast thou when I laid the foundations of the earth?" There was no Job between the Creator and the creation; no Moses writing swiftly words Divine that had to be embodied at the foot of the hill. "Where is the way where light dwelleth; and as for darkness, which is the place thereof?" Mark well, therefore, the contrast of the accounts, and the obvious reason for the amazing difference.

The next point of observation relates to the completeness of the specification as corresponding with the completeness of creation. Lay the finger upon one halting line and prove that the Divine Architect was weak in thought or utterance at this point or at that. Find a gap in the statement and say, "He forgot at this point a small loop, or tache, or ouche, and I, his listener, Moses, must fill in what he left out." We do not know the meaning of great Gospel words until we read our way up to them through all the introduction of the initial covenants. We read backwards, and thus read ourselves out at the lower end of things, instead of reading in the order of the Divine evolution and progress, upward from height to height, until speech becomes useless, and silence must be called in to complete the ineffable eloquence. Could there have been more care in the construction of a heaven than is shown, even upon the page, without going into the question of inspiration, in the building of a tabernacle? Is it not also the same in such little parts of creation as are known to us? There is everywhere a wonderful completeness of purpose. God has set in his creation working forces, daily ministries. Nature is never done. When she sleeps she moves; she travels night and day; her force is in very deed persistent. So we might, by a narrow criticism, charge nature here and there with want of completeness; but it would be as unjust to seize the blade from the ear, and, plucking these, say, "Here we have sign and proof of incompleteness." We protest against that cruelty and simple injustice. There may be a completeness of purpose when there has not yet been time for a completeness of execution. But in the purpose of this greater tabernacle—creation—there is the same completeness that there is in the specification of this beauteous house which the Lord appointed to be built in the grim wilderness.

Consider, too, that the temporary character of the tabernacle was no excuse for inferior work. The tabernacle, as such, would be but for a brief time. Why not hasten its construction—invent some rough thing that would do for the immediate occasion? Why, were it made to be taken up to heaven for the service of the angels it could not be wrought out with a tenderer delicacy, with a minuter diligence, as to detail and beauty. But to God everything is temporary. The creation is but for a day. It is we who are confused by distinction as between time and eternity. There is no time to God; there is no eternity to God. Eternity can be spelled; eternity can in some dumb way be imagined and symbolised in innumerable ciphers multiplied innumerable times by themselves till the mind thinks it can begin eternity. To God there is no such reasoning. When, therefore, we speak of lavishing such care upon a tabernacle, we mistake the infinity and beneficence of God. It is like him to bestow as great care upon the ephemera that die in the sunbeam as upon the seraphim that have burned these countless ages beside the eternal throne. We must not allow our ignorance, incompleteness, and confusedness of mind to interfere with the interpretation of these ineffable mysteries. But the tabernacle was built for eternity. So again and again we stumble, like those who are blind, who are vainly trying to pick their way through stony and dangerous places. The tabernacle was eternity let down—an incarnation, so to say, of eternity, as a man shall one day be an incarnation of God. We mistake the occasion utterly. We fall out of the pomp of its music and the grandeur of its majesty by looking at the thing, and supposing that the merely visible object, how lustrous and tender in beauty soever, is the tabernacle. The tabernacle is within the tabernacle, the Bible is within the Bible, the man is within the man. The tabernacle in the wilderness represented eternal thoughts, eternal purposes of love. Everything is built for eternity : every insect, every dog, every leaf—so frail, withering in its blooming. God builds for eternity in the thought, and in the connection, and in the relation of the thing which is builded. See how profound our iniquity in committing murder anywhere. "Thou shalt not kill; thou shalt not steal." It is one life, one property, a sublime unity of idea, and thought, and purpose. Do not segregate your life, or universe, and attempt a classification which will only separate into unholy solitude what was meant by the Divine mind to cohere in indivisible unity. We were built for eternity. Can God build for less time ? Nothing is lost. The greatest of economists is God. "The very hairs of your head are all numbered "; "Not a sparrow falleth to the ground without your Father." When we speak about the temporary, we know not what we say ; or we justly use that word, for the sake of convenience, as expressive of uses which themselves perish in their own action. But, profoundly and vitally viewed, even affliction is part of heaven ; our sorrows are the beginning, if rightly accepted and sanctified, of our supremest bliss.

Mark, too, how wonderfully the tabernacle and the human frame correspond in perfection of detail and sublimity of purpose. It is not difficult to believe that he who made the tabernacle made Adam. The tabernacle grows before our eyes and Adam is growing still. The life which God is making is Man. Do not impoverish the mind and deplete the heart of all Divine elements and suggestions by supposing that God is a toymaker. God's purpose is one, and he is still engaged in fashioning man in his own image and likeness, and he will complete the duplicate. We must not fix our mind upon our mutilated selves, and, by finding disease, and malformation, and infirmity, and incongruity, charge the Maker with these misadventures. We must judge the Divine purpose in the one case with the Divine purpose in the other. I am aware that there are a few men who have—from my point of view blasphemously—charged the Divine work, as we regard it, in creation with imperfection. There have not been wanting daring men, having great courage on paper and great dauntlessness in privacy and concealment, and who have lived themselves into a well-remunerated, respectable obscurity, who have said that the human eye is not ideally perfect. So we do not speak in ignorance of the cross-line of thinking which seeks to interrupt the progress of Christian science and philosophy. Is there not a lamp also within the human tabernacle—a lamp that burns always, a lamp we did not light, a lamp trimmed by the hand Divine, a lamp of reason, a lamp of conscience, a lamp that sheds its light when the darkness without us is gathered up into one intense and all-obstructing night ? and are there not parables in nature which help us to believe that this lamp, though it apparently flicker—yea, though it apparently vanish—shall yet throw radiance upon heavenly scenes, and burn synchronously with the glory of God's own life? You say, "Look at old age and observe how the mind seems to waver, and halt, and become dim and paralysed, and how it seems to expire like a spark." No, as well say, "Look at the weary man at night-time, his eyelids heavy, his memory confused, his faculties apparently paralysed, or wholly reluctant to respond to every appeal addressed to them; behold how the body outlives and outweighs the boasted mind." No, let him sleep; in the morning he will be young again. Sleep has its ministry as well as wakefulness. God giveth his beloved sleep. So we may by many a natural parable find no difficulty in working ourselves up to contemplations that fill us with ecstasy, religious and sublime, as we call ourselves "heirs of immortality."

Did not Moses make the tabernacle? Yes; but who made Moses? That is the question which has never yet been answered. Change the terms as you please, that inquiry always starts up as the unanswerable demand. Your hand carved the marble, but who carved the hand? Singular, if the marble was carved, but the hand carved itself. Your tongue uttered the eloquence, but who made man's mouth? Who set within him a fountain of speech? Your mind planned the cathedral, but who planned the mind? It would have been more difficult to believe—infinitely more difficult to believe—that the mind made itself than that the cathedral fashioned its own symmetry and roofed in its own inner music and meaning.

Thus perusing the specification for the building of the tabernacle, and reading the account of the creation of the heavens, and of the earth, and of man, I find between them a congruity self-confirming, and filled with infinite comfort to the heart that yearns studiously over the inspired page in hope of finding the footprints of God. The living Christian Church is more marvellous than the tabernacle in this wilderness. The tabernacle was part of a development; the tabernacle was only one point in the history. We must judge things by their final purpose, their theological aspect and philosophy. What is the meaning of the

tabernacle ?—the temple.   What is the meaning of the temple ?—
the living Church.   So we find rude altars thrown together by careless hands, symbolising worship addressed to the heavens; then
the tabernacle; then the temple; then the living fellowship.   Know
ye not that ye are the temples of the Holy Ghost ?   Know ye
not that there is a foundation laid in Zion, a corner stone, elect,
precious; and that we are built upon it, living stones; and
that God is shaping the tabernacle of humanity as he shaped the
tabernacle in the wilderness ?   Know ye not that we are builded
together a holy house unto the Lord ?   Arrest not, even in theory,
the Divine progress.   The line from the beginning up till now has
taken one grand course.   Nothing has strayed away and left the
Divine sovereignty.   The wrath of man is still in the Divine
leash, and hell is no independent colony of the universe.   There
is one throne, one crown; one increasing purpose runs through
all we know.   We wait patiently for the Lord, and when he
says from his throne what Christ said from the cross, "It is
finished," then we may be invited to say, in the terms which
God himself used when he viewed creation,—"Behold, it is
very good."

Exodus xxviii.

THE PRIEST AND HIS ROBES.

THE hand that sketched the architecture of the tabernacle is plainly visible here, for here we have the same regard for proportion, beauty, fitness, and detail. There are certain Divine ideas here which belong to all ages, and which subtly and with wondrous precision confirm the unity of the whole Biblical plan. There is here something infinitely more than ancient history. Christianity is here as certainly as the oak is in the acorn. Shall we slightly vary the figure and compare this statement to a bud ready to burst into the loveliest flower of the garden? Every detail is alive with suggestion. Beyond Aaron, above him, and round about him is Another, who is feebly adumbrated by this Divinely-attired priest.

We may perhaps collect most of the permanent doctrine of this chapter by indicating a few manifest parallels :—

The Jewish priesthood was Divinely instituted. So is the Christian ministry.

"And take thou unto thee Aaron thy brother, and his sons with him, from among the children of Israel, that he may minister unto me in the priest's office" (xxviii. 1).

Priesthood is a Divine creation. The priest himself is a Divine election. The whole idea of mediation is not human but Divine. Up to this time Moses had represented the Divine sovereignty and purpose ; but now we are coming into more delicate divisions and distributions of human life and action, and another kind of man is needed in the unfoldment of that most intricate and pregnant of all germs—the unit which holds the mystery which we call human life. The priesthood is not to be humanly accounted for. The priesthood cannot be humanly sustained. A man would hesitate to go into this warfare at his own charges and for his own self-gratification, in proportion as he feels the agony of the service

that must be rendered. Who wants to stand before his fellow-
men to speak precepts of virtue, and to call to a supernatural or
highly spiritual life, when he knows that every word he speaks is
stained by the very breath that utters it ? Who cares, being a
true-minded man, having some earnestness of purpose, and being
anxious to be really healthy in soul, to stand before the people
as a living contradiction, unable to touch the sublimity of any
prayer he offers, falling infinitely below every exhortation which
he urges upon the people ?   There is a mystery here.   This
arrangement is not to be accounted for in any off-handed manner.
There is a spirit in man—an inspiration leading to office, duty,
function, service,—a great marvel not to be trifled with. It is
because such forces are behind men, and above them, and on
either hand of them, that they go forward to be the offscouring
of all people, to be contemned, and mocked, and rebuked, and
reminded of the discrepancies which mar the poor union which
ought to subsist between their work and themselves. We claim
for the Christian ministry a distinctly Divine institution and a
distinctly Divine inspiration day by day.

Then reading further on in the story we find that the Jewish
priesthood had a double function.   So has the Christian ministry.

"And thou shalt put the two stones upon the shoulders of the ephod for
stones of memorial unto the children of Israel : and Aaron shall bear their
names before the Lord upon his two shoulders for a memorial" (xxviii. 12).

Is that all ?   Is there to be a merely external manifestation or
testimony ?   Read the completing statement :—

"And Aaron shall bear the names of the children of Israel in the breast-
plate of judgment upon his heart" (xxviii. 29).

Now the whole ministry is before us. "Aaron shall bear their
names before the Lord upon his two shoulders for a memorial."
History shall not be forgotten, deliverances shall be held in
perpetual remembrance ; marvels of the Lord wrought yesterday
shall be as the marvels wrought in the present hour.   Then there
shall be a tenderer representation ;—the names shall be upon the
heart.   There shall be a ministry of love, a pleading of sympathy,
an identification of the spirit of the man with all the difficulties
and distresses of the people.   Shoulder work : representing
publicity, courage, strength, leadership,—shoulders to which men

may look as to strong towers; and then the delicate heart-work; the sweet sympathy, the paternal or fraternal interest in all that concerns the development, and culture, and completion of poor, shattered, struggling human life. It is nothing to bear upon the shoulder—that is a kind of burden-carrying, and there is a kind of applause immediately following the completion of any athletic task,—but who can tell the heart-work of the true mediator or minister of the new covenant? A man who enters into this work with his whole soul must live a life of singular tension and agony, otherwise he is but a shatterer of words; only his shoulder engaged in the function; his heart is at liberty to run after any vanity and court the applause of any foolish idolatry. We must look at ideals; we must fasten our attention upon the thing as God meant it to be, and taking the Divine meaning of the priest-hood in the olden time and of the ministry of to-day, we have amongst us men who care for us, men with strong shoulders, tower-like men; sturdy, visible, valiant, dauntless men; men who can speak in the darkness and make their voices heard in the storm; men who know not the cloud of fear and who heed not the tempest of opposition. But we need in the same men other qualities, tenderer elements, more gracious and insinuating forces that find their way into our inmost experience, into our hearts' aching and sore necessity,—men who are taught of Heaven to speak a word in season to him that is weary; men who have the gift of consolation, who can lower the voice into a tender and helpful whisper, and who can bring all God's gospel to bear in gracious and healing application upon the wound which makes the heart sore. This is the ideal. That we do not rise to it may be a rebuke to ourselves, but it is no just criticism upon the Divine purpose. It is an ideal we should do much to sustain. We cannot tell what we owe to the men who teach us great doctrines, who pray off many a burden that strains our strength; who speak to us, even between the lines of their eloquence, things that help us to bear life's misery with a more cheerful courage. We do not know what is being done by ministry of a truly Christian type, whether in the pulpit, or in the school, or in the family, or in the market-place. No man can measure the full issue and outgoing of influence connected with the profound agonistic service on behalf of truth and humanity.

Still pursuing the story, we find that the Jewish priesthood was identified with the people. So is the Christian ministry.

"And beneath upon the hem of it thou shalt make pomegranates of blue, and of purple, and of scarlet, round about the hem thereof; and bells of gold between them round about : a golden bell and a pomegranate, a golden bell and a pomegranate, upon the hem of the robe round about. And it shall be upon Aaron to minister : and his sound shall be heard when he goeth in unto the holy place before the Lord, and when he cometh out, that he die not " (xxviii. 33-35).

The meaning is that the people were to know what Aaron was about. He was to announce himself; every motion of the body was proved by a tinkling and chiming of the golden bells. Amid all the stir and rush and tumult of the day's engagement there came a sound—a sweet, mystic sound—of golden bells. What is the meaning ?—The priest is interested for us; he is going into the holy place ; he is about his sacred work ; he is remembering us before God. The priest is not going into the holy place to perform any magical arts of his own, to make up some black art or mystery out of his own invention ; he is not stealing away with shoes whose motion cannot be heard, or with garments that do not rustle. We are to know where he is, what he is doing. He cannot stir without our knowing it ; the golden bells report the actions and movements of the priest. If those bells were quieted, and if Aaron stole about his work as if he were a sorcerer, or a magician, who had some little trick of his own to play, the penalty was death. If the bells were not heard, the priest must die. The priest is a public servant; he is not to be concealed behind a curtain working out some black craft or indulging in some Eleusinian mystery. He is a man of the people, he belongs to the people, he is the servant of the people ; all that concerns the people he must represent. How completely does the idea of the Christian ministry fructify that seed-thought, —bring to sacred and gracious maturity the opening purpose of the loving Father ! The minister belongs to the people. The minister is no conjuror. It is not only a mistake, but a wicked error to clothe the preacher, whoever he may be, with any superstitious quality or charm. We may be able to say—and must be, —" Rabbi, we know that thou art a teacher come from God ; for no man can do these miracles that thou doest, except God be with him." That is right ; words of that import may be addressed to every man who vindicates his ministerial vocation ; but the minister is the gathered-up people ; he represents the common wants of the day. When he folds his hands in public prayer it is that he may speak of the burden and stress of a thousand lives ; he must speak the language of the people ; there must be nothing whatever about his speech separating him from the great, deep currents of popular life, necessity, and heart-ache. The poorest hearer must feel as the preacher is speaking that the preacher is speaking of him, to him, for him, and is his greater self—his speaking self,—the tongue of the dumb, the eye of the blind, the completing life that takes up the meanest existence and runs it into spheral completeness and beauty. This is the ideal,—how far we fall short of it is another question. We are not now saying how far we meet the standard and satisfy it, we are asking, What is the standard ? and magnifying the grace of God in the development of spiritual education.

We find that the Jewish people had a Urim and a Thummim. So has the Christian Church.

" And thou shalt put in the breastplate of judgment the Urim and the Thummim (literally translated : Light and Perfection) ; and they shall be upon Aaron's heart, when he goeth in before the Lord " (xxviii. 30).

What the Urim and the Thummim actually were no man has been able to find out. Whether they were to be used for the purpose of ascertaining the Divine will in critical and perplexing circumstances has been a question which has excited devout attention ; but whatever the Urim and the Thummim were, there can be no doubt as to what our Urim and Thummim are. We are not left without light and perfection ; we are not destitute of means of discovering the Divine purpose in our life and progress. Our Urim and Thummim are the Old and New Testaments. Keep these in the heart ; be at home with them in all their wondrous variety of speech, of doctrine, of song, of inspiration, and of instruction of every kind ; and then you never can stray far from the path providential that makes its own course straight up to the God who started the mysterious outgoing. We have nothing to do with incantation ; we do not go to consult the witch of Endor, the sorcerer, or the conjuror ; we ask no questions at forbidden places. The whole life-course is mapped out in the Old

Testament and in the New. The Testaments are never to be separated; they are to be read together, they explain one another; torn asunder, they lose their unity and their music; brought together, you bring the flower to the root, you bring the noonday to the dawn, you unite things, forces, ministries that ought never to be dissevered. Let the word of Christ dwell in you richly. Scripture given by inspiration is profitable for all the necessities of life. If we stray, it is not for want of light; if we persist in obeying our own perverted instincts and impulses, we must not be surprised that we end in the bog of despair or in the wilderness of destitution. Do not move without consulting the oracle Divine. Let our motto be, "To the law, and to the testimony," and what cannot be confirmed by the spirit of the book is unworthy to be admitted into our life as an inspiring and directing force.

We find that the Jewish arrangement had one supreme object. So has the Christian life.

"And thou shalt make a plate of pure gold, and grave upon it, like the engravings of a signet, HOLINESS TO THE LORD" (xxviii. 36).

This motto is written in the book in large capitals. The dimmest eye can see the signet. What typography has done for the page the Holy Spirit is to do for the heart and life. There must be no mistake about the language of our prayer, endeavour, study, service, and aspiration. In the beginning they may be poor in expression, they may struggle and halt a good deal and bring upon themselves the vexation of a narrow and mocking criticism; but to the Divine eye they must be so ordered as to represent the purpose of holiness, the meaning of God-likeness. In our first, humblest, poorest prayer there must be the beginning, which, being developed in God's providence and grace, shall express the music of the eternal song. In our first Christian efforts there may be much that those who look on could easily contemn and easily minimise into something almost insignificant and trivial; but there must be in them that which is like the grain of mustard seed which God can recognise, and about which he will say, Let it grow in the right soil under the warm sun, let it be nourished and rocked by the breezes of heaven, and even that little thing shall become as a great and fruitful tree.

What, then, is the object of all this priesthood, all this ministry, church-building, and church-attendance? What is the mystery of it all? The answer is sublime; no man need blush for it; the object we have in view is HOLINESS TO THE LORD; and that is the meaning of every turn of the hand; that is what we want to write. You can mock us; we are making but poor writing of it; at present the work is done in a very feeble manner—none can know it so truly as those know it who are trying to carry it out. We know we expose ourselves to the contempt of the mocker, but if you ask us what we would accomplish, what is the goal towards which we are moving, we take up these words. We do not attempt to amend them; we cannot paint such beauty or add to the glory of such lustre; our motto, our wish, our prayer, our end is HOLINESS TO THE LORD. We are not fanatics; we know the spirit of reason; we pay homage at the altar of reason; we can think, compare; we can bring things together that are mutually related; we can construct arguments and examine evidences and witnesses, and if you ask us, as rational men—What would you be at? name your policy—this is it: that we may be holy unto the Lord. We would so live that everything within our sphere shall be inscribed with HOLINESS TO THE LORD—yea, even upon the bells of the horses would we write that sacred term, and not rest until the snuff-dishes of the sanctuary are made of pure gold, until every breath is an odour from heaven, every action of the human hand a sacrifice well-pleasing to God. This is our object: we do not disavow it, we do not speak of it in ambiguous terms; we would be holy unto the Lord.

And have we no ornaments? The ornament of the meek and quiet spirit is in the sight of God of great price. And have we no garments of blue, and purple, and beautiful suggestiveness? We have garments of praise; we are clothed with the Lord Jesus. And have we no golden bells? We have the golden bells of holy actions. Our words are bells, our actions are bells, our purposes are bells; wherever we move our motion is thus understood to be a motion towards holy places, holy deeds, holy character. We are not ashamed of this object. We know what small words can be hurled against us by the mocker and the sneerer; but holiness is an object which can neither be invalidated by argument nor forced down by violent assault; it stands like a mountain of the Lord's own setting, whose head is warmed with the sunshine of Heaven's eternal blessing. The priest has gone, Aaron has gone, all the beauteous robes have fallen away and are no longer needed; but they have only fallen off in the process of a philosophical as well as a Christian develop·ment. We need them no longer, because we have come into higher services and we represent more spiritual uses. There is a character that is far above rubies. There is a spirit which outshines the diamond. There is a holiness of which star and sun and unstained snow are but imperfect emblems. Do you see your calling then, brethren? There is no priest amongst us now. There is one Mediator between God and man, the Man Christ Jesus. We have a ministry—a human, brotherly ministry —men who explain to us as they may be enabled by the Holy Ghost the meaning of the Word Divine; men who exhort us, and comfort us, and do what they can to make us valiant in the day of danger, and serene in the hour of threatening and evil expectation. We bless God for them. We know their voices. We see God in them, above them, beyond them. They have what they have of treasure in earthen vessels, the excellency of the power is of God. We are no more children, pleased with stones that are precious, and rubies that are lustrous, and bells that are resonant; we are no longer in that infantile place in God's creation. We have left the emblematic, the symbolic, the titular, and the initial, and now where are we? With Christ in the holy place, living in his Spirit, hearing his word, worshipping at his Cross, and looking straight up to him without a man between us. We are a royal generation, a holy priesthood; we are all kings and priests. The Aaronic line is to us extinct, for the Church of the Living God constitutes the priesthood of believers.

Exodus xxix. 12.

"And thou shalt take of the blood of the bullock, and put it upon the horns of the altar with thy finger, and pour all the blood beside the bottom of the altar."

THE SHEDDING OF BLOOD.

WHAT a violent transition! We have been reading, up to this account, language of a very different kind. We have been reading of gold, and silver, and brass, and blue, and purple, and scarlet, and fine linen, rams'-skins and badgers'-skins, and acacia wood; we have been reading of oil for the light, spices for anointing oil, and for sweet incense; also of onyx, and all manner of precious stones, of rings of gold, of the cherub on the one end and the cherub on the other end of the mercy seat, and the cherubims stretching forth their wings on high, covering the mercy seat with their wings, and their faces looking one to another—and now, suddenly, violently, we are told to "take of the blood of the bullock." There has been no speech about blood hitherto. We have read of the garments of the priests, of the pomegranates, of blue, and of purple, and of scarlet, round about the hem of the sacerdotal robe, and bells of gold between them round about; we have read of the blue lace, and of the mitre, and of the embroidered fine linen; but now we read of the bullock's blood—blood upon the horns of the altar.

"And thou shalt take of the blood that is upon the altar, and of the anointing oil, and sprinkle it upon Aaron, and upon his garments, and upon his sons, and upon the garments of his sons with him: and he shall be hallowed, and his garments, and his sons, and his sons' garments with him (xxix. 21).

Sanctified by blood! Hallowed by blood of beasts! Have we fallen from some high level? Are we now upon lines lying far below the altitude upon which our imagination has folded its mighty wings? How has modern piety commented upon this blood-shedding? In some. such language as this :—" Is it to be believed that a God of love and pity would take delight in such offerings as are described in the ritual of the Jews? Is he a God taking delight in the shedding of blood, morning, noon, and night? Is that not a degrading view of God to think of him in any way participating in sacrifices so brutal and shocking? Ought we not to get rid of the word *blood?* Is it not a vulgar term? Does it not turn the mind in downward and debasing directions? Surely the mere reading of the ritual shocks the moral sense and distresses the imagination." So much for the spurious piety which has mistaken the point of view and utterly misinterpreted the whole thing. It s shocking to have to do with people who do not see the meanings of things, who continually make mistakes in the very act of priding themselves upon being correct. They want religion—but a certain kind and form of religion. They are shocked by the idea of idolatry, forgetting that they themselves are idolaters in worshipping only their own conceptions of what God requires, or might be supposed to require, at the hands of his creatures. The people who would get rid of the word *blood* would—though they do not see it— get rid of the word *sin.* They are not safe teachers; they are superficial commentators upon the dark mystery of human nature and the bright mystery of Divine love. My contention will be that without the word *blood*, as it is here found, the whole ritual would be a sham and a mockery, as without the sun the whole day would be dark and cold. But for the blood, the tabernacle would be an affair simply of filigree and upholstery,—a conception too pretty to be Divine, too mechanical to have any relation to the Infinite; this would be the frivolity of a god,— it is redeemed from frivolity by blood. Hitherto the people have been happily eager to give blue, and purple, and scarlet, and fine twined linen, and precious stones,—even a sardius, a topaz, a carbuncle, an emerald, a sapphire, a diamond, a ligure, an agate, an amethyst, a beryl, an onyx, a jasper ;—" Take them all, with pleasure !" So you might, and miss the point Divine. All this initial contribution has a meaning far beyond. Having presented all these things—so beauteous, so rich, so valuable,— further claim is made upon the donors : now *yourselves.* That was the early and necessary method of spiritual education.

The method is now reversed; but we must be just to history in
not forcing open the pages that are closed; we must patiently
and critically read the exact line to which we have come in the
light of its own time.   Mark the Divine wisdom : " Make me a
tabernacle."   " With pleasure," said Israel, in the wilderness.
" Give me gold and precious stones, purple, and scarlet, and
blue, and fine twined linen."   " Yes," was the gracious reply—
" certainly."   Does God want such decoration ?—such gilding,
and painting, and colouring ?   Not he—except educationally,
preparatorily.   The meaner gift having been laid down, and laid
down with some grace of generosity, the great claim is asserted
in some such words as these :—" You have given the donation,
now give the *donor*."   Many of us are pleased with the tabernacle
as a beautiful creation ; so many of us are pleased with life as
an opportunity of enjoyment, education, and progress, the recipro-
cation of courtesies, civilities which make life really worth living
within a narrow sense.   If we have advanced only so far, we
have not begun to live.   We do not know the meaning of life
until we know the meaning of death.   We have built a beautiful
tabernacle ; we have spared nothing of purple and blue, and fine
twined linen, and all manner of precious stones, and laces, and
beautiful things ;—how is it that *he* does not come who alone
can make the house livingly beautiful ?   Because the blood has
not been shed.   All this life-building is a trick, a gorgeous ceremonial, a subtle piece of self-adulation ; God will come by way
of death, sacrifice, agony.   Yes,—death.   This is the hard lesson ;
the preacher cannot teach it in words delicate enough, sufficiently
pungent, graphic, palpitating with the blood of his own sacrifice.
This is the reason that we have a tabernacle without a God : a
beautifully-built creed without blood, or fire, or incense ; this is
the reason that the tabernacle is rotting.   The Church has lost—
in proportion as it has lost the right conception of blood—the
one thing for which it was created.   Christianity is no longer
an agony ; it is a controversy, a speculation, one philosophy
amongst other philosophies ; but its specialty—its Cross—is lost.
Until we believe this we shall die a base death—not a death that
has life coming after it to seal it as a sacrifice—a death without
a resurrection.   We are shocked by the idea of blood.   Some
ministers are afraid of the term ; they speak of *love*, not of

blood,—as if blood did not include love and more . love at its highest point—the point of agony, sacrifice. So the church is empty, the altar is abandoned, the tabernacle is a beautiful nonentity, a marvel in upholstery,—a marvel in atheism. Churches can never live without the blood. We all know how easy it is to debase that term, to vulgarise it and make it shocking by narrow and imperfect interpretations. It requires but a dull fancy to turn that term to vulgar uses so as to offend the nostril and distress certain imperfectly trained faculties of our nature.

But we must ascend to heroic heights, and take heroic measures, and stand where base definitions can never come, and speak of blood shed before the foundation of the world—the platform of vulgarity, the world that has made vulgarity possible. This blood was shed before the world was made,—a Divine refinement, an infinite tabernacle in an infinite eternity. By whom are we to be led ? by the people who are easily shocked ? by people of perverted and enfeebled taste and faculty ? by persons who have no broad conceptions—who are afraid that words may be mistaken ?—or by another quality of soul ? The one would lead us in the direction of small moralities, little marvels in behaviour, small successes in excellent behaviour which might be measured by a school prize. The other will lead us into prayer equal to violence that takes heaven's gate by storm, and into heroism that counts all things but loss for the excellency of the knowledge of Christ Jesus our Lord. The Church has outlived itself because it has lost the profound conception of God in its creation and purpose. Only a return to God's idea can mean a true revival of piety. A revival is not an excitement of emotion, a momentary influence operating upon our sentimental nature ; a great revival —profound as truth, lofty as Divine perfectness, happy as the bliss of heaven,—can only come out of grand realisations of Divine ideas,—knowledge that does not sparkle and crackle in dying flame, but glows in eternal ardour. We can only live as we live in God.

You say that you object to the term *blood*. What do you mean by that term ? There is your mistake. You see only the red stream, the panting, quaking beast that dies under its throat-wound. No wonder you are shocked. You are looking in the wrong direction,—rather you are not truly looking at all. The ritual must be taken in its symbolic sense. What then does the shedding of blood signify ?—death ? No, there is no death in shedding of blood, as understood in its highest interpretation in connection with this old ritual. What then did the shedding of blood signify ? It signified the giving of life ;—the very opposite thought to that which ruled your thinking and debased your imagination. This is a symbolic act. The blood is taken and put upon the horns of the altar, and upon the garments of the priest, and upon the vessels of the sanctuary, and it is a blood of sprinkling by which the whole multitude is at least representatively sprinkled, and the meaning is we pour out our life in one libation of love ; it is thine, thou Giver of all existence. If we have been looking down at some poor beast dying, no wonder our Christian thinking has been driven away into dark corners and unworthy refuges. We should have been looking in the other direction,—the outflowing blood and outflowing life ; the man standing over the red stream saying, " Lord, this is what I would daily do ; give back the life to the Lifegiver ; have no life of my own, except as it is re-given to me by the God to whom I dedicate it."

Looked at physically, the spectacle is revolting ; looked at symbolically, it is full of poetry, theology, beneficence. It is the one thing we needed to express a feeling for which there was no adequate articulation. We have given the blue, and purple, and scarlet, and fine twined linen ; we have not spared the precious cut stones, and the gold, and silver, and brass ; but still we felt an aching as of a pain for which no words could be found. We were not satisfied after we had built the tabernacle, even according to the lines of the Divine specification ; we walked around it, we ventured here and there to touch it with almost worshipping fingers ; but still something was wanting ; we knew not what it was,—it required the refinement of God to introduce the term *blood* into such eloquence and beauty so ineffable ; but, having been introduced, our souls felt the completeness of the harmony ; the measure was massive, solid, full, and we are resting in God's arrangement. Have we not even now some experience of that kind ? We feel that we have done much, and yet there is a twitch at the heart, which being interpreted means : You have not done the one thing which gives value and meaning to all the other. What then is wanted ?—blood. The blood is the life—not blood-letting in some brutal sense, but life-shedding, life-giving, life-worshipping,—every pulse bearing the legend—"I am not my own; I am bought with a price."

But was there not a burning, as well as a shedding of blood ? There was. What does the burning symbolise ? Destruction of the flesh. Fire is the true and never-failing disinfectant. Chemists have devised many disinfectants of more or less questionable efficacy and utility, but fire never fails. What does that smoking heap mean ? It means that all about me that is fleshly, impure, earthly, unworthy is being consumed. We want such sanitary arrangements. This is the Divine sanitation,—not an offering of life and allowing the dead carcase to rot and scatter pestilence in the air; but a blood-oblation : the life given and the mean part handed over to fire to be turned into aspiration—the only form in which the flesh can pray.

In interpreting these ancient pages, events must never be judged out of their own time. We cannot understand the early books unless we exclude from our imagination every other book we have read. A great organist has said that, in coming to an instrument he has never tried, his first object is to forget every organ he has previously played upon ; the new instrument must stand upon its own merits and neither be elevated nor depressed by memories connected with other instruments. It is even so we must read the early books of the Bible. When we read Genesis we must not know that Exodus was ever written ; when we read Exodus we must have no idea that it is followed by Leviticus. Only in this way can we be just to the Divine method of revelation and to God's way of educating the human family. We shall thus be for the moment shocked by this word *blood*. It comes in amidst such a blaze of jewellery and such a consciousness of wealth in all directions which import civilisation, culture, luxury, even to redundance.

Whilst we have to read an event in the light of its own time, we ought not to suppose that any event is final. The caution must be exercised at the one end as certainly as at the other. We are not, therefore, yet prepared for final judgments because we have not the complete evidence before us. We must read on, and on, patiently, carefully, with all the restfulness of a judicial criticism ;

and we must add to that the singular power which is called imagination,—not as some fancy it : a base faculty that fancies things that have no existence, but the higher faculty that multiplies, that brings things into aggregation, that catches the projections of shadow and suggestive meaning amounting to an unwritten Apocalypse of viols and trumpets, and lightnings and thunderings, and beasts joining and swelling the hallelujahs of the heavens.

To what then does this " blood " point ? It points, like John the Baptist, to One who is walking, and it says, " Behold the Lamb of God, which taketh away the sins of the world." He could not have been slain openly one day sooner. It is in vain for us to ask why Jesus Christ did not come in Exodus or Leviticus. We must leave some room for God in his own universe. We must rest in the faith that there is an appointed time to man, to God, to the kingdom Divine, to the truth infinite, for revelation, incar- nation, operation. The world needed all its school days to prepare for this high learning. Now the blood of no bullock is to be shed, or goat, or lamb ; no ritual is to be performed. There is one Mediator between God and man, the Man Christ Jesus. " Ye are come . . . to the blood of sprinkling, that speaketh better things than that of Abel." It is now our blood that has to be poured out ; in other words, our life that has to be shed in daily libation. The blood of Atonement has been shed by the Son of God. He is the Propitiation for our sins, and not for our sins only, but for the sins of the whole world,—a great mystery because a great love ; a great agony because of great sin ; a great death—the greatest of deaths,—yea, the death of the Son of God. In order that we might never penally die, we are to die in Christ and to rise in Christ. If I cannot understand the Atonement, I cannot under- stand the apostacy ; if I do not understand God, it is because I do not understand myself. If I could understand the sin, I could understand the mercy. It is not for me yet to understand : my attitude is this—none happier can I have till the vail drops and the clouds depart—" Lord, I believe : help thou mine unbelief."

Exodus xxix., xxx.

THE PRIEST AND HIS CONSECRATION.

WE now study the consecration of the priest himself. Strange if God has constructed a tabernacle, given a specification for an ark, detailed the shape and colour of the priestly robes, and omitted to say anything about the priest himself. Let us see how the case stands both historically and spiritually.

We have already seen that the priest did not officially appoint himself; in no sense did he rush into the priest's office; nay, more, at the very time of his appointment to the sacerdotal function he was absolutely unaware that the dignity was about to be conferred upon him. This we saw in our comment upon the twenty-eighth chapter and the first verse : "And take thou unto thee Aaron thy brother, and his sons with him, from among the children of Israel, that he may minister unto me in the priest's office." His sons were also appointed to the same high dignity. There is nothing in this appointment that should startle students of history. It is an appointment which is taking place every day in every circle and department of progressive human life. God appoints all men to their places. The conferring of honour is an expression of the Divine sovereignty. We do not know for what purpose we have come into the world until that purpose is revealed to us by the Holy Spirit. That we have come for some purpose is a thought which should make us sober, watchful, expectant ; that should touch our every thought with the solemnity and urgency of prayer. The uppermost question should be, " Lord, what was I made for ? What is the fire which burns upon the altar of my life ?" You, it may be, have been called to be great intercessors, having power Divinely given to hold the Almighty in long converse about human life, human sin, and human destiny, and may have the wondrous faculty which is best expressed to the dulness of our minds by the act of turning back the Divine purpose, when it is one of destruction, and begetting in the Divine mind a purpose of clemency and mercy. These things are of course, in the very necessity of the Deity; but our relation to them is sometimes best expressed by an accommodation of language which permits the Almighty to be represented as if he had been overthrown by human plea, and turned to more compassionate moods by human intercession. Others have been consecrated poets, painters, preachers, tradesmen; but every man is consecrated in the Divine purpose. We can have nothing common or unclean; nothing secular; nothing that is disregarded by the Almighty. If he thought it worth while to make us, he suffers no loss of dignity by appointing us, directing us, taking care of the life which he filled with the pulses of eternity. How we fall into recklessness, and fear, and many a snare by the evil thought that the Almighty had no purpose in making us, has never spoken of us in the radiant cloud which he has gathered around him like the walls of a sanctuary, but has left us poor, blind, homeless orphans without centre, outside the infinite gravitation which binds the universe to his heart. You mock God by such wildness of conception. He gathereth the lambs in his bosom. The very hairs of your head are all numbered. There are vessels of honour and vessels of inferiority, but the great house is our Father's, and every one of us has a place in it and an appointment to fulfil, and blessed is he who with loving obedience and consent falls into the rhythm of the Divine movement, singing morning, noon, and night, "Not my will, but thine be done." Then is life a revolution round the eternal throne, and every life an opportunity for reflecting the Divine lustre upon lives that may be below it. There is a heredity of a spiritual kind, a succession priestly, artistic, philanthropic, evangelistic. Men are set in bands, classes, groups,— why not say they are fashioned into constellations?—every great grouping of stellar light and beauty having its appointed place, and though all the constellations fly so fast their wings never overlap, and there is no tumult in the infinite hurrying. We are called to this place because to this faith. To realise it is to be calm · to seize that doctrine is to **have bread to eat at all seasons,** and a vision of heaven even when the darkness of the night is sevenfold.

A very solemn view of life is presented by this incident. Aaron was unaware what was passing in the cloud. Our life is being secretly planned for us. Up in the cloud the Lord is talking about his children on the earth. He is naming them by name, appointing coats and garments, ephods, crowns, mitres, and functions of usefulness and dignity for them. We cannot hear the converse, but we are the subjects of the marvellous talk. What is to become of the old man, and the little child, and the traveller whose journey will be done to-morrow, and the warrior who lifts his great sword for the last stroke in the Master's name? We are being spoken of. Said One : " I go to prepare a place for you." God would seem to have but one thought : love to man, redemption of the creature who bears his likeness. Wait until you get the message from the mount. We may begin to feel, before we hear the actual words, that we are about to be called to some great destiny,—there are premonitions. Some of us have experienced almost miracles of prescience; we have felt the inspiration before it has fully seized us. Blessed are those servants who rise morning by morning expecting the day's message for the day's own work. Let your attitude be one of expectancy, and let the expectancy be like a prayer that pierces without violating the sacred cloud.

Notice, in the next place, the most important thought that has yet come before us. The consecration of the priest is identified with what we may imperfectly describe as the creation of sin. Mark, not the commission of sin—with that we have been but too familiar ;—but its Divine creation. That is a startling term, but my meaning of it is justified by the Bible itself. A time had come in human history when actions had to be spiritually defined, classified, and set in a new relation towards the personality and government of God. This will throw light upon many a mystery in the book of Genesis. In Genesis there was no sin as we now understand that pregnant term. That is a key to the Divine administration in the book of Genesis. Murder in the days of Cain and murder after the giving of the law were two different things. If we omit to use that all-opening key we shall feel ourselves in the book of Genesis in the midst of confusion which

defies settlement into order. You blame Jacob for coveting the
birthright of Esau, forgetting that there was no covetousness when
Jacob did so. Covetousness, in the now legal sense of the term,
was an after-creation. We must not take back with us sentiment
which has been established and cultivated by the law into the
book of Genesis, and judge antediluvian and patriarchal times by
a standard of which they knew nothing. To get a right seizure
of the genius of the book of Genesis, you must in mind detach
that book from all the other books, and read only according to the
immediate light of the particular time. It was bad for Cain to
commit murder—it would be unpardonable for us to commit it.
God did not treat the murderer Cain as he would treat a
murderer of the present day. What was punished in those
ancient times was the broad and vulgar crime about whose
horribleness there could be no doubt, and the punishment was as
broad as the crime. The two must be studied in their relation
and harmony. How did God punish antediluvian and patriarchal
crime ? By floods of water, by tempests of fire. Wondrous is
the adjustment of the answer to the aggravation ! Deceit,
covetousness, self-seeking, meanness, lying, and many other
vices, had not in the book of Genesis been defined, and consequently were looked upon in many cases as necessary weapons
of defence. The word *kill* would, in its highest sense, have
to be explained to the persons to whom it was addressed. The
word *lying* or *falsehood* would have to be expatiated upon
and made clear, by expository and illustrative remark, to the
individuals who first heard the word. They lied that they
might win ; they employed deceit as they would employ a
weapon of defence, or an instrument of assault,—a shield, or
a spear. There is what may be called a chronological morality
in the sense which is now present to our minds : hence the
wondrous speech of Christ—"It shall be more tolerable for Tyre
and Sidon at the day of judgment than for you,"—that is the
sum total of my meaning. After this interview upon the
mountain, all human actions received a new definition. The
spiritual element was introduced. Murder, incest, violence,
rudeness of behaviour—all these are left behind among the
vulgarities of the age to which they first belonged. But now we
begin to come into the heart, into the innermost places of the

thought,—yea, before the thought has shaped itself into expressibleness, criticism Divine is brought to bear upon it, and so brought that the trembling, fearing heart exclaims, " Thy word is exceeding powerful, sharper than any two-edged sword, piercing to the dividing asunder of the joints and marrow." This is the meaning of development. That great process can never be got rid of; it is the central line in revelation as it is in nature. The apostolic argument goes wholly in this direction. Look at Romans iv. 15 :—" Where no law is, there is no transgression." Where was the law in many a case which has startled and confounded us in the book of Genesis? There was no law as that term is now understood. With this view accords the testimony of 1 John iii. 4 :—" Sin is the transgression of the law." But the Apostle Paul has just said, " Where no law is, there is no transgression." See how this is confirmed by Romans iii. 20 :—" By the law is the knowledge of sin." The most distinctively illustrative statement upon the matter is made by the Apostle Paul in Romans vii. 7—this expresses the whole thought :—" I had not known sin, but by the law : for I had not known lust, except the law had said, Thou shalt not covet." So then the law created sin in its legal and spiritual sense. Until the law is revealed to a man he does not know precisely what he is doing in the judgment of God. He must learn what life is ; he must have revelations addressed to him upon morality, even though he be prepared to resent the notion of revelation upon transcendental spiritual realities.

Mark how the history accumulates, how grandly it masses itself into unity and significance. The moment when sin was enlarged and defined and made matter of law, a new agency was needed. Up to this time there has been no priest, as that term is historically understood. There was a marvellous Figure, half-God, half-man, a Symbol rather than a person, that seemed to point to mysteries yet to be revealed—himself the greatest of mysteries, for that Melchisedec had no beginning and no end, neither father nor mother, neither beginning of days nor end of life. But now we come into concrete instances, and out of our own ranks is a man selected who was to be separate from us legally and functionally for ever. Is this poetry to be lost upon us ? Is this sublime development to draw up out of our view

without leaving its appropriate impression, infinite in meaning
and in solemnity ? These are the lines which prove the inspiration of the Scriptures. A new definition of life, action or conduct,
is made up in the mount, and let us suppose there is no action
upon the earth to correspond with it, not " What an oversight ! "
but " What an offence ! " would then be our exclamation. But
as God becomes narrower in his judgments, more penetrating,
more critical, more discriminating, he adapts himself to the new
morality, the more spiritual conception and criticism of conduct.
Grace and Law were both in the mount,—even Moses and the
Lamb were both there ! Then came the mystery of sacrifice,—
blood, expiation, atonement, daily sacrifice, continual shedding of
blood, piercing criticism into every action of the human life,—a
great tumult, an infinite mystery charged with intolerable pain.

Before the law was made known to the people the atonement
was provided for sin. Behold, then, the goodness of God !
Whilst the people were at the base of the mountain, not knowing
what was being done, an atonement was being provided for the
sin which would follow upon a revelation of the more critical and
spiritual law. Is there any line in all the holy testimony which
enlarges this thought and glorifies it ? Verily there is : "The
Lamb was slain from before the foundation of the world." The
Atonement was not an after-thought, a mere expedient devised
in reply to a set of circumstances which the Divine omniscience
had not foreseen. Before the sin was committed, the Cross was
erected ; before the sinner had defied his Maker, his Maker had
become the sinner's Saviour. Who can outrun the love of God ?
"Where sin abounds, grace doth much more abound." Sin is not
an accident—something that has come into the universe without
being expected. It was foreseen from the beginning ; Grace was
ahead of it, and God will overthrow it. Instead of being surprised into despair by our sin, let us be surprised into praise by
God's prevenient love.

In the Christian dispensation both the law and the priesthood
are abolished. Sinai is but a hill left for the tourist, as the
brazen serpent is but Nehushtan,—a piece of brass intended to
be used for common purposes, and the mantle of Elijah is now

but a perished rag. We have come to another point in the Divine development of events ; now we have new heavens and a new earth. "What then ? shall we sin, because we are not under the law, but under grace ? God forbid." "We are delivered from the law, that being dead wherein we were held ; that we should serve in newness of spirit, and not in the oldness of the letter." That is the Christian position. "Likewise reckon ye also yourselves to be dead indeed unto sin, but alive unto God through Jesus Christ our Lord." We, too, have a Divinely-appointed Priest—"No man taketh this honour unto himself but he that was called of God, as was Aaron ; so also Christ glorified not himself to be made an highpriest ; but he that said unto him, Thou art my Son, this day have I begotten thee." There is one Mediator between God and man. The Aaronic thought is completed in the Christly intercession. We now come not to man, but to God through the appointed way. Jesus Christ is Priest, Jesus Christ is Advocate. "This Man, because he continueth for ever, hath an unchangeable priesthood." From the beginning to the end the line is one—heightening, broadening, glorifying, until it is lost in the ineffable lustre of the upper kingdoms.

Exodus xxxi. 1-11.

1. And the Lord spake unto Moses, saying,

2. See, I have called by name Bezaleel the son of Uri, the son of Hur, of the tribe of Judah :

3. And I have filled him with the spirit of God, in wisdom, and in understanding, and in knowledge, and in all manner of workmanship,

4. To devise cunning works, to work in gold, and in silver, and in brass,

5. And in cutting of stones, to set them, and in carving of timber, to work in all manner of workmanship.

6. And I, behold, I have given with him Aholiab, the son of Ahisamach, of the tribe of Dan : and in the hearts of all that are wise-hearted I have put wisdom, that they may make all that I have commanded thee ;

7. The tabernacle of the congregation, and the ark of the testimony, and the mercy seat that is thereupon, and all the furniture of the tabernacle,

8. And the table and his furniture, and the pure candlestick with all his furniture, and the altar of incense,

9. And the altar of burnt offering with all his furniture, and the laver and his foot,

10. And the cloths of service, and the holy garments for Aaron the priest, and the garments of his sons, to minister in the priest's office,

11. And the anointing oil, and sweet incense for the holy place : according to all that I have commanded thee shall they do.

THE METHOD OF PROVIDENCE.

WE must never forget that all these instructions were given in a mountain and were to be carried out in a wilderness. These circumstances turn their execution into a Divine miracle. In the interpretation of the sacred record, bear in mind the circumstances. If you lose sight of the wilderness, you will not see the tabernacle ; yea, though its glory—a tender glory of beauty— may gleam upon you and excite your imagination. If you detach the tabernacle from the sandy and dreary wilderness, you will fail to see all the mystery of light. The things belong to one another for instructive purposes. We do not let God have a fair place for building. We have turned the whole earth into wilderness, so that if he would build at all he must build under circumstances which act as a definite foil to every touch of beauty and every line of light. Yet God will build in the wilderness as if it were a heaven. He will not be discouraged by the stones, the sands, the bleak surroundings. We could not work under such conditions; we should complain of the environment, asking with bitterness of tone, " Who can work in a place so dreary? and what is the reward for putting up in the wilderness a thing fit for the streets of the golden Jerusalem?" God builds everything with an eye to beauty. When he rounded off the earth and sent it flying in its appointed circuit, he blessed the little thing as a man might bless his child, and said with infinite pathos, " It is very good." Now that he comes to build upon it, we have spoiled it altogether, and if he were less than God he could not lay one stone upon another on a foundation so debased and spoiled as is now the earth under our devastating and unsparing hand. Behold, as otherwhere and everywhere, the tender goodness of God! He lets down his best things upon the earth as if it were a fit receiving-house,—" He spared not his own Son." Having sent down law and priesthood, tabernacle, and ark, and prophet, and a long line of angel-visitants with messages struck in every key of eloquence, last of all he sent his Son. So there must be something in this little night-world we have never seen; there must be in the substance of things verily a mystery which, whilst it is acknowledged by philosophy, is known and esteemed infinitely by its Creator. The philosophers are quite right when they cannot see in what they term " phenomena" any reason for the wondrous revelation of Christ as the heart and image of God. There is nothing in phenomena worthy of the Cross, or fully explanatory of it; but God sees the heart of things, the innermost enfoldment, the *sanctum sanctorum,*—that entity, that pulse, which is hidden from every created eye. Instead, therefore, of finding the revelation of the Gospel to be in excess of the phenomena, I will go further and say that God must find his own balance; he must put in the one scale what is equal to the other, and doing so, he does not degrade himself—he lifts up the work of his hands and the purpose of his heart.

God would have everything built beautifully. What an image of beauty have we seen this tabernacle to be through and through, flushed with colours we have never seen, and bright with lights that could not show themselves fully in the murkiness of this air! He would make us more beautiful than our dwelling-place. He would not have the house more valuable than the tenant. He did not mean the worshipper to be less than the tabernacle which he set up for worship. Are we living the beautiful life—the life solemn with sweet harmonies, broad in its generous purpose, noble in the sublimity of its prayer, like God in the perpetual sacrifice of its life? To answer such questions in the affirmative, or in any tone hinting positiveness, is to be building a life which will outshine the tabernacle, though it were outlined by the very finger of God.

Not only will God build everything beautifully; his purpose is to have everything built for religious uses. He will not have mere beauty of form, for in the creation of form he may perpetrate an irony that would distress his own heart. His meaning is that the form shall help the thought, that images appealing to the eye shall also touch the imagination and graciously affect the whole spirit, and subdue into tender obedience and worship the soul and heart of man. What can be more ironical—and therefore to the spiritual mind more distressful—than for the stone church to be more beautiful than the living temple?—an organ out-singing the human voice?—some spectacle appealing to the fleshly eye grander than the invisible revelation, seeking the attention of the inward vision of the soul? We are the worse for the beauty that is round about us if not the better. We cannot live under beautiful environments and circumstances without being debased by them, except we rise to their appeal and put all meaner things under our feet. It is a sad thing to become familiar with beauty, —so familiar with it as not really to see its charm. It is an awful thing to have heard the Gospel so often as to feel weary under the appeal of its gracious thunder or its melting tenderness. We must watch our senses : they will victimise us if we do not; we shall be brought into a state of contemptuousness where we ought to be in a condition of worship. God, then, does not build for mere beauty of form : he always seeks to help the worshipper. He builds altars. Whatever he touches he sanctifies. How possible it is to be living amongst beauty of landscape, of art, and beauty of every imaginable kind, and yet for the soul to sink into unresponsiveness, not seeing " sermons in stones, books in the running brooks, good in everything." That is irony; that is the contradiction which makes

fools of men,—a depth below even moral degradation, for in
moral degradation there may yet remain a kind of intellectual
flicker, a species of intellectual majesty ; but in the other condition
the whole nature is depleted, debased, diabolised.   God does not
build for the gratification of taste, otherwise he would subserve
the interests of mere vanity.   There are some who are still
worshippers of the goddess they call Taste.   Be it that a thing is
in what they call *taste*, and they are satisfied.   They will not
ask whether the child is living or dead, if the form is preserved in
beauty of outline.   Taste has its right place.

The tabernacle as a work of art is never to be held in
contempt ; but we miss its meaning ; all its Divine poetry is
lost upon us, so long as we can merely admire it.   To admire
under such circumstances is to insult.   The true admiration is
worship ; the true applause is forgetfulness of the thing itself,
complete absorption in the thought it can but dimly express.
When our souls are on fire, when our blood is aflame with the
true zeal, our senses will be ordered back that our spirit may go
forward and turn the wilderness into heaven and common bread
into a type of the Lord's body.

God will not have the building put up as an expression of
mere sentiment : otherwise, he would be assisting the cause of
idolatry.   Nothing will satisfy him but a recognition of the
supreme purpose.   What is the tabernacle for ?—for worship.
What is the meaning of it ?—it is a gate opening upon heaven.
Why was it set up ?—to lift us nearer God.   If we fail to seize
these purposes, if we fail of magnifying and glorifying them so as
to ennoble our own life in the process, we have never seen the
tabernacle.   We have seen the thing which an artificer might
have made—a toy fit for a bazaar, but not the Church of God,
the holy place, the Divine tabernacle let down amongst the
dwellings of men.   Herein is it for ever true that we may have
a Bible but no revelation ; a sermon but no Gospel ; we may be
in the church, yet not in the sanctuary ; we may admire beauty,
and yet live the life of the drunkard and the debauchee.

In all his building—and God is always building—he qualifies
every man for a particular work in connection with the edifice.
Verily, God leaves nothing to Moses !   When Moses goes down
from this mountain, he will go as an errand-bearer, a messenger ;

he will simply go to carry out instructions. Nothing has been left to his own invention; he will represent God. That is the true picture of all things. We have nothing to say, if we are true teachers, but what we have been told to say. God will tell every man the message which he wishes to have repeated, and every man will tell it in his own voice and in his own individuality of tone; but the message is God's, or it is not a message at all. No man has any right, in this kind of work, to address any other man except that right is founded upon his inspiration. There is no impertinence more intolerable than for any man to stand up and tell his fellow-men to be good, to repent, if so be he is delivering something which he attributes to the heat and zeal of his own imagination. The culmination of impertinence is in what is called the pulpit—if any man shall stand up, and of his own morality tell other men to repent. The utterance must be Divine! it cannot be tolerated in the man, for we are so constituted that human nature would charge upon the man his own action as a contradiction of his speech, and would order him out to reconcile himself with himself before he found fault with the policy of the world. But when the preacher knows that he is preaching to himself, that he is putting into human utterance what he believes to be a Divine message, then though his life be before him as a mocking contradiction, calling him liar when he prays, and hypocrite when he preaches, he knows that he has not gone a warfare at his own charges, and that he is but the medium on which the infinite thought breaks into human speech. Not that the man will rest content with this. Whilst part of his supreme comfort may come to him along such lines, it will ever be his careful business with an industry that knows no relaxation to make his life equal to his speech. The point is that no teacher—Moses, Aaron, Isaiah, Paul—must stand up of his own motion to tell men to be better. Every man must speak that appealing word as the result of Divine inspiration and constraint. God qualifies every man for the work which he has to do. Aaron was not Moses, Bezaleel was not Aaron. Each had his own place, his own mission, his own work; each was Divinely chosen. When Bezaleel lifted the chisel he was performing a Divine purpose—as much so as was Aaron when he went forth with his garment distinguished by all colours of beauty and eloquent with the chime of golden bells. The one man wants the other man. The work stands still till that other man comes in. Moses, Aaron, and the sons of Aaron, and the seventy elders of Israel, are all standing still till the man with the chisel comes in; looking round upon their incomplete number, they say, "There is some man wanting." That is the true ideal of unity. Division of labour is necessary to the very bond of unity. Each man must feel that he is Divinely called and inspired to do a particular work, and he must feel that the Church cannot move in its completeness until he is in it. Then the shepherd shall be as the king, the nurse shall be almost a mother,—the lighter of the lamp shall have a distinct position as if he were in the family of Aaron, and the humblest toiler in the vineyard will erect himself in the solemn eventide and bless God that he has had some share in the day's varied toil. Who has courage to read the following words aright, and to apply them to the practical history of mankind?

"And I have filled him (Bezaleel) with the spirit of God, in wisdom, and in understanding, and in knowledge, and in all manner of workmanship, to devise cunning works, to work in gold, and in silver, and in brass, and in cutting of stones, to set them, and in carving of timber, to work in all manner of workmanship" (xxxi. 3-5).

Who can read these words as they ought to be read? How it makes ministers of God by the thousand! We have thought that Aaron was a religious man because of his clothing and because of many peculiarities which separated him from other men; but the Lord distinctly claims the artificer as another kind of Aaron. He will undertake to show a man how to work in gold, and in silver, and in brass, and in cutting stones, and in carving timber, and in all manner of workmanship. Who divides life into *sacred* and *profane?* Who introduces the element of meanness into human occupation and service? God claims all things for himself. When he hears man speak and woman sing, he says— perhaps with a father's pride (we use human terms to express human thoughts)—"Who hath made man's mouth? Have not I, the Lord?" When he sees the sculptor making a rock into an image of Moses, may he not say, "Who hath made man's hand, and given movement to his fingers and wrist? Have not I, the Lord"? Who will say that the preacher is a religious

man, but the artificer is a secular worker ? Who will say that
one man is inspired, and another man found out his own way
for himself ? If he found a low way, a mean or shallow way,
a way without perspective, and suggestion, and apocalyptic outlook and issue, verily he found it out for himself. But let us
claim all true workers as inspired men. We know that there is
an inspired art. The world knows it ; instinctively, unconsciously, the world uncovers before it.

There is an inspired poetry, make it of what measure you will.
The great common heart knows it, says, " That is the true verse ;
how it rises, falls, plashes like a fountain, flows like a stream,
breathes like a summer wind, speaks the thoughts we have long
understood, but could never articulate ! " The great human heart
says, " That is the voice Divine ; that is the appeal of Heaven."
Why should we say that inspiration is not given to all true
workers, whether in gold or in thought, whether in song or in
prayer, whether in the type or in the magic eloquence of the
burning tongue ? Let us enlarge life, and enlarge Providence,
rather than contract it, and not, whilst praying to a God in
the heavens, have no God in the heart. You would work better
if you realised that God is the Teacher of the fingers, and the
Guide of the hand. All service would look tenderer to you,
richer and larger, if you could say when it is done, " This also
cometh forth from the Lord of hosts, who is wonderful and
glorious in wisdom and in power." A new solemnity gathers
around me as I think on these things. The universe is steadier.
The whole temple is lifted up to higher grandeur. Nature
becomes a sublime totality. Prayer is clothed with broader
meaning. Labour is churched and glorified. Art turns its
chiselled and flushed features towards its native heaven. Sin
acquires a deadlier blackness, and begs to be hidden in some
deepening hell. Through all cloud and noise, all rush and strife,
God's great trumpet clears a way for the commandments which
represent his righteousness, and for the statutes which are to
become songs in the house of human pilgrimage. Realise the
unity of things. See the structural completeness of the whole
idea of the universe and of life. Verily, " the tabernacle of God
is with men upon the earth," and from the weariest wilderness
of sand there is a straight path to the city whose streets are gold.

Exodus xxxi. 18.

" . . . two tables of testimony, tables of stone, written with the finger of God."

THE TABLES OF TESTIMONY.

THOSE two tables are two revelations; first, a revelation of man; and second, a revelation of God. In this light we may profitably read the commandments, gathering from them lessons and suggestions of the most far-reaching and useful kind. Given the Ten Commandments and all the other laws relating to them, and we can have no difficulty in finding out the quality of the life to which the commandments were addressed. The statute book of a people is, in one important sense, the history of a nation. He who reads our laws reads our lives. God has written upon these two tables the history, up to that time, of the human heart. Changing the figure, are not the two stones two mirrors, in which men may see what they have done? The commandments gather up the book of Genesis, and express it in terse lines. It would seem as if the book of Genesis ought to run straight up to the twentieth chapter of Exodus, that it might complete itself. Genesis may be described as covering an experimental period of time. Men were then without written law. Nature was, to a large extent, left to work out its own instinct and its own will. The Genesis which gives us physical beauty also gives us moral ruin. The book of Genesis cannot end in itself. God would not cut us off at the end of Genesis. He would by so doing seem to cut off his own sovereignty, his own purpose, his own fatherhood. After every one of the commandments—not only the Ten Commandments, but all the other laws—God could have given a living illustration of his meaning, quoted from the book of Genesis. The commandments are not abstractions, they are concrete instances; the commandments are not metaphysical moralities, they express the disasters and the catastrophes which have been accomplished in human life. For this reason, let it be repeated, the two tables of stone, written by the finger of God, constitute the Divine revelation of human nature. Let us familiarise ourselves with this idea, and feel its rational force.

"*Thou shalt have no other gods before me.*" What an extraordinary suggestion! How impossible from what the philosophers would call an *a priori* point of view! Such an idea would never enter the human mind! So we might imperfectly and vainly reason. We would not, indeed, credit the human imagination with audacity enough to attempt to create other gods. Human imagination would rather turn in some other direction—would endeavour to flee away from the whole conception and discipline of the Divine idea, and constitute powers and realms altogether distant from the Divine throne. It required the Divine mind itself to see the possibility of this tremendous apostacy. Strange to say, the very first temptation that assailed mankind, so far as we are enlightened by the book of Genesis, was a temptation in this very direction. In effect it was: "Be gods yourselves; you have the fanciful notion that there is one God who has right of control over you, who may call you nightly to his bar, and audit the day's moral accounts; nothing can be more preposterous; eat of this lovely tree, and the film will fall from your eyes, and a new stature and sense of dignity will be given to the soul, and ye shall be as gods." The temptation was worthy of the man. We sometimes have tributes paid to our dignity from unexpected sources. To have tempted the man back into some anterior point in his development (assuming the theory of development to be true) might have been resented, but to tempt him to fall upwards was a temptation worthy of the subtlest of tempters, and worthy to be addressed to a child of the Divine creation. See, therefore, in the very first instance, how God could have quoted a concrete case in illustration of the opening commandment.

"*Thou shalt not make unto thee any graven image*"—for the purposes of worship. Again we say the idea is impossible. It does not fit into the structure of things with any sense of propriety. A man will never be so little of a man as to make an image and fall down before 't. But in the book of Genesis you find images in plenty. This very thing which we now consider to be an impossibility has been a solemn and humiliating fact in the history of the first families of the race. Rachel knew where Laban's gods were, and she stole them. So wonderful a thing is human piety : when perverted it will even steal a god.

" *Honour thy father and thy mother.*" Could a concrete instance be put after that commandment ? We have seen that when Esau married into Canaanitish relations he did that which was "a grief of mind unto Isaac and to Rebekah." Parental feeling was ignored; parental rights were scorned; parental sympathies were violated and dishonoured.

" *Thou shalt not kill* "—a metaphysical impossibility, but an actual fact. From the opening of the book of Genesis to the end, Cain has been, in himself or in his progeny, a dominating figure.

" *Thou shalt not commit adultery.*" The book of Genesis contains more terrible statements about that crime than about any other, having in it chapters which no man may read aloud.

" *Thou shalt not steal.*" If Esau has violated one of the commandments, and is quoted as a historical instance: Jacob has violated another, and may be set up in the gallery evermore.

Thus the commandments are not metaphysical subtleties; are not fanciful suppositions in the Divine mind ; are not merely ethical theories ; they are one by one expressions of what man himself has done. The Ten Commandments are not ten mysteries. The Ten Commandments do not show that virtue is divisible into ten problems; but they show that vice has discovered ten ways of breaking through the golden circle of obedience. We know the commandments. Were no names mentioned ; were the two tables of stone trumpeted by an angel from the radiant cloud, we should say at once, " These words are known down here, they need no exposition ; we ourselves are living illustrations of every one of them." This being the case, what a tremendous hold the Bible gets upon every man ! It speaks to something in the man ; it secures the consent of the conscience of every man. The inward witness does not say, " Such commandments presuppose impossibilities on the part of those to whom they are addressed "; the answer is, " We have broken these laws one by one; we have wanted other gods; we have thought that a carved image might serve instead of a living Judge; fathers and mothers we have killed as soldiers kill one another on the battle-field; we have killed, committed adultery, stolen, broken holy days, violated sacred places; the angel is not speaking through his great trumpet of thunder to populations a whole universe distant from us, he has studied our history, and he is addressing himself to our iniquities."

The commandments are also on the other side quite as distinctly revelations of God. Let us consider an inquiry to this effect :—looking at the commandments, what should we infer as to the character of God? For the purposes of this study we are supposing that we have only the commandments as an indication of the moral quality of the Legislator. With the two tables of stone before us, written in a language we can understand, what should we say is the character of the Legislator? Do we not see a wonderful care for mankind? Is there not an undertone of affectionateness in all the majestic speech? Are there not some tears amid all this awful storm? Was not the tempest devised as an accompaniment to hide the grief? Now that we are more carefully learned in all the wisdom of the heavenly kingdom may we not descry a broken heart where we once only thought of an indignant Jehovah? This is the true care for man—to care for his character, to care for his soul, to be vigilant respecting all the finer elements and qualities of his nature. To dress the body may be but to perpetrate an irony. To care for the child's physical constitution may be but a cruel sin, but to care for his moral quality, for his temper, his instincts, his soul-forces; to devote attention to his mind, to his motives, to the very springs and first motions of his life—that is care,—a care, indeed, not inconsistent with solicitude regarding matters physical and circumstances of an outward kind; but this is seeking first the kingdom of God and his righteousness. To clothe the child, so far as it is possible, with the garment of a pure character; to make the young soul heroic in all purpose and endeavour; to lead the heart to the mystery of sacrifice, and to make the innermost tenant of the human being ashamed of sin, afraid of it, regarding it as hateful— that is to show true care, true appreciation of human nature. This is what God does here. He is building up an interior heart.

He is moulding an innermost life; as for clothing, decoration, circumstance, outward importance—these are fading flowers. God cannot rest until he has made the heart right and purified the fountain of the life.

Can we fail to see a gracious condescension to the moral capacity of mankind? The Lord is pleased to speak of himself as a "jealous God." Does he mean that? Not as we mean it. This word has sometimes shocked us. It was not spoken to us. God has always spoken to the race in the language of its own day. This is the only speech that could have been understood at the time at which it was spoken. This explains many a difficulty in the earlier books of Scripture. Why persist in taking our modern education back to earlier barbarities? In this way we defraud ourselves of the richest teaching of history, and bring upon the mind a sense of confusion which interferes with the unity of worship and the completeness of sacrifice. You use to children words you will not use to them when they are fully grown men and women. You must avail yourselves of an emphasis which would be out of place in speech addressed to equals, or to those who have made considerable advance in intellectual culture. The Divine meaning could only have been expressed in the words which God used at the time. The word is not the meaning, the meaning is in the word; as the body is not the man, the man is in the body. History sheds off the body and reveals the spirit. This is the law of spiritual progress, and this is one of the innermost secrets of spiritual insight.

Can we once more fail to see how gradually men have been trained to moral pureness and dignity? The commandments are in a certain sense very rude words. They would be resented if addressed to us personally in some of their details. What man of this century, having passed through the process of Christian culture, could have addressed to him seriously the commandment, "*Thou shalt not kill*"? The man might be offended; he would suppose he was altogether unknown to the person who thus rudely addressed him, seeing that manslaughter or homicide never came within the imagination, which would have been debased or inflamed into delirium if it could have contemplated the shedding of human blood. We must begin the education of people where they themselves are. Education always goes down to the pupil, and thus lifts the pupil to its own level. It is one of the finest proofs of the gradual revelation of the Divine kingdom that from the first to the last the law pursues an ascending and widening line. How subtly the last commandment seems to link itself on to a higher kingdom. Is it not so in all development, that there is something of feature or *nexus*, something of subtle indication or fleshly possession, meaning that one kingdom has culminated, and another is just about to come down to earth? That *nexus* you do not find in "*Thou shalt not kill,*" "*Thou shalt not commit adultery,*" "*Thou shalt not steal.*" These are what we should now term broad vulgarities; but the connecting link or tentacle, just hooking itself on to something almost invisible, is to be found in the last commandment, "*Thou shalt not covet.*" That is the most spiritual word we have yet heard in all the commandments addressed to us in our social relations. The legislator is now giving us to understand that we have a spirit. He is about to prepare the way for some nobler kingdom, and truth, and thought, and relation. Thus by throwing new words into a language God prepares the way for new thoughts that are quickly to follow from heaven. God does not make great gaps which it is impossible either to leap or to bridge over; but by turning common language into uncommon uses, by striking points of departure, by the change of one hue of language, he prepares the way for the next higher kingdom, the next brighter revelation. Now that he has come so far as covetousness, he will, by-and-by, come right into the very centre of the heart and tell us that we are no longer in the infantile school, needing rude instruction about killing and stealing and other iniquities, but must have the heart cleansed, for out of the human heart proceed all those things which offend the heart of God.

Why go back to these old times? Because we want to be like those teachers who are worshipped for their comprehensiveness and their philosophical temper. The preacher can go back as well as the annalist. When a political historian spends days, and weeks, and months, in the Record Office and in the literary recesses of the British Museum, and then comes forth with his history, we call him a philosophical historian. When he enriches his pages with innumerable references to volumes we never heard of, giving page, chapter, section, and line, we call him a trust-

worthy historian.   When the social annalist would show his
country what the course of his country has been, the farther he
can go back into archaic times the more he is respected by
modern critics.   But when a preacher goes back to Genesis, he is
supposed to have gone out of the times, and to have connected
himself with forces, and ministries, and institutions which have
fallen into desuetude.   We protest against such partial criticism.
There is a philosophy of religious inquiry as well as a philosophy
of political investigation, and we insist upon having the Book of
God read as a whole.   That is our purpose for going back to its
opening pages and to its earliest characters.   The book is one.
It never goes back or overlaps itself in a backward direction, but
from first to last it maintains a line of progress and asserts a
vertebral unity which constitutes an unassailable argument for its
Divine origin.   The books of Scripture must not be broken off
one from the other as if they were separated and unrelated stones
in a heap.   If you take a book out of the Bible you take a stone
out of a temple, a star out of a constellation,—a felony that cannot
be permitted.   So we must not be deterred from going into our
records and our museums, and searching into roots, and origins,
and beginnings.   We, too, must be prayerfully philosophical and
rationalistic, turning over page by page, and turning over every
page, fearing nothing that comes up ; taking it in chronological
sequence, and persevering through all rocky places, and dangerous
paths, and mountainous districts—on and on, until we come to the
trumpets and vials, and thunders, and songs and hallelujahs of the
Apocalypse ; and having come into these completions we shall
know the meaning of the last sweet word—for when all the
thunders have died away, when the storm has spent itself on
the affrighted hills, there comes this still small voice—" The
grace of our Lord Jesus Christ be with you all.   Amen."

Exodus xxxii.

AARON'S IDOLATRY.

MOSES had been sent for to go up to the top of the mountain and speak to God. The man was sent for: he owed nothing to his own originality or invention. It is a mistake to suppose that Moses invented anything, originated or outlined anything of his own imagination. The Bible is of God, or it is not a word to be believed or received into the heart, or made the monitor of the troubled life. The minister does not make his own sermons : if he does, what wonder that they are not heard, or being heard are quickly forgotten ; that they take no hold of the life, dominating over it with sweet and gracious sovereignty, ruling it into order, and charming it into hope ? The man made it out of his own mind : he invented phrases and set them in order; the sermon is a kind of intellectual mosaic thinly sprinkled with the baptism of dew, but a human manufacture, a very clever and stirring invention—nothing more. The true minister goes up to consult the Master for a long time. He is on the mountain, and the people think he is wasting the opportunity. They say, "We are waiting, the world is waiting, and as for this man Moses and all his tribe, where are they?" They are where they ought to be—out of sight, but communing with God; away from the fray, the battle, the race, but receiving nourishment, nutriment, inspiration, comfort, and even words by which to express the Divine thought. And what is true of Moses and the minister is true of every genuine believer in God. He has his interviews with the Lord in the mountain, his periods of solitude, his seasons of withdrawment from strife, and noise, and unholy revelry; and coming back from the mountain of contemplation he touches life with a steadier hand, and does his duty with a completer obedience and more radiant cheerfulness. We should fight better if we prayed more ; we should be more

original if we were more spiritual ; we should startle the world
more if our face burned with the lustre which reflects our
interviews with God face to face.   The general is on the top of
the mountain receiving marching orders ; he is asking what to do
next ; he will invent nothing, plan nothing, start nothing, be
responsible for nothing.   He says, " I stand until I am told to go
forward ; I do the Lord's bidding ; I do not act upon my own
ingenuity."   That is the truly religious life ; that is the inner,
spiritual, Divine, immortal life : that takes nothing into its own
hands, but offers those hands as instruments through which the
Divine Being himself may operate upon the destinies of the world.
Do we love solitude ?   Do we ever go up for our marching
orders ?   Is it our habit to shut out the world and keep it far
below us that we may have every day some five minutes at least
with God—say in the morning, say early in the morning, or be it
noontide, or in the quiet eventide ?   Do we ever clip out of the
day some five minutes and say, " You shall be God's minutes ;
through you I will receive messages from the Eternal One ; I
will carve a five minutes' sanctuary out of every day " ?—for in
five minutes how much can be done !—what great speeches
made ! what oaths and vows exchanged ! what memories touched
into new vividness ! and what vows formed with solemn and
pregnant meanings !   Let God have part of every day ; then,
when his own—our own—full day comes, it will be all too short
for the interviews we wish to hold with him, and for the messages
we wish to deliver and to receive.

When Moses was away the people became impatient ; they said :

" As for this Moses, the man that brought us up out of the land of Egypt,
we wot not what is become of him " (xxxii. 1).

Were they then dependent upon one man ?   Yes, to a large
extent.   I thought every man was one ?   Not at all.   We are
dependent upon our elder brother, our strongest man, our noblest
suppliant, our wisest leader, in many of the crises and agonies of
life.   For a long time we are as good as he is ; we know no
difference between him and us ; we wonder sometimes at apparent tokens of superiority,—but suddenly we are confronted
with circumstances which classify men : we come in face of great
claims and demands which search us, and try us, and see what
our quality really is,—then we know which is Moses, which is

Aaron, which is the man of prayer, and which is the man of mighty talk. The people did not understand the discipline of keeping still. That is a difficult discipline really to understand. We understand the discipline of going on,—that suits our impatience and our littleness; but the discipline of standing still, simply waiting, doing everything by doing nothing, reducing life to a process of breathing, being nothing in the great tragedy,— who can understand that? Who is equal to that strain? Who has the patience that can simply stand still and see the salvation of God? And yet this is the way in which we are sometimes trained. Let us own our impatience in this matter. I want to be going on, and I cannot stir; I want every stroke of my arm to win a battle, and behold I cannot raise my hand to my head. So much could be done before sunset, and we are not allowed even to make the endeavour. That discipline may be accepted either in the way of fretfulness, chafing, vexation, kicking against the pricks; or it may be so accepted as to chasten the soul, clarify it, make it without flaw or stain,—a holy and beautiful thing laid in daily sacrifice upon the high altar. How shall we accept it? You want the appointment now; you want to come into your blessing to-day; you want the answer to the great question you have put immediately; and God says, "No; not to-day, nor to-morrow, nor this year, but by-and-by." How do you take that answer? Do you fret, chafe, kick, rebel? or do you say— "Even so, Father: for so it seemed good in thy sight"? If you can say that, you need no more growth in grace: you are ripe; you are matured under the blessed and all-comforting sun of God's glory, and may surely be quickly transplanted to the higher gardens. That is the last conquest of grace, the supreme acquisition of the soul,—to have no will, to be ready to stand, to go, to fight, to wait, to suffer, saying always, "Not my will, but thine be done."

And yet the people were religious all the time. They said: "Up, make us gods, which shall go before us,"—an unintended tribute to the majesty of their leader. "Make us gods which shall go before us,"—an unintended rebuke to Aaron. The responsibility did not devolve upon him. They did not say— "Come, thy elder brother is lost; be thou our leader and our king, and we will do thee homage." Moses gone—he can be

replaced only by gods! It is thus that we reluctantly and sometimes unconsciously pay tribute to our masters, and leaders, and
noblest teachers, and benefactors. One Moses gone—gods must
supply his place! Moses was one nominally, but Moses was
influentially a host. It will take a good many gods such as
Aaron can make to fill up the place of Moses. But Aaron did not
feel the rebuke ; the people perhaps did not intend it as a compliment or tribute to Moses. But you will find if you give up
the Church, you will require a good many theatres to make up its
place. You will discover that if you give up the poor preacher,
the praying man, you will be driven to many expedients to find
an equivalent in the place he really occupied. You did not think
so at the time ; you said you would find an equivalent next door—
over the way—to-morrow,—ay, it can easily be done. But when
the terrific vacancies in life occur, then we begin to feel how
much we have lost. We say, now that the old father is gone,
how we miss him ; we did not know he was so much to us until
now ; why, he did everything so quietly, easily, graciously, that
we did not know that he was doing so much ; we miss him
morning, noon, and night ; we miss him in the garden and on the
street, at the table and in all the ways of life : the sunshine all
gone : the helping story no longer told : the gracious advice no
longer available. Ay, you will have to gather a great many
people together before you find a total equal to the father whom
you did not really appreciate when he was with you. It takes
an innumerable host of acquaintances to equal one friend. It
takes a whole furnaceful of gods to equal one Moses. Do not
wait for the vacancy to occur to honour the man, the woman, the
child, the teacher, the helper, the companion ; but honour to
whom honour is due now ; and away with the cant, the hypocrisy,
the falsehood, which says, "Had we but known what Moses was
when he was with us, we should indeed have honoured and
obeyed him." If you do not honour and obey your dear old
mother now, I will not listen with complacency to the canting lie
which attempts to shed tears over her tomb. Pay her court now,
be civil to her now with a generous courtesy, wait upon her now
with filial homage and obedience ; and as for the epitaph, let any
writer of phrases invent that. You keep her out of her grave,—
no matter who writes upon the stone which marks the sod under

which she lies. Oh that we might have apt minds and good,
clear, penetrating sense in these matters! and remember that
many acquaintances are not equal to one friend, many gods not
equal to one Moses, many casual helpers and assistants not equal
to one father, and all the amusements in the world not equal to
one holy service in God's blessed house. Could we seize these
truths and make them the bread on which our heart lives and
grows, we should be sad and weak no more.

Moses came down from the mount bringing great messages
from God. What was in his heart as he carried the two tables
of the testimony? Here is writing for Israel, here is God's
gospel of law, written by God's own finger, graven upon the
tables. What a day Israel will have! What reading of the
testimony! What gluttonous eyes will devour the holy feast of
truth! Oh, what spiritual voracity will consume this word of the
Lord! Hark! what is that noise—clanging, shouting? "The
voice of them that shout for mastery?" No. "The noise of
them that cry for being overcome?" No. What then?—"the
noise of them that sing do I hear." Then they are glad with a
false gladness. Singing is religious? Often very irreligious.
But the hymn is a religious one. True, but the singers are not
religious singers; and religious songs on the lips of irreligious
singers is an irony which might make the angels weep. To hear
great Bible words sung by people who value the music rather
than the truth is an anti-climax full of sad pathos to hearts
that worship truly at the altar. I would these sinners did
not double their sin by singing God's words. Why not invent
empty phrases? Why not employ incoherent speeches? Why
not sing the unrelated words of the dictionary just as they stand
in thick columns, and let God's great words alone? Thus we are
always paying homage to the very God we deny. There are no
words like his. We borrow them to sin against them; we steal
them to make money out of them. There is no book with so
many oratorios in it as the Bible—ay, and great anthems and
swelling songs, could they but be sung aright,—sung with the
soul. It is robbery, it is sevenfold murder, to sing God's words
without God's meaning,—to laugh over them, and jest about them,
and ask how they "went" in the vocal dance. God's words sung
with God's meaning,—then make the church a place of music in

very deed; sing morning, noon, and night, for then singing will be preaching, and such preaching as will make the heart cry for the very agony of love. It is not enough that we sing : we must sing with the spirit and with the understanding, and have a right object, and a right subject, and a right soul; then the singing will be good. Moses drew near and with eyes purged by visions Divine, with a soul out of which had been taken every filament of evil, he saw the situation at once as with the burning eyes of purity, and he first inflicted judgment and then asked for explanation. Ay, that is right in great crises, in solemn eras of the soul. Moses did not first hold judgment ; his

"anger waxed hot, and he cast the tables out of his hands, and brake them beneath the mount. And he took the calf which they had made, and burnt it in the fire, and ground it to powder, and strawed it upon the water, and made the children of Israel drink of it " (xxxii. 19, 20),

and then said—How did this come? Oh the swift anger! the holy, flying, infinite judgment! There can be no explanation of sin,—that is the explanation of the judgment. When the explanation is demanded, it is but to accentuate the judgment with a keener emphasis; it is but to overwhelm the culprit with a profounder humiliation. Moses was never so much Moses as just at that moment. He cleared a space for himself, he blanched the cheek of the singing hypocrites ; they all fell back, and each man would have cried unto the rocks and to the mountains to hide him from that angry face,—symbol and prediction of a more awful situation and more poignant cry. Are we prepared for these visitations ? Have we made any calves ? Ay, many! We have been great at idol-making. Can I count the calves which we have worshipped ? My memory would not be steady enough, or persistent enough, to name all the lines in the unholy catalogue : — Pride, Fashion, Gluttony, Self-Indulgence, Wealth, Station, Influence, Appearances,—all calves of our making, calves of gold. Who does not feel a sensation of pride when introduced to a man notably rich ? Who could contradict him ? Who would not defer to him ? or who would not irreligiously worship him by affecting to despise him ? What is your calf or idol ? Mark you the earrings were very good. When Aaron said, "Break off the golden earrings, which are in the ears of your wives, of your sons, and of your daughters," the gold was excellent as earrings, but bad as gods. Do not push things out of their right position and relationship. You may make a good thing into a bad one by bad use. The thing itself—the gold—is good, the earring is well shaped and well placed and gracefully worn,—all that is right; but turned into gods it becomes an offence to Heaven. So it is with our money. It has its place and its use. Devoted to honourable business, turned over and over in honourable commerce, the more you make the better,—God bless you in basket and in store, give you bountiful harvest-fields and plenty of gold, because you win it honestly, you spend it wisely and graciously ; the more you have the more the poor have; you are treasurers and stewards, and you look into the bag which is the Lord's, and say, "There is still more here ; it belongs to the poor man and the weak man : take it, and I will make plenty more next week." Ay, that is the way to make it. It is so by that gracious grip the hand learns the cunning skill to make still more and more, even to abundance. " There is that withholdeth more than is meet, but it tendeth to poverty,"—yes, to poverty. God withers the hand that is held down in desuetude, having forgotten sweet acts of charity. Take out that hand, thou palsied man ! " I cannot !" Another—God—has sucked the life-juice out of it, and it cannot be moved ! And so with influence, so with worldly advantages, so with physical and bodily charms. Wear them for the good of others. Make everybody welcome as to the hospitable table of God; and the beauty will grow, it will be freshened with tenderer bloom every morning : for the face is made every day by its morning prayer and by its morning look out of windows which open upon heaven ; and all manly grace and nobleness—these grow as they are used for God in heaven and truth on earth. God will have us in his grip at some point if we do wrong ; or if we do right, he will have us in his holy hand, not the grip of fingers harder than iron, mighty as almightiness, but the embrace of a love that has no symbol but a mother's piety, no type on earth but the heart that would die for its offspring. Now we have a chance to make gods,—do not let us make one. The great Father is away from our eyes : let us wait for his coming. The King has gone into a far country,—what a chance we have ! He is quite as much here. We do not see him,—what a chance we have !

Let us turn it into a chance to pray, into an opportunity to double our faith; let us turn it into a chance to read more deeply the holy testimony. Then when the King returns from the far country and calls his servants together to take account of them, we shall stand before him with radiant faces, expectant hearts, blessing God in sweet pure hymns that the King has come back from his travels and is seated in his rightful place. We shall see him one day. Blessed is that servant who shall be found waiting, watching!

The Lord mourned that Israel "turned aside quickly out of the way." The word *quickly* seems to contain most of the meaning. It is always so. We go with eagerness in the wrong direction, and with leaden feet we climb the steep which leads us away to the upper places. There is but a step between us and death,—not physical death only, but moral death, intellectual death, social death. The thing nearest life is death. Even physically the strongest man is always walking by the edge of his own grave. In a moment a man may speak a word which will bring down the tower which a lifetime was required to build. One action of the hand will shatter the character of the most venerable man. A character is not destroyed a blow at a time—though even the slow process is not impossible, but the slowness is only on the social side; it is the one act done in one moment that shatters the character in the sight of God. Towards society we may go down by slow and almost imperceptible depreciation; but to the eye of God we rise or fall by one action. The departure is accomplished in a moment, and the return is but the act of one contrite prayer. A series of appalling thoughts is started by this circumstance. Life is a continual peril and can only be sustained by a continual prayer. "Hold thou me up, and I shall be safe." Never leave me; never forsake me. The higher my attainments the deeper will be my faith, if my watchfulness be not found wanting. Who can measure the time required for a stone to fall from the highest pinnacle into the lowest depth? If we would know the rapidity of the descent, we must watch the stone as it falls from its place of honour; it seems to be the work of a moment. Destruction cometh suddenly upon the sons of men. No destruction comes so suddenly as the destruction of the soul's attitude towards things Divine.

Exodus xxxii. 30-35.

30. And it came to pass on the morrow, that Moses said unto the people, Ye have sinned a great sin : and now I will go up unto the Lord ; peradventure I shall make an atonement for your sin.

31. And Moses returned unto the Lord, and said, Oh, this people have sinned a great sin, and have made them gods of gold.

32. Yet now, if thou wilt forgive their sin—; and if not, blot me, I pray thee, out of thy book which thou hast written.

33. And the Lord said unto Moses, Whosoever hath sinned against me, him will I blot out of my book.

34. Therefore now go, lead the people unto the place of which I have spoken unto thee : behold, mine Angel shall go before thee : nevertheless in the day when I visit I will visit their sin upon them.

35. And the Lord plagued the people, because they made the calf, which Aaron made.

PROVIDENCE DELAYED.

LET us look at the historical picture which has now been almost completed. Moses had been summoned to meet the Lord upon Mount Sinai. There he had tarried forty days and forty nights. On coming down the mountain, it was discovered that Aaron and the people had fashioned and worshipped a golden calf. On descending to the plain Moses broke the two tables of stone, and inflicted humiliation and punishment upon the idolaters. And strange to say—yet not strange to those who know the wondrous ways of the human heart—no sooner had Moses expended his righteous indignation than he began to pray for the very people on whom he had uttered his denunciation and his wrath. Here a very curious expression occurs :

" And Moses took the tabernacle, and pitched it without the camp, afar off from the camp, and called it the Tabernacle of the congregation " (xxxiii. 7).

But he had been in the mountain for the express purpose of receiving a specification for the building of the tabernacle ; how comes it, then, that we read of the tabernacle before it was built ? We have been expecting the erection of this glorious edifice, and,

behold, in the very agony of our expectation, we read that
" Moses took the tabernacle, and pitched it without the camp,
afar off from the camp, and called it the Tabernacle of the
congregation." This was a temporary tabernacle. Probably it
was the tent which belonged exclusively to Moses himself, and in
the urgency of his sacred passion, he anticipated the building of
the edifice which had been sketched to him in the mount, and
extemporised an altar. There is no mystery about this. We are
forced by sadness and painful surprises into new postures of
supplication and new eloquence of intercession. Moses was pre-
eminently the man to do this very thing. Now and again, though
known as the meekest of men, there flamed up out of him a
hidden fire, that burned and showed him to be just the man to
see the flaming bush where he learned his first lesson of leadership and saw what was truly his first revelation of the God of
the living. A lesson lies here. Moses will not wait for the
consecration of Aaron : he himself becomes priest before God on
behalf of the people, and pours out his soul in passionate intercession. He was priest before the anointed one; he built a
tabernacle of his own, before he had time to erect the specified
structure. These are the actions of a burning life, the eccentrici-
ties and exaggerations of men who cannot proceed by cold rule
and adapt themselves to intricate, pedantic, and slow-moving
mechanism.

In this high temper he utters the boldest prayer ever uttered
up to that time by human lips :

" I beseech thee, shew me thy glory " (xxxiii. 18).

He had been a long time upon the mountain ; he had become
acclimatised to that high region ; for a considerable space he had
been away from the commonplaces of earth and time ; and now
that he had come back again, and had been touched by the defilement of a sinful community, he bounds back and goes to a still
higher height than ever in his soul's meaning and passion, and
says, " I beseech thee, shew me thy glory." We may have
experience of a kindred kind, if so be we belong to the family of
fire. But men differ here, as otherwhere and otherwise. We
are not all children of the flame. Some run away from fire ; they
have no liking to lay their hand upon the volcano, and caress it

as if it were a friend. We must have compassion one upon another, and wait for the slow and the crippled, nor visit with too severe a censure the naturally and unchangeably cold. Strange, though cold, they fly from fire. It is not a coldness that impels towards the burning-place, but another kind of coldness that keeps away the very soul it chills from the centre of ardour—the spring and fountain of eternal heat. Moses did not utter this prayer in cold blood. Sometimes we do not know what we say in prayer. We know not how hot the soul is, and ardent the imagination, till we surprise ourselves by some burst of words that make us feel how near we have come to the violation of the screened and impenetrable sanctuary But better err in that direction than fall down in lowness of mind, pettiness of conception, smallness of purpose, and frigidity of heart. These are mountain experiences, these are the memories of a man who stepped across mountains at a time by no slow passing, but by the familiarity of a man who, having lived amid the scenes, had apparently made the scenes love him, and yield to him, and keep back from him nothing of their sacredness and wealth

Now Moses must return to Mount Sinai. Time is lost. A sinful parenthesis has thrust itself into the revelation of Divine intentions. Moses re-ascends the hill, and spends forty days and forty nights more in that high sanctuary, and the ground is all gone over again as if not one word had been said.

"And it came to pass, when Moses came down from Mount Sinai" [the second time], "with the two tables of testimony in Moses' hand, when he came down from the mount, that Moses wist not that the skin of his face shone while he talked with him" (xxxiv. 29).

What do we know about our best selves ? Men have qualities of which they are not cognisant. We may be nearer heaven than we suppose. We may be nearer God than we fully realise. Sometimes there may be between us and him but a thin film, less than a vail in thickness. We know not where sometimes we stand.

Then Moses, returning, delivered the instructions to the people. He told them what God told him ; and the people, having heard what Moses communicated to them, "did according to all that the Lord commanded." For the time being they were converted. Their conversion was not a momentary and final act. They went through a kind of process of conversion—one conversion succeeding another, repentance following upon sin with quickness and certainty.

This is the historical position in which we now stand—what are its sacred and eternal lessons? Do we not see how God's purposes are thwarted and deferred by human perversity? God's purpose was far advanced in the cloud, but the people at the foot of the mountain could not wait. At the very time when God had determined upon the election and consecration of Aaron to the priesthood Aaron was spending his time in moulding and chiselling the golden calf. Time is thus wasted. Just as the revelation was about to appear, the radiant cloud was turned aside by the wickedness of the idolatrous mob at the base of the hill. We do not know how often God has just been on the threshold, coming into the house, and has been affrighted by the overhearing of some idolatrous or blasphemous noise. We might have been crowned fifty years ago, but just as the coronation was about to take place, we were discovered in the manufacture of an idol. Your sins have kept good things from you.

It is most instructive to keep the two scenes vividly before the eye of the mind. The first scene is that of God with Moses in the cloud speaking about the consecration of Aaron, setting apart Aaron and his sons to the priestly office for ever. There the Lord detailed the mystic and symbolic garments by which the priest was to be clothed. That is the one scene. At the very moment when that scene is taking place in the cloud, Aaron is listening to the foolish clamour which insists upon having a god made, or is at that instant himself employing the graving tool upon the calf, that he may make an idol for Israel. What a solemn view this gives one of life! When we are thinking least of God, God is thinking most of us; or when God is thinking most of us, purposing for us great office and honour and service, we are farthest away in thought and love from the altar where he intended to meet us. Why is the vision delayed?— Because of the idolatry of the people for whom it was intended. Why tarry the chariot wheels of the King?—Because the people towards whom he was hastening in his golden chariot have prostituted their affections and turned their prayers to forbidden and helpless gods. Why should we blame Providence for slowness when the answer is in our own conduct ? It may suit us in some of the lower moods of our mind and heart to think of God as very slow in his action and as keeping back revelation for inscrutable reasons. On one side of life that may be true, on another side of life it is not only untrue in fact, but it is unjust in principle. Who stopped the revelation ?—Aaron. Why were forty days and forty nights wasted ?—Because of the sin of the people. Christ might have been here yesterday, but for our making of the golden calf; fifty years ago he might have had the whole country as his own, but for perfidy, selfishness, and practical atheism. We might now see some great figure in the sun, and hear some voice supernatural, in music heavenly, but that we have filled our ears with riotous noise and deafened ourselves with the thunders of our own idolatry. Do not blame God for waste of history and waste of time, and repetition of events which we thought had been accomplished. Speaking reverently, God himself might have thought that the tabernacle was just about to be begun, and Aaron in a few minutes would be called to priestly office and honour, but (still accommodating human language to Divine mysteries) he was surprised and grieved by an action on Aaron's part, which suspended the Divine revelation and held back the honour that was prepared. What we might have been this day but for the calf-making, the idolatry, the disobedience, and the sins of various names ! The Lord was just ready to make kings of us, when we made fools of ourselves. God was signing the decree that was to have given us solidity, influence, high position, and noble honour, and ere he laid down the pen of signature we smote him in the face by some new sin. Then we spoke about the mysteries of Providence, and wondered why God was so slow in his manifestations and revelations, it never occurring to the heart that had just sinned, that itself shut up the heavens and turned back a purpose which was just about to open in magnificent and beneficial fruition. When we wonder at the weeks being wasted, and the time being non-productive, and history being barren, instead of always making a providential mystery of it, let us ask ourselves the soul-dividing question, Are not we to blame for this loss of time ?

Yet even sin may be made to contribute to the good man's highest education. Moses was enriched by this very circumstance.

He never prayed in his life as he prayed for the children of Israel. When he saw what they had done, said he,

"Yet now, if thou wilt forgive their sin—";

There language fails; the sentence is not completed; it was completed in the living instance with a great choking sob which, having been overcome, made way for these continuing words,—

"And if not, blot me, I pray thee, out of thy book which thou hast written" (xxxii. 32).

He could not survive an unpardoned nation; account for it as we may, he had come so to identify himself with the people that their pardon involved his, and his heaven was involved in theirs, and to be without them was an issue not to be borne by his noble and sensitive nature. What a hold his work had upon him! He was not priest, minister, or ambassador, who could stand aside from his people and let them be divided, sundered, smitten, and accursed, saying, "I am free; take you, who deserve it, the judgment of God." We already begin to feel the formation of that spiritual fellowship which cannot be dissolved. Here is a family within a family, a life within a life, a tenderness more sensitive than all the tenderness of perishable relationship. We now begin to see what is meant by the society of souls, the masonry of hearts, the oneness of the innermost nature of man. Moses could not bear to be left whilst Israel was lost. Who could be? Can the shepherd come home at night without his flock, and be merry in the house whilst the flock is being torn by the wolf? If he could be so happy, he would be no shepherd, but a selfish hireling. Can the general return, saying, "The army is broken, slain; it was no blame of mine, and I have come to enjoy the feast and the dance, and forget the bones that whiten on the field"? If he made a speech so base he would dispossess himself of every title to be called a soldier of the true blood. A minister standing before God to receive a solitary crown, saying, "The people are lost, but I did my duty; not a man has come with me; still, I claim the heaven due to virtue"! Could he make a speech so vile, no heaven could God shape for his residence and welcome. In all our higher moods we are one. We cannot be at rest whilst there is one vacant chair at the table which might be filled. Paul rose to the same magnanimity when he said he could wish himself accursed rather than Israel should not be saved; he would be prepared to be lost if the people could be saved. We do not come into that sacred passion in any way conceived by the human mind, or invented by human selfishness. It is the inspiration of Christ—yes, it is the very mystery and the glory of the Cross. Whilst the people, with Aaron at their head, were content with their idol, Moses said, " Show me thy glory." Some sights must be purged out of our vision, for they dim the whole outview and aspect of things. To have seen sin in the right way, and yet not to have suffered in feeling, but to have risen up into a tender and truer appreciation of holiness, is really to suggest an inspired prayer. " Show me thy glory." There is logic in this passion ; there is rational sequence in all this tide of feeling, though it rolls billow upon billow, as if in a great confusion and tumult. When for a moment you have perused some debasing book, or even some feeble and inane composition, or have seen how the noble language of the fatherland can be debased into the utterance of things so jejune, so juiceless, and mean, how you have longed to take up some grand old author whose every word was a burning fire, every sentence the beginning of a revelation, every page the work of a master, that you might forget what you have passed through ; and have it obliterated from the receptive memory ! It is but a feeble picture of what Moses felt, and what we may feel, when we have seen the calf we are called to worship. We long to forget the miserable spectacle in some burst of glory worthy of a vision opened by the Almighty wisdom. So Moses was the better for this most ludicrous as well as mischievous and iniquitous event. He did not fall into the temptation. We need men of that mould and temper, who, coming down a hill of prayer and high communion, and seeing our folly, look upon it with the right eyes and burn it with their anger, and scorch it with their jealousy for God. Let us pray for such men. They are the angels of God amongst us. The Aarons of the race would fall .nto all snares and traps, and yield to all tumultuous clamour for new policies and new programmes. We need the stern, iron, burning man, the incorruptible patriot, the theologian whose soul is fastened upon central truths, the suppliant who never can lower the tone of his intercession, to keep us right, to call us back—a man so terrible that he can smite us with judgment and, ere the thunder dies, turn his very anger into prayer.

Exodus xxxiii. 2

"And I will send an angel before thee; and I will drive out the Canaanite, the Amorite, and the Hittite, and the Perizzite, the Hivite, and the Jebusite."

THE EXPULSION OF THE HEATHEN.

THE awful statements made respecting the heathen, or non-Jewish peoples, have occasioned much surprise and not a little resentment. In the twenty-third chapter are words of an exciting kind upon this subject. In the twenty-eighth verse we read : " And I will send hornets before thee, which shall drive out the Hivite, the Canaanite, and the Hittite, from before thee." If we take such words in a narrow and literal sense, we cannot fail to be shocked. It is right that we should resent them. They represent the very spirit of oppression and murder. We cannot worship a God who thus separates himself from our conscience. But if we take the words in the right sense, we shall find that they represent what is daily and necessarily taking place in human history. They set forth the very philosophy of pro gressive civilisation, and would continue to be operative even if the Bible were closed for ever. This is not a Biblical matter. It neither comes nor goes with the Bible merely as a book. It is a law. Account for it as we may, make of it what we can, there it is, inevitable, irresistible, incessant. Many of the men who have turned aside from the Bible because of such expressions, are spending their time in showing that such occurrences are part of the very necessity of history. This is the glory of the Bible. When narrowly read it drives men away from it as if a fire had scorched them. When they pursue their studies upon other ground and make their way into history, progress, human development, and all the mystery of civilisation, they come back to say that all had been foretold in sharp outline in the very book which they had once despised because they once misunderstood it. Some benevolent persons might suggest that the expulsion of the heathen peoples was a hypothetical one, that the verses so cruel in their first aspect might be read as it were subjunctively, after this fashion : " If the heathen peoples, —the Canaanites, the Amorites, and the Hittites, and the Perizzite, the Hivite, and the Jebusite,—should oppose me, and set up their will against mine, I will undertake for thee, and thou shalt have a clear course." That is not exposition which goes to the root and philosophy of things. It may cover up the mystery for a time or it may double the mystery by an aggrava- tion which was meant to be pious ; but we must find other lines and stand upon other ground, and enable ourselves by sufficient study to grasp the whole situation,—not as it is indicated in one chapter or one verse, but as it is outlined and developed on the whole field of Biblical revelation. To understand such terms we must make ourselves acquainted with the Biblical theory and method of human development. We must of all things be careful not to snatch at isolated verses and isolated expressions. The Bible must be studied and applied in its entirety.

What, then, is the Biblical theory ? We find that a point of departure was established in the selection of Abram as the typical head of a new humanity. Whilst Adam represents the outer humanity, the initial and visible man, the historical unit of the race, Abram represents the inner and spiritual humanity, the fuller thought of God in the creation of man, —the humanity that is to be, the eternal likeness of God. Understand, we are now endeavouring to discover the Biblical conception without saying whether it is true or untrue. First of all, let us grasp the philo- sophy as it is stated in the Bible. To place the matter some- what figuratively, then, it may be put thus : As Adam was made out of the dust of the ground, so Abram was made out of the dust of Adam, and as Adam had control over all the lower animals, so Abram had control over all the lower civilisations. Account for this dominion as you please ; there it is. The scientific difficulty is quite as great as the theological one. That one race does put down another is the broadest fact in history. It would be imagined from some loose and incoherent talk that the Bible created the difficulties out of which we have made moral mysteries. Were the Bible closed, the difficulties would remain just where they are. The Bible comes with a conception which points toward a large and noble construction and issue. Therein the Bible is to be heard. The Bible does not create human life ; it recognises, interprets, inspires, and directs it.

Light now begins to dawn upon the mystery. It now begins to be clear that this act was no mere act of butchery or destruction, but the gradual and solemn development of a purpose, whatever the origin of that purpose may have been. It is a fact in ethnology that some races do succumb to others. We cannot escape the fact that some races are dominant and some are servile, and that the great law of the survival of the fittest is written upon the very face of all life from the meanest to the highest. The Biblical reader is only careful that the expression, "the survival of the fittest," shall not be impoverished of its highest and richest meaning; he will seize the expression and make the highest use of it. Meanwhile, account for it as you may, with an open Bible or a shut Bible, the Canaanite, the Amorite, and the Hittite, and the Perizzite, the Hivite, and the Jebusite, are going down, or have gone down, and another type of humanity is bearing aloft the banner of advancement and conquest. Suppose we close the Bible, we do not then revive the Canaanite, the Amorite, and the Hittite ; suppose we say the Bible is not from heaven, we do not reinstate the Perizzite, the Hivite, and the Jebusite. Whatever our theory may be, it is certain that those races are going or have gone ; that they played their part and have given way to another and higher humanity. Some illustration of a collateral kind we may find in strictly personal development. Let a new life come into a man—a life associated with a new conception of duty, sacrifice, honour, or a life associated with some other new and broad and noble idea ; and what is the consequence ? Out goes his heathenism. The Canaanite, the Amorite, the Hittite, the Perizzite, the Hivite, and the Jebusite, which filled up the most of his life, are driven out by the light, and the beauty, and the purity of this new Abram,—this new conception of light. What an outgoing there is from the soul ! What superstitions and prejudices are scourged out under the mighty and redeeming influence of a new idea of life ! What new habits are established ! What broader and keener discipline is applied ! How the whole nature, which was once a wilderness, blossoms as the rose ! and the whole life, which was once a barren desert, glows with passionate blossoming ! Some idea of a collateral kind arises from that conception. It throws light upon what is meant by the erection of a new humanity that shall put down, control, absorb, destroy, or glorify all things less than itself. In all these interpretations we want time. A thousand years with the Lord are as one day. We read the verses in sweltering haste, and imagine that blow followed blow with cruel rapidity, and that weak and helpless peoples were oppressed and crushed out of existence without notice, or without chance of escape. That is our injustice towards the facts of history. Between the chapters a thousand years may lie, between the lines a millennium may elapse. The one thought governing all other thoughts is, that there is an unswerving purpose running through all the process of the ages ; and that under the development and march of that purpose all that is not of its own nature must go down. Whatever is of its own nature will be taken up, absorbed, and glorified ; but there is a stone, and one of two things happens in relation to that stone,—either fall upon it and be broken, or it will fall upon you and grind you to powder. That is the Bible of history, the Bible of prosaic, daily facts,—not a book of superstition, but pages written in the red blood of the current time.

Still pursuing the inquiry as to the Biblical theory of the unity of life and the progress of a purpose, we find that there is One spoken of in the Old Testament whose history is part of this marvel. We will not give that One a name : he shall be to us for the present a coming One, a shadow, a hint, a mysterious personality. Yet in the Bible that One is recognised above all others. Of him we read, "Thou shalt break them with a rod of iron ; thou shalt dash them in pieces like a potter's vessel." That is the text in another form of words, without one tone of the solemn music omitted. A greater than Abram must now be coming. "In the days of these kings shall the God of heaven set up a kingdom, which shall never be destroyed : and the kingdom shall not be left to other people, but it shall break in pieces and consume all these kingdoms, and it shall stand for ever" (Dan. ii. 44).

Mark the harmony ! It is possible for harmony or consistency to mass itself into the bulk and force of a noble argument. Throughout the Old Testament there is One coming whose way is marked by conquest. " I will overturn, overturn, overturn, until he come whose right it is." That is the text paraphrased in sublimer eloquence. So then the Bible is one upon this point. Adam has gone down, the new Abraham, the new humanity, is before us. There is no man so little spoken of in the Bible as Adam. He seems to have gone all but utterly out of the purview of the Biblical writers. But Abraham is a name written all over the holy book. God uses it. When does God speak of Adam ? There is a new humanity on the earth. Here is a direct continuance of the promise made to Abraham and the Israelites. It is thus something to find that we are not dealing with a local incident or a narrow purpose, but that we are on the high road of history, or in the direct sequence of a sublime development.

Is the harmony continued in the New Testament ? Is there still One coming in that later book ? We have left much behind, —tabernacle, and temple, and altar, and priesthood, and ephod, and flowing blood of ram, and lamb, and fowl of the air,—have we left behind the purpose of a new humanity ? "Then cometh the end, when he shall have delivered up the kingdom to God, even the Father ; when he shall have put down all rule and all authority and power. For he must reign, till he hath put all enemies under his feet."

This is the same principle. The Bible has never swerved ; there is a common line. We are not now saying whether the line is right or wrong, we are making no special pleading on behalf of the Bible, but are endeavouring to be just to it, and from the first until the last the new humanity is to advance and all that is of its own quality is to be taken up : all that is not of its own quality is to be destroyed. The Bible argument is a massive and beneficent development. We must read the part in the light of the whole ; we must interpret the Pentateuch by the Apocalypse. He who makes the end gracious will, could we follow him, also make the process gracious. We leave all that we cannot explain regarding the servile or anta- gonistic races to him who for a purpose created them. But there is the ethnological fact : that one type of humanity rises and cannot be put down, and another flutters in its weakness and expires in its helplessness. All this is part of a massive and large education. It is the history of every time. There is an aspect of it which affects us with sadness, but we are not to interpret things narrowly or momentarily, but broadly and in eternal lights. There are men amongst us who must go down ; there are men who cannot be put down. Were all Bibles, Churches, from this moment disregarded, the sublime and terrible fact remains of dominance and servility, the right kind and the wrong kind, and it is one of two things,—either the wrong must repent and be saved, or it must be ground to powder. For right cannot stand still. The light will slay the darkness with its million spears of glory, and a kingdom shall be established that shall explain the mystery of the conflict and the mystery of delay. We must await the incoming of that kingdom, saying, "Thy kingdom come." We need not be destroyed. I am not now speaking of the destruction of the soul in hell-fire,—all that is another mystery which must be discussed and determined upon other ground. We have to face the one fact in this connection : that the new humanity is to advance, and that every soul that sets itself against it must go down. Why set ourselves against it ? " Kiss the Son, lest he be angry, and ye perish from the way, when his wrath is kindled but a little." The whole conception amounts to this : that One called the Son of man, the Son of God, shall have the heathen for an inheritance and the uttermost parts of the earth for a possession. His garment is dyed with blood, but it is with the blood of a victor. Truly the process is, in many respects, distressing and inexplicable, but we have nothing to do with processes. The meaning of the sharp ploughing will be seen in the harvest of grain. The deep and dark foundations so long dug for and so long in being laid will be explained by the lofty edifice and the pinnacles that pierce the sun. " We know in part, and we prophesy in part. But when that which is perfect is come, then that which is in part shall be done away." God's great purpose in all this advancement and overturning is to make man in his image and likeness. From that purpose he has never swerved. We await the issue. All the parables and analogies of nature which come within our cognisance establish the purpose, and already, here and there, by help of analogue, we begin to see how possible it is that though weeping may endure for a night, yet joy comes in the morning. As for the mystery, I leave it with him whose grace I magnify. We cannot resist the supreme purpose except to our own destruction. Everything points to a grand future. Were this all, we might laugh with rational merriment at him who calls himself Creator. But we must not arrest the process or interfere with the punctuation of history, or the method of the universe : we must calmly recognise the fact that from the beginning to the end there is one purpose never halting, never swerving, mighty to destroy, mighty to save,—meant to save, intended for good, and that will never be satisfied itself until the wilderness is blotted out by the garden and the desert is forgotten in the golden harvest. In this doctrine we stand, feeling it to be strong in philosophy, actual in history, and beneficent in design.

DEATH BY HORNETS.

In a letter by an Indian gentleman living near Jubbulpore, written to the *Times* some years since, we read :—"A most melancholy accident occurred here on the 10th inst. Two European gentlemen belonging to the Indian Railway Company, viz., Messrs. Armstrong and Boddington, were surveying a place called Bunder Coode, for the purpose of throwing a bridge across the Nerbudda, the channel of which, being in this place from ten to fifty yards wide, is fathomless, having white marble rocks rising perpendicularly on either side from 100 to 150 feet high, and beetling fearfully in some parts. Suspended in the recesses of these marble rocks are numerous large hornets' nests, the inmates of which are ready to descend upon any unlucky wight who may venture to disturb their repose. Now as the boats of these European surveyors were passing up the river, a cloud of these insects overwhelmed them ; the boatmen, as well as the two gentlemen, jumped overboard ; but alas! Mr. Boddington, who swam and had succeeded in clinging to a marble block, was again attacked, and being unable any longer to resist the assaults of the countless hordes of his infuriated winged foes, threw himself into the depths of the water never to rise again. On the fourth day his corpse was discovered floating on the water, and was interred with every mark of respect. The other gentleman, Mr. Armstrong, and his boatmen, although very severely stung, are out of danger."

Exodus xxxiv. 2

"Come up in the morning . . . and present thyself unto me in the top of the mount."

MORNING ON THE MOUNT.

GOD wishes me to be alone with him. How solemn will the meeting be! Father and child; Sovereign and subject; Creator and creature! The distance between us will be infinite, unless he shorten it by his mercy! Oh, my poor broken and weary heart, think of it and be glad; God wants thee to meet him alone! He will heal thy wounds; he will shed his light upon thy tears, and make them shine like jewels; he will make thee young again. Oh that I might be on the mountain first, and that praise might be *waiting* for God! I will be astir before the sun; I will be far on the road before the dew rises; and long before the bird sings will I breathe my sweet hymn. Oh, dark night, flee fast, for I would see God and hear still more of his deep truth! Oh, ye stars, why stay so long? Ye are the seals of night, but it is for other light I pine, the light that shows the way to the Mount of God. My Father, I am coming; nothing on the mean plain shall keep me away from the holy heights: help me to climb fast, and keep thou my foot, lest it fall upon the hard rock. At thy bidding I come, so thou wilt not mock my heart. Bring with thee honey from heaven, yea, milk, and wine, and oil for my soul's good, and stay the sun in his course, or the time will be too short in which to look upon thy face, and to hear thy gentle voice. Morning on the mount! It will make me strong and glad all the rest of the day so well begun!

How shall I go before God? In what robe shall I dress myself? "All the fitness he requires is to feel my need of him." That I do feel. Without him I am lost. But when I think of him the thought of my great sin comes at the same time, and it is like a black cloud spread between me and the sun. When I

think of anything else, I am happy for the moment; but when I
think of God, I burn with shame and tremble with fear. I cannot
answer him. His questions are judgments. In his eye there
is fire that burns me. This morning I must meet him on the
mount,—meet him alone! Alone! Alone! Surely he need not
have said expressly so; for to be with God' is to be in solitude,
though the mountain be alive with countless travellers. But he
bids me come; and is not the bidding itself a promise? Would
he take me to the mount to kill me? Is it that he may bury
me in some unknown rock, that he bids me climb the steep
path? Oh, my faithless heart, these very questionings are the
beginnings of sin. Why do I question God? Why do not I
arise at once, and flee to him as my soul's one delight? It is
not my humility that keeps me back, but my pride. I am not
modest, I am guilty; I will speak plainly to myself, and set my
shameful fault in a burning light.

God asks me to meet him in the *top* of the mount. I am called
to climb as far away from the world as I can. Surely the very
place of meeting has meaning in it. For many a day I have not
seen the top of the mount. I have stood on the plain, or I have
gone to the first cleft, or have tried a short way up the steep.
I have not risen above the smoke of my own house, or the noise
of my daily business. I have said, " In my climbing I must not
lose sight of my family; I must be within call of my children;
I must not go beyond the line of vegetation; even in religion
I must be prudent." Thus I have not seen the *top*, nor have I
entered into the secret place of the Most High. Oh that I might
urge my way to the very top of the hill chosen of God! "What
must it be to be there?" The wind will be music. The clouds
will be as the dust of my feet. Earth and time will be seen as
they are, in their littleness and their meanness. My soul, move
up to the top; let no stone be above thee; higher and higher;
God awaits thee, God calls thee, God will give thee rest! God
means that the very climbing should do me good. He could come
to me, but he bids me go to him. There is mercy in the going.
There is comfort on the road. The very weariness has a promise.
The mountain is measured; God does not ask me to climb an
unknown distance; he knows my strength, and he fixes the

meeting-place within its limits. This day I will see the sacred top. The enemy will try to turn me back, but I will meet him in the strength of God, and abash him by the name of Christ Lord, help me this day to see the very top of the mount, and let my poor soul taste the sweetness of the liberty which is assured to it in Christ.

The *morning* is the time fixed for my meeting the Lord. What meaning there is in the *time* as well as in the place! This very word *morning* is as a cluster of rich grapes. Let me crush them, and drink the sacred wine. In the morning— then God means me to be at my best in strength and hope; I have not to climb in my weakness; in the night I have buried yesterday's fatigue, and in the morning I take a new lease of energy. Give God thy strength—*all* thy strength; he asks only what he first gave. In the morning—then he may mean to keep me long that he may make me rich! In the morning—then it is no endless road he bids me climb, else how could I reach it ere the sun be set? Sweet morning! There is hope in its music. Blessed is the day whose morning is sanctified. Successful is the day whose first victory was won in prayer. Holy is the day whose dawn finds thee on the top of the mount! Health is established in the morning. Wealth is won in the morning. The light is brightest in the morning. "Wake, psaltery and harp; I myself will awake early."

> Holy morning,—sacred day,
> Up the mountain I must climb;
> God invites me,—God awaits me,
> He hath fixed the place and time.
>
> Early morning,—Summer day,
> I must meet my Lord alone;
> Christ, go with me,—Christ, protect me,
> Say thou didst for me atone.
>
> Gladsome morning,—joyful day,
> On the mountain-top I'll stand;
> Spirit, help me,—Spirit, guide me,
> Spirit, lead me by the hand.
>
> Father, Son, and Holy Spirit,
> For the mount my soul prepare;
> Then the eve shall tell in praises,
> That the morn was spent in prayer.

"Come up in the morning." A tender morning light shines upon the life of the elder saints and gives it the freshness of youth. The Bible is full of morning. "Weeping may endure for a night, but joy cometh in the morning." The dew of thy sorrow shall be taken up by the sun, and God shall set it in his light like a bow of hope. "My voice shalt thou hear in the morning, O Lord, and in the morning will I direct my prayer unto thee, and will look up." "The Lord's mercies are new every morning." May we "pass over Jordan by morning light"! Of old "the morning stars sang together." "I, Jesus, am the bright and morning star." The Holy Book is full of the spirit of morning. No evening shadows darken it. Truly the day declines, but "at eventide there is light" where in the morning there has been converse with God. My soul, I would charge thee to be as those who watch for the morning. The morning makes the day. The Sabbath of the day is in the morning. Oh, may this morning bring me near to God! May it be the time of resurrection; an hour of immortality; a gleam of the upper light, a breath of the holy world! A morning misspent is a day ruined. A morning saved is a day completed. Lord, awake me at sunrise, and by the beauty of the coming light give hope for the whole day.

"Be ready in the morning." This is my Lord's command. On my part there is to be preparation. As the ground is tilled to receive the seed, so must my heart be made ready to receive the good word of God. I may not rush into my Lord's presence in violent haste; I must be calm, knowing well myself, feeling my unworthiness, and taking with me words of humility and reverence. He bids me come. That is my plea for going. Alas, what making "ready" I require! My thoughts are so worldly; my plans are so mean; my motives are so selfish; my affections are so entwined around unworthy objects. "Oh, wretched man that I am! who shall deliver me from the body of this death?" God himself must make me ready, for "the preparation of the heart" is from heaven. "I will greatly rejoice in the Lord, my soul shall be joyful in my God: for he hath clothed me with the garments of salvation; he hath covered me with the robe of righteousness, as a bridegroom decketh himself

with ornaments, and as a bride adorneth herself with jewels."
Lord, make me ready. Truly all is from the Lord. My awaking
and my preparation, my desire to go, and my ability to move—
these, Lord, are thine, and these show the might and the gentleness of thy holy hand. Being thus made ready, may I have
grace to go forth and climb the appointed hill. Doth the bridegroom hide himself in the chamber of his preparation? Doth he
not rather go forth that he may find his heart's desire and his
heart's delight? So would I be made ready, and go out to the
hill, and scale its utmost height. "Arise, let us go hence."

"Come up in the morning." "I will arise and go to my
Father." It is not to Lebanon that he calls me, nor to the top of
Shenir and Hermon, nor to "the mountains of the leopards"; it
is to "mournful Calvary"—it is to the holy, tender, mighty Cross!
Nothing shall keep me back. The orchard of pomegranates shall
not detain me, nor will I tarry by the streams of Lebanon; I will
bend my steps towards the Cross, for all my salvation is there.
We shall meet where the sacred blood flows for sin. No tainted
wind of earth blows through that solemn sanctuary. There I will
speak of my guilt, and keep back nothing that I have done. The
Lord shall see my heart of hearts, and my Saviour's blood shall
cleanse my secret thoughts. To see his holiness will be to see
my own corruption; then shall I tremble with fear, and my
strength shall be as water poured forth, but my weakness will not
be despised by the Lord. "To them that have no might he increaseth strength." He is gentle with his weary sheep. In the
green pastures he leads them, and by the still waters is their
quiet lot. He carrieth the lambs in his bosom, and he maketh his
flock to rest at noon. My Lord calls me, and I will go. When I
see him I will say, How beautiful upon the mountain are the feet
of him that bringeth good tidings! And when he bids me climb
the still higher heights, I will be "like a roe or a young hart
upon the mountains of spices." Lord, help me; Lord, pity me!

The mountain on whose top I have to meet the Lord is very
high. Sometimes, because of the poverty and feebleness of my
faith, it seems as if I could never reach the far-away height.
There are places upon the steep where I would gladly sit down,
saying, It is enough : but a still small voice comes to me asking,

What doest thou here ? The Lord is on the top of the mount, and wilt thou keep him waiting as if he were thy servant ? He hath bowed the heavens and come down; shame on thee, my soul, not to be there before thy Lord's chariot ! Oh, the seducing spirits, how they beguile me ! Oh, the cold winds, how they strike me and urge me down ! Saviour ! give thine angels charge concerning me, for thou hast made them all ministering spirits, and by their help I shall this day see the top of the sacred mount ! "Keep me this day without sin." Let me have one day's rest from evil works. Give me a sweet Sabbath of pure love and unbroken rest. One such day will make me young again. One such day shall make me forget my polluted yesterdays, and cause me by sweet foretaste to enjoy the heaven that has begun to come. Blessed are they that breathe the mountain air ! Theirs is enduring health, and the keenest joys are theirs. Bear me beyond the cold and killing fogs of earth and time, and let me breathe the pure air of liberty and heaven. I give myself to thee this day. This day I bid farewell to all that is unworthy of the Blood by which I am redeemed. Henceforward I would climb the mount of God every morning, that afterwards I may return to do the work of earth as a citizen of Holy Zion. My Father, I start for the mount this day ; may I not fail to reach the top, where thy glory rests like a tabernacle of light !

> Ready in the morning, Lord,
> Ready for the mount ;
> Till the darkness flee, Lord,
> I every moment count.
>
> Help me up the mountain, Lord—
> Help me to the top ;
> Give me strength on strength, Lord,
> When tempted sore to stop.
>
> See, I am quite alone, Lord ;
> Sinful, seeking God ;
> But I set my feet, Lord,
> In ways my Saviour trod.
>
> Not to a burning mount, Lord,
> But to Zion's height,
> Bid thy servant come, Lord,
> And change his faith to sight.

Exodus xxxv. 20-29.

20. And all the congregation of the children of Israel departed from the presence of Moses.

21. And they came, every one whose heart stirred him up, and every one whom his spirit made willing, and they brought the Lord's offering to the work of the tabernacle of the congregation, and for all his service, and for the holy garments.

22. And they came, both men and women, as many as were willing-hearted, and brought bracelets, and earrings, and rings, and tablets, all jewels of gold : and every man that offered offered an offering of gold unto the Lord.

23. And every man, with whom was found blue, and purple, and scarlet, and fine linen, and goats' hair, and red skins of rams, and badgers' skins, brought them.

24. Every one that did offer an offering of silver and brass brought the Lord's offering : and every man, with whom was found shittim wood for any work of the service, brought it.

25. And all the women that were wise-hearted did spin with their hands, and. brought that which they had spun, both of blue, and of purple, and of scarlet, and of fine linen.

26. And all the women whose hearts stirred them up in wisdom spun goats' hair.

27. And the rulers brought onyx stones, and stones to be set, for the ephod, and for the breastplate ;

28. And spice, and oil for the light, and for the anointing oil, and for the sweet incense.

29. The children of Israel brought a willing offering unto the Lord, every man and woman, whose heart made them willing to bring for all manner of work, which the Lord had commanded to be made by the hand of Moses.

THE POPULAR RESPONSE.

THE first nineteen verses of this chapter contain the speech which Moses delivered to the congregation of the children of Israel, being the words which the Lord himself had commanded. These nineteen verses are, indeed, a condensation of all that is reported in detail in the previous chapters which we have studied with some particularity. Our immediate concern is the answer of the people. Let the scene vividly present itself to the eyes of our imagination. Moses has been in secret conference with the Lord in the mountain; he has received instructions of a very detailed and critical kind; he has come down and has reported to all Israel what he has heard in the tabernacle of cloud; the proposition is now fairly before the people. Wonderful, they seem to make no reply at once. That is scarcely matter of surprise. Never was speech of the kind made to mortal ears before. It seemed to overlook all time, all faculty, all opportunity, to vex and distress every line and fibre of the human soul and the human constitution. The instruction was critical up to the point of vexatiousness, and exacting up to the point of extortion. It was a frightful claim. The people seem to have paused awhile— to have gone away from Moses and to have thought over the whole matter. The twentieth verse is therefore a verse of negation; we simply read that "all the congregation of the children of Israel departed from the presence of Moses." We have often departed from the altar; we have often left the church, saying, "Who is sufficient for these things? This altar demands much from us,—yea, it lays its voracious hand upon our whole life." So thinking, we have left the threshold of the church, silently, somewhat sullenly, with a great wonder brooding in the heart, not being certain within ourselves whether we should have returned to hear speech so exasperating and so all-claiming. Let us be charitable to the silence of men. Perhaps they may come again not the less enthusiastically that they have gone away under the silence of a great surprise. Religion is nothing if it is not great. Were it to come to us with mean petitions, we might go back to it with meaner prayers; but religion comes claiming all, and therefore entitles us to return claiming according to the same scale; so the claim of Heaven and the prayer of men balance one another in sublime and honest equilibrium. The Lord had said long ago, "Let us make man," so now he seems to say to man, "Let us make the tabernacle." As there was a plural in the creation, so there is a plural in this building. God seeks human co-operation. We forget that the tabernacle is as much for men as it is for God. We call the church "the house of God," and so it is; yet there is an obvious and deeply solemn sense in which the church is also the house of Man. We put the church away from us among the clouds which conceal the superstitions when we think of it only as the house of God. It is that first; but it is only God's house that it may be our house in some tenderer way. It is our Father's house. It is the only house in which man can truly see himself. In other houses he is flattered, but never in the house of God; in other houses man sees a picture of himself, and wonders at the delicacy of the artist who could so make colour and form speak so eloquently, but in the house of God man sees himself as he really is, and what he is he only knows who has been closeted alone with God. The ignorant man does not know how ignorant he is; so long as he keeps company with his equals, the whole earth moves tardily along one low level; but when an ignorant man comes in contact with intelligence, the intelligence need assume no attitude of superiority—need speak in no tone of dominance. Ignorance feels itself to be little, small, contemptible, feeble. Increase the intelligence, and you increase the humiliation; add to the intelligence, and you deepen the sense of disparity and unworthiness. What is true intellectually is, if one might so say, truer still morally. We know not what we are till we see the holiness of God. The house of God is the symbolic home; it is the gate of heaven; it stands—insulated by infinite sacredness, yet approachable through all holy sympathies—between time and eternity. It is neither here nor there; it overleaps both spaces. God devised the house; Man built it; the house is built for two and only two,—the one the infinite God, the other the all but infinite Humanity.

When the people returned they came back with enthusiastic haste,—hearts were stirred up, hands were wide opened, the whole life had begun, the agony and the delight of sacrifice. How the answer throbs with love! Can love be mistaken? Is there not an accent in its voice that can be heard in no other speech? Has it not a manner of its own? Does it ever cease—saying, "That is enough"? Does it keep back one bracelet, earring, jewel, skin of ram, or badger-skin? We want less argument and more love. But love *is* an argument. We do injustice to enthusiasm when we depose it from a position amongst the logical powers and authorities. Enthusiasm is reasoning on fire—ablaze with that ardour which burns but does not consume. Coldness is the deadliest enemy. Fear the cold man more than the atheist. He sends a chill through all the regions of the Church; no hymn lifts him into rapture; no view of Divine truth transfigures him or makes his raiment glisten with sparkles of light; he is outside the fire of the most burning appeal; yet for some inscrutable reason he is within the lines of the visible Church. The cold man is not brought up for excommunication, but he ought to be. We expel the drunkard, as we deem him to be such, though no drunkard may he be in heart; yet we call the cold man respectable. Our discipline needs revision. The drunkard—for whom I have no word of commendation in so far as he has fallen from sobriety—may be the better man of the two. A cold professor of religion is the deadliest enemy of the Cross. His theology is formally right; in the letter he is orthodox enough, even to satisfy geometry; but he is heterodox in soul, he is a heretic in feeling; the temperature of his heart shows that he may have the form of godliness but not the power. Were it given to me to appeal to all the ages of time and all the nominal followers of Christ, I think I should adopt the tone of a man who is afraid of coldness rather than of opposition, of iciness of feeling rather than of intellectual hostility. Herein the Church is fatally wrong. She will endorse the cold man and expel the earnest contemplatist and speculatist; she lays hands on daring yet reverent speculation, and allows the cold man to lift up his hand of ice in sign of legitimate ecclesiastical authority. Better have two men in your congregation who are in burning earnest than a houseful of men whose souls are destitute of enthusiasm. You gain in weight what you lose in number; you gain in force what you lose in show. The prayer of every devout heart should be: "Baptise me as with fire."

The answer of the people was marked by the spirit of willinghood. Some form of the word *willing* occurs again and again: "Every one whom his spirit made willing"; "As many as were willing-hearted." God will have nothing out of the reluctant hand. We may throw an offering down, but it is not taken up by Heaven. It evaporates downwards; it is not received by the condescending and sympathetic sun. There are people, blessed be God, in every Christian land, who are content to find their whole joy in doing good. They say they have no higher delight; they are inventive in beneficence; a smile irradiates the face as with an inner light when they have hit upon some new method of showing love and loyalty to God. The Church is large enough for all they are and have, and if its line leave any out side, they will extend the Church so as to include all things harmless, beautiful, tender, gracious; and so the Church roof shall be large as the firmament. This is the ideal towards which we should work. See what willingness implies. Being intelligent, it means conviction, saying, if not in words yet in actions, "This is right: this is the road that leads onward, upward, Godward, and we take it inch by inch,—here very steep, there almost dangerous; but this is the road." It implies self-denial. There are men—strange as the sentiment may sound in our ears —abasing all miracles into commonplaces, who do deny themselves that they may have another coal to put upon God's altar. There is no miracle Diviner than that extravagance of economy;— men who pinch themselves that the child may have another year's schooling, women who say nothing of their deprivations that they may add something to the success of some cause of progress and righteousness. There are men and women who have concentrated themselves upon what they believe to be a Divine work, and they are the men and women who make the noblest and brightest chapters in history. There may even be a touch of superstition in their veneration; submitted to a very close analysis, what they do may exhibit here and there a combination and admixture of elements hardly to be approved by an absolutely accurate chemistry; but the fire that is in them is a wondrous solvent and disinfectant, and is accepted of God, who is himself fire, as something kindred to his own eternal nature. Out of such conviction and self-denial there comes a process of education. We thus become used to certain methods and sacrifices. A habit is begun, continued, consolidated, and at last it expresses itself in new solidities of character. We cannot build a tabernacle in a day. The tabernacle is a symbol of life or it is nothing. This beautiful creation in the desert—something between a thought and a thing—is a symbol of that nobler tabernacle—human life, spirit, character; and we know that the element of time has much to do with the perfecting of the building. It takes a long time to make a fit tabernacle—it will take the time of eternity.

The answer was enthusiastic and expressed willinghood, and yet it involved work of every kind. A Church must go to work if it would enjoy the spirit of unity and peace.

The answer was the deepest and truest cure of all murmuring. The people had been murmuring again and again, but the moment they began to work they ceased to complain. A new music steals into the strain of the history; we hear the motion, we observe the activity, we are astounded by the energy; and what appears to be the tumult of enthusiasm and passion settles into a deep harmony of consent and sacrifice. You would murmur less if you worked more. An evil thing is idleness. It must always sit with coldness, and the two must keep one another in evil countenance. Yet we have come to such a time in the history of things when the sons of rich men have nothing to do, and therefore they do mischief with both hands. Their fathers made the money, rendering work unnecessary, and therefore the sons rot in corruption or become enfeebled through inaction. It is the same in the Church: the great wars are all over and "the battle flag is furled." Now we have come to periods of criticism, dilettanteism, easy and self-comforting speculation; we have turned theology into a box of toys or into a chest of wooden mysteries which we open from time to time trying to fit the pieces into some reluctant unity. Persecution is dead; penalty for conviction is obsolete. We have fallen upon the evil times of theological exhaustion and luxury. Verily, we are dainty in our taste now; some men we will not hear,—without knowing them, without so much as having heard their names, we turn away in implied disgust from their offered ministry. This comes of living in periods of intellectual and theological confectionery. What is to be done? Who can tell? It is easy to go with the multitude; it is comfortable to have no convictions; it is delightful to be relieved of every duty but the pleasant one of passing criticism upon other people. The tabernacle is built, the temple is finished, theology is concluded, the last volume has been published, all the standards have been erected, and we have fallen upon the evil times of having nothing to do. We are wrong; there is more to be done now than there ever was before; every wall of the sanctuary is to be heightened,—the foundation we cannot touch, that was laid in eternity; but what room there is for enlargement, for improvement, for increase of hospitality, for growth in all noblest wisdom and sympathy ! What an opportunity there is this day for the Church to stand outside her own hospitable walls and say to the sons of men, " This is your Father's house, and in it there is bread enough and to spare " ! The Church includes all other houses that are at all good, or that want to be good. What is the Church to our imagination ? Let there be one great central meeting-place ;—but that will not suffice. Round about there must be a thousand little houses,—outer dependencies having direct connection with the house-fire and with the house-comfort; so near that the voice of prayer can be overheard ; so near that now and again some gentle tone of celestial appeal can penetrate. All schools, all asylums that express the spirit of philanthropy, all houses devoted to the education and the culture of the human soul with all its varied mystery of faculty, should be included. I would let them all build against the Church, so that the Church should be one wall of the building ; and the time may come when all the outside dependencies and attachments may be turned *inside ;* then we shall know the meaning of the doctrine uttered by the sweetest of all voices : " In my Father's house are many mansions." The eternal appeal of Heaven is for service. This is the wisdom of God ; he keeps us at work,—work which he lightens with pleasure, which he intermits by many a Sabbath day's enjoyment and quietude,—work which brings its own reward ; work which is not service only but payment on the spot ; we are rewarded by the mere doing of it. When we are in the passion of the service we feel that any other compensation than that given by service itself is unequal to the sublime occasion ; it fills the soul, it enchants the spirit with highest delight ; it brings the worker every eventide into the very peace and security of heaven. The one thing to be feared is stagnation. That is to be feared with all the terror possible to the human soul. Fear no opposition, fear no atheism, infidelity, unbelief, controversy,—hail it ; welcome it ; your enemies may be turned into your friends ; but what can we do with stagnation ? That is the deadliest unbelief ;—disbelief as implying intellectual activity it is not, but unbelief as implying intellectual stagnation and spiritual death it is, and therefore it is the worst form of opposition to the demands of Heaven.

Better have a tumult than stagnation. Better that our services should be interrupted than that they should be conducted perfunctorily, beginning in coldness and ending in some deadlier chill. Better have war than death. Hear Heaven's sweet appeal for service, for sacrifice, and know that the appeal is not the demand of exaggeration, but that it is inspired by the very spirit of consideration for human feeling, and expresses the very philosophy of human spiritual education.

PRAYER.

ALMIGHTY GOD, thou dost pity the weak and encourage them that have no strength. Thou art known unto us as a shepherd. Thou dost carry the lambs in thine arms,—yea, thou dost hide them in thy bosom as if thou didst care for them with the solicitude of love. Their weakness is thine opportunity: they never know what a shepherd thou art until they are distressed by weariness. It is so with every soul amongst us. We do not know thee in our pride and haughtiness, in the abundance of our strength and wealth; we say then, There is no God. So thou dost chasten us and abase us with many an affliction. Thou dost bark the fig-tree and take away the one good plant, and turn all our clients and supporters away from our door; thou dost send a sharp pain into the head, and thou dost afflict every joint with rheum; and then we look around, and wonder, and cry, and ask for any man who can bring up the Samuel we have despised. We have run with the foot-men, and they have outrun us: we have tried our strength with the horses, and they have fled away far beyond us; now that the swellings of Jordan have next to be encountered we are dismayed. But thou wilt help us; even at the last, thou wilt not forsake us. Thou mightest well do so, for we have turned our backs upon thee, and have been pleased with any idol that could for the moment dazzle and fascinate our fancy. But thou art pitiful; thou wouldest rather save than destroy; thou hast no pleasure in the death of the wicked, thou hast no pleasure in any death that is not the precursor and condition of larger life: then it is not death but some servant of thine whom thou dost employ in thine infinite household. We are wanderers, and the darkness has come on suddenly: find a rest for us. We are mariners, and all the winds of Heaven have seized upon us, and we are rolling and staggering to and fro like drunken men: Lord, give the elements charge concerning us. We live for one little day, and we ruin the generation that comes after us by foolish careful kindness. We toil and slave, and mass our wealth, and spare our young ones from toil and labour, and, behold, we have wrecked them and made fools of them. Pity us! Our kindness is a mistake; our prevision is blindness. Give us great lessons, great comforts, great blessings, in the Lord of the Cross,—the Man who shed his blood, the Saviour of the world,— mighty to save, unwilling to destroy. Amen.

Exodus xxxviii. 8.

"And he made the laver of brass, and the foot of it of brass, of the looking-glasses of the women assembling, which assembled at the door of the tabernacle of the congregation."

OLD THINGS TURNED TO NEW USES.

THE mirrors of the period were made of burnished brass. Women having such looking-glasses at the door of the Tent of Meeting refers to an idolatrous custom. In many ancient religions women took a leading part in some of the ceremonies. This was so in Egypt. The Israelites had no doubt observed the custom and imitated it in some degree, or part of the "mixed multitude" that went up with Israel out of Egypt may have continued the idolatrous practice. Each woman had a looking-glass made of polished brass, and that mirror was used in some way in connection with idolatrous practices. When the tabernacle was being built the women gave up their mirrors and so contributed to the formation of the laver, which was made of brass, and the foot of it of brass. Thus we have old things turned to new uses, and it is for us to say whether we shall regard this incident as a piece of ancient history, or whether we shall enter into the spirit of it and realise the action in our own day and on a broader scale. We can modernise the incident; we need not allow the centuries to gather between us and the instance of consecration. We need not smile at the ancient story; we had better seize its spiritual intent and realise its purpose in our own daily behaviour.

How came the women to give up their looking-glasses to assist in constructing the laver? Because a superior spirit had taken possession of them. That is the philosophy and that the explanation of the case. That must be the philosophy and the explanation of corresponding service upon our part. This kind of action, if it is to be of the true quality and to have real virtue and merit in the sight of Heaven, cannot be done as a trick, or as an act of mechanism, or for the satisfaction of personal vanity, or for the purpose of being like other people ; it must express the fact that into our souls there has come a new principle of living, a new purpose, a nobler spirit than we have yet entertained, and the action must show that we are ruled by considerations which deprive all temporal things of the slightest permanent value. We are too prone to make ancient history ; it is a fault of ours. We might be younger if we determined not to be so old. We might see the old poetry written over again with a young hand. We might revivify all the sacred past and be rich in memory and inspiration. Is it not so that when a greater spirit takes possession of the man he is willing to attest the reality of the new occupancy by giving up that which aforetime he valued ? Great enthusiasms dispossess the soul of mean idolatries. Christ in you the hope of glory alters every standard of valuation and every test of accuracy. When a preacher has set upon his platform a little black slave-child and looking a great congregation in the face has said—Her price is so much : shall we subscribe the amount and invest the child with freedom ? what has been the reply ? Men have taken off their watches and chains and cast them into the treasury ; women have stripped their fingers of jewellery and said, "Take the baubles and buy the child's liberty with them." That is the philosophy, and until we get some such spirit as that we shall be niggards and mean men, content with little things, careful that the temperature does not rise too high ; we shall be the victims of prudence, we shall not know the sovereignty and Divinity of purest passion.

This is not to be accomplished by mere argument in words. The soul must see its own Divine sights and hear the call addressed specially to itself ; it must feel the glow of a new love, the appeal of a grand challenge ; it must answer in its own way without heeding the judgment or fearing the contempt of others. We cannot do the greatest actions in life as mere duties. Duty is a measurable term : it begins and ends ; it has appointed days, stipulations, covenants ; it goes by weights, scales, and measures. A great life can never be founded upon the mere discharge of mechanical duty. There is a conception of duty which takes up all the elements that are necessary to constitute and preserve a Divine enthusiasm; but I am dealing now with the every-day conception—*quid pro quo*, the so much for so much, and that is the spirit of the hireling, and it never can end in enthusiasm, consecration, Calvary. What then is the spirit that is to enter into us? None other than the spirit of Christ. We might use many words in describing the spirit, but all the words would focalise themselves at last in this sublime expression—"For Christ's sake." When Christ enters into a man and takes full possession of him, the world is not worth fighting for; time is so small as to be unmeasurable, and all the prizes of life are leaves that wither in the plucking. Argument can never do this; creed and dogma and written form of faith can never do it. Men cannot be followers of mere *isms*, and impersonalities, and abstract propositions. There are those who seek to quench the spirit of individuality. They do not want mere personal following to be the rule of religious life; they would have men live for an *ism*, an abstract statement. This can never be done. We are so constituted that personality rules our thinking, stirs our enthusiasm, brings to consecration our hesitating, inquiring, and reluctant will. The highest personality is Christ. We follow him, and in proportion as we follow him all things we possess are his. We feel heaven enough in the realisation of the fact that he is willing to accept and use them.

There is room in the sanctuary for everything. This is the point we have so often missed in our Christian teaching. No punishment is burning enough for the men who would belittle God's house. They are the plague of every ministry, they are the obstruction of every kingdom that is righteous and pure, are those who would limit the Holy One of Israel. What have you? You have nothing that cannot be used in the building of God's house and kingdom. Have you nothing but the little looking-glass? It can be used. Is yours, on the other hand, but one small flower which a child could pluck? It was God's flower before it was yours, and he will never consent to lose a flower; it cost him thought and care and love; he dressed the flower as Solomon never could dress himself. Are yours very great faculties? They will be small enough in relation to the kingdom which is Christ's and the house which is God's. Many a great man feels himself much contracted when he comes into the infinite kingdom of Christ. The faculties which dazzled the senate are hardly seen in the Church—always provided that the term *Church* is defined in the largest and truest way. This will be seen some time. Meanwhile, the standard of valuation is different, and men " dressed in a little brief authority," rebuke wandering people who stop public religious services. When the men who so act—as George Fox acted—begin to explain themselves, the illustrious quacks call the speech nonsense. Are you a statesman ? What a field there is in the Church for you ! Here is your opportunity—a world to liberate, a world to illuminate, a world to bless ;—*a* world ? *one* world ?—ten thousand worlds, when measured by the generations which rapidly and passionately succeed one another in the passage to eternity ! How is your statesmanship being employed ? In building paper walls ? In outwitting rivals and competitors— struggling for a prize that will perish before it is reached ? A vain and mean life ! Let the Church (truly defined) never be ashamed to claim for herself the grandest function which human genius and human strength can exercise. Have you music— some gift of touch, some gift of voice,—the faculty of rendering thought into the eloquence of music ? What a field there is in the Church for you !—for the pure man to pronounce pure words, for the soul to sing as well as the throat and the lips—to sing the world up to heaven's gate—the weary, sighing, broken-hearted world. Who will exclude the musician from the Church ? He must be brought inside, though the elder brother be offended much by the music and dancing. Better the elder brother be offended than that the passion of love and gratitude be extinguished in the soul. The elder brother must not rule us.

The time has come when men must settle this question. What spirit is to rule the Church ?—the spirit of ice—if ice can be said to have a spirit—or the spirit of fire ? The man of ice must be put out : he must be excommunicated as worse than a heretic and a most mischievous form of hypocrite. What is your talent ? Is it a faculty of amusing men ? We want you. This poor human life needs occasional recreation and gentle withdrawment from studies that would afflict it by the very profoundness of their solemnity. The child wants you—the little child all dimples, the little life all dream and laughter ; that little creature does not want the theologian, the philosopher, the dogmatist. There is every kind of life upon the face of the earth and within the compass of the government of God, and each must be attended to according to its degree and quality and compass. The Church must consecrate its laughter ; it must turn its very amusement into an instrument of religious use and blessedness. Nothing is to be turned away from the Church, except that which is impure, untrue, vicious, mean, and debasing.

Bright will be the day when all faculties which are now employed in mischief are employed in doing good. There are clever men on the bad side—men who could triumph over some of us in many departments of human skill—who are giving all their time and attention to the service of the Evil One. We want all their faculties ; we must make room for their exercise. If the men say, We cannot exercise our faculties within the lines of the Church, then somebody has taken away from the amplitude of the Church, and room must be found for every man who is willing to consecrate his faculties to the true enlightenment, advancement, comfort, civilisation, and progress of mankind.

There are others to whom an appeal may be fittingly addressed —namely, those who are using great powers for little purposes or unworthy ends. Is it worth your while to carve heads upon cherry-stones ? Taking all things into account, is it worthy of your power and dignity to be found running errands that are without a purpose, casting vessels into empty wells and drawing nothing up ? Is there nothing better for you to do than to be throwing water into a sieve all day long and finding it empty at eventide ? There may be no absolute mischief in what you are doing, but the faculties could be turned to positive beneficence— real, sound, healthy, good-doing, and when so turned the day is without a cloud, the time of cessation comes too soon, and as for he wages, they are paid in every stroke of the work.

Many entertain the hope that a day will come when all things will be turned to the building and consolidation of God's kingdom. Prophecy encourages us to take that view. As for Christ—

> "Kings shall fall down before him,
> And gold and incense bring."

All kings shall bow to him, and own hat their kingdoms are his

rather than theirs. It is promised that he shall be known as
King of kings, Lord of lords ; men shall come from the east and
from the west, from the north and from the south, with gold, and
frankincense, and myrrh, and offer them as tributes too small to
majesty so great.

Blessed will be the day when the breweries of the country are
turned into mechanics' institutes, great sanitary establishments for
the washing and cleansing of the people. Blessed will be the day
when the rich man's saloons shall be thrown open to the poorest
neighbours he has who will come to look at his articles of *vertu*,
—who will turn over his curiosities and examine them with
honest fingers, and so admire them as to be touched into desire
for broader life. Blessed—bright will be the day when in that
sense we shall have all things common ; when the strong man's
strength shall be the weak man's refuge; when the homeless
shall have a large home in the charity and love of his richer
brother ; when the one object of every heart will be to extend
the happiness of mankind,—the one question in the morning
being, What good can be done to-day ? and the one question at
eventide, What good has been accomplished ? My persuasion is
that if ever that time is to be brought about, it can only be
by the extension of the spirit of Jesus Christ. He turned
every man's faculties to use; he found a place for every man
in his *clientèle* he turned none away, saying—" In the formation
of my kingdom I never anticipated peculiarities and gifts like
yours." I know of no teacher with so keen a vision, so large
a heart, so tender a sympathy, so noble a priestliness. This I
say of him as a mere character in history without approaching
him along any theological lines ; but meeting him on the open
highway of civilisation and listening to him, 1 say, " My Lord
and my God, no man can do these miracles that thou doest
except God be with him." If I withheld that tribute from his
gentle majesty, it would be because I had suppressed the purest
passion that ever inflamed and ennobled my heart.
Taking the Christian view, all becomes larger still and brighter,
and the hope is given that one day everybody will be in the
kingdom, and every man, woman, and child will be doing their
very best to make that kingdom what God means it to be. The

great men, by heroic strength, by dauntless valour, will carry on their sublime occupation; the patient women—gentle souls, having the genius of sympathy and the faculty of interpreting by suffering—will contribute their important, their ineffably valuable share; and little children will make up the sum total of the consecration. They can say nothing, but they can laugh us out of despair; they cannot preach, but they can hug the Cross with a trust that ought to be full of significance to us. All people serving the Saviour, all houses consecrated to the Son of God, and the whole earth, casting out the devil and his hell, shall have no room in all its radiant hue but for the Christ of God. " Thy kingdom come; thy will be done on earth as it is in heaven."

NOTE.

THE Hebrew women on coming out of Egypt probably brought with them mirrors like those which were used by the Egyptians, and were made of a mixed metal, chiefly copper, wrought with such admirable skill, says Sir G. Wilkinson, that they were "susceptible of a lustre, which has even been partially revived at the present day, in some of those discovered at Thebes, though buried in the earth for many centuries. The mirror itself was nearly round, inserted into a handle of wood, stone, or metal, whose form varied according to the taste of the owner. Some presented the figure of a female, a flower, a column, or a rod ornamented with the head of Athor, a bird, or a fancy device; and sometimes the face of a Typhonian monster was introduced to support the mirror, serving as a contrast to the features whose beauty was displayed within it." With regard to the metal of which the ancient mirrors were composed there is not much difference of opinion. Pliny mentions that anciently the best were made at Brundusium, of a mixture of copper and tin or of tin alone. Praxiteles, in the time of Pompey the Great, is said to have been the first who made them of silver, though these were afterwards so common, as, in the time of Pliny, to be used by the ladies'-maids. They are mentioned by Chrysostom among the extravagances of fashion, for which he rebuked the ladies of his time, and Seneca long before was loud in his denunciation of similar follies. Mirrors were used by the Roman women in the worship of Juno. In the Egyptian temples, says Cyril of Alexandria, it was the custom for the women to worship in linen garments, holding a mirror in their left hands and a sistrum in their right, and the Israelites, having fallen into the idolatries of the country, had brought with them the mirrors which they used in their worship.—*Smith's Dictionary of the Bible.*

"HANDFULS OF PURPOSE,"
FOR ALL GLEANERS.

" And see . . . why."—Exod. iii. 3.

What serious man is always inclined to do.

What curious man is too prone to do.

What flippant man finds it impossible to do.

The spirit of the inquirer determines the result of the inquiry.—Surprises on the journey of life should awaken religious interest.—To the attentive eye the so-called continuity of law or sequence is continually interrupted.—Phenomena, so called, are as perplexing as the essence of matter itself.—There is an unknowable point in phenomena as well as in essences.—From the right heart nothing will be withheld that is good for it.—There are incidents in our life which appear to be greater than ourselves, or to challenge in us faculties which are either not present, or have not yet been awakened.—Men should not run away from great sights.—Nothing is to be gained by cowardice.—Always distinguish between flippant rashness and daring reverence.

———

" Certainly I will be with thee."— Exod. iii. 12.

The thoughts which arise in connection with this inspiring assurance are such as ought to touch our life at every point.—God is the unchanging One.—As he had been with Moses, so he promised to be with Joshua; and so from age to age he is the inspiration and strength of his moral creatures.—Take this assurance as applying to the whole service of sanctified life, and it entitles us to draw four practical inferences:—I. " Certainly I will be with thee."—*Then man is servant, not master.*—He should know his place, or he can never keep it.—As servant, he should (1) constantly *consult* his Master; (2) constantly *speak in the name* of his Master; and (3) constantly be jealous of *the honour* of his Master.—II. " Certainly I will be with thee."—*Then the work must succeed.*—What is the guarantee of success ?—(1) *Not human cleverness;* ministers may be clever, so may churches, etc. ; we may have *learned* sermons, *able* sermons, *ingenious* sermons, etc. ; (2) *not skilful organisation.* — Cards, bazaars, registers, circulars, etc., all useless as *ends.*—(3) *The word of the Lord* is the guarantee of success.—" The mouth of the Lord hath spoken it " ; " My word shall not return unto me void."—III. " Certainly I will be with thee."—*Then the servant is to be received for the Master's sake.*—" He that receiveth you receiveth me, and he that receiveth me receiveth him that sent me."—The true minister carries a blessing with him.—The Romans were to receive

Phebe *in the Lord.*—What a lesson to *ministers*—they are representatives of God !—IV. "Certainly I will be with thee."—*Then there need be no lack of grace or power.*—" If any man lack wisdom," etc.—" Lo, I am with you alway," etc.—" Ye have not, because ye ask not, or because ye ask amiss."—The servants may take counsel of one another, but not to the interruption of continuous and trustful prayer to the Master.—(1) God is with his servants for their *comfort ;* (2) for their *guidance ;* (3) for their *safety.*

Application—Notice (1) the *individuality* of the promise, " I will be with *thee* "—with the one man ; (2) the *emphasis* of the promise—" *Certainly.*" Who is with *us* in our life-ministry ?

" *I know not the Lord.*"—EXOD. v. 2.

A kind of agnosticism more prevalent than agnosticism of a scientific kind.—There is an agnosticism of the heart ; there is an agnosticism of the will.—Men reason foolishly about this not-knowing.—Men imagine that because they know not the Lord, the Lord knows not them.—This is a vital distinction.—We do not extinguish the sun by closing our eyes.—If men will not inquire for God in a spirit worthy of such an inquiry they can never know God.— Pharaoh's no-knowledge was avowed in a tone of defiance. It was not an intellectual ignorance, but a spirit of moral denial.—Pharaoh practically made himself God by denying the true God.—This is the natural result of all atheism.—Atheism cannot be a mere negative ; if it pretend to intelligence it must, in some degree, involve the godhead of the being who presumes to deny God ; the greatest difficulty is with people who know the Lord and do not obey

him. —If they who professedly know the Lord would carry out his will in daily obedience and sacrifice of the heart, their lives would constitute the most powerful of all arguments.

" *But he said, Ye are idle, ye are idle : therefore ye say, Let us go and do sacrifice to the Lord.*"—EXOD. v. 17.

A religious sentiment foolishly accounted for.—Men judge others by themselves.—When religion is of no consequence to them, they cannot imagine its being of any importance to others.—Religious exercises are supposed to be associated with idleness. This is a sophism ; this is also a vulgarity.—The popular delusion is that engagement in religious exercises takes nothing out of the strength and vigour of the worshipper.—The truth is, that an exercise of a religious kind, if it be of the true quality, leaves a man wholly prostrate—inflicting upon him the greatest spiritual and physical loss.—The reaction is of an edifying and inspiring kind ; but so far as the man himself is concerned, if he has truly worshipped, he has gone out of himself, and to that extent has exhausted himself.—We must not take other people's account of our religious inspirations.—We must not be laughed out of our enthusiasm.—Nothing is easier than to divert the mind from the right cause or motive of action, and to trouble the soul with suspicions of its own integrity.—It is useless to attempt to disprove such accusations by mere words.—Words are accounted as idle as religious exercises by the people who live a worldly and shallow life. Such people attach no moral value to words. They themselves are false in every fibre of their nature.—There are not wanting to-day journalists, critics, sneerers, who account for all religious sentiment, emotion, and activity on some narrow and frivolous ground.—Churches must not be deterred by what mockers say.

———

" *And I appeared unto Abraham, unto Isaac, and unto Jacob, by the name of God Almighty, but by my name JEHOVAH was I not known to them.*"—EXOD. vi. 3.

The different appearances of Jehovah.—The marvellous fact that he has been made known by different names. — This circumstance should put an end to all sectarian controversy.—Religion is not a matter of mere name, but of spiritual reality.—The word is unquestionably important, but only important as indicating something which is behind it, and infinitely greater than itself.—Men know the Lord under different forms and representations.—The thing to be remembered is that it is the same Lord.—The particular point of this text is that the men themselves referred to knew God by different names. At first they knew him as GOD ALMIGHTY, but they had no knowledge of the name JEHOVAH.— Does it follow, then, that the Lord was not Jehovah because the patriarchs did not know him by that designation? — We grow in spiritual consciousness as we grow in grace and in knowledge.—The mind seems to awaken to the power of describing God by new appellations, and worshipping him under enlarging and ennobling forms.—God has many a name, and he reveals himself to men by what name he pleases to adopt.— Jesus Christ has revealed himself to some thinkers as a man ; to other thinkers he has revealed himself as God the Son.—These views may be used in one of two ways—either as beginning a controversy which can

never end, or as suggesting the infinite fulness of the Being who can represent himself under names of limitation and names of infinity.—Do not let us quarrel about the mere name.—Many a man may be under the Godship of Christ, who is unable metaphysically to affirm the Godhead of the Son.—Names and words in this connection must be thoroughly well defined and understood before they are turned into weapons of controversy and assault.

———

" *They hearkened not unto Moses for anguish of spirit, and for cruel bondage.*"—EXOD. vi. 9.

How religion is sometimes placed at a disadvantage !—Men's social circumstances disqualify them for listening to sublime appeals.—Poor people are in no mood to listen to speculation ; even the word of hope falls mockingly on the ear of men who have grievous burdens to carry. — Sometimes social condition is to be improved before religious instruction can be effectively given.—The condition of the body greatly affects the temper of the spirit.—A wounded spirit who can bear ?—By long ill-usage man is disqualified for religious action. We must therefore be patient with men. We do not all start from the same point in our spiritual education. We must wait for the weak ones ; we must adapt our tone to those whose lives have been sunk in black despair. —Some news appears to be too good because of the low condition of those who receive it.—No wonder the world itself was startled almost into mockery by the announcement that God had appeared to redeem it. — Preachers should not imagine that their people are all as well prepared as themselves to go forward in the noblest pursuits.—

He is most Divine who is most patient with the suffering and the weak.— When Jesus Christ announced the forgiveness of sins, the people were shocked at the very Gospel that should have been their supreme joy.

" These are that Moses and Aaron."— Exod. vi. 27.

Particular circumstances by which men may be distinguished. — Moses and Aaron are special names to us, but they might have had contemporaries who bore the same names.—Men may have the same names and yet very different natures and functions.—Every man should have a certain name indicating spiritual education, position, and influence.—The Christian Church should be distinguished as that Church by which light is increased, charity is distributed, and life is ennobled.— Whenever any difficulty arises as to the identity of men or institutions, those men and institutions should instantly be known by the breadth of their spiritual life and the reality of their generous service to the world. —It will be of little use to be known as that Church with the long creed, that Church with the heavy purse, that Church with the brilliant intellectual ability;—all these qualifications may attach to a worldly institution: the Church of Christ is to be known as that Church which is strong in sacrifice and infinite in sympathy.

" When Pharaoh shall speak unto you, saying, Shew a miracle for you." —Exod. vii. 9.

The world has certain rights in reference to the Church. The world is at liberty to call upon the Church to prove its inspiration. —It is not enough for any Church to say that it can work miracles; it must prove the saying by the action.—Christianity is the great miracle-working power. Christianity never does anything but miracles.— The mischief is that we have affixed to the term *miracle* a narrow signification, and have declared that miracles have ceased.—This is a profound misconception.—The presence of Christianity in the world is itself a miracle. Every man who is turned from darkness to light is a living miracle.— Every life that is turned round from going in one direction to going in another direction illustrates the miraculous energy of Christian inspiration.— It is better to show living miracles than to be clever in logical arguments.— The world is not to be convinced by controversy, but by the higher kind of miracles,—change of spirit, temper, disposition, purpose; that change is known by the Scriptural name *regeneration* or the new birth—a name which ought never to be surrendered; there is none like it for range and expressiveness.—Even if the world can show miracles of its own, there must be a point of superiority in Christian miracles which will instantly and finally decide the competition.— Never disallow the power of education or of social custom to work certain wonders in human character and purpose. Nothing is to be gained by such denial. Such denial would, indeed, be unjust. — The power of Christianity is to transcend such wonders by sublimer miracles.

" If thou refuse . . . I will smite."— Exod. viii. 2.

Thus the parts of life are linked together.—Disobedience is not a self-contained act.—Man must not imagine that he has no correspondence in heaven.—What man does is important as bearing moral consequences.—Man has undoubtedly the liberty to refuse, but he has no liberty in the region of law. Law follows in its own consequences whatever man may do.—This is not to be regarded as an arbitrary infliction. The law tells equally in both ways: obedience is blessed as certainly as disobedience is punished. —Man must not therefore excuse himself on account of the supposed arbitrariness of the Divine law. It is not arbitrary: it is rational in its foundations and equal in its operations.— This is no mere threatening: it is simply the announcement of a settled ordinance of nature. It belongs as much to the physical world in degree as to the spiritual world.—If a man refuse to sow seed he will reap no harvest; if a man refuse to open his windows he will receive no sunlight into his house ; if a man refuse to take proper food and exercise his health will be smitten. — All this is not severe : it is really the active and protective side of beneficence.

" And he hearkened not unto them."—
Exod. viii. 19.

The man spoken of is Pharaoh, and the men to whom reference is made were his own magicians.—There came a time in the spiritual history of Pharaoh when he declined the teaching of his own monitors in this matter. —Paganism has its difficulties as well as Christianity. It must not be supposed that the Christian is the only religion which is disbelieved : Pharaoh gave up his own magicians. — Men sometimes give the lie to nature, disobeying every one of her laws, and seeking to invent universes of their own.—It is not uncommon also for experience to be dismissed by men who have imagined that its lessons are narrow and insufficient or hesitating in their moral deductions.—Not only have nature and experience been thus deposed, but history itself has been treated as an idle tale.—When nature, experience, and history have had to suffer these things at the hands of their supposed followers, what wonder if the men who have treated such teachers so should have treated the Gospel message with contempt and spurning ?—When a man treats all teachers in so high-handed a manner, he assumes practical godhead.—We are not at liberty to conduct our own education without hint or service from others.—If we take to this course, we shall conduct ourselves towards exhaustion. — The wise learner looks outward, upward, Godward, insisting that his earth shall be warmed by no meaner fire than the sun

---

*" And the Lord said unto Moses, Rise up early in the morning, and stand before Pharaoh."—*Exod. viii. 20.

God is always before men. However early we rise, God is waiting for us.—The Lamb was slain from before the foundation of the world. — We never can surprise God by a new necessity, or baffle him by the agony of an unexpected pain.—The Church should take a lesson from this consideration. It should watch the movements of men, and always be ahead of them and waiting for them, and surprise them by Christian appeals where such appeals are least expected.—The Church cannot begin its labours too early in the day.—The message from Heaven is always in time and in place.—Every engagement of life may be legitimately interrupted by the direct messages of Heaven.—The Church has been too particular in studying the convenience of the persons to whom it has been sent in the name of Heaven.—Interrupt everything, that the Gospel may be delivered.—Have no fear of the greatest; whatever his importance in life it is transcended by the importance of messages that are sent by God himself.

" Only ye shall not go very far away."— EXOD. viii. 28.

This was a stipulation made by Pharaoh.—He had been plagued into some concession.—This is the language of compromise — the common language of all time.—Men are generous with a reservation. This was Pharaoh's policy. — In many cases religion is to be respected, but is not to cost anything.—Some people use this language when they are giving a kind of permission to faith; they say, " It may go so far, but no farther." It is not to go very far away from what can be seen and handled; it is to be as a tethered bird unable to fly beyond its check.—Some people use the same language to the spirit of Consecration. It must not go very far away from the market-place and from the common courses of society; it must never become a passion, a heroism, a burning sacrifice.—People keep themselves very much within themselves, not knowing that self-control reaches its highest discipline in the absolute giving away of the whole life to the care and service of God.

" One plague more."—EXOD. xi. 1.

God always teaches by repetition.— One plague might have been forgotten, and another and another might have gone into oblivion. — God must so assail our lives that we can never forget the tremendous onslaught.—God

has to work a memory of recompense and judgment in the life of men.— Nothing so easy to forget as judgment when it is overpast.—So God works with repetition and severity of scourge, so that often when the pain has departed the mark of the chastisement may remain.—God can always send one plague more. The worst has never come.—Jesus Christ said : Go thy way and sin no more, lest a worse thing befall thee! — God has never dealt this heaviest stroke; the most terrible of his scourges has yet to be inflicted. God is a *consuming* fire ;— not only a thread of fire, or a string of flame, or a spark of heat, but a fire that can destroy both body and soul.— All these plagues show the greatness of the sinner as well as the resources of God.—God does not deal thus with beasts.—It is worth while saving man even by judgment.—God will spare nothing that can be turned in the direction of reclaiming and restoring his lost image.—We see as much what estimate God sets upon the value of human nature by the fear which he excites as by the hope which he inspires.

" This month shall be unto you the beginning of months : it shall be the first month of the year to you." —EXOD. xii. 2.

God is the Ruler of time.—We do not invent years and months and weeks. These are really, when searched into, the creations and appointments of the Divine power.—New days are new opportunities. New days enable us to forget the evil of all yesterdays.—Consider the dawning year in this light, and the opening day. —The true birthday of a man is the day on which his soul was born into a purer and nobler life. A birthday may be determined by a vow. The birthday of the body is the poorest of all anniversaries.—When the great idea entered the mind, inspiring and ennobling it, and filling it with Divine enthusiasm, the man was truly born.— We are entitled to date our existence from our regeneration, otherwise our memory might become an intolerable torment.—Regeneration destroys the recollections of remorse.—Man is breaking a Divine ordinance when he goes beyond the day of his re-creation, and insists upon making alive again all the iniquities that corrupted and degraded his earliest life.—Beautiful is the word *beginning*. It is one of the first words in the Bible. God himself alone could have invented that word. It is a dewy term; it is tender with the brightness of morning; it is beaut'ful with the bloom of heaven; a very holy and most helpful word.—Blessed is the man who knows he has begun his life again, and who can confidently date his best existence from a point in time which separates him from every evil and accusing memory.

"*And he called for Moses and Aaron by night.*"—Exod. xii. 31.

What men are always doing.—It is not enough to have a religion or a conviction for the daytime.—Our religious convictions must be large enough to include the whole circle of existence.—Were life a summer day and one steady pulse of health, a certain kind of religion might be made to do; were life one gloomy night and one continued consciousness of pain, another kind of religion might be wanted. Were life eternal youth or endless old age, such a condition would require special treatment.—Life is a mixed quantity; darkness—light,

youth—age, enthusiasm—coldness, wealth—poverty; all these and infinitely more elements enter into its composition; and only a religion at least as large as itself can come to such life with any hope of doing it permanent good.—Pharaoh sent for Moses and Aaron by night; ministers are most wanted when the darkness is deepest.—Darkness is always a mystery to the superstitious mind.— Moses and Aaron are always prepared to go, whether by night or by day; their message is always in season.— No invitation addressed to ministers or churches should be declined, if there is in it the faintest sign of sincerity.—A conversion wrought at night may be as good as a conversion wrought at noonday.—Nicodemus went to Jesus by night, and the blessed Christ showed the inquiring rabbi all the stars of God.—Do not put off sending until night; begin early in the day.—A whole life consecrated to heavenly pursuits will drive away the night, and it may be said of such a life as is said of the heavenly world, "There is no night there."— God uses darkness as an instrument of fear.—The ministry of Christ in the world would be incomplete if it did not appeal to the fear as well as to the hope of man.—That is, indeed, the poorest of the appeals; but it is essential in order to make up the completeness of the holy ministry, which seeks to excite the attention and save the lives of men.

"*And a mixed multitude went up also with them.*"—Exod. xii. 38.

This may be taken as a sign of mercy.—God permits men to work along the line of their impulses, even when they cannot justify those impulses by natural right or by technical argument.—Impulses to go with the people of God ought never to be repelled; out of those impulses something better may come.—We must not be too curious in inquiring into the metaphysical reasons of human action. When that action points in the right direction, we should accept it, and afterwards begin and continue the work of spiritual education. In the meantime it ought to be accounted a sign of hopefulness that men are inclined to go to church, to listen to preaching, or take any interest in spiritual activities.

This may also be taken in mitigation of judgment of a severe kind often passed upon the Church.—They are not all Israel that are called Israel; neither are they all Christians that follow the Christian standard. We must always distinguish between the true Israel and the mixed multitude. Time will separate them by teaching them.—It is of the nature of evil that it must destroy itself, and it is of the nature of life, rooted in God, that it must grow and bloom eternally.—Men are not judges.—Wherever a man proves himself to be bad and to be acting the bad man's part, he unchurches himself without any formal and penal excommunication.

There is a sense in which the Church itself is a mixed multitude. Take it, for example, in the light of spiritual attainments.—We are not all upon one level.—In the Church there are great scholars and poor learners; some are far advanced and others are toiling at the alphabet.—Take it in the matter of disposition.—It is not equally easy for all men to be religious. It is not equally easy for all men to be generous.—Where the difficulty is greatest, the sincerity may be of a very pure kind.—Take it in the matter of individual action.—Probably no

human action is free from some kind of suspicious motive.—Our motives are a mixed multitude.—We often have to go by majorities, even in our personal considerations and decisions; we have to marshal a mixed multitude of thoughts, feelings, hopes, and fears. —Herein is the delicacy of life, and herein the necessity for a discerning judgment and a sound discipline.

"Thou shalt therefore keep this ordinance in his season from year to year."—Exod. xiii. 10.

Memory needs to be vivified.—We pursue this kind of practice in our own household life.—The recurring birthday is a recurring joy.—Every child in the family has its own method of celebrating its nativity.—Great mercies should create their own anniversaries. —It is well to sanctify our time by religious recollections and consecrations.—There is no need to fall into superstition in this matter.—We may be but sparing ourselves when we relax our religious discipline on the ground that religious observances may become superstitions.—Every act of life is capable of debasement; but it does not therefore follow that life should be without action, and particularity of observance and ceremonial. The Church is a help to remembrance, so is the ordinance of the Lord's Supper.—We ourselves are at liberty to set up milestones by the road, and to set aside special days for the remembrance of particular acts of providential revelation and care.— Every line in the diary should have in it something of God.—There is a deep spiritual sense in which every day is a birthday, and every morning a new year.—They use time well who find in it many new points of newness —that is, chances of being better and opportunities of rendering wider service.—By indicating a special day, God lays down a law rather than fixes a technical statute: the law being that days may be marked according to their position in what may be termed the religious calendar—the diary of the soul.

---

*" And it came to pass, when Pharaoh had let the people go, that God led them not through the way of the land of the Philistines, although that was near ; for God said, Lest peradventure the people repent when they see war, and they return to Egypt : but God led the people about, through the way of the wilderness of the Red sea : and the children of Israel went up harnessed out of the land of Egypt. And Moses took the bones of Joseph with him : for he had straitly sworn the children of Israel, saying, God will surely visit you ; and ye shall carry up my bones away hence with you."—*Exod. xiii. 17-19.

God's mercy is continued beyond the mere act of deliverance.—God does not sit down outside the gate saying, " You are now free, do all the rest for yourselves."—Little acts follow great deeds in the wondrous economy of the Divine providence.—There is a preventative ministry in the government of life.—Near cuts to the goal are often dangerous cuts ; to go across country instead of round by the proper circuit may appear to be very clever and successful, but it is only the cleverness and the success of suicide.—Do not consider that we are out of the road because the road seems to be longer than it might have been.—Often better to be in the wilderness than to be in the battlefield.— God so orders his providence that men have services

to render which considerably assist the detection of the path of duty. The services may be of an incidental and indirect kind, and may not always be accredited with their proper bearing and influence in life.—Moses took the bones of Joseph with him. — The carriage of the bones of Joseph had much to do with the progress of Israel in the wilderness.—The solemnity of a vow was upon Israel.—A dying man had given a direct charge to the children of Israel and had received an oath, and that oath was amongst the people as an inspiration, an encouragement and a discipline.—God thus often charges our lives with sacred ministries which have an incidental bearing upon the steadiness of our course. We have made promises, or entered into engagements, or signed covenants, or done something which comes up again and again in the life and says, " You are bound to go forward ; you cannot retreat without falsehood and cowardice."

---

*" And Moses took the bones of Joseph with him : for he had straitly sworn the children of Israel, saying, God will surely visit you ; and ye shall carry up my bones away hence with you."—*Exod. xiii. 19.

A very simple thing it appears to be to us that Moses took the bones of Joseph with him.—The circumstance is full of poetry and moral significance. —Do not we all carry with us the bones of the past ? This is the very pith of history.—If we did not take the past with us the present would be a continual disappointment,—a line coming and going without bringing with it any opportunity of service and enlargement of soul.—Much depends upon our conscious and intelligent relation to the past.—We ought to have brought a good deal with us from all the centuries that are gone.— If we have come up out of them empty-handed, we have by so much turned the counsel of God to non-effect.— Every wise heart is carrying up with it memories, vows, oaths, traditions, sacred impressions, and is under the responsibility of trusteeship to the future to be faithful to all the highest claims of the past. Poor is he who has no history behind him.—He becomes the victim of every combination of circumstances; the dupe of every tempter that assails his heart with unfamiliar and lying promises.—To carry up the past may steady our whole movement and give it dignity in times of fear and depression.—However little we may be in ourselves, we are charged as messengers of Heaven to carry on certain work and to connect transient periods of time and so assist in the consolidation of human history.—On the other hand we must guard against the worship of ancestry which is founded upon mere superstition.—We do not carry the *bones* of Joseph, we honour his service and redeem our own pledge.—What *bones* all Christians have to carry !—Think of all the heroes, witnesses, martyrs, and confessors of the past, and let the humblest Christian pilgrim realise that he has it distinctly in his charge to carry forward such histories and testimonies to the age that is to follow.— Whatever Israel carried through the wilderness derived importance from the fact that it was associated with the bones of Joseph.—Those bones kept Israel from going back to Egypt.— When Israel reeled in its purpose and thought of returning to the land of tyranny the question would arise again and again, What are we to do with the bones which we promised to carry up and to protect by burial in

another land ?—By many curious lines and ties does God bind us down to the fulfilment of our destiny. —The record is not all written in plain letters ; many an invisible line now and then comes into sight to show us that under all the great letters which the naked eye can see there are writings and meanings which are only disclosed to patient waiting and scrutiny.

———

" My father's God."—Exod. xv. 2.

These words are taken from the song which Moses and the children of Israel sang when they saw Pharaoh and his hosts overthrown in the Red Sea.—It was surely an era in their history to see the Egyptians dead upon the sea-shore.—Such epochs in human life should have some moral meaning.— They should not be allowed to pass without celebration.—There is a time to sing,—surely it is the hour of deliverance from the terrible foe.— Music is the natural expression of joy. A song is the proper conclusion of a victory.—Fasting is the worship of sorrow ; singing is the worship of joy. —The words specially chosen for meditation show that the victory did not end in itself ; it touched the holy past ; it consummated the promises and hopes of ages ;—in this song, therefore, the voices of the sainted dead are heard as well as the voices of the triumphant and joyous living.

What are the ideas with which this expression is charged ?—1. "My father's God."—*Then religion was no new thing to them.*—They were not surprised when they heard the name of God associated with their victory.—Religion should not be an originality to us ; it should not be a novel sensation ; it should be the common breath of our daily life, **and the** mention of the name of God in the relation of our experiences ought to excite no mere amazement.—2. " My father's God."— *Then their father's religion was not concealed from them.*—They knew that their father had a God.—There are some men amongst us of whose religion we know nothing until we are informed of the same by public advertisement. —It is possible not to suspect that a man has any regard for God until we see his name announced in connection with some religious event.—We cannot read this holy book without being impressed with the fact that the men who made the history of the world were men who lived in continual communion with the spiritual and unseen. Religion is the *exception* in some of our lives,—it was the great and beneficent rule of theirs.—Is it possible that your *child* is unaware that you have a God ? Is it possible that your servants may be ignorant of the existence of your religion ?—3. " My father's God."— *Yet it does not follow that the father and the child must have the same God.*— Religion is not hereditary.—You have power deliberately to sever the connection between yourself and the God of your fathers.—It is a terrible power ! Let that be clearly understood, lest a man should torment himself with the thought that he must inherit his father's God as he inherits his father's gold.— You may turn your face towards the heavens, and say with lingering and bitter emphasis, " Thou wast my father's God, but I shut thee out of my heart and home ! "—4. " My father's God."—*Then we are debtors to the religious past.*—There are some results of goodness we inherit independently of our own will.—This age inherits the civilisation of the past.—The child is the better for his father's temperance. —Mephibosheth received honours for

Jonathan's sake.—**The processes of God are not always** consummated in the age with which they begin.—Generations may pass away, and then the full blessing may come.—We are told that some light which may be reaching the earth to-day, started from its source a thousand years ago.—What is true in astronomy is also true in moral processes and events ; to-day we are inheriting the results of martyrdoms, sacrifices, testimonies, and pledges which stretch far back into the grey past of human history.

The text should convey a powerful appeal to many hearts.—It is a pathetic text.—Say " My God," and you have solemnity, grandeur, majesty, and every element that can touch the reverence and wonder of man ; but say " My *father's* God," and you instantly touch the tenderest chord in the human heart : God is brought to your fireside, to your cradle, to the bed of your affliction, and to the core of your whole home-life.—The text impels us to ask a few practical questions.—1. Your father was a Christian,—are *you* so much *wiser* than your father that you can afford to set aside his example ? —There are some things in which you are bound to improve upon the actions of your father ; but are you quite sure that the worship of the God of heaven is one of them ?—2. Your father was a holy man, will you undertake *to break the line of a holy succession ?*— Ought not the fame of his holiness to awaken your own religious concern ?— Are you prepared to make yourself the turning-point in the line of a pious ancestry ?—Beware lest you say in effect, " For generations my fathers have trusted in God and looked to him for the light of their lives, but now I deliberately disown their worship and turn away from the God they loved."—This you can say if you be so minded!—God does not force himself upon you.—You may start a pagan posterity if you please.—3. Your father was deeply religious,—will you inherit all he has given you in name, in reputation, in social position, and throw away all the *religious* elements which made him what he was?—Many a battle has been fought, even on the funeral day, for the perishable property which belonged to the dead man; what if there should be some emulation respecting the worship he offered to the God of heaven?—You would not willingly forego one handful of his material possessions; are you willing to thrust out his Saviour?—4. Your *father* could not live without God,—can *you?*—Your father encountered death in the name of the Living One. How do *you* propose to encounter the same dread antagonist?—When your father was dying, he said that God was the strength of his heart and would be his portion for ever.—He declared that but for the presence of his Saviour he would greatly fear the last cold river which rolled between him and eternity, but that in the presence of Christ that chilling stream had no terror for him.—When the battle approached the decisive hour, your father said "Thanks be unto God which giveth to us the victory,"—how do *you* propose to wind up the story of your pilgrimage?

A word must be spoken for the encouragement of a class which cannot but have its representatives in any ordinary congregation.—Some of you have had *no family religion.*—Your hearts ache as you turn to the past and remember the atheism of your household and the atheism of your training. -Not a single Christian tradition has come through your family. —To-day you are asking whether it be possible for you to be saved.—I return an instant, emphatic, and impassioned YES to your heart's inquiry.—Seek ye the Lord while he may be found!— Our relation to God is strictly *personal.* —Every heart must make its own decision in this grave matter.—See to it that, though you cannot speak of *your* father's God, yet your *children* shall be able to associate your name with the God and Saviour of mankind.

"I am the Lord that healeth thee."— Exod. xv. 26.

Every man must have his own special revelation of God.—Some have never seen God in what may be called his metaphysical relations; they do not, in that sense, know God. Others know him in his relation to affliction, sorrow, and the whole of the enduring side of life. They cannot account for their deliverances except by a superior power. In their memory is the recollection of a pit out of which they were lifted, and they know of a surety that no arms could have delivered them from that pit but the arms of the Almighty One.—The infinity of true religion is thus shown by the infinity of the responses which it elicits from human nature.—One man's religion is all music—that is to say—an expression of thanksgiving, delight, and confidence in God. He has no argument, no logic, no well-connected and highly-authenticated history by which to defend himself, or on which to rest his Christian beliefs. He knows who came to him in the day of sorrow, who walked with him to the edge of the grave, who gave him heart again in the time of great loss and pain.—It is needless to argue with such a man; he is himself his own argument.— When the debater has ceased his storm of words, the man retires upon his own consciousness, and in the recesses of his memory he finds a comfort which the war of words can never reach.—This is the kind of experience open to all men.—Few can be scholars, fewer still can be poets; to only one or two has it been permitted to enter into the holy of holies; but every life has had its own difficulty, or pain, or shadow, or cross—its own awful affliction or bitter poverty.—The Christian religion is strong upon every ground, but stronger, perhaps, on this ground than any.—Every one of its believers has his own story to tell respecting the richness of Christian comfort and the cheering of the Divine light.—Every man must base his argument upon the strongest point of his own consciousness.—Let the restored blind man say, "One thing I know"; let him keep steadily to that plain story, and no band of Pharisees, how infuriated soever by malice, can unsettle his position or disturb his serenity.

" Lo, I come unto thee in a thick cloud."
—Exod. xix. 9.

This is a sample of God's daily visitation of the world.—God cannot come otherwise than in a thick cloud. The cloud is not necessary for him, it is necessary for those to whom he comes.—No man can see God and live.—Many a cloud that we blame is created for the purpose of attempering high light to our vision.—The darkness of the way is as much to be attributed to God as is the light.—He makes us stand still as well as go forward.—The cloud does not deprive us of the music of the voice. — Mere spectacle would do little for us; it is to the voice itself that we must pay heed.—Remember that the cloud only conceals God : it does not destroy

him.—Clouds and darkness are round about him; righteousness and judgment are the habitation of his throne.

" I have talked with you from heaven."
—Exod. xx. 22.

There is no mistaking heavenly music. Other voices may seem to rival it, but at points here and there it separates itself from all rivalry, and with an energy all its own appeals to human imagination.—A beautiful expression is this word, "I have talked"; it is full of simplicity and condescension; God is quite close to our ear and is conducting communication upon an almost equal level.—God sometimes thunders from heaven or causes the shining of his glory to dazzle the firmament so that no human eyes can gaze upon it.—With these dispensations we cannot interfere; it is when God "talks" with us that we may draw near and listen and ask questions and make replies.—We like to be talked to from heaven when we are in a right condition of mind; though the language is sublime it seems to appeal to something that is born within us. When we hear the heavenly speech, all earthly appeals become low and narrow and unworthy of us.—It is the same with the Book of God.— Once get into its spirit and enjoy the fellowship of its very heart, and all other books seem to be unworthy of the nature that is to be excited and hallowed by Divine communications.— God talks with us from heaven that he may lure us to heaven.—His purpose is never that we should be lower and meaner, but always that we should be higher and richer.—He stands up in the heavenly light to show us to what altitude we may rise.—It is not great superiority that is here indicated, it is a lesson to us of stimulus and encouragement.—If God has spoken to us what has he said? Where is his word recorded?—Not a syllable of the Divine message should be lost.— Let us be misers in gathering up every tone and speech of God.

"The tabernacle shall be sanctified by my glory."—Exod. xxix. 43.

Not even by the beauty which God himself had designed; not by the curious carving and cunning work of the artists whose busy fingers had made the tabernacle; not by the presence of Moses and Aaron; not by the burning of incense, or the offering of beasts, or the lighting of lamps; not by learning, pomp, splendour; not by rich and ingenious ceremonialism; only by the direct presence and ministry of the Divine Being.—If we do not see the manifestation of God in the tabernacle, we see nothing that is worth looking at in the tabernacle.— We should insist upon hearing the Word of God, and knowing the meaning of that Word, as little human as possible, whether in speech, or in music, or in spectacle;—all these we certainly need, but we need them only as mediums or vehicles; they are nothing in themselves, except as they gather up and express the immediate and living and saving presence of God.

"Aaron and his sons shall wash their hands and their feet thereat."— Exod. xxx. 19.

But we thought Aaron and his sons were ministers? So they were; but ministers are not exempt from the great law of regeneration and purification.—The man must never be lost in the officer.—Aaron was to be treated as a sinner, and not as a priest only. Aaron could assume no personal su-

periority over his fellow rebels. He had a function to discharge, an official policy to pursue; but these did not take away his sin: his feet had also gone in the evil way, and his feet must be washed in the appointed laver.—This is a law of universal application to ministers teachers, office-bearers, and leaders of men.— All mere snobbery, and self-assertion, and self-idolatry must be rebuked and condemned, and utterly driven out of the Church.—No man has any right in the Church except as he has washed in the true laver and become qualified by purity to stand in the inner place.— Wealth, considered merely as such, must be driven away; all social claim, prestige, influence, and the like, must be put down;—they have no right to be in the Church, unless they too have been washed in the appointed laver. Then they may come in, and wealth will be cleansed of its idolatry, and social influence will be humbled into heavenly modesty, and the great man shall be as the small man, and all shall be equal in the presence of God.

"And with him was——." — Exod. xxxviii. 23.

Sometimes an age is gathered up into some one great representative name.—We do not always see the under-workers; we speak of the great man and forget the small one. The Bible is always just in this particular. It does not so raise up any one man as to deny to assistants and colleagues their mete of recognition and praise. God knows every worker, however obscure. He knows who put every knob and loop into the tabernacle which he is daily building.—It is enough for the obscure man that he should work with the leader's comrade. He feels pride in his association with his great leader. — They could not exchange places.—There is a fitness of things in the allotment of service to different men, and of different men to different positions.—There should be no rivalry, envy, or bitterness : it is one tabernacle that is being built for the glory of one God, and therefore to have anything whatsoever to do with it, however humble, is honour enough for the greatest of men. —The greater the man the more ready will he be to recognise the assistance of others.—Inspiration is not to consummate in the direction of self-worship, or even in the direction of splendid service ; it takes in the co-operation, sympathy and assistance of others, and makes the most of them.—The life-tabernacle is a wondrous building ; there is room for workers of all kinds in the uprearing of its mysterious and glorious walls. If we cannot do the greatest work, we may do the least: our heaven will come out of the realisation of the fact that it was God's tabernacle we were building, and under God's blessing that we were working.